The Complete
PROJECT
MANAGEMENT
OFFICE
Handbook

The Complete
PROJECT MANAGEMENT OFFICE
Handbook

Gerard M. Hill

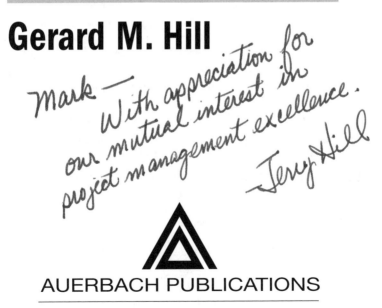

Mark —
With appreciation for
our mutual interest in
project management excellence.
Jerry Hill

AUERBACH PUBLICATIONS

A CRC Press Company
Boca Raton   London   New York   Washington, D.C.

Library of Congress Cataloging-in-Publication Data

Hill, Gerard M.
  The complete project management office handbook / Gerard M. Hill.
    p. cm.
  Includes index.
  ISBN 0-8493-2173-5 (alk. paper)
    1. Project management—Handbooks, manuals, etc. I. Title.

  HD69.P75H54 2003
  658.4'04—dc22
                                                              2003062902

Visit the Auerbach Publications Web site at www.auerbach-publications.com

© 2004 by ESI International, Inc.
Auerbach is an imprint of CRC Press LLC

No claim to original U.S. Government works
International Standard Book Number 0-8493-2173-5
Library of Congress Card Number 2003062902
Printed in the United States of America 1 2 3 4 5 6 7 8 9 0
Printed on acid-free paper

ACKNOWLEDGMENTS

In my development of this project management office model and manuscript, a number of reviewers participated in this effort, and I would like to express my grateful appreciation and recognition of their time and expertise.

First, Paul Shaltry, my colleague and friend at Catalyst Management Consulting, LLC, served as the primary technical reviewer of multiple drafts of this manuscript. His focused examination of content and his constructive chapter review commentaries ensured that initially vague information points were clarified, that use of standards and practices normally found in the project management environment were not skewed too badly, and that new and innovative ideas and approaches to PMO development and functionality were properly constructed and adequately conveyed.

Similarly, Marvin Goldstein, Director of Technical Research and Analysis at ESI International, was a key reviewer of the early content outlines as well as the completed draft manuscript. His timely examination of content flow and readability and his review comments on each chapter helped greatly to rectify weak topic areas and bolster the presentation of important business-related topics in the project management environment.

Equally vital were the technical reviews of other individuals. Larry Lambertsen, Director of Technical Solutions at ESI International, reviewed functions in the chapters on Technical Support. Mel Schnapper, a widely-recognized independent consultant having expertise in project management metrics, completed a review of the Standards and Metrics chapter. My colleague and friend Pasquel (Pat) DeFilippis validated our common client consulting experiences by reviewing the chapters on Project Management Methodology and Project Tools. Along with these reviewers, I wish to thank Gerry Jaffe and all the editors involved in the effort to translate my manuscript into a viable publication.

I would like to convey my special appreciation and regards to the many professionals at ESI International, particularly in the Product Development, Marketing, Business Development, and Technical Services and Support Departments. They individually and collectively contributed in different ways toward making this book a reality. I would also like to acknowledge the ongoing encouragement and support of my colleagues on ESI's management team. Thank you all.

Finally, this book was made possible by the love, encouragement, and support of my wife, Rita, who shined a persistent light on the path taken toward accomplishing this work.

Gerard M. Hill

INTRODUCTION

THE COMPLETE PMO: CONCEPT OVERVIEW

During the past decade, modern project management precepts have emerged to instill a vitalized, professional approach to project management across countless industries. Individual capabilities in project management have been strengthened and enlarged through a combination of developments in project management processes and techniques, implementation of training programs, and automated tools that use advanced design concepts and technology. As a result, today's project managers who practice these principles find themselves in the dual roles of a technical expert in a particular specialty or discipline as well as the business leader for the project.

The Complete Project Management Office Handbook extends these modern project management concepts and considerations into the scope of project management oversight, control, and support. It recognizes the need for an organizational entity — the project management office (PMO) — to perform in a capacity that achieves one or more of these three operational objectives. It positions the PMO as a business integrator — whether in a role that is limited to managing multiple projects as a program or expanded to serve as a business unit representing the organization's project management environment — to encompass all the people (project stakeholders), processes (methodologies and practices), and tools (automated systems and work aids) that manage or influence project performance. In either case, the PMO helps both the project manager and the relevant organization to understand and apply professional practices of project management and to adapt and integrate business interests into the project management efforts with which it is associated.

The *relevant organization* is the business unit or department that is influenced by PMO functions and that receives direct business benefits from PMO operations. As such, it is both the primary "customer" and the governing body of the PMO. In contrast, the *sponsoring organization* is that business unit or department that designs and implements the PMO capability, provides PMO resources, and holds responsibility for PMO functional and operational capability. Ideally, these two organizations are the same entity; this is normally the case when the PMO is first established. However, it is not uncommon for a sponsoring organization to establish a PMO for its own purpose and then emerge over time to serve the broader interests of a larger relevant organization or enterprise. Hence, the alignment of the PMO within the relevant organizational structure can be an indicator of its authority and responsibility and presents a major point of deliberation for PMO designers. Nevertheless, the depth and extent of PMO functional responsibility will usually guide its placement, which can be adjusted as organizational needs warrant.

The Complete Project Management Office Handbook focuses on what can be done to establish the depth and extent of PMO functional responsibility that the relevant organization requires. This is effected through two primary perspectives. First, *The Complete Project Management Office Handbook* considers five stages of PMO capability along a competency continuum. These represent progressive stages of PMO development and capability categorized specifically as a frame of reference. Each PMO stage suggests a particular level of functional capability that the PMO will have achieved if functions are fully implemented. The five PMO stages are also indicative of organizational maturity in project management, with the PMO's role and responsibilities advancing from project management oversight and control at the lower end of the competency continuum to strategic business alignment at the higher competency stages.

The second focus of *The Complete Project Management Office Handbook* is in the presentation of 20 function models that can be used to guide deliberation and development of PMO operational capability. These models suggest what capability can be realized through comprehensive implementation of each PMO function. Note that the actual implementation of PMO functions in an organization will undoubtedly be refashioned as adaptations of the function models presented in this book, depending on the appropriate use and fit within the relevant organization.

The following sections describe the PMO competency continuum, the PMO functions, and the underlying concepts regarding the context and considerations for PMO implementation.

THE PMO COMPETENCY CONTINUUM

The PMO competency continuum provides a vehicle that defines a series of PMO stages that can be examined for application in an organization.

The naming convention is relatively simple and somewhat consistent with PMO implementation efforts across most industries. However, these names provide only a frame of reference; other names can be applied as appropriate to the nature of PMO responsibilities and the business environment in which it operates.

Five general stages of PMO competency are prescribed. Figure 0.1 presents an overview of the PMO competency continuum and a description of each of its stages. These five PMO stages represent a progressive competency and advancement of functionality that can be attained to meet the needs of the project management environment and the associated business objectives of the relevant organization. It is presumed that a higher-stage PMO has already achieved the competencies prescribed for any lower-stage PMOs. Thus, if an organization wants to establish a Stage 3 Standard PMO, it will also have to ensure it has first realized the competencies prescribed for Stage 1 and Stage 2 PMOs. It is also suggested that a PMO at any stage can pursue activities at any level to address the needs within the relevant organization, which is far more important than stepping through levels of competency in sequence. Moreover, it is critical to discern the approximate level of PMO competency that the relevant organization needs. Not every organization needs to have a PMO at Stage 5. In fact, for most organizations, the Stage 3 standard PMO is probably more than adequate.

The following subsections provide a descriptive overview of each stage in the PMO competency continuum.

PROJECT OVERSIGHT	PROCESS CONTROL	PROCESS SUPPORT	BUSINESS MATURITY	STRATEGIC ALIGNMENT
Stage 1 PROJECT OFFICE	Stage 2 BASIC PMO	Stage 3 STANDARD PMO	Stage 4 ADVANCED PMO	Stage 5 CENTER OF EXCELLENCE
Achieve project deliverables and objectives for cost, schedule, and resource utilization	Provide a standard and repeatable PM methodology for use across all projects	Establish capability and infrastructure to support and govern a cohesive project environment	Apply an integrated and comprehensive project management capability to achieve business objectives	Manage continuous improvement and cross-department collaboration to achieve strategic business goals
• 1 or more projects • 1 Project Manager	• Multiple projects • Multiple PMs • Program Manager • Part-time PMO support staff	• Multiple projects • Multiple PMs • Program Managers • Director/Senior Program Manager • Full-time and part-time PMO staff	• Multiple projects • Multiple PMs • Program Managers • PMO Director • Dedicated PMO technical and support staff	• Multiple programs • Vice President or Director of Project Management • Dedicated PMO technical staff • Enterprisewide support staff

Figure 0.1 Overview of PMO Capabilities across the PMO Competency Continuum

Stage 1: The Project Office

The Stage 1 PMO is the fundamental unit of project oversight in the project management environment. The project office is created as a domain of the project manager, who is responsible for the successful performance of one or more projects. It provides the capability to ensure professionalism and excellence in applying widely accepted principles and preferred project management practices to each project effort.

However, more than one project office may exist within an organization. When this occurs, an obvious challenge lies in ensuring that each project office pursues a common approach to project management. Ideally, senior members of the project management staff will collaborate in their design and implementation of project office capability. Alternatively, a higher level PMO can be established to guide and support project office activities.

The inclusion of the project office in the PMO competency continuum is arguably an uncertain fit. By definition, it does not influence actions and activities of more than one project manager; it has no program level authority or direct strategic business relevance; and it does not fulfill the traditional role of a PMO. However, the project office implements and monitors the "rules of project performance" at the project team level, and that oversight in itself is a responsibility of PMOs at all levels. Thus, the placement of the project office at the beginning of the PMO competency continuum ensures that effective project management oversight at the project level is considered and implemented in the context of PMO responsibility.

The project office performs a variety of essential project management activities, including:

- Applying principles and techniques of modern project management, through the skill and knowledge of the project manager, to ensure that successful project performance is achieved. The project office concentrates on producing deliverables associated with project objectives, and it manages the vital signs of each project effort — cost, schedule, and resource utilization. Managing these details invariably enhances examination of project performance and facilitates the application of corrective actions to any problems that are identified.
- Serving as the direct interface to project team performance management. Because most project teams likely have a technical performance focus, the project office will introduce the elements of project management. Accordingly, the project office provides for differentiation between the technical methods, which are prescribed to create an

excellent technical product, and the project management methods, which are prescribed to ensure project and business success.

■ Applying organizational guidance in the form of policies, standards, executive decisions, etc. to each project effort. The project office also acts as the frontline point of supervision for implementing and integrating business processes in the project management environment.

■ Serving as the first level of project oversight and, often, the highest level of technical oversight. Whereas higher-stage PMOs may mandate and introduce technical methods and procedures, it is the project office that implements them in the project management environment. Indeed, at this level, there is probably less emphasis on business issues, unless the project manager has the double duty of serving also as program manager.

The project office's role is that of "implementer, applying most PMO functions." It carries the policies, practices, and guidance prescribed by higher authority — possibly higher-stage PMOs above it — into the project management environment for project team implementation. Yet the project office does not have to achieve advanced levels of functionality beyond the one or several projects it supports. Rather, a project office can exist formally in name or informally by virtue of its responsibility for project and project team performance. The formal project office can examine its roles in each of the PMO function models as a means to create a complete and comprehensive project oversight capability.

Stage 2: The Basic PMO

The Stage 2 or basic PMO is the first PMO level that deals with multiple project oversight and control. It furnishes the capability to provide aggregate oversight and control of multiple projects relative to the performance of multiple project managers.

In some industries, this stage is traditionally known as the "program office" and represents the domain of the program manager. It is possible that there could be more than one basic PMO in the relevant organization — one for each program manager. However, it is not practical for every program manager to independently build the comprehensive capability that is prescribed here. Therefore, in the context of *The Complete Project Management Office Handbook*, the basic PMO is presumed to be the highest centralized entity of project management that pursues its mission under the leadership and guidance of one designated program manager.

The basic PMO will likely have minimal staff, in some cases just one individual assigned to build the PMO's capability. Presumably, this person will be assigned full time to the PMO effort and have access to at least a few additional part-time support resources. This staffing arrangement is essential to accomplish the prescribed functionality of the basic PMO. An initiative that is fully supported financially and appropriately resourced should be able to achieve basic PMO capability and prescribed functionality within one year. This time, however, may vary based on the business commitment and culture of the relevant organization.

With an emphasis on establishing control in the project management environment, the basic PMO performs a variety of centralized project management activities, including:

- Having primary responsibility for establishing a standard approach to how project management is conducted in the relevant organization. This includes the introduction of common tools, repeatable processes, and preferred practices, ideally represented by implementation of a comprehensive project management methodology.
- Providing the means to compile aggregate results and analyses of project status and project progress as a basis for identifying and responding to project variations, evaluating project and project manager performance, and ensuring the achievement of project objectives.
- Introducing project management as a professional discipline in the relevant organization through its prescription of applicable standards, designation of qualified project managers, training and empowerment of project teams, and specification of roles and responsibilities of stakeholders in the project management environment.

The basic PMO has responsibility for implementing capability across all PMO functions. Nevertheless, most of that capability is fundamental and emphasizes establishing the foundation of a viable project management environment. As a result, the new Stage 2 PMO will likely be treading new ground within the relevant organization; functional capability advancements may initially be slow as business units become accustomed to the PMO's presence, accept transition of certain responsibilities to the PMO, and evolve with greater reliance on PMO management capability to achieve business interests associated with project oversight and control. Conversely, the new basic PMO must demonstrate its full alignment within the relevant organization and its professionalism in the practice of project management. This often requires the PMO to be proactive in planning its functionality and prepared to defend its business position.

Stage 3: The Standard PMO

The Stage 3 PMO is central to the PMO competency continuum, representing the essence of a complete and comprehensive PMO capability. While it continues to address project management oversight and control, the Stage 3 PMO introduces a new focus on support that optimizes individual and project performance in the project management environment. Its purview ranges from managing multiple projects and multiple project managers and may even include overseeing or otherwise aligning with one or more program managers.

The standard PMO can evolve from earlier efforts to construct a basic PMO. It can also be designed and implemented as the initial "from scratch" effort to introduce centralized oversight, control, and support in the project management environment. If a new PMO at the standard PMO level is to be pursued, the designers and developers must ensure that functionality prescribed for the basic PMO is incorporated into their PMO implementation plans.

Stage 3 PMO functionality is the solution for organizations seeking to implement project management as a core business competency or otherwise looking to improve project management capability or increase project management maturity. The new Stage 3 PMO necessitates minimal staffing of a full-time PMO manager or director and at least two additional full-time and part-time staff members qualified to perform and facilitate PMO functionality design and implementation. Furthermore, the extent of standard PMO functionality may warrant some part-time, possibly extended involvement from other participants in the project environment, as well as potential participation of business units in the relevant organization. As functionality is established, it is likely that a few more full-time staff members will be needed to fulfill professional specialty positions. As this PMO grows, additional full- and part-time administrative support personnel also will be required. The assignment of these resources, along with distinct executive business commitment to the effort, should enable complete Stage 3 PMO functionality to be achieved within a two- to three-year time frame. Of course, timely deliberation and planning of operational needs and priorities, along with assignment of adequate initial resources, will enable significant PMO functionality to be implemented within a matter of months. Initial standard PMO operating capability normally can be realized within the first year of the implementation initiative.

The standard PMO performs complete centralized project management oversight and control activities, with an added emphasis on introducing process and practice support in the project management environment. These activities include:

- Serving as the centerpiece of project management support in the relevant organization: a project management resource for business units, a professional practice facilitator for project managers and project team members, and a coordinator and collaborator for project stakeholders (resource managers, customers, and vendors) activity and involvement.
- Functioning as the interface between the business environment and the project management environment. The standard PMO translates, as appropriate, policy and executive guidance for project performance and implements actions and activities associated with business interests and objectives in the project management environment.
- Acting as the facilitator of project management environment process design and as a catalyst for project management excellence. This extends from attending to project management methodology and practices used to assure project success; to introducing project reporting tools and collaboration techniques; to providing executive support processes regarding matters of project governance, project portfolio management, and business performance.
- Serving as the representative of the project management environment to the senior executive of the relevant organization, and participating in or possibly convening and leading associated control boards comprising executives and senior managers. As such, the standard PMO can be the relevant organization's project management representative to business and industry affiliates, partners, and professional institutions.
- Operating as the recognized organizational entity that directly or indirectly influences resource participation on projects, to include addressing such matters as qualification, training, assignment, and evaluation.

The standard PMO has responsibility for implementing a complete capability across all designated PMO functions. It should examine the needs of the project management environment in each of the 20 prescribed PMO function models presented in this book. It will therefore be challenged to adapt each function model for optimized operational fit and maximized business benefit within the relevant organization. It should be reiterated that not every PMO needs to develop full or any capability in all 20 function areas. However, the PMO established at the standard level should at least consider every option for functionality.

Stage 4: The Advanced PMO

The Stage 4 PMO evolves from an existing, complete PMO capability and therefore is the "big brother" of the standard PMO. Its focus is on integrating business interests and objectives into the project management environment. This implies introducing common practices to be applied to both project management processes and business processes. To use a term familiar to many professional project managers, the advanced PMO helps create a "projectized" business environment.

Thus, by definition, the advanced PMO cannot be new. Rather, standard PMO functionality must be established before an advanced PMO capability can be implemented. Of course, this should not limit PMO designers and developers from incorporating advanced PMO considerations in their PMO implementation plans. Establishing the functionality and capability of the advanced PMO can be the next phase in plans for PMO fulfillment within the relevant organization. It is anticipated that this stage in the PMO competency continuum can be achieved within one to two years following establishment of the standard PMO capability.

The Stage 4 PMO has increased staffing and the potential for direct alignment of resources. In particular, the PMO staff is enhanced to include the professional and administrative resources needed to develop, implement, and manage expanded processes, programs, and functionality. The PMO director will have expanded authority to address business interests in the project management environment. Assigned PMO resources may be aligned with a few key functional units within the PMO that provide the means to integrate business and project management practices.

The advanced PMO performs comprehensive, centralized project management oversight, control, and support activities, together with expanded functionality that represents a mature and business-oriented project management organization. These activities include:

- Appearing more and more like a separate business unit. If a PMO budget has not already been established at an earlier PMO stage, the advanced PMO normally prepares and manages its own budget as a means of pursuing development and implementation of advanced project management practices and business integration activities.
- Collaborating with business units within the relevant organization and participating in the development or adaptation of practices and processes that are common to both the business environment and the project management environment.

■ Providing distinct expertise in state-of-the-art project management practices and procedures. Senior staff members are assigned full time and represent highly skilled and knowledgeable professionals who apply business acumen and advanced business and project management concepts to solutions implemented in the project management environment. These individuals help implement such functionality as mentoring services, project audits, and project recovery services. They monitor and manage project results in terms of business performance. The advanced PMO staff also can include business analysts and specialists from diverse professional disciplines, such as legal, contract and procurement management, customer service, and so forth, as needed full time or part time to achieve PMO functionality

The advanced PMO will revisit the 20 PMO functions to introduce expanded capacity and programs to manage the project management environment. Because it has a focus on integrating business interests, the advanced PMO also ensures that PMO functions are also integrated for efficient and effective implementation.

Stage 5: The Center of Excellence

The center of excellence is a separate business unit within the relevant organization and has responsibility for enterprisewide project management operations. Although lower-stage PMOs may be assigned such tasks, it is most distinct at this highest PMO level. Even so, lower-stage PMOs may have a business alignment or reporting affiliation with the center of excellence. Notwithstanding, the PMO functionality prescribed for the center of excellence has a focus on strategic business interests across the relevant organization.

Normally, there is an executive in charge of the center of excellence, and that individual should either report to or have direct access to the chief executive officer or any other top executive in the relevant organization. To that end, the center of excellence can be established within the time frame it takes an organization to establish a new business unit, which generally takes from one to two years to create a viable presence.

Although it appears at the top of the PMO competency continuum, the center of excellence is a unique project management entity. The center of excellence does not necessarily perform all of the prescribed lower level PMO functionality; but it could. There are two perspectives on how a center of excellence can be established. First, it could be created as a result of the growth and expansion of a lower-stage PMO, which would normally be the case in a small- to medium-sized organization. Conversely, it could be established independent of any existing PMOs, with the objective of providing strategic business guidance and direction to those subordinate PMOs. This would likely be the case in a large, global organization where the center of excellence provides some aspect of oversight, control, and support to PMOs serving regional business interests.

Consequently, the center of excellence assumes a strategic alignment role in the relevant organization and guides the project management environment in its continuous-improvement efforts. These include:

- Providing direction and influence for enterprise project management operations. It also may oversee subordinate PMO functionality where the relevant organization has constructed other PMO operations relative to its international, national, or other expanded geographical business focus.
- Building both project management environment and project stakeholder awareness and representation across business units, customer relationships, as well as vendor and partner relationships.
- Sponsoring and conducting studies and evaluations of project management functionality and business effectiveness, with particular focus on its own operations or those of affiliated PMOs.
- Representing the business interests of the relevant organization in the project management environment, and vice versa.

The center of excellence reviews the 20 PMO functions for strategic business implications, together with how they can be adapted, adjusted, or redesigned for optimized use, including application by other subordinate PMOs within the relevant organization.

THE PMO FUNCTIONS

The Complete Project Management Office Handbook presents 20 function models for practical application of oversight, control, and support solutions in the project management environment. These functions have a combined influence on the business environment and on the project management environment in the relevant organization. In addition, there are interrelationships among most of the PMO functions: some functional processes or procedures overlap; and some cross-function references will be apparent as each function is examined.

The 20 PMO functions are grouped within the following five function categories:

- *Practice Management*: Provides a common approach and frame of reference for conducting project management activities within an organization. This function area specifies project performance standards; establishes project management processes, tools, and practices; and creates a collaborative project management environment that includes access to project archives and a reference library. It concentrates on developing an effective organizational project management capability at the project level.
- *Infrastructure Management*: Facilitates establishing a professional project management environment. This function area examines the current state of project management; collaborates plans for the future state; and introduces the policies and oversight mechanisms needed to achieve organizational competency and maturity goals. It helps to define the project structure and stakeholder involvement necessary to support successful project performance and provides for administration of facilities and equipment needed to accomplish project objectives.
- *Resource Integration*: Manages the competency, availability, and performance of project resources. This function area enables the PMO to collaborate with resource managers to acquire, assign, and manage project managers and project team members; allows the PMO to administer training in the project management environment; and enables the PMO to shape the career progression of the project manager and support aspects of project team development.
- *Technical Support*: Provides project management advice, counsel, and support to project managers and project teams. This function area leverages the skill, knowledge, and experience of available project management experts to provide mentoring in the project management environment; provides a range of project planning, facilitation, and support activities; plans and conducts routine and special project audits and project management reviews; and provides appropriate project recovery support, as needed.
- *Business Alignment*: Introduces the organization's business perspective into the project environment. This function area oversees project portfolio management; facilitates executive involvement in project management to include overseeing project management contributions to business performance; and manages customer and vendor/contractor relationships, facilitating their roles as project stakeholders.

These function areas are, in turn, further divided into 20 specific PMO functions prescribed for comprehensive and complete coverage of PMO responsibilities in the relevant organization. Each of the 20 chapters of

The Complete Project Management Office Handbook presents a comprehensive description of one of these PMO functions. Table 0.1 provides a snapshot of the diverse activities of each function.

CONCEPTS AND CONTENT OVERVIEW

The prescribed PMO functions and associated activities are presented for due examination and consideration for individuals and organizations looking to establish a PMO capability that will enhance project performance, increase project management maturity, and integrate business interests and objectives. The proposed functions provide insight and guidance regarding the type of PMO functionality that can be pursued and suggest how they can be modeled or constructed. They suggest or prescribe possibilities, leaving it up to the individuals responsible for implementing PMO functions to deliberate and decide how to implement these model concepts in their business environment. Undoubtedly, adaptations and adjustments of the PMO function models will be the rule rather than the exception.

Similarly, it is unlikely that any individual PMO will use all of the functions or activities proffered here. There are too many unique business environments and organizational circumstances to presume that they would all fit nicely in every location and every business environment. Instead, the PMO can use the recommended function models as guidance, implementing only the particular PMO functions essential to its project management environment.

It should also be noted that the PMO function models are not particularly project management models. Whereas each PMO function model has significant relevance in the project management environment, these models represent what the PMO does, not what the project manager does. At best, the embedded prescriptions for the *project office* are activities performed by project managers when they conduct oversight as a Stage 1 PMO.

Throughout this book is the underlying premise that, overall, the PMO is a "business integration" activity. To that end, many PMO function models present concepts that not only approach, but also sometimes include, traditional business functions. It is never intended that the PMO replace organizational business functionality or functional departments. Rather, the PMO has responsibility for working with them to facilitate or adapt business functionality for use in the project management environment. The PMO function model may state that the PMO "should" or "will" do something, but that is only in the context of the prescriptive nature of this work. It is considerably more important that the PMO identify where in the relevant organization such functionality may already exist and then

Table 0.1 Overview of PMO Functions

Practice Management	Infrastructure Management	Resource Integration	Technical Support	Business Alignment
Project Management Methodology • Establish basis for project management methodology • Examine current practices • Develop project life cycle solution • Conduct methodology implementation • Manage methodology maturity	**Project Governance** • Prepare and maintain PMO charter • Develop project management policies • Develop project classification guidance • Establish project manager authority • Establish executive control board • Align business and technical committees	**Resource Management** • Acquire project resources • Assign project resources • Deploy project resources • Manage resource performance • Close out project resource assignments	**Mentoring** • Establish project management mentoring program • Engage project management mentors • Conduct project management mentoring • Evaluate mentoring program	**Project Portfolio Management** • Set up project portfolio management • Perform project selection • Integrate projects in the portfolio • Conduct project and portfolio reviews • Manage portfolio attrition
Project Management Tools • Select project tools • Implement project tools • Evaluate project tools	**Assessment** • Conduct competency assessments • Conduct capability assessments • Conduct maturity assessments	**Training and Education** • Establish training program • Manage training program • Evaluate training program	**Planning Support** • Establish project planning support • Conduct project planning support • Conduct adjunct planning support	**Customer Relationships** • Manage customer relationships • Manage customer contracts • Manage customer satisfaction

Standards and Metrics	Organization and Structure	Career Development	Project Auditing	Vendor/Contractor Relationships
• Implement project management standards • Determine project metrics requirements • Introduce and use metrics	• Set up the PMO structure • Establish project management structure • Develop stakeholder participation	• Develop project management career path • Support project management career planning • Establish professional certification	• Set up project auditing capability • Conduct project auditing • Manage project auditing results	• Manage vendor/contractor relationships • Manage vendor/contractor acquisition • Manage vendor/contractor performance
Project Knowledge Management	**Facilities and Equipment Support**	**Team Development**	**Project Recovery**	**Business Performance**
• Establish knowledge management framework • Introduce knowledge management system • Implement knowledge management system	• Establish project team requirements • Manage project facilities • Manage project equipment	• Facilitate cohesive team formation • Facilitate virtual team setup • Enable project team development • Monitor project team performance	• Develop recovery assessment process • Plan and conduct project recovery • Capture recovery lessons learned	• Develop integrated business solutions • Manage business collaboration • Manage PMO business fulfillment

develop collaborative means to have it represented in and supportive of the project management environment. The PMO should facilitate the positive influence and integration of business functionality in the project management environment. The applicable PMO function model can, in turn, be used to aid in introducing such business integration.

Likewise, when a PMO function model prescribes an action or activity for the PMO to perform, it should fulfill those efforts to the extent permitted by existing PMO competency and maturity, current business capability, and acceptance within the overriding organizational culture. The PMO function models enumerate what is needed in the project management environment to effectively conduct project management oversight, control, or support. Smaller PMOs, usually with limited staff and authority, certainly cannot begin to address the full scope of activities recommended for each PMO function model. Some larger PMOs may not be chartered to pursue certain functionality. In those cases, the PMO should adopt as much or as little of the model prescription as needed. When a PMO inherently is not able to fully implement a PMO function, it can work and maneuver within the business environment to facilitate implementation of PMO functional interests by a better-suited business unit or other functional department. In some cases, the PMO will discover that proposed functionality already exists in the relevant organization. It then becomes the PMO's responsibility to introduce it into the project management environment, to the extent possible, to align with widely accepted, professional project management practices and precepts.

Given these underlying concepts, each of the 20 subsequent chapters delineating PMO functions contains the following recurring subsections:

- *Chapter Introduction*: Presents a brief overview of applicable concepts for the given PMO function, including a specification of what capability the PMO achieves as a result of implementing the function.
- *Project Environment Interface Concepts*: Identifies the impact and general benefits to be realized within the project management environment as a result of implementing the particular PMO function.
- *Business Environment Interface Concepts*: Identifies the impact and general benefits to be realized within the business environment as a result of implementing the particular PMO function.
- *[Function Area] Activities across the PMO Continuum*: Highlights the prescribed PMO activities for implementing the particular PMO function at each of the five progressive PMO competency stages.
- *[Function Area] Function Model*: Provides a detailed and comprehensive discussion of the prescribed activities to be performed in conjunction with implementing the particular PMO functionality. This

portion of extensive content within each chapter varies significantly according to the prescribed activities of the particular function model.

■ *Postscript for the Smaller PMO*: Provides a brief statement of insight and focus for individuals associated with a more modest PMO function implementation. Following examination of the extensive and comprehensive descriptions that present the activities, concepts, and considerations of each PMO function model, this final section of each chapter suggests the fundamental capabilities that the smaller PMO can address.

CONTENTS

SECTION II: INFRASTRUCTURE MANAGEMENT

SECTION III: RESOURCE INTEGRATION

SECTION IV: TECHNICAL SUPPORT

SECTION V: BUSINESS ALIGNMENT

I

PRACTICE MANAGEMENT

1

PROJECT MANAGEMENT METHODOLOGY

A project management methodology provides a standard, repeatable process to guide project performance from concept to completion. It introduces and applies generally accepted project management techniques and practices that fit within the culture and business needs of the relevant organization. It includes identification of the roles and responsibilities associated with each process step, as well as specification of the input and output for the desired sequence of process steps. In essence, a project management methodology conveys to project managers and project team members what to do and how to do it.

The organization can begin this effort by introducing a simple series of important project management practices. It should ultimately aim for a complete and comprehensive process that specifies all essential project management activities that are performed throughout the entire project life cycle. In that regard, a project management methodology should be focused to ensure the successful achievement of project management processes: initiation, planning, executing, controlling, and closing. It is also used to apply the standards of project management, such as that contained in *A Guide to the Project Management Book of Knowledge* (PMBOK ®*). This is what differentiates the project management methodology from a technical methodology.

The project management methodology is applied to all types of projects within the relevant organization. In contrast, a technical methodology deals primarily with the technical aspects of work associated with projects.

---

* PMBOK is a trademark of the Project Management Institute, Inc. (PMI), which is registered in the U.S. and other nations.

In larger organizations, there may be one or more technical processes needed to accomplish work in different departments. Conversely, the project management methodology should be the same across all departments.

This "project management methodology" function enables the PMO to:

- Establish the standard approach to project management that is to be used by all project managers within the relevant organization
- Introduce project management practices incrementally, beginning with those that have the greatest impact on project and business success
- Achieve consensus for implementing a common project management life cycle across the relevant organization's technical and business areas
- Provide for collection of pertinent project data used in individual and aggregate analyses of project performance
- Identify and incorporate technical process methodologies into the project management methodology

The "project management methodology" function requires coordination and collaboration with key stakeholders — predominantly project managers — in the project management environment. It is imperative that any project management methodology be supportive of technical and business efforts, so it is essential to involve project engineers, product managers, and other technical and business specialists. Furthermore, because policies for methodology deployment are formulated and communicated to all project participants at the executive level, the development and deployment of a common project management methodology within the relevant organization distinctly requires executive level and senior management buy-in and support.

PROJECT ENVIRONMENT INTERFACE CONCEPTS

A project management methodology is central to the project management environment. As such, it should be responsive to the needs of all project stakeholders and guide them through the key activities of project management. An effective project management methodology conveys to all stakeholders "how we manage projects" in the project management environment. It accomplishes this by establishing a common frame of reference for everyone participating or having interest in project performance. To that end, it should support all interactions among business, technical, and project management participants. It also provides an immediate reference for those stakeholders on the periphery of or outside the immediate project involvement to inform them and set expectations about what will be achieved through specified project management activities.

Accordingly, the project management methodology introduces the relevant organization's philosophy, concepts, standard approach, and common terminology for project work. This allows cross-functional project managers and project team members to understand and share the same project management experience. Consequently, each project manager does not have to create and convey a tactical approach for each new project and for each new team member. As a result, over time, cross-functional teams become more efficient, more productive, and more successful in producing project deliverables and in accomplishing project objectives.

BUSINESS ENVIRONMENT INTERFACE CONCEPTS

Inasmuch as the PMO itself functions as an integrator for the organization, the project management methodology is a central mechanism for project and business integration. A prominent aspect of integration is using a common process across business functions. This is enhanced when each business unit adapts and incorporates its technical and business processes to fit within the methodology. This is an important concept. Once a methodology is set into place, business units having specific functional or technical areas can no longer practice old behaviors that may misalign with or be counterproductive to the project management methodology. To that end, each business unit should conform to the approved organizational standards of project management as it continues to apply essential best practices that produce the desired technical and business results.

The project management methodology provides a foundation for work accomplished across business units, including facilitation of cross-functional resource assignments. A well-conceived, well-collaborated, and properly implemented project management methodology will ensure accomplishment of all critical project management actions.

Another feature of using a standard project management methodology is that it promotes effective project collaboration and reporting within the relevant organization. A coordinated approach to project management facilitates common data collection and distribution. The result of using such a project management methodology is that project progress and performance information can be compiled and aggregated to facilitate business decisions across projects and across the organization.

PROJECT MANAGEMENT METHODOLOGY ACTIVITIES ACROSS THE PMO CONTINUUM

The evolution of the "project management methodology" function along the PMO competency continuum is characterized by:

■ Development and implementation of increasingly more complete and comprehensive project management processes and practices
■ Increased integration of technical and business process activities
■ Wider cross-functional influence at advanced stages of the continuum, in association with oversight authority and responsibility for project management methodology

Table 1.1 presents an overview of the range of prescribed PMO project management methodology activities according to each level in the PMO competency continuum.

The *project office*, as a formal or informal entity, is the fundamental agent of project management methodology implementation. Traditionally, project oversight has relied on the practices that each project manager has brought to bear, based on personal skill and experience. With the establishment of a project office, project managers can now contribute those valuable individual capabilities to the development of practices that can be applied across similar, related projects. Ultimately, these practices will form the foundation of more-structured, repeatable project management processes that can be shared across the organization.

Mid-range PMO levels of the continuum have the responsibility of developing and deploying a full project life cycle methodology that best fits the needs and requirements of the relevant organization. The PMO first ensures that a standard, structured, and repeatable process for conducting project management is established within the organization. This can begin with incremental development of only the most critical processes and later expanded to encompass a more complete methodology as the organization gains additional understanding and benefits from the initial processes. The PMO then expands its influence to develop its methodology to a comprehensive and robust level with appropriate integration or alignment of technical and business processes, according to the affiliated business units' needs.

The *center of excellence* performs any necessary methodology development, deployment, and review activities to formulate solutions and guide process collaboration across business units. As the interface with senior management, the center of excellence recommends and implements policy for development and deployment of project management methodology.

Table 1.1   Range of Project Methodology Activities across the PMO Continuum

Project Office	Basic PMO	Standard PMO	Advanced PMO	Center of Excellence
Applies effective practices for project performance and oversight; and employs standard life cycle processes when available	Introduces critical processes and practices of project management ■ Identifies and develops critical processes ■ Manages cross-project critical process use ■ Identifies best and preferred practices	Establishes and monitors use of a complete project management methodology ■ Provides full project life cycle coverage ■ Integrates technical processes ■ Conducts user training in methodology	Enhances content and monitors use of a comprehensive methodology ■ Integrates business processes ■ Optimizes alignment of automated tools ■ Facilitates use of methodology across relevant business units	Analyzes project management methodology ■ Examines process variation in business units ■ Assesses methodology use and ongoing process improvement

The fundamental objective of the PMO's "project management methodology" function across the PMO continuum is to:

- Determine and implement project management process solutions that align with the relevant organization's business interests
- Support the organization's technical work performance
- Assist project managers and project teams in achieving project objectives

PROJECT MANAGEMENT METHODOLOGY FUNCTION MODEL

This function model presents considerations for the PMO to develop a standard, cohesive process for conducting project management, to implement that process for use by the widest possible audience in the relevant organization, and to monitor and manage its use and improvement. Figure 1.1 depicts the primary activities of this PMO "project management methodology" function model. Each activity is described in the following subsections.

Establish Basis for Project Management Methodology

A frame of reference for the project management methodology is needed to ensure that all project management development participants, particularly the PMO, have and can communicate a clear understanding regarding the direction being pursued to introduce a standard project management practice. The basis for introducing a project management methodology can be formulated as described in this section.

Convene Methodology Development Team

The PMO will normally have responsibility for overseeing project management methodology development. However, the PMO must ensure that project managers and others having technical or business interests are properly represented in the methodology development effort. Therefore, a methodology development team is formed to include participants both from inside and outside the PMO to assist in development, review, and implementation of the organization's project management methodology processes and practices.

The best way to ensure effective design, development, and implementation of a project management methodology is to involve the experts, particularly those managers who can contribute one or more of the following competencies:

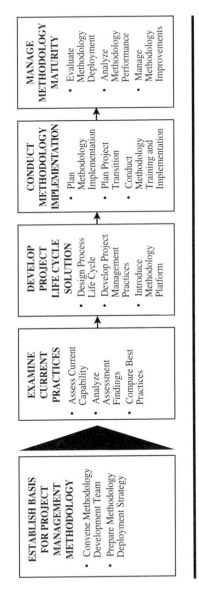

ESTABLISH BASIS FOR PROJECT MANAGEMENT METHODOLOGY
- Convene Methodology Development Team
- Prepare Methodology Deployment Strategy

EXAMINE CURRENT PRACTICES
- Assess Current Capability
- Analyze Assessment Findings
- Compare Best Practices

DEVELOP PROJECT LIFE CYCLE SOLUTION
- Design Process Life Cycle
- Develop Project Management Practices
- Introduce Methodology Platform

CONDUCT METHODOLOGY IMPLEMENTATION
- Plan Methodology Implementation
- Plan Project Transition
- Conduct Methodology Training and Implementation

MANAGE METHODOLOGY MATURITY
- Evaluate Methodology Deployment
- Analyze Methodology Performance
- Manage Methodology Improvements

Figure 1.1 "Project Management Methodology" Function Model

- Extensive personal project management experience in the industry
- Knowledge and training in advanced project management practices
- Understanding of the relevant organization's project management environment
- Experience in development of processes and practices
- Familiarity with project team dynamics
- Internal sponsorship (methodology development champion)

These characteristics should be considered when selecting individuals for participation on the methodology development team.

In addition, the PMO may want to consider using external advisors and project management consultants in their methodology development effort. Such external resources can bring cross-industry insights and experience to help the methodology development team manage process structure design, technique development, organizational issue resolution, technical and business process integration, and methodology implementation planning.

The PMO should specify and communicate the type of involvement expected of the methodology development team. It should determine whether the team will (a) serve in an advisory capacity to review and approve methodology development work that the PMO or a selected external resource performs or (b) reserve full responsibility itself for methodology development.

On average, the methodology development team should be able to accomplish its methodology development objectives with a minimum of three to five team members, to include at least one senior member of the PMO responsible for leading and collaborating the effort. Fewer people can staff the team, but this recommended team size provides smaller organizations with ample exchange of alternative thoughts and perspectives necessary to deliberate and decide on how it will conduct project management. Larger, more diverse organizations may require additional team members to represent the views and interests of all involved business units. If the methodology development team is not in itself responsible for review, additional methodology development team members can be included as necessary to serve as reviewers of completed design and development work. Regardless of team size, reviewers should represent senior management in the project management environment.

Other factors also influence the actual size of the methodology development team and should be considered when convening the team. These include available development time and deadlines for completion, level of expertise of the team leader and team members, depth and coverage of process and practice development, and extent of deployment within the relevant organization.

The PMO can define methodology development team participation requirements by preparing a responsibility matrix similar to that used for project planning. An abbreviated responsibility matrix is depicted in Table 1.2. The activities that this matrix indicates represent a project effort. To that end, project management methodology development effort should be planned and conducted as a project.

The methodology development team configuration should enable construction and implementation of a viable project management methodology within the relevant organization. An executive participant may also be identified to perform final review and approval for methodology design and to support methodology implementation.

Prepare Methodology Deployment Strategy

The methodology deployment strategy provides a roadmap for methodology design, development, implementation, and maintenance. It contains the current and emerging strategy of the organization and can therefore be revised or updated over time. As approved by senior management, it represents the PMO's current intended approach to methodology deployment. The strategy can be shared throughout the organization, as necessary, with individuals having responsibility or business interests in the project management methodology effort.

The methodology deployment strategy is composed of the following general elements:

- Methodology development responsibility statement
- Methodology development approach
- Methodology platform
- Methodology utilization policy
- Methodology maintenance responsibility statement

The PMO can adapt or expand these elements to meet the needs of the relevant organization. In general, the PMO prepares or facilitates the preparation of the methodology deployment strategy to guide and document how the project management methodology is to be established and used. Each element is described in the following subsections.

Methodology Development Responsibility Statement

The PMO prepares this statement to outline its role and responsibilities, as well as those of any other intended participants, including the methodology development team and external consultants. This statement serves as a charter for the PMO and participants to proceed with the methodology

Table 1.2 Sample Responsibility Matrix for Methodology Development Team

Responsibility by Team Member	PMO Manager	PMO Staff	Program Managers	Project Managers	Business Unit Managers	Project Consultant
Select team members	P	A	—	—	—	—
Perform make/buy decision	R	A	P	P	R	F/R
Conduct methodology design	R	P	P	P	R	F/A
Develop methodology	R	P	P	P	—	P/A
Plan methodology implementation	R	P	P	P	—	P/A
Plan methodology transition	R	P	P	P	R	P/A
Conduct methodology training	R	P	—	—	—	P/A

Note: F = facilitate, P = perform, A = assist/advise, R = review.

development effort. Inasmuch as this statement may also specify approved funding and authority to act, a senior manager or executive of the relevant organization should review and sign it. However, this responsibility statement may not be necessary if the PMO charter has already adequately covered PMO responsibilities for project methodology development.

Methodology Development Approach

Representing a fundamental plan for how the PMO expects to introduce methodology development, the methodology development steps or phases indicate the depth and extent of content and specify the scope of implementation. An organization can begin formalizing its approach to project management with initial construction of just a few key processes and practices. For the preliminary effort, it is usually prudent to select highly visible problem areas. These provide some quick benefits that will help sustain the changes introduced into the project management environment. A more complete and comprehensive project management life cycle methodology can be developed subsequently.

By identifying the range of incremental development steps that will be performed, this strategy element provides a more structured approach to project management methodology development activities. In addition, this strategy element should specify the performance and time frame for such development activities as those presented in the following sample progressive list:

- Develop a single, key project management process (for example, project risk management)
- Integrate technical methodology considerations into a key process
- Develop a key process series (for instance, for project selection: customer identification, project definition, business case, and project approval activities)
- Develop a fundamental project management life cycle process guide and flowchart
- Develop a fundamental guide for project management practice
- Link technical life cycle activities to the project management life cycle process
- Develop a complete guide for project management practices and techniques
- Integrate project management practices and techniques across the project life cycle
- Develop a comprehensive project management life cycle process with fully integrated technical activities and aligned project management practices

The PMO can prepare recommendations for these or other progressive steps of its choosing for developing a structured and repeatable approach to project management. The consideration is to identify what end-state of methodology deployment is being pursued under current and pending methodology development efforts. This element, as well as the methodology deployment strategy document, can be revised or expanded to describe the current methodology development efforts.

Inasmuch as this is a strategy statement and not a detailed plan, the timelines for these progressive methodology development activities can be very general. It would not be unusual for this strategy to indicate what is to be accomplished over a period of months or even years, with timelines specified in terms of quarters. However, when more information is known, a detailed methodology development and implementation plan can be developed for each step or phase in the strategy. In such cases, that methodology development and implementation plan can be attached to this strategy statement for easy subsequent reference.

This element of the methodology deployment strategy also defines (a) the PMO's perspective of the project management methodology and (b) what each methodology component to be developed will contain. The primary methodology components often include:

- Project management process guide: what to do
- Project management practice guide: how to do it
- Project management toolkit: the means to do it
- Project management glossary: definitions of project management terms

The PMO should specify which components will be developed and also determine whether any other methodology components are needed. Alternatively, the PMO may initially recommend creating only a few necessary project management procedures and techniques — a critical-technique component — to assist the PMO in providing early guidance for structured project management. This "component" could ultimately evolve into a larger project management practice guide that provides coverage across the complete project management life cycle as the project management environment matures.

Methodology Platform

The methodology platform addresses the means by which those responsible for project management apply the project management methodology to project work. It commonly refers to automated systems that provide access to process steps, practice and technique guidance, and an associated database of project information. For purposes of this PMO function, this strategy element considers how the PMO plans to convey the established methodology process and preferred practices that project managers and project team members will use.

The PMO, with insight and assistance from the methodology development team, as well as guidance and support from the information technology (IT)/information systems (IS) department at the onset of the effort, should determine the type of platform on which the project management methodology components will reside. Factors to weigh when selecting the methodology platform include the culture of the relevant organization, project manager familiarity with automated tools, complexity of process and practice guidance, and development or acquisition costs. Moreover, the PMO should consider the fundamental types of project management methodology platforms described in the next five subsections.

Paper-Based Documentation. Print publications are perhaps the easiest means to deploy the organization's project management methodology. The paper-based documentation platform is composed of one or more published volumes of text containing the desired methodology guidance components. It is distributed to all users and is maintained through printed updates or revisions. Within most organizations, it remains the ideal solution for the initial introduction of project management methodology.

Even in today's highly automated business environments, many organizations still use a paper-based platform for methodology deployment. Created and implemented quickly, its development can generally be accomplished at a lower cost than other means of methodology deployment. Furthermore, this methodology platform provides the requisite structure and guidance needed to achieve project objectives, including the use of standard templates, checklists, and report formats. If not developed internally, paper-based methodologies can be obtained from project management organizations and project management training and consulting firms.

Standard word-processing, spreadsheet, and database software applications are used to create paper-based project management methodology process guides, practice guides, and any other components. These software applications, commonly used by project managers and project team members, provide the PMO with a familiar vehicle for disseminating the methodology to users in the project management environment. The use of this methodology is further enhanced when associated business applications and templates reside on a common network for wide user access.

Automated Application Conglomeration. This methodology platform is a slight variation of the paper-based documentation platform. Although this approach uses standard business software applications, some project management-specific applications are now added. By definition, this platform uses a variety of software applications, but they are generally not integrated. At best, these applications are available on a network for common access to users in the project management environment, although they may also be found isolated on individual computer systems. Even though these methodology process and practice components are still accessed from standard business software, methodology guidance can now be partially provided by introducing applications that have such features and capabilities as project resource management, project cost management, and project schedule management.

Often, the "conglomeration" mode is actuated when the PMO simultaneously introduces a new project management methodology while still allowing or even facilitating the use of individually preferred project management software applications. Unfortunately, this does not always provide a fully integrated and standard approach to project management. However, it does enable guidance for deployment of a standard project management process and associated practice.

Automated Project Management Application.   This methodology platform introduces a more integrated approach to project management by acquiring one of many high-end, multiuser project management applications, which inherently provides the means to perform a variety of project management activities. Thus, the PMO must clearly define its requisite activities and features while also conducting a search for the "best fit" application. The cost of acquiring a high-end, integrated project management system is usually steep — often tens of thousands of dollars in smaller organizations up to hundreds of thousands of dollars for deployment in large organizations. Cost is therefore a distinct factor when considering an integrated project management application.

Another important factor to consider is an application's capability to manage and guide project management methodology processes and practices. Other specialized features that facilitate activities prescribed by the methodology — such as associated project team collaboration, project reporting, and scope-change management — should also be evaluated.

Note, however, that these high-end applications generally do not provide a comprehensive methodology for project management as part of product delivery. That said, some vendors do recognize the difference between a project's work breakdown structure and a project's management methodology, and these vendors have incorporated process-management and -information display capability into their products. Consequently, after acquiring the application, the PMO likely will want to "install" the organization's self-developed methodology components into the system, which prompts reflection on how such customization can be accomplished using the chosen application. The PMO needs to ensure that the selected application for automated project management will facilitate the organization's preferred approach to methodology process management and will provide adequate access and display of guidance for associated project management practices.

Automated Methodology Application Utilization. This methodology platform is characterized by the acquisition of an established, commercially available software application package to manage activities of the project management life cycle. The application contains features and functions that assist the project manager and project team in obtaining effective oversight of the processes of project management.

The automated methodology application provides an off-the-shelf solution to deployment of project management methodology. However, the software should be examined to ensure that it facilitates the performance of all project management activities required by the relevant organization. In some cases, vendors are willing to modify their product's features and functions to incorporate desired practices and processes. Note, however, that such modifications can be as expensive as constructing a fundamental automated methodology application within the organization. The PMO thus has a strong incentive to closely scrutinize off-the-shelf products to see whether the proposed platform can meet the organization's needs without the need for additional modification.

Automated Methodology Application Construction. The ideal approach to deployment of project management methodology is to construct the desired automated platform in-house. Using this approach, the PMO can control the design and development of the system's features and functions. In-house construction can be accomplished by using internal system-development resources or an external system developer. It may also be beneficial to combine the two by using (a) a team of internal developers who already know the existing system's nuances and configuration and (b) an experienced external team that helps design and incorporate the desired collection of modern project management processes and practices.

Often, the internal construction of an automated methodology application relies on a previous paper-based design. In such cases, any paper-based platform of processes or techniques that the PMO has already developed and implemented will contribute to the construction of its automated platform.

Methodology Utilization Policy

The introduction of a project management methodology is a business decision that requires overt support of senior management within the relevant organization. The way in which the methodology is promoted, anticipated, and ultimately received for use is a key success factor that senior managers directly influence. A policy statement on methodology use is an appropriate means to convey senior management support and endorsement or, better, their mandate for methodology use.

The PMO should prepare a policy statement describing the use of proposed project management methodology for review and approval by senior project managers. The best approach is to fashion the statement using a familiar format within the organization — policy, standard operating procedure (SOP), executive directive, and so forth. The means of communicating policy regarding the use of methodology may vary by organization, but the objective is the same: to demonstrate the support of senior management for deployment of the proposed project management methodology. Ideally, the most senior executive in the relevant organization will endorse the policy statement.

The PMO should consider including the following elements in the policy statement:

- Business interest in methodology deployment
- Benefits to be achieved through methodology deployment
- Executive direction for use of the methodology
- Statement of executive/senior management support and endorsement of project management as a core competency

The policy statement should clearly and briefly describe the purpose and sponsorship of the proposed project management methodology. An executive or a representative of senior management should personally introduce the policy statement as part of the planned rollout activities for the proposed methodology. In fact, the executive should personally introduce the project management methodology and identify, promote, and sustain professional behavior adjustments to support the intended use of the methodology at all levels.

Methodology Maintenance Responsibility Statement

A broad range of participants will have accomplished the initial development and implementation of the methodology. The PMO should deliberate and recommend whether a team of those same individuals (that is, the methodology development team) will remain intact to perform methodology review and maintenance activities, or whether that responsibility should be assigned to the PMO staff. In either case, a responsibility statement for project methodology maintenance should be prepared to ensure that this need is addressed.

Similar to the methodology development responsibility statement, this maintenance responsibility statement may not be required if PMO responsibilities for project methodology maintenance are already adequately covered in the PMO charter.

The PMO also should determine when specific methodology maintenance activities would be conducted. A number of items may trigger refreshing the methodology, including: changes in project metrics; results of capability assessments or maturity assessments; changes in technology; findings of research; discovery of new approaches through application and human innovation; and developments in technical processes the methodology supports. In the absence of specific triggers, however, the PMO can schedule a project management methodology review at regular intervals, normally every 12 to 18 months for a mature methodology.

Examine Current Practices

The first step in introducing formal project management processes and practices is a PMO's awareness of the starting point. The PMO should scrutinize the organization's condition in the project management environment as a prerequisite to planning and designing the type, depth, and comprehensiveness of project management methodology support that is required. An examination of current practices provides the baseline for methodology deployment. It should be assessed in conjunction with guidelines established within the relevant organization for the PMO's "Assessment" function (Chapter 6). The PMO's examination of current project management practices is presented relative to the following three activities:

■ Assess current capability
■ Analyze assessment findings
■ Compare best practices

Assess Current Capability

The PMO will gain considerable insight into the current state of project management capability by assessing the current processes and practices used in the project management environment. This examination should begin with a simple and general evaluation of functional unit and project management involvement to determine those project management processes and practices in which they are engaged. The PMO may use an external consultant experienced in assessing project organization capability or devise its own means to gain perspective relative to the following information:

- Current project management organization structure
- Individual project manager and project team alignment within that structure
- Level of upper management involvement in project management activities
- Nature of project support that functional organizations provide
- Extent of participation in project activities across the organization
- Need for information and oversight by functional and senior managers

This preliminary look at the project management environment will provide the PMO with the requisite acumen to identify any need to enhance project management awareness and support within the organization. Moreover, it will provide indicators for the design of cross-functional responsibility and involvement in project management as processes and procedures are developed.

Next, the PMO should undertake an assessment of current project management practices that project managers and teams use. This is normally accomplished through a survey instrument. However, it is preferable to conduct direct interviews with project managers at various levels in the organization as well as with project teams to gain the "group" perspective on how projects are accomplished. The interview method is preferable because it allows examiners to clarify and understand the information provided by each interviewee.

The assessment must also be established and conducted against an established and complete project life cycle process. The PMO should ensure that the project life cycle it selects for this assessment contains elements and activities that are aligned with the standards it will ultimately pursue, that is, the PMI's PMBOK. This project management capability assessment should examine the following information:

- Identify the project life cycle activities that project managers are performing
- Identify the project life cycle activities that project managers are not performing
- Identify the project life cycle activities that business unit managers are performing

- Identify the project management practices that are commonly used across all or most projects
- Identify the project management practices that are unique and used only by one or a few project managers
- Identify the project life cycle activities that involve project team members

At a minimum, the results of this assessment should provide the PMO with a basic understanding of the extent and type of project management practices currently in use. In a subsequent activity, when these data are further analyzed, they will expose more detailed gaps in the organization's current project management practices versus best practices.

In conjunction with the above assessment, the PMO also may want to pursue an examination of the human side of process performance to formulate its understanding of additional methodology deployment needs. In particular, a PMO inquiry should capture the following information from project managers and project team members:

- Interest and enthusiasm in a structured approach to project management
- Resistance and barriers to a structured approach to project management
- Personal perspectives on the need for a formal project management process
- Personal perspectives on what the use of project management methodology entails
- Personal perspectives on critical individual and group training
- Current preferences for project management practice (technique)

The results will provide user input to the methodology design and development effort.

Analyze Assessment Findings

The PMO should conduct an analysis of assessment findings to formulate a view of current capabilities. Again, this can be accomplished internally or with external assistance from project management consultants experienced in such organizational analyses. The analysis — as detailed or as simple as the PMO warrants — should be designed and conducted to provide a reasonable understanding of the relevant organization's current state of project management performance capability. Five analysis components are recommended and briefly described below.

Process Flow Analysis

Based on survey or interview results, the PMO can construct the common elements of the project management process, including those unique process elements that are not widely used. This can be achieved by preparing a preliminary process flowchart to describe what is currently being accomplished to manage projects. Although similar to and somewhat based on the project life cycle used in the earlier process assessment, this flowchart will contain only those project management activities currently performed within the relevant organization. As such, this flowchart will indicate the strengths and weaknesses of the current process relative to the standards applied.

Process Content Analysis

The process flowchart can be expanded to include the common input and output to each existing process, as well as to identify who is responsible for completing each process step. However, this analysis, in particular, will indicate what deliverables are achieved through each process step and what common results the current project management approach have accomplished.

Project Management Practice Analysis

The examination provided information about how each project manager approaches project planning, oversight, and control, that is, the practices they use. In this analysis, the PMO can identify which practices are common throughout the organization and which are unique to individuals or business units. This analysis will help contrast current practices with best practices in the organization and in industry.

Project Management Tools

The assessment should have collected information regarding how project managers and their teams accomplish the processes and practices identified in the current project management approach. The next step identifies the tools used to facilitate project management activities to determine which have common use and which are unique to individuals or business units. Tools, which are discussed in greater detail in the PMO function "Project Management Tools" (Chapter 2), include automated software applications, as well as forms, checklists, and templates that assist in performing project management activities.

Project Management Practice Support

This analysis determines the extent to which project managers, business unit managers, and senior managers are involved in and support a formal, structured approach to project management. At a minimum, the assessment results should provide preliminary indications of the "culture" in which methodology development will be pursued. They also indicate the strengths and weaknesses of support for project management in functional and technical areas of the business.

Compare Best Practices

This step in examining the current project management practice provides an additional analysis of how well the organization is performing project management in contrast to standards and best practices. Using the previously prepared analyses, the PMO can determine if and how well all essential project management process steps are being performed. This activity enables the organization to prepare a "gap" analysis of current practices against either preferred standards or a set of best practices in project management.

It should be noted that standards are inherently different than best practices. Standards represent a basis for performance: the criteria to be met and the goals to be achieved. Best practices, on the other hand, are a set of activities to be considered and pursued to the extent the user understands and values them. As such, best practices are perceptions in the eye of the beholder.

This analysis is particularly valuable when it facilitates the identification of which essential processes and practices are missing from the current approach to project management. The comparison to best practices also enables the PMO to determine where any project management practices are weak or applied in an isolated manner by one or a few project managers. Of all these analyses, this best-practice comparison, performed against a set of practices in an industry- or standards-based project life cycle, will provide immediate insight for methodology development or improvement.

Develop Project Life Cycle Solution

In its development of a unique and customized project management methodology, the PMO will focus on considerations in this activity that address the needs of the relevant organization. Methodology development is an endeavor led by the PMO, but it requires frequent and detailed input, guidance, support, and approval from a variety of participants in the project management environment. To that end, a methodology development team should be formed to represent the various business interests and assume responsibility for the development effort along with the PMO.

Project management methodology development is not a simple task. Inasmuch as the highlights presented here are intended to be a guide, they are not all-encompassing of the project management methodology development effort. This undertaking requires:

- Patience in constructing detailed process steps
- Business acumen in defining processes and practices that provide a functional fit
- Product and service awareness to ensure alignment of technical processes and interests in project management performance
- Advanced project management skills on the part of developers
- Strong executive and senior management support for the development (and subsequent implementation) effort
- Time, since an average methodology deployment effort can take from 9 to 12 months or more from concept to completion

The PMO also can use the information presented in this section to individually prepare some of the more essential project management processes and practices that may be immediately needed to give structure to its project management effort. Moreover, the acquisition and installation of a project management automated methodology platform is rarely complete without some modification of its content to better fit the processes and practices of the relevant organization. This section can assist PMOs in deliberating and deciding where system modifications can benefit the organization.

Methodology Components

The PMO should weigh the four fundamental methodology components of an effective project management methodology, which can be developed separately or as an integrated guide to project management.

Methodology Process Guide

This methodology component specifies all the steps or activities for which the project manager and project team are responsible. It usually contains a process flowchart that represents the sequence of project management activities to be performed for every project. In addition, it includes considerations for how the process can be scaled down for smaller projects or expanded for larger, more complex, and longer duration projects. This process is created for use by both experienced and novice project managers. In its fundamental form, the methodology process guide serves as a checklist of what is to be accomplished to ensure effective project management.

Methodology Practice Guide

This methodology component contains relevant guidance regarding how to perform the preferred elements of project management as presented in the aforementioned process guide. It provides a step-by-step reference that is made available to project managers, project team members, and anyone else in the project management environment involved in project planning, oversight, and control. Its content should be designed for use by the primary users (including project managers having various levels of experience) and can contain both basic and advanced practices, as may be required by different users for different classifications of projects.

Project Management Glossary

This methodology component provides a reference to standard and common terms used in the project management environment. It ensures that all project stakeholders and participants understand the language of project management. As this facilitates discussions and information exchange, it also reduces occasions for miscommunication. Glossary development proceeds out of the growth of other project management methodology components. It should therefore be expanded as each new methodology component contributes to its content.

The content of the methodology glossary is merely a listing of terms defined for use in the relevant organization. The PMO may want to consider any existing internal documentation of terminology. Alternatively, it may want to provide this component by acquiring a published document containing the requisite terms.

Methodology Toolkit

This component distinctly facilitates the standardization and repeatability that an organizationwide project management practice desires. Methodology tools consist of checklists, forms, and templates applicable to the performance of project management. However, tools also can be developed and implemented in the broader scope of organizational processes. This entails cultivating cross-functional tools and techniques that are applicable to project management or tools that support associated technical processes and business interests. It also includes incorporating automated applications for project management. A more detailed discussion of the tools that can be used to facilitate project management is found in Chapter 2, "Project Management Tools."

Design Process Life Cycle

The process flowchart provides an overall perspective of the routine performance management activities in the relevant organization. Because its guidance will apply to all projects, care must be taken to design an approach applicable to the variety of projects to be encountered. Moreover, there will likely be the need to integrate technical processes. If any one technical process is prevalent in the organization, there should be little difficulty in that alignment. However, if the methodology process is intended for wide use across several business areas, the process design will have to accommodate alignment and integration of a variety of technical processes as well as possible variations in business processes. That said, the focus of this design effort is to ensure that all essential project management processes are appropriately included in the methodology.

For the purposes of illustration and discussion, the four phases of that life cycle are:

- Project initiation
- Solution planning
- Solution implementation
- Project closure

These distinct but related phases ensure the performance of all critical project management activities and tasks. Figure 1.2 depicts the four phases of this project life cycle.

This life cycle model can serve the essential project management guidance needs of most organizations. However, in many industries and

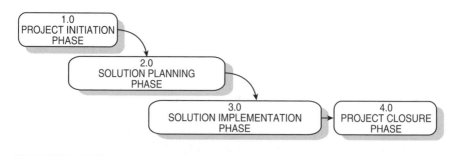

Figure 1.2   Four-Phased Generic Project Life Cycle

technical disciplines, there are definitely conditions that warrant examination of a more comprehensive project management life cycle. In some cases, the project management life cycle may contain five, six, or more phases of project management activity.

Without doubt, the PMO should consider the nature of its business when deliberating and defining the processes of the project management life cycle to be developed. The following indicators suggest the need for a more comprehensive life cycle model:

- Projects are related to product development and necessitate separate phases for design and development oversight.
- The normal project customer base is a combination of both internal and external (commercial) customers, requiring different approaches to manage internal agreements versus external proposals and contracts.
- The business processes of project selection (product or service sales), customer relationship management, and the like are not fully within the purview of the PMO or the project manager.
- The relevant organization performs different phases of projects in geographically detached — perhaps worldwide — locations, thus raising the need for "handoff" phases.
- The organization has considerable distribution of cross-functional work that is best separated by distinct project management phases.
- Senior management is involved and has specified project-review points for making project-continuation decisions that are translated into project phases.

However, if methodology introduction is a new pursuit of the PMO, it may want to begin with a more fundamental process design that can be expanded at a later time.

When using the four-phased project life cycle model, the process content described in the following subsections is recommended. The PMO and methodology development team should interpret these recommended process elements for best fit within the relevant organization. Moreover, the methodology designers should consider these recommendations as an initial and fundamental approach to methodology development. More-advanced content should be pursued as organizational maturity in project management advances.

Project Initiation Phase

The first phase of project management deals with determining what projects will be performed, as well as preparing preliminary documents to validate the project selection decision. The following critical activities should be performed during the project management initiation phase:

- *Opportunity identification and qualification:* Examines each project opportunity to ensure consistency with corporate objectives and business capability.
- *Business case preparation:* Compiles all pertinent business information about the project opportunity to facilitate a project selection decision.
- *Project definition:* This activity, which can be a separate or combined element of the business case, provides a high level description of the project in a single document (used in conjunction with financial data so that a go/no-go decision can be made).
- *Project selection:* An assessment of the relative costs and benefits of each project opportunity, usually against established criteria for selecting projects.
- *Project manager appointment:* Establishes the project's lead management role by the issuance of a "project charter" document that identifies the individual assigned as project manager, specifies the responsibility and authority of the project manager, demonstrates upper management support, and solicits the cooperation and support of other corporate organizations involved in the project.
- *Formal approval to proceed:* Provides for management's review of preliminary project documents, obtains management approval to proceed with the project effort, and specifically authorizes funding so that project planning can begin.

Solution Planning Phase

This phase is characterized by the formation of the project team, the preparation of a proposal, and the development of project plans to be used during project implementation. The following are the critical activities normally performed during the solution planning phase:

- *Project team formation:* Human resources are requested, assigned to the project, and are assembled as a viable working group. Beginning with the project kickoff meeting, project team members review and become familiar with customer requirements and project objectives; are assigned responsibilities; and then prepare to perform detailed planning activities. This activity may be repeated if both a planning/proposal team and a project team are needed during a project.

- *Customer proposal preparation:* A "planning team" (which may be the initial members of the project team) is convened to elicit, review, and validate a customer's requirements and to prepare a formal proposal document in response. The concept of "proposal" can be used even for internal customers to ensure a common understanding of the project's goals.
- *Contract or agreement execution:* This task begins with conducting customer coordination and negotiating a contract or agreement following submission and acceptance of a "proposal" by the customer.
- *Vendor/contractor acquisition:* The need for external project assistance is defined, and the organization initiates procedures for engaging vendors, contractors, and suppliers.
- *Work breakdown structure (WBS) preparation:* A WBS is developed, or project-specific details are added to an existing WBS, to serve as the foundation for project planning efforts and the project risk assessment. The WBS serves as the basis for monitoring, tracking, and controlling the project's cost, schedule, and technical performance during implementation.
- *Project plan preparation:* The project team meets to develop the project plan and any required supporting plans. The project team's involvement is essential because it must plan the details of its performance tasks. At a minimum, a project work plan is needed. The project work plan document normally contains the project WBS plus information about project cost, schedule, and resource utilization.
- *Project risk assessment:* The project team reviews the project work plan (and any other project plan elements) to determine the probability and impact of potential adverse events on project management performance and project success.

    The project team's planning efforts may include developing the following additional project plan components:
    - Risk management plan
    - Implementation/execution plan
    - Quality management plan
    - Contract management plan
    - Test and acceptance plan
    - Audit plan
    - Change control plan
    - Customer relations plan

The project planning effort may also include preparing preliminary technical designs and related documents if these are not otherwise scheduled for preparation during the implementation phase. It can also include a process stop to obtain formal approval to proceed with implementation.

Solution Implementation Phase

The solution implementation phase (sometimes called the execution phase) involves performing the technical work needed to achieve project objectives. The following critical activities are normally part of the solution implementation phase methodology:

- *Project tracking and control:* Along with monitoring and managing project schedule, cost, and resource utilization, the project manager takes corrective actions to minimize cost, schedule, and performance variance when preestablished variance thresholds are exceeded. Tracking and control activities include the ongoing management of risk, quality, and change control.
- *Customer interface management:* The project manager and project team perform these activities to deal with the customer on a day-to-day basis, manage customer expectations, and keep the customer involved and informed concerning project decisions and progress.
- *Subcontractor/vendor management:* The project manager and project team carry out these activities to tend to subcontractors and vendors on a day-to-day basis, oversee their performance and involvement, and manage the associated subcontract or agreement.
- *Contract administration:* The project manager or assigned specialist identify and perform actions needed to manage the customer contract.
- *Project documentation management:* Requirements are established for documenting, distributing, and disposing of project plans, progress reports, and lessons learned.

Project Close Out Phase

This final project management phase ensures a smooth and distinct wrap-up of project activities, both for the project team and the customer. The following critical activities are usually part of the project close out phase:

- *Customer acceptance:* A process is established for reviewing contract requirements and associated deliverables, providing for closure of customer and project issues, and obtaining written customer sign-off and formal acceptance of the project.
- *Project team dispersal:* Project team members are reassigned, and groups and individuals are recognized for their accomplishments.

- *Contract closure:* This activity (in coordination with the company's contract administration office) entails overseeing the end of contract actions with an emphasis on monitoring and managing the final customer invoice and receipt of payment.
- *Operations and maintenance transition:* This activity includes any actions (such as training, documentation, and transfer of responsibility) necessary for facilitating the transfer of processes, equipment, or systems to the ultimate user.
- *Project documentation disposition:* Materials developed and maintained during the project (such as project binder, deliverable designs, progress reports, meeting minutes, and lessons learned) are placed in permanent or semipermanent storage for retrieval and access as historical data that can be used for future project estimating and planning activities.

As the PMO designs the life cycle process, the following is the suggested content for each process element, as can be presented in the methodology process guide:

- Process flowchart with a statement of each phase, activity, and task element
- Process description for each phase, activity, task, subtask, and so forth
- Process input and output (deliverable) for each process element
- Process responsibility, assigned to the individual(s) responsible for completing the process element
- Process scalability, describing how the process element should be reduced or expanded according to project size, value, duration, and complexity

The PMO should determine whether any other elements would enhance the process presentation or benefit users of the methodology. These can be included at the discretion of the methodology development team.

Process guide development is usually performed in association with the introduction of a complete project management life cycle. However, the PMO can begin its effort with process development for specific project life cycle phases or for identified critical process series.

Develop Project Management Practices

This activity addresses the "how-to" aspect of project management. For the PMO and the relevant organization, it is the "how-we-do-it" approach to project management. The practice elements can be directly aligned with process element or prepared in a more general, life cycle approach. That is to say, the practices deployed may apply to more than one process element, and they can be described in the methodology practice guide to illustrate such application across process phases. Because the "how-to" concept may vary across business units and project types, it can be adjusted through particular technical or business methodology processes.

Suggested content of the methodology practice guide component includes presenting guidance to perform the following essential project management activities:

- Select and initiate projects
- Define a project
- Specify project needs and requirements
- Establish a project structure
- Form and manage a project team
- Develop a WBS and project work plan
- Estimate project costs
- Develop a project schedule
- Estimate project resource utilization
- Develop project support plans
- Manage project stakeholder communications
- Manage project reporting
- Manage project documentation
- Manage change and control scope
- Manage project risk
- Ensure project quality
- Manage project team performance
- Track and control project work
- Manage project deliverables and acceptance
- Manage customer contracts
- Manage customer relations
- Manage vendors and contractors
- Close a project

The components in this list provide some degree of coverage for project management activities across the entire project management life cycle. However, when first introducing a structured approach to project management with less than a full life cycle methodology, the PMO can consider and select individual components from this list for early development.

Introduce Methodology Platform

The methodology deployment strategy discussed earlier will provide guidance for how the project management methodology will be deployed for user access. Of the several methodology platforms considered, the PMO will basically treat project management methodology deployment as a paper-based document or as an automated application. The fundamental steps for introduction of these two platforms are described in the following subsections.

Paper-Based Methodology Deployment

This methodology platform compiles those methodology components in document format for distribution to users. Depending on the relevant organization's needs, it can be either a formal or informal publication. However, it is important to ensure that the methodology document is distributed to all stakeholders requiring it. Project managers and project team members, especially key project team members, and conceivably some other stakeholders in the project management environment should be included. The PMO will need to identify the distribution list.

One excellent means of methodology distribution is through participation in project management methodology training. The PMO might consider this avenue as a guide for document distribution, where those who complete methodology training receive a copy of the methodology document.

It is imperative that the PMO be aware of the effort required to produce and distribute even a simple methodology guide. This aspect of methodology deployment can affect the timeliness of methodology introduction in the organization. It may even warrant a planning effort that considers the time, cost, and resources required to accomplish the following production and distribution activities:

- Compile and edit all methodology components
- Obtain methodology development team/management concurrence on final copy
- Identify number of users and, hence, the number of copies needed
- Produce a master methodology document
- Schedule and conduct formal or informal printing or publication
- Prepare any additional methodology training materials
- Plan and conduct publication shipment to training locations

Other factors should be weighed for inclusion in this production and distribution plan as well. In the early stages, the PMO should consider involving a user group to preview and comment on project management methodology content and to establish buy-in.

Automated Methodology Deployment

After the acquired system is installed, this methodology platform is deployed by incorporating the preferred methodology processes and practices of the relevant organization. Even with an automated platform, some or all of the paper-based deployment steps identified above may be performed if published methodology documentation accompanies automated system implementation. When a new, automated methodology system is constructed or it is necessary for an existing one to be modified, that construction or modification effort must be treated as a separate project; the time, cost, and requisite resources must be addressed in planning that project.

Nevertheless, there are a number of steps to consider when planning and conducting the introduction of an automated methodology platform. These include the following prominent planning elements that encumber time, cost, and resources:

- System acquisition
  - Identification of available systems
  - Comparison of system features and functions
  - Selection of a preferred system
  - Management of system acquisition contract and negotiation
  - System shipment and setup
- System installation and testing
- System customization
  - Entry for project management methodology process life cycle component
  - Entry for project management practice component
  - Project management toolkit preparation or attachment
  - System screen customization
  - System report customization
- Project management data entry
  - Project category and handling code setup
  - Resource pool data entry
  - Project information data entry (for each project)
- Project management methodology system training
  - Prepare system-based training program and materials
  - Identify primary training participants (project managers and team members)

    – Identify secondary training participants (functional and senior managers)

    – Schedule and conduct system user training (features and functions)

    – Schedule and conduct methodology user training (processes and practices)

This list represents the highlights of what must be considered for implementation of an automated project management methodology system. It is important to reiterate that it is not intended that the PMO alone conduct such automated system implementation. In fact, the PMO should turn over primary responsibility for this kind of acquisition to the IT/IS department, which will provide full and qualified attention to this effort. However, the PMO should participate in system acquisition planning and system selection to ensure that the needs of the project management community are achieved. Similarly, the PMO staff may retain primary responsibility for guiding or performing system customization and may also be among the first to be trained in system use.

Conduct Methodology Implementation

Project management methodology implementation occurs only when an approved methodology has been developed or acquired, customized as needed to serve its project management environment, and made ready through training for the variety of users within the relevant organization. For any organization, project management methodology implementation is a significant series of activities; for large, multilocation organizations, it is a complex undertaking. Consequently, detailed planning is essential to the success of project management methodology implementation.

The following subsections describe the three primary activities that facilitate project management methodology implementation.

Plan Methodology Implementation

This activity ensures that the relevant organization is prepared for the introduction of a structured, repeatable approach to project management. It involves planning the means by which the project managers and project team members welcome the project management methodology, executive and senior managers support it, and how it is introduced for use in the project management environment.

Facilitated by the PMO, the project management methodology implementation planning effort can begin with a meeting of key implementation planners. The purpose of this meeting is to decide on what project management implementation actions will be conducted and to prepare plans accordingly.

The following seven suggested actions for project management methodology implementation warrant PMO consideration and associated planning. Adding these or any other elements to the project management methodology implementation plan should be augmented by sufficient planning guidance regarding the cost, completion dates, and the resources required to conduct each methodology implementation activity.

Executive Management Support

The involvement and validation of top executives and managers cannot be understated. Their demonstrated support is essential to the success of project management methodology implementation. Conversely, the absence, or perceived absence, of executive level commitment to the established project management process will cause inadequate and incomplete implementation. The methodology implementation plan, therefore, should specify what actions executives will take and in which activities they will participate to demonstrate support and endorsement of the project management methodology. At a minimum, a key executive should take part in communicating the project management methodology use policy developed in the methodology deployment strategy.

Formation of Methodology Users Group

The PMO should consider and recommend formation of a methodology users group. This group will likely play a very critical role in implementing the project management methodology by having direct and positive influence on its successful outcome. The PMO should include recommendations for user group participation, which may consist of selected project managers or all project management methodology users. In that respect, if a methodology users group fits the culture of the relevant organization, it should be included in the project management implementation plan.

Formation of Methodology Implementation Team

The methodology implementation team works to facilitate implementation for each project and at each methodology implementation location. The implementation team should include project management mentors, who are normally characterized by their familiarity with advanced project management concepts, a complete understanding of the methodology to be implemented, and a dedication to achieving the methodology implementation objectives. The methodology implementation team members will work side by side with project managers and project team members as the new methodology is introduced. Methodology implementation team and associated project management mentor activities can encompass:

- Facilitating project manager and project team first-time use of the project management methodology processes and practices
- Clarifying requirements and guidance contained in the methodology
- Listening to and compiling user concerns about methodology use for later analysis, which signifies that users have a voice in subsequent revisions to the methodology or in immediate actions to correct methodology errors or omissions
- Observing early methodology performance to evaluate user acceptance and effectiveness of its application on projects and, later, prepare reports of findings
- Working in conjunction with the methodology users group to understand and resolve implementation problems and issues

The methodology implementation team may benefit from the addition of external project management consultants to serve primarily as mentors. This provides independent assessment of the success of project management methodology implementation and initial methodology performance. It is strongly recommended that use of a project management methodology implementation team be included in the implementation plan.

User Assistance for Methodology Implementation

The PMO can arrange for additional methodology implementation support to users by planning the following:

- Establishment of a telephone help line or help desk to facilitate implementation of project management methodology
- Creation of an intranet Web page dedicated to implementation of project management methodology
- Use of e-mail, chat rooms, and other collaboration tools to exchange real-time, critical implementation information

Development of Methodology Feedback Mechanism

This feedback mechanism provides the capability to measure and collect information from methodology users. In cases where project management methodology implementation is conducted as a "pilot" program, such feedback will support near-term revision of the methodology. Participants in methodology implementation must be aware that their evaluation is required and that timely feedback is needed to improve the methodology before an expanded implementation takes place across an entire organization. Not only is this feedback mechanism critical in the initial methodology implementation, but it can also be used for ongoing evaluation of methodology deployment.

In planning for this mechanism, the PMO should identify the process by which user feedback can be provided, including:

■ Prescribed content of a methodology user feedback report
■ Desired timeliness and frequency of feedback reporting
■ Specification of feedback report submittal process
■ Identification of feedback report distribution
■ Process for review and evaluation of feedback reports
■ Procedure for replying to users who provide feedback reports

The feedback reporting process must be a bona fide activity that provides two-way communication because it demonstrates serious consideration of the content of each feedback report from users. The methodology implementation plan should convey both the process and the intent of the feedback mechanism to be used.

Development of Methodology Training Plan

The PMO prepares this plan to identify training for users of the new methodology. All relevant stakeholders in the project management environment should be offered the opportunity to attend. Thus, a complete project management training program would aim to provide the following participants with the level of training indicated:

■ *Project managers:* Detailed project management methodology process and practice training; and, if automation is introduced, system feature and function training
■ *Project team members:* Appropriate project management process and practice training; and, if automation is introduced, system feature and function familiarization
■ *Business unit managers:* Adequate familiarization with processes and practices and, if automation is introduced, system feature and function training as needed
■ *Senior managers:* Familiarization with methodology overview to acquaint managers with the new approach to project management

A new project management methodology is usually introduced through a formal training program that is specifically designed to present its technical, management, and business aspects. However, if formal training is not pursued, some type of methodology familiarization program must be conducted for methodology users. The type and proposed dates of project management user training for each user category are presented in this plan.

Methodology Promotion Planning

The PMO should deliberate the desired approach and specify organizational promotional programs and upper-management endorsement activities that will be used to support project management methodology implementation. In addition, internal and external publicity notices and promotions can be planned to demonstrate the organization's enthusiasm as it anticipates and conducts implementation of the project management methodology.

Plan Project Transition

Although this activity can be included in the project management methodology implementation plan, it is identified separately because of its importance to the success of methodology deployment. As a result, the PMO must provide strong leadership in planning and conducting the transition of individual projects to the newly implemented methodology.

The following five activities are recommended to assist the PMO in conducting a complete and comprehensive project transition planning effort. Because the process of conducting project transition to a new methodology can be very complex, the PMO should remove unnecessary transition burden for users through preparation of a comprehensive project transition plan that facilitates a smooth transition.

Prepare Project Transition Strategy

The PMO, with input and guidance from senior management, should lead the project management methodology implementation team in the development of a general project transition strategy. This strategy provides guidance for determining which projects to transition; which to complete using current processes, practices, and tools; and which to forgo from transition. The strategy also should address the scope of initial and subsequent implementation activities, i.e., one business unit, corporate-wide, several business units, or geographical dispersion.

The transition strategy normally includes the following information:

- The criteria to be used to classify which projects are candidates for transition to the new project management methodology
- The criteria to be used to identify the point of transition in the new methodology for projects at different junctures in the project management life cycle
- The recommended sequence and proposed schedule for project transition, i.e., by project type or classification, by business unit, and by geographical location

Review Project Status

Project managers can be led by the PMO in the compilation of relevant information for each active project to be transitioned to the new methodology. The PMO should obtain this information from current project managers and analyze it as input to project-transition decisions. Project information includes the items listed below for each project in progress or new project expected to begin during the methodology implementation period:

- Name of project
- General project information (project size, estimated total project value, and degree of project complexity)
- Planned project start and finish dates
- Actual project start date and any revised finish date
- Project location(s)
- Name of project manager and number of project team members
- List of project stakeholders (name, position, and organization)
- Where the project is in the project management life cycle
- Project manager's assessment of how well the customer will respond to changes resulting from use of the new methodology
- Project manager's appraisal of the project team's acceptance of the new methodology
- Project manager's analysis of the need and locations for implementation assistance and project management mentor support

The result of this review is the identification of projects that are candidates for transition to the new methodology.

Conduct Project Transition Interviews

The PMO arranges and conducts interviews with each project manager responsible for the projects selected for transition. The interviews are used to:

- Identify current issues with the project
- Review and examine project information that each project manager provides
- Review relevant project documentation
- Identify issues and constraints that will influence the implementation of the new methodology on the specific project
- Identify the appropriate transition time period
- Determine project managers' concerns relative to implementation of the new methodology
- Identify and plan resolutions to transition roadblocks

Perform Transition Assessment and Gap Analysis

The PMO leads a review of all project information obtained during the interviews and meetings with the project managers. Moreover, the PMO, along with the methodology implementation team, assesses each project's needs for an effective transition to the new methodology. The assessment and analysis should:

- Evaluate the application of the new methodology to each project
- Distinguish the gaps between current project documentation and documentation that the new methodology requires
- Determine, through gap analysis, the completion requirements of each project relative to the new methodology
- Categorize any special program issues or impacts regarding the new methodology implementation that should be considered in planning the business transition
- Calculate the impact of transition on project staff workload
- Identify corporation program stakeholder groups and develop recommendations for their involvement in the new methodology implementation
- Determine the need for additional resources
- Identify special requirements for project management support, training, and mentoring

Prepare Project Transition Plan

The PMO leads the implementation team in constructing a detailed project transition plan using information obtained in the above activities. The plan presents the general transition approach to be used for all projects in the relevant organization and specifies:

- The transition point in the new methodology life cycle for each project transitioning to the new methodology
- Mandatory or optional new methodology documentation to be completed for each project
- Additional resources required to facilitate project transition for each project, i.e., project data entry, document preparation and transfer work, and so forth
- The project transition activity schedule, including training for project managers and project teams, dates of transition to the new methodology, and dates of any needed project management support or mentoring

Conduct Methodology Training and Implementation

The completion of exhaustive planning by the PMO and the methodology implementation team will serve to guide project management methodology implementation activities. Per established plans, the PMO can oversee the following four project management implementation activities.

Conduct Methodology User Training

Deliver the prescribed methodology training or other methodology familiarization programs in accordance with the methodology training plan. As suggested earlier in this PMO function, completion of project management methodology training should warrant individual receipt of any methodology documentation or system access for immediate use by training program participants.

Execute the Methodology Implementation Plan

Introduce project implementation team support and accompanying project management mentoring in conjunction with the completion of methodology user training. Provide methodology implementation support as outlined in the methodology implementation plan.

Activate User Feedback Mechanism

Provide instructions to everyone involved in methodology implementation regarding the process and means to provide initial methodology use feedback. Reinforce the importance of this activity and demonstrate the value of each user's participation. Initiate feedback analysis activities, and provide replies to participating users.

Execute the Project Transition Plan

Monitor, manage, and assist project managers in their efforts to transition each project to the new project management methodology. This is particularly critical for project managers who have responsibility for more than one project transition. Ensure that PMO or methodology implementation team members are available to assist with issues or to arrange for additional resource support.

Manage Methodology Maturity

Project management methodology deployment requires ongoing PMO attention. Regardless of whether initial methodology implementation is limited to a few key processes and practices or deployed as a full project management life cycle solution, the PMO must ensure its mission is achieving the desired business objectives. Moreover, the PMO will also want to examine opportunities for methodology expansion and improvement, based on the identified needs of the users, alignment with business functions, and capability for introduction of advanced concepts in the project management environment.

Three activities, described in the following subsections, characterize oversight of the project management methodology throughout the PMO's and the organization's maturation stages in project management capability.

Evaluate Methodology Deployment

Because the PMO is responsible for overseeing project management methodology deployment, it is adequately positioned to evaluate the effectiveness of the deployment process as well as the problems encountered. Evaluation begins with the initial introduction of fundamental components of methodology processes and practices and is expanded for larger-scope, project management life cycle methodology implementation.

The PMO should monitor and evaluate several key points of project management methodology deployment:

- Readiness for using the project management methodology platform
- Completion of the methodology user training schedule
- Finalization of the methodology implementation activity schedule
- Accomplishment of project transitions to the new processes and practices
- Achievement of initial methodology performance capability
- Acceptance and satisfactory levels of initial use of the project management methodology

The PMO should track each of these items to identify and correct any difficulties that the methodology implementation team or the new methodology users encounter. In addition, problems or issues arising from this deployment and identified through conscientious evaluation can be reviewed. The lessons learned can be applied to the next stage of project management methodology deployment.

The PMO should develop procedures for conducting its methodology deployment evaluation, possibly including these in the project management methodology implementation plan. Likewise, the feedback mechanism established for methodology implementation also can be used to solicit deployment evaluation information from project managers. This evaluation can be concluded when the PMO is prepared to announce that the project management methodology deployment has been completed.

Analyze Methodology Performance

Because of its oversight responsibility, the PMO's initial decision and subsequent effort to deploy the project management methodology is a strong indication that the PMO believes there are benefits to be achieved through wide use across the relevant organization. This analysis activity facilitates the ongoing examination of the performance of project management methodology, enabling the PMO to ensure that the organization receives maximum benefits from the use of this methodology.

Methodology performance analyses should be conducted at recurring intervals that provide sufficient time to apply PMO corrective actions in response to poor methodology performance results. Upon completing the deployment of a life cycle methodology, the PMO may want to consider a quarterly examination for the first year. Then, with the achievement of favorable ongoing performance indicators, the PMO may shift to an annual examination of the project management methodology.

In analyzing the performance of the project management methodology, the PMO should accomplish at a minimum the three primary actions described in the following subsections.

Measure Methodology Use

Establish procedures to measure who and how many people in the project management environment are using the full or partial capabilities of the project management methodology. This analysis should determine whether there are any common indicators of use or nonuse, or any isolated occurrences of nonuse that need to be addressed. The PMO can prepare methodology utilization trend charts as analysis aids.

It is assumed that a PMO will seek full implementation of the project management methodology in the project management environment, particularly if the methodology provides complete life cycle coverage of the project effort. This analysis element should be designed to indicate levels of use by project managers, project team members, and other project stakeholders, as well as the extent of use across business units in the relevant organization. The PMO can then delve into the causes for any reduced use and apply actions to rectify the situation.

Evaluate Methodology Effectiveness

This analysis item may present the greatest challenge for the PMO. However, it is essential if the PMO is to determine the benefits realized from the deployment of project management methodology. The evaluation includes identification and analysis of the following example performance indicators:

- Project completion rates (on time, on budget)
- Project completion rates for individual project managers
- Project planning and associated scope change management impacts
- Efficiency of resource utilization and management
- Quality of project deliverables and customer acceptance
- Level of stakeholder communication and customer satisfaction

Other indicators designed to measure methodology contributions to project performance and achievement of the relevant organization's business interests can be added for PMO analysis.

This assessment warrants development of specific indicators to demonstrate performance within the relevant organization. Therefore, the PMO should convene a senior management meeting to establish recommended analysis criteria and solicit input on areas of management interest in developing the procedures for this analysis. Because the PMO in all likelihood will forward methodology performance analysis reports to managers throughout the project management environment, it would behoove the PMO to collaborate with senior managers on their expectations in advance.

Evaluate PMO Effectiveness

The PMO should establish a self-examination mechanism to determine its effectiveness at identifying and responding to the results of methodology performance indicators. In particular, the PMO may want to evaluate the effectiveness of its project management methodology in the following areas:

- Completeness and usability of performance and analysis procedures
- Adequacy of performance indicators used
- Quality of performance analyses conducted
- Value of the frequency of analyses that the PMO conducts

Manage Methodology Improvements

The PMO has responsibility for overseeing the initial and ongoing design and development of the project management methodology. As part of this effort, the PMO must determine how often and when any updates or revisions of project management methodology will be pursued. The PMO must then plan and conduct methodology modification per the change and improvement recommendations received from project managers, project team members, and other stakeholders in the project management environment — the end users of project management methodology.

POSTSCRIPT FOR THE SMALLER PMO

These postscript notes are included at the end of each chapter to indicate the simpler solutions that a smaller PMO might pursue to achieve some semblance of the prescribed functionality, even when there are conditions of reduced resources, inadequate funding, and limited mandate or support. However, in this first chapter on PMO functions, there is little recourse for the smaller PMO because the topic of this chapter — project management methodology —is a fundamental purpose of the PMO. Therefore, even the smallest PMO will need to focus on many of the project management methodology development and implementation activities presented in the basic PMO function model.

Nevertheless, there is a three-step approach that the smaller PMO can follow to ease the possible burdens of limited influence and staffing:

Establish Simple, Critical Procedures for Project Management

Identify the standards to be referenced and initially build simple processes for a few of the more critical project management activities within the relevant organization. Such processes might include:

- Defining the project
- Preparing the project work plan (by using a work breakdown structure with estimates of cost, schedule, and resource utilization)

- Assessing project risks
- Managing project quality
- Tracking and controlling project progress
- Reporting project status
- Conducting project close out

Processes for these or other critical activities in the project management environment should be developed and implemented across multiple projects — as many projects as project managers can support in an initial process implementation effort.

When success is achieved through implementation of initial processes, the effort can be expanded for more comprehensive coverage of process development and implementation across the project management life cycle.

Gain Increased Support to Construct and Implement More Processes

The PMOs best intentions can be undermined by a lack of support for process (methodology) implementation by key project management participants. Therefore, it is essential for the PMO to elicit the support of project managers and senior management during this effort.

Pursue the support of individual project managers by:

- Making the processes reasonably easy to use
- Giving project managers flexibility in process implementation
- Incorporating forms, templates, and checklists to accompany process guidance
- Soliciting input of project managers in developing forms, templates, and checklists
- Introducing existing methods and procedures that work well for individuals and would benefit other project managers when used more widely

Senior management buy-in can be achieved by demonstrating how a common approach to project management, applied across all projects, enables aggregate project information to be compiled to facilitate business decisions.

Expand and Incorporate Technical Processes

Expand existing processes to provide a more complete life cycle coverage of project management. After establishing the critical processes, move on to the next level and set up the essential processes of a complete and effective project management methodology.

In turn, as the methodology is completed, technical performance activities can be linked to the process.

2

PROJECT MANAGEMENT
TOOLS

"Tools of the trade" enable individuals in any profession to perform their work more effectively, efficiently, and consistently. This applies to project management, where tool utilization is similarly pursued. In today's project management environment, the project management office (PMO) can serve its constituency well by providing support and guidance regarding the selection, implementation, and use of project management tools.

The tools needed in today's project environment are predominantly automated software applications. However, there are still many paper-based tools, such as activity checklists, data collection templates, process guides, and knowledge-based desk references that also facilitate project management. The introduction and management of project management tools can be accomplished on an as-needed basis by ad hoc teams or individuals or, when aligned as a PMO function, as part of ongoing operations planning within the project environment.

The "project management tools" function enables the PMO to:

- Determine the types of tools that are needed and that fit within the project management environment
- Plan and manage project management tool selection, implementation, and maintenance
- Monitor and manage the consistent use of project management tools
- Provide training in the use of project management tools for users at various levels of expertise
- Ensure that requirements for tool integration with existing systems and processes are achieved

Professional project managers will inherently seek ways to enhance their performance, make project work proceed smoothly, evaluate project information, and manage project team activities. Whereas each project manager will choose tools appropriate for the task at hand, project managers with more experience will likely have developed a selection of preferred tools. Thus the PMO challenge will be in (a) evaluating the tools that individuals are already using and (b) achieving consensus among project managers for the selection and use of common project management tools that will provide a consistent approach within the project environment. It is essential, therefore, that this PMO function consider the project managers' insights and recommendations for project management tools. However, it is also incumbent on the PMO to do its own homework so that it can identify the needs for organizational tools and adequately research the marketplace availability or in-house development of tools to satisfy those needs. In addition, the PMO should prepare for its responsibility in overseeing tool utilization and maintenance once the tools are acquired or developed and implemented.

PROJECT ENVIRONMENT INTERFACE CONCEPTS

The key aspect of this PMO function lies in the concept that implementation and utilization of project management tools are centrally controlled activities. Although the PMO considers individual project manager requests and recommendations concerning tools used in the project management environment, it discounts or eliminates those tools that are not compatible with preferred processes and practices or that require extended effort to transfer or combine data types and results across projects for higher level reviews. The PMO's "project management tools" function helps to establish standard applications and systems used across all projects, thereby facilitating the communication of more-accurate and timely information about projects and the project environment. The PMO will need to address the challenge of providing project tools that facilitate proper user access at the right time and provide added value to the project management endeavor.

This PMO function requires collaboration with stakeholders in the project environment to ascertain their perspectives on tool needs and use. Traditionally, discussions about project management tools have focused on managing project cost, schedule, and resources — and there is still a prevalent need for those types of tools. Today, however, there is an additional need to consider tools that can implement modern project management concepts, support a project manager's broader business responsibilities, and oversee multiple projects and management of project portfolios.

The PMO can address the "project management tools" function by recognizing the various types of tools necessary to accomplish the project management objectives. However, the PMO must also examine a wider variety of tools needed in the project environment, including tools from the following categories:

- *Project life cycle management:* Tools facilitating the accomplishment of project management activities:
  - Project methodology systems
  - Project methodology process organizers
  - Process step and checklist managers
- *Project planning and oversight:* Tools providing for planning, monitoring, and managing project performance:
  - Work breakdown structure (WBS) managers
  - Project schedule managers
  - Project cost managers
  - Project resource managers
  - Task performance managers
  - Timesheets and time management applications
  - Executive dashboards
- *Project collaboration:* Tools enabling project team members and project stakeholders to communicate and to exchange and review pertinent information about each project, individually and collectively:
  - Meeting managers
  - Reporting systems
  - E-mail systems
  - On-line "chat room" systems
  - Team collaboration systems
- *Document management:* Tools facilitating development and management of project requirements and specifications, project plans, technical guidance, and other relevant documents:
  - Word processor applications
  - Spreadsheet applications
  - Database applications
  - Computer-aided design (CAD) and drawing creation and storage applications
  - Document management systems
- *Business systems:* Tools enabling the business aspects of project management to be integrated for use by the PMO, project managers, and other project stakeholders:
  - Portfolio management systems
  - Business case and requirements capture tools

- Contract and agreement managers
- Customer management systems
- Vendor, consultant, and supplier (subcontractor) management systems
- Equipment acquisition, assignment, and management applications
- Proposal management systems
- Facility management applications
■ *Project environment support:* Tools enabling the PMO or other relevant stakeholders in the project environment to examine capability, implement practices, and conduct operational planning for improvement:
  - Project management capability/maturity assessment applications
  - Knowledge management systems
  - Training management and on-line training access systems
  - Personnel and staff information management systems
  - Metrics management applications

These categories of project management tools provide some guidance for the PMO in its ongoing responsibility to evaluate and recommend tools that enhance the relevant organization's capability in project management, thus increasing the likelihood of success for project managers.

BUSINESS ENVIRONMENT INTERFACE CONCEPTS

Project management tools are selected with the principal goal of supporting project managers and their teams. However, by its nature, project management is distinctly aligned with different business functions. Project management, and associated project work, is a critical representation of the organization's business. Therefore, the project management tools used in the project management environment directly affect the creation and exchange of vital business information. In many cases, entities on the business-side of the organization will recognize that their input is crucial to project management tool selection and implementation as well. A brief review of the types of tools examined for use in the project environment, as presented in the previous section, shows how information created, collected, calculated, and stored through the use of project management tools is also a valuable asset to the business functions of the organization.

The following list highlights some examples of cross-functional business use of project management tools. Of course, the culture of each organization will determine whether the following functional roles are considered project stakeholders. Notwithstanding that label, these functional roles will have interest in the output of project management tools:

- *Executives:* Executive dashboards and portfolio-management systems facilitate senior level management decisions for project selection, continuation, and termination, as well as decisions concerning overall resource allocation. This includes the receipt and review of associated project status and progress reports. The executive role extends to participants on senior level control and advisory boards as well as business committees.
- *Resource managers:* Project resources are frequently not assigned exclusively to the PMO or to the project manager on a full-time basis. Therefore, management of the project resource matrix is necessary for project team formation. Resource managers need access to information about resource utilization, which can be provided by several types of project management tools.
- *Functional support managers:* Organizational managers in traditional business areas will find project information sufficiently relevant to their business efforts to warrant their inclusion as users of project management tools.
  - Business development and sales managers will have an interest in performing project initiation tasks and customer interface activities as outlined and managed in the methodology tool. Consequently, they will have at least some interest in monitoring project progress for customer satisfaction, perhaps using the executive dashboard.
  - Marketing managers will be looking for project and customer information to develop targeting strategies and to promote project successes in publications and news releases. They will be seeking access to project information databases across the spectrum of project management tools.
  - Human resource managers hold ultimate responsibility for ensuring recruitment and retention of qualified project managers and team members to fulfill all project commitments. These managers will have a definite interest in project management tools that capture and convey resource assignments, performance, and future commitments. Alternatively, these project management tools can also support the human-resource department's job of maintaining an appropriate supply of qualified project managers.
  - Finance and accounting managers, legal advisors, contract and procurement managers, and facility and equipment managers play various direct and indirect roles in supporting project management. Managers in these functional areas can gain useful access to pertinent information from many project management tools.

■ *Customers and subcontractors:* External parties as well as internal customers who have an interest in project information can access reporting tools from a network or Web-based applications to obtain project status and customized progress reports. Using collaboration tools, this group also can respond to and comment on project status and participate in associated on-line discussions and meetings. Moreover, automated invoice and payment systems, as might be found within a comprehensive contract or vendor-management system, would be useful to this audience.

The PMO can best serve the relevant organization by including these business function managers in its deliberations and decisions concerning acquisition or development and use of project management tools.

PROJECT MANAGEMENT TOOLS ACTIVITIES ACROSS THE PMO CONTINUUM

The progression of the "project management tools" function along the PMO competency continuum is characterized by an early capability to implement a standard toolset across projects, followed by increasing introduction and use of enterprise level business applications.

Table 2.1 presents an overview of the range of prescribed PMO project management tools activities according to each level in the PMO competency continuum.

The *project office* is the primary user of the project management tools that a higher level PMO has selected and implemented. In the absence of a higher level PMO, it may independently acquire and use the tools it needs to conduct project management. However, tool acquisition and implementation decisions are usually made in collaboration with project and functional managers.

Mid-range PMO levels of the continuum have the responsibility of introducing progressively advanced project management toolsets based on project environment needs. One primary goal is to implement tools that bolster existing project management processes and practices or that otherwise support a deliberate decision to change processes and practices according to the new tool's guidance. The mid-range PMO distinctly performs tool management when recognizing that tool introductions inherently establish a common approach to project management that will be used across all projects. As the PMO introduces more advanced tools to integrate the business aspects of project management, that common approach is then extended across the enterprise. In particular, the *standard PMO* and *advanced PMO* provide comprehensive tools that comprise the

Table 2.1 Range of Project Management Tools' Activities across the PMO Continuum

Project Office	Basic PMO	Standard PMO	Advanced PMO	Center of Excellence
Recommends new tools and applies available project management tools to achieve project oversight and control objectives	Introduces a set of fundamental project management tools ■ Identifies the organization's need for tools ■ Manages selection, acquisition, or development of tools ■ Facilitates tool implementation ■ Conducts training on the use of project management tools	Introduces more advanced project management tools ■ Conducts tool research and comparison to ensure fit within project environment ■ Monitors utilization of project management tools ■ Evaluates performance of project management tools	Introduces a viable project knowledge management system and tools ■ Establishes a project-by-project Web presence ■ Structures a complete project- and business-information database ■ Implements an executive dashboard	Oversees advanced business toolsets that extend into all business functions ■ Designs and implements enterprisewide tool solutions ■ Introduces external user access to project management tools ■ Examines and implements personal digital assistants (PDAs) and wireless tool solutions

hardware and software components of the organization's project management information system.

The *center of excellence* continues in its role as a business function responsible for integrating business performance in the project environment. It monitors project management tool selection and implementation with a concern for enterprisewide impacts and integration. It also determines the benefits and opportunities for the organization in connecting external users. As a result, it develops tool access rules and procedural guidance to bring customers and vendors into the organization's real-time project management information system.

The PMO's "project management tools" function provides project managers and project team members with timely access to pertinent information and guidance in the project environment. It also accommodates access to project information on a real-time basis per the individual needs of project stakeholders.

PROJECT MANAGEMENT TOOLS FUNCTION MODEL

The PMO's "project management tools" function model captures the process by which the PMO can introduce any tools deemed appropriate for use in the project management environment. The primary activities of the PMO's "project management tools" function model are depicted in Figure 2.1. Each activity is described in the following subsections.

Select Project Tools

The PMO is ideally positioned to lead project management tool selection through its affiliation and interface role with each project manager, project team member, and other stakeholders in the project environment — the

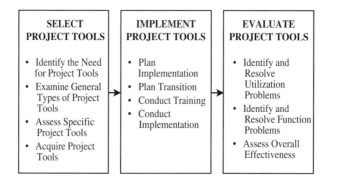

Figure 2.1 "Project Management Tools" Function Model

end users of project management tools. Inasmuch as tools are selected to facilitate project management, the PMO is wise to consult with these project participants as it considers the following steps in the process of selecting project management tools.

Identify the Need for Project Tools

Professionals in the project management discipline will likely support the need for project management tools that help to achieve project management objectives and business success. Many will have preferred products and solutions in mind when discussions arise, and thus individual contributions of knowledge about tool preferences warrant consideration. However, it is incumbent upon the PMO to establish tool selection parameters and find common benefits for the relevant organization in its ongoing search for appropriate project management tools. This includes translating individual and collective tool preferences into solutions actually needed within the project environment.

The PMO can identify the needs for project management tools in three ways:

■ Examine the current environment
■ Evaluate requests and recommendations for tools
■ Determine PMO-prescribed tools

Examine the Current Environment

The PMO can begin identifying project management tool requirements by examining the current project environment for performance results and reporting capability. This examination should identify what tools are currently being used, individually or collectively; their effectiveness in supporting project management; and their responsiveness to project management reporting requirements. Such an examination may be a casual effort or a formally planned activity that includes user surveys and tool inspections. The results of this examination should provide sufficient indications of which tools are present in the project environment, how they are being used, and user preferences for each tool.

The PMO can use these results to analyze current tool functionality and utilization. This includes a comparison to the desired state of tool use across projects and a determination of the level of tool standardization within the project environment.

Examining project management tools currently found within the project management environment enables the PMO to establish a baseline for tools utilization from which future tool standardization and functional capability enhancements can be planned. In particular, the PMO should review tool examination results against its goals for implementing best practices to see where gaps exist in the functionality of project management tools. Those gaps that are uncovered represent either the need for tool standardization or for expanded tool functionality, warranting selection of new tools.

Evaluate Requests and Recommendations for Tools

Individuals responsible for conducting project management activities may be a primary source for identifying needed tools. Project managers at the forefront of project activities are likely to be aware of tools and their functionality through ongoing efforts to improve project and personal performance. The PMO should consult these professionals to identify needs in the workplace and to establish a process for receiving and evaluating requests and recommendations for tool acquisition and use.

The ideal PMO goal is standardization of project management tools across the relevant organization. However, there are always exceptions to the rule. Individual requests or recommendations for project management tools may also have implications and benefits within the project environment. Nevertheless, individuals will need specialized tools on occasions to accomplish their jobs.

The PMO should set up a mechanism to receive requests and recommendations for new project management tools. The PMO can thereby monitor the interests and the intentions of project managers within the relevant organization. It can also collect information about project manager tool preferences as a means to maintaining an ongoing assessment of what tools are in the project environment.

Determine PMO-Prescribed Tools

The PMO should be proactive in its own examination of the need for project management tools in the project environment. It can perform this activity on a casual basis or as an event in response to project performance reviews. In essence, the PMO identifies problem areas it believes can be resolved through the acquisition and implementation of project management tools. It then conducts research to find out which tools would best be utilized and makes independent decisions to acquire and implement the project management tools that best fit the project management environment.

However, note that even PMO-prescribed tools will require some advance collaboration with the ultimate users in the project management environment. To that end, the PMO may want to establish a project management tools evaluation committee comprising participants from the project environment. This committee could review both individual requests and recommendations for project management tools as well as PMO-prescribed tools for the users.

Examine General Types of Project Tools

The PMO will need to choose from among the various types of tools that can be created in-house or that are available in the marketplace. The following subsections provide a brief overview of the types of project tools that the PMO can consider.

Paper-Based Tools

This type of tool can be created in-house under PMO guidance or purchased as a commercially prepared toolkit. These tools are commonly classified as templates, checklists, and forms. Although referred to as paper-based, this type of tool will usually have a basis in an automated software application. Paper-based tools can be created using common word processors, spreadsheets applications, and database applications. Many project management software applications also provide the means to develop paper-based tools. Some even enable users to attach externally prepared tools (documents). The manufacturers of commercially prepared toolkits usually bundle a variety of tools together to achieve specific project management objectives. Such toolkits can be obtained to guide data collection and reporting over the entire project management life cycle.

Automated Tools

There are a multitude of automated project management tools available in the marketplace. This type of tool normally resides on desktop work-stations for individual users or on a network for multiple users. For the purposes of this model, we will examine two types of automated project management tools: the simple automated tool and the integrated auto-mated tool.

In general, the simple automated tool normally resides on the com-puter's desktop to serve one user. The simple automated tool is usually characterized by singular functionality, its own database, and a limited exchange of data outside the application. This is not to say that simple automated tools cannot share information, but that is usually accomplished by an export function or a non-dynamic link. Rather, the simple tool maintains data in local computers solely for the purposes of its primary uses.

Conversely, the integrated automated tool normally resides on a network server and has multiple purposes and usually several functions that different users can access. Some users may never see or access certain functions of the integrated tool. The tool, nevertheless, maintains cross-functional data and enables cross-functional reporting and data access by multiple users. In some cases, the integrated tool will retrieve data and information automatically from other automated tools through dynamic links that are constructed at installation. However, even integrated project management tools are limited to the purposes of their several functions. The PMO should therefore also consider use of enterprisewide management systems. These are integrated automated tools designed for business use, but they could have application in the project management environment as well.

Web-Based Tools

There are valid arguments and discussions in industry regarding the use of Web-based tools versus network-based tools. Often, it comes down to individual organizational preferences and the information technology (IT) department's policies and recommendations for use of Web-based tools. The focus of this consideration, however, lies in the fact that project management applications are available on the Web. The PMO should consider these externally based tools for use in its project environment based on the relevant organization's need for Web-based tools that can be accessed via the Internet, on the expense incurred for their use, and on the reliability of the application provider.

PDAs and Wireless Tools

With new technological innovations arriving almost daily, the PMO must consider the extent to which they will infiltrate or otherwise impact the project environment. In particular, the use of personal digital assistants (PDAs) is expected to be as prevalent as the desktop computer within the next few years. The PMO must determine how it will develop or otherwise acquire project management tools for PDA use and wireless operations. Of course, this requires close collaboration with the organization's IT department, with recognition that this could be a significant system upgrade and financial investment.

Assess Specific Project Tools

The PMO should position itself as the key evaluator for introducing new project management tools. As the need for project management tools emerges, the PMO should be prepared to identify available products and assess their capability to satisfy its tool needs. The PMO should establish a process that enables specific project tools to be assessed. This begins with a general search for tools that appear to provide the desired solution. A preliminary list of available tools is then reviewed to determine how closely they are aligned with the desired solution. The resulting short list of candidate tools is subjected to rigorous examination, possibly including collaboration with the vendor, and should include the following factors:

- *Functions and features:* Criteria for tool functions and features are developed for each new project management tool identified. Each tool is then examined to determine if it has the desired functionality and preferred features.
- *Vendors:* The PMO may already have a list of vendors prequalified for use in the project environment. In this case, the PMO can review the vendor's history to ascertain product quality and service for a tool being examined. If such a list does not exist, the PMO will likely need to contact the vendors to screen them for product and service quality.
- *Implementation:* An important part of tool examination includes determining the level of effort and vendor support required for tool implementation. When a preferred tool is identified, this usually becomes a secondary issue unless tool implementation requires extended planning and technical knowledge and skill. Evaluating implementation requirements and vendor support then becomes a tool selection factor.
- *Maintenance:* Business environments today have become accustomed to automated products that generally do not appear to require extensive maintenance. This perception is often fueled by the behind-the-scenes work of the IT department. The IT people will frequently perform application checks, resolve isolated software problems, and even install new software versions in a way that is not apparent to the user population. This is mentioned because project management software requires the same level of attention. In some cases, it may require greater attention of the IT group, including routine and special requirements for data transfers.
- *Costs:* The cost of project management tools is a factor that the PMO must consider, as project management tools can, in some cases, be quite costly, particularly when intended for multiple users. The PMO should include project management tools when preparing its activity budget. If other departmental budgets are used, the PMO will have to collaborate with those functions to ensure funding availability. Cost, however, remains an important factor in the make-or-buy decision, which implies that the PMO may also consider in-house development of the project management tool.

■ *Customization:* In acquiring a project management tool, the PMO may also contemplate some alternatives. In some cases, vendors will work with their customers to modify or adapt their automated applications for better fit within the intended project management environment. Of course, this can incur substantial additional acquisition costs.

The PMO's screening of new project management tools will ensure the closest possible fit for the intended purpose of the tool. This is an activity that the PMO staff, or an ad hoc committee managed by or aligned with the PMO, can perform.

Acquire Project Tools

After completing the screening of the candidate project management tools, the PMO should be able to make a decision on the preferred tool. Weighing all the factors in the screening process should provide sufficient insight into how well the tool will fit within the project management environment. The PMO then follows several steps to acquire the tools.

First, the PMO confirms that tool acquisition (i.e., purchase) is a better alternative than in-house tool development. Information from the tool screening process is evaluated along with cost and other selection factors; tool customization options should also be considered. Finally, a make-or-buy decision is made, with a buy decision representing approval to proceed with tool acquisition. It is important to note that a project management tool should be acquired to support a valued project management/business principle or practice standard and that the tool can be clearly related to addressing project management performance/decision-making goals or to eradicating existing efficiency problems.

The next step in the process is the actual purchase of the tool. A low-cost tool may be a matter of routine procurement for the organization. Conversely, a high-cost tool (due either to multiple users or customization) may require special handling and perhaps additional approvals in the acquisition process. Accordingly, the PMO should consider these factors when planning for the acquisition. Of course, this step is subject to the vendor purchase order, making it necessary for the PMO to monitor order status and subsequent delivery.

The final step in the acquisition process is the tool receipt and installation. In managing tool acquisition, the PMO should plan for its installation either by the vendor, by the internal IT department, or even by individual users in the case of simple automated tools. Tool installation is complete when the PMO verifies that the tool has been properly configured and made accessible for the intended users.

Implement Project Tools

Installing a project management tool on the desktop computers of a few users will not normally present a major challenge for the PMO. Conversely, a larger number of users or a major system implementation warrants advanced planning and ongoing management on the part of the PMO. In either case, the implementation activities recommended below will ensure the smooth introduction of a new project management tool.

Plan the Implementation

Small tool implementations for small user groups are easily planned: simply schedule and arrange the implementation with individual users. However, major tool implementation, particularly those affecting department or organizationwide operations, will likely require additional advance planning. Implementation of a major project management tool implies a change in the way projects are managed and the way business is conducted. The PMO is inherently responsible for preparing project management environment users for such major modifications.

The PMO can consider the following planning elements for tool implementation:

- *Advance announcements:* Give staff prior notice that a decision has been made to acquire and implement a new project management tool that will prompt adjustments in current operating processes; define and include these announcements in the implementation plan and schedule of events; include vendors and customers in this notification, as appropriate.
- *Senior management endorsement:* Obtain and convey senior management sanction at appropriate points in the implementation; collaborate with senior managers to plan when and how such approval will be made; determine what types of endorsements will be needed (written policy changes, staff meeting announcements, etc.).
- *Implementation schedule:* Specify the implementation activities and prepare a schedule for their accomplishment. Beginning with tool installation, include time frames for implementation within different departments or at multiple locations; specify the system connectivity needed to provide access at various facilities and outline the data transfer activities that are required to make the system operational; identify the implementation support that the PMO will provide.
- *User training:* Specify any training required in association with the introduction of a new project management tool; include a schedule for training delivery in the implementation plan.

The inclusion of a transition plan is another element of the project management tool implementation plan. However, the transition plan is considered separately below because of its importance in the successful introduction of a new major project management tool.

Plan the Transition

The PMO will want to focus on this element of tool implementation planning because it represents a critical step in making the new project tool operational. Essentially, the transition plan requires the PMO to determine how, when, and what elements of project management data will be transferred to the new tool. If the new tool is an automated methodology system, transition planning could require an extended period of time to identify how each project in the organization will be transitioned to the new system. Any other major tool that requires populating data from all projects presents a similar extended planning process. This effort is further compounded when the new tool is transitioned at multiple geographic locations, possibly on a global basis.

The underlying premise of the transition plan is to ensure that all key participants know how and when they can begin using the new tool and what role they have in bringing it to its intended operating capability. The transition plan also will normally specify what project or business data are being transferred, how that transfer will be accomplished, and what data manipulations, if any, by the new tool must be performed to make the tool useful for real-time project management.

Conduct User Training

The complexities of using the new tool will determine the need for user training. However, the PMO should normally consider providing training when implementing any new tool and especially when introducing a major new tool. Furthermore, when a customized major tool is introduced, the PMO absolutely should consider training.

The PMO can arrange and conduct project management tool training for one or more user levels, depending on the nature of the tool and the intended access of the users. In general, frequent users will receive more detailed training, whereas infrequent users, such as executives, will have familiarization training focused on conveying understanding of tool functionality and any relevant executive access features.

The PMO can identify user levels and arrange for appropriate training programs during tool implementation planning. It is also important to identify any prerequisite knowledge needed before beginning project management tool training. For example, individual understanding of project scheduling concepts is essential before introducing a project management scheduling tool. The relevant organization should never presume that simply introducing a tool will solve "performance" problems.

Conduct Implementation

When it is time for the PMO to execute the tool implementation plan, it should address all pertinent implementation activities that the PMO will manage. The implementation plan should facilitate the accomplishment of the following three items:

- *Data transfer:* The transition-plan element of the implementation plan can be used to guide the transfer of data that will populate the new tool for operation within the project environment.
- *Operational functionality:* User training begins the process of conveying the knowledge that new tool users need. The PMO will want to monitor initial use, individually if possible, to ensure that all users achieve a complete understanding of tool functionality. The PMO can determine the depth and extent of monitoring and indicate what activities it will perform in the implementation plan. When the desired level of user performance has been achieved (as specified in the implementation plan), the PMO can declare that operational functionality has been achieved for the new project management tool.
- *User feedback:* The implementation plan should include provisions for preparing and receiving user feedback in conjunction with implementation of the new tool. This activity achieves two objectives. First, it allows users to know that any concerns about the performance of the new tool are noted and will be appropriately addressed. Second, it enables the PMO to collect individual opinions and group perspectives on the performance of the new tool, thus permitting immediate fixes of any major problems before beginning the evaluation of tool performance.

Evaluate Tool Performance

It is a truism that the PMO's work is never done. The ongoing monitoring and management of project management tool performance is just one part of that work. A follow-up evaluation of project tool performance should be based on the extent of users and the business importance of tool deployment. Major department and enterprisewide systems will require frequent performance reviews until the system becomes reasonably familiar for users and stable in the project management environment. After that, routine, recurring performance checks will be required to ensure the tool is being used properly to fulfill its intended purpose and to ensure that its functionality is maintained and optimized for best performance within the project management environment.

The PMO should establish its tool evaluation approach to include three areas of attention: utilization, functionality, and overall effectiveness.

Identify and Resolve Utilization Problems

The PMO should conduct tool utilization reviews for the most critical project management tools — those that guide the project management process and those that provide for timely reporting of project status. This type of review can be a formal survey of users or casual observation of utilization. Its intent is to ascertain whether the tool is being used for its intended purpose within the specified user group.

In particular, the PMO will want to identify why a certain tool, or feature or component of a tool, is not being utilized in a way that is consistent with expectations. Reasons for nonuse may include inadequate or no user training, tool-learning hesitation or misplaced priority of the individual user, lack of senior management endorsement or communication regarding desired tool use, limited perception of personal value or benefit by the user, limited perception of organizational value or benefit by the user, and other explanations that the PMO can discern.

Once low-utilization indicators or trends are identified, the PMO should work with project managers to rectify the situation and bring it in line with organizational expectations and mandates for tool use. The PMO may want to retain a log of the tool utilization problems encountered and the corrective actions taken as a reference for future use.

Identify and Resolve Functional Problems

The functional performance of project management tools can be examined in conjunction with a utilization review. The PMO can accomplish this by conducting random testing of tool features. Alternatively, the PMO can establish a problem log for use on each major project and then review the tool problem log, perhaps on a weekly or monthly basis. The functional problems to be encountered could range from simple system "lockup" to more profound user recognition that the tool does not possess a desired feature or perform a preferred function.

By analyzing the review findings and problem logs, the PMO can identify and isolate tool functional problem indicators and trends. As a natural follow-up, the PMO should attempt to resolve each identified problem. If recurring problems exist, the PMO may need to contact the project management tool vendor for resolution.

Assess Overall Effectiveness

The final element of the PMO's tools examination is its evaluation of overall tool effectiveness. In essence, this means determining what the tool has accomplished for the organization or the project management environment. What benefits have been achieved as a result of using this project management tool: increased project success, more timely project decisions, earlier identification and resolution of project problems, and so forth? The tool assessment should also examine the benefits to individual users. Have individual and project team efficiency or effectiveness been increased?

The PMO can use this information to substantiate continued tool use, expanded tool deployment, or as a rationale for pursuing an advanced version of the tool or an alternative replacement tool.

POSTSCRIPT FOR THE SMALLER PMO

The smaller PMO should be reasonably aware of which tools are currently available and being used and, conversely, which are currently available and not being used in the project management environment. In combination with some minor research performed by the PMO, the tools in current use can be contrasted with what is available in the marketplace. Thus, the PMO can be the source of basic tool recommendations for both individual and collective use. Even so, the small PMO can collaborate with assigned project managers and project team members to gain their insights about preferences for project management tools.

The small PMO supporting a large project management environment should consider convening ad hoc teams to identify, acquire, and implement major project management tools and systems under the PMO's guidance. Such teams also can be chartered on an as-needed basis to evaluate the effectiveness of project management tools. Alternatively, the small PMO can establish the capability to introduce small or off-the-shelf project management tools as may be routinely needed in the project management environment. In this instance, the PMO can call upon vendors to contribute their expertise in planning and conducting tool installation and implementation, which reduces or eliminates the need for the PMO to allocate resources for that task.

The small PMO can guide and influence project management tool acquisition and implementation in the project management environment or across the enterprise by being the knowledgeable source on project management tools.

3

STANDARDS AND METRICS

The PMO's attention to standards and metrics represents the management of two different types of business interests. They are combined in this function because they provide related guidance in the project management environment. That guidance is largely aligned with the concepts of project management performance.

In many ways, standards provide a basis for performance, and metrics provide for the measurement of that performance against standards. To that end, project management standards may use metrics to establish the depth and extent of applying the standards selected by the relevant organization.

The "standards and metrics" function helps the PMO to establish a common frame of reference for and among the business, technical, and project management interests within the project management environment. Standards and metrics can be considered and applied across the relevant organization to fulfill the PMO's responsibilities as a business integrator.

The "standards and metrics" function enables the PMO to:

- Identify accepted concepts and practices for use within the project management environment
- Establish consistent oversight and control for cost, schedule, and resource utilization
- Manage project, technical, and business process performance to desired standards
- Achieve compliance with industry standards, regulatory mandates, and business policies
- Conduct benchmarking related to competency, capability, and maturity goals

Standards used in the project management environment have traditionally focused on project management performance. This, understandably, is a top PMO priority: ensuring that appropriate methodologies and practices are introduced into the project management environment. Today, the PMO's expanded role as a business integrator warrants consideration and introduction of standards aligned with the project management environment that also facilitate the achievement of strategic business objectives. Instituting standards that enlarge competitive advantage, demonstrate advanced individual and organizational qualification and certification, or improve business performance is an inherent objective of this PMO's function.

Metrics serve a dual purpose. First, they provide guidance — values, thresholds, constraints, scope, duration, maximums and minimums, averages — for project, business, and technical performance. *Guidance metrics* enable the PMO to set performance requirements and expectations within the project management environment. Thereafter, metrics measurements will indicate performance results i.e., trends, achievements, discrepancies, variations, and exceptions. *Measurement metrics* represent information that can be used to establish a common understanding of status, condition, and position. This permits project and business decisions to be made in the best interests of the relevant organization. The PMO contributes to this capability by developing and deploying the metrics that are applied to the standards and practices of project management.

Metrics are established to address a particular business need. This includes such drivers as: managing to a new level of required performance, identifying individual and aggregate project performance indicators, and monitoring change within the project management environment. Over time, metrics change as new priorities and conditions are added. For example, when considering project management maturity, one set of metrics will be used to guide advancement from level-1 maturity to level-2 maturity; a new set of metrics will be needed to achieve progression from level-2 maturity to level-3 maturity. Consequently, metrics are valid for a specified period, or until a desired condition is achieved. As a result, the PMO will need to monitor and manage changes in metrics used within the project management environment.

PROJECT ENVIRONMENT INTERFACE CONCEPTS

The standards found in the project management environment should provide consistency across project and business management interests. The PMO's centralized role permits it to examine applicable standards and manage their introduction to the project management environment. Moreover, because it serves in a business integration capacity, the PMO can manage metrics associated with project management as well as those metrics that serve related business interests.

The PMO, in collaboration with its organizational sponsor, will identify the scope of standards and metrics for which it is responsible. Equally important will be the PMO's role in coordinating and conducting the implementation of approved standards and the use of metrics within the project management environment. This includes the involvement of project managers, project team members, and other project stakeholders in identifying and applying the project management standards and metrics that will be required in their day-to-day work. In addition, these groups can contribute expertise to assist the PMO in reviewing and adapting externally imposed business, technical, and regulatory standards and metrics for use within the project management environment.

An important aspect of standards and metrics is their application to benchmarking, an activity that provides a snapshot of project and business performance. Benchmarking involves assessing current processes, practices, or capability relative to industry standards or accepted best practices. The PMO will be instrumental in selecting the standards that provide the basis for such an examination. It will also formulate metrics that help both to describe any variation from that basis and to define improvement goals.

BUSINESS ENVIRONMENT INTERFACE CONCEPTS

The relevant organization will have an interest in the standards and metrics that the PMO applies. It will collaborate on project management standards and will review and endorse the introduction of cross-functional standards. The relevant organization will therefore both contribute and use many of the metrics applied in the project management environment.

Business units will be able to use the metrics defined and captured in the project management environment in conjunction with analyses of business performance, achievement of strategic objectives, and identification of the organization's competitive position in the marketplace. In many cases, the PMO can provide metrics that are directly applicable and influence business decisions in these and other important business areas.

Today's professional project managers have a broad range of responsibility that extends into the business environment. In many organizations, they fulfill key middle- and senior management roles that direct or guide business affairs. The standards and metrics that they are accustomed to using in the project management environment will also be relevant and influential in the business environment.

Many project managers have financial accountability for their projects; some have business performance responsibility as well. Project management standards help to establish the parameters of their responsibilities, and using project and business metrics provides indicators regarding how well those responsibilities are being fulfilled. The "standards and metrics" function facilitates performance analyses within the project management environment. Individuals within the project management environment need the PMO as a centrally recognized authority to select, implement, and manage the standards and metrics they will use. The relevant organization will rely on the PMO to incorporate business strategy and interests into project management processes and practices through this "standards and metrics" function.

STANDARDS AND METRICS ACTIVITIES ACROSS THE PMO CONTINUUM

The "standards and metrics" function along the PMO competency continuum is initially characterized by the introduction of standard approaches to project and technical performance management. This capability progresses to the identification and implementation of more comprehensive standards, as well as a broader use of metrics in the project management environment. At the high end of the continuum, the PMO will influence the use of standards and metrics that interface with the business unit and the organization's strategic interests.

Table 3.1 presents an overview of the range of prescribed PMO standards and metrics activities according to each level in the PMO competency continuum.

The primary user of standards and metrics established within the relevant organization is the *project office.* In the absence of a higher level PMO, it may independently specify a limited number of project management standards and metrics in collaboration with other affected project managers. The project office will not likely venture into developing and implementing business standards, inasmuch as that is a collaborative, cross-functional effort. However, it will apply business-related standards and metrics when they are integrated into project management and technical processes and practices.

Mid-range PMO levels of the continuum have the responsibility of introducing project management and associated technical and business standards and metrics into the project management environment. In particular, these PMOs will focus on selecting or recommending standards for use within the relevant organization. Thereafter, they will conduct benchmarking against those standards to identify a basis from which to plan and measure project, technical, and business performance improvement. In addition, the mid-range PMO will identify a variety of metrics by initially addressing requirements for project and technical performance

Table 3.1 Range of Standards and Metrics Activities across the PMO Continuum

Project Office	Basic PMO	Standard PMO	Advanced PMO	Center of Excellence
Applies established and approved standards and metrics to project management activities	Introduces basic standards and metrics to facilitate a consistent approach to project management	Introduces more-comprehensive standards and metrics to improve project performance	Manages standards and metrics to integrate business and organizational interests	Manages standards and metrics to help achieve cross-functional business objectives
	■ Specifies project management standards for processes and tools	■ Selects and uses preferred project management life cycle standards	■ Selects and uses preferred models for project management, technical maturity, and capability	■ Participates in or leads standards and certification activities for the organization
	■ Develops metrics for critical project management activities	■ Develops metrics for examination of methodologies and tool use	■ Develops metrics for managing project selection and strategy alignment	■ Collaborates with business unit managers to identify metrics requirements and uses
	■ Facilitates metrics for technical performance	■ Develops competency metrics for project management	■ Measures and analyzes project contributions to business performance	■ Develops standards and metrics for vendor and contractor use
	■ Measures and analyzes project and technical performance	■ Benchmarks project management practices, processes, and procedures		

metrics and then by integrating organizational and business metrics as the PMO function responsibility and capability expand.

The *center of excellence* performs the "standards and metrics" function with attention to the relevant organization's broader business and cross-functional interests. It contributes information and experience based in its selection and implementation of standards and metrics used in the project management environment to serve the broader business integration and standardization needs of the organization.

In many cases, the standards and metrics that this PMO function establishes will have direct implications on how other PMO functions are performed. Thus, the inauguration of standards and metrics in the project management environment should weigh the interrelationships of all PMO functions.

STANDARDS AND METRICS FUNCTION MODEL

The PMO's "standards and metrics" function presents the means by which the PMO can introduce the preferred ways of doing business within the project management environment. The primary activities of the PMO's "standards and metrics" function model are depicted in Figure 3.1. Each activity is described in the following subsections.

Implement Project Management Standards

Project management has advanced as a professional discipline because, to one extent or another, scholars, innovative thinkers, and experienced project managers have formulated, implemented, evaluated, and conveyed to others the concepts and practices that have demonstrated value in the project management environment. This value contributes to achieving individual success in project management and associated organizational business goals. Time-tested methods have evolved into the widely accepted project management precepts that project managers use across industries and around the world. Many of these precepts are implemented

Figure 3.1 "Standards and Metrics" Function Model

without change across industries, whereas others are modified and adapted for specific industry use. Over time, new, innovative approaches will continually emerge to provide more complete and comprehensive solutions in the project management environment.

The PMO is responsible for sorting out all of these pending solutions and for selecting those that best fit the needs of the relevant organization. Solutions become standards for the organization only when they are approved and implemented for use in the project management environment. Implementation involves a series of steps that the PMO can use to introduce standards into its project management environment.

Examine Standards Sources

The primary purpose of introducing standards is to improve project, technical, and business performance. The PMO begins this work by examining the various sources of standards that are available for consideration. Ideally, the PMO has sufficient staff experience and insight to uncover the relevant sources that need to be addressed. The following five subsections identify a few general sources of standards that the PMO can examine when initiating this effort.

Project Management Practices

The PMO should determine what standards are needed to guide the performance of project management. This includes an examination of prominent project management processes, tools, and techniques that can be introduced as standards within the project management environment. Ideally, the project management practice standards that the PMO selects will facilitate development and implementation of a complete project management life cycle methodology. However, standards introduced to assist the organization in developing and implementing component processes that are critical to its project management efforts are normally an excellent investment.

The Project Management Institute, Inc. (PMI), publishes *A Guide to the Project Management Body of Knowledge* or PMBOK®, a widely accepted and well-known project management standards reference. A small number of other project management associations also provide project management process and performance guidance. Similarly, some professional organizations have developed industry-specific project management guidance, and academia is a consistent source for new and emerging project management concepts and considerations. In some cases, business organizations have compiled and implemented best practices in project management from various sources, including their own experience. However, access to these "standards" is normally limited to participants in business or industry forums or by some other affiliation with the source organization.

Finally, a multitude of commercial vendors can provide structured project management process and procedural guidance in conjunction with the delivery of their products and services. Many of these commercial sources incorporate industry-accepted standards. However, some tend to focus on the specific purpose of their product or service and may not provide complete and comprehensive project management coverage. For that reason, the PMO should weigh its near-term and long-term needs when selecting between consultants or vendors that offer specific-focus products and services and those that provide guidance and support for the entire project management life cycle.

Project Management Maturity

The PMO should determine what standards are needed to guide its efforts to create a professional project management organization. This responsibility raises the concept of project management maturity and includes an examination of available project management maturity models that can be used within the relevant organization.

The various project management maturity models available today take a somewhat common approach that carries the organization through steps of assessment, analysis, and improvement planning. The assessment process usually involves a sample of the organization's project management population and, at times, other stakeholders within the organization. The PMO should recognize that most viable maturity assessments will delve into the "nooks and crannies" of the project management environment, i.e., project and business practices, management support, PMO guidance and support capability, project manager competency, and so forth. This enables the organization to gain an accurate and comprehensive picture of its project management maturity based on the selected standard.

Project management maturity models are also available from several of the professional organizations and commercial vendors identified in the previous section. Some models are more inquisitive and complex and require extended periods of time in their performance. Others are more cursory in scope but can be completed within a short time span. The PMO's responsibility for introducing project management maturity standards deals with the selection of a preferred model and its associated assessment process. These are used to identify the current maturity level and to construct a strategy or "roadmap" for advancing the organization's maturity in project management. Although there is no proven maturity standard or consensus of its universal application, the concept and use of a particular project management maturity model can nevertheless be meaningful for continuous improvement efforts within the relevant organization. The PMO should give serious consideration to deciding what is the appropriate level or combination of maturity level elements for its business needs. Then it can select a project management maturity model that will help achieve the desired capability.

Technical Capability

In most project management environments, the PMO will inherently have responsibility for helping to establish the technical standards associated with project work. Usually, PMOs will only need to focus on the core business and the primary technical discipline of the relevant organization, especially when that organization is a homogeneous division or business unit. In that case, the nature of work that the division or business unit performs defines the technical focus. Conversely, PMOs that have cross-functional responsibility or those that serve the entire enterprise may have to establish standards for more than one technical discipline. To that end, it is not uncommon for a PMO to begin its work in one technical department and then expand its scope of authority and responsibility into other business areas as it demonstrates success. It is for this reason that this PMO function model treats technical standards separately. Every PMO must recognize that technical standards should be integrated with the project management process or methodology to ensure a seamless approach to project management.

Industry-specific professional organizations and associations, including some that have a project management focus, are prevalent sources for technical standards and best practices, as are educational institutions. The Software Engineering Institute's Capability Maturity Model (SEI CMM) is a prime example of a technical maturity model and provider. Of course, there also are consultants and vendors who work in virtually all industry niches that can provide excellent insight (not to mention some products and services) for industry-specific technical needs. The PMO should collaborate with the relevant organization's technical professionals, including engineers, scientists, administrators, consultants, and instructors, among others, to help determine the preferred sources of technical standards.

The PMO should ensure that technical standards are properly integrated and that users do not misconstrue them as project management standards. Technical standards, processes, and best practices should guide the project participants in achieving the desired technical solution — the resulting product or service. Project management standards, however, verify that the prescribed steps are performed to manage the project. Although technical and project management standards should be duly integrated to optimize project performance, technical capability is not inherently a project management capability.

Project Management Competency

The PMO should play a major role in determining competency and skill standards for its project managers, project team members, and other relevant project participants. It should work with the human resources department and resource managers to define appropriate project management competency standards.

Whether or not the relevant organization has a formal project management career path has direct bearing on the introduction of competency standards. If a professional career progression program exists within the relevant organization, then distinct involvement of the human resources department is necessary to ensure that related compensation and employment considerations are handled properly and are aligned with the prescribed standards. In the absence of a formal career path, project management competency standards can be identified relative to a generic list of project management responsibilities rather than presented in a formal position description.

Once again, professional organizations and associations may be the prevalent source of standards for project management competency. As always, consultants and vendors are readily available to provide assistance in establishing project management competency models and standards.

Organizational Certification

Organizational certification represents achieving compliance with standards for performance across the enterprise. While such standards may be industry specific, they also may have cross-industry application. The pursuit of International Standards Organization (ISO) standards is a prime example of an organizational certification. As well, the pursuit of standards associated with government and industry awards, such as the Malcolm Baldrige National Quality Award, can be managed along the lines of organizational certification.

The extent of the PMO's responsibility within the relevant organization will guide the PMO's involvement in selecting standards for organizational certification. Most PMOs will not have to manage this type of standards implementation unless they are functioning at an advanced level. It is more likely, however, that the PMO will be called upon to participate in an organizationwide certification effort rather than take a lead role. Nevertheless, the PMO should influence or recommend pursuing organizational standards certification with regard to the interests of the project management environment. To that end, it is important that the PMO understands where project management in various organizational certification programs intersects, and how or whether project management capability is important to the certification effort.

When involved in an examination of organizational certifications, the PMO should focus on those certifications that will provide some business advantage when standards are met. Standards that facilitate added customer value and satisfaction, improved operational effectiveness, or increased revenue are good indicators of such business advantage.

Sources of organizational certification standards are likely to be prominent in the organization's base industry, or they may be well recognized by a business segment within the organization. Moreover, the industry certifying body is usually also the developer of the associated standards to be examined. Therefore, any examination of standards is easily accomplished through contact with the certifying organization.

Identify Applicable Standards

After examining the sources of standards available to the project management environment, the PMO will make or otherwise facilitate or influence decisions about the specific standards that are preferred within the relevant organization. The following six subsections describe some of the more common standards that the PMO may consider and select for use within its project management environment.

Project Methods and Procedures

The PMO should facilitate selection of a preferred project management methodology that provides a consistent and repeatable life cycle process approach to project management. If developing a comprehensive methodology is premature for the current environment, the PMO should consider beginning with simpler processes for accomplishing its most critical project management activities. This standard should guide all project managers in performing the essential activities of project management that the relevant organization requires. This standard also will serve as a reference to all other stakeholders within the project management environment — project team members, project executives, functional managers, customers, and vendors — who need either to apply or simply understand the processes of project management.

Project Management Tools

Next, the PMO should facilitate selection of the preferred project management tools used in the project management environment. This particularly represents the specification of a cross-project management information system that is used by all projects to capture pertinent project information. It also includes oversight for selection of all tools being used in the project management environment and distinguishes standard tools from those having limited use by selected individuals. This selection of standard tools should ensure that project management and business interests in project data collection, reporting, aggregation, and sharing are well served. All in all, the PMO also should ensure that the selected tools will not overly burden project managers and other users but will expedite timely and accurate project information management.

Project Performance

The PMO should facilitate the selection of performance standards for project management. This means defining when a project starts and ends, what constitutes satisfactory progress, what constitutes a successful project, and what status or conditions warrant some level of additional management intervention. Project performance standards also reach into the specification of project selection (and termination) criteria, which is normally contained in project portfolio management guidance. In some cases, performance standards are industry- or market-driven; in others, business processes of the relevant organization are the predominant influence. The PMO will want to select standards that produce project outcomes that help achieve strategic business objectives.

Technical Performance

The PMO may facilitate or otherwise assist in the selection of technical performance standards. The caveat to this standards selection effort is the consideration of whether the PMO is also the technical leader in the primary discipline used on projects. Sometimes it is, and in such cases, the PMO has a primary role to define the accompanying technical performance standards. However, in cases where the PMO has purview over multiple disciplines, it can still facilitate technical standards selection, but it then relies on the technical leaders in each discipline to recommend and substantiate the preferred technical performance standards.

Individual Performance

The PMO should facilitate the selection of individual performance standards. This usually focuses on performance of the project manager but may also include performance of project team members. Selected performance standards can be incorporated into position descriptions, particularly if a professional project manager career path has been established. Otherwise, more general standards for individual skill and experience can be applied at the time of project assignment.

Product/Service Quality

The PMO may facilitate the selection of product/service quality standards. Again, the consideration of primary versus multiple technical disciplines comes to bear. In either case, the PMO should ensure that appropriate quality management standards are in place in the project management environment. An added point to consider is organizationwide quality certification. The PMO must ensure that any certification standards being pursued or achieved are clearly integrated into project, technical, and individual performance guidance.

Introduce Preferred Standards

Although the process for introducing preferred project and business management standards into the project management environment is not particularly complex, it does warrant discussion to ensure proper positioning for users and effective implementation within the organization. The PMO will know how to work within the nuances of its environment and can follow the following general steps when introducing standards.

Stakeholder Concurrence

It is essential that key stakeholders within the project management environment — project sponsors, project managers, project team members, and business unit managers — acknowledge and accept the standards that the PMO introduces. Moreover, the final decision to implement new standards normally resides at the executive level. Not only should the PMO be able to demonstrate benefits of a standard for executive consideration, but the PMO also should be able to win endorsement from the user community. Consequently, the list of key stakeholders should be expanded to include technical experts for technical standards and functional managers for standards having heavy business impacts.

Key stakeholders can be included at various junctures in the standards identification, review, and deliberation process. The various stakeholders may have differing interests and levels of influence in the selection of standards. However, successful standards implementation requires all stakeholder groups to be represented in the standards selection process.

Standards Implementation Planning

The PMO can either conduct or facilitate standards implementation planning. The extent of planning required depends on the impact that standards introduction will have on the business of the relevant organization and activities within the project management environment. In some cases, standards implementation planning may be as simple as a page change or as complex as a new approach to business. Whereas one takes less than a few hours to complete, the other may take more than a few days just to get planning underway.

In general the PMO will want to consider the following planning elements for standards implementation:

- *Identify the standards "owner":* Identify who will be responsible for managing the implementation and monitoring the use and effectiveness of the preferred standard. This may be someone either aligned with the PMO or external to it. Include and assist the "owner," as appropriate, in preparing the remaining elements of the standards implementation plan.
- *Specify the standard:* Prepare a brief description of the standard to be implemented for use in notifications.
- *Notify of decision to implement:* Determine the timing, method, and content of the notification of new standards to stakeholders and any other relevant internal or external audience. Identify whether any special promotions and advertising need to be included in the notification.
- *Check current practices and guidance:* Conclude whether any current standards are being modified or replaced by the introduction of the new standard. Include planning to address any impacts.
- *Identify the standards reference locations:* Resolve where the new standards will reside (for example, in documents, in electronic files, on Web pages, on a big sign at the entryway, and so forth). Plan for incorporating changes or adding the new standard to these media locations.
- *Identify the standards implementation team:* Determine if this is a simple standards introduction or one requiring more than one person to implement. Specify the activities that will identify (and form, if necessary) the implementation team.
- *Prepare the standards implementation work plan:* Ascertain what activities will be performed to implement the standard, and incorporate cost, schedule, and resource requirements. Assign or facilitate the standards implementation team to perform primary planning.

- *Specify any necessary standards training:* Decide whether implementation of a new standard warrants any significant training for those individuals who will be tasked to implement it, as well as those who will apply it.
- *Obtain final decision to proceed:* Determine whether a final decision is required to proceed with implementation of the standard. Specify who makes that decision and when it is made.

Standards Implementation

The PMO will perform or monitor standards implementation in the project management environment. This task can be performed for a distinct project management standard or a technical or business-related standard that must be integrated into the project management approach.

If an authority outside the PMO is conducting the implementation, the PMO should be a collaborative partner for that portion of standards implementation that affects the project management environment. In such a case, the PMO should accomplish the following:

- Review the standards implementation plan for the PMO's required implementation actions to include identifying the need to assign one or more resources to the implementation effort.
- Determine when standards implementation begins and ends, noting that implementation could be a simple and immediate event. Manage PMO involvement in the implementation effort.
- Identify what standards monitoring requirements will be required during and after implementation. Assign one or more resources to the monitoring effort.
- Report the achievement of standards implementation to the vested authority.

If, however, the PMO is implementing a standard within the purview of its own authority, it can conduct its own planning (treating a complex effort as a project) and monitor and manage implementation from that perspective.

Conduct Benchmarking

Implementing standards in the project management environment is a business decision that warrants monitoring and measuring. Benchmarking provides for initial and subsequent measurements to verify whether applicable standards are being achieved. It provides a comparison between the current state — of practices, procedures, policies, products, tools, people skills, and other bases for measuring effective project performance — and what should or could be. In the project management environment, assessments often represent benchmarking based on the inherent standards of the assessment model used.

There is another prevalent context in which benchmarking is conducted relative to industry and specifically relative to other organizations in the industry, either competitors or business leaders believed to use best practices. However, this type of benchmarking, at the very least, suggests an informal acceptance of the competitor or business leader as having a "standard" that warrants comparison. This is a valid benchmarking endeavor for the PMO to pursue, particularly when the organizations examined are known to be top performers that justify the "standard" reference. It is similarly a bona fide effort when performing benchmarking against several organizations in an industry to indicate the standing of the PMO and its relevant organization relative to the rest of the industry. In contrast, cross-industry benchmarking has been selectively attempted and can be an enormous challenge when pursued independently. In that regard, the PMO may want to seek out industry partners to conduct collaborative benchmarking activities that provide mutual benefit — at a minimum a learning experience, at best a solid industry performance indicator — for each participating organization.

Many areas of the project management environment can be benchmarked. The PMO may simply consider focusing its benchmarking efforts on the more prominent standards it has introduced into the project management environment.

Benchmarking identifies the difference or "gap" between the current state and the preferred standard. Benchmarking allows the PMO to establish or quantify the position of its current state as a reference for future measurements that indicate advancements toward achievement of results associated with the preferred standard.

The following are suggested simple steps for the PMO to consider and expand further when conducting benchmarking activities within the project management environment:

- Identify the standard (including best practices or organizations) to be examined.
- Specify the capability and resources required for the benchmarking effort.
- Plan the benchmarking approach and activities.
- Conduct benchmarking data collection.
- Perform benchmarking comparison analyses.
- Reset the benchmark point by recalibrating from any previous benchmarking of the standard.

These steps are designed to focus the PMO on establishing benchmark points. It is presumed that additional planning to achieve the standard will be conducted, but that can be done within the context of implementing the preferred standard. It is possible, however, that the PMO could use benchmarking simply to evaluate its own position against a preferred standard and then decide not to further pursue actions to achieve that standard. Of course, this is not the practice when the PMO is benchmarking to establish a baseline or recalibrate its position for a formally selected standard. In that case, planning or replanning associated with introducing the standard should be carried out.

Benchmarking acts like a bridge between standards and metrics. In many ways, benchmarking is the measurement that links standards and metrics. The concepts and considerations of using metrics in the project management environment are presented in the next section.

Determine Project Metrics Requirements

The PMO will be involved in determining which metrics are used in the project management environment. In many cases, it will have responsibility for identifying the metrics that are applied to project, technical, and business performance or are captured from measurements, such as tracking efforts, assessments, and audits. To that end, the PMO is responsible for metrics comprising the various sets of data that represent and quantify either its prescriptive practice guidance or result from its directed measurements.

As in the business environment, metrics have a wide variety of uses in the project management environment. In general, metrics can be used in the project management environment to:

- Facilitate decisions (for example, go/no-go criteria, project selection/continuation, and so forth)
- Specify project classification
- Provide common understanding of project and activity status
- Manage project performance
- Convey a concept or model
- Monitor consistency and improvement
- Determine trends
- Ensure compliance
- Ascertain capability
- Identify performance goals

Although this list offers a few primary uses of metrics, PMOs can likely identify more uses relative to their business interests. Recognizing how metrics can be used permits the PMO to determine which metrics are required within its project management environment.

This PMO function model focuses on three metrics requirement areas: process improvement metrics, project performance metrics, and business management metrics. A discussion of each follows.

Identify Process Improvement Metrics

The PMO will likely have responsibility for a number of interrelated processes that are relevant to project management. It needs to develop guidance and measurement metrics for these processes. A high level perspective on process improvement metrics is provided for the following prevalent processes that are integral to the project management environment.

Project Management Methodology

The PMO should develop and capture metrics for using the methodology and for determining its effectiveness (and thus the extent of need for improvement). This task includes identifying such factors as:

- Frequency of activities (reporting, auditing, plan reviewing, risk monitoring, etc.)
- Levels of activity participation (such as project manager, team members, project executives, customer, etc.)
- Process scalability (i.e., conditions of process element use/nonuse)
- Extent of project management information collection (required forms and template use, required data items, data entry timing, etc.)
- Process review frequency (quarterly, annually, for each project, etc.)

Normally, most metrics are embedded during development and implementation of project management methodology, making them manageable in that context.

Technical Processes

Technical processes are ideally integrated within the project management methodology and are based on the specific nature of technical work performed. To ensure proper alignment with project objectives, however, technical process standards will likely warrant a separate set of metrics. The PMO will need to collaborate with its technical experts to define any process metrics within a technical discipline or industry. It also can examine some general metrics considerations, such as particular technical process applicability to the type of project, specification of preferred technical tools and models, and technical information management. Again, presuming that there is close alignment with the project management methodology, technical process metrics can be introduced in conjunction with methodology development and implementation and managed accordingly.

Business Processes

Business processes also should be integrated with the project management methodology, depending on the organization's operating requirements. However, these processes may contain some unique standards that must be addressed, particularly if they are not fully integrated into the project management methodology. Because individuals within the project management environment may not always themselves perform the business processes, the PMO is responsible for extending its collaboration with functional managers to create any necessary business process metrics. This usually involves factors of when, where, and how the business aspects of project management will be performed, as well as who will perform them. Some business process metrics to consider include providing for timing and responsibility for transition from "sales" to project management; scope and contract-acceptance criteria and change management criteria; customer interface and issues management protocols; vendor and contractor selection criteria; and project financial and contractual close out requirements. Although business processes and associated metrics can be incorporated into the project management methodology, the PMO must ensure that business unit managers at least concur with, if not endorse, the business processes to which the methodology and the associated metrics are aligned.

Resource Management Processes

Because it has a responsibility for resource integration, the PMO should establish close communication and collaboration with the human resources department when it defines metrics for resource management processes within the project management environment. Some resource management process metrics that the PMO might consider establishing include resource assignment responsibility and criteria; performance review responsibility; content and timing criteria; project management and technical training eligibility criteria; management protocols for resource performance issues; and resource sourcing criteria (such as internal resources versus external contractors). Where appropriate, resource management process metrics can be incorporated into the project management methodology.

PMO Support Processes

The PMO should define the necessary metrics that constitute how it conducts its own support activities within the project management environment, i.e., the functions of the PMO. The PMO may develop operating processes to help achieve its prominent functions, which would justify considering metrics. In general, the PMO can evaluate the effectiveness and efficiency of each PMO function it implements. This would include establishing metrics in such areas as PMO staff workload coverage; criteria and guidance for project support priorities; reporting frequency, content, and criteria; and level of process redundancy within the relevant organization. Individual PMO functions, however, may warrant a more detailed examination of metrics needs and requirements.

Identify Project Performance Metrics

PMOs at all stages will have a vested interest in project performance. Indeed, in some cases, project performance oversight is a primary purpose for the PMO's existence. In that respect, it needs to develop guidance and measurement metrics for such performance. In discussing project performance metrics in this section, much of the metrics implementation can be associated with the development and implementation of the project, technical, and business processes with which these metrics are aligned. Thus, many of these metrics will be incorporated into the project management methodology or technical and business processes that the PMO constructs. In other cases, the PMO will develop metrics for internal use in its functional processes. This section highlights the metrics that should be considered in several process areas.

A high level perspective on project performance metrics is presented for the following five key project performance elements.

Budget

The PMO should provide metrics for developing and managing a project budget to include both guidance metrics and measurement metrics. Beginning in the planning effort, the PMO can offer a list of standard cost estimates for common activities. In some instances, this is derived from internal lessons learned, or the PMO can validate and implement industry-standard budget estimates. The PMO should prepare funding authorization guidance that explains what routine funding limits can be considered, as well as the criteria for elevating budget authority. This might include metrics for standard funding of each project phase based on project classification. The PMO also can specify metrics for contingency funding stipulated as a percentage of the project budget. As a project approaches the implementation phase, the PMO should supply budget metrics that guide project cost management and reporting. This includes metrics for using earned-value cost concepts, cost variance models, and budget trend analyses and forecasting indicators. The use of budget performance metrics ensures that every project remains within cost or that corrective actions are taken in response to indicators that identify when a project budget is experiencing difficulties. In addition, the PMO can use budget metrics to compile aggregate project cost and budget results, plus indicators for all projects within its purview.

Schedule

The PMO should provide metrics that aid in managing and controlling the project schedule. Guidance metrics are applicable in such areas as: suggested duration estimates for common activities examined during the early project planning phases; preferred depth of activity coverage within a work breakdown structure (WBS); and identification of the number and types of activities that can be concurrently scheduled based on project classification. Similarly, schedule measurement metrics are essential in tracking schedule performance during project implementation. The PMO will want to consider those metrics that are applied to earned-value schedule concepts, schedule variance models, and schedule management analyses. Using schedule performance metrics ensures that every project remains on schedule or that corrective actions are taken in response to indicators that identify when a project schedule is experiencing difficulties. Again, the PMO can use schedule metrics to compile aggregate project schedule results and indicators for all projects within its purview.

Resource Management

The PMO will want to consider the use of metrics that help ascertain the performance of resource management on projects. At the outset, there are comparable guidance and measurement metrics for resource management on projects similar to those for budget and schedule. These include such metrics as the suggested number and type of resources for common activities, learning-curve diagrams for resource estimating, and resource-acquisition timing indicators. The PMO should examine these metrics plus any others that contribute to effective project planning and expedite the assignment of necessary project resources. Later, during project implementation, the PMO should consider metrics such as resource-utilization trends and variances, assignment completion rates, and resource availability. Similar to the previously mentioned metrics for budget and schedule performance, resource performance metrics also allow the monitoring of planned and current status of resource utilization and, if necessary, the application of enabled corrective actions when indications of resource performance difficulties surface during a project. In the case of resource performance, the PMO also gains effective oversight of resource utilization across projects when appropriate metrics are introduced.

Another aspect of resource performance — the acquisition, assignment, and management of the human facet of project management — warrants PMO attention for metrics. With the help of guidance and measurement metrics, project managers and the PMO will be able to properly staff projects and manage individual performance. Metrics in this area include focusing on resource pool or other internal source availability rates, hiring needs versus use of external contractors, resource manager participation in preparing and assigning resources, individual performance trends and analyses, and team cohesion and performance indicators. The PMO should devise the metrics necessary to properly integrate resources into the project management environment, consistent with the resource allocation and assignment processes of the relevant organization.

Risk Management

Risk management is an inherent component of project management, and virtually all effective PMOs and project managers acknowledge the need to manage project and business risks. The PMO needs to confirm that perspective by developing the necessary guidance and measurement metrics to facilitate effective project and business risk management.

The common risk management process calls for identifying, prioritizing, and responding to risks that could affect projects. In some project management environments, risk is distinguished between events having potential adverse impact and those having potential positive opportunities. In that regard, the PMO should develop and implement metrics that address the relevant organization's process and business approach to risk.

Metrics guidance for risk management can include such items as specification of standard risk events and responses; preferred response strategies for major types of risks; frequency of risk examination and analysis; frequency and type of risks encountered on common projects, along with the preferred solution that can be incorporated in the project planning phase; common risk impacts on project performance; costs of proactive versus reactive risk response strategies; and ranges of risk fund allowances per the project classification. The PMO needs to ensure that project managers and risk managers have sufficient guidance to deal with the risks that are identified and the risk events that are encountered.

Metrics measurements assist the PMO in oversight of projects, but measurement results also contribute to the development of metrics guidance that can be used on subsequent projects. The PMO will want to consider such metrics as the average number of risks identified on each project (by project classification), the number of risk events that actually occurred (whether identified or not in advance), the number of risk events (identified and actual) associated with project teams and individual project managers, and the cost of responding to risk events (on average and by project). Moreover, one of the more underappreciated aspects to risk management involves managing the value of the project, as outlined in the business case. Metrics should track the reliability and validity of the business case value calculations during the project. Together, this collection of metrics should enable the PMO to identify and assist the project manager in responding to potential risk impacts on a real-time basis or in analyzing overall risk management performance and improving practices and individual competency on future projects.

Quality Assurance

Quality assurance performance tends to be aligned with the technical aspects of the work performed. The extent of PMO involvement in technical oversight determines the nature of the quality assurance metrics that the PMO introduces into the project management environment. However, every PMO has inherent responsibility for quality on all projects, regardless of its technical oversight and alignment. Quality assurance metrics remain, therefore, within the PMO purview.

Quality assurance guidance metrics can include such considerations as identification of quality standards criteria (as may be influenced by organizational quality certifications or internal policies); frequency of customer deliverable specification and project scope reviews; allowable variations in product/service quality; and content and frequency of quality assurance reporting, including criteria for special reporting or elevation of quality issues.

Quality assurance measurement metrics should include such items as quality variance values at interim checkpoints, number of project/contract scope changes requested and approved affecting deliverable specifications, quality difficulties or defects associated with particular project teams and individual project managers, average customer acceptance rates and timing, and contribution of lessons learned from quality performance. Quality assurance also applies to the project management aspects of performing the project work and producing its prescribed deliverables — products and services.

A PMO that is heavily involved in the technical aspects of the project will want to convene its senior technical experts to define more detailed metrics for use in performing technical activities and in achieving customer product and service specifications.

Identify Business Management Metrics

In its role as business integrator, the PMO will want to (a) ensure that applicable business management metrics are introduced into the project management environment and (b) provide applicable project information to project stakeholders having direct responsibility for business management. The PMO should introduce metrics that provide for this mutual exchange. It should attempt to build these metrics gradually, leveraging commonly supported elements first and then demonstrating the success of early metrics before increasing the range of business management metrics that are implemented in the project management environment.

A high level perspective on business management metrics is presented for the following four key project elements.

Contract and Agreement Metrics

The PMO should provide metrics to ensure that contract formats and content are achieving strategic business objectives. This includes metrics for pricing strategies, customer payment management, invoice distribution, and customer prequalification. Of course, the PMO should also adopt metrics for contract change management to maximize and control the legal aspects of project management.

Customer Satisfaction Metrics

The PMO should develop and implement metrics that enable the relevant organization to ascertain customer and customer-group satisfaction with project deliverables and to identify the opportunities for long-term customer relationships. In particular, the PMO should apply metrics that help identify and rectify customer problem areas with minimal impact on marketplace perceptions of project performance.

Project Portfolio Management Metrics

The PMO is ideally positioned to convey project information between senior management and the project management environment. It should use this advantage to construct metrics that facilitate project portfolio management. This includes defining metrics that assist in formulating decisions about project selection, continuation, and termination. It also includes developing metrics that help to review aggregate project performance, identify strong and weak project performance areas, and assess ongoing alignment with strategic business objectives.

Financial Metrics

Although the consideration of financial performance metrics may be a part of any of the previous business management areas, it is often aligned with project portfolio management. It is highlighted separately here to enable examination of such factors as revenue generation, expense trends, and bottom-line analyses. A separate examination of financial metrics also may be expanded to provide the PMO with the analysis and insight to implement or recommend improvements in areas of project cost estimating, project pricing strategies, project expenditure allowances, vendor and contractor cost qualification criteria, and project staffing costs.

Introduce and Use Metrics

Once it has developed the necessary metrics for the project management environment, the PMO must ensure their integration into appropriate processes and their use according to design. The latter is particularly important to the PMO because it normally designs the use of metrics to guide and measure results across a collective set of projects within its purview, and it should ensure that metrics are applied consistently to all projects.

Because the PMO will predominantly seek a big-picture view of all projects, it should introduce metrics to serve project managers while also fulfilling its purposes of oversight, control, and support, based on its charter. To that end, there are three primary activities that should be accomplished to introduce metrics into the project management environment: preparation of a metrics measurements plan, comparison of metrics performance, and establishment of corrective actions. Each is discussed in the following subsections.

Establish Metrics Measurements Plan

When the PMO designates a metric, it should be prepared to monitor and manage it at a higher, aggregate level of examination. Therefore, the PMO should be cognizant of and track all of the metrics it has constructed — both guidance metrics and measurement metrics — for use within the project management environment.

The focus of the metrics measurements plan is on measurement metrics, which are used to track project, technical, and business performance, and to provide timely indications about project conditions or status. Measurements that use prescribed guidance metrics also enable the PMO to examine and enhance its guidance metrics.

The PMO should actively monitor and manage metrics that it prescribes in the project management environment. This can be accomplished by developing a metrics measurements plan for the project management environment. This plan will help the PMO organize and manage the prescribed metrics plus their individual and collective values to the relevant organization.

The following are suggested elements of a metrics measurements plan for the project management environment:

- *Measurement sources:* Prepare a brief description of the metric and its intended use; identify what project data are used to measure the metric.
- *Measurement levels:* Specify the level of detail and type of data to be obtained from the metric to be used; identify any special competencies or authority needed to obtain measurements for the metric.
- *Measurement frequency:* Indicate how often metric measurements are needed and used, e.g., the time frames for each project phase.
- *Measurement performers:* Identify who is responsible for conducting measurements relative to each prescribed metric. (This may be integrated into the project management methodology, or into the technical and business process, or identified separately when there is no associated process.)
- *Measurement consumers:* Designate who should receive data or reports containing project management environment measurements based on prescribed metrics; clarify when further measurement analyses are needed.

In essence, the measurement plan for the project management environment compiles all prominent metrics for which the PMO is responsible. It allows the PMO to consider how and when the metrics are applied, and it enables ongoing examination of the values of the metrics that are implemented. The PMO can refine or adapt the contents of this measurement plan to fit the needs of the relevant organization.

Compare Metrics Performance

The metrics measurements accomplished per the measurements plan should provide appropriate and sufficient data to evaluate each metric or set of metrics used in the project management environment. This enables the PMO to perform comparative analyses on project, technical, and business performance in areas in which metrics have been installed.

Beginning with an analysis of metrics from specific project efforts, this activity can include both in-progress analyses and postproject analyses.

Thereafter, aggregate analyses of metrics across all projects are conducted. These analyses examine the application of guidance metrics and the results of measurement metrics to identify how well projects are achieving specified objectives. In conjunction with the real-time project oversight that it performs, the PMO also examines project performance trends resulting from the introduction of particular metrics.

A metrics review is then conducted at intervals (specified by the PMO) to ascertain how well-chosen metrics are benefiting project efforts and the organization's business interests. This includes examining how consistently metrics are being applied to projects and the reasons why they are not being applied according to prescribed procedures. This review also closes the circle of this PMO function in that it identifies what progress has been made toward achieving any associated standards in the project management environment.

Establish Corrective Actions

Like standards, metrics are applied to improve performance in the project management environment. The PMO has a vantage point in its examination of cross-project results of standards and metrics implementation. Thus, it can provide remedies — on projects immediately and in the total practice over time — as described below.

Project Corrective Action

The PMO should examine metrics from project status reports and other sources to determine whether there are any troubled projects that warrant its intervention. If any adverse indicators are discovered, the normal PMO response is merely to confirm that the project manager is attending to the problem. If, however, indicators are more severe, the PMO may want to delve into the details with the project manager at a regular or special meeting and provide recommended corrective actions.

Along with this immediate response to a specific project, the PMO can also use its cross-project perspective to evaluate the preferred corrective action responses to the variety of metrics indicators it reviews. The PMO can then incorporate these corrective actions into the project management methodology as a reference for future use by all project managers.

Practice Corrective Action

The PMO, in its examination of metrics, will be able to discern where strengths and weaknesses exist in processes and procedures used within the project management environment. Similarly, it will be able to determine when metrics are appropriately applied or bypassed in favor of individual solutions. The PMO can take corrective actions at the practice level to bolster preferred metrics application within the project management environment. This type of corrective action could also be achieved through adjustments to the project management methodology. However, rather than being a simple effort, methodology modification might affect processes, which would then have to be adapted to ensure the proper use of metrics.

POSTSCRIPT FOR THE SMALLER PMO

This model has presented some advanced concepts and complex practices that provide for comprehensive management of standards and metrics in the project management environment. It is not likely that the smaller PMO will have either the staffing or the authority to construct such an elaborate function. Therefore, it may be appropriate for the PMO to focus simply on the following two fundamental activities to fulfill its responsibility to manage standards and metrics within the project management environment.

First, identify a practice standard for project management. This effort alone may require considerable time and collaboration with project stakeholders, and particularly project managers, to achieve consensus in selecting a preferred standard. Prominent issues will likely include contemplating how the standard will be deployed in terms of process guidance, whether project management and technical processes will be integrated or linked, who will develop it, and how long it will take to be deployed. If necessary, start by developing only a few of the more critical processes, but prepare plans for a full life cycle methodology in the foreseeable future. As initial PMO activities go, establishing a standard for conducting project management is somewhat of a priority. Once established, it then becomes a practice standard then serves as a frame of reference for many other activities in the project management environment. It also provides the basis by which the PMO prescribes additional project management guidance and monitors and manages project performance.

Second, focus on project performance and ascertain what information project stakeholders need to do their jobs. Construct a few primary metrics that enable stakeholders to make decisions and take actions consistent with their responsibilities within the project management environment. Consider the following responsibilities for the more-prominent stakeholders:

- *Project manager:* Makes daily decisions to keep individual projects on track and reacts to problems and issues encountered. Metrics are constructed to help manage cost, schedule, and resource utilization, accompanied by metrics to facilitate risk and quality management. In most cases, these supporting metrics are embedded in the project methodology.
- *Project sponsor, project customer, and the PMO:* Evaluates project progress based on reports from the project manager. Metrics are constructed to provide quick indications of project progress, what problems and issues remain unresolved, and whether plans and expectations for project deliverables are still valid.
- *Project executive:* Evaluates project performance from a business perspective. Metrics are constructed to address customer satisfaction, ongoing business case validation, and appropriateness of fit within the portfolio. In particular, metrics for selecting, continuing, and terminating projects are needed for this stakeholder.

These are perhaps the most important metrics to key participants in project management. They provide a solid start for the "standards and metrics" functional responsibility in a small PMO.

4

PROJECT KNOWLEDGE
MANAGEMENT

The emerging concepts of knowledge management are a prominent topic of debate: what it is, what it does, and who should use it. For the purposes of this PMO function, knowledge management will be examined as coordinating organizational knowledge and information to enable increased project management capability and to achieve business value from that capacity. This concept elevates fundamental communications in the project management environment from mere data transfer to the conveyance of ideas, perceptions, experiences, and interpretations that transcend the simple exchange of information. When using knowledge management concepts, the traditional aspects of project management reporting and project information management are properly retained but are generally adapted to be more timely, comprehensive, and widespread among stakeholders and relevant to business interests.

Because the PMO is responsible for establishing the project information management capability in the relevant organization, it can now employ the features of project knowledge management to achieve its objectives. The "project knowledge management" function enables the PMO to:

- Develop an approach to project performance reporting
- Construct an effective project management information system
- Facilitate collaboration among project managers, project teams, and project stakeholders
- Manage activities of virtual and geographically dispersed project teams
- Implement a robust project management knowledge reference library

- Capture and utilize individuals' wisdom, perspective, intuitions, and experiences
- Promote a learning organization among project managers

The PMO's knowledge management efforts should create a well-informed project management environment that operates efficiently, communicates effectively, and responds knowledgeably in providing customer and business solutions.

PROJECT ENVIRONMENT INTERFACE CONCEPTS

The PMO is charged with facilitating, if not directly handling, much of the project information that crosses desks, influences meetings, and enters boardrooms throughout the relevant organization. The PMO undertakes a major initiative and broad role that combines elements of oversight, control, and support in developing and implementing a project knowledge management capability. When properly constructed, the knowledge management system will be a tremendous benefit and distinct service in the project management environment and throughout the relevant organization.

The PMO's "project knowledge management" function establishes the processes and means for reporting project progress and status. *Progress* is the specification of the advancements made in achieving planned project activities and objectives, i.e., cost, schedule, and resource utilization management. *Status* is a determination of what that resulting progress signifies relative to project management effectiveness, contractual obligations, customer satisfaction, and business interests. The knowledge management system enables the generation and distribution of project performance information so that these status factors can be examined, interpreted, and, as necessary, acted upon by a wide range of project stakeholders.

Moreover, the PMO will use this function to provide procedures and tools that facilitate project teams' ongoing efforts to communicate, collaborate, and become a more cohesive unit, with particular consideration for those project team members not physically collocated. This activity includes establishing capability for such things as project level reporting, project task assignment and management, technical solution deliberation and discussion, task performance review and hand-off, and time management. In addition, this may also include acknowledging external vendor and contractor participation in project activities and providing them with appropriate access to selected areas of the knowledge management system. Furthermore, project management communication and collaboration can be extended to senior management by implementing an "executive dashboard" tool that provides real-time, business-critical information at a glance.

The knowledge management function can provide the modern, presumably electronic answer to the traditional "project binder," where all project information resides. This function allows the PMO to introduce and integrate preferred tools that help the PMO, project managers, and other project stakeholders to develop and manage project information and documentation. Accordingly, the project management information system tool is a prominent knowledge management component. It is used to capture and distribute project data, such as cost, schedule, and resource utilization; develop and access project plans and documents; and maintain issues, meeting agendas and actions, and other important project logs.

Similar to the need for a standard "project binder" is the consideration for project archives, which includes possible alignment with a project management reference library. This enables access to such information as lessons learned, technical solution guidance, and, perhaps, interactive discussions of prevalent business or technical topics and personal insights in "chat rooms." It also may address on-line training for project stakeholders across the relevant organization. Consequently, this PMO function can be used to establish and integrate the preferred project management reference capability for use within the project management environment.

BUSINESS ENVIRONMENT INTERFACE CONCEPTS

Early project management information systems were influential in information exchange and communication within the project management environment. The PMO's knowledge management function introduces new capability that improves upon and expands that influence throughout the relevant organization while still maintaining the essential information needed within the project management environment. Knowledge management recognizes the organization's project information needs and drives the development of a solution that integrates project information with business interests. When this capability is implemented, the interactions between business units and individuals in the project management environment become more efficient and effective.

Individuals and business units that were previously unaware that they were project stakeholders will now be able to access the project knowledge management system for their own business purposes. Indeed, it is quite likely that any required project information will now be exchanged with routine efficiency.

Business units, in particular, that have interactions with customers, vendors, and contractors will gain more information and insight into these relationships. For example, business managers responsible for sales will be able to examine project performance and customer satisfaction; resource managers responsible for project team members will be able to review resource commitments; and senior managers responsible for business performance will be able to determine progress toward achieving strategic objectives.

The information and knowledge management tools needed in the business environment are essentially the same as those described above for the project management environment. Some additional packaging, data calculation and compilation, and distribution methods — usually by electronic means — may be all that is necessary to provide benefits to the business environment.

PROJECT KNOWLEDGE MANAGEMENT ACTIVITIES ACROSS THE PMO CONTINUUM

The "project knowledge management" function along the PMO competency continuum is represented by increased capability to collect and share project management information and knowledge and a greater efficiency to accomplish it thanks to the introduction of on-line knowledge management application tools. Moreover, the PMO competency continuum reflects a progressively broader scope of project management information and knowledge access to entities outside the project management environment. In particular, the more developed PMO levels extend project management information and knowledge for sharing and integration into business operations of the relevant organization. There is also the potential for extending knowledge management system access, on a selective basis, to external project participants such as customers, vendors, and contractors.

Table 4.1 presents an overview of the range of prescribed PMO knowledge management activities according to each level in the PMO competency continuum.

The *project office* applies the information and knowledge management tools and practices that are available for use in the project management environment. In the absence of a higher level PMO, the project office will collaborate its needs with key project participants to establish a common approach for reporting project progress and status, as well as to identify a preferred tool to facilitate reporting.

Mid-range PMO levels of the continuum have the responsibility of introducing on-line project information and knowledge management practices, ideally supported by on-line tools and applications. A prominent PMO effort at this level is "building" a project management information system (PMIS) that allows the PMO to achieve an effective project management information and knowledge management capability. In addition, there is increased focus on knowledge management as the preferred solution for practices and tools.

Table 4.1 Range of Project Knowledge Management Activities across the PMO Continuum

Project Office	Basic PMO	Standard PMO	Advanced PMO	Center of Excellence
Uses established project knowledge management tools to prepare and manage project plans, reports, and documents and to collaborate on project team performance	Introduces essential project information management capability ■ Develops project management reporting and collaboration procedures ■ Provides tools for managing project information ■ Creates methods for compiling and using project postmortem information and feedback	Introduces tools and practices for managing project knowledge ■ Installs a project management methodology tool ■ Builds a project management information system (PMIS) ■ Constructs a project document archive and reference library having on-line research and access features	Expands knowledge management tool functionality for business use ■ Develops Web-based project team knowledge spaces ■ Implements a Web-based project team collaboration tool ■ Installs an on-line project portfolio management tool ■ Introduces an on-line executive dashboard	Analyzes capability of project knowledge management system ■ Examines business value and benefits of project knowledge management ■ Recommends advanced tools and knowledge management capabilities

The *center of excellence* participates in this effort in an advisory role to the project management environment and possibly lower level PMOs, as well as to the business environment. It furthers the functional effort by focusing on the implementation of advanced knowledge management tools and their interconnectivity for greater efficiency of communication and collaboration within the project management environment.

This PMO model promotes the timely transition from information system management to the expanded project management communication and collaboration capability found in the context of the emerging knowledge management discipline.

PROJECT KNOWLEDGE MANAGEMENT FUNCTION MODEL

The PMO's "project knowledge management" function model presents a capability to communicate and collaborate within the project management environment and with stakeholders in the business environment of the relevant organization. The model addresses project management information handling, particularly through the progressive implementation of knowledge management tools and techniques. However, this model does not attempt to introduce all concepts and considerations of the knowledge management discipline in an exhaustive manner. Rather, the PMO can use this model to guide the introduction of those knowledge management components that are aligned with project management communication and collaboration exchanges.

The prominent activities of the PMO's "project knowledge management" function model are depicted in Figure 4.1. Each activity is described in the following subsections.

Any PMO implementing a knowledge management capability must consider the culture of the relevant organization while knowledge management is being planned. In this case, organizational culture represents

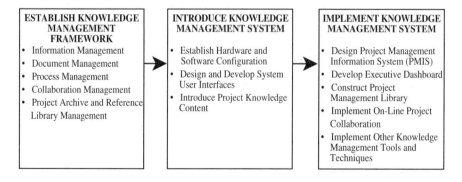

Figure 4.1 **"Project Knowledge Management" Function Model**

the manner in which people within the relevant organization interact, together with the responsibilities and actions they accept as appropriate. Instituting knowledge management affects the organizational culture and brushes up against people's beliefs and values. This condition must be considered while the elements of an effective project knowledge management system are discussed and deliberated. Afterward, people, for the most part, will gain an understanding of knowledge management concepts, as well as an appreciation for how their personal use of knowledge management ultimately contributes to business interests and objectives. The PMO can facilitate this acceptance by proceeding with implementation at a pace acceptable to the organizational culture.

Establish Knowledge Management Framework

The PMO, in close coordination with business unit managers and particularly the unit responsible for information systems (IS), should design a strategy for implementing knowledge management within the project management environment. This entails creating a knowledge management framework that will guide the development of near- and long-term capabilities of knowledge management used in the project management environment. Three complementary tasks — develop an approach, identify tools, and prepare a project knowledge management plan — should be performed in conjunction with establishing a knowledge management framework.

The PMO should take the lead in defining how data, information, and knowledge will be collected, stored, and retrieved to facilitate project management and to achieve its own functional responsibilities. It must develop a perspective on how such data and information is transformed into knowledge, and it must develop the means by which knowledge material is produced, maintained, and applied to benefit the relevant organization.

When establishing the framework for knowledge management, the PMO must have sufficient understanding of knowledge management concepts in order to achieve proper initial planning and subsequent implementation of advanced tools. First, the PMO should begin by recognizing that knowledge proceeds from — but is distinctly different from — data and information. *Data* usually results from quantitative measurement. *Information* adds meaning, relevance, and purpose to data. *Knowledge*, therefore, represents information that has been transformed by human experience or interpretation. It contains such added values as judgment and understanding about a matter or topic.

For the most part, knowledge is an organizational asset generated by people. It is codified or categorized to facilitate placement and application within the workplace, and then it is transferred or otherwise made available for use by other people. A number of automated tools can and should be used to facilitate the critical practices of knowledge management.

This discussion is hardly intended to be a primer in knowledge management, but it does provide a fundamental frame of reference for what needs to be performed to introduce knowledge management into the project management environment. In lieu of having an internal knowledge management development capability, the PMO may need to seek the advice and services of qualified vendors and consultants, particularly as it approaches implementing advanced processes and capabilities.

The PMO can begin its efforts to construct and implement a project knowledge management system by examining the communication and collaboration requirements within the project management environment. This examination can be as detailed or as abbreviated as the PMO's scope of responsibilities warrants. The following are key components of a knowledge management system and framework for which the PMO can determine needs and develop an approach for implementation.

Information Management

Most PMOs should likely begin their efforts at the information system level and then expand as more advanced knowledge management capabilities and tools are introduced over time. To that end, each PMO must decide how pertinent project management information will be exchanged, distributed, or otherwise managed, and then identify those participants who will be responsible for the information management processes that are established.

The PMO addresses this knowledge management element as a means to develop concepts that will guide the direction of project management information handling within the relevant organization. The PMO should identify the elements of information management that are described in the following three subsections.

Information Users

Determine who needs project management information in the relevant organization. Four broad categories of information users can be examined:

- *Project participants:* Project managers, team members, and technical staff
- *Project oversight managers:* PMO, sponsors, executives, control boards, etc.

- *External project stakeholders:* Customers, vendors, and contractors
- *Business managers:* Business unit managers (sales, contracting, human resources, etc.)

Begin by reviewing or identifying prominent project information needs among these groups. Compile the types of information required as the basis for subsequent specification of information content and processes for collecting and distributing information. Include needs for project management information archives and library services.

Information Systems

Review existing information systems and examine system architecture options for introducing new, automated mechanisms for information handling. Relative to those activities closely aligned with the PMO's "project management tools" function, this includes identifying what information systems approach is preferred in regard to four general types of systems:

- *Paper-based approach*: Project management information is collected and distributed by hand and is possibly supported by fundamental word processor, spreadsheet, or database software applications.
- *Automated approach*: One or more automated systems provide integrated collection of project management information as well as automated access and distribution for network-based information users.
- *Web-based approach*: This is a variation on the automated approach that simply uses the Internet or an intranet as the preferred platform for project management information collection and distribution.
- *PDAs and wireless approach*: This is yet another variation on the automated approach that expands the reach of the information system to mobile use via personal digital assistants (PDA) and other devices.

After identifying what systems or information management methods currently exist, the PMO should then prepare its recommended approach for the level of automation and interconnectivity to be used for information management. This can include recommendations for one primary system tool for capturing project information and serving as the central application of the project management information system. The resulting approach will be appropriately coordinated within the relevant organization and will guide the introduction and implementation of new information systems used in the project management environment. (Refer to the PMO "project management tools" function for conducting tool selection and implementation based on the developed approach.) Moreover, the chosen approach will provide the basis for other knowledge management system features yet to be considered.

Information System Access

The referenced users identified above must be revisited to ascertain their requirements for information system access. The same users who have project management information needs are also likely to be the ones who will contribute to information collection and analysis. In a sense, this represents a circular exchange where one user group accesses the input of another user group. The PMO should determine the general nature of input required from each group (or individual roles within a group) and then ascertain their access requirements across one or more information system platforms to be implemented. In addition, it is important to identify any information system training that will be provided to users at different access levels as new information system platforms are introduced.

Document Management

The project management environment inherently generates documents. Documents represent bundles of data and information having interrelated content. As an element of knowledge management, the PMO will benefit from developing a document management approach. Thus, the PMO must devise the means to facilitate project document management.

In developing this document management component, the PMO will identify primary documents and how they will be used and managed, which is complementary to the information systems element described above. The PMO can begin this examination by identifying the types of documents that reside within its project management environment. This includes:

- Project management plans
- Project management reports
- Technical documents
- Business documents
- Project records and logbooks

These documents will be examined more closely for content development in the later section on establishing the project management information system. However, for our purposes here, the PMO's focus is on developing an approach to how such documents in the project management environment will contribute to the knowledge management effort. In particular, the PMO must determine whether a separate need exists for an automated document management system or, perhaps, even a content management system. The PMO must also ascertain the types of documents used in the project management environment. Next, it must determine the preferred means by which authorized project management participants and stakeholders can generate, store, and retrieve the necessary project management documents.

The following subsections present three levels of document management capability that the PMO may wish to consider in constructing its approach to knowledge management.

Attached Documents

In this approach, pertinent project management documents are electronically appended to a feature or function of the primary information system, such as the document files attached to e-mail messages.

Document Managers

This technique uses an automated system specifically designed to handle multiple documents. The word processors on most computers have a file management capability that simply displays document filenames, size, and location on the system. Accordingly, the PMO can establish standard file directories and use an existing word processing system as the document manager. However, larger, more complex documents may be encountered and used in the project management environment, including CAD files, engineering drawings and specifications, and software engineering output. These examples may justify the PMO's consideration of specially designed tools or applications that facilitate large or complex document management. Of course, such tools and applications increase cost because more-advanced document handling features are included in the package.

Content Managers

This type of tool is used when there is a need for extensive use of recurring document content across many documents. Essentially, content management provides data sets — chapters, paragraphs, drawings, and even words — that are available for reuse and insertion in multiple documents. This is accomplished through the data-set management capability of the content management system. An example of how content management can be applied in project management is the use of templates and repeatable content for project management plans. Most word processors can manager templates. However, the technical and business aspects of project management may warrant some consideration of content management. The requirements for developing customized products or other technical solutions may indicate a need for a content management system that "translates" technical information to design and specifications documents. In addition, the complexity of associated contracts may require content management system support to address the multitude of content options in individual customer and vendor contracts. Most organizations would consider the acquisition of a content management system to be a major operating expense — starting at a low six-digits figure — that demands validation of need. At the same time, content management systems can often be used for multiple purposes across the relevant organization as a means to justify the hefty cost. Furthermore, if the PMO designs a comprehensive knowledge management system, there may also be applications for the content management system in the project archives and library.

Process Management

Process guidance, like much of the other information in a project management environment, has traditionally been paper-based. However, the advancing capabilities of information systems have increased access to and management of process guidance through automated means. In the project management environment, the issues of process management deal directly with the "project management methodology" function. The PMO's methodology management function ensures that all essential elements of project management, including links and integration with technical and business processes, are accomplished. Thus, the knowledge management aspect of methodology management provides for the efficiency of an automated platform on which the methodology resides.

In defining the needs for the project management methodology platform, the PMO should consider:

- Access by:
  - Project participants
  - Other stakeholders in the relevant organization
  - Customers and external vendors
- Translation and integration of methodology process management system content in:
  - Project management Web-based information pages
  - Executive dashboards
  - Project management information systems
  - Business systems
- Coverage and capture of project management life cycle activity information

The approach that the PMO deliberates in this knowledge management component identifies how the project management methodology will be made available within the project management environment. This PMO effort should therefore determine (a) what systems it will reside on, be connected to, or interface with, and (b) what information will be transferred to which project management participants as a result of that placement.

Collaboration Management

Collaboration within the project management environment presents the need for both facilitating processes and systems. The *process* factor is normally addressed through methodology and technical process implementation; the *system* factor then becomes prevalent in knowledge management as the means or mechanism used to convey process guidance. However, there are adjunct factors that also must be considered in establishing an effective collaboration capability. The PMO should examine this knowledge management component with consideration for:

- *Collocation or geographical separation of project teams:* The PMO should list all work locations of the project teams within its purview. This will enable a simple analysis of physical constraints on collaboration and initially indicate the types of tools needed to facilitate collaboration within the project management environment. This includes consideration of:
  - Single-location teams, where all team members work in the same facility — commonly typified by "walking distance" personal contact
  - Multiple-location teams, where team members perform different aspects of project works at different facilities — generally represented by some need and anticipation for short- or long-distance travel for routine or recurring personal contact
  - Virtual teams, where team members work at home offices or at global or local business facility locations and do not plan or anticipate routine personal contact
- *Types of collaboration required:* The PMO should determine the nature of collaboration needed within the project management environment and consider:
  - Project performance reviews
  - Technical performance reviews
  - Project team coordination and development meetings
  - Project stakeholder meetings
  - Project team member assignments and coordination of task status

- Project team time use and approval activities
- Technical and business innovation forums
- Project Web-based knowledge-space reference pages
- Cross-project collaboration, coordination, and information exchange forums

■ *Complexity of technical and business elements:* The PMO will need to recognize the impacts of more-complex project solutions resulting from contract innovations, the introduction of new technology, or simply the complexities of the established technical solution and business interests. In this regard, the PMO can examine the:
- Nature of collaboration required
- Level of management involvement
- Inclusion and availability of technical expertise
- Participation by external stakeholders (and their collaboration capabilities)

Identifying the working locations of project participants, along with considering the types of required interactions and the complexity of project efforts, will help the PMO begin to discern the needs for collaboration tools and techniques. As this information emerges, the PMO can begin developing its approach to the collaboration component of knowledge management.

Next, the PMO will formulate the best means to achieve preferred project management collaboration. In particular, the PMO will identify what types of system applications or activities are necessary to facilitate collaboration efforts, which includes considering the following collaboration mechanisms:

■ *E-mail:* A message creation and distribution system, as well as a virtual standard in today's business organizations for communicating and tracking project information.
■ *Instant messaging:* Also a real-time message creation and distribution system, but which limits real-time access to communication and collaboration only to those participants currently connected to the system. This capability is provided through certain types of on-line Web-based communication applications, selected Internet service providers, as well as some mobile telephone and paging systems.
■ *Face-to-face meetings:* Real-time personal interactions used to facilitate deliberation and discussions regarding technical, business, and project management topics.

- *Telephone conferencing:* A means to provide real-time deliberation and discussion among participants. Because this system may constrain the number of active participants by relegating other conference attendees to listening-only status, it is not practical for more than a handful of participants.
- *Video conferencing:* Similar to telephone conferencing, but it is enhanced by visual display of participants, as well as referenced displays and diagrams. These enhancements can incur considerable additional equipment costs, which the needs of the relevant organization may warrant, particularly if videoconference equipment and costs are shared across business units.
- *Web-based collaboration:* The systems and tools in this collection all perform project-related communication and collaboration within the context of their connectivity to the Internet or an intranet. Some may be associated with network-based applications and are differentiated by the features offered. They include the following generic tools:
  - Web-based presentation systems, which enable on-line audio-visual presentations to audiences of various sizes. Some systems provide for reruns of stored presentations.
  - Web-based communication systems — either an integrated feature of Web-based presentation systems or separate — enable interactive participation in on-line presentations and meetings where larger audiences require a participant–moderator capability.
  - Dedicated and open chat rooms, which provide both real-time conversation mode and forum-type conversation "threads" on various pertinent topics.
  - Task management systems, which provide for on-line assignment of project tasks to team members and others while also tracking and managing task progress.
  - On-line work spaces, which facilitate document and work-in-progress reviews by various project participants. Such work spaces can also transfer or exchange partially completed work products for use by other project participants. (This represents specialized use of project of knowledge spaces, which is reiterated in the next section about project archives and reference library.)
  - On-line time management systems, which enable the collection and management of individual participant time on project work. This feature may be integrated with other on-line systems, particularly task managers.

The PMO should gain an understanding of the relevant organization's collaboration needs and examine practical tool and system solutions in formulating its approach to the collaboration management element of knowledge management.

Project Archive and Reference Library Management

The capability to access and use lessons learned from previous projects is an essential activity of effective project management. Through the construction of a project archive (that is presumably on-line), users are able to access pertinent information elements for review or for application to new project planning efforts. Similarly, a project management information library, enhanced by knowledge management tools and features, can assist project teams in their individual and collective performance efforts.

Applying the following general tools can help in creating and managing the project archive and reference library capabilities of this knowledge management component.

Project Information Storage Database

The project information storage database is the on-line project information center that contains critical information about past and present project work. It may be the primary tool selected for the project management information system that also has the capability and capacity to retain and access information on previously conducted projects. In particular, it addresses the project work breakdown structure (WBS), the project work plan (cost, schedule, and resource utilization), and the project risk management plan. This inherently provides indications of the accuracy of project estimates and allows standard estimates to be adapted for particular project use. This storage database may contain important project information components, such as project performance feedback and lessons learned, or this information may be captured using a project management knowledge space, described below.

Project Management Knowledge Spaces

This system tool extends the reference library features for accessing real-time and relevant project information and project management knowledge. Able to cover any imaginable topic the PMO may want to pursue, this tool includes user contributions in the form of project documents, technical papers, and on-line threaded or real-time discussions that essentially serve to expand the understanding of points and topics presented. After the project management information system, the use of knowledge spaces may be an organization's single most valuable tool. Because it can also be a significant cost item, it warrants PMO consideration of the following types of knowledge space use:

- *Technical knowledge space:* Provides access to technical papers and presentations that have value in the project management environment. This material can be compiled and stored on internal systems or provided via an Internet address for access at the source location. One or more knowledge spaces can be constructed to address multiple technical disciplines.

- *Project team knowledge space:* Provides on-line capabilities to exchange ideas in a discussion forum, display the project work plan and track project progress, attach project plans and documents for project team members to access, as well as conduct planning and document-review and -approval activities.

- *Project management forum:* Provides on-line capabilities to exchange project management concepts and ideas, identify and discuss current practices and solutions applied to project efforts, deliberate best practices in project management, and reference other relevant on-line forums. This is a cross-project knowledge space that all project stakeholders in the relevant organization can access.

- *PMO knowledge space:* Provides the PMO staff with a working knowledge space similar to that furnished to project teams. It can be used to assist in creating and managing PMO functions.

- *Vendor/contractor knowledge space:* Provides a means to identify and select vendors and contractors for project work assignments, manage their contractual responsibilities, and track their performance for ongoing consideration in subsequent work assignments.

- *Customer knowledge space:* Provides a means to capture information about customers for use in the project management environment. Such concerns as customer project history, customer performance issues, and customer evaluations, in particular, can be captured and examined for future reference.

- *Project management and industry news:* Provides access to news articles (normally as Internet addresses to Web pages) that are pertinent to the project efforts that the relevant organization conducts.

- *Project management publications:* Provides a general review of project management and technical books, and possibly incorporates a recommended reading list. This knowledge space also may contain a listing of relevant magazines and periodicals and may include an Internet address for on-line access to reviews or entire manuscripts.

■ *Project history knowledge space:* Provides for Web-based display of relevant information from past projects, per information captured or derived from the project database — project descriptions, project classification, project results, etc.

■ *Project management training:* Provides for Web-based review of internal and external training courses relevant to project partici-pants. This consists of descriptions of optional and mandatory training and provides on-line registration capability.

These are a few ways in which knowledge spaces can be developed for use in the project management environment. The PMO should consider pursuing these, together with other types of knowledge spaces, to achieve a full-capability project archive and reference library.

Project Archive and Reference Library Options

The project archive and reference library can contain the following optional features:

■ *Project management knowledge database:* An internal/external on-line system that enables project management information, technical guidance, and practice reference materials to be identified, col-lected, and stored as needed, or referenced for random access by users in the project management environment. This may not nec-essarily involve one system but, rather, a collection of several systems that provide access to project management concepts and techniques, white papers, sample tools and templates, on-line publications and project management news, and similar reference materials. The project management knowledge database may be a combination of the project information database and the project knowledge spaces and may possibly include other knowledge management access capabilities and features, which are also described in this section. In essence, this database represents the conceptual location for the project management reference library materials to be introduced for use in the project management environment, since this material will have to reside in a stored format somewhere.

■ *Search capability:* The on-line project management reference library and knowledge management system should include the capability to search internal knowledge databases, as well as exter-nal sources on the Internet, to locate needed information. In particular, automated search capability can be established to automatically seek information on the Internet using keywords, phrases, or even names of vendors, contractors, or competitors.

■ *Executive dashboard:* This may be a separate tool connected with the project management information system, or it could be presented in a knowledge space format. Inasmuch as information in this space will likely need to access the project database, creating this reference is a matter of PMO preference, with consideration for the capability that the primary project information database tool can provide.

■ *E-training:* This library feature presents internal and external online project management and technical training programs that are accessible to users.

■ *Commercial project management portals:* Many project management library features described in this list are available through this option. While some features are free, some have additional cost, usually in the form of an individual or organizational subscription fee. Most portals permit users to access various types of project management and technical information and publications; some include project management tools and templates that are available for download; and still others provide project team "knowledge spaces," "chat rooms," and discussion forums. This is a good alternative for the PMO to consider when it does not plan to pursue its own internal knowledge management system.

It is important to note that the automated focus of this discussion of project archive and reference library options does not preclude continued development of the traditional library, such as books, papers, and publications. In that regard, the PMO may wish to maintain a physical library in conjunction with its automated knowledge management system capability.

Introduce Knowledge Management System

The preceding section discussed defining the knowledge management concepts and practices for the relevant organization. The discussion that follows considers the planning required to introduce the preferred approach. This includes identifying the configuration of recommended hardware and software; specifying what system customization or "buildup" is necessary; and preparing for project knowledge content entry, transfer, and connectivity with other systems. These activities are described in the following subsections.

Establish Hardware and Software Configuration

The PMO should collaborate with the information technology (IT) department to examine and select an appropriate project knowledge management system architecture. However, it is the PMO's responsibility to ensure that the hardware and software selected will achieve the intended project knowledge management objectives. Actual hardware and software tool acquisition and implementation can be conducted within the PMO's "project management tools" function. The present activity, however, describes the prerequisite steps for identifying the preferred configuration of hardware and software to be used in the project management environment.

All in all, this effort provides insight into what hardware and software is needed to implement the preferred approach to knowledge management in the project management environment. It further identifies the hardware and software configurations that will be introduced in conjunction with project knowledge management system implementation.

The PMO will outline the results of the knowledge management framework examination presented earlier to identify the means by which it will introduce project knowledge management capability. It will then specify the types of software applications that are recommended to achieve the preferred approach in each of the knowledge management component areas. This entails considering and making decisions in the following three areas:

System Integration

The PMO should recommend what project information system capabilities will be sought as well as whether there will be one primary system or multiple systems that can be linked to manage:

- *Project information:* Management of cost, schedule, and resource utilization; often includes graphical depiction of project timelines and resource matrices, project reporting features, as well as executive dashboard project and program depictions
- *Project management information:* Management of activities performed across the project management life cycle; often includes checklists, templates, and information tracking forms to facilitate management and approval responsibilities
- *Project portfolio information:* Management of decisions and deliberation related to project selection, continuation, and termination as well as project prioritization; often includes on-line access to business case information and current project status

- *Project collaboration:* Management of on-line interactions among project team members and other relevant stakeholders within the project management environment; often includes task assignment and progress reporting, time management, and communication and discussion features
- *Project reference information:* Management of on-line access to project and business documentation (plans, policies, etc.), project management archives and library services, and internal and external project management information services

The PMO will have to determine which type of system will best serve its immediate project information management needs while also considering system expansion in the future, as may be identified in long-term plans.

System Connectivity

In collaboration with the IT department, the PMO should identify how its project information systems will operate in conjunction with its other systems (if there is more than one system) and with other current and planned business systems. Although the IT department may manage considerably more aspects and issues, these are a few of the key connectivity issues that the PMO may wish to know about and perhaps influence.

- Electronic data interchange requirements
- Software residence locations on networks
- External access requirements and capability
- Mobile computing interfaces (PDAs, wireless, dial-up modems, etc.)

Once necessary coordination has been accomplished, the PMO should rely on the IT department to fulfill system connectivity requirements.

System Customization

The PMO, in conjunction with guidance from the IT department, will need to determine what system customization and buildup should be accomplished and who will perform that work: the system vendor, the IT department, or resources within the project management environment. Planning in this area usually addresses customization that aligns the system with current processes and practices. However, it may also include customization that affects the capability for system interconnectivity. Normally, the IT department will lead or perform operating system configuration while the PMO will perform software application customization.

Design and Develop System User Interfaces

To assist users in accomplishing their work in the project management environment, the PMO will need to plan how users will access and use knowledge management systems. This may include a range of considerations from simply adding the final touches on current system user screens to creating new system user interfaces.

The PMO will need to identify the preferred user-interface features (in Web-based and standard-screen formats), and then plan and conduct system user-interface design and development activities to include the following areas:

- *Web-page screen design*: Provides the preferred, standard information content and screen appearance in a logical and relevant manner for user access
- *Automated Web-page generation*: Provides automated data calculations, introduction of new information from linked database systems, and report templates for display of information on pre-designed Web-page screens
- *Search-engine criteria specification*: Provides automated capability to build up the project management information library (database) through automated searches on the Internet
- *User access levels*: Provides access level definitions for the various types or categories of system users and administers security/password features of the system
- *User personalization*: Provides options for individual users to customize screens, reports, and screen content according to personal preferences or needs

The PMO can facilitate the design and development of these user-interface features to optimize system capabilities and maximize system benefits for users.

Introduce Project Knowledge Content

The capability and configuration of the total project knowledge management system will guide content management. However, the PMO will want to prescribe how all systems will capture, store, and organize relevant information. For each knowledge management framework component, it should specify its plan for achieving the following content-handling attributes.

Content Capture

This element specifies the means by which information is introduced into the project knowledge management system. To a large extent, project management data and information captures will be a manual-entry process. The project manager, team member, or designated project administrator will enter data and information content into the system when they become known or at specified recurring time frames. Automated calculations or electronic data transfers from other systems may generate some content as well. As a result, the PMO should be able to identify the source of required knowledge management system information, particularly if there will be any requirements for individual manual entry. Such requirements must be conveyed to system users.

Content Storage

This content management element specifies where the data or information resides. This may be a moot point if the project knowledge management system is totally automated and requires no manual database or storage setup or access outside of IT department management. However, defining this element becomes more essential when users of the knowledge management system create electronic files and documents and have the associated responsibility for addressing their storage locations. The PMO should identify preferred databases and other electronic file storage locations and then convey the electronic or on-line system storage addresses to system users.

Content Organization

This element of content management addresses the relationships between and among knowledge management data elements. It provides for examination of data and information to ensure time relevance and content compatibility. Time relevance means making sure that two or more data elements used in calculations, presented in reports, or introduced into discussions and deliberations are of the same time period and, therefore, relevant to one another. Content compatibility means verifying that each data element used, particularly those retrieved from connected systems, is what it is supposed to be. To illustrate this latter point, one knowledge management system component may access a data element from a connected system that uses a data field identifier called "Project ID." For a given value of "Project ID," that data field identifier must refer to the same project in all systems. The PMO must be reasonably assured that all data and information are checked and properly organized for time relevance and content compatibility as they are introduced into project knowledge management system components.

Implement Knowledge Management System

The specific features of the project knowledge management system will be designed and implemented based on prerequisite deliberation and decisions that define the knowledge management framework for the relevant organization. The PMO can consider the following guidance for designing and implementing project knowledge management system components.

Develop Project Management Information System (PMIS)

The PMIS represents the fundamental capabilities of information capture and exchange within the project management environment. It is the traditional term and approach applied to project data and information handling. As such, it retains high importance within the context of this PMO "project knowledge management" function model. The PMIS includes several elements that the PMO must consider to ensure effective communication within the project management environment. The PMO has responsibility for implementing these elements using the one or more project knowledge management system components selected and installed for use. The PMO should adapt its project knowledge management system to deliver as many of the following six features and capabilities as the selected project management information system provides.

Project Plans

The PMO should design and implement the means to prepare and access project plans, which include the following:

- *Project plan*: The document that defines the project and guides project management activities, and includes:
    - Project definition: Project scope, objectives, preliminary schedule and cost; identification of project manager, sponsor, and key resources; etc.
    - Technical solution elements: Technical approach steps and detailed description of how project objectives will be achieved, including identification of techniques and technologies used
    - Project business case: Customer information, customer needs and expectations, technical capability to perform the project,

strategic business interest, assumptions and constraints, business risk, feasibility and cost-benefit analyses, etc.
- Business solution elements: Costs, fees and expenses, vendor costs, contract terms and conditions, etc.
- *Project work plan*: The project work breakdown structure (WBS), with cost, schedule, and resources identified and appended for each work element.
- *Primary project management support plans*: Documents that are prepared to expand on concepts and provide routine project management guidance. The following plans can be considered individually or combined and prepared as one project management support plan:
  - Risk management plan
  - Communications management plan
  - Scope management plan
  - Schedule management plan
  - Cost management plan
  - Procurement management plan
  - Quality management plan
  - Staffing management plan
- *Secondary project management support plans*: Documents that are prepared to expand project management guidance, as needed, with regard to organizational policies, achievement of business objectives, industry practices, project complexity and risk factors, and the experience level of the project team. The following plans can be prepared on an as-needed basis and appended to the project management support plan:
  - Budget management plan
  - Business case management plan
  - Customer support plan
  - Cost estimating plan
  - Project documentation plan
  - Facilities management plan
  - Financial performance plan
  - Project auditing plan
  - Marketing plan
  - Performance review plan
  - Project structure plan
  - Staff training plan
  - Staff integration and transition plan
  - Materials acquisition plan
  - Standards compliance plan
  - Vendor/contractor management plan

- Transportation plan
- Project close out plan
- Operations transition plan

Project Reports

The PMO should design and implement the means to prepare and access project reports, which includes the following general types:

- *Project progress or tasking reports:* Normally prepared by project team members to indicate progress toward accomplishing assigned project tasks, with distribution to the project manager
- *Project status reports:* Commonly prepared by project managers to indicate the current project status relative to planned cost, schedule, and resource utilization; to identify problems, issues, and their resolution; to specify deliverables and achievement of project objectives; to confirm contract compliance or note contract modifications; and to address accomplishment of business objectives; with distribution to the project sponsor, executive control board, and the PMO
- *Project portfolio reports:* Customarily prepared by the PMO and containing aggregate results or indicators of project performance, business case fulfillment, and recommendations for project continuation or alternative actions (such as project audits, temporary hold, termination); with distribution to the executive control board
- *Project audit reports:* Usually prepared by the lead auditor (which is sometimes the project manager) to present the findings and recommendations of a project or technical audit; with distribution to the project sponsor and the PMO, as well as to other project stakeholders as deemed appropriate

Project Management Documents

The PMO should design and implement the means to prepare and access project management documents, which includes the following:

- *Project charter:* Specification of project management authority, funding allowance, and authorization to proceed with project management and technical life cycle activities. This document may be incorporated as an element of the project definition document, as deemed appropriate within the relevant organization.
- *Scope change management documentation:* Management of project scope change requests, change request reviews and analyses, scope change approval, and change notice actions

- *Project issues log:* Identification and resolution management of project customer, project sponsor, and project team issues; may include the consideration and documentation of problem management
- *Contact log:* Identification and management of important project stakeholder contacts
- *Actions log:* Identification and management of critical project or technical activities (including postmeeting action management) that are not otherwise covered in project planning documents

Technical Plans and Documentation

The PMO should design and implement the means to prepare and access project technical documents, which includes the following:

- Technical requirements document
- Technical specifications document
- Engineering and technical site survey
- Technical standards and procedures
- Technical design document
- Technical review document
- Technical testing and validation plan
- Product quality control plan
- Configuration management plan
- Construction and engineering plan
- Health and safety plan
- Inspection plan
- Logistics support plan
- Make-or-buy plan
- Manufacturing plan
- Field support plan
- Product life cycle plan
- Regulatory compliance plan
- Systems integration plan
- Tooling plan

Contract Documentation

The PMO should design and implement the means to prepare and access project contract documents, which includes the following:

- Customer technical and business proposals
- Customer contracts

- Customer contract modifications
- Customer deliverable acceptance documents
- Customer invoices
- Vendor/contractor proposals
- Vendor/contractor contracts
- Vendor/contractor contract modifications
- Vendor contractor document submittals and reports
- Vendor/contractor deliverable acceptance documents
- Vendor/contractor invoices

Meetings and Collaborative Events

The PMO should design and implement the means to prepare and access information and documents concerning project meetings and similar collaborative events (for example, technical reviews, performance reviews, technical solution discussions, etc.), which include the following:

- Meeting agenda preparation
- Meeting scheduling (date, time, location, and method, such as in person, on-line, via phone)
- Notification of meeting participants
- Meeting actions and follow-up responsibilities

This PMIS element can also be considered relative to the subsequent discussion of on-line collaboration, if that becomes a prevalent meeting method.

Develop Executive Dashboard

The executive dashboard can be viewed as a condensed and graphical representation of the project status report in real time. Its name corresponds to instruments on an automobile's dashboard panel, which may vary from graduated dials to displays of specific values. Despite the naming convention, executives are not the only project stakeholders who can benefit from accessing such information. However, the project information needs of the executive are usually the primary factors in the design and development of the executive dashboard.

The PMO should identify the requirements and construct an executive dashboard solution that provides appropriate project information to prominent users. The PMO can consider the following sample information elements in designing and developing an executive dashboard capability that serves key project stakeholders of the relevant organization:

- Primary dashboard indicators
  - Project status*
    - Green indicator: project is proceeding according to plans
    - Yellow indicator: project has some variation but it falls within allowable tolerances
    - Red indicator: project has some critical variations from plans
  - Project milestones
    - Identified milestone
    - Milestone achievement status (completed/not completed)
  - Project deliverables
    - Identified deliverable
    - Deliverable achievement status (delivered/not delivered)
- Secondary dashboard indicators
  - Project risk management performance
    - Risk events (for past project periods to date, perhaps by life cycle phase)
    - Risk response implementation (yes/no)
    - Risk control effectiveness (percentage of impact reduction)
  - Project issues management
    - Issue type (per such categories as customer, project team, vendor/contractor, etc.)
    - Issue description statement
    - Issue resolution statement
    - Issue status (open/closed)
  - Customer invoice status
    - Invoices submitted (invoice ID, date, amount)
    - Invoice amounts paid (invoice ID, date, amount)

This sample listing represents a few common executive dashboard content elements. The PMO can decide which of these or other information elements are needed for the dashboard it will implement in the relevant organization. In that regard, the dashboard should contain sufficient information to give users an adequate high level perspective of project status and its performance. It should also provide links to more-detailed project information according to individual user needs. For example, the dashboard can be prepared as an automatically refreshed Web page or by using a predefined display scheme that the deployed knowledge management system provides.

---

* Note that these status indicators can be presented for the overall project or for each of the three critical work plan elements: cost, schedule, and resource utilization.

Construct Project Management Library

The project management library is an on-line reference tool that virtually all stakeholders in the project management environment can use. Although selected content may warrant access control, a large part of this project knowledge management component should be accessible to project managers, project sponsors, and project team members.

The PMO can use the inherent capabilities of the project management information system and supplement them as necessary with other knowledge management system components to provide a complete and comprehensive project management library facility that contains the information elements described below:

- *Project lessons learned:* Information and recommendations from previously completed projects that can be applied to current project planning efforts. For easy reference, lessons learned can be captured and organized into the following categories:
  - Customer feedback
  - Project manager feedback
  - Project team feedback
  - Project cost, schedule, and resource estimating results
  - Technical and technology feedback
  - Executive feedback and guidance
- *Project archives:* A repository for project management plans and technical documents that can support postproject analyses and studies, provide reusable technical and project management solutions, and review project management and technical process effectiveness. Project archives also can be aligned with the project team knowledge spaces described in the next section.
- *Policy guidance:* A reference to applicable policy and governance information that has application in the project management environment. This may comprise policies that direct the use of project management and technical methodologies, tools and practices, standard business objectives for every project, and industry and government regulatory guidance and mandates.
- *Industry news:* A reference to current news articles and publication content that deals with pertinent business, technical, and project management topics. This can be managed as a collection of industry-relevant news and information that is either captured and stored for later network database access by users or is represented by links to specified Web pages that are compiled and categorized for subsequent user access via the Internet. This information collection effort can include automated and manual information searches based on relevant key words, as well as monitoring and

participating in on-line business, technical, and project management forums, chat rooms, or Webinars.

■ *Papers and presentations:* An on-line repository for relevant internal and external technical papers and presentations dealing with business, technical, and project management topics. Information that is submitted at professional conferences and conventions or obtained from those sources or individuals can be categorized and stored for access in the project management environment.

■ *Project audits database:* An on-line repository of the different project and project management audits that the PMO conducts. In general, this is essentially a document repository, but some PMOs may want to construct a more rigorous audit quantification system that provides a more detailed automated analysis capability. The project audits database will necessarily have restricted user access and can be used for subsequent internal studies in the project management environment.

Implement On-Line Project Collaboration

The PMO can maximize collaboration in the project management environment by implementing knowledge management tools. In the context of this PMO function, collaboration means enabling project team members and other stakeholders to communicate and exchange information that helps to achieve project objectives.

The PMO can use three prominent tools to facilitate project team collaboration:

Project Team Knowledge Spaces

This is an on-line information center — often represented in Web-page format — that is established for every major project. However, other configurations can also be used. For example, the project manager, cohesive project teams working multiple projects, and even business units can also set up team spaces. Possible content for such knowledge spaces includes:

■ Project charter
■ Project definition and other descriptive information
■ Project status information
■ Project logbooks
■ Project reports
■ Participant contact list (telephone, location, e-mail address, etc.)
■ Customer information, including links to customer Web sites

- Vendor/contractor information, including links to vendor/contractor Web sites
- Links to relevant industry news and information Web sites
- Links to project plans and technical documentation (see handover spaces, below)
- Links to relevant project management information portals
- Links for project management methodology access (such as process and practice guidance, as well as forms, checklists, templates, etc.)
- A dedicated project team chat room to chronicle project management and technical discussions pertaining to the project (see also general discussion rooms, below)

The project team knowledge space is an on-line location that provides quick and easy access to project information that the project team and other stakeholders require. This tool's Web-based nature makes it accessible to geographically dispersed project team members.

Product Review and Handover Spaces

This is an on-line repository of project and technical documentation that authorized individuals can access. Represented by on-line work spaces where project and project management deliverables are created and stored, it can be used to:

- Store and access project plans, including retrieval for review and approval
- Store and access technical documents, with particular emphasis on retrieval and use of documents by different project team members (possibly at different geographical locations) for iterative design and development of project deliverables
- Store and access project deliverable electronic files and documents for quality review and approval, both internally and by customers
- Store and access vendor/contractor electronic file and document deliverables
- Provide simple or extensive feedback from technical and management reviews, as well as next-step guidance for iterative design and development activities
- Facilitate access to iterative deliverables for use in concurrent engineering of other project deliverables

The product review and handover space can be used to convey any deliverable design and development documentation that project team members need, including access to actual project deliverables that are constructed in electronic formats.

General Discussion Rooms

This is an on-line collaboration feature that traverses the project management environment. It can be developed for a wide audience, like all stakeholders within the project management environment or for a specified user group, such as all project managers. It presents a capability for ongoing exchange of knowledge and information about project management, which can be conveyed in formats such as live on-line chat and threaded topic forums. One or more on-line discussion rooms can be developed to provide such capabilities as:

- Forum for exchanging project manager knowledge and information
- On-line project management mentoring through an "ask the expert" forum
- Forum for discussing new techniques and emerging technologies
- Real-time distribution of lessons learned
- Forum for organizational news and announcements about current and new projects

The introduction of general discussion rooms emphasizes a cross-project and cross-business unit collaboration capability within the relevant organization.

Implement Other Knowledge Management Tools and Techniques

This PMO "project knowledge management" function generally retains the traditional considerations of strong project communication while presenting a relatively new focus on intensive collaboration or interaction within the project management environment. To that end, this PMO function model does not presume to provide a comprehensive examination of emerging knowledge management concepts and practices. However, there are a few more knowledge management tools and considerations that the advanced PMO may want to consider in its evolution. The list below briefly describes a few:

- *Project management methodology system access:* Provides interconnectivity between knowledge sources and the processes and practices of the preferred project management methodology system.
- *Customer information knowledge spaces:* Provides capability for customers to have their own Web page on the relevant organiza-

tion's knowledge management system as a means to access information (such as project status, reports, and deliverables) relative to the customer project being conducted and possibly including an interactive communication capability, together with contract and invoice information.

- *Vendor/contractor knowledge spaces:* Provides capability for preferred vendors and contractors to have their own Web page on the relevant organization's knowledge management system as a means to access relevant project information, as well as to provide information about their participation and progress.
- *Project portfolio management system access:* Provides interconnectivity between knowledge sources and the processes and practices of the preferred project portfolio management system.

POSTSCRIPT FOR THE SMALLER PMO

The smaller PMO has a somewhat equal advantage in implementing the knowledge management function. In terms of cost and capability, the smaller PMO can normally compete with its larger counterparts in providing comparable knowledge management tools and practices to satisfy the needs of its relevant organization. This equality is based on the consideration that every project management environment requires some level of communication and collaboration, and each organization commits some level of cost and effort to achieve the capability it needs.

Communication costs noted that there are three fundamental project knowledge management capabilities which the smaller PMO should consider to provide adequate communication and collaboration capability within the project management environment:

- Identify and implement one standard project management information system (PMIS) — one that (a) facilitates input from the project manager and project team members while providing them with access to important project management information and (b) provides senior management access to project information needed for business decisions.
- Acquire and install an efficient (preferably Web-based) project team and project stakeholder collaboration tool, if not already integrated as a component of the PMIS. Project managers need to communicate with project team members, vendors and contractors, the project sponsor, and relevant executives; and project team members need to communicate with one another. However, they all not only need to communicate, they also need to collaborate and exchange their concepts, ideas, and knowledge. Thus, this tool becomes a

critical need for geographically dispersed or virtual project team members.

▪ Establish a basic project management archive capability. It is imperative that lessons learned be captured from each project conducted and be made available for review and consideration when planning similar, subsequent projects. It is additionally important to have a reference to how well project management plans have performed in order to adjust planning on future projects. The PMO should determine the best way to collect and retain this information as a part of the automated knowledge management system it constructs.

The smaller PMO will do well to facilitate appropriate levels of contact among participants within the project management environment by ensuring that they have the necessary knowledge management tools that effectively accomplish communication and collaboration objectives.

II

INFRASTRUCTURE MANAGEMENT

5

PROJECT GOVERNANCE

The PMO is responsible for ensuring that the preferred business practices of the relevant organization are properly conveyed for use within the project management environment. The "project governance" function provides the authority and guidance necessary to enable the PMO and other project stakeholders to pursue project management objectives in a manner that is consistent with business interests and operating standards. It also provides for the ongoing examination of how well authority and guidance are being applied within the project management environment, where the PMO serves the dual roles of examiner and examinee.

This "project governance" function enables the PMO to:

- Establish its authority to develop, implement, and manage project management practices and associated business interests within the relevant organization
- Introduce and apply organizational and business standards, policies, and directives within the project management environment
- Confer authority and responsibility for project performance to project managers
- Facilitate executive and senior management involvement in project management
- Convene management and technical advisory boards, councils, and committees to collaborate decisions and provide guidance relevant to the project environment

The PMO ensures that project management and PMO functions are conducted within accepted boundaries of established business practices and guidance. At the same time, it translates business requirements and develops methods for conducting business within the project management environment. Furthermore, it can also contribute project management practices to influence how business objectives are achieved outside the project management environment. This is the two-way nature of the PMO's "project governance" function.

PROJECT ENVIRONMENT INTERFACE CONCEPTS

The PMO should be the centrally recognized authority for project management within the relevant organization. This centralization provides for consistent leadership and management across all projects, in contrast to each project being an independent work effort accomplished as dictated by individual or departmental interests and priorities. The PMO provides the common level of project management oversight and control that spans all projects. Recognition of the PMO as a central authority facilitates: a consistent and repeatable approach to project management based on preferred standards and practices; translation and integration of business interests from a single and reliable source; technical guidance for achieving accuracy in project planning, tracking, and forecasting; and aggregation of project performance results for timely management review.

The PMO presents project management and project manager interests to senior management. It has a primary role to interface with executive and senior managers to convey not only project performance results, but also to identify the needs of the project environment that will make it more technically viable, more professionally competitive, and more aligned with advancements in the project management discipline. The PMO's authority coincides with its responsibility to keep senior management informed about the state of capability within the project environment.

The PMO's "project governance" function prominently includes efforts to work with executives and senior managers to solicit and implement their guidance regarding oversight and control of project performance and project management activities. This is generally accomplished through mutual participation on advisory boards and in decision-making forums. This is the PMO's direct interface with business managers at all levels in the relevant organization. It is the primary means to identify, consolidate, and translate organizational business decisions into actions or directives requiring implementation in the project management environment.

The PMO also is ideally situated to develop, guide, and possibly manage the distribution of authority given to project managers. More specifically, the PMO can pursue expansion of project manager authority levels promoted by concepts of modern project management. It can assist in defining the qualifications associated with increasing levels of authority, and then collaborate with functional managers to identify individuals demonstrating skill, knowledge, and experience aligned with those qualifications. The PMO also can coordinate with project sponsors to assist them in developing project charters that specify authority for each project undertaken. Some PMOs may take on the responsibility for issuing project charters.

Of course, the PMO also needs a charter to conduct its business. This PMO function facilitates the creation of a PMO charter along with its coordination and approval at the executive level.

BUSINESS ENVIRONMENT INTERFACE CONCEPTS

The PMO's "project governance" function demonstrates to business managers across the relevant organization that they retain control and influence over their business objectives and interests. To a large extent, it may even provide the means for business managers to expand their control and influence into the project management environment to ensure that business interests are being achieved. Two primary types of governance are recommended to provide this interface between business managers and the PMO.

The first type of governance is an executive control board. This board comprises representatives of senior management within the relevant organization. For enterprise level PMOs, this board would ideally include the chief executive officer. This board, or possibly a single executive on the board, is the senior manager responsible for the PMO's performance and serves as the approval authority for the PMO's charter. The head of the PMO will normally report to this board or, more specifically, to a designated executive on this board. This business alignment and oversight at the executive level ensures that all important business interests and objectives are conveyed and implemented within the project environment. If project portfolio management has been introduced, this executive control board would be the guiding body for its implementation. To that end, board composition would be the CEO and executives who hold or otherwise influence project portfolio management.

The second type of governance needed may include one or more technical or business advisory committees. In some cases these technical-based and business interest groups already exist within the relevant organization and can be used intact. For example, the PMO may be tasked to introduce a business standard for which an oversight committee has already been established. It can either call on this committee simply to provide established guidance, or it can determine whether committee participation is desirable and feasible and seek to provide PMO representation on the committee. In other cases, the PMO may seek specialized guidance either from business managers, project managers, or technical managers (or some combination of these) to achieve a particular objective. In this case, the PMO would convene the necessary committee to review, guide, and advise in technical and business matters applicable to the project management environment.

PROJECT GOVERNANCE ACTIVITIES ACROSS THE PMO CONTINUUM

The "project governance" function along the PMO competency continuum is initially characterized by activities that establish the PMO as a business activity having central authority and responsibility for project management across the relevant organization. This includes an acknowledgement of accountability to higher authority throughout the advancing stages of PMO development. However, it also illustrates progressively independent authority to "govern" in the project management environment without being burdensome to executives and senior managers.

Table 5.1 presents an overview of the range of prescribed PMO project governance activities according to each level in the PMO competency continuum.

The *project office*, in the form of the project manager, is the first line of authority for project management. The project charter is the instrument that conveys the necessary authority to manage project work. It also is the instrument that can specify what information or feedback is required from the project manager to the PMO and, ultimately, to the responsible executive or executive control board.

Mid-range PMO levels have the responsibility of introducing the capability and asserting appropriate authority within the project management environment. In particular, the mid-range PMO is responsible for using its authority to implement the business and technical policies and guidance deliberated and decided by executives and senior managers who have vested interests in project performance. Throughout this level of PMO operations, the PMO will play an influential role in developing and recommending project management policies and guidance for senior management review and approval. The PMO may evolve to hold its own authority to prescribe policy and guidance without excessive senior management review, although it continues its close collaboration with senior management representatives from business units.

The *center of excellence* takes on a business unit-type approach to project governance. It is concerned with oversight and the delegation of authority within the project environment, but with a distinct cross-functional business interest and perspective. It will look at what authority different participants need, and how that authority can be placed at the appropriate level of management to maximize effectiveness for all business operations.

Table 5.1 Range of Project Governance Activities across the PMO Continuum

Project Office	Basic PMO	Standard PMO	Advanced PMO	Center of Excellence
Conducts project management using authority conveyed by a project charter	Introduces essential business authority and policy guidance for use in project management ■ Establishes the PMO charter ■ Develops policy guidance needed in the project environment ■ Identifies project managers' scope of authority ■ Specifies project classification	Ensures that business and technical guidance is properly conveyed to the project environment ■ Establishes an executive control board ■ Convenes and uses business and technical advisory boards and committees ■ Monitors project environment for use of business and technical guidance	Manages authority for direct interfaces with organizational business managers ■ Collaborates on preparation of policy, practices, and guidance used by project managers ■ Establishes requirements for cross-functional business support ■ Identifies project sponsors' scope of authority	Develops and contributes practice guidance for use across the relevant organization ■ Recommends adaptation of business processes ■ Assesses practices of the executive control board ■ Establishes cross-functional task forces for major practice renovations

The PMO's "project governance" function undoubtedly will be established consistent with the existing culture and distribution of authority that exists within the relevant organization. That considered, it remains only to be said that the PMO, at whatever stage it is introduced, must have sufficient authority to influence the activities of the project management environment and to undertake and achieve the business objectives for which it was created.

PROJECT GOVERNANCE FUNCTION MODEL

The PMO's "project governance" function model presents the capability to define and construct a viable, if not a superb, project management capability within the relevant organization. It does this through authority granted and supported by senior management. It also requires a moderate amount of ongoing senior management involvement at critical junctures in the PMO's efforts to implement an effective and professional project management capability. As the PMO demonstrates its own capability and success, the early reliance on senior management decisions and approvals can be somewhat reduced, but it will never be eliminated. In project governance, the PMO is the extension of executive and senior manager authority within the project environment. That necessitates ongoing PMO coordination and collaboration at senior management levels across the relevant organization.

The prominent activities of the PMO's "project governance" function model are depicted in Figure 5.1. Each activity is described in the following subsections.

Prepare and Maintain PMO Charter

The PMO is created to oversee, control, and support the project management capability of the relevant organization. It is normally designed relative to the existing business and cultural norms of the organization. Some PMOs may vary from those norms, and in such cases, it may require a concerted effort to introduce and manage the required organizational changes. Whatever the conditions, the PMO should pursue its mission based on a PMO charter that is documented and approved at the highest management level within the relevant organization.

The PMO charter is a "living document" that can be updated and adapted to organizational changes, growth of the project management environment, or PMO expansion as a business unit. As a document, the PMO charter should be no more than a few written pages in length. A two-to-three page PMO charter document should be sufficient to present all of the credentials and guidance that will be needed.

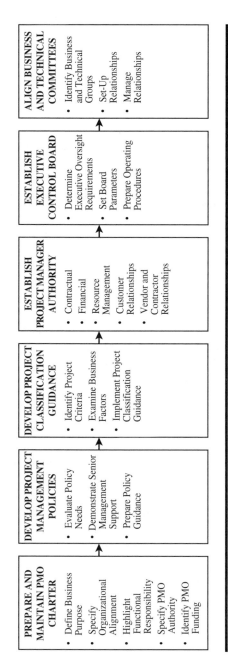

Figure 5.1 "Project Governance" Function Model

PREPARE AND MAINTAIN PMO CHARTER
- Define Business Purpose
- Specify Organizational Alignment
- Highlight Functional Responsibility
- Specify PMO Authority
- Identify PMO Funding

DEVELOP PROJECT MANAGEMENT POLICIES
- Evaluate Policy Needs
- Demonstrate Senior Management Support
- Prepare Policy Guidance

DEVELOP PROJECT CLASSIFICATION GUIDANCE
- Identify Project Criteria
- Examine Business Factors
- Implement Project Classification Guidance

ESTABLISH PROJECT MANAGER AUTHORITY
- Contractual
- Financial
- Resource Management
- Customer Relationships
- Vendor and Contractor Relationships

ESTABLISH EXECUTIVE CONTROL BOARD
- Determine Executive Oversight Requirements
- Set Board Parameters
- Prepare Operating Procedures

ALIGN BUSINESS AND TECHNICAL COMMITTEES
- Identify Business and Technical Groups
- Set-Up Relationships
- Manage Relationships

The PMO charter is constructed to:

- Describe its purpose relative to the achievement of business objectives
- Show its organizational alignment with other business functions or units
- Guide its development of functional capability
- Confer appropriate authority to accomplish its mission
- Identify PMO funding

The following sections describe the preparation of these five elements within the PMO charter.

Define Business Purpose

The PMO, while dedicated to the pursuit of excellence in project management, conducts its efforts with a somewhat higher purpose — to ensure that project performance contributes to improving business performance. How this will be accomplished is an element of the PMO charter that should be explicitly stated. If the PMO's business purpose is not stated, it could be viewed as an ad hoc attempt to fix an isolated or temporary condition within the project management environment.

Consider the following five points of discussion when formulating the statement of business purpose of a PMO.

Project Contributions to Business Revenue

Project management in many organizations directly represents the product or service that generates revenue — either directly for customer-specified work or indirectly as a matter of products on-the-shelf. Likewise, the PMO could concentrate on internal project work that is also indirect but still supports the generation of revenue by making the business environment more efficient and effective. The PMO charter should address these as business concerns that the PMO will manage. Avoid placing specific financial objectives in the PMO charter, as these can be identified elsewhere after the PMO functionality and authority have been established and tested. Rather, indicate why a business solution is being placed under the purview of the PMO.

Reduction in Project Disarray

The PMO can be instrumental in introducing the critical practices needed to gain control of an otherwise disorderly collection of projects. This is not to say that all projects are in disarray, but that a sufficient number of projects across the relevant organization have performance results that warrant some additional professional oversight and guidance. Project disarray can be identified by a variety of indicators — a change in the types of projects being conducted, reduction in force, excessive turnover and replacement of project managers and project team members, changes in senior management, reactions to customer satisfaction issues, and much more. Specify what responsibilities the PMO will have for improving project management performance and what centralized oversight, control, and support will be included in its responsibilities.

Project Management Competency

Is project management a core business competency? Should it be? The PMO may be established to build both organizational and individual competencies in project management. At the individual level, the PMO could provide training and education consistent with an individual's responsibility within the project environment. This would be done in conjunction with the identification and introduction of best practices in project management that allow them to translate their new skill and knowledge into immediate and effective solutions in the workplace. Similarly, at the organizational level, the PMO can lead the pursuit of increased organizational maturity in project management. Indicate in the PMO charter what responsibilities the PMO will have for improving or enhancing individual competency and organizational maturity in project management. This point of discussion could include the PMO's potential purpose of providing project management technical support — the options for project management mentoring, facilitation of project planning, conduct of formal and informal project audits and reviews, etc. In addition to being a primary resource for project management expertise that nearly all stakeholders in the project management environment can access, particularly project managers, the PMO may also have responsibility for technical process performance. If so, then that should also be specified in the PMO charter.

Project and Business Integration

The PMO's role as a business integrator has been mentioned many times. The PMO charter should indicate how that role would be played out within the relevant organization. In general, it means identifying what the PMO will do to facilitate the integration of appropriate process and business relationships between the project environment and business unit activities. In a broad sense, this represents a variation on the concept of project disarray resulting from internal inconsistencies and multiple perspectives on how business processes are conducted. The PMO charter can address the PMO's responsibilities for bringing business and project stakeholders together under common practices and objectives.

Strategic Business Objectives

When properly designed and designated, the PMO can be an extension of senior management within the project environment. It will carry the results of executive deliberation and decisions for implementation by project managers, and it will return compiled and analyzed results of project performance back to senior management for subsequent deliberation and decisions. This is particularly characterized by a project portfolio management process that ensures that executives are involved in making project selection, continuation, and termination decisions. Of course, that is done in the context of ensuring that all current and pending projects are aligned with the strategic business interests of the relevant organization. The highlights of any such strategic alignment responsibility can be presented in the PMO charter.

Specify Organizational Alignment

This element of the PMO charter specifies how the PMO will relate to other business functions in the relevant organization. This can be an easy determination for a smaller PMO operating within a relatively flat organization, or it can be an extensively coordinated determination with politically charged implications for a larger PMO or one in which operating units tend to function independently. There are three practical points of information that are needed to specify the PMO's organizational alignment.

First, the PMO must have an executive sponsor. Ideally, this sponsor is the most senior person in the relevant organization — the CEO if the PMO is supporting the enterprise. Business needs will help determine whether the PMO is aligned at a level that warrants direct reporting to the executive sponsor, or if it is to be aligned lower in the executive sponsor's business unit. The PMO charter should identify the executive sponsor and the executive or senior manager to whom the PMO reports, if these are not the same person.

Second, the PMO should be designated at a recognized business unit level — work group, branch, department, division, etc. This designation will inherently demonstrate the PMO's peer business unit relationships within the relevant organization. This designation will either facilitate or constrain the PMO's ability to accomplish its business purposes, but nonetheless it should be presented in the PMO charter.

Third, and somewhat related to the business unit designation above, is the identification of the individual slated to head PMO operations. The individual selected for this position must have the appropriate position title to manage PMO operations consistent with the business unit designation and the responsibilities assigned, i.e., PMO manager, PMO director, etc. The incumbent head of the PMO should be named in the PMO charter, along with confirmation of the position title.

Highlight Functional Responsibility

The PMO charter should indicate what PMO functionality will be established for new PMOs, or what will be added or eliminated for existing PMOs.

First, a review of the PMO functions is needed to determine applicability to the needs of the relevant organization and the stated purposes of the PMO. Presumably, a team responsible for PMO planning will accomplish this. Planners must be cognizant of the workload impacts — both in function implementation and function operations — as choices of preferred functions are made. However, with the assumption of qualified resources being assigned to the PMO, a wide range of functionality can be addressed. More important is the depth or extent of that functionality. Many of the functions presented in this PMO model can be adapted for simple implementation and use. The PMO can specify these as "initial" or "fundamental" capability. Other PMO functions, those directly aligned with the PMO's business purposes, can be cited as more comprehensive functions and planned accordingly.

Following this PMO function review, a list of preferred functions can be identified for inclusion in the PMO charter. This can be presented as a general statement of activities to be performed by the PMO, and this might include an item for developing a PMO design document and schedule for implementing the PMO. This more detailed plan is not normally a part of the PMO charter.

Specify PMO Authority

The PMO charter provides the PMO and other business units with an understanding of PMO responsibilities. It is therefore very important to outline the authority granted to the PMO to enable it to achieve its business purpose.

A new and usually smaller PMO may not require as much authority as one that has broader responsibilities. In many cases, the specification of organizational alignment is sufficient to define what the PMO can and cannot do based on the implicit authority of its position within the relevant organization. However, if there are unique authority needs, these should be addressed in the PMO charter.

There are five particular areas of PMO authority that should be considered for inclusion in the PMO charter, as needed:

- *Business and contract management:* Define what the PMO is authorized to do with regard to leading cross-functional business efforts and establishing internal and external contracts. In particular, external contract management has business implications for which the PMO may require signature or review authority. Specify what role the PMO has in business and contract management.
- *Financial management:* Define what financial responsibility the PMO has with regard to financial management. Specify what it is authorized to do regarding the commitment and allocation of funds; any requirements for management and reporting of revenue or cash flow resulting from external, customer work; and preparation and management of an internal business unit budget.
- *Resource management:* The PMO will likely work with resources obtained and "owned" by resource managers across the relevant organization. Specify what authority the PMO has to interact and direct the work efforts of individuals assigned to project teams within its purview. As well, consider any authority needed to redirect individuals to additional projects, project-related training, or follow-on work. This section also may include guidance on how the PMO is involved in selecting the project manager and the project team members as well as responsibility for individual performance review activities.
- *Customer relationship management:* Determine the PMO's authority for interactions with customers. Specify whether the PMO is the next level of issue resolution above the project manager, whether the PMO is involved in customer invoicing and payment management, and what role the PMO plays in ensuring customer satisfaction.
- *Vendor/contractor management:* Define how the PMO will interface with vendors and contractors in the project environment. Specify its level of authority in vendor and contractor selection; establishing and managing vendor/contractor contracts; and whether it is involved in vendor/contractor invoicing and payment management, including oversight of acceptable performance and approval of deliverables.

Identify PMO Funding

This section of the PMO charter may or may not be required as a matter of organizational practice. If parent organization funds and the associated budget are being used, this section may simply identify one or more expense codes that can be used by participants in PMO activities.

Conversely, if the introduction of the PMO is treated as a business initiative, then a separate budget is likely needed to appropriately place boundaries on progressive steps of PMO development and implementation. In this case, a funding statement should be presented to identify any initial or updated funding to be applied to PMO development and operations. This inherently implies that PMO development and operations costs will be tracked and managed.

Establishing and operating a PMO is not a casual expense item. If such an effort is treated as a routine business activity without recognizing the investment costs, the relevant organization may not get the expected value or anticipated results from the effort. The specification of funding in the PMO charter provides an acknowledgement that there is a cost associated with the pursuit of excellence in project management.

Develop Project Management Policies

Business guidance is prevalent throughout most organizations. Proper oversight of the project management environment warrants similar attention. The PMO must develop necessary policy guidance to ensure that all participants and stakeholders understand the business aspects of project management. The PMO actually only recommends policies; it is senior management, presumably the executive control board, that approves the PMO's recommendations and issues the policies for implementation by the PMO. By agreeing to guide project management policy, senior management is endorsing the use of project management as a preferred if not core competency within the relevant organization. Such endorsement is vital to the success of nearly all project management endeavors.

The PMO can facilitate development of project management policy using the three steps described below.

Evaluate Policy Needs

The PMO should examine areas of the relevant organization where development of project management policy will provide benefit without undue burden on individuals or business units. However, it is likely that "growing pains" will be experienced before benefits are realized, so some difficulties should be expected. The PMO can minimize any adverse impact by developing a complete understanding of the organization in conjunction with policy development.

The PMO should evaluate project management policy needs in the following areas:

- *Cultural reception:* Identify the prevalent culture of the relevant organization and indicate how that will influence the introduction or expansion of professional project management capabilities.
- *Organizational change capability:* Examine the change initiatives of the relevant organization to determine (a) how well individuals and business units have responded to the specification and (b) the results of change.
- *Current business practices:* Review business practices to ascertain how they fit with the preferred practices of project management. In particular, identify any business practices that appear contrary to best practices in project management.
- *Current project management practices:* Review project management practices, the methodology, and any linked technical processes and determine whether they represent benefits to project performance and associated business practices in the relevant organization.

This evaluation should enable the PMO to gain insight to the policies and senior management endorsements that are needed to support project management activities. The PMO should then use this information to develop required policies for review and approval by senior management.

Demonstrate Senior Management Support

It is essential that all participants in the project environment — project managers, team members, business unit managers, customers, and even vendors and contractors — understand the business interest and operational importance placed on project management within the relevant organization. This must be expressed by managers at all levels, and particularly by senior management. Before issuing written policy guidance, the PMO can assist executives and senior managers in conveying their positions on project management as a vital business initiative and an integrated component of their business operations. The PMO can facilitate this by illustrating the need and encouraging executive and senior managers in a few action areas:

- The PMO charter is endorsed and signed by the senior executive in the relevant organization. This is followed by personal endorsements of PMO operations by that executive in formal meetings and informal gatherings.

- Senior management participates in reviews of project performance commensurate with its position and responsibilities, and it routinely provides guidance to rectify performance problems and applauds performance excellence.
- Senior management demonstrates ongoing awareness of initiatives to improve project management capability, perhaps commenting on them in interviews and written articles. In situations of major initiatives that affect the entire organization, senior management convenes large group meetings to make formal announcements, issue press releases, and establish expectations for cross-functional participation and contributions to the efforts.
- Individual promotions in the project management environment are associated with the successful completion of initiatives that produce improved project performance or integration of project management and business practices.
- Consideration is given to making project management a core competency within the relevant organization. This is an executive decision that is a policy statement in itself.
- Policies created and implemented in the relevant organization that have application to the project environment are signed by the appropriate executive and endorsed by all members of the senior management team.

These actions by senior management will convey the business relevance of project management. They will do as much for policy implementation as will the written policy document.

The extent to which senior management support of project management appears lacking in the relevant organization provides an additional indicator to the PMO of the work that lies ahead. Any senior management support is needed and welcome. If there is a noticeable lack of support, the PMO can encourage buy-in by senior management by developing better ways to demonstrate the benefits of what can be achieved through the use of effective project management practices.

Prepare Policy Guidance

The PMO, as senior management's representative in the project management environment, examines the policy needs and senior management positions on the issues to develop policy guidance that can be implemented to support the efforts encountered within the project management environment.

There are four prominent areas in which the PMO will want to consider developing policy guidance, as summarized below:

■ *Business interest:* This type of policy guidance conveys the use of project management for purposes of achieving business objectives. This approach highlights the fact that project management and business processes and practices must be aligned and integrated. Such policies usually specify or mandate the use of a preferred process. They also indicate whether it is primarily a business process introduced into the project environment or a project management process introduced for use by business units.

■ *Project management as a core competency:* This is a specific policy that transcends all business units in the relevant organization. It establishes that business will be pursued with a high degree of reliance on individual capabilities in project management. This is a business decision that can only come from the most senior executive in the relevant organization.

■ *Enterprise continuous improvement:* This is a policy area that enables expansion of project management practices both within the project environment and throughout the relevant organization. It also represents expansion of PMO responsibilities, possibly across business units. Policies in this area specify or mandate the use of practices that provide more comprehensive oversight, control and support of project management activities. This approach is often aligned with pursuits of increased organizational maturity in project management.

■ *Project management practices:* This policy area indicates the required use of the established project management methodology within the project environment and, possibly, across the relevant organization. It also specifies the preferred business practices, tools, and standards that are applied in project management, and it presents requirements for use of project classification guidance. As well, it can specify requirements for project audits and reviews.

It should be noted that policy development operates within a different context than the "mere" guidance offered by standards, operating procedures, or regulatory documents. These can be prepared and implemented by the PMO, often on its own authority and perhaps with some level of senior management approval. However, the preparation of project management policy guidance presented by this PMO model is one of developing an "executive directive." That means that an executive within the relevant organization is establishing official business direction, and in this case, one that requires application of project management practices or principles.

The PMO should prepare its policy guidance in close collaboration with project managers and business unit managers, as the policy may influence them. This effort is one that requires ongoing coordination during development to ensure that all parties are aware of adjustments and modifications that may have occurred since a previous review. This culminates in a meeting for group acceptance of the recommended policy. Then the PMO presents the policy recommendation to senior management for signature and endorsement. When signed, the PMO will then conduct business according to the established policy, implementing procedures, conducting initiatives, and preparing further guidance as necessary to carry out policy.

Develop Project Classification Guidance

It is important for project management stakeholders to have a common frame of reference regarding the types of projects being performed. The establishment of a project classification scheme addresses this need. This determination is placed under the "project governance" function because it has distinct business implications. It is also placed here because it requires senior management review and may require an associated policy statement.

The specification of a classification for every project will assist the PMO in describing the important characteristics of each project, and it will allow stakeholders to immediately associate project importance to the business. Project classification, when constructed while considering the business interests of the relevant organization, will be an aid in the following areas:

- Selecting, prioritizing, and managing projects in portfolio management
- Aligning projects with business objectives
- Identifying business and technical risks that may be encountered
- Calculating levels of project work performed in different technical areas
- Providing general indications of duration, resource requirements, and complexity
- Identifying and assigning project managers with appropriate skill and experience
- Qualifying team members for participation in the project effort
- Selecting vendors and contractors for participation in the project effort

For some PMOs, this information could very well be the project performance indicators that it tracks and manages. The list is sufficiently condensed for use by senior managers, who may or may not have adequate time for detailed reviews of project performance results. Nevertheless, the use of a project classification scheme will convey a significant amount of information in a few words.

The PMO is responsible for creating and implementing a project classification scheme under this PMO function. Project classification criteria are developed to describe the project in terms of the business interests and the project work effort. This PMO function model prescribes a relatively simple, yet fairly complete, project classification scheme. It applies the four factors of business interest, project size, project value, and project complexity to classify projects.

The PMO can consider the following categories for inclusion in its project classification scheme:

- *Nature of business interest:* This category refers to the importance of the project to the organization and suggests four criteria:
  - *Base project:* A project that is usually short-term in duration, generally noncompetitive, and frequently concerned with providing an administrative or simple technical solution. This represents many of the internal projects conducted within an organization.
  - *Tactical project:* A general-interest project that is usually short- to medium-term in duration (although some may be long-term), tactical or operationally oriented, and concerned with developing established products or providing well-defined services.
  - *Growth projects:* A market-based project that can be short- to long-term in duration, tactical or operationally oriented, and concerned with developing a product or service having market growth objectives. It is performed as a result of emerging market demand, a response to changing business conditions, or a response to changing technology. It is usually concerned with delivery of new products or services or with modifications to existing products and services.
  - *Strategic project:* A market-based project that is usually long-term in duration, integrated with the organization's strategic business plan, and concerned with developing a product or providing a service that meets critical strategic business objectives. It is concerned with providing products and services to key customers, selected market segments, and new markets.
- *Project size:* Size is based on the amount of resource labor hours, the number of resources (project team members), and the approximate duration required to complete the project. The PMO will have to calibrate the size values for this criteria category to adequately represent the types of projects it conducts. Some sample values that can be used to describe project size include:

- *Small:* Up to 1000 labor hours, one to three project team members, and less than 2 months duration
- *Moderate:* Between 1000 and 2500 labor hours, two to five project team members, and up to 6 months duration
- *Intermediate:* Between 2500 and 5000 labor hours, up to ten project team members, and 6 to 12 months duration.
- *Large:* Over 5000 labor hours, usually more than ten project team members, and more than 1 year duration.

▪ *Project value:* The estimated cost or value of a project is critical to defining the project classification, as it indicates what financial gain or loss is at stake by undertaking the project effort. Again, the PMO will have to calibrate the project-value figures for this category to adequately represent the range of project values it encounters. Some sample figures that can be used to describe project value include:
- *Low value:* Up to $250,000
- *Moderate value:* $250,000 to $1 million
- *Intermediate value:* $1 million to $10 million
- *High value:* $10 million or more

▪ *Project complexity:* Project complexity is based on the following sample elements that may produce complications for the project effort. These sample elements can be adapted by the PMO to address specific matters of importance to the relevant organization. Each of these elements will also require a rating that serves as an indicator of complexity. In general, the PMO can start with simple ratings such as low, medium, high, and very high to describe the impact of these elements on a given project. More detailed calculations can be introduced as needed.
- *Number of business units:* The number of business units participating in the project, including cross-functional participation and external vendors and contractors, their locations considered, will affect project performance and project management requirements.
- *Technology factors:* The amount of technology that is introduced into the project will have an effect on the capability to provide the intended technical solution. This includes consideration of new technology, current technology, the likelihood of technology changes, and technology training requirements.
- *Risk:* This element considers the business risk produced primarily by external business influences and the technical risk associated with new product development, recurring project work, and development of new technology.
- *Strategic importance:* A project becomes more complex when it becomes more important to business success. This element

examines the alignment of the project with strategic business objectives, the level of importance associated with marketing efforts, and business factors such as net present value and results of cost-benefit analysis. Strategic importance can also be defined by executive mandate or demonstrated interest.

These four project classification categories should be sufficient to identify projects in most types of organizations after criteria values that are more appropriate to the organization are constructed to replace the samples shown. The PMO should create a tool or matrix that allows these elements to be combined and evaluated together.

The project classification can then be used to identify the type of project being undertaken. It provides a common frame of reference that allows all key participants to recognize the type and nature of each project, and it facilitates decisions along the way. As well, the nature of the content of this sample project classification scheme illustrates why this should be addressed within the PMO's "project governance" function.

Establish Project Manager Authority

The concepts of modern project management prompt continuing expansion of the project manager's responsibilities. The PMO must be a proponent for providing project managers with adequate project and business authority to allow them to accomplish their jobs. Of course, this can only be pursued with consideration for existing business practices, project management guidance, and cultural norms of the relevant organization. The PMO may find, however, that if project managers demonstrate responsibility toward achieving business objectives, appropriate levels of authority will be provided.

The PMO's role in this governance activity will be decided by its own level of authority, as presented in the PMO charter. If sufficiently vested, the PMO can serve to specify the level of project manager authority while also serving as the granting authority. Otherwise, the PMO's primary objective in this function element is to prepare recommendations for project manager authority levels for review and approval by the executive control board. The latter may be the more frequent approach taken by most PMOs.

Similar to the elements in the PMO charter, the PMO can examine the relevant organization's business interests, the stakeholders in the project environment, and project management performance requirements to identify the types of authority needed by project managers. It can then prepare its recommendations for project manager authority.

The following are examples of project manager authority the PMO will want to include in its deliberations:

■ *Contractual authority:* The PMO must determine whether project managers have any signature authority relative to customer contracts. Presumably, the organization's sales management team will sign any master contract. Conversely, the PMO may want project managers to have certain levels of authority to deal with such things as contract modifications and statements of work.

■ *Financial authority:* The PMO will use its knowledge about the nature of the business to guide the extent of financial responsibility given to the project manager. That, in turn, will indicate the level of associated financial authority needed by project managers. This consideration may require collaboration with the accounting department to ensure granted authority is recognized. It deals with such things as customer invoice management, vendor and contractor invoice management, and in some cases, special or additional employee compensation, such as bonuses or rewards.

■ *Resource management:* The PMO will likely operate in an environment where project team members are introduced to projects in a matrix format. This may present a need for broad collaboration within the relevant organization. Project resources working in a matrix format are assigned to resource managers. They are "borrowed" by project managers to work on specific project efforts, and then returned to the purview of the resource manager. The PMO must develop recommendations regarding how resource management authority can be shared between the resource manager and the project manager. Again, the business culture will influence this deliberation, but in some cases a new approach to project resource management can be designed as a result of the PMO's effort.

■ *Customer relationships:* The PMO will recognize that there are many business elements in the organization that influence each customer relationship. It needs to determine what role project managers will pursue as a part of the total business effort. Authority issues here deal with such things as customer contact protocols, customer satisfaction, and resolution and elevation of customer issues. This deliberation is particularly important when the project manager and project team perform work on site at client facilities, where they are the primary representatives of the relevant organization.

■ *Vendor and contractor relationships:* The PMO will likely want to be involved in any prequalification of vendors and contractors, and it may have an established process for doing this within its performance of PMO functions. However, once vendors and contractors have been validated, the PMO may find it to be of benefit to allow project managers to select them for specific work on projects.

The PMO can examine this list of project manager authorities and add to it based on the business interests and needs of the relevant organization. Following this review, the PMO should develop its recommendations for project manager authority. Key stakeholders in the project environment, and of course senior management, should review these recommendations. Then, senior management approves these authorities, and the PMO can then implement them in the project environment.

The PMO may want to consider varying levels of project manager authority. That is to say, project manager authority increases as each individual progresses to more advanced project management positions. Conversely, project manager authority can be specified for individuals who have project performance responsibility, where every project manager is given the same authority level based on standard project management practices rather than on position within the organizational hierarchy.

Establish Executive Control Board

The PMO in most organizations will be responsible to an executive team — the executive control board — that provides business guidance and direction for application within the project management environment. A key participant on this board will be the PMO's executive sponsor. This person will interpret and convey the deliberations and decisions of the executive control board to the PMO on a routine basis. However, there also may be occasions when the PMO participates in meetings and interactions with all members of the executive control board.

This executive level body may already exist within the relevant organization, perhaps operating under a different naming convention. It might be called the management oversight committee or, in a technical organization, the systems control group. It is the PMO's responsibility to identify and facilitate its inclusion in this senior management board's business matters. In some cases, a new or smaller PMO may not have sufficient functional responsibility to warrant a direct interface with this senior management board. It then will normally report to a senior manager who does. In the rare case where a central, executive oversight group cannot be readily identified, it will fall upon the PMO to seek or facilitate creation of such a body for the purpose of providing executive level business guidance and direction to the project management environment.

Whether an executive control board currently exists or not, the PMO will need to orient either current or new control board members to the needs of the project management environment. The PMO's role, as is often the case, is one of facilitating the executive control board in its role and responsibilities to lead and endorse effective project management. The PMO can perform the following three activities to establish either a new or existing body as the executive control board.

Determine Executive Oversight Requirements

The PMO begins this effort by examining the needs of the project management environment to determine the project, business, and technical oversight requirements. In conjunction with this examination, the PMO also collaborates with control board members or the PMO's executive sponsor to gain an understanding of the depth and extent of oversight that such a board would prefer to have within the relevant organization's normal mode of operations.

The PMO should examine the following prominent functional areas under its purview to prepare an initial list of oversight responsibilities for consideration by the executive control board:

- *Methodology development:* The control board should consider whether its review and approval are needed to authorize and fund project management methodology development. The board's endorsement will certainly be needed, but it may defer development responsibility to an appropriate technical board or committee, or even to an individual executive or the PMO.
- *Knowledge management:* This function provides for the exchange of project management and project performance information in the form of status reports, project work plans, and technical deliverables. This function also deals with implementing an "executive dashboard" that summarizes all project management information on-line at a glance. The control board will need to determine the type, frequency, and receipt method for project information it needs to keep itself informed so that it can make timely business decisions.
- *Project governance:* The control board or executive sponsor will be the issuer of project management policies. The board must determine the scope of policies it will consider as a group, and which policies will be deferred to the executive sponsor.
- *Organization and structure:* The executive control board may want to be included in deliberation and decisions regarding how project managers are functionally aligned, and assigned, to project efforts. This could be particularly important if the PMO is recommending

a change to the current organizational structure and practices. This also may be only a one-time consideration that still warrants senior level involvement.

■ *Resource training and education:* The executive control board may want to be included among those initially trained in project management practices and principles. It needs sufficient understanding of project management, although not the intensive training of project managers and team members, to effectively oversee and use the project management environment to achieve its business objectives. The board will have to decide on the training it will receive and, through PMO recommendations, the training other project management participants will be given.

■ *Project auditing:* The executive control board may want to influence, and possibly control, project audit efforts. It must determine whether it will be involved in constructing the criteria or simply approve the PMO's recommended criteria for conducting project audits.

■ *Portfolio management:* This function may be the most critical and essentially requires participation by the executive control board. Unless otherwise delegated, the executive control board inherently has responsibility for project portfolio management within the relevant organization. It should be involved in establishing both the process and the criteria that will be used to assist it in making project selection, continuation, and termination decisions that affect the outcomes of business.

■ *Business performance:* The executive control board will likely want to influence how the PMO supports its business initiatives and strategic business plan. Considerations in this functional area enable the control board to direct the PMO in specific business integration activities within the project environment.

These are only a few samples of the functional considerations the PMO can formulate in preparing control-board oversight requirements. It is suggested that the new PMO start with just a few of the most important requirements and then add additional responsibility to the executive control board over time. It can also be noted that the size, culture, and business objectives of the relevant organization may influence delegation of some of these requirements to other technical or business committees that may be better positioned to deal with them.

Set Board Parameters

The PMO's next step is to help set the parameters for the executive control board's project management oversight activities. This will provide an operating basis and a common understanding of responsibilities among board members and business units.

The PMO should address the following elements when preparing the parameters for executive control board operations:

- *Purpose:* The purpose of establishing the executive control board for project management oversight is stated in the language and style of the relevant organization. The control board will be an active and positive influence on the project management environment when a well-defined purpose for its existence is established.
- *Roles and responsibilities:* The roles and responsibilities of key participants in project management oversight are defined. This includes identifying the PMO's executive sponsor on the board, if that person has not already been identified. It may also include specification of those executives having project portfolio management responsibility.
- *Membership composition:* It is a very good thing to know exactly who are the members of the executive control board. It is equally important, both for the board members and the PMO, to know whether alternative board members are required for meetings, activity coordination, and decision-making purposes. The identification of board members facilitates communication and collaboration requirements.

Prepare Operating Procedures

The executive control board will fall into an effective routine in a shorter period of time when operating guidance is prepared for use by board members and those conducting business with the board. The regard for executive time is a prevalent issue in organizations across most industries. In many cases, the issues are minimized through adequate advance planning for executive participation. In this activity, the PMO prepares the recommended operating procedures for conducting executive control board activities with a focus on accommodating board member participation. The board then will review and implement these procedures.

The PMO should consider the following elements in its preparation of procedural guidance:

- *Preparation and deliberation:* Procedures should specify the responsibility of board members to prepare for each meeting. This could include reviewing the agenda, reading point papers, or examining status reports. The procedures also can specify the required advance distribution times (e.g., one week for point papers, three days for the agenda, etc.) in order for matters to be considered at an upcoming meeting.

- *Meeting frequency and timing:* Procedures should prescribe a recurring meeting time, either monthly or quarterly, so that board members can plan on participation. The duration of every meeting also should be standard for planning purposes. The procedure might also indicate the conditions and means to conduct special, interim meetings.

- *Collaboration process:* Procedures should identify the preferred methods of collaboration outside of scheduled meetings. This is particularly important when a board member is reviewing a document and requires additional information. The procedure might specify that the document producer serve as a primary contact for additional information, or that the PMO serves as a clearinghouse for such requests and will manage getting a response to the requester. This procedural area may also specify the means of individual collaboration using e-mail, telephone, or informal meetings.

- *Action management:* Procedures should identify how control-board action items will be managed — both those actions assigned to board members and those referred to the PMO or other business unit. This can include guidance on who can make assignments and completion dates, how progress is tracked and managed, and who closes action items.

The PMO will have to discern from its internal experience what procedures are needed and how they are conveyed to the executive control board and others having affiliation with the control board's activities.

Align Business and Technical Committees

The PMO's responsibility for some if not all areas of project management will warrant interaction with existing business and technical committees within the relevant organization. This is similar to the role of the executive control board, but here the PMO is soliciting guidance from specific business activities and technical leadership groups. In larger organizations, there may be several such groups. In smaller organizations, the executive control board, as defined earlier, is the group that also manages business and technical issues and guidance.

The primary objective of this activity is to ensure that the PMO has the necessary input and guidance from relevant committees so as to effectively incorporate their interests, and sometimes their mandates, into the project management practices. The PMO can use the following three steps to conduct initial alignment with relevant business and technical groups: (a) identify business and technical groups, (b) set up relationships, and (c) manage those relationships.

The PMO will likely have insider knowledge of business unit activities to adequately identify business and technical working groups and committees. This can be assured by the PMO with some additional examination of the organizational structure to uncover any "hidden" or newly formed groups. Some groups will be more deliberating and directive in their purpose, while others will be aligned with managing initiatives or leading forums. The PMO should identify all such business and technical groups in the relevant organization, and possibly in any parent organization as well.

In larger organizations, there may be multiple technical disciplines represented across business units. It is particularly important to recognize major technical components, especially if they have a technical guidance group. This will ensure that they are included in the committee relationships that the PMO will establish under this activity.

The PMO should then review each of the boards, committees, and action groups it has identified to understand their roles and responsibilities and their purposes within the relevant organization. It will then decide which groups on the list will be pursued for business or technical alignment. For the most part, the PMO should recognize that in this process it is primarily seeking sources of business and technical guidance that it can then integrate into project management operations. That is to say, the PMO will align itself with such groups to ensure that it thoroughly understands and is accurately conveying technical and business needs and interests of the relevant organization into the practices of project management.

The PMO should initiate contact with business and technical managers who head the groups identified for PMO alignment. In some cases, the PMO will simply request representation on a relevant board or committee, and this represents a peer relationship. In other cases, the PMO will be establishing an oversight responsibility for the identified group and a reporting requirement to the PMO. This type of business unit relationship should be examined carefully to ensure that operating procedures are properly developed, that other board responsibilities are not usurped, and that the PMO retains reasonable control of the project management environment. This latter type of oversight relationship may require executive control board review and sign-off acceptance by the PMO sponsor.

The PMO can then proceed to participate in the business and technical group relationships it has established and their associated activities. In many cases, the management of such relationships is a matter of routine information coordination. For oversight relationships, the PMO may have to prepare and participate in mandatory meetings and carry away action items.

POSTSCRIPT FOR THE SMALLER PMO

The "project governance" PMO function specifies many activities that provide oversight and guidance or otherwise specify the business influence of the project management environment. This function is somewhat laden with bureaucracy that is beyond the capability of the smaller PMO. However, even the smaller PMO must ensure the creation of a project management environment that is responsive to business needs and interests and whose behavior is consistent with the same senior management expectations and business guidance that is applicable to all business units within the relevant organization.

Here is a list of some of the more important project governance activities on which the new or smaller PMO can focus:

- Develop a PMO charter and get it approved at the highest executive level. This guides the activities of the PMO and its oversight of the project management environment. It represents the PMO's operating orders, and it designates responsibility and authority to act within the relevant organization.
- Identify the PMO executive sponsor and establish an "executive control board." The smaller PMO will likely have initial focus on technical work performance within the project environment and will distinctly need senior management participation to add insight and guidance to the business dimensions of its operations. This board also will inherently address any policy development that is needed to support project management activities. Successful integration of business interests will pave the way for an expansion of PMO responsibilities and influence within the relevant organization. It is good for the project management environment to have such representation.
- Develop a project classification scheme. This promotes a common understanding of project activity within the project environment and across business units. It does not have to be complicated, but it must accurately define the prominent types of projects conducted within the purview of the PMO.
- Identify and recognize the roles of key business and technical management groups within the relevant organization. Know where to go to get pertinent guidance. Appropriate oversight relationships will likely emerge as needed.

The bottom line of project governance is to ensure that project management is conducted according to the prescribed processes and procedures, as endorsed by senior management and aligned with business needs and interests.

6

ASSESSMENT

Organizations improve business and project management performance by analyzing three interrelated factors — people, processes, and practices. Some organizations tend to focus on only one of these factors and likely become very good in that area, sometimes to the detriment of the other two factors. However, as organizations become more project-based and pursue project management from an enterprise perspective, an integrated approach is needed to manage all three factors throughout the relevant organization. This highlights the need for assessments to ascertain current position and progress toward enterprise level project management goals.

In the project management environment, initial assessments are conducted to establish a baseline for the current state or conditions. In turn, assessment results facilitate the formulation of strategies and action plans to guide advancements or improvements in the current state or condition. Then, follow-up assessments are performed at intervals to measure improvements or advancements relative to the initial baseline state or conditions.

The term "project management assessment" appears to have some variation in meaning across industries and even among different sources within the project management discipline itself. For the purposes of this PMO function model, project management assessments are conducted to evaluate three facets within the relevant organization — competency, capability, and maturity.

This model also distinguishes between assessments and audits. Where assessments measure conditions, audits measure performance resulting from those conditions. (See the PMO "project auditing" function in Chapter 15.)

This "assessment" function enables the PMO to:

- Identify project management assessments than can be used within the relevant organization
- Evaluate conditions of project management competency, capability, and maturity.
- Develop strategies and action plans to improve project management performance
- Validate the use of project management standards and practices within the enterprise

This PMO function is another facet of project management oversight within the relevant organization. It represents the PMO's ability to influence growth and advancement of project management competency, capability, and maturity — ideally across the entire enterprise.

PROJECT ENVIRONMENT INTERFACE CONCEPTS

The PMO's role in conducting assessments spans a broad range of activities that evaluate project management competency, capability, and maturity — all based in accurately identifying the current conditions and then implementing action plans to improve upon or otherwise advance those conditions to achieve continuous-improvement objectives.

First, the PMO can assist in determining individual project management competencies within the project management environment. Such assessments are useful in accurately aligning project team members with project tasks and responsibilities, indicating potential for professional advancement, and identifying requirements for additional training in project management and related skills and knowledge.

Second, the PMO can facilitate identification of overall project management capability within the relevant organization. This assessment is helpful in developing and implementing standard and repeatable project management methodology processes for use across business units; improving project management efficiency and effectiveness; and implementing applicable technical and business factors of people, processes, and practices.

Finally, the PMO can facilitate the identification of project management relative to the integration of business and project management practices within the enterprise. This assessment is helpful in aligning project performance with strategic business interests and objectives, involving executives and other stakeholders in the business aspects of project management, and establishing the PMO as an enterprisewide business influence.

BUSINESS ENVIRONMENT INTERFACE CONCEPTS

The PMO will initially prescribe and conduct assessments primarily within the project management environment. However, as organizational capability and maturity in project management become viable business considerations, assessments will expand to include the participation and contributions of business units that interface with the project management environment. At the highest level of maturity, the PMO will normally interface with all remaining business units in the relevant organization.

The broader assessments of the relevant organization, possibly the entire enterprise, will enable business managers and project managers to join forces in pursuing the challenges of business and the achievement of strategic business objectives. The more each manager knows about the other's interests and needs, the more they can be made compatible. Assessments will help to identify commonality of purpose and establish overall management commitment to excellence in project management.

In many organizations, projects represent a prominent aspect of business revenue. Therefore, it is quite appropriate to evaluate how well an entire organization influences project performance, project management efficiency, and management effectiveness. It is likewise essential to ensure that executive level decisions are applied in a timely manner to guide projects toward the achievement of business objectives. If executives aren't attending to projects as a prominent source of business revenue, who is? Assessments conducted by the PMO can and should include evaluations of the level of involvement of executives and senior managers in project management. It is likely that these organizational leaders are already attending to critical business responsibilities, but they may not be fully engaged with a major component of the business — project management. Assessments and the resulting action plans are not intended to change their demonstrated successful approach to business. Rather, they are intended to enlarge their perspective of project management contributions to the achievement of business objectives.

ASSESSMENT ACTIVITIES ACROSS THE PMO CONTINUUM

The PMO's "assessment" function represents an effort to understand the current state and plan the future state of competency, capability, and maturity within the project management environment, the relevant organization, and the enterprise.

Table 6.1 presents an overview of the range of prescribed PMO assessment activities according to each level in the PMO competency continuum.

Table 6.1 Range of Assessment Activities across the PMO Continuum

Project Office	Basic PMO	Standard PMO	Advanced PMO	Center of Excellence
Participates in project management assessments	Conducts essential evaluations ■ Evaluates project manager skill and knowledge ■ Evaluates project management processes ■ Evaluates technical processes	Conducts complete assessments ■ Assesses project management competency ■ Assesses project management capability ■ Assesses project management maturity	Conducts advanced examinations ■ Examines project oversight ■ Examines project sponsorship ■ Examines project governance ■ Examines relationships among project stakeholders	Collaborates the results of assessments throughout the enterprise ■ Analyzes the benefits of improvements ■ Recommends assessment types and frequency

In the absence of a higher level PMO, the *project office* examines and improves general capabilities in project management as best can be achieved by the project manager and project team members. However, it primarily will be a contributing participant in assessments that are prescribed and conducted across all projects.

Mid-range PMO levels have the responsibility of leading project management assessments to determine competency, capability, and maturity. They will review and select or recommend the assessment models to be applied, plan and conduct the assessments, and prepare action plans for achievement of project management improvement strategies.

The *center of excellence* performs in an advisory and support role to evaluate and quantify the improvements achieved within the relevant organization, and to collaborate the expansion and use of project management assessments across the enterprise.

PMO assessment activities usually include three components — the identification of an assessment tool or model, the evaluation or assessment, and the action plan to advance competency, capability, and maturity. Assessment has alignment with the PMO "standards and metrics" function (see Chapter 3), as assessments are generally conducted to determine how well standards are being achieved. There also is likely to be some general link to other PMO functions as assessment results identify strengths and weaknesses in various areas of project management oversight, control, and support.

ASSESSMENT FUNCTION MODEL

The PMO should become the resident expert in assessments associated with project management. That means (a) knowing the types of assessments that can be utilized to achieve desired improvement in project management performance and (b) facilitating the accomplishment of those assessments to begin the improvement efforts.

The prominent activities of the PMO's "assessment" function model are depicted in Figure 6.1. Each activity is described in the following subsections.

CONDUCT COMPETENCY ASSESSMENTS	CONDUCT CAPABILITY ASSESSMENTS	CONDUCT MATURITY ASSESSMENTS
• Identify Competency Assessments • Conduct Competency Assessments • Implement Competency Improvements Plans	• Identify Capability Assessments • Conduct Capability Assessments • Implement Capability Improvements Plans	• Identify Maturity Assessments • Conduct Maturity Assessments • Implement Maturity Improvements Plans

Figure 6.1   "Assessment" Function Model

Conduct Competency Assessments

The PMO should conduct competency assessments first from the perspective of helping individuals to ascertain their own level of skill and knowledge as a beneficial step in professional development. Then, it can view competency assessments from the perspective of making project team performance more effective. Finally, it must also pursue competency assessments relative to business interests, whereby the strengths and weaknesses are identified and actions are taken to improve individual competency contributions to the achievement of business objectives.

The PMO can address competency assessments as presented in the following three activities.

Identify Competency Assessments

For the purposes of this model, competency is a measure of individual technical or professional skill and knowledge, and in some cases includes determining the ability to apply that skill and knowledge within the project management environment. In general, competency is not a direct measure of experience. However, to the extent that experience contributes to the retention of skill and knowledge, experience can influence increased competency. As well, it is possible that someone with less experience could demonstrate greater competency in the comprehension and application of skill and knowledge than someone with more experience, particularly when new concepts, practices, or standards are introduced. Therefore, the PMO will need to be precise in selecting the assessments used to evaluate competency in the project management environment.

Competency assessments are normally conducted with reference to a specific skill, knowledge area, or performance standard. The following are a few relevant methods that the PMO can consider for use in evaluating individual competency in the project management environment:

- *Project management competency assessment:* An evaluation of individual skill and knowledge of concepts, practices, and principles of modern project management. This assessment is most applicable to project managers; however, the PMO also may consider its use for project team members and other project stakeholders as well.
- *Technical competency assessment:* An evaluation of particular technical skills and knowledge needed by members of the project team having responsibilities for achievement of the technical work elements of the project. The PMO will have to determine the nature of technical competency to be measured, and select assessment

tools for the various technical disciplines aligned with project efforts.

■ *Professional certification:* In lieu of specific competency assessment tools, the PMO can consider professional certification credentials as an indicator of technical or professional competency. Of course, it will have to identify the basis by which such awarded credentials evaluate skill and knowledge, and determine whether that is an acceptable indicator of competency within the relevant organization.

For the most part, unless the relevant organization is in the business of developing project management competency assessment models and tools, the PMO will be wise to obtain such competency assessments from external sources. These sources normally administer the assessment, compile and analyze assessment results, and provide recommendations for improvement — as comprehensive a support package as is needed and arranged by the PMO.

Conduct Competency Assessments

This activity presents an overview of the primary activities the PMO will normally perform in conducting competency assessments. It can review and consider the following steps as it prepares to evaluate competency in the project management environment:

■ *Collaborate need for competency assessment:* Achieve concurrence and approval of key managers in the relevant organization before proceeding with the assessment.

■ *Select the competency assessment instrument:* Determine the project management or technical standards to be measured and select the assessment instrument that will measure individual competency against those standards. Plan and coordinate arrangements for assessment administration to include likely participation by the assessment instrument vendor.

■ *Announce the competency assessment:* Prepare an announcement that describes the need for the assessment relative to planning and achieving business interests, and not as a measure of individual performance. Emphasize the confidential nature of individual assessment results, and indicate how the PMO and senior management will review results from a group perspective.

■ *Notify assessment participants:* Notify selected assessment participants of the arrangements for taking the assessment. Dates, times, and location will need to be conveyed for paper-based assessments;

date and time periods, Web addresses, and access passwords will need to be conveyed for on-line assessments.

■ *Conduct the assessment and analyze results:* Monitor internal or vendor activities through the assessment process, normally concluding with the delivery of a report of analyzed competency results (and possibly recommendations for improvement).

■ *Review results and formulate strategies:* Distribute the competency assessment report for review by the PMO and key managers in the relevant organization. In turn, convene this group to deliberate and discuss strategies for overall competency improvement, to include such things as:
  – Enrollment in project management training programs
  – Enrollment in technical training courses
  – Project management mentoring
  – Process guidance improvement
  – Policy guidance improvement

■ *Prepare the action plan for competency improvement:* Develop an action plan with specific activities, responsibility assignments, and completion dates to implement the selected strategies for improving individual and overall competency within the project management environment.

Implement Competency Improvement Plans

The action plan for competency improvement can range from uncomplicated to complex in nature, and the PMO will normally have responsibility for its implementation. In the case of competency improvement, there will usually be involvement by the human resources training unit, as training solutions are the common response to competency issues. Along those lines, project managers will undoubtedly serve competency improvement efforts by helping to define training needs for themselves and their project teams. They would also likely be involved in implementing any nontraining solutions contained in the action plan. Action plans that address nontraining solutions are highlighted in the capability and maturity sections of this function. This competency section will focus on implementing the training solution.

The PMO's responsibility to conduct or otherwise manage the implementation of the training solution for competency improvement is characterized by several key steps:

■ *Specify the training requirements:* Per the weaknesses identified in the competency assessment, determine the type of training required to improve individual contributions to project management efficiency and effectiveness and project performance.

■ *Identify and select the preferred source of training:* Review internal and external sources of training program delivery, confirm that they have existing courses or programs that will fulfill current training requirements, and select the training provider that will best serve the interests of the project management or technical competency improvement effort.

■ *Arrange delivery of the desired training courses or program:* In collaboration with the training provider, determine the training courses or program to be delivered and schedule them for delivery in the project management environment.

■ *Administer training program enrollment:* Notify training participants of the availability of training or of their specific selection for attendance. Publish and distribute the schedule, delivery dates, and location for each training program, and include information that identifies the benefits of attendance and convey PMO and relevant organization encouragement to enroll and attend. Specify the procedures for on-line or manual training program enrollment.

■ *Conduct the training program:* Monitor training program delivery, to include participant registration, attendance, and completion. Review instructor and participant evaluations of each training program conducted.

The PMO should evaluate how well the training solution has translated into competency improvement in the workplace. It should be able to informally discern some level of individual and group performance improvement soon after training has been completed by individuals. As well, it can conduct another formal competency assessment after some reasonable period of time, perhaps annually, to obtain quantifiable competency improvement information and measurement.

Conduct Capability Assessments

The PMO should conduct project management capability assessments to ascertain what is being done to achieve a professional level of project management in the relevant organization. The desired level of capability is normally indicated by the preferred standards of project management or internal policy guidance. The project management capability assessment helps to identify how well those standards are being met.

The PMO can address capability assessments as presented in the following three activities.

Identify Capability Assessments

For the purposes of this model, capability is a measure of (a) what people, processes, and practices are currently in place in the relevant organization and (b) how well they contribute to the achievement of project management objectives. Project management capability assessments often involve a cross-examination of the business environment and the project management environment.

The following is a list of several of the more prominent project management capability assessments that the PMO can consider for use in the relevant organization:

- *State of project management assessment:* A comprehensive examination of the project management environment to determine capability derived from organizational structure and project resource alignment, project management methodology deployment, and senior management oversight and involvement in project management. These three assessment components can be examined separately, each requiring about the same time it takes for the complete assessment, but they provide extremely valuable insight to the PMO when combined and performed concurrently under this type of assessment.
- *Project organizational structure assessment:* An examination of how project management responsibilities are aligned within the relevant organization, and of how project resources are acquired, assigned, and managed within the project management environment. It also usually includes an evaluation of the reasonableness of project manager and project team member workload in terms of the number and types of projects assigned and individual ability and competency to accomplish the required work.
- *Project management methodology assessment:* An examination of the completeness of the current methodology process used in the course of managing projects. This assessment has a particular focus on identifying gaps in essential project management activities (consistent with the specified standards), and it includes an evaluation of how well currently prescribed processes and practices are being accomplished.
- *Senior management oversight assessment:* An examination of leadership activities in the relevant organization, possibly including the PMO role, to ascertain the current level of senior manager awareness of project management capability and involvement in project management oversight, control, and support. This assessment can also be used to identify executive and senior management strategies

and perspectives for desired capability within the project management environment.

■ *Standards compliance assessment:* If not inherently covered by performing the project management methodology assessment, this examination can identify additional standards that are applicable within the project management environment and then evaluate their integration and achievement.

■ *Technical capability assessments:* An examination that ascertains how well technical aspects of project work are being accomplished. It includes an evaluation of applicable technical processes and procedures, and therefore requires an assessor with particular technical expertise that is aligned with the technical nature of projects under consideration. The PMO may have to define the basis or standard that applies to the technical processes and procedures being examined. Where there are multiple technical disciplines present in the project management environment, appropriate technical standards must be defined for each technical discipline. Note that many organizations are familiar with the Software Engineering Institute's capability maturity model (SEI-CMM) that is widely used to guide and establish capability in software development (and related technical areas). In the context of this PMO model, the SEI-CMM is a technical standard and approach that warrants examination using a technical capability assessment. It is not a project management process or standard because of its distinct technical content and focus, and it is not a project management maturity model because it does not extend guidance to all types of projects or facilitate enterprisewide coverage. However, it is recognized as a technical-based capability maturity model that appears preeminent in its purpose, and it is that capability that is evaluated within this technical assessment category.

■ *Strategic integration assessment:* An examination of the processes and procedures associated with project selection, integration, and ongoing management review relative to the achievement of strategic business objectives, e.g., project portfolio management. It includes an evaluation of (a) an evaluation of the project portfolio management used and (b) the frequency and nature of executive involvement in the project portfolio management process or other similar activity at this strategic level.

The PMO can consider these assessments, or it can devise or acquire others that enable it to obtain indications of project management capability within the relevant organization.

Conduct Capability Assessments

A capability assessment helps the PMO to establish a frame of reference about current conditions in the area examined. It can use that frame of reference to make decisions regarding the direction to be taken to improve or enhance the current capability.

This activity presents an overview of the primary activities the PMO will normally perform in conducting capability assessments. It can review and consider the following steps as it prepares to evaluate project management capability in the relevant organization:

- *Identify type of capability assessment needed:* Review observations and project performance indicators to isolate any particular problem areas that warrant closer examination, and select the appropriate assessments that will provide more detailed insight in those areas. As well, review the broader option for establishing an assessment baseline that will provide a complete examination of capability within the project management environment, and select an approach like the "state of project assessment" to conduct the examination.
- *Collaborate need for capability assessment:* A capability assessment represents an intervention in the project management environment that will require the time and participation of project managers, project team members, and other project stakeholders across several if not all projects. Due to this impact, the PMO should obtain buy-in from affected managers and concurrence from other key managers in the relevant organization before proceeding with the assessment.
- *Identify the capability assessment team:* Determine the internal or external resources that will be used to conduct the capability assessment. Capability assessment accuracy and adequacy comes from the deliberations and judgment of highly qualified professionals in project management. The PMO can certainly develop that professional competency internally, but it also can call upon external, prequalified professionals who can bring full project management assessment capability, and a proven assessment process, on relatively short notice to fulfill the PMO's capability assessment needs.
- *Announce the capability assessment:* Prepare an announcement that describes the purpose for the assessment relative to planning and achieving business interests, and not as a measure of project manager or project team performance. Emphasize the cross-project nature of the examination to illustrate that no one project or person will be singled out during the assessment. Focus on the benefits

of learning the status of current project management capability relative to industry standards and best practices.

■ *Plan and prepare for the capability assessment:* Use the guidance and experience of the capability assessment team to complete assessment planning and preparation activities:
  - Identify assessment stakeholders in the relevant organization
  - Determine the assessment scope and purpose
  - Establish the assessment period
  - Identify relevant project managers
  - Identify other assessment participants
  - Specify preferred project documentation and sample size for review
  - Develop a meeting and interview schedule
  - Notify and arrange individual assessment participation

■ *Conduct the capability assessment:* A capability assessment requires identification and verification of what conditions currently exist in the project management environment. Note that if the PMO does not itself conduct the capability assessment, it should monitor assessment team activities throughout the on-site assessment process. The capability assessment team will work on-site to lead and perform the following fundamental activities:
  - Initial meeting with management or assessment sponsor
  - Assessment interviews
  - Project document reviews
  - Interim information compilation and analyses
  - Meeting with management or assessment sponsor to discuss preliminary findings

■ *Prepare and present capability assessment results:* The capability assessment team will conduct a final analysis of information and prepare a written report of assessment findings and recommendations. Often, the capability assessment team will also prepare a summary of findings and recommendations for oral presentation to management, and sometimes to the relevant assessment participants in the project management environment.

■ *Review results and formulate strategies:* Distribute the capability assessment report for review by the PMO and key managers in the relevant organization. In turn, convene this group to deliberate and discuss strategies for overall capability improvement. The nature of the assessment and its associated findings and recommendations will enable the PMO to focus on one or more capability development areas. Some of the more common strategies for improvement will lead the PMO to consider the following activities:
  - Further detailed examination of capability or competency

- Project management and technical training
- Project team member and project team development activities
- Project management or technical process development
- Project management methodology development
- Project management tool implementation
- PMO function expansion
- Project management mentoring
- Implementation of knowledge management system
- Implementation of portfolio management system

■ *Prepare the action plan for capability improvement:* Develop an action plan with specific activities, responsibility assignments, and completion dates to implement the selected strategies for improving project management capability within the relevant organization.

Implement Capability Improvement Plans

The action plan for capability improvement in the project management environment will likely be more complex than not. In any event, capability improvement plans tend to have durations on the order of weeks or months. This is because there are usually some new or significant concepts being introduced, and they usually require sufficient time for advance design planning and coordination actions, followed by the actual solution development and implementation effort.

To that end, there is no specific activity guidance that can be offered in advance of knowing the type of capability improvement effort being pursued. However, note that many of these improvement initiatives can be planned and conducted in the same manner as other projects. Nevertheless, here are a few general guidelines the PMO can consider as it attends to project management capability improvement initiatives:

■ *Establish a core oversight team:* Convene a core team of end users to conduct deliberations and make decisions regarding the planning and design of the preferred solution. This team is needed whether the initiative is being led by internal project management experts, perhaps the PMO, or external project management consultants. This team will ensure that end users in the project management environment are adequately represented as the project management experts present design and content considerations for the preferred solution. Above all, ensure the members of this core team are available at critical design and decision points in the early stages of education development.

■ *Apply professional project management expertise:* Identify and engage qualified professionals in project management to introduce capability improvements in the project management environment. The PMO should involve experienced professionals who can comprehend and convey the concepts and practices of modern project management and their integration with technical and business interests. If this expertise is not readily available within the relevant organization, the PMO may need to consider the use of external resources that can bring essential project management experience and expertise to the initiative. An added value of using external expertise is that qualified consultants should bring experience that expedites achievement of the initiative.

- *Obtain executive support:* Obtain executive support for the initiative, and facilitate continuation of that support through completion of the initiative. First, executive support will be needed to provide adequate funding for the capability improvement initiative. Presumably, the PMO will be able to show the benefits and business advantage to be achieved by the initiative in order to gain the necessary funding. Second, executive support may be needed to influence the prescribed use of any new processes, practices, or procedures introduced into the relevant organization, possibly across business units. The PMO should attempt to have this type of support demonstrated at the onset of the initiative, but particularly at the point in time when the solution is ready for implementation. Executive influence is an effective response to most types of resistance encountered.

- *Prepare users for solution implementation:* Make the project management environment, and for that matter the relevant organization, ready for solution implementation. In particular, individuals and teams responsible for applying a new process, tool, concept, or activity need to become familiar, and possibly competent, in using the prescribed solution within their work effort. During solution development, keep people informed about what is planned. As the time for implementation approaches, provide information updates and training, as necessary. During implementation, project management mentors provide an excellent means to transfer skill and knowledge regarding use of the prescribed solution.

- *Solicit early user feedback:* Provide the means for users to evaluate and respond to capability improvement initiatives. Users often will be the first to discover unintended nuances in the new process or inaccuracies or something missing in the worksheet, etc. In most cases, these represent relatively minor adjustments that can be made to correct deficiencies and then credited to individual feedback. As well, there could be situations of user uncertainty and resistance, and having a feedback mechanism provides a means for users' concerns to be heard and acknowledged as a step toward their ultimate acceptance of the solution.

Conduct Maturity Assessments

The PMO should conduct a project management maturity assessment to ascertain the level of attained achievement of certain capabilities — prominently, project management and business integration in the relevant organization.

Project management maturity assessments provide guidance that allows organizations to pursue continuous improvement in managing and developing project management capabilities within the relevant organization. This is accomplished through use of a project management maturity model that specifies progressive and broader capabilities associated with increasing levels of maturity.

While capability assessments address performance in the project management environment, maturity assessments examine that performance plus the alignment of organizational operations and business influences on project management. The lower levels of project management maturity do tend to focus on achieving the essential capabilities implemented for use at the project level, as covered in the previous section on capability assessments. In turn, the middle and higher levels of project management maturity begin introducing a broader strategic perspective, one that suggests that project management is a core business competency and a way of doing business. The highest levels of project management maturity are characterized by demonstrated executive involvement and support, extended business unit participation, integrated customer and vendor/contractor associations, and defined pursuits that foster continuous improvement within the enterprise and contribute project management innovations to industry.

The PMO can address project management maturity assessments as presented in the following three activities.

Identify Maturity Assessments

A project management maturity assessment is a significant undertaking for any organization. The maturity assessment, even in smaller organizations, can incur several weeks of work for a small assessment team. This is because of the depth and extent of the examination performed. It is an examination that delves deeply into the project management environment. The maturity assessment is an intervention of discovery — going places some project managers have not gone before. In the wake, discoveries are illuminated and adjudged to identify merit or, sometimes, shortcomings. Known shortcomings can be rectified; unknown shortcomings cannot.

The maturity assessment, however, is also a guiding light that helps achieve business advantage in the marketplace, effectiveness and efficiency in the workplace, and professional recognition in industry and everyplace. The discoveries resulting from an effective project management maturity assessment can be used to formulate strategy and develop a comprehensive roadmap in pursuit of project management excellence.

The PMO will have to select a project management maturity model as its frame of reference for an organizational maturity assessment. The marketplace offers several project management maturity models. The PMO can consider the following points and features in selecting an appropriate project management maturity model for use in evaluating the relevant organization or enterprise:

- *Defined maturity levels:* The model defines and describes the conditions and capabilities required for each progressive level of project management maturity. This includes (a) specification of the indicators used to judge attainment of those conditions and capabilities and (b) the acceptable thresholds to be achieved for each indicator. This makes the model reusable and the results repeatable and consistent for the same and similar conditions and capabilities discovered throughout the relevant organization.
- *Adequate organizational coverage:* The model presents an organizational perspective of project management capability. It is the organization that is evaluated for project management maturity, not just the capability at the project level. Therefore, the assessment should include participation at the highest management levels in the relevant organization and across the various relevant business units.
- *Prescribed assessment process:* The model identifies and describes the action steps for conducting a project management maturity assessment. It enables the user, i.e., the PMO, to plan assessment activities, prepare informational announcements, schedule and arrange participation, and assign and manage staff responsibilities.
- *Essential technical guidance:* The model provides detailed guidance to the assessment team regarding technical content reviews, i.e., what project documents or materials to examine, what to look for, and how to interpret what is discovered. Similarly, interviews and questionnaires are prescribed and standardized to ensure consistency of (a) information collection across the selected group of interviewees and (b) responses presented by interviewers.

■ *Comprehensive assessment report:* The model provides clear and complete assessment documentation to substantiate the discovery and analysis of findings and to support the determination of the adjudged maturity level. Information tools, assessment templates, and evaluation forms used for information collection and analysis are identified, and where appropriate and possible, attached to the assessment report.

The PMO may wish to specify other features for the project management maturity model that will be used within the relevant organization.

Conduct Maturity Assessments

The selection of a viable project management maturity model will allow the PMO to plan and conduct the maturity assessment. However, to the extent that the PMO has competency to conduct a maturity assessment, it may still want to consider the value of a third-party assessor who can provide an impartial and unbiased examination of the enterprise. In some commercially available maturity models, consultants are trained and certified to comprehend the models and to use the associated assessment process and materials. Unless the PMO desires to identify qualified individuals for such training and certification internally, the use of prequalified consultants will likely expedite the accomplishment and ensure greater accuracy of the project management maturity assessment.

In lieu of third-party maturity assessments, the PMO may want to consider use of abbreviated self-assessment instruments based on the preferred maturity model. This usually consists of completing questionnaires (normally on-line), but also removes the elements of personal interviews and examination of relevant documents by expert assessors. Nevertheless, a maturity self-assessment will provide a baseline and a basis for the PMO to conduct improvement initiatives.

The following are several common steps that the PMO can anticipate encountering in the course of conducting a comprehensive project management maturity assessment:

■ *Form the assessment team:* The activities associated with an organizationwide project management maturity assessment will likely be a small team effort. There is certainly benefit to having multiple opinions expressed during the assessment process. If an external team is used, there will still be a need for active, internal participation. This team should be convened to accomplish initial assessment planning, arrange for participation in the relevant organization, and conduct and manage assessment activities.

■ *Conduct initial assessment meeting:* The initial assessment meeting is conducted to plan the assessment effort. The assessment team will review the assessment model and process, assign team member responsibilities, and walk through assessment activities.

■ *Administer prequalifying participant questionnaire (optional step):* This step is performed when the population of the relevant organization is sufficiently large to warrant identification of a representative sample of the total population. Prequalification is accomplished by administering a preliminary questionnaire to the population as a means to determine the population sample on which to focus. Additional assessment team meetings may be needed to review questionnaire results and select the sample to be used.

■ *Conduct assessment:* Assessors will likely convene at intervals during the assessment period to review and compare interim assessment results and to deliberate and discuss issues and accomplishments. The qualified assessment team members who have responsibility for performing the assessment proceed to conduct the following activities:
  – Conduct interviews with management
  – Conduct interviews with project managers and project team members
  – Examine relevant project management documents and materials
  – Examine relevant organizational documents and materials

■ *Compile and analyze maturity assessment information:* Upon completion of on-site activities, assessors will "retreat" to survey and evaluate the assessment information collected from questionnaires, interviews, and document reviews. The assessment team will then develop and deliberate assessment findings and assign a project management maturity rating based on weighing criteria and other guidance provided by the maturity model used.

■ *Prepare assessment report:* The assessment team describes its effort and presents the results of its evaluation in a written maturity assessment report. The report commonly includes the following major sections:
  – Executive overview
  – Assessment approach (model and process used)
  – Assessment finds (categorized statement of condition)
  – Assessment recommendations
  – Report attachments — data collection forms, analysis worksheets, etc.

Prepare Maturity Advancement Plans

The development of action plans for advancing project management maturity within the relevant organization will be influenced by the maturity level assessed. As alluded to earlier, lower maturity ratings will warrant fundamental project management capability enhancements, e.g., use of standard methodology and repeatable processes across all projects, introduction of standards, and implementation of tools and techniques. In contrast, advancements at mid and high levels of maturity will address broader organizational issues, e.g., strategic alignment and project portfolio management; organizational change; and centralized project management oversight, support, and control activities (i.e., PMO function implementation).

For the most part, the same general steps for capability improvement plans are applicable to maturity advancement plans. The following points present a few distinguishing features of maturity advancement plans:

- *Senior management involvement:* While senior management involvement and support is always sought throughout capability improvement efforts, it becomes more essential to maturity advancement efforts. In order to achieve higher levels of project management maturity, per comprehensive maturity models, executives must demonstrate involvement, support, and leadership as a measure of advanced project management maturity.
- *Broader stakeholder involvement:* The project manager and project team members are distinctly involved in capability improvement, and they continue their focus on capability development within the project management environment as an important contribution to organizational maturity. As well, other project stakeholders also take on a contributing role in the achievement of project management maturity. Notably, customer and vendor/contractor participation in the project management environment is characterized by close alignment of business policies, processes, and practices. This suggests that stakeholders are involved in defining some of the solutions needed for maturity, including participation in the development and implementation of maturity advancement plans.
- *Cross-business unit collaboration:* In a mature project management organization, support units adapt and integrate business procedures for use within the project management environment. Other business units having responsibilities in different technical disciplines all establish links and integration with the standard project management methodology prescribed by a central authority (i.e., the PMO), but in collaboration with the variety of technical users throughout the relevant organization.

- *Continuous improvement:* In capability improvement efforts, the desired capability is measured, achieved, and maintained. Maturity advancement extends present capability through an ongoing, continuous-improvement effort that addresses: What can be done next? How can current capability be enhanced? What new techniques and technologies can be introduced? What project management innovations have been created internally that can be contributed to industry or the project management discipline? Project management maturity is not maintenance of current capability. It is growth and improvement of current capability. Yesterday's best practices may not be tomorrow's business solutions.:
- *Strategic enterprise application:* The pursuit of project management maturity has strategic importance throughout the enterprise. Maturity advancement plans, even for achieving lower level project management maturity ratings, recognize this. Project management capability is pursued and solutions devised with consideration for how the entire relevant organization benefits. Project management maturity advancement plans are consistent with and contribute to strategic business objectives of the enterprise.

The PMO may or may not control the implementation of maturity advancement plans. It normally will be responsible for plan implementation within the project management environment. It may be charged with plan implementation progress monitoring across the relevant organization — until the next maturity assessment is conducted.

POSTSCRIPT FOR THE SMALLER PMO

The smaller PMO is not likely to have the strategic focus of its larger counterparts. Its primary responsibility is to establish a reasonable professional level of project management capability. To that end, the smaller PMO needs to have a fundamental understanding of current capability relative to standards or relevant industry practices, with particular focus on competitor capability within a given industry.

Here are a few basic activities the smaller PMO can pursue to evaluate its project management environment:

- *Competency:* Conduct formal or informal evaluations of competency through observation and performance reviews. If possible, select and administer an instrument to measure project management competency of project managers and at least the key project team members. Review competency measurement results and recommend or facilitate project management training programs for those who need them.

■ *Capability:* Identify the applicable project management practice standards that will best serve the project management environment. Conduct a gap analysis or, if possible, a state-of-project management assessment to ascertain current conditions and capability. If necessary, set a course to achieve closer alignment with preferred practices.

■ *Maturity:* The smaller PMO may not have the scope of responsibility that would necessitate a maturity assessment, although such an effort might be warranted if the PMO were serving a moderately sized relevant organization. Nevertheless, the smaller PMO, in its pursuit to establish essential project management capability, can do so with the proviso that it considers the impacts and influences of its solution implementations on the entire relevant organization or enterprise. The smaller PMO could become familiar with a preferred maturity model and should first address capabilities that advance project management maturity at lower maturity levels. Later, it can implement effective solutions that set the foundation for greater project management maturity when the relevant organization or enterprise establishes the strategic direction to do so.

Larger and additional assessment responsibilities of the smaller PMO can be introduced as its mission grows and as the value of professional project management capability is recognized within the relevant organization.

7

ORGANIZATION
AND STRUCTURE

The organizational alignment of project managers in the relevant organization is a business decision. That alignment represents the extent of authority and responsibility conveyed to project managers to enable them to achieve business objectives in the project management environment. In conjunction with project team structure, organizational alignment contributes to project management capability within the relevant organization. In particular, it determines the influence and interactions the project manager will have with project team members and other stakeholders in the project management environment. Organizational alignment also addresses the PMO's position of influence in the relevant organization, from which PMO oversight, control, and support activities are derived.

Project structure aligns project team members, and other stakeholders, with the project manager and with the PMO. It defines their roles and responsibilities, but just as important, project structure specifies accountability — presumably to the project manager and, ideally, in relation to and with regard for PMO guidance. The effectiveness of project performance is a function of individual accountability. Therefore, project structure can facilitate or diminish project performance.

This "organization and structure" function enables the PMO to:

- Establish PMO structure and organizational alignment
- Develop project management alignment within the relevant organization
- Prescribe project team member roles and responsibilities
- Define the stakeholders in the project management environment

Function implementation will necessitate development of strong executive level support. This is needed in association with the PMO's ability to accurately define project management organizational and structural needs, demonstrate appropriate business alignment and fit, and achieve buy-in within the relevant organization.

PROJECT ENVIRONMENT INTERFACE CONCEPTS

The PMO should take the lead role in defining and establishing its own functional capability by developing the organizational alignment with the other business units, as prescribed by the PMO charter. It can then ensure the implementation of capability through specification and introduction of PMO staff members who will implement the functionality needed to achieve business objectives in the project management environment. The PMO can then define, recommend, and implement the project team organizational alignment and structure that will enable desired project performance and project management capabilities to be achieved. Finally, the PMO will be instrumental in identifying all other stakeholders inside and outside the relevant organization for the purposes of facilitating and administering their varying levels of involvement and participation.

BUSINESS ENVIRONMENT INTERFACE CONCEPTS

Most executives and some business unit managers likely will have an inherent interest in the alignment of activities in the project management environment. The PMO will be able to describe that alignment and convey it throughout the relevant organization. It will facilitate executive and senior management involvement in organizational alignment decisions and provide advice regarding the impact and influence of their decisions.

The specified project management and project team organizational alignment will suggest and develop formal and informal professional peer relationships — another facet of business communication and coordination. Organizational alignment can be created with intended business unit and peer relationships in mind. Perhaps such alignment can be used to achieve a stronger integration of business and project management objectives.

ORGANIZATION AND STRUCTURE ACTIVITIES ACROSS THE PMO CONTINUUM

The "organization and structure" function along the PMO competency continuum provides project management capability by establishing an efficient and effective organizational alignment and project team structure that (a) facilitates business and professional interactions among stakeholders and (b) presents sufficient project team and PMO representation within the relevant organization.

Table 7.1 presents an overview of the range of prescribed PMO organization and structure activities according to each level in the PMO competency continuum.

The *project office* uses established organizational guidance to align and structure the project team to achieve project objectives. The project office itself represents the first level of organizational alignment and structure above the individual project team member.

Mid-range PMO levels take on a progressively more active role in (a) specifying organizational alignment and structure of project managers and project teams and (b) defining the relationships of project teams to each other, to the PMO, and to the relevant organization. In general, project team alignment with the PMO is pursued through increasing levels of PMO competency. As well, the mid-range PMO will normally seek to progressively expand its business role and recognition as a business unit in its alignment within the relevant organization.

The *center of excellence* conducts analyses and examinations of the project team structure and alignment within the relevant organization. It is continuous in its efforts to establish the project team and PMO structure and alignment that will maximize capability in the project management environment.

The PMO "organization and structure" function is significantly influenced by organizational culture and established business and operating procedures. This PMO function model suggests that ultimately establishing the PMO as an integral business unit having broad influence over project management policies and direction will increase overall project management capability and maturity within the relevant organization. However, it is the PMO's responsibility to demonstrate the business effectiveness that warrants such business alignment.

The PMO "organization and structure" function is likely to be achieved in conjunction with other PMO functions. Prominently, project team alignment and structure issues will be affected by the activities of the PMO's "resource management" function (see Chapter 9), and vice versa. Relevant organizational interest in any of the PMO functions under the "business alignment" category (see Chapter 17 to Chapter 20) will likewise influence PMO alignment and structure, as those functions represent a distinct focus on business and project management integration activities. However, it is the business objectives and authority established in the PMO charter (see PMO "project governance" function, Chapter 5) that will guide the PMO's ability to influence organization and structure activities within the relevant organization.

Table 7.1 Range of Organization and Structure Activities across the PMO Continuum

Project Office	Basic PMO	Standard PMO	Advanced PMO	Center of Excellence
Manage the preferred project team structure	Establish essential project roles and relationships ■ Specify standard roles for project team members ■ Facilitate internal business unit relationships ■ Identify project stakeholders	Introduce project management structure ■ Evaluate project management structure options ■ Implement the preferred project team structure ■ Implement the preferred PMO staffing structure	Expand project management and business alignment ■ Develop PMO organizational alignment ■ Align project managers with the PMO ■ Manage broader stakeholder alignment and participation	Review and analyze project organization and structure ■ Analyze effectiveness of project management organization ■ Examine effectiveness of project team structure ■ Identify capability associated with current structure

ORGANIZATION AND STRUCTURE FUNCTION MODEL

The PMO should establish a viable position of authority and business function alignment within the relevant organization — for itself and for affiliated project teams. Otherwise, a business entity other than the PMO, which does not have the same level of vested interest in achieving project management excellence as the PMO, and which is presumably less qualified than the PMO to lead professional project management activities in the project management environment, will apply general experience and rules of thumb rather than practices of precision to guide project management efforts.

This is not intended to suggest that other business units are unable to accomplish project management. Rather, it is intended to emphasize that the PMO is established for that very purpose, and it should be given the mandate, through appropriate organizational alignment, to represent, lead, and otherwise influence the activities of the project management environment.

To achieve the desired level of influence, the PMO will have to demonstrate greater capability and business benefits than have been shown by the business units it supports. To that end, this PMO function is likely to be one of the more difficult PMO functions to fulfill. However, it can be accomplished in due course under managed and collaborated PMO growth and expansion efforts within the relevant organization.

The prominent activities of the PMO's "organization and structure" function model are depicted in Figure 7.1. Each activity is described in the following subsections.

Set Up the PMO Structure

The PMO should conduct initial planning to establish its structure, and then ongoing planning to expand its structure and reach the desired level of organizational alignment. The PMO can use the suggested guidance presented in the following three subsections to set up the PMO structure and operational alignment within the relevant organization.

Figure 7.1 "Organization and Structure" Function Model

Identify Staff Needs for PMO Functions

The PMO charter is the guiding document for this effort, as it contains the specification of PMO responsibilities for the PMO functions to be pursued. The PMO charter should adequately convey the functionality to be established. In this activity, the PMO will have to translate functionality into staffing requirements.

It is fairly common that the core staff of a brand new PMO is made up of one or two senior project managers, individuals deemed competent to organize the efforts within the project management environment. Furthermore, this full-time PMO staff may be the one that is expected to remain in place for the foreseeable future, with no anticipated staff additions. This condition prompts two considerations. First, this small PMO staff must accurately estimate current and near-term (i.e., one year) workload requirements to ensure that it can achieve performance expectations with limited resources. Second, the core PMO staff should conduct an early and active search for reliable, part-time assistance, particularly in technical areas.

The PMO will need to set up functional capability according to the PMO charter. It can begin by reviewing and prioritizing its responsibilities and activities in each of the 20 PMO function areas designated for implementation. Presumably, a new PMO will not tackle all 20 PMO functions at the onset. Rather, the several most important functions will be introduced and accomplished by the core PMO staff. Then, for each selected PMO function, the core staff will highlight the anticipated work requirements and identify the staff position responsible for its accomplishment. In essence, a PMO staff responsibility matrix is constructed.

PMO staff planning should be an ongoing effort unless the PMO has become stagnant in its growth and expansion efforts. However, both initial and ongoing PMO staff planning activities can benefit from a general analysis of PMO staffing requirements from a staff-category perspective. The PMO can define staff needs according to three primary PMO staff categories.

PMO Business Staff

The PMO business staff is represented by the designated PMO manager and by any designated PMO function managers or other operational leaders in the PMO. Usually, the limited cadre of initial PMO staff members in a new PMO will all have business-staff responsibilities. The depth and extent of business-staff responsibility will increase as the PMO and the project management environment become more mature. General business-staff responsibilities for small and large PMOs alike could include:

- Managing PMO operations and PMO staff performance
- Establishing PMO functionality for oversight, control, and support of project management
- Collaborating with business units to integrate business needs, interests, and objectives
- Collaborating with technical discipline managers to integrate technical management
- Advising executives and senior managers in professional project management practices
- Contributing to management of customer and vendor/contractor business relationships
- Monitoring and managing project performance
- Maintaining and tracking project cost, schedule, and resource utilization

These PMO business-staff responsibilities transcend virtually all of the 20 PMO functions, so they have some applicability regardless of which functions are selected for implementation.

PMO Technical Staff

The PMO technical staff is represented by individuals aligned with the PMO who develop, implement, and manage professional project management practices within the project management environment. It also may include experts in the one or more technical disciplines pursued within the relevant organization.

The initial staff members of a new PMO will fulfill this technical-staff role on a full-time basis. Other project management and technical discipline experts in the project management environment can contribute their skill and competency on a part-time basis. If PMO growth and expansion is anticipated, part-time technical-staff roles could be transitioned to full-time PMO positions. Of course, project managers and technical leaders are prominent candidates for full or part-time PMO technical-staff positions. The PMO may also want to consider qualified project team members to fill PMO technical-staff roles.

General PMO technical-staff responsibilities for either full-time or part-time PMO staff members could include:

- Developing, implementing, and managing project management processes and practices
- Integrating technical discipline and business processes and practices
- Performing project management and technical audits and reviews

- Researching, recommending, and implementing project management tools and systems
- Developing and implementing project management and technical discipline standards
- Analyzing and implementing improved project management capability solutions
- Facilitating project manager and project team activities — planning, mentoring, etc.

Unless the PMO is a mature organization, it will likely have to rely on part-time PMO staff support that is aligned with a specific event or purpose over a prescribed period of time. A common approach to part-time PMO staffing is the creation of a task force or development team from among qualified resources available within the project management environment. Per the sample of PMO technical-staff responsibilities cited above, it can be seen that senior level project and technical managers will be prime task-force candidates. These ad hoc teams will contribute a valuable service to the relevant organization and to the PMO as it heads up and provides business and technical direction to the team's efforts.

PMO Administrative Staff

The core PMO staff will likely have primary responsibility for accomplishing administrative activities that accompany their work in PMO business and technical management areas. However, to the extent that the PMO's administrative burden can be reduced, the more effective it will be in providing timely project management capability improvements. Like administrative aspects of project management, the PMO will have to identify prominent needs and requirements, substantiate the cost, and acquire the necessary resources.

It should be noted that PMO administrative staff responsibilities tend to have a broader connotation beyond that of administrative assistant, although such an individual would be an invaluable PMO staff member. More so, the PMO administrative staff will likely require some fundamental comprehension of project management concepts and practices, which makes this an ideal role for emerging project manager candidates and talented project team members.

General PMO administrative staff responsibilities for either full-time or part-time PMO staff members could include:

- Collecting, compiling, and distributing recurring project management progress reports and other documents from various project managers for PMO and senior management review

- Preparing project performance analyses for PMO and senior management review
- Preparing and managing PMO business and technical correspondence
- Coordinating and administering training in the project management environment
- Performing project schedule management using an automated tool and creating master schedules of all projects for PMO and senior management oversight
- Establishing and maintaining the project management library and archives and any associated on-line project knowledge management system capability
- Supporting PMO task force efforts by coordinating, compiling, and producing documents and materials resulting from task force efforts
- Coordinating arrangements and scheduling routine project audits, mentoring services, and project planning support and facilitation

Per the set of sample PMO administrative staff responsibilities presented, it can be seen that, at times, there may be little distinction between administrative staff and technical staff. This category of PMO staff responsibilities is presented to illustrate the workload that can be encountered to warrant additional PMO staff assignments.

Introduce PMO Staff

The initial core PMO staff will usually be positioned through executive mandate (or through other similar senior management action) to establish the PMO capability. This one-, two-, or perhaps three-person team will be charged with creating the preliminary PMO design and implementing initial PMO functional capability. Ultimately, the PMO will need to enlarge its staff, via introduction of full-time or part-time resources, if full project management capability and maturity are specified as business objectives within the relevant organization.

The PMO can use the PMO staff responsibility matrix cited earlier to contrast business, technical, and administrative staff responsibilities against the current capacity to fulfill them. In turn, the PMO should identify any prescribed functional areas that are not adequately covered and specify the staff resource(s) needed to close the responsibility gap relative to the required PMO functionality.

This staffing plan may be an element of the PMO charter for a newly formed PMO, but its review and preparation should be a recurring activity, possibly annually. A staffing plan worksheet can be developed and can include the following elements for examination:

- Current PMO resources assigned
- PMO functional areas not adequately covered
  - Functional area identification
  - Functional performance absent or lacking
  - Impact of inadequate functional coverage
  - Resource(s) required to fulfill functional coverage
- New or expanded PMO functionality to be implemented
  - Functional area identification
  - Functional performance to be achieved
  - Requirement for function implementation — mandate or natural expansion
  - Intended impact of function implementation, e.g., business benefit
  - Resource(s) required for function implementation
- Adjusted PMO staff requirements

This sample worksheet can be used to compile requirements and justification that will be presented to senior management for approval and allocation of resources to the PMO.

The PMO staffing plan is presented to appropriate authority within the relevant organization for review and approval. The PMO will have to decide if other affected business units will also receive copies of the PMO staffing plan for purposes of coordination and collaboration. One example of this is found in coordination with the human resources department. Another example is when the staffing plan includes requirements for a part-time PMO task force involving representatives from various business units and resource managers. Those entities should be aware of and included in coordination for specific or general PMO resources.

The PMO also may want to personally present its staffing plan and associated strategy to senior management and other key participants as a means to further solicit their support and ensure proper conveyance of needs. This may include being available for executive or senior management team meetings at which PMO staffing deliberations will take place.

The final step is that of acquisition and assignment of approved resources to complement the PMO staff. The PMO will usually coordinate with the HR department for any full-time staff acquisitions and with resource managers for part-time acquisitions.

Analyze and Establish PMO Relationships

The PMO should be recognized as a viable business entity that represents the interests and activities of the project management environment. In some cases, PMO recognition within the relevant organization will facilitate relationship development, and in others, relationship development will foster PMO recognition. The PMO will need to examine which perspectives can be pursued to establish the necessary organizational relationships it needs to conduct business effectively.

In general, PMO recognition is usually achieved through the combined influence of three factors:

- *Executive mandate and support:* The PMO is established and maintained under executive direction as the means to undertake centralized oversight, control, and support within the project management environment.
- *Business need:* The PMO emerges from a fundamental technical or business support team, possibly a methodology development team or capability assessment task force, to acquire broader responsibility and authority within the project management environment.
- *Distinct business contribution:* The PMO grows and expands when it is viewed as a contributor to the achievement of business objectives (revenue generation), improvement of project management capability, or realization of customer satisfaction.

These are prominent factors to be considered and analyzed when defining the PMO's role and position within the project management environment, and in establishing its relationships with other business units within the relevant organization or enterprise.

Internal and external business relationships also will be established according to the overall responsibilities of the PMO, consistent with its stage of maturity, i.e., its level of progression along the PMO competency continuum. Less-mature PMOs will usually have limited need for far-reaching business relationships, and most will be internal. More-mature or advanced PMOs will operate more like a business unit and will require business relationships comparable with peer business units within the relevant organization.

An analysis of current PMO recognition, current PMO responsibilities, and current PMO business unit peers will provide insight to the business relationships that warrant pursuit. The following are a few key points for examination and analysis of PMO business relationship needs.

- *Appropriate technical representation:* The PMO will need to integrate the expertise and participation of technical departments — design, manufacturing, product development, etc.
- *Alignment with senior managers and decision makers:* The PMO will implement policy guidance conveyed by executives, senior management teams, and oversight committees.

■ *Affiliation with internal business-support units:* The PMO will need support to initiate and conduct customer projects and to manage business processes within the project management environment. Some representative affiliations could include:
  – Information systems
  – Human resources
  – Procurement and contract management
  – Business development
■ *Affiliation with project resource managers:* The PMO may not have project resources directly assigned and thus will rely on resource managers to provide project managers and project team members.
■ *Affiliation with external project stakeholders:* The PMO will need to conduct business associated with project performance that could extend outside the relevant organization:
  – Customer relationships
  – Vendor/contractor relationships
  – Regulatory agency relationships

A review of these points of examination will enable the PMO to identify and pursue the appropriate business relationships needed to accomplish its mission.

Establish Project Team Structure

The PMO has a vested interest in achieving the prescribed level of oversight, control, and support in the project management environment. All that it can accomplish is influenced by the degree of formal alignment of project managers and other project resources within its purview. Likewise, the structure by which project team members are aligned under a project manager influences the project manager's ability to oversee, control, and support the performance of project team members. The third consideration of project team structure includes defining the extent to which external participants will be regarded as members of the project team. This refers primarily to customers and vendors/contractors, but it also includes potential designation of other participants within the relevant organization as members of the project team.

Essentially, the project team structure is defined to include the project manager and project team members, the integration of external participants into that team, and the relationship each project participant has with the PMO. These considerations are addressed in the following three subsections.

Specify Project Team and PMO Relationship

The nature of project team alignment with the PMO is generally associated with the PMO's stage of development along the PMO competency continuum. That is, it is more likely that there will be formal affiliation of project managers and project resources with the PMO when the PMO is operating at an advanced stage. Notwithstanding, there appears to be a prevalent approach in many organizations where project managers and project team members are not aligned with the PMO, regardless of the PMO's stage of development. However, at least some professionals in the project management discipline would agree that greater project effectiveness is achieved when all project resources are aligned to some degree under the PMO, and this function model recommends that at least project managers be aligned to some extent with the PMO.

The concept of project resource alignment presented here means the PMO has some range of control over project resource assignments, activity schedules, and performance. A generally acceptable range of control extends from *reasonable influence*, where project resources inherently respond to PMO oversight and guidance as a natural approach to project participation, to *direct assignment*, where the project resource reports to the PMO director, an aligned project manager, or other manager associated with the PMO.

The following are four progressive configurations that the PMO can consider in specifying its relationship with project managers and project team members. The PMO can identify variations of these configurations to better describe resource alignment in its project management environment. This specification is valuable because it can be associated with impacts on project performance. As well, it can indicate conditions that limit or facilitate advancements in project management capability and maturity.

No Alignment of Project Resources

This configuration is one in which the PMO has no apparent influence or control over resources assigned to perform work within the project management environment. This is normally associated with the smaller PMO operating at the basic stage of development. However, it is not unusual for a standard PMO to also encounter this condition. The following list identifies a few of the prominent impacts of this condition on the PMO and the project management environment:

- Strong and extended-period communication and collaboration will be needed to develop and implement project management governance and guidance, project management standards, and common project management tools and systems.

- Recurring executive and senior manager involvement may be needed to direct and monitor timely project resource input for cross-project reporting and adherence to the standards of report content for PMO review, analysis, and aggregation.
- The ability to implement preferred practices can be limited by individual professional interests and conflicting business and professional priorities encountered outside the project management environment.
- Training for project manager and project team members arranged through business units or individuals could be inconsistent with preferred project management practices.
- Capability to identify cross-project needs and reassign project resources on short notice to priority projects may be limited.
- Resource utilization across multiple project assignments may not be effectively planned and tracked when there is no central oversight, resulting in resource overcommitments and undercommitments to project efforts and project task work that is based on personal schedules and availability instead of business priorities.
- Project resource performance evaluations can be inconsistent across the various reporting officials serving as performance evaluators.

Indirect Alignment of Project Managers

This configuration is one in which the PMO develops active working relationships with project managers who are directly aligned with business units. In turn, those project managers will usually accept and apply PMO governance and guidance when an advantage is identified. As well, some of these project managers will demonstrate a willingness to participate with the PMO in developing and implementing standards and practices in the project management environment. This provides a reasonable level of PMO influence, albeit very limited control over project resource assignment and performance. The following list identifies a few of the prominent impacts of this condition on the PMO and the project management environment:

- Project management practices may vary across different project efforts, and project team members will need to differentiate the approach and preferences used by the project manager on each project to which they are assigned.
- The PMO will likely need to compete for project manager time and influence with the project manager's reporting official in the business unit.

- The capability to develop a cadre of professional project managers within the relevant organization may be limited by an inherent focus on the technical aspects of project performance rather than on effective implementation of modern project management practices.
- Modest levels of affiliation with the PMO will facilitate communication and an exchange of ideas and concepts among project managers who share the PMO as a central point of coordination and collaboration on project management practices.
- Project managers will gain a better understanding of the PMO's support capability in the project management environment, particularly identifying PMO support available for use on their projects. Ideally project management efficiency and effectiveness will improve as a result of the PMO relationship.

Direct Alignment of Project Managers

This configuration is one in which project managers work for the PMO when assigned to lead efforts in the project management environment. For the most part, they will receive their assignment from the PMO, and they will be responsible to the PMO for successful project completion and the associated achievement of project objectives. In turn, the PMO will monitor project progress and project manager performance. Note, however, that direct alignment does not necessarily require direct assignment to the PMO, although that would be the preferred condition. Moreover, this alignment of project managers does not infer alignment of project team members, which is discussed in the next section on project team structure. The following list identifies a few of the prominent impacts of this condition on the PMO and the project management environment:

- This influential position of the PMO can be used to ensure that business interests and objectives of the relevant organization are integrated and managed across all projects.
- The PMO will be able to prepare performance reports that are consistent across all designated project managers, but it will likely have to coordinate and manage the incorporation of its individual performance evaluations with those of the business unit if project managers are not directly assigned to the PMO.
- The PMO will have greater ability and a more effective means of introducing a viable and repeatable project management methodology process that is mandated for use by all project managers. Similarly, common project management practices and tools will be more likely to achieve widespread use.

- The PMO will need to establish the capability and infrastructure to properly manage aligned project managers, whether that group is small or large, and that need is increased if project managers are assigned directly to the PMO.
- The PMO can qualify and assign project managers to projects consistent with their skill and knowledge, not just because they are available. The PMO can also prescribe and provide technical and professional competency improvement activities for individual project managers to broaden their availability for more types of projects.

Direct Alignment of All Project Resources

This configuration is one in which all project managers and project team members are assigned to the PMO as a component of the PMO staff. There may be a distinction made between these project resources and members of the PMO staff working in specific function or support roles. However, once resources are assigned to the PMO, that distinction may be reduced as resources become available for work assigned on projects or on PMO functional efforts. The following list identifies a few of the prominent impacts of this condition on the PMO and the project management environment:

- The PMO can hold central accountability for the assignment and performance of all resources in the project management environment.
- The PMO can identify and commit the specific project resources that are qualified to perform approved project efforts.
- The PMO can analyze skill and competency requirements, prescribe professional development activities, and forecast project resource strength in specific technical and professional competency areas in advance of needs.
- The PMO can monitor and manage resource utilization across all projects and redirect resources to critical tasks as warranted by project needs and business priorities.
- The PMO can effectively implement standard, repeatable processes within the project management environment.

Define Standard Project Team Structure

The project team structure is primarily a function of project resource ownership and project manager authority, as prescribed by most project management standards applied in industry today. Project manager responsibility for achieving project performance objectives must be supported by an appropriate level of authority to control project resource utilization, assign and manage project task performance, and enforce accountability of project team members. Otherwise, the designated project leader is merely serving as a project schedule coordinator or project report administrator and cannot reasonably be held responsible for project outcomes.

The PMO should be influential first in evaluating the effectiveness of the current project team structures that exist within the project management environment. Then it should define and recommend the project team structure that fits within the established organizational culture and serves the project management needs and interests of the relevant organization.

This PMO function model examines project team structure in a manner that is generally consistent with most prominent standards. It presents three models for the PMO to consider in defining and establishing a project team structure:

- Functional project team structure
- Matrix project team structure
- Integrated project team structure

These structures represent a progressive state of project team cohesion that could exist or be established within the relevant organization. Upon examination of these different structures, many professionals in project management would likely agree that the most effective project team structure is probably represented by a combination of a prominent integrated project team structure, with a matrix project team structure applied for some elements of project participation when needed. In reality, most PMOs will probably implement structures that represent a variation of one or more of the structures presented.

Functional Project Team Structure

This represents a project team structure where the project manager has little or no authority over project resources. Instead, project resources are aligned with the resource provider, usually a functional manager in a business unit, who has primary authority over assignments and management of project resource contributions to the project effort. Other likely conditions resulting from this project team structure include:

- A project manager may be designated, but that individual probably fulfills only a portion of the responsibilities normally associated with professional project management. Decisions affecting project performance often are made outside the purview of the designated project manager by one or more functional managers, business managers, and technical managers.

■ Direction, guidance, and the ability to apply effective project management processes and practices can come from various sources. The oversight of multiple functional managers could result in an inconsistent approach to project management and the uncertainty of project outcome. This condition of authority shared across functional managers also may indicate that there is no central project management authority below the executive or senior management level.

■ Functional manager position and business experience may serve in lieu of formal project management skill and competency to guide project management activities and affect project progress and outcome.

■ Project resources serve under the direction and conditions of a functional manager, who — instead of the designated project manager — will evaluate their performance and influence their career progression. At best, a designated project manager will coordinate the efforts of these assigned resources and achieve resource performance results primarily through personal attributes of influence and persuasion.

■ Technical managers may be called to perform as project managers solely because of their demonstrated technical skill and competency rather than on capability and experience to manage the full range of project management life cycle activities.

Matrix Project Team Structure

This represents a project team structure where the project manager has limited authority over project resources, which are now aligned with the project manager for purposes of project work. Some project management standards distinguish between a strong matrix structure and a weak matrix structure. In a strong matrix structure, the project manager has significant authority and control over project resources during their project assignment. In a weak matrix structure, the resource provider (i.e., functional manager) retains primary authority and control of the resource but fulfills resource commitments to the project manager. Other conditions that are often associated with this project team structure include:

■ The role of the project manager is distinct and presumably associated with an individual qualified on the basis of skill and experience in project management concepts and practices. It is a role that is generally recognized and appropriately regarded by all project resources and functional managers within the relevant organization.

- The project manager will normally evaluate project resource performance as an element of project management. If the resource's project assignment is an extended one, the project manager may be solely responsible for conducting the annual performance review. If the assignment is shorter, the project manager is usually requested to provide an interim resource performance review for the assignment period, and that is entered into the individual's personnel records and serves as contributing input to performance reward and career progression decisions.

- The qualification and designation of project managers as the central point of project management responsibility facilitates the introduction of common and repeatable project management processes and practices. In turn, this capability is readily conveyed to those project resources in the matrix team structure, and they become increasingly effective in their accomplishment of project responsibilities across all project assignments.

- The assigned project resource normally cannot be assigned to other project tasks or other projects without the concurrence and commitment of the resource provider. Similarly, if there is a precise period of performance specified for a particular project matrix team resource, untimely completion of associated project tasks could affect project resource availability.

- The resource provider or functional manager who "owns" the resource can assert control or influence to remove or replace the resource assigned to the project. In turn, project managers will need to collaborate with resource providers at regular intervals to ensure current resource commitments and planned resource assignments are fulfilled in a timely manner. This is a small administrative burden that is encountered primarily when a weak matrix team structure is applied.

Integrated Project Team Structure

This represents a project team structure where the project manager has primary authority over project resources, which are usually aligned through a direct and full-time assignment to a project manager or to the PMO. Certain project management standards refer to this as a "projectized" project team structure. This model uses the term "integrated" to represent the full-time, ongoing alignment of project team members, project managers, and the PMO in the project management environment. In the next section, the further integration of external project participation will again be considered. Other prominent conditions for this project team structure include:

- A distinct central point of authority and responsibility for project management and project performance is established at the project level and at the PMO level.
- Accountability and actions for integration of strategic business objectives into project management efforts becomes less cumbersome. Executives and senior managers can influence project management direction toward achievement of business objectives without having to personally manage projects.
- The project management needs of all business units can be served. Professional project management processes and practices can now be applied to all applicable business and technical interests within the various business units of the relevant organization.
- Project management resources can be developed and grown within the culture of the relevant organization as they are acquired. This structure promotes measurement of project management skill and knowledge alongside technical capability as a qualifier for professional advancement.
- Project resources have reduced task performance and scheduling conflicts. These results stem at least from their full-time alignment with a central project management authority and, possibly, by having one supervising project manager.
- Project resource utilization planning and management should be more effective. Project resources can be assigned within the project management environment to respond to projects having business priority, to fill in temporary resource vacancies, to apply specialized skills, and to contribute to the development and implementation of PMO function areas. Any nonproject time can be accounted for in developing capabilities within the project management environment.
- Project resources have common performance standards across all projects to which they are assigned. Project managers contribute to establishing these standards and are instrumental in applying them to all project efforts.

Define Extended Project Team Alignment

The PMO will need to examine its culture and business environment in making decisions regarding extended project team alignment. This involves the need to determine how closely other project participants who are external to the relevant organization are aligned with the project and with the project manager. Specifically considered are three project stakeholder groups — customers, vendors/contractors, and regulatory agents. Other stakeholder groups presented in the next section can also be considered, as the PMO deems appropriate. Project performance benefits when representatives from these groups, as well as specifically assigned project team members, know and recognize who are members of the project team.

The PMO can create a default approach for the inclusion of extended project team members. However, unless the nature of project work is so homogenous and the same project stakeholders tend to be present on recurrent projects, each new project will warrant independent examination regarding the need for extended project team alignment.

The consideration of extending project team begins with understanding the conditions that warrant project team alignment. This is followed by establishing protocols for project team participation and alignment. Then the value of combining tasks and work activities in a common project work plan or keeping them in separate plans is examined.

An overview of these factors is presented for PMO consideration for each of the stakeholders who could be aligned as extended participants of the project team. Decisions concerning stakeholder alignment should be made in collaboration with applicable stakeholders to obtain their concurrence. Alignment consideration should account for current and potential business relationships, particularly with customers and vendors/contractors. To that end, also see the information presented in the chapters on the PMO "customer relationships" function (Chapter 18) and the PMO "vendor/contractor relationships" function (Chapter 19).

Customer Project Team Alignment

Some customers will collaborate on the project's technical solution and the plans to achieve it, and then they will essentially remain uninvolved outside of routine status meetings and progress report reviews. This is probably not characteristic of a project effort that warrants customer inclusion as part of the project team.

Conversely, some project work inherently requires ongoing customer involvement in the development and delivery of the project's technical solution. This bears consideration for having one or more customer representatives on the project team. In some cases, the customer may even have its own intact project team to be integrated. Presumably, there will be a customer contact or customer project manager who will serve as the point of integration.

The PMO or project manager should establish the protocol for this relationship early in the project effort, at or before the project kickoff meeting. In particular, the parties will need to decide how project team members will be assigned responsibilities and perform work together. A common approach is for the two project managers to coordinate their plans and then collaborate on the nature and extent of participation by necessary project resources. A related protocol point is establishing how technical or other subteams having combined participation will be managed, including specifying who will be the subteam leader. Finally, an important point of protocol is made when the customer distinguishes between being a project team participant and being a representative for acceptance of project deliverables obligated under a contract or agreement.

Many project managers find it useful to have key customer activities included in their work plan. Even subtle customer activities associated with the project take time — a few days for a document review, allocation of time for meeting preparation and attendance, a period for customer deliberation and decision, etc. The project work plan should account for these types of customer "deadlines" and activities. In many cases, the project work plan can become the customer's work plan, and the inclusion of assigned tasks for the customer will allow everyone to see the sequence of activities for which they are responsible. Besides, if it is not specified in the work plan, how will everyone know that it is an important and timely project activity, or even an activity on the project's critical path?

Vendor/Contractor Project Team Alignment

The vendor/contractor is too often a forgotten entity in some project management environments. If not specifically aligned as part of the extended project team, the vendor/contractor must be distinctly aligned with the project manager. This is a subtle difference in some cases, but it is one that should be examined to determine whether the vendor/contractor project manager works solely with the project manager, or whether the vendor/contractor participants are integrated with the project team.

The prescribed protocols for this project relationship are very similar to those indicated for the customer project team, only now with reversed roles. Here the project manager can determine the level of vendor/contractor integration, the preferred approach to technical leadership and project team resource management, and the point of contact for vendor/contractor deliverables.

The PMO should prescribe conditions and standards for alignment, but the project manager will need to make the final decision regarding the integration of any vendor/contractor work plan with the primary project work plan. The conditions that normally warrant full integration of project work plans are associated with technical activities where vendor/contractor participants work side by side with primary project team members, serving as technical leads, technical experts, or technical assistants. In other project situations, the vendor/contractor may have responsibility for one or more deliverables that it prepares independent of any participation with the primary project team. That condition probably just requires that a single line item be included in the project work plan to represent the vendor/contractor effort relative to other project activities. Of course, the project manager or a designee on the project team must actively manage that work plan line item.

Regulatory Agent Project Team Alignment

The introduction of a regulatory agent as an extended participant on the project team may initially seem awkward. However, the purpose of identifying the extended project team in the first place is to ensure that the project manager is able to account for and manage all prominent project activities, with appropriate alignment of key participants. In some project management environments, a regulatory agent can be a prominent participant at critical junctures in the project management life cycle.

A regulatory agent is often thought of as an external government representative. However, as described in the next subsection on other project stakeholders, the regulatory agent role could originate within the relevant organization or as an external representative. Usually, a regulatory agent is introduced into the project at points of product development or delivery. The decision to formally recognize regulatory agents as extended members of the project team will be determined by the protocol required and by mutual agreement between the regulatory agent and the project manager.

The points of protocol for regulatory agents may be preestablished by the regulatory agency by the nature of its oversight role and the type of project. The PMO should thoroughly understand these protocols for all regulatory agents and convey associated requirements to project managers and project team members.

It is wise to include regulatory agent activities associated with the project as elements of the project work plan, as would be done for any other key project participant. This enables the regulatory agent to identify preferred points of activity and, if necessary, to coordinate adjustments as a matter of protocol or convenience. Equally important, the participation of a regulatory agent on the project work plan serves as guidance and a reminder to the project manager and project team members about the need for timely completion of project activities.

Other Stakeholder Project Team Alignment

The alignment of extended project team participants is a factor for PMO consideration based on relevant organizational culture and business needs.

The PMO and others within the project management environment benefit by specifying and recognizing the standard composition of an active project team within the relevant organization. In that regard, this PMO function model does distinguish between members of the active project team, including primary and extended members, and other project stakeholders. Per reference to the listings in the following section, the PMO can add or exclude any project stakeholder roles as active participants on the project team.

Develop Stakeholder Participation

Who are the project stakeholders in your project management environment? This is determined by the PMO as it attempts to optimize communication among project participants and to maximize the benefits of stakeholder participation. This section recommends the identification of project stakeholders and describes the role that each can perform relative to project management activities and project performance. The following subsections describe six primary categories of project stakeholders.

Internal Project Team Stakeholders

This stakeholder category represents those project participants that are directly involved in conducting and managing the project effort. This group is responsible for producing required project deliverables and for achieving specified project objectives. In some project management environments, the project team can also be augmented by full- or part-time participation of PMO staff members. The following subsections describe the various stakeholders in this category.

Program Manager

This individual is responsible for oversight of multiple projects, usually a collection of projects that are interrelated by similar business interests, technical solutions, or customer base. This position usually serves as the reporting official of the project when it exists in the project management environment, and therefore it bears the responsibility for project success. Related position titles include "manager of project managers," "program director," and "project director."

Project Manager

This individual is responsible for conducting project management activities through all phases of the project management life cycle, managing project resource utilization and performance, and fulfilling project deliverables and objectives. Related position titles include "project leader," "project coordinator," and "project administrator."

Project Team Member

This individual is responsible for planning and performing work to accomplish project deliverables and to complete selected project management activities, as delegated by the project manager. This position reports to the project manager, either directly or through another project team member serving in an interim management or technical leadership position. The project team can comprise a variety of technical and managerial roles. Some of the more common roles include:

- Assistant project manager
- Technical leader
- Technical staff member
- Technical specialist
- Professional staff member
- Task leader/supervisor
- Craft specialist/laborer

In some project management environments, the project team may be augmented by full-time or part-time participation of PMO staff members.

Internal Oversight Stakeholders

This stakeholder category represents those project participants that provide senior level direction and decisions to guide project management toward the achievement of business interests and objectives. The following subsections describe prominent stakeholders in this category.

Project Executive (Sponsor)

This individual is the senior manager responsible for project performance, with the power to authorize project selection, continuation, and termination and project funding. In some organizations, these responsibilities are deferred to a committee of executives or senior managers. However, this role still retains responsibility for the alignment of projects with strategic business objectives, as can be performed using an effective project portfolio management system. A related title for this position is "project sponsor." This role can also be fulfilled by the executive head of a business unit or, in some smaller organizations, by the CEO.

PMO Director

This individual is the head of the project management office having responsibility for establishing and conducting project management oversight, control, and support across all projects in the relevant organization, and thereby for each project at hand. The PMO director advises and collaborates with the project executive and other executives and senior management teams regarding overall project management capability as well as individual and collective project activities and status. Program and project managers may report to or otherwise be aligned with the PMO director, per the organizational structure established for the project management environment. Related position titles include: "PMO manager," "chief project officer" (CPO), "chief technical officer" (CTO), and "vice president for projects."

Executive Control Board

The executive control board is the group of executives or senior managers within the relevant organization that deliberates and decides on the capability instituted in the project management environment; determines project selection, continuation, termination, and funding (when deferred by the project executive or by business mandate); and thereby has vested interest in individual project performance. Related titles for this board include: "project management oversight committee," "project control board," and "executive management team."

Technical Advisory Boards

Technical advisory boards are groups, usually having some executive level representation, that convene to deliberate and decide technical processes and practices applied in the project management environment and in association with technical elements of project performance. Such boards could have special technical purposes, and there could be a board aligned with each major technical discipline within the relevant organization. These groups would collaborate decisions and activities with the PMO to achieve integration with project management processes and practices and thereby would have a vested interest in technical aspects of real-time project performance. A variety of groups by different titles can be established to represent technical discipline interests, including the following few examples:

- Product development control board
- Technical process control board
- Configuration management team

- Engineering design committee
- Scientific analysis committee
- Test and acceptance procedures committee
- Construction management board
- Manufacturing process control board
- Technical achievement advisory council

Internal-Support Stakeholders

This stakeholder category represents those project participants within the relevant organization that serve as adjunct or part-time project team members. Their particular business, technical, or project management skill and expertise may warrant concurrent short-term assignments on several small to medium projects, or they could be assigned as full-time project team members on longer projects. The following subsections describe stakeholders in this category.

PMO Staff Member

This stakeholder group reports to the PMO director to establish and implement PMO functionality, develop project management capability in the relevant organization, and support project managers and project teams to achieve fulfillment of project deliverables and accomplishment of project objectives. Support is provided relative to the established functional capability of the PMO. See the PMO "career development" function (Chapter 11) for a full list of PMO staff positions.

Project Resource Manager

This is the individual to whom personnel who are competent to perform business, technical, and project management activities as members of a project team are assigned. This stakeholder is responsible for collaborating with the PMO and project managers to fulfill requirements for qualified project resources according to commitments made. In turn, project resource managers should solicit and incorporate project manager evaluations of project team member performance into performance reports for each assigned individual. Related titles for this position will vary by organization and industry.

Business Unit Managers

These stakeholders are the individuals who head the business units or departments in the relevant organization, including their designees who routinely provide business support to project managers and the PMO. Because of their interest in business outcomes on each project, they are viable project stakeholders. On larger projects, they could assign individuals with particular business expertise as members of the project team on a full- or part-time basis. Some examples of business unit support stakeholders include:

- New product expert
- Human resources manager
- Business development manager
- Legal adviser/counselor
- Procurement/contracts manager

Customer Stakeholders

This stakeholder category represents those project participants that have responsibility for ensuring that project outcomes fulfill the intended business purpose or need of the customer's organization. These stakeholders are members of the customer's organization. The specified stakeholders in this category are not always active participants on every project. However, at least one of them is normally identified as a primary point of contact for each project effort. Stakeholders in this category are described in the following subsections.

Customer Executive

This stakeholder is the senior manager in the customer environment who authorized project selection and funding and who holds strategic level responsibility for project success. Although not always visible in the customer's project management environment, this stakeholder is undoubtedly present and working behind the scenes. This is also the point of contact for executive level discussions, if needed.

Customer Project Manager

This stakeholder is responsible for providing project oversight and control on behalf of the customer's interests and perspectives for project success. This individual, along with relevant customer project team members, will normally be involved in developing technical requirement and specifications, participating in the preparation and approval of project plans, and tracking project progress through acceptance of project deliverables. When present, this customer stakeholder serves as a point of contact and coordinates and collaborates directly with the project manage to ensure project success.

Customer Project Team Member

These stakeholders are responsible for performing technical, business, and project management activities on customer-initiated projects that may be performed in conjunction with the project at hand. In some cases, joint project management plans are prepared, and customer project team members join the primary project teams in task efforts. In other cases, customer project team members represent the customer project manager to establish an oversight presence. On many projects in different industries, there is no customer project team in the project management environment.

Customer End Users

These stakeholders are responsible for implementing the project's technical solution in the customer's business environment. They may act in lieu of or in deference to the customer project team to test, approve, and accept project deliverables.

Customer Business Manager

This stakeholder is the default customer representative and point of contact for project efforts. This role normally has responsibility for initiating the project request, managing the associated project contract or agreement, and receiving and approving project deliverables. This role is the one usually encountered on a majority of customer projects across industries, and it is used in lieu of a customer project manager and project team on projects where deliverables do not require intense technical oversight, scrutiny, and test and acceptance activities.

Vendor/Contractor Stakeholders

This stakeholder category represents those project participants who have responsibility for ensuring that project outcomes fulfill the offering of the vendor/contractor. These stakeholders are members of the vendor/contractor organization. The specified stakeholders in this category are not always active participants on every project. However, when vendors and contractors are involved in the project, at least one of them is normally identified as a primary point of contact for each project effort. Stakeholders in this category are described in the following subsections.

Vendor/Contractor Executive

This stakeholder is the senior manager in the vendor/contractor organization who holds business responsibility for the offering. It is this individual who normally warrants quality of products and performance as well as the fulfillment of any associated contract or agreement. This stakeholder is also the point of contact for executive level discussions, if needed.

Vendor/Contractor Project Manager

This stakeholder is responsible for leading the vendor/contractor project team in conducting assigned project tasks and in achieving the prescribed technical solution to fulfill the vendor/contractor's offer. When present, this stakeholder serves as the vendor/contractor point of contact and coordinates and collaborates directly with the project manager to ensure successful completion of the vendor/contractor effort.

Vendor/Contractor Project Team Members

These stakeholders have responsibility for performing technical, business, and project management activities on assigned projects. In some cases, joint project management plans are prepared, and the vendor/contractor project team members join the primary project teams in task efforts. In other cases, vendor/contractor project team members work independently to accomplish assigned project tasks. A vendor/contractor project team may or may not be established for each vendor/contractor offering.

Vendor/Contractor Business Manager

This stakeholder is the default vendor/contractor representative and point of contact for project efforts. This role is also prevalent when there is a particular product or service acquired, in lieu of technical development work associated with the project effort. It is the position usually encountered in business interactions with a vendor/contractor organization.

Other Project Stakeholders

This stakeholder category represents those project participants that have primary interests in fulfillment of all or part of the project objectives. These stakeholders can be associated with the relevant organization or be introduced from an external organization. The stakeholders in this category are not always active participants on every project. The nature of each project will determine the need for their participation. Stakeholders in this category can include:

Regulatory Agents

These stakeholders normally perform inspections or examinations within the project management environment to ascertain quality or compliance. This includes regulatory agents from business units within the relevant organization who primarily address product- and service-quality issues. It also can include external representatives who focus on compliance issues such as those from industry or technical standards organizations or government regulatory agencies.

Business Partners

These stakeholders have interests in recouping investments associated with project efforts. They are not normally visible in the project management environment, but they may be encountered through integrated activities with the business environment.

Industry Partners

These stakeholders have interests in achieving technical and technology solutions that advance industry standards, enlarge markets, or promote associated professional disciplines. They could be visible in the project management environment when one or more projects are involved in developing or implementing a solution of interest to the partnership. In general, industry partners may be business partners, but business partners are not inherently industry partners.

Executive Management Team

These stakeholders represent the highest level of executive management in the relevant organization. This stakeholder category includes the CEO, CIO, CFO, etc. It would be rare for these stakeholders to be visible in the project management environment, unless the enterprise is a small business. Therefore, this stakeholder group normally defers oversight responsibilities to the PMO or project executive (sponsor). The absence of visibility, however, does not mean lack of interest. These stakeholders undoubtedly will have some measure of regard and support for project contributions to business, and thereby they have an interest in the business results achieved within the project management environment.

POSTSCRIPT FOR THE SMALLER PMO

The efforts of the smaller PMO should focus on introducing professional project management concepts and practices into the relevant organization, including promoting an organization and structure that will facilitate excellence in project management.

Organizations are structured to conduct business according to the traditions and best practices that are best known to them. Many technical and business entities are already structured and are well embedded in the relevant organization, but some of them do not inherently address all the needs associated with an effective project management environment. Conversely, an effective project management organization and structure naturally pursues integration of technical and business functions, practices, and activities.

To that end, the smaller PMO can address a few fundamental organizational alignment activities in the relevant organization to advance awareness of the benefits to be gained from having an effective project management organization and structure:

■ First, establish the professional roles of the project manager and the project team members as best as can be accomplished. Draw awareness to who is a project manager and who is not by defining the role and responsibilities of a project manager within the relevant organization. Similarly, define any standard project team roles, particularly those having delegated project management responsibilities. When project team members know their specific roles and responsibilities, they will tend to become more effective and efficient in their work environment.

■ Examine the project participation by individuals in business units. Identify the scope of project support that is provided — support to a few types of projects or to all projects. Determine where the PMO can serve as a central coordinator for those activities to streamline the process or to optimize participation across projects. As well, determine whether business unit participation is included in project planning and listed in the project work plan. Identify project information that can be compiled by the PMO for distribution to business units to help them plan and conduct their portions of project work and to achieve their business objectives.

■ Identify the project stakeholders in and around the relevant organization. Determine who is involved or otherwise has business interests in different aspects of project performance. Examine each stakeholder individually to see how well their business interests are achieved per their current alignment with projects. Develop recommendations for improved alignment of various stakeholders with relevant project efforts.

8

FACILITIES AND EQUIPMENT SUPPORT

Project managers have traditionally held general responsibility for obtaining and using the facilities and equipment required for each project effort. On larger, possibly geographically dispersed projects, the project manager could enlist the assistance of specialized business units within the relevant organization to obtain such resources, e.g., facilities management, procurement, and contracting departments. Under the concepts of this PMO function, the PMO will examine the opportunities in which it can intervene to oversee facilities and equipment within the project management environment. In so doing, it will facilitate better alignment of facilities and equipment acquisition, assignment, and disposal based on project requirements, thereby reducing a large part of the project manager's burden in this area of responsibility.

This "facilities and equipment support" function enables the PMO to:

- Establish a common project work space configuration
- Monitor, manage, and control facilities and equipment acquisition, use, and disposition within the project management environment
- Optimize specific facilities and equipment utilization and assignment across projects
- Reduce facilities and equipment expenses for individual projects

The PMO will be able to achieve these functional objectives by working closely with (a) project managers, to help them identify requirements for facilities and equipment as part of their physical resource planning, and (b) business units that currently provide this type of support to project managers. In turn, the PMO can establish the procedures necessary to requisition facilities and equipment for each project effort. This PMO function is inherently needed more in organizations that have significant or specialized project equipment needs and extensive project facilities requirements.

PROJECT ENVIRONMENT INTERFACE CONCEPTS

The PMO can use its comprehensive understanding of project management requirements to plan and support facilities and equipment needs in the project management environment. This ranges from addressing individual project needs to establishing cross-project support capability for facilities and equipment.

In many cases, the relevant organization will have an existing capability to provide facility and equipment support, likely as two separate business functions. The role of the PMO is to bring that support into close alignment with project needs while serving the business interests of advanced planning and reduced costs. To that end, the PMO serves as an interface for project managers with such business support units, thereby reducing the project manager's need to attend to such matters.

The PMO's oversight of facilities and equipment can provide an important accounting function. If the nature of business is one that requires reusable specialized equipment — e.g., heavy equipment for construction, gauges and testing equipment for laboratories, and toolkits for hardware maintenance — the PMO can be the source for planning and allocating equipment use at the times needed by different projects. Likewise, equipment needs for anticipated project work across multiple projects can be procured in bulk to realize cost savings, in contrast to expensing equipment for individual projects at no cost benefit. Similarly, the PMO's perspective across projects will enable it to examine facility acquisition and assignment opportunities that maximize cost savings to the relevant organization, locally and worldwide.

Finally, the PMO performs a combined oversight and support role by ensuring that facilities and equipment within the project management environment adequately support project teams in their pursuit and achievement of project objectives. This includes identifying and acquiring the computing hardware and software needed to get the job done, as well as monitoring the needs for office space and office fixtures, furnishings, and equipment needed by project team members. Again, this PMO support reduces the administrative burden and allows project managers to spend more of their time on direct project management efforts.

This PMO function is merely one of coordination for collocated project teams, where the business unit to which they are assigned inherently provides the necessary office space and equipment for the project team member. Conversely, where project teams are more transient — separate facilities needed at various locales for specific client engagements, global-reaching projects requiring travel, frequent turnover of personnel assigned to the project effort — the PMO can play a facilitating role in helping project managers achieve project objectives while also monitoring business interests in the process.

BUSINESS ENVIRONMENT INTERFACE CONCEPTS

The PMO can accomplish the "facilities and equipment support" function by being a coordinator and collaborator in the business environment. The intent is not to replace any current business unit functionality but, rather, to influence processes that are conducive to effective and efficient management of facilities and equipment within the project management environment. However, if there are no existing business-area processes that address facilities and equipment management to support project efforts, then the PMO can play a lead business role in its accomplishment of this PMO function.

Presuming that there are current business functions within the relevant organization that address facilities and equipment, the PMO's primary responsibility will be to monitor the support provided to the project management environment. To that end, the PMO can collaborate with in-house facilities and equipment support providers to help them achieve a better understanding of how their support activities impact project management requirements. Subtleties taken for granted in the project management environment are not always evident to nonpractitioners, and current support processes may not necessarily be conducive to effective project management. For example, the classification and priority of a new project may influence equipment assignment, rather than an earlier-dated requisition request. Likewise, facilities that are available and can house two or three project teams may not be appropriate for such use if one of the project teams has contractual obligations for separate facilities to avoid a conflict of business interest. The PMO can monitor these conditions and help current support providers understand the concepts and considerations of project management.

FACILITIES AND EQUIPMENT SUPPORT ACTIVITIES ACROSS THE PMO CONTINUUM

The "facilities and equipment support" function along the PMO competency continuum provides increasing involvement in facilities and equipment management, as is applicable to projects within the relevant organization.

Table 8.1 presents an overview of the range of prescribed PMO facilities and equipment support activities according to each level in the PMO competency continuum.

The *project office* is responsible for requesting and managing the facilities and equipment needed to accomplish each project effort. This responsibility inherently falls within the purview of the project manager, who must identify and submit requirements for facilities and equipment support to the PMO or other supporting business unit.

Mid-range PMO levels help project managers to identify and achieve facilities and equipment support requirements on individual projects. The mid-range PMO also will manage an effort to optimize the use and assignment — and potential reuse and reassignment — of project facilities and equipment across multiple project efforts as a means to make facility and equipment acquisitions and deployment more cost effective for the relevant organization.

The *center of excellence* will continue its focus on business performance by conducting strategic level analyses of the facilities and equipment support activities as a means of improving its effectiveness within the project management environment.

This PMO function implements the capability to provide effective facilities and equipment support within the project management environment. This includes establishing processes for the PMO and project managers alike to apply to the support effort. To that end, facets of that process can be prescribed and incorporated into the project management methodology, as presented in the PMO "project management methodology" function (see Chapter 1).

FACILITIES AND EQUIPMENT SUPPORT FUNCTION MODEL

The PMO's primary role can be either that of facilitator or that of manager of facilities and equipment support within the project management environment. If business units within the relevant organization already conduct such support, the PMO should facilitate alignment and integration of business and project management processes. If such support is not readily present or fully supportive of interests in the project management environment, the PMO can be more proactive in implementing facilities and equipment-support solutions, but always consistent with established practices and coordinated with appropriate existing business-support functions.

This PMO function is generally applied within organizations that have large project team populations. It centralizes the management of facilities and equipment across multiple project efforts, thereby alleviating some of the management burden of individual project managers. The project manager is still responsible for identifying facilities and equipment

Table 8.1 Range of Facilities and Equipment Support Activities across the PMO Continuum

Project Office	Basic PMO	Standard PMO	Advanced PMO	Center of Excellence
Identifies and uses facilities and equipment needed to accomplish the project effort	Ensures reasonable facilities and basic equipment are available to the project team ■ Monitors needs for project team facilities and equipment ■ Recommends configurations for project team office space and equipment	Provides support for project team facilities and equipment ■ Identifies requirements for facilities and equipment ■ Monitors assignments and utilization for facilities and equipment ■ Manages disposition of facilities and equipment	Expands support capability to include facility acquisition ■ Forecasts facility requirements ■ Evaluates facility acquisition and use options ■ Establishes facility contracts	Analyzes needs and uses of project facilities and equipment ■ Conducts optimized-use and cost analyses of project facilities ■ Performs optimized-use and cost analyses of project equipment

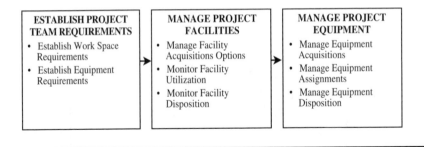

ESTABLISH PROJECT TEAM REQUIREMENTS	MANAGE PROJECT FACILITIES	MANAGE PROJECT EQUIPMENT
• Establish Work Space Requirements • Establish Equipment Requirements	• Manage Facility Acquisitions Options • Monitor Facility Utilization • Monitor Facility Disposition	• Manage Equipment Acquisitions • Manage Equipment Assignments • Manage Equipment Disposition

Figure 8.1 "Facilities and Equipment Support" Function Model

requirements, but with this PMO function, the manager can submit a request for fulfillment to the PMO. In turn, the project manager resumes responsibility for managing assigned use of project facilities and equipment. At a minimum, the PMO can perform oversight and provide facilities and equipment support, as needed, even for organizations with smaller project team populations.

The prominent activities of the PMO's "facilities and equipment support" function model are depicted in Figure 8.1. Each activity is described in the following subSections.

Establish Project Team Requirements

The PMO serves in a capacity to (a) examine and validate project team work space requirements in conjunction with project managers' input and requests, (b) manage fulfillment of requirements either through direct action or by passing the requirements to the appropriate business unit within the relevant organization, and (c) monitor fulfillment actions. As well, the PMO can represent project management environment work space needs to facility managers and to senior management. This activity enables the PMO to ensure that project team performance is supported by adequate work space and equipment needed by individuals responsible for project management and task performance.

The PMO may have to apply special consideration and adjust the prescribed approach if work space setup support is provided to geographically separated work teams or those operating in a virtual team environment.

Establish Work Space Requirements

The PMO should evaluate existing working conditions to determine whether the work space for the project team members is sufficient for current and near-term project team requirements. In general, this is an evaluation that can be formally or informally conducted by the PMO on a recurring, perhaps annual, basis. It provides the PMO with sufficient insight to workplace conditions to enable meaningful deliberation and discussions in support of the work space requirements to be pursued.

The PMO can then proceed to develop a set of recommended work space features that are desired within the project management environment. Things to consider include:

- *Preferred individual work space dimensions (area):* The size of various work spaces needed, consistent with organizational standards, roles and responsibilities of project team members, and nature of project work.
- *Preferred work space enclosures:* Requirements for office space for different purposes, including offices for managers or others requiring levels of privacy due to the nature of their work; enclosed rooms for meetings, storage, or library; offices, cubicles, or open work space for project team members; laboratory rooms or enclosures; and work space for visiting project participants. As well, this work space feature considers break rooms, needs for special ventilation or other type of climate control, utility (e.g., electricity, water, etc.) requirements, the need to accommodate access for handicapped participants, and the necessity to fit any (furniture-size) project equipment.
- *Furniture and furnishings:* Presents the need for desks, workbenches, work stations, chairs, tables, bookcases, lamps, etc., again consistent with organizational standards, the roles and responsibilities of project team members, and the nature of the project work.
- *Work space access requirements:* Identifies the need to control access to the project team work area or facility. This also includes a description of any information, security, or work-safety-based protective requirements for individuals, equipment, and materials associated with project work efforts. This feature specifies access requirements and provides the preferred (or required) means of access control.

The PMO can compile and recommend the acquisition and assignment of project team facilities that have the preferred work space features, or it can validate that current facilities are adequate to support the projects involved.

The PMO should monitor facilities utilization and configuration during and between recurring work space examinations. The following are several facility utilization factors for the PMO to consider as it provides ongoing management of facilities and equipment support:

- Project team number and average size
- Project team member population
- Project manager population
- Project manager alignment with number of project teams
- Project team (and team member) locations

This effort will produce results that vary significantly by organization and by industry. In some cases, a handful of project managers will be aligned with a few project team members, and generally all are collocated in one facility. In other cases this may expand to configurations of many project managers, hundreds of project team members, and multiple project team locations. The simpler configuration will likely require the PMO to be more attentive to details of the support provided. The latter configurations provide more opportunity for the PMO to play a larger role in managing facilities and optimizing their use across the larger number of project teams.

The PMO should prepare a fundamental recommendation document for work space requirements by project team or a general recommendation by individual. The more advanced PMO may incorporate this document into a broader organizational facilities plan for how project team facility requirements will be implemented across the relevant organization.

Establish Equipment Requirements

The PMO should develop fundamental guidance and recommendations for the equipment needed by individual project managers and project team members, per the technical and professional nature of the types of project work they are tasked to perform. This might be identified as a project team member equipment package. Then, the PMO also should identify equipment shared by all members of the project team — usually within a business office environment. Finally, the PMO should identify any special equipment needed by one or more project teams to accomplish project objectives.

An overview examination and checklist for these three types of equipment requirements are presented below. Each PMO must consider the history of project team equipment provisioning and current needs as it specifies its requirements and recommendations for each equipment group within the project management environment. As well, it is not presumed that such equipment support is not currently provided by another business unit. For example, the IT department will usually support individual and group office equipment, and other business units will support specialized equipment. However, now the PMO uses the information it compiles to improve and optimize equipment assignment and utilization support across project teams.

Individual Equipment Requirements

The PMO can consider items in the following list in creating a standard equipment package for the project team. Note that some project teams and team members are generally office-based, while others may be field-based. The PMO's recommendations should take into account the different equipment needs of these project participants.

Computer. Today's project management environment inherently requires consideration of individual computer equipment, which includes:

- Desktop computer
- Laptop computer
- Personal digital assistant (PDA)
- Computer docking station/cradle (for laptops and PDAs)

Consideration of this equipment includes any necessary peripheral equipment such as monitor, keyboard, modem, network card, CDROM/diskette readers, etc. Assignment of this equipment also implies connectivity to a network within the relevant organization for purposes of internal and external communications and access to the Internet.

Software. This is a standard set of software that can be prescribed for users on the project team, including the following items:

- Business suite applications (e.g., word processor, spreadsheet, database, presentation manager, etc.)
- Communications applications (e.g., e-mail, Web browser, contact manager, collaboration tools, etc.)
- Project management applications (e.g., cost-schedule-resource manager, task manager, project information dashboard, methodology process manager, etc.)
- Document reader applications (e.g., text-file reader, drawing/CAD-file reader, etc.)

Although not particularly an equipment item, the PMO may want to consider access (and any associated cost) to Internet technical and business Internet locations in association with use of any Web-based applications, including membership requirements. As well, access to the Internet and to the home office network is a feature to consider.

Individual Office Equipment. This is a general set of equipment that facilitates individual project work performance and business communications that can be considered, including the following:

- Desktop telephone
- Mobile telephone (cell phone)
- Mobile pager
- Two-way radio
- Voice-mail recorder/mailbox
- Desk, chair, and associated office furnishings
- Individual work document and media storage containers (file cabinets)

The specification and assignment of individual office equipment, to a large extent, will be influenced by the culture and practices of the relevant organization. The PMO should carefully examine its recommendations for any equipment that exceeds those norms.

Individual Special Equipment. This is a set of equipment determined by the nature of business and project requirements that is considered for assignment to individuals because of personal or professional need or frequency of use, including the following:

- Personal health and safety devices
- Toolkits
- Measurement devices
- Writing instruments
- Calculators and special computing devices
- Equipment and document travel cases
- Special work apparel/clothing

The PMO will need to examine special equipment utilization to determine whether assignment to individuals is warranted.

Project Team Office Equipment Requirements

The PMO can consider items in the following list in creating equipment recommendations for a standard project office, i.e., for a collocated project team. The items below generally represent office equipment types that can be shared by all project team members. However, in some cases they also may be issued as individual equipment:

- Document printer (computer peripheral)
- Electronic plotter (computer peripheral)
- Power-surge protectors
- Facsimile machine
- Reproduction/copy machine

- Document scanner
- Workbench or laboratory table
- Technical manuals (issued as equipment in some environments)
- Team work document and media storage containers
- Meeting room table, chairs, and associated furnishings
- Drawing and writing boards
- Audiovisual equipment
- First-aid/emergency kits and equipment
- Trash receptacles, including document-destruction equipment

This listing provides a preliminary consideration for items that create a basic "project office" equipment configuration. The PMO should collaborate with project managers to determine if there are any other team office equipment requirements unique to current or planned projects.

Special Equipment Requirements

The PMO can consider the generic items in the following list as a guide for preparing its recommendations for special equipment that is normally shared across project teams. It will certainly have to examine the nature of project work and collaborate with relevant project managers to finalize these requirements. As well, these items generally represent "nonoffice" equipment that is assigned for project team use on an as-needed basis and subsequently returned to centralized control for scheduled use by another project team:

- Personnel transportation vehicles
- Heavy equipment (e.g., construction equipment and vehicles, large hardware/product installation equipment, etc.)
- Unique (and sometimes very expensive) calibration and measurement devices
- Special-purpose tools/toolkits
- Additional/spare computing equipment and peripherals
- Mobile operations equipment
- Field operations equipment

Again, the PMO should collaborate with project managers and technical team leaders to establish a specific special equipment requirements list for the relevant organization.

Manage Project Facilities

The PMO begins this effort by identifying facility needs and requirements across the various projects. The PMO can then concentrate on developing the processes for their acquisition, utilization (assignment), and disposition. This necessitates having a fairly comprehensive understanding of project team strength, project team locations, and project durations for all current and upcoming projects across the relevant organization.

The PMO can then proceed to review current facility utilization to determine whether it is sufficient for project team needs or whether it can be optimized for multiple project team use. As well, the PMO should identify pending projects with known or anticipated start dates as a means to plan upcoming facility needs.

Presumably, there will be an existing facilities management function within the relevant organization. If so, the PMO plays a role to ensure that the needs of the project management environment are met through coordination of the project facility requirements with the planned facility assignment actions of the facility manager. Conversely, the relevant organization may not have a facilities management function that specifically addresses project team requirements. In this case, the PMO should become a more visible influence on facility oversight within the project management environment. PMO involvement is likewise appropriate in situations when project facility management is associated with distinct customer engagements, where facility costs are associated with one or more project efforts, or where customer-provided facilities require a measure of project manager oversight.

The depth of facility management processes used by the PMO can be adjusted to fit the needs of the relevant organization. However, it is essential to note that the activities prescribed below are not intended to replace any organizational facilities management function or to make the PMO an expert in facilities management. Rather, this guidance is provided so that the PMO can assist or guide the project manager — while collaborating with the in-house facilities management experts — in conducting project facilities management with regard to the interests of the project management environment.

The following subsections prescribe three fundamental areas of project facility management that the PMO can consider when establishing project facilities support processes within the relevant organization.

Manage Facility Acquisition Options

The PMO, with an eye on all projects within the relevant organization, should review the different facility acquisition options that have been undertaken to provide current project facilities, examine effectiveness to date in supporting project facility needs, and develop recommendations for the approach to future project facility acquisitions.

The PMO can consider the benefits and drawbacks of the following four acquisition methods when evaluating and recommending facility needs for current and future projects.

Collocation

This approach to facility acquisition is likely the most common situation the average PMO will encounter. It simply represents planning and acquiring work space for the project team in existing facilities within the relevant organization. This is the default facility assignment for individuals who are assigned to business units but who also contribute time on one or more project teams. Their work space is relatively permanent, regardless of the project work they may be assigned. The PMO usually plays a negligible role in influencing business unit work space assignments.

However, the PMO's attention to the collocation method could also mean acquisition of work space within existing relevant organization facilities for use by project teams, where members of a cohesive project team are collocated in a common office or work space. As this is a preferred project management practice, the PMO's role is to recommend and facilitate such arrangements, as needed by project teams.

The PMO may also encounter another collocation arrangement — that of collocation at an existing customer's facility. This is a common practice, but it does require the attention of the project manager and oversight of the PMO to ensure that any associated contractual obligations for facility use and management are satisfied.

In this facility acquisition method, the PMO plays a primary role in helping the project manager to identify work space that is available for collocation of project team members. Normally, there is no direct cost to the project effort when acquiring collocated facilities for the project team. However, there is a cost to be accounted for in the overhead of the organization supplying the facilities.

Lease

This approach to facility acquisition is often used by rapidly expanding project teams to accommodate the influx of new project team members. It is also a solution for setting up project team operations at locations that will be staffed for only a fixed period of time, usually the duration of the project. The PMO's role in this acquisition method is to validate the need for and the conditions of the facility lease. This involves close collaboration with the project manager to deliberate acquisition options and decide on a course of action.

A few of the more prominent issues to consider in deliberating leasing arrangements for the project team include:

- *Leasing cost:* Will the cost be expensed as a project budget item or as overhead?
- *Leasing period:* What is the period of the lease relative to the period of the project; can the lease be terminated if the project is terminated early; can the lease be extended if the project is extended?
- *Leasing conditions:* What facility maintenance and management responsibilities are incurred by the lease; do they represent significant cost items for the project?
- *Leasing contract:* Who will manage the leasing contract and monitor associated compliance; what are the lease payment arrangements; who will make payments and when; what are the penalties and remedies for noncompliance?
- *Facility renovation:* Does the lease account for any required renovation or reconstruction within the facility; what effect do such requirements have on the leasing cost or the period of the lease?

The PMO should be involved in lease deliberations that accommodate project team operations, but it must always seek the advice and council of experts and professionals within the relevant organization, e.g., legal department, contracting department, etc.

Purchase

This approach to facility acquisition is one that normally represents a business decision to conduct a capital program. It is characterized by a cash outlay or other funding approach to obtain the preferred existing building or structure. The PMO will need to understand the ramifications of recommending this type of project facility acquisition. However, it can confer with strategic planners and facility management experts during its prerecommendation deliberation.

In general, the PMO should be involved in project facility purchase decisions when long-term facility requirements are identified. Its primary role will be to validate or support the need for a facility purchase. This approach may be considered when there is a need for permanent offices for project team members, or when a particular project or program has a definitive need and an appropriate funding source has been identified to warrant the facility purchase.

Build/Develop

This approach to facility acquisition has PMO deliberation impacts similar to those encountered in a purchase. It too is a business decision that is likely to be a capital program. However, deliberation requirements are enlarged by the need to evaluate architectural, engineering, and construction facets of the acquisition method. The result of this effort is the construction of a new facility.

The PMO will primarily serve in an advisory capacity for this type of project facility acquisition. It should be involved to represent the interests of the project management environment and to participate in facility space allocations for project teams. This method of facility acquisition is normally considered in response to the longer-term strategic needs of the relevant organization.

Monitor Facility Utilization

This activity provides the PMO with the means to examine facility utilization across all projects within the relevant organization. It has three fundamental objectives that are presented below.

Ensure Adequacy of Facilities

The PMO should ensure that current facilities adequately support the effectiveness and efficiency of project team work efforts. This includes examining conditions of both separated and collocated project team members and ascertaining impacts on project performance. In particular, the PMO should identify where project team members have work spaces away from each other to the detriment of project performance capability.

The insight from this examination will enable the PMO to devise an approach and formulate recommendations for project facility management within the relevant organization. In turn, the PMO will also gain a fairly complete understanding of project team facility requirements. This will be a valuable PMO information asset, even if PMO recommendations are not immediately implemented. This information will allow the PMO to advise project managers across the relevant organization regarding planning for utilization of the project team facility. It also will allow the PMO to advise senior managers and to contribute to senior management decisions regarding facility requirements that support effective project performance.

Optimize Facility Utilization

The PMO's examination should prompt an analysis of ways to optimize facility utilization for the project team and its members. This is not likely to be a concern for the PMO serving a small number of collocated project teams. However, the PMO that has a larger number of project teams located across an expanded area, perhaps one with global responsibility, will benefit from reviewing the following facility utilization considerations:

- Identify availability of work space in currently assigned project team facilities
- Identify overcrowding in work space in currently assigned project team facilities
- Identify projects having multiple locations for assigned project team members
- Identify projects that have dedicated, collocated work space for project team members (i.e., project office configuration)
- Identify disparity in project team facility assignments (i.e., number of project team members versus available work space for key projects)
- Identify project team facilities approaching end of assignment and those available for reassignment
- Identify facilities where associated leases or contracts have become a management burden, so as to warrant early or at least timely termination of use
- Identify facilities where maintenance requirements and associated costs have expanded beyond desired limits

An examination of these factors should provide indicators of opportunities for optimizing the assignment of facilities used by project teams. This could include:

- Collocating multiple project teams in the same existing facility to dispose of unneeded facilities and reduce overall facility costs in the project management environment
- Moving project team members from dispersed business unit work spaces to a dedicated project office environment
- Making work space available at existing facilities in dispersed geographical locations or regions for individual project team members or small teams associated with different projects
- Acquiring project team facilities in a dispersed location to accommodate individual project team members or small teams associated with different projects

The PMO does not necessarily have to recommend or make abrupt facility assignment changes, but it can compile indicators that can be applied to improved facility acquisition and assignment management in the future.

Plan Future Facility Utilization

The PMO should have the combined awareness of current facility availability and knowledge of new projects about to begin. This information can be used to conduct facility planning to support each project effort. The PMO can work with the relevant project manager to identify project team facility needs and then recommend and pursue a course of action for acquiring and assigning preferred project team facilities.

The PMO might consider establishing a tracking system for such facility management, which is particularly valuable if there is frequent project facility turnover within its purview. Even if the PMO does not directly own or manage a facility, it will enhance its support capability to project managers by knowing the availability within existing facilities and the acquisition options that are immediately available to the project. Ideally, a PMO involved in facility management activities will be proactive in preparing a plan that recommends the facility acquisition and assignment course of action for upcoming projects.

Monitor Facility Disposition

In conjunction with monitoring and tracking facility utilization, the PMO can develop plans and recommendations for facility disposal, i.e., what to do with the project team facility (or work space) when the project team is finished using it.

The end result of monitoring facility disposition is that the PMO must have reliable information regarding the availability or nonavailability of existing facilities that have been used by project teams. The PMO's tracking process can be formal or informal, but it should represent an appropriate level of effort that will enable the PMO to support project managers' requests for project team facilities within the relevant organization.

The PMO active in management of project team facilities should be prepared to make or recommend facility disposition decisions, including the following prominent options outlined in the following subsections.

Continuity of Use

An "established" project team is recognized as a group that pursues one or more project efforts as a coherent group and does so on a more or less ongoing basis, taking on new projects as they emerge. In such cases, there is no particular need to dispose of the facility or discontinue its assignment to the established project team. The PMO identifies the approximate period of extended use, or it designates the facility as a "permanent" facility assignment for the established project team, and tracks its utilization accordingly.

Reassignment

An existing project team is preparing to disperse at the end of the current project effort and will vacate the facility. The assignment to that project team will be discontinued, and the facility will be made available for utilization by another project team. The PMO identifies the planned discontinuation of facility assignment, coordinates end-of-use date with the project manager, and includes the facility in considerations for assignment to another project team based on period of availability and the project team's needs. The PMO tracks its reassignment, and if facility reassignment cannot be specified in a reasonable period of time, alternative facility disposition actions should be considered.

Administrative Return to Landlord

A currently assigned project team will no longer have need for facility use, and conditions of occupancy require the return of the facility at the conclusion of the current assignment. If the facility is considered for follow-on use after the current project team vacates, the PMO or project manager may have to renegotiate an extension to continue facility use. Otherwise, this situation warrants return of facility (or work space) control to the relevant organization or customer's facility manager, and this usually includes a variety of administrative activities to document that return transfer of responsibility. The PMO should track the transfer activities that are conducted to ensure that all conditions of use and facility close out have been satisfied. It can then remove the facility from its facility tracking list.

Conclusion of Leasing Arrangement

This disposition option arises from either dispersal or relocation of the project team from a leased facility. If the facility is considered for follow-on use by another project team, the leasing agreement is simply reviewed to ensure that such an assignment is covered, and any needed adjustments to the lease are then negotiated and implemented to accommodate the new project team. Lease close out could be compounded by the need to address issues of lease compliance and duration of use, and the project manager or PMO should use available legal advisors and facility management professionals to lead that type of encounter. Otherwise, the facility is simply returned to the landlord, and the PMO monitors lease close out activities to ensure a timely and distinct return of property responsibility. It can then remove the facility from its facility tracking list.

Deactivation

Deactivation occurs when a vacated project team facility becomes unavailable for reassignment but is not otherwise disposed. This results when facility managers take action to shut down the facility pending management decisions for its further use. Or, the facility could be taken out of use for major maintenance, refurbishment, or add-on construction. The PMO will need to track the status of a deactivated facility and bring it back to consideration for project team assignment when the facility is again activated for utilization, assuming that it is again made available for project team assignments.

Transfer of Ownership/Property Sales

A project team facility, vacated or not, may become slated for sale. The PMO should be positioned to learn about such organizational decisions as a means to assist in project team relocation, if necessary, or to simply recognize nonavailability of a particular facility for future planning of project team work space.

Destruction

Similar to a facility sale, a project team facility, vacated or not, may become slated for destruction. Again, the PMO should ensure that it is notified of such organizational decisions regarding facilities used by project teams. The PMO will then note future nonavailability of the facility, but it may also want to pursue any intentions to replace the facility through construction of a new facility. The PMO can then track facility availability accordingly.

Manage Project Equipment

The primary purpose of PMO involvement in equipment management is to optimize the use and assignment — and potential reuse and reassignment — of project equipment across multiple project efforts as a means to make equipment acquisitions and deployment more cost effective for the relevant organization. For example, a single, expensive piece of equipment (e.g., special tool or precision measurement device) can be obtained and shared across projects to reduce the expense instead of replicating equipment purchases for each project. Savings can be realized if a centralized authority such as the PMO can manage and control that equipment. Similarly, project expense can be reduced when multiple pieces of equipment (e.g., laptop computers) can be purchased in volume. The PMO can be instrumental in achieving these types of benefits.

There are three primary activities prescribed for PMO involvement in equipment management. The PMO can use the guidance provided for these activities to establish a process for managing and tracking equipment acquisition, assignment, and disposition within the project management environment.

Manage Equipment Acquisition

The PMO should establish a process that enables it to manage or otherwise influence equipment acquisition for project team use. Equipment acquisition includes both equipment purchases from external sources (vendors and retailers) and internal transfer of equipment within the relevant organization for use in the project management environment.

This activity focuses on the PMO's efforts to acquire equipment for use by project team members. The following fundamental process steps are recommended.

Inventory Current Equipment

This process step provides information regarding what equipment is currently available for assignment within the relevant organization. This includes equipment that is under PMO control pending assignment, equipment that is under the control of other business units and available for assignment, and equipment that is currently assigned to projects or project team members. In other words, the inventory identifies equipment that is known to exist within the relevant organization that is or can be assigned to project efforts. The equipment inventory should include some basic essential information about each item, for example:

- Equipment nomenclature (e.g., equipment name, brand, description, units, etc.)
- Equipment type (e.g., technical, office, tools, vehicle, heavy equipment, etc.)
- Equipment purchase information (e.g., purchase date, vendor/retailer, cost, etc.)
- Equipment information (e.g., tag number, current value, disposal method, etc.)
- Equipment maintenance record (e.g., warranty, maintenance action, date, etc.)
- Equipment storage location (e.g., PMO, business unit, facility name, etc.)
- Equipment status (e.g., ordered, received, available for use, assigned, disposed, etc.)

The inventory list and associated equipment information can be as detailed as needed to help the PMO achieve its responsibilities for managing project equipment. This inventory will also aid in subsequent analyses of equipment acquisition needs by indicating what equipment is currently on hand vs. what needs to be acquired.

Identify and Acquire New Equipment

This process step guides PMO activities regarding how equipment can be acquired for use within the project management environment. The level of PMO authority in approving and funding equipment purchases will dictate the need to extend this process for use at higher levels of funding authority. Note also that equipment acquisition is not necessarily a purchase. It also includes the process that makes equipment within the relevant organization available to project teams. This means that the PMO will collaborate with other business units to identify equipment and to negotiate potential equipment assignments for project team use. However, sometimes equipment purchases will be achieved through the efforts of another business unit, sometimes per PMO requests and with PMO follow-up tracking of the acquisition.

Presumably, the business units of the relevant organization are already providing timely equipment acquisition support to satisfy project requirements. For example, construction projects are likely already getting heavy equipment support from that department; project team members are getting computer equipment from the IT department; and precision equipment is made available for projects by still another department. In such cases, the PMO is simply trying to quantify and document equipment availability for assurance purposes and with consideration for the interests of the project management environment.

This process should include the PMO's consideration of the following steps:

- Use equipment utilization analyses to identify needs for equipment replacement or refurbishment.
- Use equipment utilization analyses to identify needs for additional or new types of equipment.
- Review equipment requests from project managers and project team members to identify needs for additional or new types of equipment.
- Convene a formal or informal equipment acquisition review group to validate new equipment acquisition requirements; forward the acquisition request either to the appropriate funding authority or to the business unit that routinely acquires and manages the type of equipment requested.

■ Conduct negotiations and manage internal equipment acquisitions.
■ Track the internal equipment acquisition progress, any purchase activity, and equipment receipt.

Update the Equipment Inventory

This process step prompts the PMO to add any newly acquired equipment to the equipment inventory list maintained by the PMO.

Inventory management is usually a part-time task, or one associated with a PMO staff role. Inventory management should not be burdensome. Therefore, when possible, an inventory list should be generated by a business unit that normally monitors equipment acquisition. The PMO's equipment inventory list can be compiled using such transferred information.

Manage Equipment Assignments

The PMO will likely defer responsibility for management of major equipment assignments to the relevant business units. However, it probably should be cognizant of equipment assignments just as a matter of building its awareness of transactions within the project management environment. However, in some organizations, the PMO may be assigned responsibility for management of project team equipment, particularly the standard equipment associated with the technical nature of project work efforts.

This activity addresses PMO equipment management relative to the several recommended steps presented below. Project managers and project team members, as well as the PMO, will perform these steps implemented within the project management environment.

Identify and Issue Standard Equipment

The PMO should identify essential equipment needs of project team members in the relevant organization. When new personnel are introduced as project team members, the PMO can automatically prepare and issue a standard equipment package to those individuals. This is an action that is normally accomplished for personnel assigned full time to project teams and not for casual or part-time project team members. The latter can obtain any needed equipment through the subsequent equipment assignment steps described below.

Manage Equipment Requests

The PMO should develop an equipment request process that can be used to identify any special project equipment needs. This can include a form prepared by the project manager and submitted for PMO review and action during the planning phase of the project management life cycle. This process can be incorporated into the activities specified by the project management methodology. The process should specify how equipment needs can be requested at the discretion of the project manager or individual team member.

Manage Equipment Request Actions

The PMO can review, validate, and record the equipment request. If the request contains equipment under the control of the PMO, it can authorize the assignment. If the request is for equipment available outside the PMO, it can either forward the request to the appropriate business unit equipment provider and track request fulfillment, or it can return the reviewed request for project manager action. If the PMO merely tracks equipment requests and does not become involved in authorization or fulfillment, this process step can be shortened to having the project manager provide the equipment request to the PMO at the same time it is submitted to the equipment provider.

Monitor Equipment Assignments

The PMO should establish the means to identify and track equipment assignments, including equipment fulfillment actions not conducted by the PMO itself. This involves documenting what equipment has been assigned to which project team or individual. It includes specification of the assignment date for all equipment as well as specification of the planned return date for "borrowed" equipment. It may also include specification of pending assignment dates for selected types of equipment. This information can be used to analyze equipment utilization and to forecast future equipment needs within the project management environment.

Manage Equipment Disposition

In general, the PMO will need to identify equipment assignments as either permanent or temporary. Permanent equipment will normally remain with individuals throughout their tenure with the relevant organization or with the project team or project office (assigned to the project manager) as long as it is engaged in conducting one or more projects. Some permanent equipment may be replaced over time, and the PMO will want to note such changes in major assignments of equipment. Otherwise, permanent equipment is usually not returned to PMO or other business unit custody until the individual's association with the project has ended or the project team has dispersed.

Temporary equipment will normally be provided to individuals or project teams for a specified period of time, after which it is returned to the original custodian upon completion of use. It should be noted that temporary equipment could be assigned for extended periods of use, which further warrants keeping track of such equipment assignments.

The equipment assignment process should include instructions to users regarding the preferred disposition of equipment upon fulfillment of its purpose. Individuals and project managers should confirm the disposition actions with the PMO or the equipment custodian as the equipment-assignment period ends. The disposal option applied for each equipment assignment should be noted by the assignment-tracking process and annotated on the equipment inventory list, as appropriate. The following subsections present several options for equipment disposition that can be applied within the project management environment.

Equipment Discard

This form of disposal is used when equipment issued does not require return to the PMO or central custodian. This disposal option is normally used for equipment that results in sufficient wear and tear, or other reduction in performance over time, so as to preclude the need for its return. The project manager or individual then has responsibility for equipment removal, destruction, or other form of disposal. The discard option should be cost effective for the type of equipment affected; otherwise a more cost effective disposal method should be considered.

Equipment Return

This form of equipment disposal requires accounting and return to the PMO or equipment custodian. This method could include an examination of the equipment to ensure that it was properly maintained and used. In particular, this method requires the user to return the equipment for reuse by another person or project team. The PMO or custodian will normally track equipment returns by annotating the inventory list to show equipment status as accounted for and available.

Equipment Transfer

This form of equipment disposal is more or less an administrative exercise associated with equipment assignment tracking. It is used when individual accountability for equipment is transferred as a result of personnel changes, but it does not necessarily represent a change in the purpose of equipment assignment. For example, this disposal method usually pertains to equipment assigned to project managers for project team use, and it is applied when one project manager is transferred and replaced by another. The new project manager then receives accountability for the assigned equipment. This method of disposal does not normally apply to equipment assigned to individual project team members.

Equipment Loss

This form of disposal accounts for premature loss of assigned project equipment due to misplacement, theft, or inadvertent damage or destruction. These conditions obviously make the equipment unavailable for use and may require replacement action. This disposal method is identified to the PMO or equipment custodian as soon as the event is identified. This allows any relevant guiding policies to be implemented (e.g., investigation, law-enforcement notification, security-control notification, etc.) and for the equipment assignment process and inventory list to be updated. Certain conditions of equipment loss, per project needs and business priorities, may trigger the assignment of replacement equipment.

POSTSCRIPT FOR THE SMALLER PMO

The activities of this unique PMO "facilities and equipment support" function are ones that are generally performed by existing business units. Only the more advanced PMOs, particularly those having a global or enterprisewide scope of responsibility, are likely to need an intensive facilities and equipment control program. However, all PMOs should develop a fundamental facilities and equipment support capability as a means to make equipment acquisition, assignment, and disposition decisions in the project management environment that are responsive to project needs and to the business interests of the relevant organization.

To that end, the smaller PMO serves as a representative of project management environment equipment needs, and it should concentrate on the collection and analysis of equipment utilization information as the basis for that representation. It can perform facilities and equipment support, and thus achieve the necessary representation, by addressing the following suggested activities:

- The PMO should develop a general perspective on the needs of the project management environment facility so that it can analyze current project facility use and forecast future project facility requirements.

- The PMO should develop insight, if not a specific list, of prominent equipment used by all project teams. It should be able to discern, through collaboration with project managers and project team members in the field, whether present equipment adequately supports each project. It can then lead efforts in the business environment to identify and acquire equipment that is required or that will improve project team performance.
- The PMO should review the current assignment processes for project facilities and equipment. It can identify facility providers and equipment custodians and then collaborate with them to optimize processes for project management and business benefit. In turn, the PMO should incorporate the established approach for acquisition of facilities and equipment into the project management methodology that is deployed within the project management environment.

RESOURCE
INTEGRATION

9

RESOURCE MANAGEMENT

Resource management in the project management environment takes on as many different configurations and approaches as there are organizations and PMOs. Mostly, project resources are introduced to projects through matrix management, where a resource manager in the relevant organization "lends" individual resources to project managers for specific project efforts. In some organizations, resources are assigned directly to the project manager, who then serves as the resource manager. To a lesser extent, a few organizations have all project resources assigned to the PMO.

Regardless of the approach used across industries and organizations, there are two fairly common and generally accepted views about project resource management. First, the human resources (HR) department serving the relevant organization has ultimate responsibility and overriding authority for resource management, and it directs, guides, or otherwise facilitates the resource manager in managing and supervising organizational resources. Second, the PMO must be able to influence the quality and availability of resources used on projects, and it should be able to oversee or at least monitor resource assignments and performance in the project environment. These two premises will be applied to this PMO "resource management" function model.

The "resource management" function enables the PMO to:

- Assist the HR department and resource managers in acquiring and qualifying resources
- Develop guidance for managing project resource assignments and performance
- Evaluate overall effectiveness of project resource performance

The PMO will accomplish these activities through close coordination and collaboration with the HR department and relevant resource managers.

PROJECT ENVIRONMENT INTERFACE CONCEPTS

The PMO can be the primary interface between the project management environment and the resource managers in the relevant organization. This takes some of the burden for resource acquisition away from project managers until their input and decisions are ultimately needed. The PMO's understanding of project management and technical disciplines, combined with frequent examinations of project performance, enable it to guide or recommend management processes for project resources. It can take responsibility for interacting with resource managers to establish the resource acquisition and assignment processes that can then be used by all project managers.

The PMO also can serve as the interface between the project environment and senior and executive managers for matters involving management of project resources. A PMO that is involved in resource management will be more adequately prepared to assist senior management in its responsibilities for resource allocation, for example in such processes as project portfolio management. The more advanced PMO also can be involved in forecasting resource requirements to ensure that senior management has the resource strength to meet the demands of projects expected to be undertaken in an upcoming period of time.

The PMO can assist and guide project managers in their deliberation and selection of project resources, making recommendations from an informed perspective. In particular, the PMO might have insight of resource availability that can be introduced to resource planning efforts. It also can serve to develop and present project resource performance standards and requirements that are applied across all projects and used by all project team members. And finally, by developing procedures for project manager use, the PMO can guide project managers in dispersing project teams at the completion of a project or in managing individual departures from the project team during the project.

The PMO can facilitate the introduction of part-time and temporary project team members into the project management environment. In particular, it can develop procedures for project managers to use that help individuals acclimate to the project assignment. In some organizations, this may be rote for project team members who are accustomed to participating in one or more projects outside their business unit. However, the PMO may consider reviewing and formalizing this process to ensure an effective approach for all parties involved. In other cases, the process for introducing new project team members may simply be incomplete, thus warranting further PMO examination. The need to introduce individuals to project assignments applies as well to full-time resources, where the PMO can contribute a standard approach for what is accomplished to deploy resources on each project.

BUSINESS ENVIRONMENT INTERFACE CONCEPTS

The PMO can serve as an implementer of HR department guidance in the project management environment. This is an effort that business units in most organizations already perform, and it is applicable to the PMO whether it is itself a resource manager or is simply coordinating the activities of resource managers within the relevant organization. This ensures that resource oversight above the project manager's supervisory level continues even when resources are no longer in their assigned business unit. Of course, this may not be needed if the project manager's resource management authority is limited by a weak matrix-type project team structure, where resources continue to report to their primary resource managers. However, there are arguably indications that such a structure reduces resource management effectiveness for both the project manager and the resource manager.

The PMO is ideally situated, and presumably authorized, to coordinate project resource use with resource managers across the relevant organization. It can serve as a source of information and endorsement for resource managers who are essentially external to the project management environment. A prominent role would be for the PMO to educate resource managers on project resource needs, demonstrating that "loaned resources" are not a loss to the resource manager but, rather, a gain to the relevant organization's project efforts. It can further illustrate how the matrix management approach is intended to serve the project management environment as well as the business unit. As well, the PMO can assist in monitoring both project manager and resource manager commitment of resources to project efforts. It also can formalize the process and monitor individual resource commitments to project assignments according to the practices established in the relevant organization.

RESOURCE MANAGEMENT ACTIVITIES ACROSS THE PMO CONTINUUM

The "resource management" function along the PMO competency continuum is characterized by expanding influence and control of project resource assignments and performance. The PMO's responsibility ranges from facilitating and monitoring resource assignments from an awareness perspective to being involved in managing project resource acquisition, assignment, deployment, performance, and assignment close out.

Table 9.1 provides an overview of the range of prescribed PMO resource management activities according to each level in the PMO competency continuum.

Table 9.1 Range of Resource Management Activities across the PMO Continuum

Project Office	Basic PMO	Standard PMO	Advanced PMO	Center of Excellence
Identifies project resource needs, coordinates project resource acquisition and assignment, and manages project resource performance	Provides guidance for utilization of essential project resources ■ Establishes basic procedures for requesting and assigning project resources ■ Prepares routine reports documenting project resource assignment and utilization	Introduces oversight capability for project resources ■ Implements practices for acquisition of project resources ■ Collaborates requests and assignments for project resources ■ Implements guidance for project resources performance management	Manages standards of performance for project resources ■ Develops formal procedures for deployment of project resources ■ Conducts competency assessments for project resources ■ Monitors and evaluates performance of project resources	Collaborates with HR and business units to determine resource utilization requirements ■ Forecasts utilization of project resources ■ Identifies needs and recruits project resources

The *project office* uses established organizational practices to request, assign and manage project team resources. In the absence of a higher level PMO, it will need to communicate and collaborate requirements directly with resource managers and gain their commitment to provide the project resources needed for each project effort. The project office will further collaborate with resource managers to determine responsibility for reporting project resource performance.

Mid-range PMO levels have the primary responsibility of establishing processes that facilitate the identification, acquisition, assignment, and performance management of project resources. The processes may vary for project management environments where resource managers control project resources in contrast to those assigned "full time" to project managers or to the PMO. In either case, the mid-range PMO is responsible for guiding the way for project managers to obtain the project resources needed to accomplish project objectives. As well, mid-range PMOs will normally play a larger role in establishing and managing project resource performance standards, including the assessment of project resource competencies to ensure effective and successful project performance.

The *center of excellence* represents a PMO level that pursues a well-prepared cadre of project resources available for assignment to short- and long-term project efforts. It operates somewhat like a business unit to identify long-term resource needs and conducts project resource recruiting and acquisition activities in conjunction with practices established by the HR department. It will ensure that competent project resources are available to conduct all projects aligned with the relevant organization's strategic business objectives.

This PMO function is focused to ensure the availability and assignment of qualified project resources to conduct project work. This function must be viewed as a component of the overall project resource integration effort.

RESOURCE MANAGEMENT FUNCTION MODEL

The "resource management" PMO function model enables the PMO to be involved in project resource management to the extent that the relevant organization requires or allows resources to be managed using a structured, project management-based approach. In some organizations, the PMO will evolve to become recognized as the "manager" of project resources; in others, the PMO simply will influence and monitor how project teams are staffed to achieve project objectives. In this range of roles, one of the most important contributions the PMO will make will be to support project managers in their efforts to acquire competent resources and manage their availability and performance on projects.

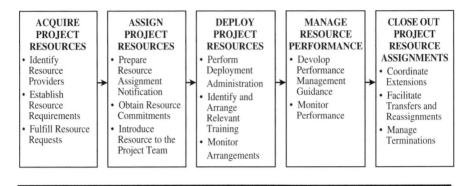

Figure 9.1 "Resource Management" Function Model

The prominent activities of the PMO's "resource management" function model are depicted in Figure 9.1. Each activity is described in the following subsections.

Acquire Project Resources

The PMO will play a vital role in this first activity of resource management — ensuring that qualified people are available for project assignments. Project resource acquisition can either be performed by the PMO or delegated to project managers, depending on the practices within the relevant organization. In either case, the PMO should establish a guiding process for acquiring project resources, and that same process should apply to include situations where the PMO is the resource manager. Development of the resource acquisition process requires close collaboration and coordination with affected resource managers to gain their insight and acceptance of the process. The acquisition process also warrants input or review from the HR department to ensure that the process adheres to all regulated or required personnel management actions and practices.

Advanced-stage PMOs also will establish more intricate ties with the HR department's recruiting and screening activities as a means to influence, if not manage, the process for introducing newly acquired resources into the project management environment.

The PMO should establish a process or otherwise influence the approach used to accomplish the three project resource acquisition steps described below. The PMO may consider facilitating this process with a standard form or template, ideally one that is accessible on-line and that provides the resource request information, specifies the project resource requirements, and documents commitment to fulfill the request. As appropriate, the PMO will either manage the acquisition-request document or be included on information copies as the acquisition process progresses.

Identify Resource Providers

The PMO should ensure that providers of project resources are identified and that these sources know who they are and the nature of their responsibilities to provide resources to project efforts. The four primary providers of project resources are described below:

- *Human resources department:* The HR department is the primary source for new personnel. It performs recruiting and hiring of qualified personnel in response to resource needs and requests from resource managers in the relevant organization. It also is positioned to recognize staffing needs through attrition planning and can hire or transfer resources to fill authorized allocations. The PMO can work with the HR department to confirm resource needs for itself and for the project management environment. The advanced PMO will likely analyze project resource allocations and performance, and it can assist the HR department in understanding project resource needs and utilization.
- *Resource managers:* The resource manager, by whatever reference name is used in the relevant organization, is the primary provider of project resources in most organizations that follow a matrix management structure for project efforts. Personnel assigned to resource managers may have a split and simultaneous responsibility to both their resource manager and the project manager associated with their project assignments. This condition is compounded when the individual has full-time responsibilities for work assigned by the resource manager and part-time responsibilities assigned by the project manager. The PMO has inherent responsibility to minimize this impact on individuals serving in the project management environment. It can urge implementation of a stronger, project manager-based matrix, as presented in the PMO "organization and structure" function (see Chapter 7), but that normally represents a significant organizational change that must be fully examined and approved at senior management levels. In the interim, the PMO can work with resource managers to define and implement an effective project resource acquisition process that reduces real and perceived adversity for both the resource manager and the project manager. Close collaboration can resolve many of the issues and implications that the PMO may encounter in this effort. Then, resource managers become recipients of project resource requests and are adequately

prepared to provide resources based on an understanding of their roles and responsibilities as specified in the established project resource acquisition process.

- *Project management office:* The PMO's role as a resource provider is a concept that is just beginning to emerge in some organizations that have a more mature project management environment. This centralized oversight capability optimizes the assignments of available resources and significantly reduces disarray and disjoint responsibilities for individuals. This concept also prompts consideration of full-time resource assignments to individual project managers, where the nature of project work permits such a structure. In either case — with resource alignment focused on either the PMO or the project manager — the PMO retains strong influence to ensure that (a) the right resources are available to support project efforts and (b) the PMO develops the capability to evaluate resource performance over time. If the PMO becomes a recognized resource provider, it can introduce a resource acquisition process that addresses this authority and capability.

- *Vendors and contractors:* Vendors and contractors are external resource providers. They are called upon, routinely in some organizations and less frequently in others, to perform work using skills and knowledge that is not available or not a core competency within the relevant organization. It is addressed in more detail in the PMO "vendor/contractor relationships" function (see Chapter 19). It is mentioned here simply to recognize that this resource provider is available within the project management environment. It is not a part of the internal acquisition request process for project resources.

Once the PMO has determined who has assigned and capable resources available and who has the authority to release them to project work efforts, it can construct the project resource request process that will be used by all resource managers.

A final point to make deals with the request and assignment of qualified project managers, who are also project resources. It is suggested that the PMO should distinctly be a participant in identifying and requesting project managers from their resource managers. Ideally, project managers will be assigned or otherwise aligned with the PMO and, therefore, will be available for assignment to projects through the PMO. However, the unique requirements of different types of organizations across industries will determine whether such an alignment structure is needed or warranted.

Establish Resource Requirements

The PMO's representation of the project management environment positions it to be involved in the identification of project resource requirements. At a minimum, the PMO should be included in coordination of project staffing requests and the resulting actions to fulfill resource requirements. Ideally, the PMO will review project resource requirements for accuracy and fulfillment capability within the relevant organization, and it will make decisions regarding the need or requirement to seek external project resources. As well, the PMO can be an interface with resource managers to resolve resource requirement issues and with the HR department to identify resource acquisition needs. In turn, the project manager will routinely prepare resource requirements as a part of the project initiation activities that are included in the project management methodology (see Chapter 1).

The identification of project resource requirements implies that there is a generally accepted capability within the relevant organization to fulfill those requirements. Assurance of this capability is a primary PMO responsibility, with consideration for the specified PMO scope of activities and associated authority. In essence, the PMO should be able to identify all available project resources in the relevant organization. It can then anticipate emerging project resource requirements and contrast current staffing levels against projected resource needs. This activity allows the PMO to take action within its authority to fulfill resource requirements or to advise senior management of necessary resource acquisition actions. PMO staffing requirements are likewise included in the resource requirements of the project management environment.

There are four primary types of project resource requirements that the PMO can identify and manage within the project management environment. The following is an overview of each:

- *Project management staffing requirements:* A project manager will be needed for every project conducted within the relevant organization. In some organizations, an individual project manager will be assigned to lead more than one project. This should prompt oversight by the PMO to ensure that qualified project managers adequately cover all projects and that unreasonable project loads are not imposed on individual project managers.
- *Technical discipline staffing requirements:* A variety of technical resources may be needed for different projects conducted by the relevant organization. The PMO can work with technical leaders to identify qualified personnel and specify their availability for particular types of project work. The PMO may want to prepare

more detailed subcategory references for the types of technical positions normally required on projects conducted within the relevant organization.

■ *Adjunct discipline staffing requirements:* The introduction of non-technical staff, those personnel who do not perform work directly related to achieving project objectives, is too often an assumed capability and presumed availability. The PMO can attempt to identify these adjunct project team participants and enable them to be specified in project requirements. This includes such participants as representatives from HR (the project may require a large influx of new recruits), the legal department (the project may have regulatory components that require specialized attention), procurement (the project may have large product or contractor purchasing needs), R&D (the project may necessitate the introduction of new technology), etc. As well, adjunct disciplines include any support personnel that assist the project manager in project coordination and administration activities. The PMO should attempt to have them included in resource requirements specifications.

■ *PMO staffing requirements:* The PMO is a central participant in the project management environment and needs staffing to accomplish its assigned responsibilities. This presents staffing requirements that must be addressed, even if the PMO is a small two- or three-person operation. Such requirements are not normally aligned with projects but, instead, with PMO responsibilities. To that end, key PMO staff positions are usually full-time positions, although some part-time PMO assignments could be pursued in conjunction with requests to resource managers. PMO staff assignments must be identified as requirements within the project environment.

A more detailed examination of the types of project resources to be considered is presented in the PMO "organization and structure" function (see Chapter 7).

The purpose of this activity (establish resource requirements) is to prompt the PMO to develop procedures for identifying project resource requirements as a component of the project resource acquisition process.

Fulfill Resource Requests

The final step in acquiring resources is that of obtaining them from the resource managers. The PMO should develop a process that can be used by project managers seeking project resources from resource managers within the relevant organization. The process should address the following fundamental steps, which are normally incorporated into the project management methodology:

- *Submit project resource request:* Forward the prepared project resource request to the PMO for record and to the resource manager having the appropriate resources that are needed for the project effort. The PMO may serve as clearinghouse for such requests to identify the resource manager and forward the request.
- *Conduct project resource request review:* The resource manager may independently review the request for content — type and number of personnel needed, period of project assignment, and any other relevant information needed to understand the project resource requirements. If desired, the resource manager can meet with the project manager or the PMO to clarify project resource requirements and to negotiate the conditions of the pending commitment of resources.
- *Obtain resource manager commitment:* Project resource fulfillment is achieved at the point when the resource manager signs off on the project resource request, indicating a commitment to provide the specified resources as specified in the request (or subsequent modifications to the request). This step should be performed even when the PMO is the resource manager. It allows all involved parties to track and manage resource commitments.

The PMO may have direct or indirect involvement in performing this process. It should be included in distribution of the resource commitment document. This type of documentation is essential to effective resource acquisition, and it is particularly needed in organizations that use a weak matrix project structure, where the signed resource commitment is the basis for the project manager to advance with planning resource utilization.

The result of this process is the commitment of required project resources that are now allocated and available to work on the specified project at times agreed to by the resource manager.

Assign Project Resources

The second activity of resource management follows closely behind the resource commitment received in the resource acquisition step. The PMO should establish the resource assignment process, again usually as a component of the project management methodology, for use by project managers and individuals assigned to the project management environment.

The process contains the preferred steps for performing notification and introduction of the resource to the project. It should address the needs of the relevant organization and contain the following elements:

- *Prepare resource assignment notifications:* This provides a formal notification of project assignment that is presented to the selected resources. Ideally, it will specify as much information about the project and the individual's associated responsibilities as is available at the time of preparation. In particular, it provides the assignment period and identifies key dates for resource participation, with a focus on initial meetings and activities. This notification enables the individual to schedule and plan for participation, which is particularly important if the resource has concurrent commitments to other project work or business activities.
- *Obtain individual resource commitments:* The assignment notification document should provide a means for the individual to acknowledge receipt and essentially accept the project assignment. This step often may warrant a personal meeting between the individual selected and the project manager to clarify the level of participation needed, establish performance expectations, and elicit personal commitment to the project effort. The selected individual will then sign off on the notification to complete this step.
- *Introduce resources to the project team:* The resource assignment process is finished when the individual is first introduced to the project at a kickoff meeting or other mid-project team event. The project kickoff meeting serves as an introduction for all initial project team members. If the resource is being introduced to the project at an advanced project stage, then an individual introduction to project team members should be accomplished. Resource introductions should include identifying the individual's role and responsibilities on the project. In conducting group introductions, team building exercises may be appropriate to enable participants to become a more cohesive team. The resource introduction step validates individual participation on the project team and reinforces individual commitment to the project effort.

The project manager can use assignment notification documents to prepare for and conduct more-detailed project planning in terms of resource utilization.

Deploy Project Resources

Project resources assigned to specific project efforts make their way to the location where the project is to be conducted. This could simply be a trip down the hall, a short drive to a nearby facility, or sometimes cross-country or cross-continental travel. The PMO can monitor the recurring needs to deploy project resources and establish processes to make deployment activities more efficient.

Project resource deployment means getting the project team member to the work location fully prepared to begin the work effort. It is important to distinguish between *simple* deployment and *global* deployment. The smaller, internal project doesn't normally require much effort to deploy resources. If an assigned resource on an internal project "moves" from a permanent workstation, it is probably just to attend a meeting down the hall. Conversely, if a resource is assigned to a project effort that requires frequent travel or semipermanent relocation, perhaps to global locations, there will be considerably more logistical and preparation activities to consider. Traditionally, these activities have been performed by services available within the relevant organization. However, such services are often delivered without the central oversight that is needed (a) to bring the service results together at one point in time for the individuals involved or (b) for project managers to have confidence in deployment success.

It is important to recognize that project resource deployment is more than just travel arrangements. It means ensuring that the individual is personally and professionally prepared to take on the project assignment and that the project is ready to accommodate the resource through adequate setup of required facilities and equipment — down the hall or across the globe.

The PMO can develop procedures to facilitate needs for both simple and global deployment activities. Project resource deployment activities can be incorporated into the project management methodology. Simple deployments are covered by a relatively quick examination of deployment needs and a brief check to ensure that required actions are being accomplished. More-complex global deployments can also be addressed for those organizations that have a broader deployment perspective. Of course, there are deployments that fall in between these two extremes, and the PMO should develop project resource deployment practices that satisfy the standard types of projects encountered within the relevant organization.

There are three recommended project resource deployment activities for the PMO to consider. Each is described in the following subsections.

Perform Deployment Administration

The PMO should define considerations that will be addressed on every project to ensure that the individual is ready to perform project assignments at the specified project work location. This includes a project-by-project examination of the items and issues highlighted below:

- *Project work space:* If the assigned individual is not working from a permanent location, a project work space should be assigned. This may be a work space belonging to the relevant organization or one arranged at or near customer facilities. The PMO "facilities and equipment support" function model (see Chapter 8) addresses overall planning in this regard, and this activity implements those arrangements at the individual project team member level. If the assigned individual can perform project assignments from a permanent office workstation, then there are no particular requirements for this deployment element.
- *Standard and special equipment:* The assigned individual may require certain equipment to perform required project or project management tasks. This element ensures that all necessary equipment is provided. Again, The PMO "facilities and equipment support" function model (see Chapter 8) addresses overall requirements for standard and special equipment used in conducting specific project efforts. This activity ensures that individuals have the equipment they need, either through advance issuance or by having it on site for use at the specified project location.
- *Project and customer special requirements:* This element of deployment deals with conveying information about the project and the customer's environment that are unique or warrant reminders as a matter of good business practices. Normally, project resources will obtain all the information needed about the work they are about to perform in project kickoff meetings, planning sessions, and technical requirements reviews. This element of deployment extends into consideration and dissemination of special information or awareness needed by project team members. The PMO should survey managers in the project management environment to help identify what items will be examined and accomplished to address project and customer special requirements for each project. This may deal with such matters as:
  - Customs, cultures, and conditions associated with travel to foreign locations
  - Customer facility and equipment utilization guidance
  - Project and customer communication protocols
  - Impacts on project work of time-zone differential at different customer facilities and project locations
  - Special time-accounting and reporting practices for project work

- Special vendor/contractor sourcing requirements for the project
- Medical and immunization requirements for overseas customer and project locations
- Handling and protection of technology and business confidential information
- Project deliverable review and authorization authorities
- Group travel arrangements

■ *Regulatory requirements:* The concept of regulatory requirements in the context of this model refers to the influence or guidance asserted by governmental authority. This administrative process should ensure that appropriate project team members are cognizant of regulatory requirements applicable to project performance and deliverables. It could prompt a review of relevant "regulations" at junctures in the project effort. It may also warrant the introduction of special team members, such as legal advisors or examiners, to ensure that regulatory requirements are being properly addressed. However, consideration of this administrative element is primarily used to inform project participants of applicable regulatory conditions and laws, particularly when traveling to foreign countries.

■ *Security requirements:* As may be required by the nature of project work, administrative activities can include considerations related to handling and use of government- or business-classified information and material. It could provide for acquisition or confirmation of individual security clearances as well as review of security practices and procedures applicable to the project effort.

The specification of deployment administration activities will prompt PMO consideration of how these actions are currently performed in the relevant organization and help identify areas where they can be made more efficient.

Identify and Arrange Relevant Training

The second element of project resource deployment is focused on ensuring that each project member completes any required training prior to beginning the assignment or, as needed, during the project effort. The PMO should establish the process for identifying individual requirements for training and then develop the means to arrange, conduct, and complete training within the schedule of project activities.

The introduction of a standard training curriculum for project participants is discussed in the PMO "training and education" function (see

Chapter 10). That training is pursued as a matter of routine individual qualification. The training addressed for deployment is that immediately needed to perform the work at hand. It may include programs from the established curriculum, or it may include special internal or external training programs associated with achieving project objectives and meeting project requirements.

The PMO should consider the following types of training for possible inclusion in deployment preparation activities:

- *Project management training:* Identifies training associated with project management activities. This type of training could be needed by individuals who are taking on new project management responsibilities, such as serving as a task leader, or by experienced project managers who need training in new project management practices and processes required by the customer or the relevant organization for the current project.
- *Technical skill training:* Identifies training needed by project team members to expand their technical skill and knowledge for the current project effort. This could include the need to attend a training program offered by the customer in order to gain relevant information that will be applied in the course of project work. This type of training also could be used to provide or enhance critical skills of project participants who are assigned to the project on short notice. As well, unique project activities may warrant special project team training that provides the ability to understand new technical concepts, use special equipment, or otherwise qualify for project assignment.
- *New technology training:* Identifies training associated with use or implementation of new technology concepts, tools, and equipment. This may be a standard preproject training event in some organizations where new products are routinely manufactured. In particular, the project teams associated with implementation of new products require ongoing training to ensure their knowledge and understanding of the product and its capabilities or application in the customer environment. In a related sense, this type of training also could apply to tools and equipment the project team uses in conjunction with normal project work efforts, and it also addresses technology updates or replacements that might require additional training for project team members.

In conjunction with facilitating the "just-in-time" training described here, the PMO may also be able to assist in forecasting training needs based on anticipated project work.

Monitor Travel Arrangements

A project management environment that deals with extensive travel requirements may warrant the PMO to establish a moderate oversight capability regarding travel associated with project work. This in no way implies that the PMO should become a "travel service." Rather, the PMO should monitor issues and matters of project-related travel to determine efficiency and to ensure that project resources are where they should be in a timely manner. In particular, the PMO can establish procedures that facilitate:

- Confirming individual travel plans associated with acceptance of project assignments
- Coordinating group travel arrangements
- Monitoring vendor/contractor travel plans and expenses

This project-resource-deployment element should not overburden the PMO, but it can be applied to contribute to the overall effort of ensuring cost-efficient operations within the project management environment.

Manage Resource Performance

The PMO should play a lead role in developing a standard approach to managing project resource performance. This is an approach that should be agreed to and implemented by project managers and resource managers alike, and one that is fully understood by individuals assigned to every project effort. The PMO will guide and assist project managers in their efforts to manage resource performance. In its oversight capacity, it also will monitor project resource performance results and indicators provided by project managers and take or recommend actions to improve individual and overall resource performance. The prescribed involvement of the PMO in resource performance management is described in the following two subsections.

Develop Performance Management Guidance

The PMO should be instrumental in collaborating the approach that project managers will take in managing project resources assigned to their projects. To that end, the PMO will work with project managers and resource managers to identify the performance management responsibilities of each. Then the PMO can develop the guidance needed by project managers to manage the performance of project resources.

The elements of performance guidance that the PMO can consider developing to support project managers include the following:

- *Planning:* This element provides guidance to the project manager regarding how to prepare for managing resource management, including individual and team performance-planning activities. Per the nature of project work and the length of individual assignments, the PMO will be able to construct recommendations regarding the type of performance planning that the project manager should pursue.

- *Monitoring:* This element gives the project manager insight as to the frequency and types of performance observations that should be accomplished. This may include a range of approaches from very general observations to stricter monitoring required to ensure quality, achieve standards, or comply with contractual or regulatory obligations.

- *Mentoring:* This element provides tools and guidance for project managers to use in managing the performance of project team members. It includes such activities as listening, facilitating, guiding, illustrating, etc., and it provides recommended means to optimize the performance of project team members. As well, it could also include guidance for calling upon PMO-based mentors, as described in the PMO "mentoring" function model (see Chapter 13).

- *Assessing:* This element guides the frequency and types of performance evaluations for which the project manager will have responsibility. It will also prescribe actions to be taken in situations of weak performance and participation. This is one particular area in which collaboration with resource managers is essential. A standard approach to assessing, reporting, and responding to individual performance should be established and then confirmed with each resource manager as project resources are released for use in the project management environment.

- *Rewarding:* This element recommends ways to recognize the participation of project team members. In particular, it prescribes what can be done to reward individuals who have contributed to project success through innovation, demonstrated commitment, and performance excellence.

The PMO can also be available to assist project managers in their resource performance management activities.

Monitor Performance

The PMO, having either general or specific oversight responsibility for performance results in the project management environment, should collaborate with project managers to obtain necessary performance reports and indicators to provide timely advice and guidance as well as to review other factors within its purview in order to maximize performance excellence.

The PMO will normally be a recipient of project management performance reports, and that should include access to individual performance reports. It should establish a recurring examination of project resource performance results by applying the following three monitoring steps:

- *Reviews:* Regular reviews of project performance are conducted from the perspective of identifying individual performance strengths and weakness, and individual contributions to the project effort. They can be accomplished through examination of specified elements in project reports, discussions with project managers, and PMO observations of individuals' project activities.
- *Analysis:* Performance indicators are examined to identify individual and project team trends. Trend analyses can be examined for individual performance across projects as a general indicator of demonstrated competency. Analyses also can be done to compare individual performance within a project team. Performance analysis should be conducted within the norms of the relevant organization and in conjunction with HR department guidelines for monitoring and managing individual performance.
- *Improvement:* The PMO can provide significant contribution to the project management effort in collaborating with project managers and resource managers to prescribe performance improvement remedies.

Performance monitoring can be delegated to project managers, with exception reporting of critical indicators provided to the PMO as they are identified.

Close Out Project Resource Assignments

The PMO ensures that necessary and appropriate actions are taken to close out individual assignments to projects. This is important because it specifies a point in time when the assigned resource is no longer responsible for project work. This importance is compounded for individuals who must manage participation in multiple projects. Closing out the assignment not only relieves individuals of project responsibility, but also makes them available for consideration as resources in a subsequent project assignment. To that end, the PMO is concerned with establishing the capability to determine an individual's current project workload and period of availability for the next project assignment. This can be accomplished in conjunction with assisting or guiding the project manager in managing the disposition of assigned project resources.

There are three primary types of project resource close out actions that the PMO should address:

- *Coordinate extensions:* This action is a response to the established project resource close out date, ideally in advance, and provides for extending the individual's continuing participation in the project past the original performance end date. This action could be expedited by developing a process for coordinating the extension with any involved resource manager and, possibly, with another project manager who will be affected by delays in the individual's current assignment. This is a process that must be used sparingly and controlled to address only the most extenuating circumstances, particularly when a specified team member is needed for immediate assignment to a subsequent project effort. The PMO can build the authorization criteria for this action into the assignment extension process it creates.

- *Facilitate transfers and reassignments:* This action represents the routine response to project resource departures from the project team. Here the PMO prepares the process for releasing resources from current project responsibilities in order for the individual to return to the operational environment or for assignment to another project. This process should address the individuals leaving a project at various junctures in the project life cycle as well as those groups of individuals who close out the project as a cohesive project team upon completion of project objectives. The PMO can play an important role in assisting the project manager to identify, confirm, and announce subsequent project team member assignments as a matter of reducing individual concerns about their next role in the relevant organization. This concern may not be as much of a factor for individuals who simultaneously hold operational positions. It can be a primary concern for individuals who rely on project assignments to maintain their tenure within the relevant organization.

- *Manage terminations:* This action represents the release of a project team member from the project and from the relevant organization. There are three primary reasons for project resource terminations: (1) a business decision has been made to discontinue the individual's position; (2) there is no follow-on project assignment currently available for the individual; and (3) a decision has been made in conjunction with HR department guidance to release the individual based on inability to achieve performance standards or other personnel-based action. The PMO should define the process needed by project managers to handle termination of project team members, including the involvement of the HR department and resource managers, and the specification of PMO responsibilities in such matters.

The close out actions enable the PMO to gain insight into project resource utilization and to help in the overall planning for project resources and resource strength requirements.

POSTSCRIPT FOR THE SMALLER PMO

The smaller PMO can play a vital role in resource management by facilitating and monitoring resource utilization within the project management environment. This includes the following three prominent activities:

- *Develop a standard process for how resources are assigned to projects:* A resource assignment process may already exist and can be confirmed and documented, or a new and efficient process can be developed. The process should identify resource providers and specify how resource requests are accomplished to obtain resources for project work assignments.
- *Identify roles and responsibilities of project managers and resource managers:* The use of matrix management to provide project resources implies that there are at least two people involved: the project manager and the resource manager. The PMO should ensure that participants in this relationship understand their roles and responsibilities with regard to managing resources assigned to the project management environment. Ideally, such roles and responsibilities are documented for standard implementation across the relevant organization.
- *Monitor resource utilization within the project environment:* The PMO can demonstrate value within the relevant organization by providing an ongoing monitoring of resources used within the project management environment. This essentially means knowing who is assigned to what projects and for how long. This information allows resource assignment decisions to be made in a timely manner. Whether or not the PMO makes such decisions, it can be a contributor. It also allows the relevant organization to understand current project resource strength and to determine whether more or fewer resources are needed for upcoming project efforts. Project resource monitoring also means identifying qualified project resources that are not currently assigned to specific projects.

If the smaller PMO can help the organization implement appropriate project resource utilization and management activities, the business units will recognize the value of PMO support.

10

TRAINING AND EDUCATION

Training and education is the underpinning of an effective project management environment. It provides individuals with the skill, knowledge, and competencies needed to implement project management guided by technical and business concepts and practices.

Project management has been emerging in the last few decades as a distinct professional discipline, to the point where institutions of higher learning currently offer a range of credentials from basic certificates to advanced degrees in project management. This suggests that organizations can pursue such professionalism to enhance their own capability and credibility in project management. To exaggerate the point, would you want a doctor, or an accountant, or an automobile mechanic to work on something you own without the best of credentials? Likewise, it better serves the business interests of an organization to avoid relegating its project management practice to untrained individuals.

The pursuit of training and education is a business decision that an organization deliberates relative to helping it to achieve strategic business objectives. The PMO, with its charter to advance the practice of professional project management, plays a key role in advising the relevant organization regarding training and education within the project management environment. Its purpose is to ensure that project participants throughout the relevant organization, from the most senior project manager to the part-time project assistant, apply a professional approach to the practice of modern project management consistent with their levels of responsibility.

This "training and education" function enables the PMO to:

- Specify the competencies needed within the project management environment
- Identify current competencies within the project management environment
- Develop training and education programs to achieve competency objectives
- Conduct and manage training and education programs

The PMO normally will implement training and education programs in collaboration with established training managers within the relevant organization. In some cases, as the need presents itself, it may establish a separate PMO position of project management training manager.

PROJECT ENVIRONMENT INTERFACE CONCEPTS

The PMO has continuous insight within the project management environment to enable it to discern the competencies and capabilities being displayed and then to contrast that with competency objectives that it helps to establish. It can measure the skills and knowledge of individuals in the project management environment for comparison with business and industry standards. Then it can recommend or apply training solutions to fill any gaps leading toward those objectives that are compatible with the culture and needs of the relevant organization. However, it must facilitate organizational participation in training or risk falling behind the proverbial power curve in areas of business efficiency, professional caliber of staff, and marketplace competitiveness. In conjunction with project management training, the PMO also can monitor and manage related technical training that is applied within the project management environment. Finally, the PMO can examine the results of training in the project management environment and adjust training requirements and methods as needed over time.

BUSINESS ENVIRONMENT INTERFACE CONCEPTS

Today's business environment is linked to and involved in the project management environment more than ever before. To that end, project management training is no longer limited to just project managers and project team members. There are quite a few adjunct project staff and other stakeholders in and around the relevant organization who would gain tremendous benefit from participation in training conducted in the project environment. To say the least, today's senior managers and executives need to be familiar with project management concepts and practices in order to make critical business decisions related to project management efforts. The PMO has responsibility for identifying such business environment participants and then constructing and implementing a training program of relevant project management topics to meet their needs.

The ensuing benefits and success from training in the project management environment can have strategic significance for the relevant organization. When training benefits are properly captured, the PMO can use them in capability statements and other business and marketing documents to advertise the competitive advantage that the relevant organization has gained by establishing a formal training program within its project management environment.

TRAINING AND EDUCATION ACTIVITIES ACROSS THE PMO CONTINUUM

The "training and education" function along the PMO competency continuum represents a structured approach to improving or increasing professional capability within the project management environment. The PMO's responsibility ranges from simply identifying what professional-grade training and education programs are available and encouraging enrollment, to the more complex capability of designing, implementing, and administering a comprehensive training program for the project management and business environments of the relevant organization.

Table 10.1 provides an overview of the range of prescribed PMO training and education activities according to each level in the PMO competency continuum.

The *project office* nearly always has direct interface with project team members, and it is positioned to identify preferred content of individual training, with consideration for both technical and project management training. This level of oversight will make or influence decisions regarding which project team members could or should attend available training. In the absence of a higher level PMO, the *project office* should conduct a general search of training available for participants in the project management environment and then use those training resources when an individual project team member demonstrates need or otherwise warrants specific training.

Mid-range PMO levels have the responsibility of establishing a complete and comprehensive training program for use within the relevant organization. It normally begins this effort with some type of training needs survey or a more detailed current competency assessment. Then the PMO will identify either internal or external professional training resources as a basis

Table 10.1 Range of Training and Education Activities across the PMO Continuum

Project Office	Basic PMO	Standard PMO	Advanced PMO	Center of Excellence
Manages project team member participation in optional and required training	Identifies needs and facilitates participation in training courses ■ Initiates surveys and assessments to identify training needs ■ Identifies internal and external training providers ■ Introduces basic project manager training courses ■ Integrates project technical training	Establishes and manages a formal training curriculum ■ Defines training requirements ■ Develops and implements a comprehensive training program for project managers, team members, and executives ■ Evaluates project environment training results	Expands training capability and oversight role ■ Extends project training to other stakeholders ■ Introduces training in advanced topics ■ Manages training records in project management environment	Uses training results in strategic business initiatives ■ Includes vendor and contractor participation in training programs ■ Applies training credentials in customer and other business proposals ■ Applies training credentials in advertising and marketing

for developing an initial or complete training curriculum for the project management environment. In a more mature organization, the mid-range PMO will identify competency requirements for project resources and specify training courses that will help individuals to achieve those competencies. Training program administration is an important element of this function model. To that end, the mid-range PMO will ensure that managers and other individuals in the project management environment are made aware of requirements and availability of the training program curriculum that the PMO establishes. It also will provide oversight, management, and documentation of participant enrollment, attendance, and outcomes in training courses as a means to measure and examine success and benefits of the training program.

The *center of excellence* is characterized by the examination of training programs from a strategic business perspective. It will review and align training program results to achieve maximum competitive business advantage for the relevant organization. Based on its own success with training, it may encourage or require vendor/contractor business partners to participate in training offered through the PMO or in a similar project management training regimen.

This PMO function provides the relevant organization with the capability to improve or increase individual skill, knowledge, and competency for work conducted within the project management environment. This model PMO function highlights some prominent considerations for the PMO that is involved in establishing a comprehensive training program to fulfill the needs for project management training and education.

TRAINING AND EDUCATION FUNCTION MODEL

The PMO's presence in the project management environment often makes it a common referral resource for a variety of project management matters, including training. The PMO will have or can readily develop insight as to what training is needed in the project management environment, and it should be proactive in preparing the preferred training solutions. This will enable the PMO to respond to routine inquiries about available training and to use prequalified, professional level training resources to deliver a curriculum that has been developed to meet the unique needs of the relevant organization.

The "training and education" function model makes the PMO a centralized resource for training and education within the project management environment. The concepts presented in this functional model can be applied even when there is a designated training department in the relevant organization. In such cases, the training department can review this function model as a means to examine the needs of the project

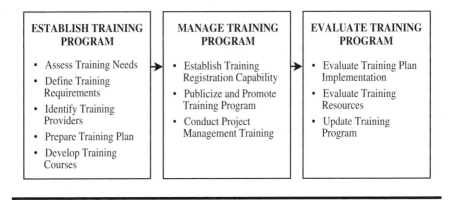

Figure 10.1 "Training and Education" Function Model

management environment, in collaboration with the PMO. Alternatively, the PMO can establish a staff position of training manager, which will apply established practices and collaborate with the training department to introduce an appropriate training curriculum for the project management environment. In either case, the PMO should be able to influence the content and context of training developed and conducted for the benefit of participants within the project management environment.

The prominent activities of the PMO's "training and education" function model are depicted in Figure 10.1. Each activity is described in the following subsections.

Establish Training Program

The development stage of the PMO and the maturity of project management capability in the relevant organization will guide how formal and comprehensive the project management training program will be. As well, the number and types of potential trainees across the relevant organization will influence the topic focus and approach to training. This activity of the "training and education" function model presents recommended steps the PMO can pursue to determine these factors and to construct a training program that will result in discernable project management efficiency and effectiveness. This, in turn, should contribute to improved business performance.

The several prescribed steps for establishing a training program in the project management environment are described in the following subsections.

Assess Training Needs

The PMO will have to develop at least a fundamental understanding of the current capabilities and competencies of individuals in the project environment in order to determine what types and levels of training are needed. An initial perspective on training needs can be accomplished through surveys, meetings, and even informal conversations with project managers and other project stakeholders. Their project management experience and insight about individual and group skills, knowledge, and competencies could be sufficient to identify some fundamental training needs. In particular, the PMO could convene a select group of managers to discuss and deliberate current performance capabilities and to identify discernable project management training needs related to individual comprehension of concepts, application of processes, use of tools, etc. The PMO then can compile the information collected to plan and present basic training solutions.

The more mature project management environment may warrant a more formal assessment and examination of training needs. The PMO can arrange for project management competency surveys and assessment instruments to be administered to project participants to establish a baseline or frame of reference against accepted industry competency standards. The results of such an assessment can be analyzed to ascertain specific training needs. The PMO, in collaboration with the appropriate executive committee or control board, can determine whether the training needs assessment will be conducted with stakeholders outside the immediate project management environment.

The PMO can examine training needs using a simple or more formal approach, depending on its established role and capabilities. In either type of training needs examination, there are several recommended points of consideration. They include the following training needs assessment elements.

- *Project management competency:* Identify the overall and individual competency of project managers. Determine where strengths can be enhanced and weaknesses reduced through general and specific training solutions.
- *Leadership and managerial capability:* Identify the overall and individual effectiveness of soft skills within the current project management environment. Determine where project manager experience is a factor, and identify areas and individuals where training can be used to enhance or improve individual leadership and management capability.

- *Technical skills and knowledge:* Identify the overall and individual competency of technical staff members. Examine technical requirements, determine availability of technically skilled individuals, and determine where technical training is needed. In particular, identify where technical skills and knowledge training can be integrated with project management training.

- *Executive and senior manager awareness:* Identify the current involvement and awareness of project management concepts and practices among executives and senior managers in the relevant organization. Determine any gaps and review the types and levels of familiarization training or orientation programs that can be conducted to achieve necessary awareness in the ranks of senior management.

- *Contractor participation:* Identify the extent to which the relevant organization desires or will require vendor and contractor participation in project management and technical skill training. Include vendors and contractors in training needs assessments, or issue requests for them to conduct their own assessments.

These elements represent the points of examination addressed in a training needs assessment. Assessment results in each of these areas can be analyzed to determine specific types of training required within the project management environment. The PMO may want to consider having such an assessment performed by an external resource that has experience in individual and organizational project management environment assessments. This would lend the credibility of a third-party assessment and save time and cost associated with constructing a validated project management assessment tool and an accompanying process for conducting the assessment. Of course, the PMO can use this list of training need assessment elements to construct and conduct a simple, informal training needs assessment.

Define Training Requirements

The PMO will gain insight into training requirements from the results of any formal or informal training needs assessment. The PMO will want to identify any particular individuals requiring training to ensure their effectiveness as a project team member. The PMO also can pursue an effort to specify overall training requirements for the different types of participants within the project management environment.

The PMO will want to consider establishing training requirements in the following areas:

- *Project manager development:* The training afforded project managers will rely on the competencies associated with project manager authority and responsibility levels. The PMO should consider defining training requirements for entry, standard, and advanced project manager levels. This results in specifying training courses applicable to those levels. It is presumed that project managers will bring appropriate experience to their project oversight efforts. Project managers can also be considered for selected types of technical training, particularly advanced technical or technology training.
- *Project manager certification:* In addition to routine project manager training, the PMO may also consider training that facilitates or otherwise supports internal and external project manager certification. This consideration represents identification of special training programs that focus on helping project managers to achieve the skills, knowledge, and competency that qualify them for professional certification.
- *Professional development:* The aspects of technical and business training should be integrated into project management training where possible. In some cases, separate training programs or courses will be needed to enable the individual to advance within a particular professional discipline or career pursuit. The PMO should address these additional training requirements relative to its authority to respond to the needs of the affected individuals and the business interests of the relevant organization.
- *Team member development:* Project team members are too often neglected in the delivery of project management training. It is through the combination of training and on-the-job experience that project team members gained the skill and knowledge to advance to become project managers. That consideration known, the relevant organization will benefit from capable project team members who readily understand the concepts and practices of project management in which they participate. The PMO should identify training requirements for project team members, which could include some or all of the basic training courses available to project managers. The more the project team members know about the project management process, the more projects will be conducted with efficiency.
- *Executive familiarization:* Perhaps more than project team members, executives and senior managers are discounted from consideration for project management training. It is conceded that they do not require the detail of project management competency that is used by project managers. It also is recognized that members of senior management inherently do not have available time for

detailed training. However, an organization would be remiss in excluding executives and senior managers from gaining insight and understanding of modern project management concepts and practices. The PMO should identify training requirements, normally in the form of shorter one-half to one-day familiarization training or orientation programs, for executives and senior managers in the relevant organization. If possible, participation in longer training programs is recommended.

■ *Stakeholder familiarization and training:* The PMO staff, adjunct project staff, and business unit participants are key stakeholders that would benefit from training conducted in the project management environment. The PMO staff will likely require participation in both standard and advanced project management training as a means to ensure a common frame of reference for the oversight, control, and support that they will provide. They also may require specialized training associated with PMO functions, such as process development, tools selection, etc. Individuals who serve in adjunct project roles may also benefit from project management training. This includes such people as are found in the HR department, legal department, procurement department, and others that participate in project activities on less than a full-time basis. The PMO should define training requirements for such stakeholder involvement.

■ *Vendor/contractor integration:* Small vendor/contractor organizations (i.e., individual or two-person operations) can be included in training requirements defined for the project management environment. This is particularly appropriate when vendors/contractors serve in a recurring role in project efforts over time. The PMO should design and convey vendor/contractor training requirements that are consistent with the training requirements specified for its own project managers and project team members.

The PMO should compile the training requirements, by group, in a document that can be referenced when preparing the training plan for the project management environment. This requirements document can become an attachment to that training plan.

Identify Training Resources

The PMO should facilitate the introduction of resources, normally internal or external business entities, to conduct training in the project management environment. Training resources should be identified and selected per the skill and experience in project management training that they can offer, including the capability to deliver a wide range of basic and advanced courses that will satisfy the needs of the different stakeholders in the relevant organization. Training resource selection also should consider any application of course completion toward diplomas, degrees, continuing education units, and professional certification.

As well, the training resource should be able to contribute expertise and assist the PMO in planning the training program, including determining which courses will provide maximum benefits in the project management environment, identifying frequency and location of course delivery, and ensuring assignment of qualified course instructors. Similarly, the PMO will have to set up training program administration — participant registration, fund transfers for internal resources and payments to external resources, and course completion and training record management. The PMO may want to include this administrative element in the responsibilities it assigns to the training resource.

The primary purpose of this activity is to identify what resources are available and will be used to conduct training within the project management environment. There are three primary resource types to consider, as described in the following subsections.

In-House Training Resources

The PMO can examine the offerings and capabilities of any education center, training department, or corporate university currently serving the relevant organization. In larger organizations, this internal resource will likely have multiple classroom locations for training program delivery, as well as some capability for off-campus course delivery in work facilities.

The primary factor in selecting an in-house training resource is the consideration of whether or not it has sufficient range and depth of offerings in project management to serve the needs of professionals in the project management environment. Of course, a comprehensive in-house training resource will likely have the capability to develop courses to meet the needs of its patrons, but not all organizations favor this approach because of the time it takes to develop and test the several required courses, the unique expertise in modern project management required for course developers, and the general need to maintain course materials as new project management concepts and practices emerge for inclusion in updated training materials.

Nevertheless, the in-house training resource can be an important partner with the PMO in establishing some fundamental project management training courses. It also can be called upon to assist the PMO in selecting and managing any preferred external project management training resources.

External Training Resources

The PMO can examine the offerings and capability of commercial project management training resources. These external vendors normally provide training at facilities in various national and international locations, and therefore are excellent options to in-house training centers that do not have that geographical capability. External training resources also extend efforts to learn about your business interests and technical frame of reference, and thereby integrate such information in instructor awareness and delivery from the podium as a standard feature of training.

The primary factors in considering an external training organization is the range of available project management training courses, the ability to customize those training courses for use in the relevant organization, and the ease and ability for participants to translate skill and knowledge received in the classroom into immediate applications and solutions in the workplace. Most but not all external project management training resources offer a wide range of professional project management training courses to achieve the learning needs of all stakeholders in the project management environment. Some external training resources offer a few levels of customization and course development to accomplish alignment of training with current processes or specific industry or professional-discipline practices. A few external resources provide accompanying mentoring and consulting services that are consistent with the training course content to help the PMO to implement newly acquired skills and knowledge in the project management environment.

The PMO can collaborate with the internal training management department to identify and select an appropriate external project management training resource. In particular, the PMO may need to prepare or otherwise participate in developing a budget and acquiring funding to obtain such external training services. This warrants an examination of preferred external training resources to establish not necessarily the lowest cost of project management training, but the greatest return on the investment of training funds for the relevant organization.

Public Training Resources

The smaller PMO, particularly those just starting operations, may want to consider available project management training courses that are available to the public. Some of the external project management training resources referenced above also conduct such public programs. The difference in the public program is that it does not particularly focus on the current technical processes and industry practices of each course participant because they come from a variety of cross-industry organizations. However, public training is an excellent means to either start up project management training or to gain insight to the approach and capabilities used by external training resources under consideration for selection as a preferred training resource.

Prepare Training Plan

The PMO can use the results of previously presented training program activities to prepare a plan that will guide delivery of training in the project management environment. The training plan will identify what training courses are available, as may be required or optional for different participants, and include the course presentation schedule, location, and assigned instructor. As well, the training plan should include an outline or description of each course offering, the recommended audience, the applicability in the project management environment, and any personal qualification or achievement awarded as a result of participation. Each course description should identify the internal or external training resource responsible for course delivery and the means to contact them. The training plan also should include the process by which individuals can register for attending the project management course.

In particular, the PMO should examine options and develop the training plan to identify the different training program structures available to participants in the relevant organization. This includes consideration of the following standard training program categories:

- *Core project management courses:* Identify the several essential project management courses that are recommended or required for all project managers and, possibly, for project team members. Specify any preferred presentation order for course attendance, and indicate any certificate associated with completion of the course and curriculum.
- *Advanced and optional project management courses:* Identify the several project management courses that will be available to those individuals who have completed the core curriculum and to those who need advanced or specialized training otherwise not covered by the core curriculum. This also may include training in use of project management tools and project management methodology user training.
- *Technical courses:* Identify the courses designed to support technical work activities associated with project efforts. This also may include any just-in-time training that satisfies business interests or provides technical qualification.

- *Professional development courses*: The extent of PMO authority and the nature of individual assignments to the project management environment may prompt consideration for including professional development courses in the project management training plan. This inclusion may be the primary means for staff members to review and select professional development training provided by the relevant organization.
- *Executive courses and workshops*: Identify those project management courses, workshops, seminars, and forums that are applicable to senior management involvement in and understanding of the project management environment. This category of training should include at least one course or workshop that enables executives and senior managers to gain familiarization with the modern project management concepts and practices being implemented by the PMO within the relevant organization.

The PMO can collaborate with the internal or external training resources to obtain training course descriptions and other training plan content. In some cases, it can use the training resource to lead training plan preparation activities.

Develop Training Courses

Training course development is an activity that should be performed in conjunction with the preparation of the training plan. The training plan can be finalized when all course development decisions have been made. To accomplish training course development, the PMO will likely need to work with internal or external training resources to identify requirements, collaborate training course development solutions, and review and approve customized course material. A review of each preferred course is necessary to determine if it will be presented using its current format and content, if it is to be customized to meet the specific needs of the project management environment, or if it requires a design and construction effort for it to be presented as a new course.

First, the PMO will need to consider and plan the format and content for training course delivery. This includes the activities conducted to select methods of course delivery from among the following prevalent types:

- *Instructor-led classroom training:* This is the traditional approach to training that facilitates interaction among participants and promotes their discussion and exchange of ideas in a classroom setting. It allows various instructor-led, adult learning techniques to be used, e.g., lecture, discussion, facilitated exercises, etc. This is generally recognized as a quick method for the completion of training.

■ *Instructor-led e-learning:* This is the traditional method of class-room instruction translated for on-line use. Normally, this type of e-learning experience represents a combination of independent participant coursework combined with routine real-time availability of a qualified instructor to conduct on-line and telephone discussions as well as to respond to student inquiries and to make points of clarification through on-line (e.g., e-mail) contact.

■ *Standard e-learning:* This method represents the use of on-line training courses that take the participant through a series of learning objectives using automated procedures. This may include e-mail access to an assigned instructor.

■ *CD-ROM-based instruction:* The use of the CD-ROM approach to training represents independent performance of training steps that generally result in the achievement of learning objectives for the participant. This method allows for presentation of project management topics that participants can pursue at their own pace. It generally does not provide interaction with a qualified instructor for questions and inquiries.

Once the preferred format of instruction has been identified, the PMO can deliberate and decide on actual training course development that is needed. Not all instructional delivery formats lend themselves to customization and modification. However, most external training resources can adapt instructor-led classroom training to satisfy individual customer needs by incorporating an awareness of processes and practices in the relevant organization.

In particular, the PMO will need to examine course development options from a time and cost perspective. The following are three primary options for the PMO to consider:

■ *As-is course format:* The PMO acquires the training product more or less off-the-shelf from the internal or external training resource. It is ready for use, as is, and it can be scheduled for delivery and presented upon achieving sufficient participant registration.

■ *Course customization:* The PMO should understand that significant modification of training course materials is a process that may be as time-consuming and costly as new course development. However, minor modifications (e.g., simple content additions and deletions) may not have an excessive impact on time and cost. The PMO will have to evaluate its need for integrating current project management practices, technical concepts, and organizational policies into such training, and determine if that warrants the added cost.

■ *New course development:* The PMO is making a significant business investment in deciding upon or recommending the new-course development option. A quality three-to-five-day course will generally take months to design and develop the concepts and content. Then there is additional time required for testing, post-test revisions, and preparation of any associated handouts and job aids. The costs of such an effort are a distinct budget item.

For the most part, there are many excellent project management curricula in the marketplace today, and the PMO should consider this as a first option if training is not otherwise obtained from internal training resources. Likewise, the PMO has inherent interest in providing training for immediate application in the workplace. Only as-is and minor customization course development options provide timely solutions to pressing project management needs. Major customization and new course development should be a part of longer-term strategic plans for the relevant organization.

Manage Training Program

The PMO should be prepared to oversee any training program it establishes for the project management environment. Of course, it can obtain assistance from the internal or external training resources it engages, but it will still need to provide leadership to the effort. The several activities of training program management are described in the following subsections.

Establish Training Registration Capability

In conjunction with implementing a comprehensive project management training program, the PMO must ensure the means for individuals to identify available training courses and to register for them. Ideally, this is done on-line, through either the relevant organization's Web site or by using a link to the training resource's Web site. Once at the registration Web page, anyone in the relevant organization can schedule attendance at an upcoming training event. If a manual, off-line registration system is to be used, the PMO will have to make arrangements for its operation.

Some desired features of a training program registration capability include:

■ *Individual access provisions:* Individuals authorized to register for training should be provided with an access code for on-line registrations, and the training resource should be given an authorized list for manual registrations. This ensures that only authorized project stakeholders in the relevant organization are able to perform registration.

■ *Individual contact information:* The registration process should be able to capture adequate information about the registering individual to enable future contact and to track completed training in an individual training record.

■ *Registration acknowledgement and reminder:* The registration process should provide the individual with an acknowledgement of successful registration. Such notification should also go to the individual's supervisor and to the PMO. In some cases, course registration may be made far in advance of the scheduled course delivery date, and this warrants a follow-up reminder at some designated time, usually a few weeks before the course delivery date.

■ *Course payment:* Where appropriate, the registration process should generate billing information for an external training resource or a funds-transfer listing for an internal training resource. Such documentation may be a time-based report that is produced perhaps monthly for all who have registered in a given period, and not necessarily an individual transaction.

■ *Training information and materials:* The registration process should generate distribution of any advance information or training materials needed by the registered student. In particular, information about getting to the training location, class start and end times, and any other relevant information should be provided to the student. In some cases, the advance material will include precourse reading requirements and associated text materials. Some of these items can be combined with registration acknowledgement; others may be delayed until a specified period before the course presentation date.

■ *Registration withdrawal:* The registration system must have the capability to remove individuals from registered status in the event that they are unable to attend as scheduled. This action includes steps for supervisor and PMO notification, retraction of billing or fund transfer actions, and return of any pertinent advance materials.

The PMO should maximize the involvement and participation of the internal or external training resource in establishing the training program registration capability.

Publicize and Promote Training Program

Establishing a comprehensive project management training program is of no value to the relevant organization if participation is weak. The PMO should be proactive in its development and dissemination of project management training information that promotes attendance in preferred and optional training courses.

The following list contains a few suggestions regarding how the PMO can publicize and promote its project management training program:

- *Training program catalogs:* The PMO should arrange for a training catalog or other similar publication to be prepared and distributed with information about the core project management curriculum along with any advanced or optional courses available to stakeholders. This publication should include information about individual benefits and certificates and any requirements for the accomplishment of training associated with professional advancement in the relevant organization.
- *Senior management announcements:* The PMO should arrange for the most senior managers in the relevant organization to announce availability of the newly developed project management curriculum. Such announcements should demonstrate support for the training program as a business interest and request endorsement of managers at all levels in the relevant organization.
- *Web page listing:* The PMO should arrange for information about the project management training program to appear on the internal Web site used by project stakeholders in the relevant organization. If an automated registration process is available, a link to the training program registration page should be provided to accompany the Web page listing.
- *Training success announcements and events:* The PMO should use Web pages, internal memos, and even public press releases to announce significant training accomplishments by individuals. Achievements of completing all courses in the core project management curriculum, a promotion associated with the completion of a training event, or an "aced" course would warrant such an announcement. If there is a certificate to be earned as a result of training, a monthly or quarterly luncheon could be held to recognize such individual accomplishments.
- *Project manager roundtables:* Any meeting or event with several project managers in attendance should be used (a) to promote the established project management training program and (b) to reit-

erate the request for an endorsement of the training program among project team members.

Again, the PMO should collaborate with the involved internal or external training resource to gain insight to other training program publicity and promotion methods. As well, it can elicit training resource participation and support in meeting this challenge.

Conduct Project Management Training

The PMO will be responsible for ensuring that project management training is accomplished as specified in the training plan. While the training resource will have responsibility for actual delivery of the training course, the PMO will need to monitor that delivery as well as a few other aspects of project management training, as recommended in the following list:

- *Monitor attendance:* The PMO should review recent and registered attendance in project management training courses at recurring periods of time, perhaps monthly. This review will indicate whether expected levels of participation are being achieved. The PMO should compare current attendance numbers against projections used to justify the training course delivery schedule. The PMO can then make subsequent course delivery decisions in collaboration with the training resource based on registrations and projected attendance.
- *Review student evaluations:* The PMO should regularly examine the course evaluations of students who have completed each course. This will enable the PMO to determine whether the training program, course by course, is attracting stakeholder interest and satisfying individual training needs and expectations. Minor adjustments can be made to course delivery fairly easily when overall course evaluation results identify a weakness, content gap, or other undesirable pattern in the training approach.
- *Maintain participant training records:* The PMO can take responsibility for managing the training records of individuals working within the project management environment. In being copied upon registrations, and likewise upon course completions, the PMO can enter training information for future reference by individuals and by managers involved in selecting project team members. The PMO can delegate this responsibility to project managers or resource managers.
- *Prepare and distribute course completion certificates:* The PMO will ensure that all successful training participants receive the proper

certificate of course completion. This is an activity that can be performed by the training resource, but it warrants monitoring by the PMO. The PMO also can be involved in special recognition events for individuals.

■ *Monitor unsuccessful course participation:* Presumably, most courses in the project management training program will have some form of learning measurement — a quiz, an examination, or a demonstration of skill. The PMO will want to identify any individuals who are not successful in completing any courses attended. First, the PMO should find a means of encouraging individuals to retake any "failed" course, usually at no additional cost. As well, the PMO will want to identify any individual trends in failed course completions, particularly in the core or basic courses. Continuing trends showing an individual's inability to complete course learning may warrant special mentoring or counseling and affect consideration for advancement. The PMO can delegate this interaction with the affected individual to the relevant project manager or resource manager, as appropriate.

■ *Manage training mandates and withdrawals:* The PMO will be responsible for managing mandates for training course attendance in the project management environment. This may include mandates for an individual or a group of individuals to take a single training course or to complete an entire curriculum. Such business decisions that dictate mandatory training require the oversight of the PMO. Likewise, business decisions may halt delivery of one or more training courses. The PMO will be similarly involved in conveying this decision and in managing associated registration withdrawals.

As suggested throughout this discussion of the "training and education" function model, it is to the PMO's benefit to transfer as much of the training program management responsibilities as possible to the vested internal or external resource. In turn, the PMO should establish a recurring schedule for receipt of training program status reports from the training resource, and it also should schedule a regular meeting with the training resource to discuss training program progress and benefits.

Evaluate Training Program

The PMO has ultimate responsibility for assessing the impact and benefits of the project management training program within the relevant organization. The process of evaluation includes the three activities presented in the following subsections.

Evaluate Training Plan Implementation

The PMO should, from time to time and at least annually, review its training plan to ensure that it still represents the best means to achieve project management training objectives. Some suggested elements of this evaluation are highlighted in the following list:

- *Training course selection:* Determine whether the proper courses are represented in the core project management curriculum. If a core curriculum has not yet been established, decide whether it is time to introduce one. Examine the advanced and special courses in a similar manner: determine whether it is time to add an advanced curriculum. Identify any changes to course content, or consider the possibility of customizing the course. Specify any changes to the training plan that are needed with regard to course selection and content.
- *Course performance:* Review course performance and analyze benefits achieved from course and curriculum delivery. Examine the training program from several perspectives. First, identify any increased capability in achieving business objectives. Specify any discernable improvements in project management effectiveness, as demonstrated by on-time, on-budget project performance results. Compile and review observed improvements in individual and project team performance resulting from training, e.g., greater cohesion, less disarray, increased individual capability to achieve assigned tasks on time, individual professional advancements as a result of new project management skill and knowledge, etc.
- *Training course delivery schedule:* Review attendance at mandatory and optional training courses, and determine whether the current course delivery schedule and frequency continues to satisfy the needs of project stakeholders within the relevant organization. Examine any courses having weak attendance, particularly courses slated for attendance by senior management. Determine whether a better course schedule or additional publicity and promotion is needed for sparsely attended courses.

Compile the results of this evaluation, and then review and recompose the project management training plan for improved effectiveness in the next training period.

Evaluate Training Resources

The PMO should examine the performance of internal or external training resources in conjunction with its recurring evaluation of the project management training program. Such performance reviews can include the following elements:

- *Instructor performance:* Assess how well instructors have performed in the classroom or in e-learning encounters.
- *Administrative performance:* Evaluate training resource contributions to course registration, course completion, and course delivery processes.
- *Course evaluation review:* Examine overall results of course evaluations (a) to determine where students observe strengths and weaknesses and (b) to ascertain effectiveness of instructional methods used as perceived by course participants.
- *Course development review:* Evaluate any new course or course customization efforts underway and evaluate the timeliness and cost against the development plan.
- *Business contract/agreement review:* Examine the contract or agreement that was used to provide training resource course delivery and associated services. Determine where any terms and conditions warrant change reviews, establish costs for the upcoming training period, and confirm continuation of the internal or external training resource as a training program provider.

The PMO can perform the elements of training resource evaluation at any time, but it should complete a full examination at least annually.

Update Training Program

The final step of this PMO functional effort represents a renewal of the project management training program to produce additional benefits from training course delivery while removing or reducing disarray in training program implementation. This includes attending to the following items:

- *Training requirements update:* The PMO should revisit its previous examination of training requirements for the project management environment. It will need to determine whether the current training needs analysis is still valid (or, more precisely, useable) or whether another detailed examination of requirements is necessary. Essentially, the PMO will need to confirm or modify its training participant forecast for the upcoming training period.
- *Training resource update:* The PMO should revisit its relationships with internal and external training resources (the people who actually deliver the training courses). In this regard, the PMO can evaluate the performance of each resource as a basis for deciding

whether the business relationship will be continued into the next training period, modified, or discontinued.

- *Training plan update:* The PMO should review the training requirements and the results of participation of the training resources, focusing on the details of the training course and the curriculum delivery — course title, instructor, dates of delivery, locations of delivery, etc. This PMO effort includes defining and implementing a basic or advanced project curriculum if one did not previously exist. It also addresses plans for any new course development or course customization to be started or completed in the upcoming training period.
- *Training program administration:* The PMO should review and improve the various administrative practices used to facilitate the training program. This includes such matters as course registration, handling of student inquiries, training record management, etc. As needed, the PMO can adjust practices and activities, introduce new ones, or even redirect responsibility for their accomplishment.

This training program update activity allows the PMO to refresh course content and approach to make it more beneficial for the relevant organization and more satisfying for training course participants.

POSTSCRIPT FOR THE SMALLER PMO

The smaller PMO may not have the readily available funding or resources needed to establish a comprehensive project management training program. Similarly, a less mature project management environment may not recognize the immediate need for an elaborate approach to project management training. However, the smaller PMO should convey the necessity of project management training at every opportunity. It can begin to recognize training needs within the project management environment through simple and informal surveys, and it can identify the availability of training courses that would provide benefits to project participants. Furthermore, it can research and compile publicly available project management training and workshops as a means of providing early training solutions within the relevant organization. As organizational needs come into focus, the PMO can facilitate the implementation of a basic project management curriculum conducted on site.

11

CAREER DEVELOPMENT

Career development represents the activities associated with achieving professional advancement aligned with progressive expansion and application of individual skill, knowledge, and experience in project management. The career development effort usually involves additional consideration of universally accepted professional performance standards as well as organizational requirements for business skill and acumen, technical and analytical competencies, and supervision and leadership capabilities. For many individuals, rewards and benefits associated with personal achievement, professional recognition, and increased income opportunities are a significant part of the career development equation.

The PMO should facilitate activities to establish a career path for individuals within the project management environment. This inherently implies gaining acknowledgement and recognition of project management as a professional discipline within the relevant organization. In some cases, this PMO effort is welcomed as a means to add structure to the roles and responsibilities of project managers and project team members. In other cases, it presents a challenging initiative for the PMO to manage — to gain the attention of key project participants, the involvement and support of the HR department, and the consideration of senior management toward implementing a project management career path.

This "career development" function enables the PMO to:

- Achieve professional recognition for project managers and project team members
- Facilitate project managers' career planning and professional development efforts
- Provide career motivation and direction for project management participants

- Prepare advancing professionals for expanded business roles and responsibilities
- Contribute to the organization's retention of highly qualified professionals
- Enhance the organization's competitive stance in the marketplace

The PMO cannot implement a project management career development program alone. Rather, it serves primarily as an advocate and performs in a prominent role to contribute and facilitate knowledge and understanding about professional project management. This PMO effort distinctly requires collaboration with the HR department, which brings capability and insight of personnel management practices in the relevant organization to guide career-path construction, implementation, and management. Ideally, it is a joint development effort, but one that is ultimately a responsibility of the HR department. However, it is likely that the PMO will have visible responsibility for ongoing management of career development activities within the project management environment.

PROJECT ENVIRONMENT INTERFACE CONCEPTS

The PMO's efforts to manage a professional project management career path will provide the human element of attention needed by professionals in the project management environment. The PMO becomes a resource for advice and guidance in helping individuals, particularly project managers, to develop personal strategies and plans that are used to advance their professional status and stature within the relevant organization.

The PMO's participation in preparing career progression guidance, if not a leading effort, at least ensures that the interests of individuals in the project management environment are adequately represented. It will bring to the forefront and manage the current and preferred skill-set requirements for project managers and project team members at various career levels. It does this per its ongoing awareness and involvement in project management industry news and events, its associated implementation of project management performance standards, and its integration of relevant organization business needs and interests.

The identification of career levels within the project management environment presumably delineates individual skill, knowledge, and experience. This delineation across progressive levels of professional advancement also contributes to a new ability to easily identify individuals who are qualified to participate or manage different types of projects, per project classifications assigned. This may not be an imminent need for the smaller PMO, where everyone knows who "can" and who "should not" be assigned to one of the few project efforts. Conversely, in any larger organization, where project team members and project managers are not as well known personally or where they are separated by resource managers, an objective indication of professional capability is essential to successful resource performance within the project management environment. A project management career path provides credentials that confirm the appropriateness of individual assignments to projects.

As well, the PMO can develop and implement the preferred standards of performance for each progressive level of career advancement. This includes specification of any internal or external professional or technical certification required for advancement.

BUSINESS ENVIRONMENT INTERFACE CONCEPTS

As the underwriter of career advancement in the project management environment, the PMO will be able to guide and lead individuals in their professional pursuits with consistency and alignment to the business needs and objectives of the relevant organization. In the absence of a formal project management career path, individuals would tend to associate with a closely related technical discipline, which may or may not have project manager development as a primary focus, and therefore limits their professional growth. Or they will opt to find their own ways and means to professional growth using resources available to them individually and not necessarily in a direction aligned with business interests.

The relevant organization also can use this PMO function to ensure that comparable career advancement opportunities are extended to individuals working in the project management environment. This is particularly important if the relevant organization historically has high retention rates and promotes from within. It will want to ensure that it helps prepare that group of individuals working in the project management environment to be competitive for advancement opportunities in other areas of the business. Establishing a career path for individuals in the project management environment places them on equal footing with other professionals within the relevant organization.

CAREER DEVELOPMENT ACTIVITIES ACROSS THE PMO CONTINUUM

The "career development" function along the PMO competency continuum represents an increasing recognition of project management as a professional discipline. At early PMO stages, it facilitates a professional capability, and at advanced PMO stages it mandates it. Thereby, this PMO function is an instrument for instilling and managing professionalism within the project management environment.

Table 11.1 provides an overview of the range of prescribed PMO career development activities according to each level in the PMO competency continuum.

The *project office* applies experience in the relevant organization, combined with general knowledge and information about professional project management, to guide and advise project team members in their individual pursuits of professional advancement.

Mid-range PMO levels introduce increasingly formal processes and practices of professional career development, including specification of the prescribed and HR department-approved progression of advancement for project professionals in the relevant organization. Its work is characterized by close collaboration with the HR department in setting up and managing a career path for project professionals. More advanced PMOs will ensure that business needs and interests are integrated into the career development program, and they will administer higher levels of individual assistance in areas of career planning and management support.

The *center of excellence* is characterized by its ongoing or specific examinations of results from the project professional career development program. Its findings from studies and analyses can be applied to improving the career development program within the relevant organization.

This PMO function addresses as many personal needs of professionals as it does business needs of the relevant organization. The unstated purpose of this function is to ensure that a professional approach to project management is pursued, and that can only be done when the participants in that effort are bona fide professionals in their own right. This function introduces and manages professionalism in the project management environment.

CAREER DEVELOPMENT FUNCTION MODEL

The PMO's role in project management career development is one that facilitates recognition of project management as a professional discipline. This recognition is warranted in conjunction with the implementation of new professional performance standards, expanded professional responsibilities, and integrated professional business activities — all elements associated with the concepts and practices of modern project management. This recognition is needed (a) to distinguish those individuals who are pursuing professional project management skill and capability from those who are not and (b) to identify those who are qualified and charged with implementing modern project management concepts and practices from those who are not.

The PMO must carefully examine how project management career development can be applied within the relevant organization. It can apply

Table 11.1 Range of Career Activities across the PMO Continuum

Project Office	Basic PMO	Standard PMO	Advanced PMO	Center of Excellence
Assists project team members plan and review career advancement activities	Introduces project management as a professional discipline ■ Facilitates the identification and designation of project managers ■ Encourages professional certification ■ Recommends individual career planning actions ■ Examines options for formal career-path development	Manages a project management career development program ■ Defines a career path for project professionals ■ Prepares career-path position requirements, job descriptions, and compensation ■ Incorporates technical and professional certification requirements ■ Develops a career guide for project professionals	Expands support capability for project management career development ■ Implements a professional development plan and review process ■ Provides project management career planning and counseling assistance ■ Facilitates cross-functional professional job transfers and advancement opportunities	Monitors business interest fulfillment and value from career development ■ Conducts studies and analyses to monitor project manager and team member retention ■ Conducts studies and analyses to ascertain career-path-designation contributions to performance

Figure 11.1 "Career Development" Function Model

the consideration that professionalism suggests the need for credentials to distinguish someone who has been trained and demonstrates competency in a particular discipline. However, it will likely see that project management degrees, diplomas, and certificates are not necessarily among the prominent credentials of most people in the organization. The PMO's job then is to determine the best way to introduce project management professionalism in conjunction with recognition of other professional credentials.

The prominent activities of the PMO's "career development" function model are depicted in Figure 11.1. Each activity is described in the following subsections.

Develop Project Management Career Path

A project management career path gives structure and affiliation for project managers and for all project participants. The PMO should endorse and pursue this function as a means of introducing appropriate recognition and differentiation of these participants.

The PMO can be instrumental in bringing professional recognition to the project management environment through recommendations and actions that establish a project management career path. The activities listed below highlight a complete process for developing the career path. However, even partial completion of these activities represents advancement toward identifying individuals within the project management environment. The four prescribed activities for establishing a project management career path in the relevant organization are described in the following subsections.

Establish Project Management as a Professional Discipline

The PMO is charged with introducing concepts and practices of modern project management in the relevant organization. This must be accompanied by identification and recognition of the people who participate in that effort. This is a business-perspective issue as much as it is an individual recognition issue. By establishing position titles affiliated with pursuits within the project management environment, the relevant organization places emphasis on and demonstrates the importance of developing and applying competency in project management.

The PMO can help the relevant organization make project management a critical if not core business competency by identifying and endorsing the professional attributes of those individuals working within the project management environment, including the PMO staff. This exposure of professional attributes has an ultimate goal of establishing a progressive project management career ladder by which individuals can be assigned positions and responsibilities aligned with their skill, knowledge, and experience in the project management environment.

To that end, the PMO will need to build an understanding of this concept of project management professionalism. It will have to identify the needs and benefits of a formal project management career path within the relevant organization. It will have to gain buy-in from participants and decision makers alike.

There are three primary areas in which the PMO can take steps to establish project management as a professional discipline.

Develop Basis for Executive Support

The senior managers in the relevant organization must be see business value in the concept of establishing a career path for project management. Therefore, the PMO should meet with individual executives, or perhaps the executive control board, to present its case for adopting such a career structure. This case presumes that the relevant organization is pursuing modern project management as a competency higher than casual business interest, or that at least the business strategy calls for examination of such options. Otherwise, there may be no foundation for professional position designation or need for individual advancement in the context of project management.

Conversely, if the relevant organization is primed for such a change, the PMO should prepare a preliminary examination of the opportunity as a basis for executive consideration. It can include the following sample items and information points in its examination of a project management career path for presentation to senior managers in the relevant organization:

- Purpose for establishing a project management career path in the relevant organization:
  - Alignment with comparable positions in other business areas
  - Alignment with comparable positions in other organizations (partners/competitors)
  - Endorsement of modern project management as a core competency
  - Fulfillment of regulatory requirements or business needs
  - Implementation of organizational restructuring initiatives
- Benefits of establishing a professional career path in project management:
  - Increased staff retention based on defined professional advancement opportunities
  - Easier identification of individuals for specific project assignments
  - Improved morale and motivation within the project management environment
  - Specified training, certification, and skill/knowledge requirements for each level
  - Enhanced collaboration and information sharing among peers and within peer groups
  - Clearer definition of professional responsibilities within the project management environment
  - Professional affiliation for traditionally "nonprofessional" project team members
- Impacts on current "project managers" and other project team members:
  - New position designation issues
  - Responsibility change issues
  - Scope of control and influence issues
  - Compensation issues
  - Professional recognition issues
  - Professional certification and position qualification issues
- Impacts on the relevant organization:
  - Organizational change issues
  - Personnel action and administrative issues
  - Customer reaction issues
  - Partner and vendor/contractor-reaction issues

The PMO will need to examine these points and others that it deems applicable to develop its position for implementing a well-conceived project management career path. No such organizational effort will be without issues to resolve. However, the PMO should be able to show that the benefits warrant the change and outweigh the adverse issues and impacts it has identified.

The results of this examination in hand, the PMO is then ready to begin introducing the project management career-path concept for deliberation at the senior management level. Early in this effort, the PMO is attempting to gain executive level support to enable it to pursue a wider career-path examination with other influential business units. If events progress in favor of establishing this career path, the PMO will ultimately return to senior managers for final approval of the career-path structure and to obtain authority to proceed with its implementation.

Secure Human Resources Department Ownership

The HR department has been mentioned once or twice with regard to resource management within the project management environment. Establishing a career path is another area in which the HR department absolutely must be involved. Realistically, it may have to take the lead on the career-path development effort because of the personnel actions and impacts that will be encountered.

The PMO should begin its interaction with the HR department with a joint examination of the opportunities and advantages a project management career path will offer. The preliminary examination discussed earlier is a good point of departure for bringing in the HR department to the deliberation. Issues and disadvantages will naturally emerge in discussions as detailed consideration of a project management career path is undertaken. Ideally, preliminary executive support for the career-path concept will already be percolating. In some cases, the PMO can gain HR department support first, as a catalyst for senior management consideration. Ultimately, the HR department will need to "own" this pursuit, and the PMO can facilitate that ownership by expressing and demonstrating its commitment to being an involved partner in the total project management career development process.

The HR department will own the career path as a part of its personnel management function. The PMO can participate with the HR department in setting up and managing the career path, lending expertise in several areas:

- Job descriptions and responsibilities
- Skill, education, and experience requirements
- Compensation and benefits research
- Position-transition analysis and plan
- Training and certification requirements
- Travel requirements

- Location requirements
- Analysis of recruiting and retention mechanisms
- Analysis of staffing strength

In some organizations, the HR department will have to lead and guide preparation of these career-path elements and merely solicit PMO assistance or review. In others, the PMO may play a key role in their development. The essential point of this activity is to achieve HR department buy-in and participation in establishing a project management career path.

Solicit Project Manager Acceptance

Professionalism in the project management environment is characterized by the demonstrated capabilities and attitudes of the individuals charged with project performance success. Specific concepts of professionalism are sometimes said to be in the eyes of the beholder, and one beholder must be the project manger in the relevant organization.

The PMO should collaborate with all or many of the project managers that would be directly affected by the introduction of a formal career path. In a mature project management environment, these same project managers might be pursuing the PMO for the same reason: to establish professional identity within the relevant organization. In either instance, the PMO should regard project managers' input throughout the career development effort.

In particular, at the onset of the career-path development effort, the PMO will need to collaborate with project managers to convey its intentions for establishing a career structure, present its preliminary ideas and concepts, and solicit project manager participation in formulating and implementing the career-path model ultimately agreed upon by all participants — PMO, project managers, HR department, and executives. Similar to the collaboration with the HR department and executives, the PMO will want to meet with project managers to communicate the benefits and responsibilities it envisions in its preliminary career-path model. This allows individual project managers to review and respond to the preliminary model and to identify personal and organizational implications of a project management career path that they believe must be considered.

The organizational culture and its project management maturity will influence the ease of overall career-path acceptance within the project management environment. The PMO's concerted efforts in working with project managers, or a representative group, will influence individual support and acceptance of career progression concepts and considerations. The PMO needs to obtain the support and acceptance of relevant project managers in order for the career development effort to be successful.

Define Professional Advancement Model

The professional advancement model is what defines who's who in the project management environment. Knowing this facilitates project resource allocation activities, project resource task assignments, project performance measurement and reporting actions, project communication and collaboration processes, and of course project management responsibilities.

The most fundamental model is one that identifies those individuals designated as project managers within the relevant organization. If no other position is specified in the career progression model, this one position must be examined and assigned to those deemed qualified to lead project efforts. There should be a distinction regarding who is a project manager in the relevant organization. This project manager position can specify levels based on responsibility or seniority, but the designation implies one thing: that an individual is qualified to manage projects in this organization. Ideally, the organization's project manager designation also implies individual capability and pursuits within a professional discipline.

A second fundamental consideration is that of determining who are the professionals in a project management environment. This PMO function model suggests there are a variety of individuals who are involved in professional project management activities. In particular, virtually all project team members are project stakeholders in most organizations. They have direct or indirect influence and responsibility for elements of project success, and they perform work or otherwise contribute to the achievement of project objectives.

This concept can be examined with reference to the following brief considerations. Any project team member, or even other project stakeholders, may have professional project management career alignment if they:

- *Participate in project planning activities:* They need to convey technical expertise as well as associated identification of technical solution cost, schedules, and resource utilization.
- *Prepare or compile project status or progress reports:* They need to understand project status and correctly interpret conditions to properly structure report content.
- *Lead or perform technical or business activities associated with projects:* They need to recognize how their activities are integrated and affect project performance outcomes, and they need to be able to apply specified project performance tracking models and procedures.
- *Manage resources used in the project environment:* They need to know how resources are identified, assigned, and used on

projects, and they need to recognize their own responsibilities for resource commitments to the project effort.

■ *Report to a project manager:* They need to have at least a basic understanding of their reporting official's professional project management role and responsibilities.

■ *Hold responsibility designated in the project management methodology:* They need to recognize how their contributions are integrated into the overall project management effort, and they need to apply the preferred project management practices and techniques.

■ *Contribute professional business expertise to project management:* They need to know how and when to provide timely and meaningful input on such topics as legal advice, finance and accounting guidance, customer service management, contract management, etc.

■ *Hold business responsibility for project success:* They need to understand fundamental concepts of modern project management as a means of evaluating project and project manager performance and applying results to business decisions.

These represent the more prominent roles in the project management environment, usually assigned to full-time or part-time members of a project team. Obviously, some roles will have more distinct and more frequent involvement in actual project management activities than others. However, the more mature organization will have a broad scope of project participants that warrant some role designation.

One exception to requiring involvement in professional project activities might include any groups of project team members designated as skilled or unskilled laborers. Participants in such groups usually are not required to pursue the professional aspects of the project management discipline. Another exception might be traditional administrative support personnel. However, this exception group should not include project and PMO administrative personnel who have distinct project support responsibilities.

Following an examination to identify the key participants, the PMO can then develop a preliminary project management career progression model to align roles and responsibilities in the project management environment. This model should represent the various preferred position designations that will be used in the relevant organization to define individual participation.

It is important that the PMO recognize that position naming conventions can be modified to meet the needs of the relevant organization. The following subsections present a suggested, first-glance consideration for the PMO to deliberate in defining and establishing professional advancement levels in the project management environment.

Entry and Support Level Positions

Every project manager has to start somewhere. The PMO can use this career level to identify professional potential and to provide basic project management skill and knowledge development. Activities at this level will prepare individuals for expanded responsibilities in project management as it provides the fundamental experience needed for progression within the project management environment.

Participants at this career level could include those with recently completed formal education who are just beginning their professional careers in a business environment. It also could include individuals with varying levels of business experience who are transitioning into a professional project management environment, or who find the project management environment growing around them. The focus of activities at this career level is on supporting project management efforts.

The following are position options at the entry and support level that the PMO can consider:

- *Project assistant:* Performs traditional administrative duties to include graphics design and document preparation and reproduction; schedules and arranges meeting facilities and participant attendance; maintains telephone and visitor logs; prepares and manages project correspondence and shipping of project deliverables.
- *Project coordinator:* Facilitates collaboration among project team members and across project teams, business units, and other project stakeholders; manages project team information and knowledge exchange, including the project team on-line knowledge space; manages project facilities, equipment, and supplies (acquisition and assignment).
- *Project administrator:* Monitors, receives, and compiles reports from project team members to the project manager; manages change control, project plan updates, project document storage and control, and project issues and action logs; monitors and manages project deliverable due dates, risk mitigation actions, and contractual obligations; manages customer and vendor/contractor invoices and payments.
- *Project business analyst:* Performs specialized project management activities such as schedule development and management, budget preparation and oversight, and resource workload management; provides project estimating and planning support and expertise;

analyzes cost, schedule, and resource utilization performance and variations; contributes expertise to project management planning in areas of specialty, e.g., risk, quality, procurement, etc.

Although consolidated in this category list, the PMO should distinguish between entry level and support positions. The positions highlighted above are usually appropriate *entry* positions in an organization because they provide a starting role for individuals with only fundamental project management skills. Conversely, a *support* position designation may warrant a fully qualified individual on specific projects. In some cases, even qualified level professionals may serve in support roles on larger projects. The PMO should recognize that a support position is not necessarily a junior role on the project, and it should consider that in its development of a project management career-path model.

Qualified Level Positions

The capabilities identified above for positions at the entry and support career level are presumed for qualified project managers, who will likely perform all of those duties themselves, as needed, on small- to medium-sized projects. Therefore, they do not have to be repeated for qualified level positions. However, there are several roles at the qualified level that may warrant inclusion in the professional advancement model the PMO constructs.

The following are positions at the qualified level the PMO can consider:

- *Project technical staff member:* Performs technical or skilled work to achieve project objectives. Includes such roles as engineer, scientist, analyst, researcher, developer, etc.
- *Technical task leader:* Leads technical task efforts; supervises work of project technical staff members and ensures quality in the timely development of project deliverables.
- *Project leader:* Performs in a manner similar to the technical task leader, but with an emphasis on completion of essential project management actions in addition to technical performance management. This role may be assigned to lead smaller project efforts.
- *Assistant project manager:* Monitors and guides project and team performance; represents the project manager in meetings and communication with internal and customer managers; performs other project management activities as assigned by the project manager. An individual in this role is likely a qualified project manager but is assigned in an assistant capacity because of the size, value, or complexity of the project.

- *Project manager:* Conducts project management activities using preferred organizational practices and established processes contained in the project management methodology; demonstrates leadership in the project management environment; holds accountability for project cost, schedule, and resource utilization performance and the achievement of project objectives and business goals.
- *Senior project manager:* Performs in the same manner as the project manager but is recognized for achievement of advanced training and education credentials, extended project management experience, or demonstrated success on previous projects. As well, this professional level represents competency to oversee the larger project efforts conducted by the relevant organization.

Project team members and task leaders may be assigned to roles on multiple projects, requiring them to be effective task and time managers. Project managers and senior project managers are also likely to have multiple project responsibilities in small- to medium-sized organizations. The capability to handle this type of responsibility should be considered by the PMO when defining specific position descriptions.

Business Level Positions

Ideally, the capabilities described for the previous two levels of the project management career path are aligned with individuals serving in positions at the business level. Business level roles in project management represent a wider management perspective, usually including responsibility for oversight of multiple projects or management of large and extended project engagements. Therefore, some capability and comprehension of modern project management concepts and practices is distinctly needed. However, in some organizations, the perceived need to assign relatively senior managers to these roles sometimes precludes the completion of formal project management education and training and the associated experience gained at the qualified level.

To that end, business experience or identified individual business management potential is a prime qualifier. To be successful at the business level, qualification must include some hands-on capability and experience in understanding modern project management concepts, applying project management methods, using common project management tools and terminology, and leading project teams. As well, the PMO should recognize that technical expertise and advancement does not necessarily imply advanced project management capability.

The following are positions at the business level that the PMO can consider:

- *Program manager:* Manages the performance of multiple project managers, oversees multiple project performance, and lends business guidance to collections of related projects. Alternatively, a program manager may be assigned to oversee a long-term program characterized by multiple-discipline technical task performance requirements, large and evolving program/project team compositions, and usually a single customer with participation of the customer's several and diverse business units.
- *Program director:* Manages the performance of program managers, and possibly some project managers, usually on a regional, nationwide, or global basis. Responsibility may focus on a product line or market segment. The director position ensures business interests are appropriately addressed in project and program technical solution deliveries and in associated customer relationships.
- *PMO director:* Holds responsibilities that may include those of a program director, but also includes responsibility for establishing a centralized project oversight, control, and support capability within the relevant organization. The PMO director should also demonstrate capability to manage the PMO as a separate business unit if PMO maturity and business needs warrant such an entity within the relevant organization.

The positions aligned with the business level of the project management career path are focused on (a) identifying, developing, and implementing processes and practices that enhance and expand project management effectiveness and capability within the relevant organization and (b) guiding and managing project performance to achieve strategic business objectives.

Executive Level Opportunities

Executive level project management — involving vice presidents, CEOs, CFOs, CIOs, and others at the strategic decision level — is catching on. It would be nice to have a prevalent cross-industry need for chief project officers (CPOs). These do exist in some global organizations, but the term "CPO" is not widely used. Nevertheless, there is now a precedent for elevating the professional project manager to the executive levels in an organization, and the organizations that do so are also those generally at the highest levels of project management maturity.

Executives distinctly need business competencies, but they also need to understand and apply project management competencies. A home-grown vice president who emerges from the project management career path is desirable, but not essential. More important is that executives can associate their professional background and experience to the project management career ladder they are joining.

The following are positions at the executive level that the PMO can consider:

- *Vice president of project management:* Heads the relevant organi-zation's project management center of competence that serves business interests on a regional, national, or global scale; lends leadership and guidance to PMO development initiatives and to the infusion of modern project management tools and practices; often holds associated responsibility for achieving strategic business objectives.
- *Director of project management:* Holds responsibilities and author-ity similar to that of vice president of project management, but is so named when an executive position cannot be established.
- *Vice president of business unit operations:* The project management career path should provide for cross-functional professional posi-tion opportunities. Project managers at senior levels gain tremen-dous business experience that, along with relevant education and training, prepares them to lead business unit operations. The PMO should examine how opportunities outside the project management environment can be introduced into the professional project man-agement advancement model.

Executives will be introduced from within the organization and from external sources. The PMO should collaborate with current executives to develop the future roles and responsibilities of executives in the project management career path.

Construct Position Descriptions and Qualifications

The PMO, in collaboration with the HR department, will develop a preliminary structure for project management career progression using example positions presented in the previous section or using other posi-tion-title naming conventions that fit in the relevant organization. Then, for each of the positions identified, the PMO will prepare the associated position description and qualification specification.

The preparation of this position information will allow the PMO and HR department to examine and fine-tune the position titles and preferred characteristics for each position in the career path. It will enable different position levels or categories to be distinguished and delineated.

The PMO should consider the following elements in constructing position information:

- *Position title:* This element represents the naming convention used to identify the professional position and level, and it lends some reference to the nature of the associated role and responsibilities.
- *Role and responsibilities:* This element identifies the performance objectives to be achieved and suggests the nature of work to be performed. It also may include specification of the reporting official and identification of any other positions that report to this one.
- *Scope of authority:* This element can provide direct or indirect reference to authorities associated with the position, including consideration of authority in areas of finance and spending; staff assignment, management, and termination; contract and agreement signatory and management; and any other authority granted by the relevant organization.
- *Experience requirements:* This element identifies the preferred level of professional experience required to be effective in performing work associated with the position. This is usually stated in terms of years.
- *Education and training requirements:* This element identifies the preferred types and levels of formal and informal education and training required for this position. This is usually stated in terms of diplomas or degrees earned, but it also may include professional or technical certification requirements that must be achieved to qualify for the position.
- *Salary, compensation, and benefits:* This element identifies the salary range for the position. It may include a brief comparative analysis of professional salary for similar positions in the industry and within the relevant organization. This element also specifies any other compensation or benefits offered in association with the position, e.g., standard compensation package used throughout the relevant organization, business or sales commissions, stock options, retirement plan funding, bonus opportunities, education and training scholarships or assistance, etc.

As these elements for all positions in the project management career path are completed, the PMO and HR department can perform a collective review of all specified positions to ensure the continuity of progressive salary, compensation, and benefit offerings.

If individuals filling current positions in the relevant organization are to be transferred to the new career structure, the HR department also will likely need to perform a compensation analysis on each individual. This is needed to ensure that individual compensation and benefits are not lost or reduced in the transition without due consideration, and that if such decisions are made, they are based on solid business needs. As well, any potential increase or expansion in compensation or benefits resulting from implementing a new career structure should be examined to discern business interest and value.

The effort to develop a project management career path is not likely to be a secret unless extensive information safeguards are in place. Therefore, individuals in the project management environment and throughout the relevant organization likely will learn about the effort before it is officially implemented. It may be wise for the PMO and HR department to prepare and distribute appropriate information about the initiative at timely intervals during the development process. If those individuals who will be directly affected can be identified, they should receive special and more-detailed progress reports.

Integrate Career Path into the Organization

The PMO will largely turn over responsibility for career-path integration activities to the HR department, complementing its activities as needed. The following steps are presented for PMO consideration in situations where career path integration support may be needed:

- *Position alignment with staffing structure:* The position descriptions will provide adequate information to align positions in the project management career path with the organizational chart. This will result in identifying reporting flow, peer relationships, and business unit alignment.
- *Position transition planning:* The approach to how any current professional, technical, or administrative positions will transition to the new project management career structure must be deliberated and decided, and appropriate plans created to manage the effort. This includes consideration of such matters as:
  - *Identification of affected individuals:* A list should be created to specify whose, how many, and what types of current positions will be affected.
  - *Identification of transition impacts:* The known and potential impacts on individuals and on the relevant organization should be specified and accompanied by the preferred approach to reducing adverse impacts.

- *Specification of new positions:* The new position to be transferred to individual members of the current staff, as well as to any imminent incoming staff, will be identified and conveyed to those individuals. In some cases, this may include a moderate or large change in the person's role and responsibilities. The time and location for conducting group and individual notification sessions should be specified.
- *Preparation for transition:* This activity will accomplish required review and adjustment of personnel files and finance and accounting records, and it should be included in the transition plan.
- *Determination of transition date:* A variety of factors — including such things as transition impacts, the HR department's calendar of recurring personnel events, and compensation payment schedules — should be examined to identify any primary or secondary transition dates.
- *Promotional activities:* The relevant organization should identify promotional events in the transition plan. This includes such things as internal announcements, public statements and press releases, associated individual promotions, and anything else the relevant organization cares to do as an uplifting introduction of a professional project management career path.
- *Authorization of transition:* The transition to a new professional project management career path is not a casual activity. To say the least, it is one that requires a business decision to explore and then a final decision to implement. The transition plan should indicate the authority that will be used, the proposed date(s) for final review and approval of the initiative, and a date to conduct career-path cutover.

■ *Staff notification activities:* The manner and timing in which all staff, but particularly affected staff, is notified about the career-path transition should be included in the transition plan. This activity represents the execution of the associated transition plan element. It generally will include:
  - Initial, general announcement of the career-path development initiative
  - General announcement of the anticipated cutover date or timeframe
  - Group or individual notification of affected personnel (with follow-up meeting dates if not conducted individually to respond to likely inquiries at time of notification)

- Individual review of applicable personnel and finance records by affected personnel
- Final, general announcement of cutover date

■ *Initiative promotions:* The types and timing of promotional activities will be specified in the transition plan. This activity represents the execution of those plan elements. The introduction of a new and robust professional project management career structure should be given appropriate pomp and ceremony, both internally and with customer and industry recognition.

■ *Career-path cutover:* The actual career-path cutover event can be as festive or as uneventful as is appropriate within the relevant organization. A small gathering to recognize the new career structure and to congratulate individuals with new titles (and perhaps new responsibilities) is usually an appropriate activity. As well, a few other things could potentially be pursued at career-path cutover:

- Personnel record reviews for affected personnel
- New individual professional objectives and development plans
- Press release or other public announcement
- Meetings with new supervisors, as is applicable to new structure
- New business cards for affected personnel

An effective and collaborated planning effort between the PMO and HR department will ensure a smooth and efficient transition.

Support Project Management Career Planning

The PMO can perform a vital leadership role in the project management environment by establishing capability to guide or otherwise assist individuals in their professional pursuits within the project management discipline. It can use the experience and insights of assigned managers and other resources to build this support capability.

Three primary activities are recommended for PMO consideration in defining and implementing a project management career planning support capability. These are described in the following subsections.

Provide General Career Guidance

The PMO can assist professionals by facilitating availability of career guidance activities. The larger PMO may have one or more staff members responsible for this effort on a part-time or full-time basis. Smaller and medium-sized PMOs can convene a volunteer force from among senior managers to develop and implement this capability.

The areas of project management career guidance that can be considered include:

- *Career planning:* Collaborating with individuals in their examination of career opportunities in project management, with reflection on role and responsibility opportunities at progressively advanced career levels. Ideally, the project management career path established by the relevant organization will provide a frame of reference, but industry standards and references also can be used to examine career opportunities. Then assistance can be provided to identify individual career objectives and to specify the actions and activities to achieve those professional pursuits. As well, individuals can be encouraged to establish a schedule for recurring review of their professional development plan, whereby they can note achievements and modify professional objectives, as needed.
- *Training and education:* Conveying industry and organizational standards and requirements for training and education to enable individuals to acquire preferred skill and knowledge in a learning environment. This includes examining the need for formal education that result in diplomas and degrees, continuing and advanced education and training benefits, and recognition through professional certifications, which usually adds the element of professional experience as a certificate award factor.
- *Personal progress reviews:* Examining the indicators of personal performance, particularly the perspectives of task supervisors regarding the demonstration of professional competencies and capabilities. This allows individuals to set a measurement point with regard to their level of professional performance, identify skill and capability gaps, and renew objectives to overcome them and continue advancement in the project management discipline.
- *Career counseling:* Advising project managers, project team members, and other participants in the project management environment in formulating career development objectives, defining personal educational and career development pursuits, and performing self-evaluations of progress and potential in project management. This includes developing mentor-protégé relationships that help individuals understand and meet the challenges of a professional career by providing contact with individuals who are experienced and have traveled a similar path to achieve career success.

Promote Business Skill Development

The concepts and practices of modern project management present a broad range of project management responsibilities that warrant development of business skills and knowledge. The PMO can be instrumental in helping individuals to prepare for meeting the challenges of expanding professional responsibilities, consistent with individual career pursuits and stage of professional development. This activity can be treated within the context of career guidance discussed above, but it is an area of professional development that may already be a part of the relevant organization's professional development offerings. In this case, it just has to be brought into the project management environment.

The following three subsections are critical elements of business skill development that will benefit project managers, particularly those at or approaching senior professional levels.

Strategic Perspective

Project managers need to have sufficient strategic perspective on business activities in the relevant organization and in their industry. This perspective normally seems to emerge for individuals in technical disciplines as they approach mid-career in association with appointments to early senior level positions. Some individuals are unsure what to do with newly acquired business information, while others learn how to use it aptly in their business endeavors. The latter is likely to have a professional advantage in the industry and in the relevant organization and advance at a quicker pace. The PMO should examine opportunities to infuse standard and viable business concepts and practices into its operations, where possible. It should also research the availability of business-related education and training programs, workshops and seminars, and senior level mentors that personnel in the project management environment can use to assist in professional growth.

Business Function Familiarity

Project managers need to understand business operations outside the project management environment as a fundamental requirement of professional development. Ideally, project managers will encounter opportunities for temporary cross-business unit assignments by which they can learn and enlarge their understanding of business functionality. However, even such simpler endeavors as professional reading, pursuing business education and training, and discussions with peers in other business units will provide a level of learning that will be valuable toward achieving professional career objectives.

Interpersonal Relationship Management

Project managers at all levels need to recognize the impacts of their personalities — behavior and attitude — in the business environment. Only those that have stronger personality traits that facilitate business pursuits will be effective in their business efforts and in their professional advancement. The good news is that individuals can learn accepted and proven methods for managing professional relationships and for leading teams that produce results. This is inherently needed to achieve success in the project management environment. It is mandatory to achieve success in the business world. The PMO can design such training into the career development program it creates.

Implement Career Planning Support

This activity represents an expansion of the more general career planning support highlighted earlier. Here the PMO gives consideration to establishing a more formal process to facilitate career planning. Likewise, the relevant organization may already have a professional development planning process in place, perhaps one that is used in conjunction with annual performance reviews. The PMO could ensure that project management career-path participants use it to maximize career progression advantage and opportunities.

A more formal process for career planning can include the following elements:

- Review of prior-year performance goals and achievements
- Review of prior-year education and training goals and achievements
- Preparation or update of individual career development plans
  - Initial-year career objectives
  - 3 to 5-year career objectives
  - Long-term career objectives
- Specification of review points for achievement of objectives
- Joint review of the career development plan by mentor and protégé
- Finalization of annual career development plan
- Implementation of annual career development plan

The PMO can facilitate this career planning process by using instruments already available within the relevant organization. Likewise, it can create or customize planning tools and templates for particular use within the project management environment.

Establish Professional Certification

Professional certification represents validation of individual skill, knowledge, and experience and perhaps a few other attributes required by the certifying body. The certifying body is usually an external professional or educational institution that has vested interest in the advancement of project management or an aligned discipline. However, more and more, organizations are developing their own project management certification programs to qualify individual competency. This is usually done in addition to external professional certification, but in some cases an organization will have only the internal program as the official and primary pursuit.

Two primary activities associated with PMO involvement in professional project management certification are presented in the following subsections.

Develop Project Management Certification Program

Certification of professionals within the project management environment is an excellent way to ensure a consistent level of project management performance within the relevant organization. Certification is based on standards selected by the PMO to guide the development and implementation of project management concepts and practices. Those same standards may often be used to measure and manage individual professional growth and capability within the project management environment. A certification program, at a minimum, provides a snapshot at a point in time of individual qualification to perform all or portions of the job at hand. If the certification requires follow-on updates, or recertification at intervals, that snapshot is extended across time to add even more validity to individual competency.

Project management certification is a program that should be a priority for PMOs at all stages of maturity. Project management certification programs come in two primary forms: external certification and internal certification. The PMO can consider the benefits of each as a prerequisite to defining the type of certifications that will be pursued within the relevant organization. In some organizations, both forms of certification are used. The external certification serves to obtain a third-party validation of professional competency, usually based on examination of individuals against widely accepted standards. An internal certification program allows the PMO to consider industry-specific issues as well as applicable organizational and business interests. A brief discussion on each form of professional certification follows.

External Professional Certification

The concept of external certification in the context of this PMO function deals with verification, validation, or confirmation of professional or technical capability and related characteristics and credentials by an independent institution. It does not refer to certificates or "certification" resulting from the completion of training.

The PMO will want to consider recommending or mandating individual professional certification in project management using an established independent examination and certification body. In particular, the Project Management Professional® (PMP®) certification program developed and administered by the Project Management Institute® (PMI®) is a widely accepted, internationally recognized certification program. The PMP designation lends validation and confirmation to individual project management knowledge and experience. It represents a third-party, cross-industry program that applies the principles and practices contained in PMI's *A Guide to The Project Management Body of Knowledge* (PMBOK®). Other examples of institutions that provide certification programs related to project management include the Gartner Institute, Gartner certified associate programs; the Association for Project Management (UK), Project Management Capability Test (PCT); and the Singapore Computer Society (Singapore), National IT Skills Certification Programme.

A few benefits from selecting and implementing an external certification program include:

- Reference to globally available project management standards
- Access to an established and validated certification process
- Application of an established and widely used competency measurement capability
- Independent confirmation of individual certification credentials
- External management of certification administration

Using an external certification program for professionals in the project management environment provides recognition of individual achievement and contributes to an enhanced perception, if not distinctly demonstrated, competency within the relevant organization.

Internal Professional Certification

Internal certification usually deals with validating individual achievement of specified criteria, which may include some combination of training, demonstration of performance, testing or measurement of competency, and experience. An internal certification program will normally monitor progress and confirm individual accomplishments toward certification based on achievement of all criteria.

The PMO involved in developing and managing an internal professional certification program will likely do so in collaboration with the HR or training department, which provides capability in defining required competency levels, constructing competency measurements, and administering such programs. The PMO can contribute to this effort in the following areas:

- *Define relevance of certification:* Specify what the certification will do for the individual and how it will benefit the relevant organization, e.g., satisfy a business requirement, increase opportunity for advancement, qualify for a position, enable expansion of responsibility, etc.
- *Specify certification program target group:* Identify who should pursue certification as a mandatory or optional activity. Identify who will be authorized to enter into the program and who will be authorized certification upon completion.
- *Determine certification program implementation approach:* Examine impacts and determine how the certification program will be implemented to account for individual completion time limits or constraints, multiple and repeat attempts, options for any "grandfather" clause if the program is mandatory, and whether or not there is an official program registration process.
- *Construct certification criteria:* Determine the skill, knowledge, and performance objectives to be achieved by individuals, as well as any other business or professional qualifications (e.g., experience, tenure, career level, manager recommendation, etc.) required for individual participation.

These activities help to develop an internal certification program. They are also valid points of consideration for introducing external certification programs.

A few benefits from developing and implementing an internal certification program include:

- Internal control of the certification criteria and process
- Specification of certification criteria that have direct alignment with business interests and strategic objectives
- Incorporation of qualifications for advancement consistent with existing programs within the relevant organization

- Ability to consider and include multiple standards as the basis of certification

The PMO will need to carefully consider the relevant organization's commitment to any internal project management certification program. It is better to pursue an external certification program than to develop an unprofessional, uninspiring, or underused internal certification program. Perhaps the organization would prefer to consider simply establishing some competency criteria in lieu of a full-blown certification program. The PMO also might want to consider and recommend an internal program that complements an existing external certification program for implementation within the relevant organization.

Facilitate Technical and Professional Certification

The PMO will likely operate from a particular industry or technical-discipline frame of reference (e.g., information technology, pharmaceuticals, construction and engineering). It is appropriate, then, for the PMO to provide or support the pursuit of technical and professional certification opportunities by individuals within the project management environment. These certification programs provide considerable value to the relevant organization, and the PMO should promote, endorse, and recognize them as accomplishments within the project management environment.

The following is a list of some of the actions the PMO can initiate to help individuals in the project management environment achieve certification:

- Provide training courses and programs that help individuals to achieve the skill and knowledge required for certification
- Conduct or arrange for technical study groups; provide meeting facilities, primary and guest speakers and instructors, and equipment access for participating individuals
- Incorporate technical or professional certification in professional development objectives, and recognize individual achievements in performance reports and appraisals
- Conduct public recognition of individuals who have achieved relevant and specified technical and professional certification — internal and public announcements and news articles, awards ceremonies, bonus or other rewards programs, salary increase, increased eligibility for promotion or advancement, etc.

The project management environment will benefit through enlivened technical discussions and by PMO encouragement for pursuit of individual technical and professional certification.

POSTSCRIPT FOR THE SMALLER PMO

The smaller PMO will very likely rely on the HR department to lead efforts in areas of project management career development. In some cases, such PMOs will have little influence over the career development of project resources that are assigned to separate business units and who participate in the project management environment on an as-needed basis. However, to fulfill its role and responsibilities of leadership within the project management environment, there are two particular activities the smaller PMO can plan and conduct to advance project management career development.

First, the PMO should plan its approach and present an initiative to specify the role of project manager within the relevant organization. Ideally, this will be an officially designated position title, i.e., one that appears next to the individual's name on a business card. However, an acceptable alternative is to identify those individuals serving in a "project manager" role in addition to their assigned position title. The smaller PMO can construct a case for this recognition and designation, collaborate across business units to build support, and then introduce it for executive level and HR department deliberation and decision.

Second, the PMO should urge individuals within the project management environment to pursue professional project management certification. This can easily be accomplished as a one-on-one effort, as recurring reminders in group meetings, and through dissemination of information on the preferred project management certification program. It is in the smaller PMO's best interest to increase competency in project management and to demonstrate that competency by increased participation in project management certification.

12

TEAM DEVELOPMENT

The project team is the fundamental staffing unit within the project management environment. When there is more than one person assigned to a project effort, a project team is formed either formally or informally. As project size and complexity grows, so does team size and complexity. A two- or three-person project team will benefit from team development activities. A larger, more diverse, and possibly geographically separated project team distinctly requires team development support to ensure project success.

The PMO can facilitate team development by establishing the procedures that help project teams to be formed and that help govern their development and performance. As well, the PMO can help project managers to develop and apply project team leadership and management concepts and practices consistent with industry standards and with the relevant organization's guidance for resource management.

This "team development" function enables the PMO to:

- Establish practices for developing cohesive project teams
- Develop guidance for performance of geographically separated teams
- Introduce team development tools and techniques for use by project managers
- Monitor and manage project team performance improvement initiatives

The PMO will be able to achieve this functionality by working closely with key project managers within the relevant organization to incorporate their input and recommendations surrounding project team development needs. It also can gain insight from ongoing examination of team activities from the perspective of project team members, who are charged with contributing to cohesive team performance.

PROJECT ENVIRONMENT INTERFACE CONCEPTS

The PMO can use this function to prepare individuals for project team assignments and work efforts. By establishing a standard approach to team formation and development activities along with the associated expectations for team member contributions to team cohesion, the PMO will enable project teams to be more effective and more efficient in their pursuit of project objectives.

This PMO effort will capture experienced project managers' skill and insight to prepare recommended practices that can be applied to leading project teams. This information can be incorporated into project management methodology guidance or conveyed by other means for use by all project managers, including novices and those with less experience.

The PMO's examination of project team development will address many aspects of human behavior and the dynamics of professional interaction in the workplace. It will highlight for project managers and project team members alike the preferred interpersonal skills that work best within the project management environment. In particular, project managers will benefit from a more complete understanding of project team dynamics, leadership responsibilities, and problem-resolution actions that are appropriate to the project management environment. The PMO will be able to lend customization to these matters by adapting practices and procedures to account for organizational culture and other factors in the relevant organization.

Project team members generally want to contribute their best to project performance and to the associated dynamics of team development. The PMO can construct motivational threads in processes to facilitate a vested interest that prompts individuals to maximize their efforts and participation in team development objectives.

BUSINESS ENVIRONMENT INTERFACE CONCEPTS

Project team members are likely performing their project work as a part of a matrix project organization. That means they complete their project assignments and then return to their business unit to conduct normal operational tasks or they proceed to another project. In either case, these individuals bring a little more awareness of teamwork and team dynamics to their next job as a result of this PMO function. An effective project team development approach applied today will make individuals more productive on their next project assignment or on their next task back in the business unit.

The need for the PMO to facilitate project team development is a part of its ongoing collaboration effort with the HR department. The HR department remains a prominent and knowledgeable resource to support developing individuals and teams within the relevant organization. This allows the PMO to utilize any established HR department practices in team development in the project management environment. As well, the PMO has access to project management industry standards for project team development. In some cases, the PMO may implement a team development approach that also can be used in business units outside the project management environment.

Finally, in a reiteration of sorts, the benefits that individuals gain through team development activities in the project management environment will be applied in their subsequent interactions across the relevant organization. Individuals also will be better prepared for professional advancement within the relevant organization.

TEAM DEVELOPMENT ACTIVITIES ACROSS THE PMO CONTINUUM

The "team development" function along the PMO competency continuum represents an increasing capability to lead, develop, and manage the full performance potential of teams in the project management environment.

Table 12.1 provides an overview of the range of prescribed PMO team development activities according to each level in the PMO competency continuum.

The *project office* has front-line responsibility for team formation and development activities. It will apply the leadership and skill of individual project managers to quickly build viable project teams that are focused on achieving project objectives within the constraints of cost, schedule, and resource utilization.

Mid-range PMO levels have the responsibility of influencing the development of leadership capabilities in project managers at all experience levels, and in guiding and supporting their approach to project team development. This includes ensuring that project managers are proactive in attending to issues of team development, which the PMO influences by incorporating required team formation and team development activities into the project management methodology. It also includes providing a variety of tools and techniques that are available to project managers to assist in their project team development efforts. Advanced PMOs also will use this function to help individual project managers to define and develop leadership capabilities. In some cases, the advanced PMO will monitor and manage development of individual project manager leadership capabilities through observations and the use of survey instruments, with subsequent prescriptions for improvement, as appropriate.

The *center of excellence* represents an advanced-stage PMO that is concerned with measuring and quantifying business performance. It will

Table 12.1 Range of Team Development Activities across the PMO Continuum

Project Office	Basic PMO	Standard PMO	Advanced PMO	Center of Excellence
Manages individual integration into project teams and participation in team development efforts	Introduces concepts of project team dynamics ■ Incorporates project team development guidance into methodology ■ Recommends remedies and reconciliation actions for distressed team performance	Establishes and manages practices for project team development ■ Implements tools and techniques for project team development ■ Facilitates and manages project team development activities	Expands practices to develop project manager leadership skill and capability ■ Specifies project manager team development and leadership skill requirements ■ Monitors project managers' team leadership skill and capability	Conducts research and analysis of team performance ■ Performs formal and informal examinations of project team performance ■ Recommends project team composition

therefore examine project team performance from a business perspective and recommend team development activities that adapt project team performance to serve business interests. As well, it will examine team compositions and individual contributions to project team efforts and then recommend preferred individual assignments relative to achieving desired team staffing schemes.

This PMO function has a focus on oversight of individual capability to lead and develop effective and efficient project teams. To that end, PMO responsibilities may be closely aligned with associated leadership training prescribed in the PMO "training and education" function (see Chapter 10).

TEAM DEVELOPMENT FUNCTION MODEL

The central role of the PMO in the project management environment makes it a visible support player for the project team development. To the extent that the PMO is established to provide guidance and support to project managers, this function becomes an important one in its array of activities. Implementing this function requires the PMO to instill leadership in the cadre of assigned project managers and cohesive team work in the project management environment.

The prominent activities of the PMO's "team development" function model are depicted in Figure 12.1. Each activity is described in the following subsections.

Facilitate Cohesive Team Formation

An effective project management environment creates project teams that are productive early on in each project effort. The PMO can play a key role in preparing individuals and facilitating work groups to maximize their performance potential. In particular, the PMO should provide support

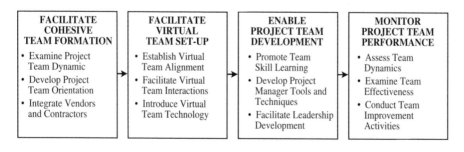

Figure 12.1 "Team Development" Function Model

and guidance to project managers who, in turn, apply their leadership capabilities to form and manage cohesive project teams.

The three prescribed steps the PMO can take to facilitate cohesive team formation in the project management environment are described in the following subsections.

Examine Project Team Dynamics

The PMO can assist in ongoing efforts to assign appropriate and compatible project team members by participating in or prescribing steps for an early review of project staffing requirements. Specifically, this effort calls for an examination of project team dynamics that is conducted relative to an established project team or with regard to pending composition of a project team.

The PMO can support the project manager in this activity by developing and conducting a more-or-less standard approach to the examination of project team composition from the team dynamics perspective. The objective is to determine the characteristics of the current or proposed project team composition and then to ascertain how those characteristics will affect project performance.

An examination of the following elements of team dynamics will provide preliminary insight as to the effectiveness of the project team and allow for leadership measures that can be applied to reduce or remove the impacts of any deficits in team composition.

- *Project classification review:* The level of project team cohesion and experience required should be aligned with the nature and type of project conducted. Classification factors to be considered include:
  - Strategic importance
  - Marketplace or internal visibility
  - Introduction of new technology
  - Business and project risk
  - Project duration

  The identification of these factors will assist the project manager or PMO in determining whether project team composition is appropriate to meet the business demands of the project. As well, this examination area will enable team formation and development activities to prepare the project team for challenges associated with project classification.
- *Technical requirements review:* The diversity of technical skills needed to achieve project objectives is considered, with particular focus on identifying skill and experience in the prominent technical

areas. This review will ensure that individuals working in technical areas not only have the requisite technical experience, but also have the necessary ability to provide interpersonal leadership that facilitates the integration of all participants across technical disciplines. This examination area will allow identification of team formation and development activities needed to prepare the project team for such interactions.

- *Project management review:* The size, technical diversity, and depth of project experience of the project team is reviewed to identify the anticipated oversight requirements relative to project manager leadership skill and experience. Logically, either the project manager is selected to manage the project team, or the project team is determined by the technical and management leadership skill sets of the project manager. Realistically, available project manager and project team member resources are going to be assigned to the project effort. Therefore, this examination enables both the favorable and adverse aspects of the pending project leader-team member relationships to be identified and addressed in a proactive manner.

- *Project team member and subgroup review:* This factor addresses an examination of individual contributions and interactions in project team activities — technical skill, project team experience, professional attitudes and behavior, and ability to work effectively and accomplish project objectives within the project team. On smaller project teams, most if not all project team members can be reviewed for their exposure and activities within the project management environment. On larger teams, time limitations usually require a focus on the key project team roles from both a technical and business leadership perspective. This examination will facilitate identification of fundamental strengths and weaknesses of the project team, as characterized by individual contributions to project team dynamics.

This examination should result in a fundamental understanding of the group dynamics to be encountered within the specified project team. This will enable the PMO to analyze conditions and prescribe guidance, and the project manager to plan and apply leadership techniques that will expedite team formation and maximize team member interactions.

Develop Project Team Orientation

Cohesive project teams demonstrate effective personal interactions and group behavior that enable work to be accomplished in a steady and progressive manner. This often results from team members who gain familiarity with the working patterns and priorities of others around them on the project team. However, there are a few other factors observed in the project management environment that also can be considered in developing project team cohesion:

- Respect for the strengths and weaknesses of each team member, with individual interactions that focus on drawing out strengths
- A common understanding and buy-in of project performance objectives and consistency of project team member motivation to achieve them
- Ability to make decisions, resolve problems, manage conflict, and demonstrate leadership both individually and collectively
- Type and frequency of communication, including dealing with the proximity of project team members and their frame of reference to standard processes and practices

The PMO and the project manager can collaborate to identify general team cohesion issues and characteristics found in the project management environment as well as those anticipated for each new project team. From this deliberation, a project team orientation program can be constructed to meet the general and specific needs of project teams within the relevant organization.

A project team orientation program can be used to provide insight and guidance that will prepare individual project team members for team assignments. Although such an orientation program will normally be delivered to a group, it is not necessarily a team building exercise. Rather, it is an individual learning and awareness "workshop" that enables individual team members to contribute to developing and maintaining team cohesion.

The PMO can lead the effort to design and create such an orientation program. The program should not be overly time-consuming, perhaps an hour in length, as a reminder to professional participants of the advantages to be gained by applying effective group dynamics skills. The program also should point out the team performance expectations of the relevant organization. Finally, the program should highlight some of the prominent concepts of team building and group dynamics that most participants will be familiar with through personal experience or as a result of professional or technical training that addresses teamwork concepts. Additional specialized training in this topic area can be extended to individuals who require a more comprehensive understanding of group dynamics — fundamental concept training for team members new to the workforce and advanced concept training for new project managers and those who are in initial team leadership roles.

The team orientation program can be as formal or informal as warranted by the organizational culture and the needs of the project management environment. There are two primary approaches that can be taken by the PMO in its development and delivery of this orientation program: a one-time program and an as-needed program.

First, a project team orientation program can be constructed for one-time delivery to new project team members, with "refresher" attendance on an individual basis as requested by the project manager. This program has a focus on preparing each participant for project team interactions. Such a one-time program also may be a part of the organization's project management or other professional training program. This one-time attendance option is good for project teams that have more or less the same recurring project team composition across multiple projects.

Second, the project team orientation program can be made available to specific project teams at the request of the project managers. This approach would be valuable for project teams having a significant number of individuals who have not worked together before. It may also apply to very large project teams comprising multiple subteams.

The bottom line of this effort is to introduce or review concepts of individual and group behaviors that promote effective project team performance and reduce or remove adverse behaviors and barriers to effective project team performance. Realistically, the elements of this orientation program could be included for brief review in the project team's initial kickoff and planning meeting.

Integrate Vendors and Contractors

Vendors and contractors will often become active players in project team activities. If this is the case, then consideration must be given to ensuring their participation in team building activities and their contributions to project team cohesion. The need for such cohesion becomes more critical when there are multiple vendors and contractors that must interact on projects within the relevant organization. Many professionals will agree that the last thing a project manager needs is to be in constant conflict-resolution mode because vendors and contractors were not properly integrated, and therefore are conducting project work based on a separate set of team interaction guidelines and performance expectations.

The PMO and project manager again should collaborate on the intended involvement of vendors and contractors to determine the extent of their integration as participants on the project team. The PMO is involved because it can contribute insight gained from its performance of the PMO's "vendor/contractor relationships" function (see Chapter 19), which should provide knowledge about the vendor and its operating practices. The project manager is involved to weigh that knowledge about the vendor against project objectives, team composition, and work performance goals to determine the actions needed to introduce and orient each outside vendor and contractor. On some projects, extensive vendor and contractor integration may not be required. On others, they play a critical and interactive role alongside other project team members in producing project deliverables.

Vendor and contractor integration, very simply, is the action taken to make them a part of the project team. This action normally is the responsibility of the project manager, although the PMO can assist in certain areas. Essentially, the project manager determines the extent of project team participation to be achieved and then acts to establish vendor and contractor expectations and requirements for the desired level of project team integration.

The PMO can develop or recommend several vendor and contractor project team integration activities for use by project managers:

- *Project team orientation:* The orientation program described earlier also can include participants from external vendor and contractor organizations.
- *Kickoff meetings:* Vendors and contractors can participate in project kickoff events to demonstrate affiliation and alignment as a full participant with other project team members.
- *Contract and agreement highlights:* The extent of required and optional vendor and contractor project team involvement can be specified in contract or agreement documents.
- *Vendor and contractor meetings:* The project manager can meet individually with vendor and contractor managers to define and develop individual roles and protocols for project team participation.
- *Vendor and contractor interviews:* The relevant organization can ensure achievement of desired project team cohesion by selecting individuals from vendor and contractor organizations who possess the requisite team interaction skills and experience. The desired individual skill and attributes can be examined through interviews with vendor and contractor representatives.
- *Public announcements:* Significant partnerships with selected vendors and contractors can be endorsed, and joint project team efforts can be recognized through public announcements, press releases, published business news articles, and internal distribution of news.

Vendor and contractor integration activities should also address any limitations or constraints on vendor and contractor project team participation. The project manager responsible for implementing the policies and practices of the relevant organization normally determines this aspect of vendor and contractor integration, and thereby manages any limitations or constraints.

Facilitate Setup of Virtual Team

Today's business world, and thereby its associated project management environment, is no longer constrained by physical buildings or boundaries. Customers and competitors, not to mention suppliers and civil and legal regulators, can be across the globe or just down the street. Virtual project teams are formed to address associated business needs and objectives of work accomplished by the relevant organization.

Consideration of virtual project teams should begin with acceptance of one fundamental premise: The business needs of the relevant organization and the personal and professional needs of the individual team member are not significantly changed because of "virtual" work performance. Rather, it is the conditions under which business is pursued and individual work is performed that are changed.

The PMO's involvement in team development very well may be highlighted by its responsibility for supporting geographically separated or virtual project teams. The context of this function does not purport to be a total solution or even a primer in "virtual team" management. There are volumes of documented expertise on this topic in the published and public domains. Rather, this section identifies the PMO's responsibility to address virtual team participation in the project management environment with consideration of some of the more prominent issues of virtual team management.

The three primary activities that will guide the PMO's efforts are presented in the following subsections.

Establish Virtual Team Alignment

The PMO must ensure that members of a virtual project team maintain strong affiliation with the relevant organization and its business purpose. It can do this by establishing the interface processes and alignment activities needed to maintain ongoing affiliation of the virtual team.

The PMO can collaborate with project managers, as well as with virtual team members, to conduct the necessary organizational interface and alignment activities. The following subsections describe a few of the prominent considerations and activities to be addressed in this effort.

Statement of Purpose

The virtual project team should have a statement of purpose prepared to guide its work on one or more projects. If there is only one project, then the statement of purpose will likely be captured in the project definition or the project charter. The nature of virtual teamwork may also merit including an explanation of alignment with business objectives — why the project was selected — to provide additional insight for isolated or independent project team members.

Virtual Team Process Implementation

To the extent possible, virtual team members should be familiar with and use established standards guidance, project management and technical methodologies, and routine business practices. This is particularly important if the virtual team members are aligned with or support one or more traditional teams. However, variations to standards and process deployment may be warranted, but any adjustments made should be duly considered, documented, and communicated to all involved participants.

Virtual Team Structure

All team members need to know how they fit into the structure of the relevant organization, and virtual team members need similar alignment. Virtual team members should be provided information that specifies key points of contact: their virtual supervisor/project manager, their business unit affiliation, and their primary support resources: administrative, technical, and technological.

Team Assessment

The manager of the virtual project team should perform interval assessments of team performance and effectiveness, such as a project audit in the virtual environment. Likewise, the PMO should assist or otherwise conduct examinations of the technical and administrative processes deployed for virtual team use in a manner similar to that applied when examining project management methodology utilization.

Team Member Recognition

Members of the virtual project team should be considered for rewards and recognition consistent with the practices of the relevant organization. This allows all virtual team members to feel a little more aligned with the business unit and its objectives. Such individual successes also represent a measure of success for the entire virtual team by demonstrating how the virtual team efforts are achieving the specified purpose.

Facilitate Virtual Team Interactions

The project manager may be operating either partially or fully within the virtual environment, and therefore will likely encounter new challenges in managing virtual team activities and interactions. The PMO can anticipate and plan how to handle such emerging issues and lend guidance to project managers in the following three areas.

Socialization of Virtual Team

Members of the virtual project team will have limited personal contact with the project manager, other team members and stakeholders, and other business units. This lack of personal interaction must be considered, and the need for team member socialization must be recognized. The following subsections list a number of activities that the PMO can recommend to reduce the impact of isolated or independent team member work efforts resulting from assignments in the virtual environment.

Face-to-Face Time. Opportunities for the project team to convene in person should be identified and conducted. Project kickoff meetings are ideal venues for face-to-face time needed by virtual team members. Other events should be planned and conducted to enable team members to become personally acquainted as a basis for developing quality, professional interactions.

Routine Business Communication. The PMO should examine needs and recommend the frequency of voice contact for routine communication between the project manager and the team members and for contacts between project team members. For example, routine and recurring contact could be pursued to accomplish weekly telephone status meetings.

Augmented Business Communication. The PMO and project manager should encourage frequent interactions among project team members as a matter of accomplishing project tasks. It is likely that the technology selected for the virtual team will facilitate information exchange, but this can easily be augmented by follow-on personal contact via telephone to discuss receipt and content of transferred information.

Team Member Introductions and Orientations. Individuals joining the virtual team subsequent to project kickoff activities and associated in-person meetings need to be introduced to teammates and to the virtual team processes being deployed. At a minimum, any new virtual team member should receive an in-person orientation from the project manager

— whether the member travels to the project manager, or vice versa. As well, the new individual should be introduced to other virtual team members at the next scheduled group telephone conference. A current, experienced team member might be selected to serve as a primary point of contact, or even serve as a mentor, during the initial weeks as the new team member becomes acquainted with virtual practices. It is important to facilitate all opportunities for virtual project team members to know one another at the onset of the project and as new members are introduced.

Management of Trust Issues. Trust issues emerge from isolated and independent virtual teamwork and limited interactions, and these are a prevalent aspect of virtual team socialization. Virtual team members do not have the luxury of frequent interpersonal interactions, as do traditional project team members. It is not uncommon for issues of trust to arise regarding team member performance (particularly work hand-off quality expectations among team members), conveyance and understanding of project manager perceptions regarding individual work performance and acceptance, and business unit recognition and treatment of the virtual team member. The project manager must be cognizant of these issues and, in collaboration with the PMO, develop a proactive means to identify and resolve them.

Virtual Team Collaboration

The geographical separation of project team members working in a virtual environment prompts a significant need for effective collaboration relative to the project work effort. The following subsections show some of the prominent collaboration issues that influence the performance of the virtual team and that the PMO should address.

Communication. The number of team members, their job requirements, and the need for information exchange and discussions must be examined to determine communications requirements for the team and for individuals. The primary goal in establishing communications requirements is to reduce or remove communication delays regardless of team members' time zone, organizational alignment, or physical location. Managing this challenge warrants developing and distributing an effective project communications plan.

Task Flow. The consideration of passing completed project work from one virtual team member to another, or to a group of reviewers, warrants creation of a task flowchart. A task flowchart will show individual team members where they fit in the work-flow scheme and guide them in the transfer actions and activities for completed work. Who to send completed work to, when to send it, and how to send it are essential components of the task flowchart.

Assignments and Responsibilities. Project team members need to be informed of work performance expectations in a timely manner, and a mechanism to confirm their receipt and understanding of assignments and associated responsibilities must be incorporated into the process.

Team Member Training. Like any intact project team member, virtual team members will need training from time to time. This includes skill and competency training in their professional discipline; training in products, processes, and practices of the relevant organization; and training associated with the introduction of new tools or technology. Virtual team members should be included in training plans created for the project management environment. Training courses for virtual team members can be scheduled to accommodate necessary local or long-distance travel, or alternative training methods such as on-line programs can be incorporated into the training plan for their use.

Lessons Learned Exchange. "Lessons learned" is a special example of the virtual team's communications needs, and it is highlighted because of the benefits to be derived from an effective and timely exchange of such information. This item warrants consideration and use of the Web-based collaboration tools outlined in the PMO's "project knowledge management" function (see Chapter 4), e.g., a project team "chat" room would serve these interests.

Governance of Virtual Team

The presumably limited contact between the project manager and virtual project team members, working more or less independently and, in some cases, in isolated conditions, provides a need to ensure some reasonable level of oversight and control of work performance and participation in team activities. The PMO should consider needs for developing and implementing governance activities and establish the virtual team governance solutions described in the following subsections.

Standards. Project management and technical process standards should be identified and communicated for use by virtual team members. As well, business standards related to quality, productivity, and performance can also be conveyed.

Operating Procedures. The "ground rules" for project team members should be specified. This includes addressing such personal aspects as team member work hours, team member availability, and participation in required teleconferences, on-line meetings, and other work-related activities. It also includes procedures and guidance for reporting and managing technical problems and issues, equipment failures and outages, and local disruptions to work.

Team Member Supervision. All virtual team members should be notified of who is responsible for oversight of their work performance and productivity. This item also identifies the preferred means for contact and availability of the supervisor, and it includes arrangements for initial and recurring contact with the supervisor. Ideally, performance and productivity expectations established by the supervisor will be included in the initial notification.

Team Member Administration. Each virtual team member should be advised regarding whom to contact (or expect contact from) with regard to administrative matters. This includes such things as personnel actions, time reporting, benefits management, travel, and of course salary and payments.

Introduce Virtual Team Technology

Effective communication and collaboration is essential for any project team, and it is absolutely vital for a virtual project team. Fortunately, communications technology is rapidly evolving to facilitate virtual team needs. The Internet alone is a powerful tool that enables real-time communication and collaboration as well as on-line access to software applications.

The PMO should be involved in planning technology support for use by virtual project teams. This effort can be integrated with the establishment of tools as specified in the PMO's "project knowledge management" function (see Chapter 4), its "project management tools" function (see Chapter 2), and its "facilities and equipment support" function (see Chapter 8). In particular, the PMO should address the following technology needs of the virtual project team in its overall plans:

- Telephony lines and equipment (telephone and fax capability)
- Computer hardware (desktop and laptop computers and supporting peripheral equipment)
- Project management software
- Technical development application software

- Communication and collaboration tools (Web-based and server-based)
- Connectivity hardware and software (Internet access, server access, and e-mail access)

Enable Project Team Development

The PMO can be a vital resource that assists project managers and, for that matter, individual team members in developing enhanced team performance capability. It works under the premise that a fully developed project team will be more effective in achieving project objectives than a less cohesive team.

Project team development is generally seen to occur on two levels: individual learning and group development. First, individual learning about effective interpersonal interactions, group dynamics, and leadership provides the general concepts, knowledge, and understanding about oneself and others that the individual can bring to team efforts. Then, group development represents the application of individual learning about effective team development and performance within the context of team member interactions.

The following three subsections discuss the activities that the PMO can pursue to enable project team development within the relevant organization.

Promote Team Skill Learning

The PMO should foster a project management environment that promotes individual learning and group application of effective team development practices. All professionals having project team affiliation have applied team skills through a combination of learning and personal experience. The PMO should provide guidance regarding preferred team skills, including consideration of the following:

- *Leadership:* All project team members — as each progresses from project team member, to project task leader, to project manager and higher in the project management environment — should be aware of their individual leadership styles, comprehend the influences and impacts of other styles, and learn to apply effective leadership techniques.
- *Interpersonal skills:* Individuals contribute to project team development when they demonstrate capability to work effectively with other team members. Interpersonal skills often tend to be relegated to second-class status compared with competency in primary

technical or professional disciplines. The nature of project team-work necessitates that the PMO introduce a renewed emphasis on interpersonal skills in such areas as:
- Effective communication
- Interpersonal conflict resolution
- Team problem solving
- Consensus building
- Group dynamics

■ *Work/professional-enhancement skills:* The PMO should consider endorsing and providing skill-development opportunities in the following extended-capability areas:
- Time management
- Stress management
- Supervision
- Decision making
- Meeting management

The PMO can address these important areas of team development through a variety of means, including some that have presumably already been established in other PMO functions, such as training, team building exercises, mentoring and coaching, peer-feedback activities, and access to project management and technical library materials.

Develop Project Manager Tools and Techniques

The PMO can support the project manager's leadership and team development efforts by creating one or more team development tools and techniques that can be applied within the project management environment.

The following are a few examples of such team development tools and techniques:

■ *Team building exercises:* Construct or acquire workshops to achieve team building objectives
■ *Assessment of team development stage:* Develop the means and methods to measure the current stage of project team development, e.g., forming, storming, norming, performing, adjourning, or some other preferred team development stage model
■ *Communication and collaboration assessment:* Develop the means and methods to conduct a formal or informal assessment of project team communication and collaboration effectiveness
■ *Motivational techniques:* Examine and apply motivational techniques applicable to the organizational culture, e.g., group-performance monetary rewards and bonuses, cross-project team

performance indicator tabulation (awards program), and team social events

■ *Team recognition techniques:* Apply current business practices or devise new ways to convey project team recognition and conduct recognition activities

Facilitate Leadership Development

Project management leadership is a critical component of recurring project success. Advanced project management leadership capability is an essential ingredient for recurring success of large and complex projects. To that end, it is imperative that the PMO attend to leadership development within the project management environment. The PMO will need to examine ways to develop individual leadership capability, with consideration for specific leadership training programs, progressive assignments that enable individuals to demonstrate increasing leadership capability, and formal and informal mentoring in the "art and science" of leadership.

The component skills of leadership are identified differently by a variety of practitioners. For the purposes of application within the project management environment, each PMO will have to define desired leadership skills based on the values and culture of the relevant organization, as well as the influences of professional and technical disciplines, industry norms, and requisite skills for individual levels of leadership responsibility.

The following is a list of leadership skills for PMO consideration. Of course, each PMO should examine which are aligned with the needs of the relevant organization and which are appropriate for different levels of performance responsibility, e.g., project executive, project manager, project team member. As well, the PMO can add additional leadership skills not included in this list.

The following four categories of leadership competency and associated skill areas are presented for individual and organizational consideration, and the PMO should select and facilitate their development.

Personal Leadership Skills

Leadership is often said to emerge from within the individual. This competency category is represented by several skills inherent to personal behavior that prepare the individual to develop the self-awareness, confidence, and interactions needed to be an effective leader of others:

■ Interpersonal communication
■ Listening
■ Interpersonal behavior

- Stress management
- Personal and professional ethics
- Awareness of management and leadership style
- Awareness of personality characteristics
- Emotional stability

Process Leadership Skills

Leadership skill in dealing with work processes facilitates reasonable control and influence within the work environment. It also provides a focus on the group leadership needed to achieve results from project team efforts. There are several skill sets that help to accomplish this:

- Motivating
- Team building
- Organizing
- Planning
- Decision making
- Delegating
- Conflict management
- Time management
- Problem solving
- Negotiating
- Meeting management

Business Leadership Skills

The nature of business warrants oversight and direction that drives all project team members and other stakeholders toward achievement of business goals. A few leadership skills will facilitate that effort:

- Strategic perspective
- Derivation of tactical solutions
- Cultural and political awareness
- Diversity management
- Customer relationship management
- Vendor relationship management
- Industry and market knowledge
- Business acumen
- Management of organizational change

Technical Leadership Skills

This category is intentionally separate to show that (a) technical competence alone is not the sole basis for effective leadership and (b) technical leaders sometimes need to address skills in the earlier categories as they progress in their career and advance in the organization. However, technical competence is a distinct factor in overall leadership capability, and it includes varying degrees of competency — from general technical familiarity to technical expert — that can provide the necessary technical leadership skills for project and business efforts.

- Specialized technical and professional knowledge
- Technical and professional certification
- Presentation skills (e.g., preparing and presenting abbreviated topic content)
- Effective writing (e.g., technical reports, white papers and manuscripts, correspondence)
- Effective speaking (e.g., conveying concepts, achieving buy-in, making announcements)

Monitor Project Team Performance

The PMO's responsibilities to the relevant organization warrant an ongoing examination of project team performance, with particular attention to reviewing the effectiveness of project team development activities and initiatives.

The following subsections present three recommended activities to assist the PMO in planning and accomplishing project team performance monitoring.

Assess Team Dynamics

The PMO should establish a formal or informal method of examining the activities and interactions of the project team members as a means to determine strengths and weaknesses encountered by the particular composition of the team. Aspects of team dynamics to identify could include:

- Observed or measured project team "stage of development"
- Frequency and type of discernable favorable behavior (e.g., collaboration, effective communication, listening)
- Frequency and type of discernable ineffective behavior (e.g., personality conflicts, disagreements, disgruntlement, adverse emotional reaction)

- Situations of demonstrated leadership by individual team members (e.g., consensus building, encouraging and facilitating others' achievements, volunteering for special or additional duties that contribute to project success)
- Situations of demonstrated indifference by individual team members (e.g., withdrawal from team activities, frustration, limited active participation, missed deadlines)
- Variation of project team member responses to project manager leadership and management styles
- Variation of project team member personality traits demonstrated in the project management environment

The PMO can use this type of examination to ascertain how well project team members work together, perhaps identifying preferred project team composition for future efforts. As well, the PMO can evaluate formal and informal assessment findings to prescribe team activities and team development solutions for use by the project manager in creating a more effective work group.

This type of assessment should be pursued from a positive perspective — a focus on making the project team more effective rather than a practice to identify poor performance. To that end, such an assessment of team dynamics may be transparent to project team members.

Examine Team Effectiveness

This activity is primarily assigned to the PMO because of its cross-project alignment. An examination of project team effectiveness looks at the "hard numbers" of project performance: cost, schedule, and resource utilization. This normally comes out of routine and recurring project reporting and control activities. However, in the context of this PMO function, the next step is to contrast the results of project team dynamics assessments with project performance results.

From this examination, the PMO should be able to identify indicators in the following areas:

- Relationship of project team "stage of development" with project progress and timely achievement of deliverables, including quality of deliverables and extent of rework
- Characteristics of effective individual and team behaviors in the project management environment, in terms of contributions to project success
- Impacts of project team dynamics on customer satisfaction and acceptance of project deliverables

■ Implications of vendor and contractor participation on project teams, in terms of results from cohesive involvement or independent activity

The PMO can define additional indicators to examine project, technical, and business aspects of project team effectiveness. All indicators can be analyzed to gain a better understanding of which project teams are most effective based on the group dynamics in effect. Then the PMO, in collaboration with project managers, can create team composition models and construct team development programs to maximize the strengths and minimize the weaknesses of all teams working within the project management environment.

Conduct Team Improvement Activities

The PMO can use results of project team performance assessments and analyses to determine areas that warrant improvement and work with project managers, individually and collectively, to plan and conduct team improvement activities.

Team improvement activities can be applied in response to assessment findings, as appropriate to the culture within the relevant organization. The following list identifies several solutions that can be considered for implementation within the project management environment:

■ *Training:* Individual and group training courses (including on-line learning) can be provided to offer insight and understanding into group dynamics and interpersonal skills.
■ *Team spirit exercises:* Activities focused on team building can be conducted to promote personal interactions for the purpose of reducing or eliminating "drudgery" and instead concentrating on team spirit and enthusiasm. This activity area can be a formal facilitator-led event or an informal social event.
■ *Lessons learned:* Appropriate "lessons learned" sessions could be conducted as ad hoc or facilitator-led events to obtain team member feedback and discussion of future direction that the team can take to reduce or remove ineffective group behavior. The "lessons learned" aspect of this activity prompts participants to consider the impacts incurred and presumably to address team interactions, including processes, to rectify situations encountered.
■ *Self-evaluation/self assessment:* Individuals and groups can be provided opportunities to examine the dynamics and impacts of personal and group behavior, group processes, and the general effectiveness of each. There are a significant number of different

survey and assessment instruments that can be obtained for use in this type of activity.

- *Team member role reviews:* Team member responsibility and authority may need to be examined to clarify individual roles on the project team. This activity is conducted to identify where role ambiguity or uncertainty is creating blockages in project teamwork progression. This is an activity that can be performed informally by the project manager or more formally with PMO, mentor, or facilitator assistance, and it can include discussion and deliberation with individual team members. Results of this examination are provided to individuals or the project team for action, as appropriate.

- *Mentoring/coaching/counseling:* This activity can have either an individual focus or a group focus, as warranted by the situation at hand. Mentoring and coaching offer a personalized approach to interpersonal skill development when provided as a one-on-one activity. Conversely, counseling activities tend to be viewed as placing responsibility for corrective action on the individual, per discussion of the problem to be rectified. The project manager, with the support of PMO guidance and recommendations, will normally conduct counseling for project team members.

- *Technical qualification examination:* The project manager or the PMO conducts this activity to gain insight to problems that could be caused by inadequate technical skill of one or more project team members. In this activity, several individual performance indicators can be examined, including the capability to handle the assigned workload, the competency to perform technical tasks, and the ability to manage and meet work schedules and deadlines. Identified weaknesses must be addressed with the individual to determine whether the person is underqualified for the position (i.e., needs more skills training and experience to perform the assigned work) or is not achieving results at the present level of qualification (i.e., factors other than personal competency are affecting performance).

- *Executive/senior management intervention:* The primary aim of this activity is to demonstrate senior level interest in removing roadblocks to effective project team performance. Senior manager appearances and comments in the project management environment, and in association with a particular project team, is one means of reinforcing business interest in the project at hand and conveying the need to immediately resolve any disruptive team conditions or interactions that threaten project success.

Of course, many of these activities can be used as proactive team building and team development measures. Their early use will preclude the need for later implementation to rectify or correct weak project team interactions and reduced project team performance.

POSTSCRIPT FOR THE SMALLER PMO

The role of the smaller PMO in this function is to provide as much support as possible to the project manager, who ultimately has responsibility for project team development. To that end, there are three primary activities that the smaller PMO can pursue.

- *Project manager leadership training:* The PMO can identify training course availability for project managers to enhance their personal leadership effectiveness. This activity can range from simply identifying training courses that individual project managers can pursue on their own (a useful approach for an environment with just a few key project managers) to arranging on-site course delivery (for organizations with a larger cadre of project managers). The focus of this training should be on leadership skills needed within the project management environment. However, other training classes dealing with team building and interpersonal skill development will also be useful. As well, the PMO may want to consider including training opportunities for project team members who are advancing in responsibility within the project management environment.
- *Team development process guidance:* The PMO will likely be developing or maintaining at least a fundamental set of project management processes, if not a complete project management life cycle methodology. It can then introduce team development guidance into the established project management process at the point where project team formation is conducted. In particular, methods for developing team cohesion, specifying individual team member authority and responsibility, and establishing personal commitments to the project work effort should be included in the process.
- *Resolution of distressed team performance:* The PMO, as a centralized business function, becomes a repository for both general management practices and lessons learned in the project management environment. It therefore plays a role in collecting, developing, and providing remedies for distressed project teams. This can be either in the form of content made available to the project manager and project team in the project management library or in the form of PMO-led interventions in project team meetings per advance collaboration with the project manager.

The primary objective of the smaller PMO is to make each project manager successful in managing team interactions and performance.

IV

TECHNICAL SUPPORT

13

MENTORING

Mentoring provides the means to impart the art and science of modern project management through transfer of a mentor's knowledge, skills, and experience to a protégé or group of protégés in the project environment. In most project management environments, the prominent protégés are project managers and project team members. The mentors are highly skilled and generally senior level individuals who bring to bear their broad experience in project management, and possibly professional certification, in the guidance and assistance they provide to protégés.

Mentoring within the project environment presents a powerful means to transfer not just project management skills and knowledge, but also leadership techniques, business values, and professional ethics. A strong project management mentoring program is an excellent way for the PMO to support professional development for project managers and promote the consistent use of sound practices across project teams.

This project management "mentoring" function enables the PMO to:

- Promote and demonstrate use of preferred or best practices in project management
- Endorse professional development standards through mentor qualification
- Identify mentoring opportunities advantageous to business and project purposes
- Provide quick-response, expert guidance to support real-time project management needs
- Facilitate introductions of new project managers through recruitment and advancement
- Build confidence and camaraderie among project managers and project team members

Project management mentoring can be a significant investment within the relevant organization. Sometimes the returns on this investment are almost immediate. Other times, the realization of project management mentoring benefits takes a longer time as the protégé gains confidence in applying new tools, techniques, and perspectives learned from the mentor. The benefits to be realized are in the individual professional development that occurs through the mentoring processes undertaken. A project manager becomes more capable on the current project and uses this expanded capability on the next project.

The success of project management mentoring certainly depends on each mentor's personal skill. However, success also relies on the participation, interest, and learning abilities of the project manager and project team member protégés in the mentoring process. To that end, it is important to note that the mentor is not assigned to perform project management. The mentor should not direct the project team, assume project outcome responsibility, or make project management decisions. These activities must remain with the project manager, who is ultimately responsible for project success. Rather, the project management mentor provides advice, guidance, experience-based recommendations, facilitation, concept support, and personal encouragement.

The project management mentoring program should not lead to undue reliance on project management mentors or their availability. Project management mentors are needed only until either the protégé's individual need for mentoring support subsides or until the supported activity, event, or situation prompting mentor involvement has passed. A mentor's assignment should always be viewed as a temporary one, and successful mentors will always be working themselves out of a job on every assignment.

This function requires senior management support and endorsement as a primary success factor. As a minimum demonstration of support, a senior level sponsor is needed to establish and maintain a viable project management mentoring program.

PROJECT ENVIRONMENT INTERFACE CONCEPTS

The presence of project management mentors in the project environment is representative of a concerted effort to reach for advanced maturity and performance excellence in project management. It draws attention to the level of regard that project management elicits as a professional discipline within the relevant organization.

Establishing a project management mentoring program enables the PMO to facilitate:

- *A quick and focused application of project management skills*: An assigned mentor will help the project manager and project team to begin using appropriate project management skills quickly and correctly. The mentor can guide the project manager toward the practices and techniques that are most appropriate for the current phase of the project and the current stage of team development. This eliminates wasted time on inappropriate and nonproductive activities.

- *Introduction of new techniques and best practices*: Because mentors are professional, experienced project managers, they are continually updating their knowledge and skills, and they bring that expertise to the protégés they serve. Their independent study of best practices particularly makes mentors valuable players when new tools, advanced techniques, or revised processes are being introduced into the project environment.

- *Dramatic reduction of trial-and-error approaches*: Too often, new project managers waste time trying things that do not work and then trying something else again and again until they finally come up with the best way to approach a job. Mentors can guide and coach project managers in applying the right techniques at the right time, thus achieving the right results the first time.

- *A quick and focused start for new projects*: A qualified mentor can help the project team overcome the "what are we supposed to do first?" syndrome that is often encountered by ad hoc teams. Mentors know the process for moving a project through its entire life cycle and can particularly provide an accurate perspective on startup activities.

- *Early development of project manager confidence*: Mentors help increase a project manager's self-confidence when they demonstrate how to take advantage of new knowledge and skills. Increased self-confidence leads project managers to take active ownership of their projects at an earlier stage in their professional development.

- *Maximum return on investments in training*: Mentors encourage and assist project managers and project team members in applying the new skills and knowledge that they received in the classroom or other type of training program. They facilitate transfer and translation of concepts and principles learned in the classroom directly to the project workplace for immediate application and value to the project effort.

- *Maximum return on investments in project management software*: The practice of installing a software application package and then leaving it for casual use, underuse, or no use by project personnel is revisited. The mentor helps project managers and project team members take advantage of the full value of the features and capabilities of project management software application packages. Mentors provide guidance in using the software to perform the mechanical work of project management, leaving project managers with more time to actually manage the project.

Project management mentors apply established standards and help "set the goals bar" for individual success and achievement that characterizes the project management environment.

BUSINESS ENVIRONMENT INTERFACE CONCEPTS

Project management mentors are resources for new and developing project managers. They provide coaching, serve as sources of information, and apply experience to guide and reassure project managers in their application of skill and knowledge. The mentoring effort ensures that no project becomes an experiment in failure and that no project manager is tested to a level of uncertainty or incompetence. This inherently ensures that business objectives are consistently achieved, even through the efforts of newer project managers, both those who are just joining the organization as well as those who are advancing upward to the project manager ranks.

Project management mentors, in working with protégés from across the organization, gain a business perspective that few other senior managers will see — the interaction and productivity of cross-functional teams. Mentors often will observe and in some cases facilitate cross-functional project management activities that enable them to discern where strengths and weaknesses may lie relative to business unit influences. This information is not necessarily for compilation and reporting back to the business unit or to functional and senior management. Rather, it is for the mentor to take steps that encourage continuation of practices that are good for business and to rectify situations that reduce business effectiveness immediately, at the personal level, and within the context of the respected mentor-protégé relationship.

Of course, the mentor's role in the organization does facilitate the identification and exchange of such information as recurring project management business issues, resource utilization indicators, and project performance trends. Mentors can and should compile this type of information for broader examination and discussion, when appropriate.

As well, the project management mentor, as a senior professional, properly holds responsibility for advising other senior managers and executives in the art and science of project management. This is particularly valuable for executives who have project management oversight respon-sibility but limited formal training in the discipline and its recent advances. They need the advice and guidance of project management mentors on the details and intricacies of project management as input to their project management support and business decisions.

MENTORING ACTIVITIES ACROSS THE PMO CONTINUUM

The progression of the "mentoring" function along the PMO competency continuum is characterized by increasing use of internally qualified senior project management mentors, combined with more personalized mentor-ing services as the project environment matures.

Table 13.1 provides an overview of the range of prescribed PMO project management mentoring activities according to each level in the PMO competency continuum.

The *project office* tends to be the primary user of the mentoring services provided by a higher level PMO. In the absence of a higher level PMO, it may independently acquire the services of a project management mentor, usually on an outsourcing basis. As well, the head of the project office — often a senior project manager — may be called upon to serve as a mentor to other project managers.

Mid-range PMO levels of the continuum have the responsibility of designing and establishing a mentoring support program that fits the needs of the relevant organization. This includes at least a fundamental capability to provide project management mentoring support to new project man-agers. This level of support evolves to dedicated and personalized men-toring of all project managers as PMO capability matures. In mature management project environments, mentoring services can be extended to include one-on-one transfer of skill and knowledge related to business issues, leadership development, and individual project manager goal achievement as mentor-protégé pairs become more defined.

The *center of excellence* develops, recommends, and implements policy for project management mentoring. It manages an advanced mentoring program that includes recurring evaluation of mentor effectiveness and mentoring program achievements.

The PMO's project management "mentoring" function provides project managers and project team members with access to qualified and expe-rienced senior managers in the project management environment.

MENTORING FUNCTION MODEL

The PMO's project management "mentoring" function model prompts considerations for how and when to use seasoned and skilled senior level

Table 13.1 Range of Mentoring Activities across the PMO Continuum

Project Office	Basic PMO	Standard PMO	Advanced PMO	Center of Excellence
Requests and uses available to project management mentors to assist the project manager and project team in their achievement of project objectives	Introduces project management mentoring on an as-needed, ad hoc basis ■ Mentoring focus is on support of critical project management practices ■ Mentor source is primarily external consultants ■ Mentoring process tends to be informal	Establishes a more formal project management mentoring program ■ Menu of mentor support services is developed for project life cycle support ■ Mentor source includes internal and external consultants ■ Mentoring process is more formal	Develops expanded scope of project management mentoring activities ■ Mentor source is primarily internal senior staff ■ Mentor-protégé pair alignment with individual project managers evolves ■ Mentor services are expanded to include personal and professional development for project managers	Performs mentoring program oversight and guidance ■ Policies and guidance for mentor programs is developed ■ Mentor program evaluation and examination is accomplished

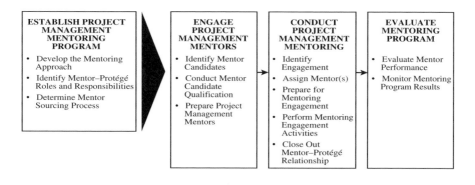

Figure 13.1 "Mentoring" Function Model

project managers to assist other project managers, project teams, and project executives who are new to the professional discipline or new to the organization. This model offers options for a formal or informal program structure for mentoring and for the scope of mentoring a PMO can pursue.

The primary activities of the PMO's project management "mentoring" function model are depicted in Figure 13.1. Each activity is described in the following subsections.

Establish Project Management Mentoring Program

The PMO should collaborate with senior managers in the project environment, first to gain their insight on the value and purpose of project management mentoring, and then to solicit their ideas on the extent to which the PMO should pursue the "mentoring" function. This collaboration effort can be an informal survey or discussion with individuals and groups, or a more formal functional design activity. As well, the PMO should prepare and distribute its own recommendations to set the frame of reference for discussions. When sufficient input has been received as guidance, the PMO can begin its work to establish a viable project management mentoring program, as outlined in the following subsections.

Develop the Mentoring Approach

Project management mentoring should be recognized for value that goes beyond the simple measures of time spent to conduct mentoring and the immediate benefits to the project effort. Although these elements are important, in mentoring program design the PMO must ensure that a larger purpose is served, i.e., that the organization develops increased capability in the performance of project management through the broad transfer of skill and knowledge in the project management environment. To a certain extent, this even transcends the discipline of project management. Therefore, in preparing an approach to project management mentoring, the PMO will first have to consider the type of mentor-protégé relationships that will be pursued. Then it can examine how to initiate and conduct project management mentoring that best fits in the current project management environment.

Define the Mentor-Protégé Relationship

The assignment and use of mentors in the project management environment is an excellent way for the relevant organization to gain the greatest leverage from its investments in project management training, methodology development, and other professional development activities. The PMO must determine the depth and extent of the mentor-protégé relationships that will be created as a result of establishing a project management mentoring program.

The professional interaction between mentor and protégé (project manager) or group of protégés (project team members) is an advanced one that provides for one-on-one collaboration, discussion, and information exchanges. The following three subsections describe the progressive types of relationships that the PMO should consider in defining this interaction between mentor and protégé within the project environment.

Project Relationship.   The protégé can expect to gain guidance, knowledge, and skills to succeed on the current project. The primary responsibility of the mentor is to convey experience and insight to assist the protégé in the accomplishment of project objectives. This is usually done by providing personal instruction and facilitation for the protégé to achieve hands-on learning and understanding of the application of effective project management practices. This relationship tends to be more formal because of the focus on specific support objectives, and it is generally temporary, as completion of work efforts normally tend to discontinue the relationship. However, the benefits of the learning experience can continue long after the protégé and mentor have parted ways, as the protégé further develops professional habits and uses self-empowerment resulting from the mentoring received. In some cases, the mentor can be recalled at a subsequent time to repeat or reinforce information and practices.

This is probably the most common type of mentor-protégé relationship across most organizations and industries. It tends to be cost effective and can be applied in a just-in-time manner to meet specific project or project manager needs. This type of mentor-protégé relationship also enables use of either internal senior project managers or external senior project management consultants as mentors.

Practice Relationship. The protégé can expect all of the mentoring support identified above on an as needed, project-by-project basis. However, in this practice level relationship, the protégé, normally a project manager, also will receive extended and more personalized mentor support. In this type of mentor-protégé relationship, the mentor helps the protégé address individual learning of project management skills and competencies, and provides advice and counsel on related career development needs, possibly including preparation of a personal career development plan. As well, mentoring at this relationship level should include expanded topics of consideration such as leadership, customer service, vendor management, etc.

This mentoring relationship also would be applicable to project team members, particularly those individuals seeking self-improvement and progression within the project management environment. Of course, this works best when the relevant organization also provides a project manager career ladder to pursue. However, professional development for project managers and project team members also can be accomplished on an individual basis and without formal career progression within the organization.

In this type of relationship, the protégé has ongoing access to mentoring support. There may be a mentor request and scheduling process, but that should not be unduly complicated. As well, the PMO's pool of mentors that are made available to assist project managers can be formed in one of two ways. In the first approach, all mentors in the PMO pool are available to all project managers. Each mentor is trained to deliver the full range of mentoring services from project support to individual competency development. The second approach provides similarly qualified mentors, but now they are assigned to specific project managers. This enables each mentor to provide dedicated assistance and support to the protégé. In this type of ongoing relationship, the PMO maximizes the protégé's benefits by providing a trusted coach to use as a "sounding board" for ideas, issues, and career-planning deliberation. Normally, such mentors would be internal senior project managers. External senior project management consultants could perform some of these mentor duties if engaged for extended periods.

Professional Relationship. The protégé can expect the same mentoring support and guidance as for the previously described project and practice types of mentor-protégé relationships. However, this type of relationship is likely to be unique in most project environments because of its expanded focus. It addresses not only project management competency, but also business competency. This mentor-protégé relationship is one that prepares the protégé for advancement within the relevant organization. It brings to bear mentoring that includes a full range of business and professional development topics — accounting and finance, global business development, business unit management, and other topics relevant to the emerging executive.

Mentors in this type of relationship obviously must have appropriate experience and positions within the relevant organization. The PMO may have to consider looking outside the project management environment to identify qualified senior managers as mentors for this advanced type of relationship, particularly if that project management environment is itself still maturing toward becoming a separate business entity. However, such mentors should be identified from within the relevant organization.

Structure the Mentoring Engagement

It is sometimes said that there is no mentoring process, per se. Each mentoring engagement is unique and tailored to the needs of the organization and the protégés involved. However, there are some common activities among all mentoring engagements that require conscious deliberation and planning by the PMO. The PMO should construct a standard process for examining the following or similar items to provide structure for each mentoring engagement:

- *What is the purpose of mentoring support?*: There is frequent temptation to view mentors as "more project management bodies" and assign them to active project management roles. While this practice may relieve immediate staff demands or shortfalls, it does nothing to transfer the skills and knowledge of the mentor back into the project management environment. However, due consideration can be given to the fact that in some situations, business decisions must be made to assign a generally highly qualified project management mentor to manage a portion of a high-profile project for which there is a particularly urgent need for the mentor's skills. The PMO should establish the mentor's purpose for each engagement that is supported.
- *Who are the protégés that the mentor(s) will support?*: It is important to specifically identify the recipients of mentoring support: project managers, project teams, project executives. In particular, it is important to ensure that these individuals are aware of their roles as protégés to enable the professional mentor-protégé relationship to be established early in the assignment. It also allows

the mentor to prepare for the engagement by knowing who the protégé is in advance.

- *How many mentors are needed?*: The PMO must ultimately assess needs and compile metrics to determine the level of mentor coverage needed for various types of projects and types of protégés. However, typical assignments have indicated one mentor can support between four and ten project managers. This includes direct support to the individual project manager and general support to the associated project team. The exact number of mentors needed relies prominently on an examination of the capability of project managers, the nature and size of their projects, project visibility and urgency, and the stage of project team development. A rule of thumb is to start conservatively, with one or a small number of mentors for the number of projects and needs at hand. Additional mentors can be assigned as needed.
- *What is the planned duration of mentoring support?*: The intended period of mentoring support must be identified to maximize the effectiveness of mentoring services. The protégé must know how long to expect mentoring support as part of planning and scheduling the required mentor's time, and as a matter of reliance on mentor availability. The mentor must know the anticipated duration of the engagement to properly plan and conduct support activities that fit within the allotted time frame and avoid partially completed mentoring efforts. Mentoring support schedules can always be adjusted if the engagement is completed earlier or later than contemplated, but with awareness of impacts against the original schedule. To that end, the PMO may schedule mentors for successive assignments, so planning each engagement facilitates mentor availability for subsequent assignments.
- *What skill or knowledge will be conveyed by the mentor to the protégé?*: This may be a difficult question to answer, and it may be deferred until the mentor arrives to provide support. However, early determination of this information will enable the mentor to better anticipate the nature of the intervention. Moreover, such information could help the mentor identify needs for technical publications or other references for use as mentoring-engagement support materials.

The PMO should develop a structured approach to project management mentoring engagements that includes indications of what mentor preparation activities are needed, the time frame in which mentoring will be performed, and the protégé audience to be encountered.

Develop Mentoring Support Activities

The PMO must identify the types of mentoring activities that it will provide. Mentoring support options should cover the full range of project management topics, consistent with the PMO's capability and maturity to conduct project management and deliver mentoring support. Advanced PMOs also may extend mentoring support into areas of professional development for project managers and project team members. As well, mentoring support can be used to provide advice and counsel to executives, senior managers, and other stakeholders that are in or interface with the project management environment.

The PMO should identify the type of mentoring support requested or required for each mentoring engagement. The assigned mentor uses this information to establish the scope of the engagement. Then, the mentor should begin each assignment by working with the protégé (or groups of protégés) to review the relationship purpose, outline how they will work together, and identify and agree upon what they expect to accomplish. The mentor will normally take the lead on this initial collaboration activity.

The following are several types of mentoring support that the PMO can provide in association with this PMO function. It should communicate those mentoring support options it makes available to the project management environment of the relevant organization after it has established the capability to deliver each:

- *Project management competency development*: The mentor helps the protégé to develop skill and capability in applying established practices and principles of effective project management. This includes assisting the protégé in performing process steps and using tools within the context of project management activities. This can be accomplished as a one-on-one effort or in a workshop setting for a group of protégés.
- *Group facilitation*: The mentor either will help protégés, particularly project managers, to plan and conduct project team activities, or the mentor may personally facilitate those activities. The latter is more common at the beginning of the mentoring effort and could lessen as the protégé gains confidence and capability under the mentor's guidance. This type of mentoring is prevalent in support of project and solution planning activities, project team formation and development activities, progress review and collaboration meetings, project close out and lessons-learned feedback sessions, and some customer/stakeholder meetings.
- *Protégé review and critique/collaboration*: The mentor will review and critique protégé performance as a natural part of most

mentoring engagements. The protégé should recognize the value of feedback as an important professional development experience. At times, mentoring support may be requested to perform specific reviews of project management performance or project management deliverables. This is an effort that is separated from review of technical deliveries.

■ *Project assessment*: The mentor will provide guidance and assistance to assess project progress and achievement of project objectives. This can be done upon project completion or at interim points in the project management life cycle. Similarly, mentors can participate in departmental or organizational assessments of project management capability and maturity, particularly serving as experts for analysis and interpretation of assessment results.

■ *Executive counsel*: The mentor will meet with executives and senior managers to facilitate their understanding of modern project management concepts and to collaborate on strategies for developing a comprehensive project management practice within the relevant organization.

■ *Professional development*: The mentor in this case is uniquely qualified to assist individuals in their planning and performance of professional development activities. Generally, the protégé is assigned within an advanced project management environment in which there is a discernable project management career path. To that end, the mentor will provide advice and guidance regarding the protégé's pursuit of project management training, technical training, professional certification, career planning, and other professional advancement activities.

The PMO's capability to deliver different types of mentoring support will be a factor of the skill and competencies of available resources, of which senior project managers and senior project management consultants are the prominent groups. The PMO should consider each of the above mentoring support options and develop those within its capability. Other mentoring support options needed by the relevant organization can be added by the PMO as necessary.

Identify Mentor-Protégé Roles and Responsibilities

The PMO's work to establish a project management mentoring program should clearly define the respective roles and responsibilities of the primary participants, the mentor and the protégé. This enables the participants to understand the activity and become involved in the give and take of the ensuing professional interaction.

The PMO can use the following suggested content for mentoring program roles and responsibilities as guidance for creating its own. These roles and responsibilities should be communicated within the project management environment, but particularly to project managers and project team members about to encounter the mentoring experience. Mentors will gain understanding of their roles and responsibilities in associated mentor training activities and will review them prior to each mentoring engagement.

The roles and responsibilities for project management mentors are presented first, followed by the roles and responsibilities for protégés.

Mentor Roles and Responsibilities

The mentor brings to the engagement requisite knowledge, experience, and a commitment to the professional practice of project management. The primary responsibility of the mentor is to help the protégé focus on what is important in the context of performing project management. The mentor helps the protégé to identify and achieve project objectives and, at times, personal and professional goals. Mentors are particularly observant to identify when protégés hit "roadblocks" and appear unable to move forward to the next step or activity. Mentoring interventions are applied to reduce and remove such problems and to allow appropriate progress to be achieved.

A mentor is a seasoned professional project manager who serves as an advocate of the protégé and a role model in the discipline of project management. The mentor helps solve immediate problems alongside the protégé but, more importantly, helps the protégé to learn concepts and apply new project management skills and knowledge that enables the protégé to carry on independently in future endeavors. The mentor generally works with an individual project manager, although the mentor also will work with associated team members to help them improve the team's overall performance.

The professional demands placed on mentors require them to act in various capacities in their interactions with protégés. Some prevalent mentoring roles include: coach, counselor, teacher, adviser, facilitator, guide, master, expert, leader, and dedicated project management professional.

The PMO should devise its own set of mentor responsibility guidelines, consistent with organizational culture and needs within the project environment. Consider the following list of suggested mentor responsibilities. Mentors will:

- *Set and maintain realistic expectations*: The mentor will normally be the one who controls the pace of the mentoring relationship, especially at the outset. In this capacity, the mentor has to be the arbiter of what can reasonably be expected from the protégé. This includes managing expectations for the relationship, for protégé achievement, and for mentor involvement. Caution must be used to avoid setting expectations too high, as that will only frustrate all involved. Conversely, setting expectations too low wastes time and causes similar frustration. The mentor is ultimately responsible for fine-tuning and managing expectations in the mentor-protégé relationship.

- *Be reasonably available to assist with protégé needs*: The mentor should ensure that the protégé understands how to make contact, and the mentor should be reasonably available to meet the protégé's planned and unplanned needs. The ground rules for what is "reasonable" availability should be mutually established. This should be based on the scope of the mentoring engagement and with regard for the mentor's additional professional duties and responsibility to other protégés.

- *Be on time for protégé meetings and appointments*: Protégés are professional project managers whose time is critical and in high demand. They should be treated accordingly. Being on time for meetings and appointments with protégés is an indication of mentor reliability. It also demonstrates respect for the protégé, which is a vital characteristic of an effective mentoring relationship.

- *Maintain appropriate frequency of contact with the protégé*: The mentor will have to apply good judgment in determining the frequency of contact with the protégé. This will often be a challenge. The mentor must be available to the protégé, yet must allow the protégé room to grow. The mentor must try to find the right timing and schedule to both develop the relationship and provide time for the protégé to apply learning from the previous contact with the mentor.

- *Provide empathetic listening and support*: The mentor must demonstrate understanding of the protégé's particular situation, otherwise the protégé is unlikely to participate fully in the mentoring activity. Mentors, as coaches, should discern when to provide a friendly ear to protégé issues and concerns. The mentor should lend emotional support, when appropriate.

- *Be courteous and considerate*: Application of "the golden rule" is a desired trait to carry into the project management environment.

- *Be open to protégé's needs and opinions*: The ultimate purpose of mentoring is to meet the protégé's needs. Therefore the mentor must always keep those needs in mind and also recognize that those needs will evolve and change as the protégé develops professionally. Furthermore, the protégé, like the mentor, is a professional and thus will have opinions or ideas that must be duly considered, evaluated, and adopted if appropriate. In particular, mentors should recognize that the protégé's previous experience has led to the formulation of opinions that have value equal to the mentor's recommendations. In situations of "deadlock," the path provided by the protégé should be strongly considered.

■ *Distinguish different protégés*: A mentor will typically work with several protégés at one time. It is important that mentors do not characterize each protégé as similar to another and then work with them from a set of common generalities. Every protégé is an individual with separate bases of learning and professional experience. By keeping the distinctions of every protégé separate, the mentor will be able to build a strong relationship with each.

■ *Be willing to apply extra effort*: The project manager's job is usually one of continuous extra effort. This may require mentoring support at off hours or late time frames. To facilitate achievement of effective mentoring services, the mentor may have to be flexible in schedule at times. As well, the mentor, as a role model, must be willing to demonstrate extra effort that helps achieve mentoring relationship objectives.

■ *Alert protégés to issues and opportunities*: Mentoring is not a passive role. The mentor, applying advanced skill and experience, must always be on the lookout for impending issues and problems or be ready to apply insight to an approaching opportunity. Per the nature of the engagement, the mentor should intervene immediately when an urgent reaction is necessary. However, the mentor also can provide indicators and allow time for the protégé to discover problems, issues, and opportunities when possible.

■ *Share success and failure experiences*: Learning can be a frustrating process. Sometimes protégés encounter mistakes that lead to a reduction in self-confidence. Protégés appreciate hearing that the lessons they are now learning are par for the course, and that the mentor's professional development was not so dissimilar. The mentor should use personal experience — both successes and failures — as a teaching tool that helps to expedite the protégé's professional development.

■ *Give and receive constructive feedback*: Feedback is a critical element of the mentoring process. The mentor should provide consistent and frequent feedback on protégé performance and progress. The approach to this information exchange may be gentle and tactful or, if appropriate, somewhat forceful. Of course, the mentor also should be poised to receive replies and feedback from the protégé. This will help the mentor to identify and understand the protégé's more prominent needs. It will also enable the mentor to formulate the most effective approach for interactions and to apply any behavioral adjustments needed in the relationship.

The PMO should deliberate and decide what the mentor responsibilities will be in the relevant organization. With consideration for the list above, the PMO can begin to examine mentor responsibilities by asking the question, "If I were the protégé, what would I be looking for from *me?*"

Protégé Roles and Responsibilities

The protégé must be an active and highly involved participant for the mentor-protégé relationship to be successful. Sometimes, the mentor's initial efforts are too focused merely on developing the protégé's involvement in the mentoring engagement. The creation of protégé roles and responsibilities should help to reduce the likelihood of this initial mentoring support constraint. This is important because both protégé and mentor need to step off smartly and quickly to obtain maximum benefit from the interaction.

A protégé is usually both a student of project management and a business or technical professional. Some protégés may have years or decades of experience in their technical fields or business practices, but little formal exposure to the concepts and content of modern project management. Therefore, it is challenging for many such protégés to pursue new professional directions or to consider alternative approaches to their work efforts. The protégé's role in the project management environment is one that requires examination of what can be learned and applied to achieve new successes.

The PMO must construct and communicate the responsibilities of protégés in a mentoring engagement. It can begin with consideration of the following suggested protégé responsibilities. Protégés will:

- *Welcome the mentor's interest and guidance*: Protégés distinctly have professional experience and many have achieved senior manager status through their career-long professional efforts. The mentoring experience is not intended to dismiss or diminish the protégé's professional advancements. Rather, mentoring support is usually arranged to provide insight and guidance in new areas not yet encountered or experienced by the protégé. For example, the protégé, as a senior project manager, may fully understand a particular project management concept or practice, but that same individual may have limited experience in facilitating a team to perform that activity. The mentor will assist. Likewise, project managers who are new to the discipline or new to the organization may require the insight that a project management mentor can provide. Protégés ranging across the full spectrum of professional experience and seniority should recognize that resistance to the mentor's efforts would likely cause the engagement to fail. Instead, protégés are encouraged to welcome an assigned mentor and to draw every benefit from the mentoring relationship.

- *Be proactive in learning*: The protégé should be proactive in taking responsibility for all learning activities and not wait to be led to new knowledge and skill. The protégé should use the mentor as a learning resource, actively soliciting specific knowledge or insight from the mentor when needed.

- *Accept and react to constructive feedback*: The protégé should be open to constructive feedback and accept information that the mentor provides without interpreting it as a personal evaluation. Feedback is the primary deliverable of the mentoring engagement, and it is a key mechanism by which a protégé will learn to apply new skills and knowledge. Likewise, the protégé can provide feedback to the mentor regarding how well the protégé understands and accepts the guidance provided, and what will be done to apply the content of what is learned from the mentor.

- *Identify and examine needs and deficiencies*: The protégé must be open and sincere in the identification of needs and deficiencies related to the purpose of the mentoring relationship. The protégé should work with the mentor to jointly examine causes and formulate solutions for improvement. The protégé must be open and honest in this examination in order to gain maximum benefit from the mentoring support. In the absence of openness, the mentor can proceed only on what is observed or perceived. The protégé's openness will close the information gap in that approach and allow the mentor to likewise openly share personal, experience-based solutions.

- *Provide mentoring process feedback*: Protégés should share with mentors their perceptions about the mentoring relationship and process. In particular, they should frequently review the expectations set early in the mentoring engagement. Protégés can and should share personal reactions to the mentoring process as a means of improving the mentor-protégé relationship and maximizing the opportunity for a successful mentoring engagement. Issues and concerns should be discussed and resolved for mutual benefit. Any solution that allows the mentor to continue providing support and the protégé to be successful in the learning experience is a good resolution of issues and concerns.

- *Be proactive in contributing ideas*: The protégé should use the mentor as a sounding board to test ideas and premises that can be applied to the work effort. The protégé should particularly demonstrate this capacity after several learning experiences with the mentor. Initially, the mentor may solicit the protégé's ideas. As the relationship matures and the protégé develops new skills and knowledge from learning, the protégé should be proactive in contributing concepts, ideas, and solutions to the work at hand.
- *Address failures along with successes*: The protégé should make every effort to build confidence in the mentor to enable discussions regarding professional successes and failures. Recognizing that the extensive experience of the mentor is a result of the mentor having similar personal experience, this information sharing should be viewed as an opportunity to learn from the mentor's failures and successes — without having to personally repeat them as many times in one's own career. As professionals, the protégé and mentor together cannot shirk this responsibility, which is a key element of the mentoring relationship.
- *Facilitate the mentor-protégé relationship*: Protégés comprise half the mentor-protégé equation. They are equal partners with the mentor, and both should be working toward enhancements, improvements, and innovations that influence professional success for the protégé. If the mentor-protégé relationship is to be successful, the protégé must contribute to developing mutual respect, trust, and openness as the foundation for this professional relationship. A viable starting place for such relationship development is a common commitment to the achievement of mutual goals.

Determine Mentor Sourcing Process

The PMO must identify the process by which mentors are assigned to support different project management and protégé needs and activities. Four processes are presented for consideration. The first three processes represent internal sourcing of mentors. The fourth process is for external sourcing of mentors. Each is briefly described in the following subsections.

Create Mentor Positions on the PMO Staff

This approach to mentor sourcing provides for one or more full-time, permanent mentor positions on the PMO staff. The PMO will hire or transfer in qualified senior project managers for this position. The primary responsibilities of this position will be to provide professional mentoring services as prescribed by the PMO.

The assigned mentor(s) also will be available to conduct and administer the PMO's mentor program — for the startup effort and for ongoing management and oversight. The position may even manage one or more of the alternative mentor sourcing activities described below. However, the greatest benefit of this mentor sourcing approach is probably realized by the delivery of highly qualified and dedicated mentoring support to project managers and project team members, not to mention opportunities to provide advice and counsel to senior managers and executives across a full range of project management topics.

The high quality and dedication aspects of this approach are achieved because there is a focus on project management excellence that is inherently built into the position description. The assigned mentor(s) will have the time and the purpose to develop professional self-capability in project management that ultimately will be shared throughout the relevant organization. Mentors assigned to the PMO will be able to fully develop their critical skills of listening, coaching, facilitating, problem solving, etc. They will concentrate on examining ways to apply state-of-the-art practices, conduct reading and research to learn about new and emerging concepts, collaborate with others in the industry and in the project management discipline to share insights and innovation — and then convey all of their knowledge and skill to protégés in the project management environment.

Establish a Rotational Mentor Program

The preferred approach for mentor sourcing is to have senior project managers serve as mentors on a full-time basis. If a permanent PMO staff position is not established, the PMO can consider the alternative approach of selecting and assigning senior project managers as mentors for a specified period of time: three months, six months, or even a year.

The value in this approach is that mentors bring their own personal experiences in the relevant organization to the mentoring relationships. Yet, the full-time nature of the assignment allows each mentor to concentrate on developing the necessary mentoring skills, performing reading and research, and establishing the focus needed to achieve the prescribed mentoring objectives. Then, mentors can return to their primary duties upon completion of "temporary service" in their mentoring role. Ideally, their departure from this temporary assignment is accompanied by adequate recognition and possibly professional advancement that represents the organization's regard for such mentor assignments.

Establish a Pool of Qualified Mentors

The PMO can use this process when sufficiently qualified senior project managers are assigned and available within the relevant organization.

Simply stated, the PMO reviews organizational staffing, identifies candidates for mentor positions, validates their experience and other qualifications, and recruits or otherwise arranges for their assignment to the PMO on a part-time, as-needed basis. Selected participants then remain in standby mode until called upon by the PMO to perform mentoring services.

Participation in the mentor pool may be a collateral duty for selected senior project managers or program managers already in the project management environment. Therefore, caution must be used to separate their primary duties of day-to-day oversight of projects and project managers from their role as mentors. The latter requires a more open and collaborative relationship than is normally associated with a supervisory figure.

This approach to sourcing mentors presents the PMO with the burden of (a) scheduling around the availability of qualified staff to serve as mentors and (b) conducting ongoing recruitment. As well, the part-time nature of the assignment inherently limits the time for individual mentor preparation and participation in each mentoring engagement. The PMO should note that this type of mentor sourcing works best for short-term mentoring assignments. Notwithstanding that consideration, a part-time mentoring capability is better than no capability.

Acquire Senior Project Management Consultant Mentors

This project management mentor source represents acquiring and assigning senior project management mentors from an external consulting firm that has established credentials to provide such project management services. This approach to mentoring particularly warrants consideration when there is no other established mentoring capability in the PMO. It also may be the best solution for the PMO's short-notice, short-term mentoring needs and, arguably, a better approach than part-time internal mentors.

The PMO benefits from this alternative sourcing approach in that external mentors are prequalified senior project managers, and they are ready to perform in the role at the time and place specified by the PMO. As well, they normally do not have the organizational or industry biases that may be associated with internal mentors. These externally sourced mentors are continually in preparation for the technical and interpersonal aspects of mentoring. However, while external mentor sourcing can provide for highly qualified resources, the drawback is that these individuals may not fully understand your organization or your operations at the onset of support. Although most professional consultants will work very hard to gain this information and insight very quickly, expect initial mentoring advice and guidance to have primary focus on generally-accepted project management processes and practices, and not necessarily on your processes and practices.

The PMO's consideration and selection of this mentor sourcing option should include a review of a few business and administrative items, as suggested in the following list:

- Identify and validate the qualifications and credentials of the preferred project management consulting firm in advance of actual need. Begin a relationship with the consulting firm as a matter of setting up the mentoring capability, and possibly use consultants to help define and structure your mentoring program.
- Ensure that the selected firm provides mentoring services that are consistent with the content of any related project management training in the organization and with the project management standards used by the PMO. There should be a focus on the transfer of this knowledge and skill to the participating protégés.
- Establish an agreement or contract for one-time or ongoing project management mentoring support, so as to have qualified mentors "on call" with reasonable advance notification.
- Specify the period of performance, the purpose and scope, and the number of mentors needed for each mentoring engagement. Include this in the agreement or contract, or in a separate statement of work (for attachment to established contracts).
- Specify and discuss any interim and end-of-engagement reporting requirements with the assigned mentor, and consider the recommendations provided. Frequent verbal reports and discussions of progress may be preferred over written engagement reports to optimize the consultant's time.
- Arrange an end-of-engagement feedback meeting with the mentor and the PMO staff and any other appropriate managers to obtain insights from the mentor, discuss lessons learned, and plan any subsequent mentoring support requirements.

The PMO can deliberate and decide the best course of action for mentor sourcing as it plans and establishes the PMO "mentoring" function. The sourcing approach selected will be influenced by the size of the project management environment and by the number of projects in which mentors are needed, by the qualifications of personnel available to serve in a mentoring capacity, by the number of mentors required, and by the funding available for internal or external mentoring support.

A final consideration for the PMO in constructing a project management mentoring solution is the location and placement of mentors. An examination of project environment needs will determine whether the PMO will require mentor travel to dispersed business facilities. If so, this becomes both a logistics management issue and a budget management activity that must be addressed in deciding on the structure and setting up this PMO function.

Engage Project Management Mentors

The PMO is responsible for identifying, qualifying, and preparing the mentors who will serve in the project management environment. It must establish a process that is used to introduce senior level project managers into the project management "mentoring" function. This can be a simple process of examining individuals already available to the PMO or a more tedious effort of recruiting either internal or external resources. The following three activities lend guidance to the PMO's development of a process that meets the needs of the relevant organization.

Identify Mentor Candidates

The PMO should accomplish this activity step as a matter of determining what resources are available for consideration as mentors. Ideally, mentor candidates will turn up from an internal search among senior project managers within the relevant organization. The next level of search should be at any higher or parent organization level. Finally, external resources can be considered for hiring into the mentor position. These approaches all require some level of advertising and recruiting, which can be a time-consuming activity that warrants support of the human resources department.

It should be noted that qualification and assignment of mentors in this activity is conducted to fill full- or part-time mentor positions managed by the PMO. It does not refer to external sourcing or use of mentors provided by consulting firms. The use of external project management consultants as mentors relies on the external provider to identify and qualify its own individual mentors. Of course, if external mentor sourcing is used, the PMO may want to examine the credentials of external project management mentors as a part of that acquisition.

The mentor candidate identification process should facilitate the preliminary collection of candidate information. Whether the PMO actively solicits individuals or conducts a more formal recruiting program, each candidate should complete a mentor application that is constructed and made available by the PMO. The mentor application should contain sufficient information to enable the PMO to decide whether to schedule an interview with a candidate.

The following represents information content that the PMO can consider for inclusion in the project management mentor application:

- Candidate identification and contact information
- Candidate professional résumé (or application fill-in blocks) highlighting:
  - Current professional position and responsibilities
  - Biographical information
  - Educational background
  - Mentoring experience
  - Professional organization affiliations/certifications
- Candidate letters of recommendation
- Availability for full-time/part-time mentoring
- Statement of interest in becoming a project management mentor

The PMO should consider whether a formal application is needed and then adjust the desired content to fit the organization's needs if an application is developed.

Mentor candidate identification is accomplished when the PMO decides to interview individuals based on a preliminary screening of their mentor application or other preliminary information. The PMO should provide early notification to those applicants not selected for the mentor candidate qualification process.

Conduct Mentor Candidate Qualification

The PMO can qualify mentor candidates through various means, including detailed candidate application reviews, personal interviews with candidates, and reference checks. An important element of this PMO activity is to establish criteria for mentor qualification. The following mentor qualification criteria can be considered for elaboration and use by the PMO. The criteria are presented relative to four qualifying categories:

- Professional experience
  - Years of experience in project management
  - Scope of experience in project management
  - Depth of experience in project management
  - Focus of experience in technical discipline and industry
- Education and training
  - Formal degree programs
  - Professional development programs
  - Technical training programs
  - Project management training programs

- Interpersonal skills for mentors
  - Communication (listening)
  - Collaboration
  - Confidence in abilities and personal experiences
  - Genuine interest in others' success
  - Problem solving
  - Leadership
- Mentor potential in project management environment
  - Professional certification
  - Ongoing study and research in project management
  - Business knowledge and skills
  - Group facilitation skills

The PMO can use the items in the preceding list as a general reference for examining mentor candidates, or it can construct a detailed checklist that incorporates specific criteria to be applied in a comprehensive candidate qualification process. A PMO pursuing an advanced mentoring capability that supports broader mentoring responsibility in areas of professional development and executive counseling must identify additional qualification criteria for those mentoring capabilities.

Consider a final thought on mentor qualification: the PMO should carefully examine its criteria for mentor selection. It will likely be challenging, particularly in a growing project management environment, to find mentors who can meet all desired criteria. That is why external sourcing may be a viable option for the new PMO. However, the organization may have candidates that meet the most critical criteria. A project management mentor can be selected from among the most-qualified candidates. Then, once selected, mentors become eligible to participate in project management mentor preparation and training activities. Any additional mentoring skill and capability can be addressed by mentor preparation.

Prepare Project Management Mentors

The mentor qualification process is completed when available mentor preparation and training activities have been accomplished. The level of the relevant organization's need and the PMO's ability will guide which mentor preparation and training activities are pursued.

It is recommended that, at a minimum, a project management mentor familiarization program be developed and presented to newly assigned mentors in order to enhance their readiness for the mentoring engagements ahead of them. This familiarization program conveys the PMO's perspective on the mentoring program, i.e., its purpose and its practice parameters.

It contains fundamental guidance regarding individual performance in the mentoring role and highlights the primary responsibilities of a mentor within the relevant organization. This program will normally include the following training and information elements:

- Review of the project management mentor position description
- Discussion of recommended mentor professional development activities
- Identification of tools and information resources available to mentors
- Examination of the types of mentoring support offered by the PMO
- Presentation of the preferred mentoring approach to various types of protégés
- Overview of key mentoring-engagement process steps
- Requirements for reporting and collaborating mentoring activities
- Identification of other available mentor preparation and training activities

This familiarization program is likely to be a one-half-day to one-day activity in most organizations. However, multiple-day training can be provided per development of the program content. The program is constructed and presented by the PMO to ensure project management mentors assigned to full-time or part-time mentoring duties have sufficient understanding of the mentor-protégé relationship and the PMO's perspective on work to be accomplished through mentoring engagements.

Other mentor preparation and training activities also can be pursued per the capability and interest of the PMO to do so. This would include more-formal mentor skill training that is available from commercial sources, specific training that has a focus on developing and managing the mentor-protégé relationship, and a variety of training or workshop programs that deal with interpersonal skills, personal and team communications, and technical process facilitation. Of course, the PMO must ensure that all mentors either have attended or can demonstrate comprehensive awareness of project management training attended by protégés. This facilitates a common frame of reference for all participants.

As well, if the mentor also has responsibilities for special types of mentoring, e.g., professional development or executive mentoring, it would be wise to have mentors attend training or workshops to enhance their capability in those areas. Nevertheless, do not lose sight of the fact that the focus of mentoring is on project management. The mentor is a senior project manager who has awareness of the relevant organization and should already be able to provide reasonable guidance to project managers and team members in their career pursuits related to the project management discipline. Similarly, mentors working with executives and senior management level peers do so to convey the concepts and practices of project management and to assist the executive protégé in developing a more comprehensive understanding of the issues and implications of project management within the business. This mentoring relationship with upper management is focused on deliberating and deciding on courses of action that can be taken. Actually, this executive interface role is one normally performed by the head of the PMO, with or without formal mentor credentials, although other assigned mentors could assist from time to time.

Conduct Project Management Mentoring

The PMO can define a process for conducting project management mentoring that is consistent with its sophistication for delivery of mentoring services. There should be a general preferred approach that mentors take when conducting a formally established mentoring engagement. The process elements in the following subsections can be reviewed and used or modified by the PMO to develop a mentoring-engagement approach that best fits within the relevant organization.

Identify Engagement

The PMO or other authority may specify the need for mentoring support for certain types of projects or particular categories of project managers. This results in a PMO-directed mentoring engagement. The PMO also may set up a process for managing and responding to requests for mentoring from project managers or functional managers overseeing project managers and project work. This provides mentoring services on an as-requested basis. In either case, engagement identification includes specifying the type of mentoring support to be performed and the desired outcomes. Engagement identification activities should assist the PMO in determining which mentor(s) to assign to the effort while enabling the assigned mentor(s) to construct initial plans for the mentoring event. When using external mentoring services, much of this engagement identification step is likely to be addressed in association with the established contract or agreement.

Assign Mentor(s)

The PMO examines mentoring requirements to assign a mentor with appropriate qualifications to the engagement. In some cases, this may include mentor-protégé matching to ensure that there is potential for an effective working relationship. Then, the PMO notifies the selected mentor of the pending engagement as the basis for the mentor to begin preparation for the engagement. It is suggested that the PMO include some lead time in its mentoring offerings to allow adequate preparation. Once the engagement is started, the mentor can determine whether an "on call" response capability will be provided, or whether the mentoring engagement will proceed only according to meetings, activities, and interactions specified in the mentoring engagement plan.

Prepare for Mentoring Engagement

The mentor will spend adequate time preparing for the new mentoring engagement and the new mentor-protégé working relationship. Mentor preparation activities should include development of a mentoring engagement plan that outlines the mentoring approach that will be used and the activities that will be performed. An external mentor may use the guidance contained in the applicable contract or agreement in lieu of a separate mentoring plan. As well, the mentor may meet with the protégé's sponsor to obtain further clarification of mentoring needs and may meet with the protégé or lead person of a group of protégés as a matter of becoming acquainted.

Perform Mentoring Engagement Activities

The mentoring engagement begins with a meeting between the mentor and protégé(s) to review the purpose and approach to the mentoring engagement. It then continues with the planned ongoing activities and mentor facilitation that allows skill and knowledge to be transferred. In conjunction with mentoring, and with consideration for the time frame of mentoring, the mentor may prepare recurring reports to highlight progress and capability achieved. These reports are shared with the protégé(s) and may be forwarded to the PMO for review.

Close Out Mentor-Protégé Relationship

A close out meeting should be conducted between the mentor and protégé(s) to review activities and to recognize the value of the time and effort spent together. It also is appropriate to provide feedback to the mentor regarding the effectiveness of the program.

Evaluate Mentoring Program

The PMO should play a key role in overseeing the results of the project management mentoring effort it constructed. It can best ascertain the effectiveness of mentoring by establishing a routine process for evaluating the mentoring program. There are two primary activities to accomplish in evaluating the mentoring program, as outlined in the following subsections.

Evaluate Mentor Performance

The PMO can review mentor reports and protégé feedback to determine the effectiveness of program delivery for each assigned mentor. The PMO should particularly elicit feedback from protégés by formal or informal means. In turn, the PMO can review the recent series of mentoring engagements for each mentor as a means to evaluate individual mentor performance. Mentor performance trends can be examined to identify individual strengths and weaknesses, and successful mentoring engagements can be shared with all mentors as a matter of lessons learned.

Monitor Mentoring Program Results

The PMO can contrast project performance results for project managers and project teams with mentors and those without mentors. This will be a key indicator of whether project performance is enhanced by the presence of a mentor. As well, the PMO can examine increases in project team effectiveness, improvements in project manager leadership, and additional skills and capabilities of project team members.

POSTSCRIPT FOR THE SMALLER PMO

Establishing a formal mentoring program can be a significant undertaking for a small to modest-size PMO. Unless fully qualified resources are plentiful, a formal mentoring program is not likely to be a high priority when establishing PMO functionality. However, that should not sway a PMO of any size from pursuing the benefits of providing such professional development services within the project management environment.

The smaller PMO should establish formal or informal means to make one or more professional project management resources available at least to project managers. The head of the PMO or other senior project manager might initially serve in this capacity. The consideration is to provide a point of contact for project managers to turn to with fundamental questions and concerns. In a sense, if you have a PMO, you already have a project management mentoring resource.

14

PLANNING SUPPORT

Project success is inherently aligned with and dependent upon effective project planning. Project plans establish a common frame of reference for the performance of project management and technical activities, and they provide a road map that guides the project team to fulfillment of project objectives. In turn, project tracking and control ensure progress toward project success by measuring actual project accomplishments against planned activities at regular intervals. When differences between the planned and actual events are deemed significant, corrective actions (project controls) can be implemented. That is the essence of project management. Of course, project planning must be timely, accurate, and complete, per the needs of each project. That is where project planning support provided by the project management office (PMO) becomes a valuable instrument within the relevant organization.

The PMO "planning support" function is arguably the second-most-important PMO function after methodology development (see Chapter 1) that can be offered by the PMO in support of project managers and project team efforts. It provides guidance and assistance to project teams in their development of the essential planning elements needed for every project, and it enables them to become more self-reliant in their application of project planning concepts and practices. Project planning support is a function in the project management environment that is readily accessible to all project teams. It is constantly there, and ideally it is responsive to even short-notice calls for support.

The practice of modern project management can inundate project managers with responsibility for developing extensive plans that address virtually all aspects of project and technical management. That, of course, is appropriate for lengthier and more complex projects. However, the PMO can play a role in identifying the critical plans needed for most projects in the relevant organization, and it can identify those plans appropriate to smaller, less complex projects. This "planning support" function enables the PMO to:

- Establish a preferred, common approach to project planning across all projects
- Reduce the time and effort of project team planning activities
- Facilitate meeting and workshop activities to prepare effective project plans
- Introduce project planning process tools for use by project teams

Planning support is characterized by a considerable amount of PMO involvement in project team planning activities. The focus of this function is primarily on helping teams to prepare the project work plan — an essential ingredient for getting a project underway quickly and managing its progress. The work plan is likely the one project plan component that is required for every project regardless of size or complexity. After establishing the capability to prepare work plans, additional project plans and planning support activities can be introduced as the PMO grows in its own capability and capacity to expand such functionality.

PROJECT ENVIRONMENT INTERFACE CONCEPTS

The planning element of project management can be pervasive in the project management environment, and it is often a challenge to pursue for project managers across many industries. The introduction of this PMO function very simply provides the support capability to help project managers overcome most of the project planning challenges they will encounter by reducing them to a structured and repeatable process.

Planning support is a PMO function that helps project teams find that too-often elusive starting place for their project work effort. The project planning process developed and implemented under this PMO function can serve to reel in "fast starters," who appear to disregard formal planning (a) because they "already know the technical solution and approach" to be taken without collaboration with the complete project team or (b) because of perceptions that there is not enough time to both plan and do the project work. It identifies issues and impacts that may be unique to an otherwise routine project effort, and it provides a single frame of reference for all project team members, who should be pursuing common project objectives. The PMO will be instrumental in constructing a time-efficient process that provides effective project planning guidance while addressing ways to adjust embedded perspectives on older, outdated planning practices within the relevant organization.

In the absence of project planning guidance and support, project teams may flounder with concepts of what project planning accomplishes, how it is structured and conducted, and what constitutes a viable project plan. This leads to dissimilar plan content and structure within the project management environment and, thus, to inconsistency in project management within the relevant organization. PMO efforts in establishing this function can rectify those conditions.

Project planning support is maximized when the PMO carries a portion of the responsibility and burden for implementing the planning process, at least until project managers and project teams gain familiarity and confidence in performing the prescribed activities. It can demonstrate its own expertise, or acquire external services, to facilitate the project planning effort. Effective facilitated planning sessions have been shown to reduce the average time for project planning from several weeks to a matter of days.

BUSINESS ENVIRONMENT INTERFACE CONCEPTS

Personnel in the business environment who are not regular project team members will gain a better frame of reference for their participation on projects. In particular, they will be able to contribute their technical or professional expertise to the project planning effort without special skill or advance knowledge about project planning when the PMO develops (or acquires) the capability to facilitate the project planning session.

A common approach to project planning suggests that there will be more similarities than differences in the content of all project plans when a prescribed approach is used. That generally reduces review time as reviewers become familiar with the content and format. However, it particularly enables accurate and timely aggregation of similar project planning information and data for all projects in the relevant organization. This means that all projects can be examined and contrasted from a normalized perspective, project performance within a program or a portfolio can be summarized, and decisions can be made regarding overall project performance in the relevant organization.

PLANNING SUPPORT ACTIVITIES ACROSS THE PMO CONTINUUM

The "planning support" function along the PMO competency continuum represents a primary PMO support activity in the project management environment. Associated responsibilities expand from simply providing project work plan guidance and tools to specifying and facilitating a comprehensive collection of adjunct project plans, as required in the project management environment.

Table 14.1 provides an overview of the range of prescribed PMO planning support activities according to each level in the PMO competency continuum.

The *project office* is the frontline user of the project planning processes developed and implemented within the relevant organization. In the absence of a higher level PMO, the project office should examine best practices in project planning to devise its own repeatable approach. Ideally, this approach will be coordinated and collaborated for use across multiple project offices that exist in the relevant organization.

Mid-range PMO levels have the responsibility of developing and implementing a viable planning process and accompanying tools to serve the needs of project teams. Initially, this effort focuses on introducing and managing the project work plan — the essential project planning document that guides project team activities toward achieving project objectives. As PMO capability advances, the planning process is expanded to include other adjunct project plans needed within the project management environment (e.g., communications plan, vendor/contractor management plan, quality management plan, etc.). Above and beyond the responsibility for establishing the planning processes, a PMO matures when it also can facilitate project teams in their preparation of at least the fundamental plans used to conduct the project management effort.

The *center of excellence* pursues an oversight role through ongoing analysis of the established project planning capability. In turn, its findings can be used to develop improved planning activities, recommend better planning support tools, and identify best practices through ongoing research relative to specific needs of the relevant organization.

Planning support activities should be conducted in conjunction with process guidance prescribed in the PMO "project management methodology" function (see Chapter 1). In essence, this PMO function represents the development and implementation of the planning components of the project management methodology, with the added features of PMO involvement and facilitation of the prescribed planning processes in specific project planning efforts.

PLANNING SUPPORT FUNCTION MODEL

Project planning activities are fairly straightforward for project teams that have worked together over extended periods of time. The same activities can be confusing at times for project team members who do not routinely work together or for those who do not have a solid frame of reference in concepts of modern project management. Furthermore, a group planning

Table 14.1   Range of Planning Support Activities across the PMO Continuum

Project Office	Basic PMO	Standard PMO	Advanced PMO	Center of Excellence
Conducts project planning using the established process	Conducts simple project planning support ■ Identifies project work plan format and content ■ Prescribes the standard project planning process ■ Introduces basic project planning-support tools	Develops capability to facilitate primary project planning ■ Conducts project preplanning collaboration ■ Conducts work plan facilitation ■ Offers follow-on project work plan support	Expands capability to conduct project planning efforts ■ Specifies adjunct project plan requirements ■ Facilitates development of adjunct project plans ■ Expands project planning process and tools for adjunct plans	Conducts project planning analyses to identify planning effectiveness ■ Examines completeness of project plans ■ Examines use of project plans ■ Examines efficiency of the project planning process

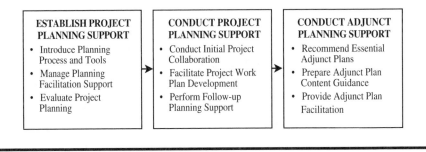

Figure 14.1   "Planning Support" Function Model

effort is ideally one of collaboration — an exchange of ideas, pros and cons, and preferred approaches that ultimately represents a consensus of the project team regarding the direction to be taken to achieve project objectives. An effective project planning capability can minimize the conditions of reduced team cohesion and maximize the benefits of team collaboration.

The PMO can influence project planning capability and fulfill its role as a support provider by attending to the planning needs of project teams in the relevant organization. This simply means establishing the processes, tools, and practices for project planning and, as needed, taking an active role in facilitating their implementation in the project management environment. It can accomplish these objectives through development of the PMO "planning support" function.

The prominent activities of the PMO's "planning support" function model are depicted in Figure 14.1. Each activity is described in the following subsections.

Establish Project Planning Support

The PMO should assume responsibility for establishing the foundation and essential approach to planning support within the relevant organization. It can examine and consider the three actions described in the following subsections to establish a project planning capability that best fits within the project management environment it serves.

Introduce Planning Process and Tools

The PMO should construct a common approach to project planning that can be used across all projects within the relevant organization. This "standard" can provide planning-activity familiarity for project team members over time, make cross-functional teams more effective as everyone learns and responds to the same preferred activity steps, and even enables nonproject stakeholders to benefit from the use of project plans that have a recurring, consistent content and format.

The five following subsections present some fundamental steps prescribed for PMO consideration and inclusion in its project planning process. The PMO should add sufficient additional detail and identify particular tools that it will introduce or otherwise use to help accomplish the preferred project planning steps.

Review Project Guidance Materials

Every project planning effort should begin by establishing a comprehensive understanding of the nature of the project, identifying its purpose (what it will achieve) and examining the needs and expectations of the primary customer as well as other project stakeholders. This knowledge and awareness is conveyed to all participants in project planning through a review of the materials that have been created or acquired to guide the project effort. A few of the more prominent materials that normally will be available to project teams engaged in planning preparation activities are listed below. The PMO can add or remove recommended guidance items as the project planning needs of the relevant organization warrant.

- Customer's statement of work
- Requirements document
- Technical specifications document
- Preliminary survey documents
- Technical solution description
- Project definition worksheet
  - Project manager, sponsor, and other key stakeholders
  - Project scope statement
  - Project objectives
  - Project deliverables
  - Initial (order of magnitude) project budget
  - Major project activities and rough schedule
  - Key and critical project team resources
  - Assumptions and constraints
  - Preliminary evaluation of project and business risk
- Project charter (statement of authority and funding)

Tools for Reviewing Guidance Materials. It would appear that many of the project guidance materials require text document management. To that end, the PMO can examine its requirements, particularly for internally generated materials (e.g., project definition worksheet, etc.), and devise standard forms, templates, and checklists that facilitate the collection and handling of information needed for this preplanning review. The PMO also can consider using commercial or internally developed automated tools that capture the needed information either in a database, or in a document management system, as a means to provide planners with ready access to the project guidance materials. There are commercially available systems available to accomplish these purposes.

Construct Project Work Plan

The project work plan is an essential instrument of project management that specifies all project work activities and aligns factors of cost, schedule, and resource utilization with each specified work element. The PMO can prescribe in its process that a project team construct a project work plan for every project undertaken. The following items are generally accepted as critical or key components of the project work plan:

- *Work breakdown structure (WBS)*: A specification and breakdown of project work activities, normally to the work-package level, i.e., the lowest level of work breakdown, where work-element cost, work duration, and resources required to accomplish the work are assigned.
- *Cost*: A specification of the estimated cost to be incurred as a result of completing the work element to which it is aligned.
- *Schedule*: A specification of the estimated time required to satisfactorily complete the work element to which it is aligned.
- *Resource utilization*: A specification of resources, usually by name or type, that are needed to accomplish the work described for the work element to which it is aligned.

Tools for Work Plan Construction.   The PMO again can consider developing any paper-based forms that can be used to facilitate work plan construction. However, there is a plethora of automated tools available in the marketplace to make this process step very efficient. In particular, the PMO can examine automated project schedule managers, and there are other "enterprise" systems that also can accommodate preparing the components of the project work plan.

Refine Project Estimates

The purpose of this process step is to provide estimates of cost, schedule, and resource utilization for each work element in the WBS. This enables the project team to specify the initial project budget at a reasonable level of accuracy, develop a project schedule with confidence in the work duration indicated for each work element, and prepare a reliable project staffing plan allocating appropriate resource skill and knowledge so that the specified project can be completed within cost and schedule constraints.

The required levels of accuracy for these estimates are metrics that the PMO must determine. In some project management environments, professional estimators who are skilled in the product or service deliverable being offered are used to provide the desired level of project estimation accuracy. In many cases, however, the responsibility for accurate project estimation falls upon the project manager and project team members.

Tools for Project Estimation.   Nearly all tools used for project work plan development inherently enable associated project estimates to be specified. Automated tools, in particular, will likely have database power to collect work estimates and possibly even produce reports that represent the project budget, project schedule, and project staffing plan. The PMO may want to consider some specialized tools for use in the project estimating step. These are tools that actually help planners to formulate the estimates needed. One example is the creation or acquisition of a database application that specifies standards for time and cost, usually industry-specific, for various types of project work efforts. There are also automated tools for calculating work efforts based on the skill and experience of assigned resources. Finally, and in conjunction with the PMO "knowledge management" function (see Chapter 4), the PMO can develop access to and use of prior projects' "lessons learned" that have been captured from previous project close out activities and, presumably, are in an automated lessons-learned knowledge space.

Conduct Project Risk Assessment

The project work plan is usually not considered ready for implementation until it undergoes a risk assessment and a subsequent risk-response strategy has been developed for each identified risk. The PMO should ensure that this step is included in the project planning process. The results of this step can then be incorporated into the subsequent preparation of a risk management plan, as specified in the next section dealing with primary project support plans.

The risk assessment step involves looking at a variety of variable factors that could hinder or otherwise adversely impact project performance or successful project completion. It is recognized that some industries and organizations also align "project opportunity" assessments with the project risk management effort. That is not specifically prescribed by this process step, where the focus is on discovery of potential adverse impacts. Project opportunities certainly can be addressed in subsequent preparation of adjunct plans for each project if that is an activity desired by the relevant organization.

The PMO should define the preferred approach and scope of project risk assessments. The suggestions below represent a few areas for risk examination using the project work plan and any other pertinent information available to the project team during the planning effort.* Upon completion of the risk assessment, risk-response strategies that have prescribed actions should be integrated as work elements in the project work plan.

- *Internal risks*: Those risks that the project manager or project team can control through response strategies dealing with resource assignments, schedule development, and cost management:
  - Technology
    - New or untested technology
    - Availability of technical expertise
    - Customization (design risk)
    - Availability of material
    - Manufacturing (production) capabilities
    - Subcontractor or vendor performance
    - Transition from design to production
  - Schedule
    - Resource availability
    - Schedule constraints
    - Dependencies
    - Inadequate planning
    - Insufficient information
  - Financial issues
    - Funding or customer budget
    - Estimate accuracy
    - Contract labor rate
    - Material cost change
  - Legal issues
    - Patent rights or infringement
    - Data rights
    - Government policies
    - Contract ambiguities
- *External risks*: Those risks that are generally beyond the control or influence of the project manager or project team. They include

---

* The risk-assessment categories were obtained from *ProjectFOCUS®: A Project Management Methodology*, ESI International, Arlington, VA, January 1999.

risk events dealing with market shifts, customer decisions, or government or regulatory actions:

- Unpredictable external events
  - ■ Regulatory changes
  - ■ Natural hazards
  - ■ Environmental impact
  - ■ Public interest
- Predictable but uncertain external events
  - ■ Market changes
  - ■ Inflation
  - ■ Taxation
  - ■ Exchange rates

Tools for risk assessment: The nature and impact of risks normally encountered in a particular industry or technical environment will influence the types of tools that can be used in conjunction with the risk assessments performed. A common tool for PMO consideration is the manual or automated checklist that project planners can use to evaluate risks, similar to the preceding lists, but generally with considerable more detail. These checklists are usually based on established risk assessment models, which can be created by the PMO or acquired from commercial sources. It is not unusual for acquired risk models to be customized for use within the relevant organization. As well, there are also a number of "enterprise" applications that will help the PMO address specification and management of project risks, and there are add-on applications that can be used in association with several commercially available project scheduler software applications.

Develop Project Support Plans

A project support plan, sometimes referred to as an adjunct project plan, is a formal or informal document that adds definition and direction to the project effort. The combination of the project work plan and all project support plans constitutes the project plan.

The PMO will need to examine requirements within the project management environment to determine which support or adjunct project plans are needed. It can evaluate its needs relative to primary support plans and secondary support plans, as presented in the final section of this chapter.

All project support plans should include a brief description of the means by which the plan can be modified, who can authorize changes to the plan, and a listing of project stakeholders who will receive the original plan and any subsequent plan updates and revisions.

A note of particular importance is offered with regard to preparation of both primary and secondary project support plans, as well as the project work plan. The planning effort takes time that must be accounted for in the course of project management. Therefore, it is important that all plan development efforts required by a specific project be included in the project WBS and work plan. Each plan development effort will have cost, schedule, and resource utilization components that need to be specified as a part of the total project effort.

Manage Planning Facilitation Support

The PMO can offer enhanced support to project team planning efforts when it achieves the capability to provide, or otherwise arrange for, project planning facilitation. This means having one or more qualified professionals work directly with the project manager and project team members in their development of the project work plan and any other primary and secondary project support plans that may be needed. The delivery of support for project planning facilitation can be characterized by the three activities described in the following subsections.

Identify the Nature of Planning Support

The PMO should determine its own capability as well as that available from external professional sources to specify a menu of project planning support services that will be made available within the project management environment. This can include such services as:

- *Project planning workshop facilitation*: A facilitator-led program that takes the project team through the iterative steps for developing a project work plan. Ideally, this workshop is presented as a rigorous planning effort that can be accomplished in a matter of days, rather than a drawn-out period of weeks or months that can result in disjointed and inconsistent planning. The shorter period allows key project team members to assemble for a one-time planning session that establishes the fundamental work plan. The essence of workshop content is described later in this chapter in the "conduct project planning support" activity. As PMO capability and resources become available, the PMO can extend this type of workshop into support for primary and secondary project support-plan development.
- *Project mentoring*: The use of qualified project management mentors is a natural follow-on to the project planning workshop. This allows the facilitator or participating mentors in workshop activities to remain with the project manager and project team to help refine

the project work plan, develop other project support plans, and facilitate project work plan implementation. This effort includes (a) monitoring and encouraging the project team in its finalization of required plan content and (b) facilitating individuals and small groups in their deliberation and validation of planning elements. It also could involve demonstrating the use of project planning tools that are currently available within the project management environment or creating new tools that reduce the project team's planning burden. See the PMO "mentoring" function (Chapter 13) to learn how to establish a full-scope project management mentoring program within the relevant organization.

▪ *Project plan review and validation*: The PMO can provide a valuable service by offering to review and validate project plans that have been constructed by project teams. This type of review would be used to examine plan content, clarity, and comprehensive coverage of intended guidance. This effort could include meetings with individual planners to obtain an understanding of concepts and calculations used in plan development. It should distinctly provide recommendations for plan improvement, if needed.

These planning support services can be provided either by qualified PMO staff resources or through arrangements with external providers of professional project management services. The availability of these and any other planning support services provided by the PMO should be communicated widely within the project management environment.

Establish Capability to Provide Project Planning Support

The PMO's ability to fulfill project planning support requests will be influenced by the PMO's identification of qualified resources to conduct each planning support effort and by resource availability. The PMO should either establish a program to qualify and prepare internal resources to conduct project planning support, or it should identify prequalified external resources that can bring the requisite professional capability and project planning experience into the PMO's project management environment. See the PMO "mentoring" function (Chapter 13) for further consideration of these two resource options.

Establish Procedures for Introducing Project Planning Support

The size of the relevant organization, the nature of project work, and the number of projects will influence the need for project planning support and the procedures for requesting and providing such support. A checklist item in the project management methodology can prompt the project manager to review needs for project planning support and provide instructions for requesting support from the PMO. As well, the PMO may want to develop a means to monitor upcoming new project initiation activities as a means of anticipating planning support requirements. This includes possible PMO deliberation to offer project planning support to more-needy project efforts. In some cases, per policy and governance procedures in the project management environment, the PMO may independently determine that a facilitated planning session is mandated for certain projects. Similarly, the PMO may want to influence project recovery efforts by requiring the use of a facilitated program for the project recovery planning effort.

Otherwise, under routine conditions, the PMO will simply develop a process to accommodate and fulfill project planning support requests. The following are some sample steps the PMO can consider for such a process:

- Review and specify required project planning activities — project manager
- Determine associated need for project planning support — project manager
- Submit a project planning support request — project manager
- Review and prioritize the project planning support requests — PMO
- Coordinate arrangements for planning support — PMO and project manager
- Conduct project planning support activities — PMO
- Evaluate project planning support results — PMO and project manager

Again, these steps can be incorporated into project management methodology guidance.

Evaluate Project Planning

There is a significant amount of evaluation associated with the PMO's ongoing role in project and project management oversight, and the need is no more evident than in the realm of project planning. While evaluation of project planning can be formal or informal, per the PMO's capability and functional mandate, it should be conducted to ascertain what parts of the planning process work and what parts can be improved to provide greater project planning effectiveness.

To that end, the PMO will need to examine project planning processes, content and format, the effectiveness and efficiency of facilitated project planning sessions, and the availability and use of project support plans. This examination can be an ongoing and progressive collection and analysis of process use information that is evaluated at three or four intervals during the year. It may also be a distinct examination that is conducted one or more times a year, possibly in association with an annual review or following a recent process revision.

The PMO can develop and conduct project planning evaluation in three areas, as described in the following subsections.

Evaluate Project Planning Process

The project planning process warrants separate examination even though it will likely be an integrated piece of the project management methodology. The impact of project planning on project performance warrants such exclusivity.

The PMO should first ascertain the extent of process use. A few simple evaluation points will provide a preliminary indication of process use, and the PMO can expand this checklist if more-precise information is needed:

- Determine who uses the established project planning process.
  - Identify how many project managers know the process exists and how many use it.
  - Determine how many project team members know the process exists and how many have used it.
  - Evaluate the percentage of the project management environment population that has used the established project planning process.
  - Deliberate the influence or impact of process utilization across project managers.
- Determine the frequency of project planning process use.
  - Identify the total number of new projects initiated in a specified recent period.
  - Identify how many of those projects applied the established project planning process.
  - Deliberate the influence or impact of process utilization frequency across projects.

The results of this evaluation can be represented, in general, by high, medium, and low process use. In turn, the PMO can identify and rectify causes of low process use.

Another PMO perspective on process evaluation in this area can be obtained by determining how well the process is serving the needs of users, which is often characterized by an examination of the depth of use. In this area of examination, the information being sought is represented in one more fundamental checklist. This checklist can be used in conjunction with a review of selected project work plans, PMO observations, and user feedback regarding benefits perceived as a result of using the established project planning process:

■ Identify any particular project planning process elements that are routinely not used.
■ Identify any particular project planning process elements that are almost always used.
■ Determine any reduction in planning times as a result of using the established project planning process.
■ Determine whether the project planning process facilitated full project team participation in planning.
■ Evaluate individual users' perspectives on added value achieved through use of the established project planning process.

These two checklists suggest a review of process utilization for project work plan development, but a similar examination can be conducted for any project support plan guidance that has been implemented.

The results of this first evaluation activity are intended to provide the PMO with rough indicators of the efficiency of the established project planning process.

Evaluate Project Performance Contributions

The PMO should evaluate how well the established project planning process contributes to successful project performance on a regular basis, perhaps annually. This aspect of process evaluation considers what project performance improvements have been achieved as a result of planning process implementation. The PMO should devise an examination and analysis approach that suits the needs of the relevant organization. For a simple evaluation, the PMO can obtain some general indicators by referencing the following points of inquiry:

■ Identify whether cost, schedule, and resource-utilization variance has been reduced at one or more points in the project management life cycle as a result of process implementation.
■ Identify whether enhancements in project team performance are evident, e.g., reduction in planning time, reduction in rework, timely task completion, improved project team communication and collaboration, etc.
■ Identify whether customer and executive stakeholder satisfaction has improved.

- Identify whether project team members and other planning participants are better prepared for subsequent project planning sessions after first using the process.
- Identify whether there is a reduction (from normal) in the number of scope changes encountered during the project effort. Determine whether any required changes are handled more efficiently.
- Identify whether short-term project team members are more productive during their abbreviated project participation periods as a result of having adequate project plan guidance.

The results of this evaluation activity are intended to provide indicators of the effectiveness of the project planning process.

Evaluate Project Planning Support

If the PMO offers project planning facilitation support by internal or external resources, it should also examine the results of such services. If facilitation is a recurring practice used to assist project team planning efforts, then the contributions to project performance can be included in the general evaluation of performance described in the previous section. If facilitation is an infrequent event, then the PMO simply weighs the contribution relative to the level of effort expended by facilitation.

However, the PMO also should examine how well project planning facilitation support activities are being accomplished. This evaluation relies a great deal on feedback from planning session participants. With that information in hand, the PMO can consider the following basic evaluation points and add others as needed:

- Demonstrated technical competency and capability of the project planning facilitator(s)
- Demonstrated workshop and facilitation skills and experience of the facilitator(s)
- Appropriateness of the duration of the project planning session
- Appropriateness of the participants selected for attendance; notable absentees
- Appropriateness of participant contributions to the planning effort
- Completion of planning session objectives, e.g., a preliminary project work plan

The results of this evaluation will provide insight to the effectiveness of facilitated project planning sessions and to the capabilities of the assigned facilitators. In general, most facilitated sessions will normally expedite and enhance the project planning process and improve the plan content through participant information and skill contributions. Therefore, the occasion of a poor outcome for a planning session tends to be associated with facilitator performance. This evaluation will be valuable in developing the full capability of individual facilitators and in improving the overall approach to the delivery of effective facilitation.

Conduct Project Planning Support

The PMO reaches a mature stage when it can offer project planning facilitation and support within the project management environment. This is because facilitation represents a more or less consistent and repeatable approach to project planning, which is an important characteristic for this component of the project management methodology. Likewise, to the extent that the PMO has created the planning process and integrated it within the established methodology, it should be able to effectively demonstrate its application under live project planning conditions.

This section of the model highlights the primary activities that are accomplished in facilitating project work plan development. This represents implementation of the project planning process and associated content described in the previous activity.

The PMO can examine the following steps as a means for accomplishing project planning support and then develop the preferred approach it will use to assist project teams in preparing their project work plans.

Conduct Initial Project Collaboration

The first step in project planning support involves accomplishment of several requisite planning workshop preparation activities. This includes:

- *Ascertain workshop need*: The PMO coordinates with the project manager to obtain preliminary information about the technical nature and business objectives of the project and about the skill and experience of the project team. This provides a basis for determining the scope of the planning workshop and the number of facilitators needed. As well, the PMO will request and arrange for receipt of any available project materials that will be used to help facilitators prepare for the planning session, e.g., project charter, any completed project planning documents, requirements documents, business case, etc.
- *Arrange planning session*: The PMO coordinates with the project manager to specify the dates for workshop presentation, usually a three- to five-day period, and identify the project team members who will participate in the planning session. Project team participation should be sufficiently broad, if not the entire team, in order to properly address and obtain knowledgeable input on all planning

requirements. The project manager will normally be responsible for notifying team members of their participation requirements and ensuring their full-time attendance.

■ *Arrange session logistics*: The PMO coordinates with the project manager to determine the facility and location to be used for the planning session. The PMO will normally be responsible for coordinating arrangements for facility use. This includes reserving meeting rooms, specifying preferred meeting room setup, arranging access for all participants, identifying points of contact for on-site support, and anticipating any advance arrival of workshop and participant materials.

■ *Identify and assign workshop facilitator(s)*: The PMO will identify qualified resources and arrange for facilitators who are experienced in conducting project planning sessions to be assigned to lead the workshop activities. This includes any lead time required to request and arrange for either internal or external project planning workshop facilitation services.

■ *Prepare workshop materials*: If the PMO maintains the materials used for delivery of project planning workshops, it should begin efforts to publish sufficient copies for the anticipated level of participation. It will then make materials available at the workshop location in advance of the workshop start date. This might require shipping for workshops conducted at locations away from the PMO's home facilities. If the internal or external facilitators maintain their own materials, the PMO should monitor their handling of this workshop-materials preparation step.

■ *Conduct facilitator preparation for workshop*: The PMO will transfer project materials received from the project manager to the assigned facilitator(s) for review. The facilitator(s) will use the project materials to develop a preliminary understanding of project scope and objectives. This facilitator preparation effort usually takes one to three days.

■ *Conduct preworkshop conference*: The planning workshop facilitator(s) and the project manager will convene to discuss the planned workshop activities, thus allowing the project manager to convey (a) personal perspectives on the project and project team and (b) expectations for workshop outcomes. This meeting can be planned for a one- to three-hour period and can be done in-person or by telephone. It is recommended that this meeting be scheduled and conducted not more than one week nor less than one day in advance of the workshop start date. Consistent with established responsibilities, the PMO can be a participant in this advance collaboration meeting with the project manager and workshop facilitator(s).

The PMO can prepare and use a planning workshop checklist to manage and monitor the timely accomplishment of all prescribed project planning, workshop planning, and collaboration activities.

Facilitate Project Work Plan Development

The PMO will already have established the preferred content for the project planning workshop. This activity now focuses on the delivery of that content by the assigned facilitator(s), with participation by all or part of the project team.

This aspect of PMO project planning support includes the accomplishment of activities needed to develop a viable project work plan. The following are suggested project planning workshop activities:

- *Workshop introductions*: The facilitator(s) should be introduced and become acquainted with project team participants at the beginning of the workshop. This is an opportune time to allow individual participants to introduce themselves, their project role, and their expectations for the workshop. The latter must be tracked and addressed by the facilitator(s) over the course of the workshop. The facilitator(s) will then introduce the workshop objectives and provide an overview of workshop activities. It is also usually appropriate to provide an overview of the concepts of modern project management that will be used over the course of the workshop as a means of developing a common frame of reference for all workshop participants.

- *Project definition preparation*: The project definition process begins by specifying the roles of the project sponsor and project manager and then conducting an abbreviated review of project requirements. This is followed by facilitated activities that establish project scope and objectives, identify key resources, and examine project assumptions and constraints. This effort will necessitate that workshop participants bring current knowledge and information about the project and that they be active contributors to preparation of the project definition. In addition to the items already listed, a group perspective on the overall project work effort is achieved through participant deliberation and specification of the major phases of the technical work to be performed, which in turn serves as a basis for conducting subsequent project planning activities.

- *Project planning*: The facilitator(s)' first activity in project planning will be to lead development of a project work breakdown structure (WBS). Using the project definition as guidance, the process of deliberating and deciding on the project work identifies the elements to be included. This activity normally leads participants through a rigorous and iterative planning process in which they are guided from the phase level perspective of the project to the creation of work packages. The next step of project planning is the preparation of the project work plan. In this activity, participants estimate and incorporate cost, schedule, and resource utilization information for each work element in the WBS. It is recognized that often there is limited or no information currently available to accurately complete each work plan element. However, that should not preclude the planning effort, and this planning session still will be of value simply because it enables participants to identify what they do not know and must find out. The facilitation then usually proceeds through successive plan development stages to refine the WBS and each work plan element. The result of this effort is a preliminary project work plan that can be used to begin the project work effort.

■ *Project risk assessment*: The prescribed process for assessing and responding to project risks should be an inherent part of any project planning effort. To that end, facilitator(s) should lead participants in identifying prominent project risks and formulating initial risk-response strategies. As project risk-response strategies are created, any proactive strategies should be incorporated into the project WBS and work plan for assignment to a responsible individual. Workshop participants can then include a preliminary project risk management plan as an item resulting from the planning effort.

The PMO should develop the means to evaluate the project planning workshop facilitator(s) and the planning process, and that will likely include soliciting feedback from workshop participants. Participant assessments are best accomplished immediately following completion of the workshop. However, in some environments, the PMO may want to defer individual evaluations of the planning session until attendees return to their work locations, where they can apply the results of their planning efforts and recognize the significance of their workshop accomplishments.

Perform Follow-Up Planning Support

There is a potential need for follow-up planning support for most major projects. The PMO should consider the need for such services within the relevant organization. Follow-up support essentially equates to providing project management mentoring services, as outlined in the PMO "mentoring" function (see Chapter 13). However, there are distinct objectives to be pursued when mentoring is associated with project planning activities. As well, when mentoring is conducted following a project planning workshop, it is not unusual for other mentoring service needs to emerge.

The PMO will have to determine whether this follow-up support activity can be offered in the relevant organization and then develop the methods and means for delivering follow-up planning support. Typical postplanning support activities include:

- *Project plan refinement*: The facilitator(s) can continue working with the project manager and project team members to refine the preliminary project work plan created during the project planning workshop. This activity concentrates on inserting any deliberated results or decisions coming from the planning workshop that were not accomplished due to time constraints or participant availability. It is also an excellent means of conducting a postplanning session review of the overall plan, i.e., a walk-through to validate plan content.
- *Subteam facilitation*: This is an extension of project refinement, but it focuses on work with subteams of the project team to facilitate *new* inputs to the project WBS and work plan to fill in technical performance details, add project management and business activities, or integrate vendor and subcontractor project plans.
- *Project plan tool use*: Project team members can receive guidance in the entry of project data and in the management of the WBS and project work plan elements using the prescribed automated tool.
- *Project support plan development*: The timeliness and effectiveness of the project work plan preparation effort can be carried forward to allow facilitation of other support plans needed to accomplish the project. This effort will rely on the PMO's capability to provide both facilitation and the requisite technical expertise relative to the specific nature of the support plans needed.
- *Project support plan reviews*: In contrast to facilitating their development, the PMO can provide expertise in reviewing and validating project support-plan documents as they evolve from the efforts of the project team.
- *Project plan presentation*: The facilitator(s) can collaborate with the project manager to assist in the preparation, and sometimes delivery, of presentations of the project work plan or simply presentations of the overall project management approach. These are presentations that could have a variety of project stakeholder audiences, including senior management within the relevant organization, customer project managers and senior management, and vendor and contractor project managers and senior management.

The PMO must take care in establishing provisions for follow-up support to project planning efforts. It is imperative that the assigned facilitator or mentor not be perceived or otherwise commandeered as a member of the project team. First, that would impact the PMO's capability to provide ongoing support to multiple projects underway in the project management environment (presuming the PMO does not have a limitless supply of qualified and skilled facilitators and mentors). Second, the underlying purpose of such support is to transfer project management skill and knowledge to the project manager and project team members so that they become increasingly self-reliant over time and therefore no longer need PMO facilitator/mentor support.

Conduct Adjunct Planning Support

The project work plan is the central planning document in the arsenal of project management plans. It guides the accomplishment of tasks needed to fulfill project deliverable requirements. However, projects often also need additional direction regarding the accomplishment of project management activities, technical performance activities, and communication and relationship management activities. This additional guidance can be accommodated through the preparation and use of adjunct project plans.

The PMO's role warrants taking a lead role in identifying and implementing the adjunct planning capability within the project management environment. The three activities described in the following subsections will assist the PMO in deliberating and deciding its approach to adjunct planning support.

Recommend Essential Adjunct Plans

The PMO can consider such factors as organizational policy and practices, customer requirements, industry practices, project complexity and risk factors, and the experience level of the project team when recommending the need for adjunct project plans. The fundamental purpose of these plans is to provide sufficient additional guidance and direction to enable project goals to be achieved.

The PMO will need to examine requirements within the project management environment to determine which adjunct project plans are needed. It can evaluate its needs relative to primary support plans and secondary support plans, as described in the following two subsections.

Primary Support Plans

Primary support plans are those adjunct project plans that need to be prepared for every project conducted within the relevant organization.

Their content may vary according to project size, value, and duration, but their purpose is generally applicable to all projects. The following list presents six adjunct project plans that are recommended for PMO consideration:

- *Risk management plan*: Specifies the activities for managing risk throughout the project management life cycle. It identifies the project team members and other stakeholders responsible for managing various types of project risk, and it compiles the identified project risk events and response strategies established through a project risk assessment and through other ongoing efforts to identify and manage risks.

- *Communications management plan*: Describes the methods for gathering, distributing, and storing various types of project information. In particular, it specifies the content, format, and frequency of required and optional project reports. It also identifies and possibly presents a schedule for project meetings. If not created as a separate plan, it can specify project document requirements and control procedures. This plan also identifies all project stakeholders and, to the extent possible, specifies their roles and responsibilities as well as their physical locations and various means of contact. As well, this plan indicates the protocol for project communication, specifying the preferred and authorized interactions and communications among project team members, senior management, the customer, vendors and contractors, and other project stakeholders. Finally, this plan can include instructions for identifying problems and escalating project issues to the project manager, the PMO, and senior management.

- *Scope management plan*: Describes the management and control of project scope. It particularly includes specification of the preferred change-management process as an integral component of scope management. It also specifies individual responsibility for managing scope, and it specifies "dos and don'ts" for project team members as guidance for avoiding unintentional modifications to the work effort that represent scope changes. This plan can contain a checklist for evaluating indicators of drifting scope.

- *Quality management plan*: Describes how the project team will implement its quality policy and practices on the current project. It includes the identification of quality requirements for direct and indirect project deliverables, specifies the technical reviews and threshold values of quality control, and identifies the quality assurance activities to be accomplished as a matter of ensuring successful technical performance. It also can identify scheduled and ad hoc technical and project management audits that may be conducted as a part of the project oversight effort. It can reference applicable technical standards and specification documents as well as adjunct plans having greater quality-process and procedural details. Where possible, individuals and organizations responsible for quality management should be identified. Finally, this plan should specify the procedures for customer acceptance of project deliverables.

■ *Vendor/contractor management plan*: Describes how external resources will be integrated into the project effort, including specification of their primary point of contact and key roles and responsibilities that will be fulfilled. If not otherwise provided in a separate support plan, the procurement process for vendor and contractor acquisition can be incorporated in this plan. This plan also can reference and highlight key information elements for each vendor/contractor agreement or contract. In particular, this plan will specify the deliverables to be accomplished by the vendor/contractor, the methods that will be used to accept vendor and contractor deliverables, and the process for receiving and approving invoices associated with vendor/contractor deliverables. Finally, this plan should prescribe the management activities that will be accomplished to ensure effective and timely vendor and contractor performance on the project.

■ *Staffing management plan*: Describes the project resources needed, allocated, and assigned to the project effort. The plan is constructed to help the project manager and technical team leaders to identify the number and type of resources needed to accomplish the project effort; when, how, and from where they will be sourced; and what steps will be taken to manage their timely acquisition and assignment. It frequently contains a project resource responsibility matrix to show alignment of individuals with project work responsibilities. This plan may reiterate the location and methods of contact for each project team member. As well, a portion of the plan should specify how the project team and individual team members would be dispersed following completion of their assigned project duties.

Secondary Support Plans

Secondary support plans can also be prepared, and they tend to be those adjunct project plans associated with technical or functional organization requirements, such as a manufacturing plan or software testing plan. The term "secondary" is used relative to the practice of project management and does not signify importance relative to the technical effort of the project. However, there also are a fair number of secondary project support plans that constitute guidance for project management activities.

The following list presents a wide variety of secondary project support plans that can be considered by the PMO for use within the relevant organization:

- *Auditing plan*: Specifies the scheduled and unscheduled technical and project management reviews to be conducted. This plan can be an extension of or included in the quality management plan.
- *Budget plan*: Presents the annual budget for the company, division, or relevant organizational unit for consideration in this project planning effort.
- *Business case plan*: Specifies the analysis and presentation of business assessments providing the justification to pursue the project opportunity.
- *Configuration management plan*: Describes the procedures used to apply technical and administrative direction and oversight to identify, document, and control application of the functional and physical characteristics of any item or system.
- *Cost management plan*: Presents the procedures for tracking and managing cost variance and provides guidance for general oversight of the project budget, including management of cost changes.
- *Construction plan*: Provides information for coordinating, communicating, and directing the construction of a capital facility in terms of scope, quality, time, and cost.
- *Contingency plan*: Identifies alternative strategies to be used if specific risk events occur. This plan can be an extension of or included in the risk management plan.
- *Customer relationship management plan*: Specifies the steps to be taken to manage customer expectations and involvement in the project effort.
- *Customer support plan*: Describes the activities designed to assist the customer with a product or service after acceptance.
- *Cost estimating plan*: Specifies the information and steps necessary for conducting an effective estimate of the related elements of cost, schedule, and resource utilization. This can be an extension of or included with the project work plan.
- *Documentation plan*: Specifies the design, storage, and disposal of reports, information, records, references, and other project data.
- *Engineering design plan*: Describes the project deliverable in the form of specifications, drawings, data flow diagrams, or any other methods that can be used to provide detailed information on how to build the product.

- *Equipment disposal plan*: Tells how equipment and material used on a project will be disposed of at the conclusion the project.
- *Facilities management plan*: Designates the facilities required to support execution of the project and the actions and responsibilities associated with acquiring, managing, and maintaining project facilities.
- *Financial performance plan*: Stipulates business unit performance goals for a given financial period (or a given project).
- *Health and safety plan*: Outlines the performance standards and requirements designed to protect project team members.
- *Inspection plan*: Presents the design for the examination or measurement of work to verify whether an item or activity conforms to specific requirements.
- *Inventory management plan*: Presents the design for the use and control of materials required to execute the project.
- *Logistics support plan*: Presents the design for the acquisition and movement of materials and personnel required to conduct the project.
- *Make-or-buy plan*: Explains the procedures for analyzing whether a particular product or service can be produced or performed cost-effectively by the performing organization or should be contracted out to another organization.
- *Manufacturing plan*: Provides the scheme for building the product or deliverable resulting from the project effort.
- *Materials procurement plan*: Describes sourcing of raw or prefabricated materials to support execution of the project.
- *Operations plan*: Defines interface roles and responsibilities between the project team and the relevant organization's business units.
- *Peer-review plan*: Structures the content and method of peer technical reviews of the deliverable product.
- *Portfolio management plan*: Identifies pending and approved products of the relevant organization; defines the prioritization of approved products and projects, including the current project.
- *Procurement management plan*: Describes management of the procurement processes, from solicitation planning through contract close out.
- *Product life cycle plan*: Defines how the technical product will evolve into a new offering.
- *Project organization plan*: Defines the management structure for the project and how it interfaces with the relevant organization. This plan can be an extension of or included in either the project charter or the project definition statement.

- *Regulatory compliance plan*: Explains how the work of the project will be managed to conform to applicable government regulations or industry standards.
- *Resource utilization management plan*: Presents the procedures for tracking and managing resource utilization variance, and provides guidance for how to measure and manage project team member assignments and performance.
- *Schedule management plan*: Presents the procedures for tracking and managing schedule variance, and provides guidance for general oversight of the project schedule, including management of schedule changes.
- *Staff training plan*: Specifies training to be undertaken by designated or potential project team members so that they can achieve qualification of project skill, knowledge, and competency requirements.
- *Staff transition plan*: Addresses staff replacement issues and migration from the project to other assignments within the organization. This plan can be a part of or an extension to the project staffing plan.
- *Strategic business plan*: Sets the organizational business direction and context for decision making in the development and execution of the project.
- *Systems integration test plan*: Defines operating requirements and standards for combined elements of a system or the system as a whole.
- *Technical plan*: Describes how the scope and deliverables of the project will be achieved from the perspective of the technical or professional work to be performed.
- *Testing plan*: Defines the method and criteria for checking the conformance to requirements of the deliverable product or its components.
- *Tooling plan*: Provides the design for manufacturing equipment used to produce product components.
- *Transportation plan*: Defines how the product will be transported through distribution channels to reach the customer's points of product acceptance.
- *Verification plan*: Provides for the evaluation of the correctness of the output (deliverable) of various stages of product development based on the criteria for that stage.
- *Warranty and field support plan*: Provides for replacement and repair of parts and extended services associated with product delivery.

The generic titles in the preceding list are proffered to give the PMO some perspective on what can be accomplished relative to project planning. Undoubtedly there are numerous technical and business planning components that are unique to industries and organizations that are not listed here. The PMO should define those and create the preferred format and content guidance for their preparation in the planning process.

Prepare Adjunct Plan Content Guidance

The PMO's collaboration of needs for adjunct project plans in the project management environment and subsequent selection of required plans would influence the planning workload of each project team. To that end, the PMO will want to ensure that only essential adjunct planning requirements are specified and that adequate guidance is provided for preparing and using adjunct project plans. Not every project manager will recognize the need for a particular adjunct plan, and more likely, individuals will have a different perspective on its content and purpose even when fundamental concepts are known. Therefore, the PMO should determine several guidance features in association with specifying the need to prepare each adjunct project plan:

- *Purpose*: Specify the reason for constructing the adjunct plan and how it will be used in the course of the project and in the life cycle of project management. Indicate its alignment as a project management plan, technical plan, administrative plan, or any other categories that provide perspective to users on the project team and other project stakeholders.
- *Preparation requirement*: Determine and specify whether the adjunct plan is a primary support plan that is required for every project or a secondary support plan that is prepared only for certain types of projects. Identify the criteria or conditions that will determine when the adjunct plan must be prepared.
- *Responsibility*: Identify who, in terms of a project team or project stakeholder role, is responsible for developing the adjunct plan, reviewing and approving the adjunct plan, and managing adjunct plan implementation.
- *Content specification*: Identify what information will be contained in the adjunct plan and provide format requirements or recommendations, as necessary. This includes specifying the major sections of the plan and describing the prescribed content for each section in sufficient detail so as to preclude misunderstanding or incorrect interpretation.

- *Template or sample plan*: Provide a template or form that can be used to construct or otherwise guide construction of the adjunct plan. As well, consider available automated applications and associated databases and features that can be used to provide content and fulfill adjunct plan preparation requirements.
- *Plan distribution*: Identify the project team members and other project stakeholders who will routinely receive copies of the adjunct plan; indicate who has authority to issue copies to individuals not on the distribution list.
- *Plan modification*: Identify who is authorized to make changes to the plan and what types of modifications require initiating a formal change-management process.

To repeat a reminder found throughout this book, the introduction of requirements and processes for preparing adjunct project plans should be incorporated into the project management methodology (see Chapter 1). The methodology will be the primary repository for the feature descriptions resulting from this PMO activity.

Provide Adjunct Plan Facilitation

This activity represents a special capability of the PMO to provide facilitation support to project managers and project team members for the preparation of adjunct project plans. It is an activity similar to that described earlier to facilitate project work plan development. It should be distinguished from the general follow-on type of facilitator/mentor planning support for adjunct plan development by the nature of the preparation required and the formality of the facilitation process used. In essence, formal adjunct plan facilitation requires the development of a structured program or workshop and associated workshop materials.

An adjunct plan facilitation workshop involves coordination and preparation time for both the project manager and the facilitator, and possibly some project team members. It also involves development of workshop materials that can be used to expedite the planning effort, a primary reason for having a facilitated planning session.

The decision to proceed with this service offering is as much a business decision as a project support decision because of the expense and the effort that will be consumed. Therefore, it is particularly important that only adjunct plans that are frequently required be included for consideration in a facilitated workshop. More precisely, the PMO should examine primary project support plans for workshop consideration, because they are required for every project.

As well, the use of external professional services may be a more appropriate means of fulfillment. If development costs and time are a factor, professional project management consultants, already well-versed in the technical or project management aspects of the adjunct plan, is a viable solution for PMO consideration. Use of external consultants is also a means of introducing new concepts of planning and prescribed industry content into the scheme of adjunct plans.

Once the PMO establishes the capability to deliver adjunct project planning facilitation, it should ensure that availability of that support is widely publicized within the project management environment. That ensures that the cost of development and delivery, or the expense for an external service provider, is optimized through maximum use of the workshop. Likewise, it will have to develop procedures for requesting and fulfilling adjunct plan workshop requirements.

POSTSCRIPT FOR THE SMALLER PMO

A primary objective for the smaller PMO is to ensure that adequate and appropriate project planning is routinely accomplished by all project teams for all projects. The project work plan and various project adjunct or support plans comprise the project plan. The most efficient approach is to direct the PMO's initial attention to the project work plan because it contains the essential planning elements needed to effectively guide project management:

- Project definition (scope, objectives, etc.)
- Project WBS (specification of project work tasks)
- Project management key elements
  - Cost (budget)
  - Schedule (work task durations and dependencies)
  - Resource utilization (staffing plan)
- Project risk examination

The development and implementation of a standard and repeatable project work plan preparation process is something the PMO should pursue in conjunction with its project management methodology development efforts. The PMO also can address preparation of adjunct or support-plan guidance in association with methodology development or as required by the needs of the relevant organization and specified PMO responsibilities. However, adjunct or support-plan guidance is generally prepared after development of the work plan process is completed.

In association with deploying an effective approach to project work plan development, the smaller PMO also can contribute insight and expertise in the identification and use of automated software application tools that facilitate project work plan development and use. In many cases, tools currently found in the project management environment can be configured for use in project planning activities.

15

PROJECT AUDITING

Auditing is an activity that has unique connotation and context across various industries and within different professional disciplines. A common aspect of auditing across multiple venues appears to be the concept of examination: observing, identifying, evaluating, determining, etc. The uniqueness of auditing across different venues lies in what, specifically, is being examined. Still, there is similarity in that most auditing efforts examine overall efficiency, quality, and value of outcomes resulting from use or nonuse of a process, practice, policy, or capability.

The PMO has an inherent interest in and responsibility for conducting examinations within the project management environment. To that end, prescribed auditing activities will seek to identify the efficiencies, qualities, and values associated with projects and project management. Of course, this normally extends into examination of business and technical aspects of project work as well.

This model also represents that audits are not assessments. We will use the term "assess" from time to time as a general reference to activities within the auditing process, but not as a distinct descriptive of the auditing process. Assessments, in the context of this model, measure and specify competency, capability, maturity, and perhaps other relevant conditions within the project management environment. In contrast, audits measure outcomes resulting from those features and conditions. An audit in the project management environment, in general, will measure results and identify the contributing causes to those results.

This "project auditing" function enables the PMO to:

- Monitor project management contributions to the achievement of business objectives
- Identify and respond to weak or troubled project performance
- Conduct quality management activities

- Maintain professional and practice standards within the project management environment
- Ensure compliance with organizational policies, industry certification requirements, government regulations, and contractual obligations.

The PMO's focus is on implementing auditing processes and procedures that measure results related to project performance. This inherently implies making judgments about those results, generally in terms of acceptable, marginal, and unacceptable. In turn, the PMO will need to construct corrective actions for results judged to be marginal or unacceptable. Ideally, the PMO also will construct favorable recognition actions for results judged to be acceptable.

PROJECT ENVIRONMENT INTERFACE CONCEPTS

The PMO should develop and implement auditing practices in the project management environment as a means to achieve required levels of project management oversight, including individual performance, project performance, and program or portfolio performance. The PMO should demonstrate or otherwise influence a high degree of professionalism and collaboration in conducting such audits, which are inherently needed to ensure proper examination of project performance and project management activities.

A viable project auditing program will first and foremost enable the PMO to identify troubled projects that may require special attention or even transition to project-recovery mode. However, project audits should also contribute significant value in identifying minor irregularities that can be "fixed" on the spot, thus precluding the need for major project recovery actions or reactions.

As well, the PMO can use audits to ensure that established standards and practices are adhered to across all projects within the relevant organization. Audits will serve as reminders to all project stakeholders that such standards and practices exist, and that there are expectations that will be applied within the project management environment. This includes examination of the proper application of business and technical standards and practices as well as those having specific project management connotations.

The PMO is responsible for ensuring adequate oversight and control within the project management environment, and auditing can help fulfill a portion of that responsibility. The PMO can introduce auditing from an internal perspective relative to operations within the project management environment, i.e., those audits the PMO performs or controls. It also can identify the need for appropriate external or third-party audits, which are provided by business units within the relevant organization or by auditors in industry or commercial venues. The PMO lends expertise to deciding the types of audits and the auditing sources that are required within the project management environment.

BUSINESS ENVIRONMENT INTERFACE CONCEPTS

The business units within the relevant organization distinctly bring professional expertise to the project management environment on a part-time, as-needed basis or as full-time stakeholders. In particular, business units influence the achievement of business standards and interests in association with project performance. They also often represent centers of technical expertise within the relevant organization. Therefore, they are ideally prepared to conduct project-related business and technical audits in the project management environment through arrangements with the PMO. A prominent auditing requirement found in many organizations is that of quality assurance, and the business unit responsible for quality management activities should normally be involved in collaboration with the PMO.

Establishing an auditing capability in the project management environment also advances business interests. The use of project audits can be promoted as a means of providing current and potential customers with assurance of project success. Similarly, the inclusion of audits in the project management process can be touted in marketing and advertising or in proposals to demonstrate differentiation from competitors.

Above all, auditing conducted in the project management environment ensures the efficiency, quality, and value of project work. This contributes to the bottom line of the business and represents an investment toward achievement of strategic business objectives.

PROJECT AUDITING ACTIVITIES ACROSS THE PMO CONTINUUM

The "project auditing" function along the PMO competency continuum provides for progressive levels of internal and external examination of project and business performance. It represents project review activities that are conducted for the purposes of oversight and control at specified points in the project management life cycle. It also represents reviews that are conducted in response to project management, technical, or business indicators that trigger the need to examine all or a portion of project performance in greater detail.

Table 15.1 presents an overview of the range of prescribed PMO project auditing activities according to each level in the PMO competency continuum.

Table 15.1 Range of Project Auditing Activities across the PMO Continuum

Project Office	Basic PMO	Standard PMO	Advanced PMO	Center of Excellence
Conducts project audits and reviews as prescribed by the project manager	Prescribes and conducts simple project reviews ■ Establishes basic project health checks ■ Monitors project technical reviews	Establishes project auditing capability across projects ■ Implements preproject reviews ■ Conducts project phase reviews ■ Conducts other essential project, business, and technical audits ■ Implements postproject reviews	Expands auditing efficiency through training ■ Provides auditor and team training ■ Provides project manager self-audit training ■ Provides auditing familiarization training to project stakeholders	Conducts project audit analyses to improve auditing effectiveness ■ Evaluates current audit capability ■ Examines use of external auditors ■ Recommends project audits

The *project office* will normally focus on reviews initiated and conducted by the project manager or project team, who use any guidance provided by a higher level PMO or by business units within the relevant organization. These reviews are intended to validate reported project status and to identify any unreported indicators that threaten successful continuation of the project effort.

Mid-range PMO levels will develop and implement project auditing processes that can be used to provide reasonable assurance of project success throughout the project management life cycle. This involves (a) the specification of audit points for standard project audits and (b) the identification of criteria for triggering project audits within the project management environment. The mid-range PMO will examine and identify the fundamental audit and review needs of the relevant organization and then implement auditing processes and procedures in response to those needs. Conducting project audits and reviews is an inherent feature of project management, and the advanced level PMO may consider establishing a training program that addresses concepts and practices in project auditing for selected project stakeholders.

The *center of excellence* will focus on ensuring that the auditing capability established within the project management environment is efficient and effectively serves the interests of project and business managers alike. It contributes business perspectives to decisions about which audits and reviews are needed and which are not while also recommending the addition of certain types of audits and the removal of others. The center of excellence is also adequately positioned to identify and evaluate external auditors who can assist the PMO in deliberating its project audit and review needs, in developing auditing processes and procedures, and in conducting relevant project audits and reviews as third-party participants.

The project auditing activity is another area that interfaces with process guidance prescribed in the PMO "methodology management" function (see Chapter 1). In particular, audit and review activities prescribed for the project manager or project team, and the procedures for accomplishing them, should be incorporated into the project management methodology. As well, other audits to which the project, project manager, or project team members are susceptible should be identified.

Project auditing also has alignment with the PMO "standards and metrics" function (see Chapter 3), as audits are generally constructed and conducted to validate compliance with standards that are (a) identified in association with project management activities and (b) imposed by business needs, interests, and objectives. There is likely to be some general link to several other PMO functions to the extent that project audits and reviews are applied to measure their application and performance results.

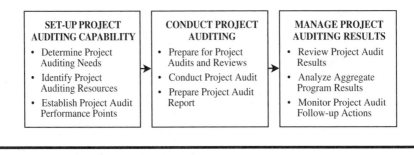

SET-UP PROJECT AUDITING CAPABILITY	CONDUCT PROJECT AUDITING	MANAGE PROJECT AUDITING RESULTS
• Determine Project Auditing Needs • Identify Project Auditing Resources • Establish Project Audit Performance Points	• Prepare for Project Audits and Reviews • Conduct Project Audit • Prepare Project Audit Report	• Review Project Audit Results • Analyze Aggregate Program Results • Monitor Project Audit Follow-up Actions

Figure 15.1 "Project Auditing" Function Model

PROJECT AUDITING FUNCTION MODEL

The PMO can lead development and implementation of auditing activities prescribed for use within the project management environment. It can choose the extent to which it is actually involved in conducting audits and reviews, but it should be a participant in reviewing and deliberating results as a basis for ascertaining the overall health and effectiveness of project management within the relevant organization.

The prominent activities of the PMO's "project auditing" function model are depicted in Figure 15.1. Each activity is described in the following subsections.

Set-Up Project Auditing Capability

The PMO can be instrumental in defining the proper types and levels of review and audit activities conducted within the project management environment. However, appropriate and timely planning is essential to achieving a viable auditing capability. The auditing capability needs a process and an organizational basis for maximum effectiveness.

The PMO can consider the activities in the following three subsections when establishing or refining a project audit capability.

Determine Project Auditing Needs

The frequency and nature of project audits and reviews is a matter of the relevant organization's need for oversight and assurance of project management capability and the alignment of support for business interests. To that end, the PMO will want to identify the needs for audits and reviews and then select the preferred ones for incorporation into the PMO's arsenal of management tools.

Across industries, professionals in project management will encounter the term "project audit." Unfortunately, across industries, and sometimes within organizations, there are different interpretations with regard to what a project audit is and what it accomplishes. This function model offers a "project management audit" as a primary examination tool for PMO consideration and then goes on to identify and define other types of audits and reviews applicable to the project management environment.

The PMO should examine the following subsections for audits and reviews that can or should be implemented within its project management environment.

Primary Project Management Audits

Primary project management audits represent a few essential audits that can be considered by the PMO and prescribed for use within the project management environment.

Project Management Audit. Despite being broad in scope, this audit provides a fairly comprehensive examination of project management performance. Although the project manager or project team can perform this audit, it is highly recommended that this audit be conducted by the PMO or some other third-party to accomplish an impartial and objective appraisal from an unbiased perspective. This is a formal audit that may take one or more qualified auditors a full day or more to complete, depending on project size, and with additional time needed for associated analysis of findings and report preparation.

This audit is accomplished through discussions and interviews with the project manager, technical leaders, and at least a sampling of project team members in conjunction with a hands-on review of pertinent project documents. It normally includes examination of:

- Project work plan and support plans created to guide the project management effort:
  - Completion of required planning documents (per project classification)
  - Adequate inclusion of prescribed plan content
  - Appropriate inclusion of preferred practices and industry standards
- Effectiveness of project work plan and support-plan implementation:
  - Accomplishment of project work efforts according to applicable plans
  - Demonstrated tracking of actual project results against work plan elements
  - Timely identification and response to variations in work plan elements

- Use of approved change-management procedures for modifying plan content
■ Oversight of project resource management and task performance:
  - Identification of assigned project resources and their contributing competencies
  - Management of resource task assignments and task completion status
  - Accessibility and use of the project work plan and applicable support plans by project resources
■ Oversight of project vendor/contractor management and task performance:
  - Identification of roles and responsibilities of vendor/contractor project team
  - Management of vendor/contractor assignment and deliverable status
  - Accomplishment of vendor/contractor deliverable approval and acceptance
  - Performance of vendor/contractor contract administration activities
■ Fulfillment of customer contractual obligations:
  - Accomplishment of adequate deliverable quality assurance activities
  - Achievement of timely presentation of deliverables and customer acceptance
  - Performance of customer contract administration activities

This general project audit is applicable to larger and longer-duration projects that are already underway beyond the initial planning stage. It is an audit that can be performed as often as quarterly until the project reaches the close out stage.

Project Performance Audit (Project Health Check). This audit represents a detailed examination of the financial and business aspects of the project. In particular, earned-value analysis or some other preferred method of financial examination is applied, business case elements are reviewed, and the project risk management plan and activities are evaluated. This is a formal audit that will generally take one or more fully qualified auditors three to five days to identify conditions, analyze findings, and prepare a fundamental project performance audit report, depending on the size of the project and the scope of the audit. Validity of the audit is significantly enhanced when conducted by the PMO or other external, third-party auditor.

This audit can be conducted independently or in conjunction with a *project management audit* to review and validate the financial and business conditions of the project, with emphasis on evaluating and confirming the ability of the project to achieve specified objectives. This audit normally includes examination of:

- The business case used to manage selection and continuation of the project:
  - Relevance of business purpose and alignment with business interests
  - Achievement of staffing aligned with the resource allocation plan
  - Confirmation of trends toward achieving cost-benefit analysis results
  - Achievement and acceptance of project deliverables
  - Identification of customer relationship status and pertinent issues
- Cost specified in the project work plan:
  - Review of cost tracking and reporting methods and accuracy
  - Identification and evaluation of cost performance (i.e., planned versus actual)
  - Identification and evaluation of cost variance
- Schedule specified in the project work plan:
  - Review of schedule tracking and reporting methods and accuracy
  - Identification and evaluation of schedule performance (i.e., planned versus actual)
  - Identification and evaluation of schedule variance
- Resource utilization specified in the project work plan:
  - Review of resource utilization tracking and reporting methods and accuracy
  - Identification and evaluation of resource utilization performance (i.e., planned versus actual)
  - Identification and evaluation of resource utilization variance
- The project risk management plan:
  - Achievement of project risk identification, analysis, and prioritization
  - Documented review and update of project risks at appropriate intervals
  - Specification of risk response strategies for high-priority risks
  - Inclusion of proactive risk response strategies in the project work breakdown structure (WBS)
  - Preparation of contingency plans and acquisition of funding for reactive risk response strategies

This *project performance audit* is applicable to virtually all projects of discernable value and duration that are already underway beyond the initial planning stage. It is an audit that can be performed as often as quarterly until the project reaches the close out stage. The PMO can also use this audit in conjunction with project portfolio management reviews.

Preproject (Planning Phase) Audit.   This audit validates project readiness for implementation. It is usually performed by the project manager and project team, but it can also be accomplished by the PMO or other external auditing team or third-party auditor. This audit presumes that requisite project selection activities have been accomplished and normally includes examination of:

■ Initial project management documents and activities:
  - Finalization of the project definition
  - Validation of the project budget and resource allocation plan
  - Preparation of the project charter (specification of project manager authority)
  - Authorization of project funding (if not in project charter)
  - Executive (sponsor) approval to proceed with project implementation
■ Initial technical documents and activities:
  - Review of customer requirements documents
  - Review of technical specifications documents
  - Review of technical survey documents
  - Preparation of project quality management plan
  - Identification of technical plans needed for the project
  - Preparation of initial technical plans required by methodology or policy
■ Initial project management planning documents and activities:
  - Preparation of the project work plan
  - Preparation of the project risk management plan
  - Preparation of the project communication plan
  - Identification of project management plans needed for the project
  - Preparation of initial project management plans required by methodology or policy
■ Initial project team documents and activities:
  - Preparation of the project responsibility matrix and staffing plan
  - Appropriate participation in project kickoff and planning meetings
  - Specification of project team member reporting requirements
  - Determination of project team readiness to begin project execution

- Initial vendor and contractor documents and activities:
  - Coordination and acceptance of vendor/contractor technical approach
  - Specification of vendor/contractor reporting requirements
  - Execution of vendor/contractor contract or agreement
  - Determination of vendor and contractor readiness to begin project execution
- Initial customer documents and activities:
  - Acceptance of technical solution by customer
  - Specification of customer reporting requirements
  - Execution of customer contract or agreement
  - Confirmation of customer readiness to begin project execution

This *preproject audit* is applicable to virtually all projects of discernable value and duration. It is an audit that is performed as people and plans become ready for project execution. In a sense, it is a "gateway" audit that facilitates transition from the planning phase to the project execution phase. Here, the planning phase emphasizes development of initial project management and technical plans necessary to describe the project's game plan. Additional project plans can be prepared in conjunction with project execution.

Postproject (Close Out Phase) Audit.   This audit confirms project readiness for closure. It is usually performed by the project manager and project team, but it can be accomplished by the PMO or other external auditing team or third-party auditor. This audit normally includes examination of:

- Customer acceptance of project deliverables:
  - Receipt of interim and final customer acceptance statements
  - Completion of customer's evaluation of project performance
  - Preparation and submittal of invoice(s) to customer
  - Receipt of customer invoice payment(s)
- Project lessons learned:
  - Review of project financial and business performance
  - Review of project management plan content and effectiveness
  - Review of technical plan content and effectiveness
  - Review of project team performance
  - Review of customer feedback and evaluations
- Vendor/contractor close out activities:
  - Evaluation of vendor/contractor performance
  - Receipt of vendor/contractor invoices(s)
  - Payment of vendor/contractor invoice(s)

This postproject audit is applicable to virtually all projects of discernable value and duration. It is an audit that is performed when all project activities have been completed, deliverables have been accepted, and the project is ready for closure. This audit is the "gateway" audit that facilitates and, to a large extent, indicates project closure.

Review of Project Management Methodology.   This audit examines the use and validates the content effectiveness of the established project management methodology. The PMO or a qualified external third-party auditor normally accomplishes this audit. It is a review that transcends individual projects and project managers to gain a perspective of the application of project management processes and techniques across all projects within the relevant organization. This audit normally includes examination of:

- General content of project management methodology:
    - Contains adequate descriptions of process (what to do) and practice (how to do it) for project management phases, activities, and tasks
    - Designates the roles and responsibilities of project team members and other stakeholders for participation in the accomplishment and oversight of project management activities and tasks
    - Provides adequate tools to facilitate the accomplishment of methodology process elements, e.g., automated tools or paper-based forms, checklists, templates, etc.
- Process content of project management methodology:
    - Presents a discernable process relationship and flow that advances the project through phases of initiation, planning, implementation/execution, and close out
    - Specifies all essential project management activities and tasks within each phase (per project management standards and practices used)
    - Incorporates essential technical planning and performance activities in each phase (per technical standards and practices used)
- Methodology utilization by project managers and project teams:
    - Identifies and reviews project management methodology phase, activity, and task use on a representative sample of projects in a specified time period
    - Determines causes for nonuse of selected methodology elements
    - Examines user feedback regarding methodology use
    - Identifies project management benefits or liabilities that can be associated with the use of project management methodology

    – Identifies business benefits or liabilities that can be associated with the use of project management methodology

This review of project management methodology can be accomplished annually to ascertain its completeness, effectiveness, and use.

Additional Project Management Audits

The category for "additional project management audits" includes a wide array of audits that can be considered by the PMO to achieve more-detailed examination of project performance elements or to ascertain conditions within the project environment.

The PMO can construct and perform audits to meet a variety of needs. The following list presents a few suggestions for additional project management audits that may be of value within the relevant organization:

- *Customer satisfaction audit:* An examination of the customer business relationship that identifies how well the customer perceives the project to be progressing toward the achievement of desired objectives.
- *Project recovery audit:* An audit similar to the combined content of the project management audit and the project performance audit, but with focus on the indicators of unsatisfactory project performance.
- *Project support plan review:* A review of the guidance prescribed by any of the individual project support plans. The PMO or a third-party auditor usually conducts this audit to provide an unbiased perspective on plan content, comprehensiveness, and usability.
- *Project resource utilization audit:* An examination of fulfillment of resource allocations and the timely assignment of resources for the accomplishment of specific tasks. This audit does not examine resource performance. The PMO or a third-party auditor usually conducts this audit to provide an unbiased perspective on issues and activities surrounding resource support by resource managers and at the executive level and includes examination of the effectiveness of project managers in assigning resources.
- *Project team performance audit:* A review of project work assignments and their alignment with individual technical and professional competencies of project team resources. The PMO or a third-party auditor usually conducts this audit to provide an unbiased perspective on individual capability issues, appropriateness of individual assignments, and the effectiveness of project manager and technical leader supervision.

■ *Vendor/contractor audits:* An audit or review using any of the previously described project or project management audits, but one that is conducted within the vendor or contractor project management environment. This type of audit is normally authorized and conducted in one of two ways. First, the vendor/contractor can request assistance from the PMO in conducting an examination of its project management position and contribution to the overall project, and sometimes the PMO will encourage this. Second, the provisions of the applicable vendor/contractor service contract or agreement allow the PMO to independently initiate and conduct project management audits within the vendor or contractor project management environment.

These and other unique audits can be prescribed and performed when project performance conditions indicate the need for such examinations in the project management environment. The PMO should maintain the documented process of any new audit for future use and refinement.

Technical Audits

Technical audits are an inherent part of project management responsibilities. However, technical audits are distinctly aligned with the nature of the product or service delivered to the customer and with the particular technical skills and competencies found in the project management environment. Individual PMOs will need to define technical audits that are appropriate to and associated with the business operations of the relevant organization.

The following list presents a few generic types of technical audits that are applicable across different project management environments for PMO consideration:

■ *Technical approach review:* A thorough review of the technical solution prepared to produce required project deliverables and to achieve overall project objectives within the specified scope of work. It is normally accomplished early in the project planning effort, and sometimes in conjunction with the preproject audit.

■ *Quality assurance audit:* An examination of the project quality assurance plan; associated test and acceptance plans; and quality control procedures, scheduled activities, and accomplishments. This type of audit is often aligned with responsibilities of quality management business units within the relevant organization. A general review of the project quality assurance plan also may be performed during the preproject audit.

- *Project gateway review:* One of a series of reviews conducted at technical transition points or phases in the project, e.g., design, build, produce, test, etc. The gateway review examines the readiness to proceed with the next major technical activity, including:
  - Verification that all requisite technical activities have been properly accomplished
  - Determination that technical leaders and project team resources needed to conduct the technical work prescribed in the next technical phase are available and ready to begin the assignment
  - Confirmation that the executive (sponsor) and customer agree to proceed to the next technical activity
  - Receipt of required funding for the next technical activity
- *Structured walk-throughs:* A technical review, usually conducted by a group of technical experts, including project team members, customer representatives, and external technical advisors, to validate a technical process or procedure, a technical design or approach, or a technical performance outcome normally associated with a project deliverable.
- *Technical reviews:* An examination of technical content, usually conducted by project team members, to adjudge satisfactory completion of technical tasks that contribute to preparation of project deliverables. The PMO, in collaboration with technical leaders in the relevant organization, can construct procedures for required technical reviews within the project management environment.

The PMO should prescribe routine technical audits for inclusion in the project work plan.

Identify Project Auditing Resources

The PMO may have responsibility for project auditing in the relevant organization, but it will likely not have the staff depth or broad skills to conduct all required audits within the project management environment. To that end, it will have to evaluate project auditing requirements and designate preferred auditors and auditing teams.

An inherent issue in identifying project auditing resources is the need to qualify auditors. Audit training and experience are prominent factors in qualifying auditors. As well, requisite technical or project management competency is a primary factor for consideration of auditor qualification by the PMO. Qualified auditors can then use the PMO's prescribed approach to conduct audits.

In addition to the PMO, there are four types of resources that can be used to conduct audits in the project management environment. These are described in the following subsections.

Project Managers and Project Team Members

Project managers have responsibility for continuous monitoring and management of project status and progress. They inherently conduct informal audits as part of their ongoing practice of project management. They can similarly be given responsibility for performing particular project audits specified by the PMO as project conditions warrant or as project audit points are encountered. The key here is that they will distinctly use auditing guidance and processes prescribed by the PMO to make the performance of designated audits consistent across all projects.

Individuals serving as senior project managers have demonstrated their understanding of project management concepts and principles; they are more or less well versed in the nuances of project management within the relevant organization; and they presumably have the experience required to use and comprehend primary project condition indicators. This qualifies the more senior project managers to conduct audits on projects other than their own. The key here is for these resources to demonstrate an ability to achieve an impartial, business-oriented review of people, performance, and practices according to the procedures of the particular audit to which they are assigned.

As well, project team members who demonstrate technical or project management competency also can be used to conduct formal and informal project audits. They can assist the project manager in performing audits on their current project. Since they usually bring particular technical expertise, they can even lead certain technical audits and reviews. In some cases, individual expertise may warrant their assignment to auditing teams that are convened to examine projects other than their own within the project management environment.

To the extent that the PMO relies on project managers and project team members to conduct project management and technical audits, consideration for training them in effective and efficient auditing practices is warranted. Particular consideration should be given to training of individuals designated as leaders of primary audits within the relevant organization.

Internal Auditors

The PMO can canvass the resources available within the relevant organization to identify and qualify individuals from business units who can participate as auditors in the project management environment. In some cases, organizational policies and procedures, or the inherent responsibilities of individuals in certain business positions, will designate auditor status.

The following is a sample listing of a few roles in the relevant organization that can be considered for participation as technical and project management auditors:

- Senior managers, in any position (ideally ones that interface with project management)
- Quality assurance managers
- Quality control managers
- Finance managers and specialists
- Business analysts
- Senior engineers and scientists
- Senior technical specialists

Auditing team assignments for these internal resources should have some alignment between their primary specialty or professional credentials and the type of audit being conducted and their responsibilities for that audit. One important criterion in qualifying internal resources is that there must be at least one influential individual on the auditing team who can demonstrate advanced qualification in the application of concepts and content of modern project management practices.

Again, if the same internal resources are assigned to auditing duties on a recurring basis, some training in auditing practices, as well as training in project management practices and principles, is recommended for consideration by the PMO.

External Collaborative Auditors

The PMO can preclude an internal search to identify and qualify auditor candidates through use of external collaborating resources, such as project management auditing consultants. This approach is particularly cost effective when the frequency or type of primary audits conducted within the project management environment does not warrant an effort to fully qualify and train internal personnel in project management auditing practices and procedures. However, it can also be beneficial in organizations that desire to take advantage of third-party expertise and impartiality in conducting audits in the project management environment.

In taking this approach, the PMO will have to manage external auditor qualification and selection. This can be accomplished by following a few recommended steps:

■ *Identify the field of external project management auditor candidates:* Prepare a list of auditing consultant candidates by examining project management capabilities and credentials; contrast candidate offerings against the anticipated range of auditing needs in the project management environment; and identify other areas of project management expertise the consultant has brought or can bring to the relevant organization.

■ *Discuss and evaluate the auditing process and approach of each candidate:* Meet with auditing consultant candidates to determine the fit and effectiveness of each candidate's project management auditing process and identify the particular benefits to be achieved by their selection. Distinguish those consultants who offer only general business and management auditing capability from those who demonstrate complete comprehension of modern project management principles and practices as an inherent part of the auditing process.

■ *Select and assign the preferred external auditing resource:* Make a decision regarding which of the auditing consultants will be introduced into the project management environment. If there is an identifiable need for the variety of project audits to be conducted by the selected consultant, arrangements should be made to schedule consultant participation. In particular, the PMO should note that there might be value represented by reduced service costs when multiple project management auditing assignments for the auditing consultant can be identified within a specified period.

These steps for selecting an auditing consultant are rudimentary, but fulfilling them can be a time-consuming effort for the PMO. The PMO should anticipate project auditing needs and — with consideration for the time involved in identifying and introducing external resources into the relevant organization — conduct the necessary internal coordination so that it can evaluate the external auditing consultants, select an appropriate candidate, and assign the task in a timely manner.

External Regulatory Auditors

The second type of external resource the PMO might encounter is the regulatory auditor. This auditor, who may or may not have expertise in the full range of project management knowledge and practices, has a bona fide need and appropriate authorization to conduct an examination within the project management environment. Generally, such an auditor is introduced in association with government regulatory requirements or through a government customer's contract provisions. However, in some cases, the PMO may be obligated to accept an auditor into the project management environment as a result of contractual provisions in a non-governmental customer's contract or agreement. This auditing possibility makes it an essential PMO job to review and understand the contents and provisions of every customer contract or agreement.

The regulatory auditor should provide an agenda and identify the scope of the audit to be conducted. PMO assistance may be needed (a) to schedule and arrange for participation of project managers and team members in auditor fact-finding meetings, document reviews, and other presentations and (b) to facilitate the auditor's administrative activities within the relevant organization. Otherwise, there is normally no formal responsibility for the PMO or the relevant organization to perform the audit steps prescribed by the regulatory auditor's process.

The PMO is responsible for ensuring that relevant executives and senior managers are aware of any scheduled audit by an external regulatory auditor. Advance notification of upcoming external regulatory audits also should be conveyed to project managers and project team members.

Establish Project Audit Performance Points

The PMO can establish audit performance points to specify when or under what conditions an audit will be conducted within the project management environment. There are three types of audit performance points that will be identified: the routine project audit point, the triggered project audit point, and the discretionary project audit point.

Routine Project Audit Point

The routine project audit point is a designated point in the project management life cycle or in a technical process at which a specified type of project or technical audit or review is conducted. This type of audit is normally identified in the project WBS and work plan, and its performance is anticipated as a routine part of the project management effort. It may include virtually all of the primary project management audits defined earlier, as project duration permits, and many of the technical audits and reviews associated with the nature of the project deliverables. The PMO should define and incorporate the process for conducting any routine project audit points into the project management methodology and associated technical processes.

Triggered Project Audit Point

The triggered project audit point is an unscheduled audit or review conducted in response to a project performance indicator, or "trigger," that suggests a more detailed examination of some aspect of project or technical performance is warranted. While a triggered project audit point is not necessarily anticipated at any specific point in the project, it should not present any major surprises to the project manager or project team. In a sense, it is a normal response to a highlighted condition in project performance. In fact, triggered project audit points can be identified in appropriate project plans and include the particular conditions under which such audits will be pursued.

Discretionary Project Audit Point

The PMO also may seek and obtain the authority to conduct audits at its own discretion, where a project audit performance point is not specified. Presumably the PMO will apply superb judgment to guide decisions that initiate such unanticipated audits in the project management environment. Moreover, unannounced project audits should not always have a negative connotation. There may be circumstances under which the PMO, in collaboration with project managers, wants to examine project team performance and participation under project audit conditions. Likewise, the PMO may need to conduct a minor audit across all currently active projects as a matter of specific information collection and analysis. Finally, the PMO may want to test a newly formed audit team in their performance of an auditing process.

Conduct Project Auditing

The PMO will need to develop guidance for conducting audits within the project management environment. Audits and reviews conducted as routine project management activities are normally unobtrusive and short-lived events, and procedures for their conduct should be adequately described in the project management methodology or applicable technical process. Audits and reviews deemed more critical or comprehensive and conducted outside of routine procedures will likely warrant some additional time for planning and preparation, performance of audit activities and analysis of results, and compilation of findings in an audit report. This is particularly the case when internal or external third-party auditors are introduced into the project management environment.

The PMO can address these needs — incorporating aspects into project management methodology guidance and preparing general guidance for third-party participants — by reviewing three primary activities that can be accomplished to fulfill project auditing requirements.

Prepare for Project Audits and Reviews

The PMO should specify the key audit preparation activities to guide its efforts when leading project audits. Project managers and project team members responsible for conducting routine internal audits and reviews on projects can apply this same PMO guidance, as contained in the project management methodology. However, the PMO often can defer audit preparation activities when either internal or external third-party auditors are taking the lead role in conducting a more formal audit or review in the project management environment.

Nevertheless, the following three project audit and review preparation steps are listed for PMO consideration and further development for use within the relevant organization.

Identify and Convene Auditor/Auditing Team

The PMO should prequalify lead auditors, particularly for formal audits. To that end, project managers would be considered "prequalified" to conduct routine audits by virtue of their position of responsibility and their training and experience in the concepts and practices of modern project management. Similarly, internal auditors coming in from other business units are likely prequalified by virtue of their roles, e.g., quality management, finance, etc. Therefore, it is usually the external auditor that requires some level of prequalification by the PMO. However, the PMO will need to maintain a list of available auditors from all internal and external sources, their particular audit or review area specialties, and general requirements for arranging for their services and participation.

As audit requirements are identified, particularly triggered and unannounced audits, the PMO can use its list of prequalified project auditors to select, request, and assign them to the audit activity at hand. In the case of internal or external third-party auditor participation in recurring, routine audits across multiple projects, the PMO can schedule and arrange for their services in advance of the need. In some project management environments, the PMO may want to prepare and publish a project audit schedule that extends out several weeks or months.

Convening the auditor/audit team will normally begin with an initial on-site audit meeting that the PMO may want to attend for the purposes of introducing audit participants and to ensure the proper specification of objectives in planning auditing activities. The PMO can also facilitate arrangements for work space and individual meetings for external auditors. This PMO participation may be required less over time as the PMO becomes familiar with auditor/audit team performance.

Plan the Audit

An initial audit meeting is recommended to identify audit participants and to plan (or review plans) for conducting the type of audit prescribed. Normally, the project manager should be included in this initial planning session to gain insight to planned activities and requirements for personal and project team member participation.

The audit planning session will be used to accomplish the following:

- Specify the type of audit to be conducted
- Identify the lead auditor and audit team members
- Review auditor/audit team preparation activities
- Request timely receipt of project documentation for advance examination
- Determine schedule and review auditor/audit team on-site activities
- Identify audit responsibilities of the project manager and project team members
- Identify any pertinent issues or problems that might be encountered
- Determine schedule and review audit report preparation activities

Audit planning is needed to establish a common frame of reference for all audit participants. This activity usually can be accomplished in less than one-half day, and in extenuating circumstances it can be achieved by means of a telephone conference for most common types of audits.

Conduct Auditor/Audit Team Preparation

The auditor/audit team will need adequate time to prepare for on-site auditing activities. To that end, it is particularly important that project documents and other requested materials be provided in a timely manner. The PMO may be able to facilitate or otherwise monitor the transfer of project documents and materials required for auditor review in this preparation step.

The nature of the project and the type of audit to be conducted will determine the time needed for audit preparation activities. In some cases, it can take up to two or three weeks to prepare for an on-site audit. The time needed can usually be determined and specified at the initial audit planning session.

The auditor/audit team will perform a number of activities to prepare for the project audit:

- Specify the scope and purpose of the audit
- Review project documents and materials per the type of audit prescribed

- Identify project documents that do not exist or are not available for review
- Identify individual and group audit interview requirements
- Prepare or review existing audit checklists to guide investigation activities
- Prepare and distribute an agenda for audit meetings and activities
- Coordinate final plans with PMO and project manager

The PMO can rely on established practices of internal and external third-party auditors to provide the necessary detail for these preparation steps. It may want to develop more-comprehensive audit preparation procedures for audits conducted in association with project management audits conducted by the PMO.

Conduct Project Audit

The auditor/audit team, in collaboration with the PMO and the project manager, should begin its on-site audit activities in a meeting with affected participants, likely the project team members. However, the project executive (sponsor) and other relevant project stakeholders also can be invited to attend. To the extent possible, this meeting should review the planned auditing activities and procedures, and it should also serve to reduce any anxiety and concerns about the audit. Participants in this meeting need to recognize that the pending audit is a natural and routine business activity designed and applied to ensure business success.

The audit will then proceed with a detailed examination of the project or elements of the project. It will include some combination of the following audit activities, per the type of audit conducted:

- *Interviews:* Auditors will meet with individual project team members and other project stakeholders, normally of their choosing (to remove bias), to discuss processes, activities, and performance of the project effort as a means of obtaining insight into the prevalent project conditions or to evaluate specific project condition indicators.
- *Observations:* Auditors will view project team meetings, group interactions, and individual work performance to identify contributions and influences on the current project condition.
- *Further document reviews:* Auditors will examine project documents and materials not previously examined, including individual documents and notes used to construct technical solutions, accomplish assigned tasks, and prepare project status reports. Auditors also may meet with individuals to receive clarification of content

for project documents and materials examined during the audit preparation period.

■ *Analysis:* Auditors will meet independently at intervals, generally at the end of each audit day for multiple-day audits, and throughout the day for shorter audit periods. These meetings will enable them to share information, identify common threads of findings, and formulate concepts of project conditions. This analysis meeting also will be used to identify topics of interest and points of focus for next-day/next-period audit activities.

■ *Initial audit feedback:* The auditor/audit team will meet with the PMO, the project manager, and any other relevant project stakeholders to provide initial feedback regarding findings identified during the audit period. It should be noted by the lead auditor that there may be some variance in the details presented in the audit report, but the essence of the project conditions identified should be adequately conveyed in the report.

The specific audit activities to be conducted will evolve during the audit. The auditor/audit team will begin using the audit agenda and activity schedule to guide their activities. They will use preliminary audit findings to finalize their approach.

Prepare Project Audit Report

The project auditor/audit team will normally depart from the project management environment to prepare an audit report of findings and recommendations. Note that some audits are routine and are not necessarily conducted in response to any particular indicator of poor project performance. That considered, the auditor/audit team may well be able to report only a few findings. Indeed, the auditor/audit team may deem that overall adequate-to-excellent project and project management conditions will be presented in the audit report.

The following elements are recommended for inclusion in a typical project audit report:

■ Executive summary:
  – Overview of the audit type and purpose
  – General description of the project's condition
  – General identification of the cause(s) of the condition
  – Summary of recommendations (prescription for project continuation)

- Audit approach:
  - Overview of the activity steps performed by the auditor/audit team
  - Overview of audit methods used
  - Identification of auditor/audit team members
  - Identification of other audit participants
- Audit findings:
  - Specific statements of fact resulting from the audit examination, usually indicating an adverse situation or condition
  - The impact, influence, or contribution of each finding to project performance
  - Apparent or actual cause of the audit finding, usually representing: a flaw or gap in established processes or procedures; a departure from established policies, standards, or management guidance; an incomplete or ineffective activity; or inadequate or incompetent task performance
- Audit recommendations:
  - Recommended actions and activities to remove or reduce findings and their cause
  - Suggested points of leadership and responsibility for each recommendation
  - Statement declaring the likelihood of project success after considering recommendations

The PMO can develop and use variations of this audit report content structure.

Manage Project Auditing Results

The PMO should be a recipient of all project audit reports. This enables it to properly accomplish its ongoing oversight role within the project management environment. In some cases, the PMO may be the primary repository for project audit reports, i.e., the project management library (see the PMO "knowledge management" function in Chapter 4). Nevertheless, it does have responsibility to maintain an awareness of project performance and project management capability within the relevant organization. The three activities described in the following subsections can be considered to help the PMO achieve its oversight objectives.

Review Project Audit Results

The PMO should conduct its own review of project audit reports as a matter of maintaining its awareness of conditions within the project management environment. This review should be timely and can be achieved in conjunction with an oral presentation by the auditor/audit team.

The PMO's review of audit results has three particular objectives that extend beyond the general need for awareness of the project management environment. These are described in the following subsections.

Identification of Troubled Projects

The PMO should identify, in collaboration with any other reviewers, whether the indications of project performance warrant special attention, up to and including the initiation of a project recovery effort. Short of that indication, the PMO can examine audit results in the following areas:

- Findings that can be resolved by the current project manager
- Findings that cannot be resolved by the current project manager, perhaps as a result of larger organizational policy or process issues or as a function of the PMO
- Findings that warrant PMO or PMO-arranged support of project manager efforts
- Identification of recurring difficulties for a particular project manager
- Identification of difficulties encountered across several projects

The PMO's review of each audit report will allow it to (a) assess trends within the project management environment and (b) be proactive in formulating solutions that resolve major and recurring issues and problems that adversely affect project performance.

Examination of Audit Completeness

The PMO can use the audit report as a basis for evaluating auditor/audit team performance. It should examine the report to determine whether the audit was complete and comprehensive and to verify that it achieved the objectives and expectations established. Points of examination can include:

- Consistency of reported audit findings with known conditions
- Clarity of findings statements that represent the adequacy and depth of auditor examinations and analyses
- Apparent constraints or roadblocks encountered by the auditor/audit team that reduced its ability to delve into certain aspects of project performance

- Apparent unanticipated intrusion or interference by the auditor/audit team in the project management environment
- Consistency and completeness of audit recommendations with reported findings

The PMO will presumably have selected a qualified project management audit consultant to conduct the audit. This is the PMO's opportunity to build a professional relationship with the audit consultant and to bring the needs of the project management environment, as well as the business interests of the relevant organization, to light so that future auditing efforts will be more closely aligned with PMO needs and expectations. This consideration works well for both internal and external third-party auditors.

Formulation of Follow-On PMO Activities

The PMO can examine each audit report to determine whether there are any required follow-on PMO actions that are either directly associated with report recommendations or indirectly associated with rectification or resolution of audit findings. The PMO should consider the following possible action areas:

- Review impact of policy guidance
- Review content and utilization of project management methodology
- Review content and utilization of technical processes
- Consider acquisition or replacement of project management tools
- Review training of project manager and project team members
- Review performance of project manager

Other needed PMO actions can be developed and pursued as dictated by the particular results of the project audit.

Analyze Aggregate Program Results

One means by which the PMO can develop and maintain its awareness of overall project performance is through ongoing reviews of similar audit-type results. This requires examining the aggregate results of audits across all projects, including current, completed, and terminated projects. It provides another way for the PMO to identify and monitor trends and the effectiveness of remedies applied to correct deficiencies in project performance.

A simple example of a tool that can be used to monitor audit trends and remedies is a cross-tabulation worksheet. This worksheet can be constructed to enable the PMO to list audit findings by the type of audit conducted and the appearance of related findings across multiple projects. The worksheet can be expanded to include instances where a particular remedy was applied to projects, and an indication of improvement can be noted for all projects. In essence, this worksheet provides a current picture of the prevalent problems or deficiencies, the prescribed fixes, and the results of applied fixes. The PMO can update this worksheet as each new project audit report is received and reviewed.

Another benefit of performing aggregate analyses of audit results is that senior management and other project stakeholders can use them to review the overall project performance capability within the relevant organization. In particular, the PMO will be formulating and applying remedies to correct deficiencies, and an aggregate trend analysis will quantify the rate and nature of project performance improvement achieved, which can then be reviewed by senior management.

Aggregate analyses also will be beneficial for review by project managers, who can use them in planning meetings to incorporate remedies into the technical and project management approaches and activities. They can also apply and monitor remedies identified by other project audits during project execution or implementation phases, thus allowing them to recognize and perhaps avoid similar deficiencies or problems.

The PMO's examination of audit results from the larger perspective of all projects enables it to monitor and manage improvements in overall project performance.

Monitor Project Audit Follow-Up Activities

The PMO, as facilitator of the "project auditing" function in the relevant organization, should also ensure that the full value of auditing is achieved by monitoring the conduct of audit follow-up activities. This includes oversight of corrective actions applied at the project level as well as at the PMO's functional level.

This effort begins with a review of the audit recommendations to determine which will be accepted for immediate action, which will be placed on a long-term improvement activity list, and which will be deferred (but not discarded). This review should include collaboration with project managers, senior managers, and other project stakeholders, depending on the nature of the proposed remedy. In the course of review and collaboration — a single meeting or an ongoing series of communications — follow-up actions should be deliberated, decided, and assigned to responsible individuals.

The PMO can identify, track, and monitor several elements to ensure timely achievement of follow-up activities resulting from project audits:

- *Activity statement:* A simple statement of the effort, e.g., adjust status report frequency
- *Activity description:* A more detailed description of the effort that specifies the corrective actions to be taken, presents any required steps for effort or implementation, and indicates what objectives will be achieved when the corrective action is applied
- *Activity completion date:* The date by which the corrective action should be completed
- *Activity interim review date(s):* The date(s) when activity progress will be reported to the PMO
- *Activity manager:* The designation of the individual responsible for accomplishing the activity description
- *Activity close out date:* The date when the corrective actions have been completed

The PMO can use this information to monitor the progress of corrective action implementation and, as necessary, suggest, implore, assist, and mandate accomplishments. Once the remedy has been deliberated and decided, the activity manager can prepare this information, and the PMO can concentrate on monitoring progress at key dates.

POSTSCRIPT FOR THE SMALLER PMO

The smaller PMO will generally find itself in a support role more than in an oversight role, and therefore it is likely that no formal PMO-based auditing function is established or currently planned within the relevant organization. However, even in a support role, the PMO can be a key contributor to project performance improvement, and it can achieve that through the use of less-formal project examination methods.

The following list identifies a few ways in which the PMO can examine and monitor performance within the project management environment in the absence of a formal "project audit" function:

- Review project status reports and progress reports to obtain insight into project performance information. Compile information and analyze trends on individual projects and across all projects within the PMO's purview.
- Examine conditions and establish a few simple indicators of the effectiveness of project performance, and request that project managers include that information in their monthly reports. Alternatively, go out and meet with project managers on a recurring basis to discuss the prescribed indicators.

- Develop a professional relationship with individuals in business units that conduct audits within the project management environment, e.g., quality management. Request collaboration on their audit findings and recommendations as a routine action. Then, review their audit reports and perform trend analyses on individual and groups of affected projects.
- Convene a group of senior or otherwise prominent project managers to gain individual and group perspectives on project performance issues, e.g., general problems, deficiencies, and inconsistencies. Facilitate their discussion and deliberation for remedies to the top issues identified.

There is another activity the smaller PMO can consider, particularly if there are one or more obviously troubled projects in the relevant organization. In lieu of establishing the full project audit functionality, the PMO can coordinate its needs and gain approval to obtain the services of an external, third-party project management audit consultant. This will allow a comprehensive examination of the identified projects and the subsequent application of appropriate remedies that will enable them to become viable and more likely to achieve successful completion.

16

PROJECT RECOVERY

Projects are selected and performed because of their inherent business value. Therefore, barring any business decision to terminate a project, every project warrants the opportunity to succeed. In most business environments, a project is expected, if not mandated, to succeed. However, there may be times when project success will seem fleeting, and corrective actions beyond the routine are needed to return the project to a path toward success. The rigor and formalities of an effective project recovery process is a recognized approach to turn around straying and troubled projects.

The PMO should take a lead role in developing and influencing project recovery actions within the project management environment. Similar to project management methodology development, the PMO can conceive and implement a project recovery solution that best fits the needs of the relevant organization. Project recovery implementation can be relatively simple once the more difficult and more complex development of capability to respond has been established. To that end, the approach and description of this PMO function is not extensive; it provides essential activities for PMO consideration and implementation. However, the impact of developing an effective project recovery capability will have significant positive business impact.

This "project recovery" function enables the PMO to:

- Distinguish routine project corrective actions from defined project recovery efforts
- Specify recommended composition and attributes of a project recovery team
- Prescribe the criteria and process for implementing a project recovery effort
- Build a library of project corrective actions for use by project managers

Project recovery is a specialized tool used within the project management environment to (a) examine why routine project management practices are not producing desired project performance results and (b) prescribe the corrective actions needed to return project management oversight and control to a routine state. Establishing that capability is the objective to be undertaken by the PMO.

PROJECT ENVIRONMENT INTERFACE CONCEPTS

Project recovery implies that there is a variation in project performance that is significant enough (within a particular project management environment) to warrant special attention by the PMO and probably senior management. At first glance, it would seem that project recovery is needed because of some sudden and massive failure somewhere in the process, in the people assigned to the project, or in the support system, so now the PMO and management experts are needed to "clean up" the situation. Unfortunately, that is always a possibility. However, project recovery is more likely to be needed because of slower and less discernable deterioration in project performance that suddenly becomes apparent.

To instill confidence, the PMO can develop recommendations for ongoing senior management involvement through such mechanisms as project and portfolio management reviews, as a means of monitoring project performance before trouble occurs and project recovery is needed.

The PMO also serves as a resource for project managers, possibly in conjunction with mentoring or risk-planning support activities, helping them to identify critical project performance indicators that can be examined and managed during project execution to avoid the need for formal project recovery actions. However, when project recovery is needed, the PMO can also assist in forming and preparing the specially qualified teams needed to spearhead the project recovery effort, often from among the cadre of highly qualified project managers it has developed.

Similarly, the development of a PMO "project recovery" function also should do as much to preclude its formal implementation as it does to guide corrective actions when specifically needed. The PMO will be able to assert technical influence over projects through development of a project recovery capability. The "project recovery" function uses technical and business concepts based in routine project management activities, only now those activities are performed with more rigor and closer attention to process details. Therefore, much of the project management process and content that is examined and implemented within the context of project recovery can be simultaneously applied as well to project management standards (Chapter 3), methodology (Chapter 1), planning (Chapter 14), and mentoring (Chapter 13) functions, to name a few.

BUSINESS ENVIRONMENT INTERFACE CONCEPTS

It is a generally accepted perspective that troubled projects are not the result of one single problem but, rather, are a combination of multiple neglected indicators of poor project performance. To that end, the need for project recovery warrants an examination of contributing processes and practices that could span the involvement of other business units within the relevant organization. The PMO plays an important role in collaborating such an investigation across business units, as well as recommending or otherwise facilitating remedies for any adverse factors uncovered outside the immediate project management environment.

The PMO also can facilitate senior management and business unit understanding of the problems encountered by project managers, serving as a representative of the project management environment. It will ensure that a professional examination of troubled projects is undertaken and that accurate information about troubled projects and their causes is conveyed to the business environment. In turn, the PMO is centrally positioned to receive and implement executive and senior manager guidance regarding the initiation and conduct of project recovery activities.

PROJECT RECOVERY ACTIVITIES ACROSS THE PMO CONTINUUM

The "project recovery" function along the PMO competency continuum establishes expanding capability to identify and resolve project management problems and issues that threaten the stability of project performance or the successful outcome of projects within the relevant organization. This places the PMO in a key role of assuring that project management is at least sufficiently effective to detect and discern its own limitations. It does this to varying degrees according to the stage of PMO development.

Table 16.1 presents an overview of the range of prescribed PMO project recovery activities according to each level in the PMO competency continuum.

The *project office* is at the forefront of project control and has direct responsibility for identifying project problems, issues, and other difficulties using criteria established for all projects. It can achieve this by following prescribed processes for project management, with a particular focus on elements that include reviewing and reporting project performance. The project office will normally apply standard remedies to minor project performance variations. However, when the situation warrants, the PMO will use established criteria and guidance to elevate problems and issues to a higher level PMO or to senior management for review. It is usually

Table 16.1 Range of Project Recovery Activities across the PMO Continuum

Project Office	Basic PMO	Standard PMO	Advanced PMO	Center of Excellence
Monitors project performance indicators to detect potential for major problems	Creates preliminary guidance for project control ■ Manages a list of indicators for troubled projects ■ Compiles and validates general remedies used to correct project performance ■ Specifies procedures for elevating issue projects	Develops capability to conduct project recovery activities ■ Builds qualified project recovery teams ■ Develops assessments based on project recovery results ■ Specifies project recovery actions ■ Evaluates project recovery results	Expands capability to conduct project recovery efforts ■ Provides project recovery training for recovery team members ■ Introduces project recovery management and tracking tools	Analyzes project recovery to promote goals of continuous improvement ■ Analyzes results for project recovery processes and utilization ■ Develops project indicators and remedies to avoid need for project recovery

the authority above the project office that determines whether project recovery actions are warranted.

Mid-range PMO levels will apply their authority and expertise to establish a fundamental to advanced capability to deal with troubled projects. This capability includes specifying criteria and defining what constitutes a troubled project within the relevant organization, forming a qualified project recovery team and process to assess and rectify the problems encountered (and return the project to a standard state), and evaluating the effectiveness of the project recovery intervention. It also introduces the tools needed to manage project recovery efforts.

The *center of excellence* continues its pursuit of continuous improvement within the project management environment. It will conduct analyses to determine the use and effectiveness of the project recovery process. It also will conduct root-cause analyses as a basis for developing indicators that can be used to identify potential for troubled projects and to prescribe solutions that reduce the number of troubled projects encountered within the relevant organization.

This PMO function serves as the focal point for identifying problems and then prescribing and implementing remedies to correct troubled projects. To that end, it inherently will have significant interface with and draw on capability already established in several other relevant PMO functions, as is highlighted in the function model presented below.

PROJECT RECOVERY FUNCTION MODEL

Project managers routinely identify problems and apply corrective actions on an ongoing basis throughout the project management life cycle. This normally represents minor or routine adjustments needed to bring around veering alignment with project cost, schedule, and resource utilization. Routine corrective actions also may address scope, risk, quality, customer service, and a variety of other issues. Conversely, when such factors have reached unacceptable thresholds, when they no longer respond to routine corrective actions, or when they become too numerous to control, a more formal approach is warranted — project recovery.

The PMO should be instrumental in defining when and how project recovery actions will be introduced in the project management environment. Presumably, using a formal process to fix a troubled project will be an infrequent activity and will likely draw attention to the effort on several fronts — project team, management, customer, etc. Devise a precision approach for quickly assessing the need for project recovery and then implement a solution that brings the project back on track. The ultimate goal is to return the project to a routine state of project management at the earliest possible time.

In a sense, project recovery represents a specialized approach to conducting a project audit, with the anticipated need for follow-on project planning support. To that end, features and capabilities developed in those PMO functions can be applied to the project recovery effort. This includes the examination (audit) of a project that has given indications of poor performance to determine what actually is wrong, followed by planning and implementing a revised project plan (and usually an adjusted, more rigorous project management approach) when it is confirmed that a project in fact needs special, project recovery attention to be successful.

The PMO needs to develop the approach to project recovery that will be used within the relevant organization. It can consider the prescriptive steps described in this function model to develop the project recovery approach used — by the PMO or other project recovery body — to guide project recovery actions within the project management environment.

The prominent activities of the PMO's "project recovery" function model are depicted in Figure 16.1. Each activity is described in the following subsections.

Develop Recovery Assessment Process

The PMO should apply awareness of the relevant organization's culture, consideration for the nature of projects, and an understanding of business interests to establish an effective approach to assessing the need for project recovery. The PMO can focus on developing four process steps to guide project recovery assessment activities within the relevant organization. These are described in the following subsections.

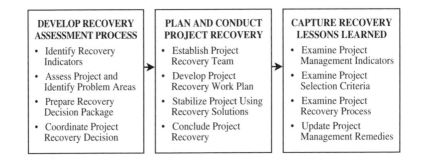

DEVELOP RECOVERY ASSESSMENT PROCESS	PLAN AND CONDUCT PROJECT RECOVERY	CAPTURE RECOVERY LESSONS LEARNED
• Identify Recovery Indicators	• Establish Project Recovery Team	• Examine Project Management Indicators
• Assess Project and Identify Problem Areas	• Develop Project Recovery Work Plan	• Examine Project Selection Criteria
• Prepare Recovery Decision Package	• Stabilize Project Using Recovery Solutions	• Examine Project Recovery Process
• Coordinate Project Recovery Decision	• Conclude Project Recovery	• Update Project Management Remedies

Figure 16.1 "Project Recovery" Function Model

Identify Recovery Indicators

The PMO should evaluate and prescribe the indicators that can be used to identify the need for a project recovery assessment. Such indicators will be used to define a troubled project in the relevant organization. Having such indicators not only addresses project recovery needs, but when routinely monitored, these indicators can also serve as a general means of project control. Essentially, the PMO will need to examine indicators and specify what criteria can be applied to the project under examination to distinguish it as one that is on a troubled course and thus warrants consideration for formal project recovery actions.

It should be noted at this juncture that the PMO is simply trying to identify the general indicators that can be used to bring attention to a potentially troubled project. It is not yet assessing the underlying cause of any problems. The PMO can consider indicators in the following areas, add more indicators pertinent to the relevant organization, and assign significant threshold criteria by which each indicator will be monitored:

- Scope:
  - Alignment of project plans (and deliverables) with official scope changes
  - Variation in stakeholder versions (or perspectives) of the scope statement
  - Frequency and cause of project scope changes
- Cost:
  - Variation in planned versus actual cost
  - Reliability of cost estimates
- Schedule:
  - Variation in planned versus actual schedule
  - Reliability of schedule estimates
- Resource utilization:
  - Variation in planned versus actual staffing
  - Reliability of resource utilization estimates
- Quality:
  - Level of defects or discrepancies in deliverables undergoing internal review
  - Level of defects or discrepancies in deliverables presented to the customer
- Risk:
  - Reliability of the most recent project risk analysis
  - Frequency of occurrence of unforeseen project risk events
- Other general indicators:
  - Reliability of vendors and subcontractors
  - Nature and impact of corrective actions taken to date

452 ■ The Complete Project Management Office Handbook

  - Timeliness, completeness, and accuracy of project status reports
  - Management satisfaction and confidence
  - Customer satisfaction and confidence

Monitoring these indicators on an ongoing basis is inherently a part of tracking and controlling project performance, and these are indicators that can be used to that end. However, the PMO should distinguish assigned criteria between routine control thresholds and those used to identify troubled projects.

In general, when the threshold for a troubled project has been identified, the PMO or relevant management group (e.g., executive control board) should make a decision regarding whether or not to conduct a project recovery assessment. The decision to assess implies that the project has reached unacceptable levels, that routine corrective actions are deemed inadequate to correct the situation, and that project recovery action is to be pursued.

Assess Project and Identify Problem Areas

The project recovery assessment represents a detailed examination or audit of project performance. It can be conducted by the PMO or by a qualified ad hoc team in the relevant organization. It is also a consideration that the assessment team could be a replacement for the current project team. A project recovery assessment is normally not conducted by the current project manager to ensure that a fresh and unbiased perspective of the project condition is achieved.

Conducting this assessment formally places the project in recovery mode. This status needs to be identified to warrant and explain the likely interference with routine project operations and the intervention of the assessment team that will be forthcoming. It also will help anticipate and explain the cost to be incurred by the project recovery effort.

The PMO or other assessment team can use the evaluation areas prescribed below to examine and identify the causes of poor project performance. This examination should include consideration of all examination areas listed, including those not necessarily aligned with initial poor or weak performance indicators. This is because the project will undoubtedly undergo replanning, and all aspects of project performance should be included as a basis for improving current project status and conditions and to provide greater opportunity for successful completion of the project.

There are five major areas of project performance that can be examined as a part of the project recovery assessment, and these are described in the following subsections. The PMO can use this list as a reference in developing a more specific approach to project recovery assessment content and activities for use within the relevant organization.

Assess Application of the Current Project Management Methodology

This examination area evaluates how well the prescribed activities of project management have been accomplished. It includes consideration of:

- Timely and accurate achievement of key project management planning deliverables:
  - Project definition (requirements, scope, objectives, deliverables, etc.)
  - Project charter (project management authority, funding, etc.)
  - Project work breakdown structure (WBS) and work plan (cost, schedule, and resource utilization)
  - Resource responsibility matrix (requirements, competency level, tasks, etc.)
  - Adjunct project plans (risk, quality, communication, etc.)
- Timely and accurate achievement of key project management execution deliverables:
  - Project team formation and management activities
  - Customer agreement or contract execution
  - Management reviews and stage/gateway activities
  - Project tracking, controlling, and reporting
  - Customer involvement and deliverable-acceptance activities
- Timely and accurate application of appropriate technical management components:
  - Technical solution development (technical design, standards application, etc.)
  - Technical reviews and stage/gateway activities
  - Introduction of tools and technology

The examination of these methodology assessment factors should identify any critical project management activities that were not performed (or not performed effectively) as a basis for specifying contributions to poor project performance. In a general sense, the assessment should also examine the appropriateness of the content and process of the project management methodology used for the project under consideration.

Assess the Current Project Management Support Structure

This examination area evaluates how well or poorly the project management support structure of the relevant organization has contributed to project performance. It includes consideration of:

- Executive and senior management participation and support
- Business unit involvement and support activities
- PMO involvement and support activities
- Accomplishment of required training for project team members
- Availability, assignment, and use of project management and technical tools
- Availability, assignment, and use of technical equipment and new technology
- Functional alignment of project team (resource manager implications)

The examination of these support-structure assessment factors should provide sufficient insight to determine any impacts that the current support structure had on project performance. This includes examination of attentiveness (actions taken) and inattentiveness (lack of involvement or support) that contributed to the current project performance conditions.

Assess the Current Business Interests and Issues

This examination area evaluates the influence of the relevant organization's business interests and issues as contributions to project performance. It includes consideration of:

- Project priority (e.g., business importance, internal visibility, customer retention)
- Project contributions to strategic business objectives (i.e., business case changes)
- Adequacy and availability of properly skilled staff
- Timeliness of project resource allocation and assignment decisions
- Customer sales process and engagement-management issues
- Customer reactions to project performance

This examination area evaluates the implications of any changed business perspective or unattended business interest that is associated with project performance.

Assess the Current Project Work Plan

This examination area evaluates the fundamental drivers of project performance. These factors tend to be the primary points of examination, which is usually warranted because of their direct impact on project performance. It includes consideration of:

- Project scope and WBS:
  - Initial validation of project scope with the customer
  - Formal documentation and collaboration of project scope changes
  - Frequency of project scope changes
  - Occurrence of scope creep outside of a formal change-management process
  - Identification of internal and external events affecting scope change
  - Customer decisions, indecision, and unilateral changes in requirements
  - Incidental influence (expansion or reduction) of project team on work efforts
  - Scope representation in the WBS (e.g., work-flow gaps, critical activities, etc.)
  - Collaboration, coordination, and approval of all WBS changes
- Project cost:
  - Accuracy of project cost (budget) estimates
  - Cost variation history
  - Cost tracking and controlling practices applied
  - Current status of project cost
- Project schedule:
  - Accuracy of project schedule (time) estimates
  - History of schedule variation
  - Schedule tracking and controlling practices applied
  - Current status of project schedule
- Project resource utilization:
  - Accuracy of project resource utilization (staffing) estimates
  - History of variation in resource utilization
  - Resource utilization tracking and controlling practices
  - Current status of project resource utilization

This examination area addresses the core aspects of effective project management to ascertain how well they have been managed to date and to identify underlying causes for unusual variations and unacceptable project performance. The factors considered in this examination area are normally a direct responsibility of the project manager. Therefore, interviews and discussions with the project manager may be an important part of this assessment component.

Assess the Current Project Team and Key Stakeholders

This examination area evaluates the actions and interactions of the current project manager having responsibility for project performance as well as the associated project team (in whole or part) for their contribution to the current state of project performance. It includes consideration of:

- Project manager:
  - Workload
  - Competence and experience relative to project size, type, value, etc.
  - Technical skill and capability to provide technical oversight
  - Authority and control (e.g., excessive or insufficient)
  - Response to business guidance
  - Personality and professional behavior constraints
- Project team:
  - Workload
  - Technical skill and experience relative to assigned project tasks
  - Composition and cohesion (i.e., stage of development)
  - Member reductions, additions, and intermittent appearances
  - Response to technical and management guidance and direction
  - Conflicts and unresolved interpersonal problems
- Vendor and contractor participation in the project effort:
  - Achievement of contractual obligations
  - Appropriate participation in prescribed project team role
  - Demonstration of continuing vested interest
  - Accomplishment of required reports and participation in required communication
- Customer participation in the project effort:
  - Achievement of contractual obligations
  - Appropriate participation in prescribed project activities
  - Demonstration of consistent guidance toward stable project objectives
  - Responsiveness to requests for clarification, scheduled document and deliverable reviews, and scheduled project activities

This examination area prompts enhanced awareness of the project recovery effort and should be pursued carefully and with a professional approach. It delves into an evaluation of personalities and competencies of individuals who hold responsibility for successful project performance. This effort should focus on fact-finding and not on personal attributes, although it is likely that personal attributes will be indirectly identified and examined as a part of the project recovery assessment.

Prepare Recovery Decision Package

The PMO should provide guidance for confirming the project recovery decision either for use under its own authority or for presentation for senior management review and approval. Conducting a project recovery assessment presumes that a subsequent project recovery effort will be undertaken. This activity step enables a final review of the project status to be accomplished and provides an opportunity to confirm the need for project recovery.

Recovery action review and approval is facilitated when the PMO constructs a standard document and approach to the decision process, i.e., a project recovery decision package. The following elements are suggested for inclusion in the project recovery decision package.

- *Project recovery assessment activities*: A presentation and written discussion regarding the project recovery assessment. This section can be as detailed or abbreviated as is required by the decision maker and in alignment with the established business document preparation practices of the relevant organization. It includes the following information points:
  - Assessment team composition
  - Identification of areas of project performance examined
  - Overview (statement) of assessment findings
- *Statement of project condition*: The results of further analysis of project recovery assessment findings are compiled and presented for reviewer consideration. They include:
  - Project performance problems and their root causes
  - Impacts of project performance problems (i.e., business, industry, customer, etc.)
  - Project performance improvement actions needed to achieve project success
- *Project recovery recommendation*: A recommendation concerning what to do with the project as a result of the current project condition is prepared. The recommendation should be consistent with project recovery assessment findings and with the subsequent statement of project condition. The default recommendation is to proceed with the project recovery effort. However, at this final decision point, there are still at least two alternative solutions. The three possible recommendations are:
  - Continue the project and proceed with project recovery. The condition of the project and its continued business interest and importance warrant proceeding with project recovery actions.
  - Continue the project without formal recovery action. The condition of the project can be rectified through minor corrective

actions and does not warrant the cost and effort incurred by a formal project recovery action. This recommendation validates that the project has continued business interest and importance.
- Terminate the project. The condition of the project is so severe that a recovery effort does not warrant the expense, or project continuation is not otherwise in the best business interest of the relevant organization.

The project recovery decision package is then presented to senior management decision makers for review and approval of the recommended action. In the interest of the likely pursuit of project recovery actions, this review and approval step should be expedited by the PMO. Following the project recovery decision, or alternative course of action, the PMO can prepare to lead the effort that implements the decision, beginning with the next and final step of this project recovery assessment process.

Coordinate Project Recovery Decision

The PMO can perform or otherwise facilitate coordinating the project recovery decision within the project management environment, and that effort may include some collaboration with key individuals in the business environment. In some cases, project stakeholders in the business environment will be involved in the deliberation and decision process.

The following are points of coordination to consider following a project recovery decision:

- Project manager and project sponsor (if not already involved in the decision process)
- Project team members (notification normally is achieved through the project manager)
- Vendor and contractor engagement managers (other appropriate key points of contact)
- Customer engagement manager (other appropriate customer points of contact)
- Business unit representative
- Resource managers
- Other project managers

Once all key participants are notified, the PMO can proceed with implementing the decision, presumably a project recovery effort.

Plan and Conduct Project Recovery

The PMO's reaction or influence in response to a decision to proceed with project recovery should be immediate and with a distinct purpose: to fix the problems encountered by the troubled project as soon as possible and to return the project to a routine state of project management operations.

In the following subsections, a four-step approach to conducting project recovery is presented for consideration.

Establish Project Recovery Team

The responsibility for bringing around a troubled project falls to the project recovery team. The project recovery team can be an incisive team striking immediately at the root causes of the troubled project, or it can be a replacement project team that addresses a comprehensive approach to project recovery activities. The project recovery team can be formed using a preorganized and pretrained group of highly experienced, highly qualified project professionals who are "on-call" for the purpose of conducting project recovery. Otherwise, convening the project recovery team is similar to any project team formation effort, but with more focus on ensuring that critical project management skills and experience are introduced as needed by the troubled project.

The disposition of the current project manager and project team members will vary by organization and industry and by the extent and nature of the project recovery effort. In some cases, the current project team will remain intact as recovery activities are pursued, such as in the case of the incisive team where the current project manager temporarily gives up the reins of the project. At other times, a large portion of the project team is disbanded, reassigned, and replaced by the project recovery team. It should be noted that unless the project team is only a handful of people, there does not have to be 100% replacement of all project team members. Rather, it is the key technical, business, and project management leadership that is refreshed under the project recovery mode of operations. In some cases, only the current project manager is reassigned. Most individuals would likely recognize project management replacement as a drastic measure, but that only serves to highlight the significance of a project recovery effort.

The PMO should play a primary role in defining project recovery team roles and responsibilities, which will serve as the basis for convening a project recovery team when one is needed. The following five subsections identify the important participants in every project recovery effort.

Senior Management

Senior management should have appropriate involvement and oversight in all projects conducted within the relevant organization. Under project recovery conditions, they play an even more active and critical role that is warranted by the additional expense committed to achieving the project recovery effort. Senior management has undoubtedly been involved in the decision to pursue project recovery for the project at hand, and executives and senior managers will strongly influence the ability to rectify the project problems that were encountered. Their decision to recover the troubled project is likewise a decision to accommodate the fixes necessary to get the project back on track.

The more pertinent project recovery responsibilities of senior management include:

- Funding the project recovery effort
- Allocating new or additional resources required for the project recovery effort
- Adjusting project portfolio priorities and decisions to accommodate project recovery
  - Evaluation of impacts on other projects resulting from project recovery needs
  - Temporary or permanent reassignment of key project professionals
  - Review of strategic business interests affected by project recovery actions
- Participating in project recovery status reviews and updates
- Supporting and facilitating PMO development and implementation of process guidance in the project management environment to avoid recurring needs for project recovery

The PMO should serve as a primary advisor to senior management during project recovery activities, and it can take a lead role in ensuring that senior management is aware of its responsibilities and is appropriately involved.

Project Recovery Manager

The project recovery manager will serve as the new project manager during the project recovery period, and in some cases, for the remaining duration of the project. This is distinctly a role in which experience counts, and some specialized training in project recovery would be beneficial as well. At the very least, the project recovery manager should be among those individuals with the most impeccable qualifications in project management capability to be found within the relevant organization.

The PMO would be well advised to identify candidates for project recovery manager before the need for such an assignment surfaces. This allows the PMO and the selected individuals to achieve at least some fundamental preparation for the role and responsibilities associated with rectifying what ails troubled projects.

The following are primary responsibilities that are associated with the project recovery manager serving as the new project manager:

- Gaining early awareness of the project condition:
  - Review of the project recovery decision package
  - Review of current, viable project planning documents
  - Review of current, viable project tracking documents and reports
- Managing project recovery team formation:
  - Inform current project team members of approach to project recovery
  - Select new project recovery facilitators and core managers
  - Introduce and integrate current and new project team members
  - Establish guidance and responsibilities for operating in project recovery mode
- Preparing the revised business solution:
  - Review and update project financials
  - Review and reassess project risks
  - Review and update the project definition statement
  - Develop revised business case
  - Incorporate project recovery assessment recommendations
- Preparing the revised technical solution:
  - Structure the new technical approach
  - Develop a project recovery work plan
  - Incorporate project recovery assessment recommendations
- Collaborating project recovery activities with the customer:
  - Inform the customer of the status of the project recovery effort
  - Obtain customer input to business and technical plan updates
  - Prepare a project recovery proposal for submittal to the customer
  - Manage the customer relationship under project recovery conditions
- Managing the project recovery effort:
  - Facilitate frequent senior management involvement in project recovery review and approval activities
  - Closely monitor and manage project recovery team performance, with particular focus on accurate and timely project reporting

- Direct and manage vendor and contractor replanning and performance under project recovery conditions
- Conduct timely project recovery business and technical review meetings
- Prepare timely project recovery progress reports to senior management
- Manage costs and expenses associated with project recovery
- Recommend return to normal project management operations

The PMO should develop a more detailed key activity checklist for project recovery to guide and assist the project recovery manager in accomplishing essential project recovery activities.

Project Team Members

The project recovery team normally comprises a combination of the individuals currently assigned to the project effort and the influx of hand-selected team members who will facilitate the project recovery effort. Some current project team members may depart for a variety of reasons that are not necessarily related to the root causes of the troubled project. Such factors as the timing of the recovery effort matching the individual's planned departure date, the need to replace someone on another project who is now assigned to the recovery effort, or the need to reduce the cost associated with project recovery are examples of such departure reasons. However, it should be recognized that there also might be some current members of the project team who are released because of their weak performance.

New members of the project team likely will be introduced during the project recovery effort to bring needed technical and project management skill and experience, as well as to revitalize an effort that is deemed to have continuing strategic business importance to the relevant organization. New team members should be selected because they have demonstrated capability and desire to address the challenges of the project recovery effort. In general, it will likely be mid level managers, established technical leaders, and others who have demonstrated leadership within the project management environment who will be hand-selected to fulfill just a few of the critical project roles during the project recovery effort.

Again, the PMO can be proactive in identifying candidates for critical project recovery team roles in advance of the immediate need for such assignments. It might even consider the same project managers who are also candidates for the role of project recovery manager. The consideration in using the same candidates is to get the best and most competent project and technical professionals on board immediately, with as little preparation as necessary to achieve early results, and then return them and the project back to routine operations as quickly as possible.

The following are several of the key responsibilities of individuals assigned as members of the project recovery team:

- Recognize the effort as one of project recovery and business importance
- Advise the project recovery manager in areas of professional and technical expertise
- Conduct and communicate risk management activities in areas of responsibility
- Provide frequent and timely project status reports
- Perform assigned project tasks in a timely manner
- Collaborate immediately with the project recovery manager on issues and problems

The PMO should devise a means of recognizing members of the project recovery team. It can do this during the assignment, but it is particularly important at the conclusion of a successful recovery effort.

Vendors and Contractors

Different organizations will likely have different perspectives regarding the alignment of vendors and contractors as members of the project team. Regardless of their capacity and involvement, these external resources, when aligned, will be important stakeholders in conducting the project recovery effort. They warrant sufficient attention and examination if they are to be included in the project recovery effort.

Vendors and contractors who remain on the project will need to be aware of the project recovery operating conditions, and they will need to become an active participant in achieving project recovery objectives. New vendors and contractors introduced after the initiation of project recovery activities will likewise have to become acquainted with the demands and constraints of the approach to project management conducted under recovery conditions.

Essentially, this means preparing vendors and contractors for the rigorous oversight and control they will encounter, ensuring that they have assigned competent and experienced personnel to critical tasks prescribed by the project recovery plan, and gaining their support and commitment for the duration of their involvement in the recovery effort. On major projects, the PMO can support the project recovery manager by serving as a facilitator for the advance qualification and preparation of vendors and contractors. Otherwise, the PMO can construct guidance and recommendations for managing vendors and contractors under project recovery conditions, and these recommendations can be used by subsequent project recovery teams.

Customers

The customer is arguably the project stakeholder experiencing the greatest impact from the need for project recovery. The customer's expectations for project success have undoubtedly been diminished, faith in the competency and capability of the performing organization has likely been stirred, and reliance on future project success is at best uncertain. It is therefore imperative that the customer be involved in the project recovery effort to the extent that the customer desires without being an adverse influence or a hindrance to the timely deployment of a recovery solution. Perhaps the preferred role of the customer, at least from the perspective of the relevant organization, is that of active participant.

There presumably will be early business meetings with the client to identify project failure and to deliberate the alternatives, and the results of such interactions will factor heavily into the decision to proceed with a recovery effort. Therefore, by the time project recovery actually begins, the customer is essentially poised for participation in the recovery effort to be undertaken. However, the participation needed and the specific role of the customer may not be clear at the onset of recovery activities. The PMO and the project recovery manager should address initial participation and ongoing customer involvement in the project recovery effort.

If, perchance, the customer was a contributor to the troubled project, the recovery plan will identify how those root causes of problems can be rectified, and the customer relationship can be discretely managed to implement necessary corrections.

Otherwise, the customer should be actively involved in several key project recovery activities:

- Review of and concurrence with the recovery plan
- Participation in meetings to discuss project recovery progress
- Participation in technical review meetings (particularly when changes to project scope, deliverable specifications, or delivery schedule are discussed and deliberated)
- Review and acceptance of deliverables
- Celebrations of project success

The PMO can develop a customer information package that specifies recommended points of customer involvement in the project recovery effort. This information-style package presented to the customer can also provide reassurance by highlighting the activities undertaken by the relevant organization to ensure effective management of the recovery effort and ultimate success of the project.

Develop Project Recovery Plan

The project recovery plan represents the renewed approach and commitment by the relevant organization to the project recovery effort. It will likely require more detail, or at least more supporting documentation and analyses for its content, than that normally required for routine project planning. Above all else, the project recovery plan must be a mechanism that demonstrates that the relevant organization knows how to manage projects. Nevertheless, there is still room for deliberation regarding the content actually needed in the project recovery plan.

The following four items represent the suggested minimum content for a viable project recovery plan:

- Revised project work plan:
  - *Work breakdown structure (WBS)*: Incorporates tasks and actions to rectify adverse findings and implement prescribed solutions identified in (a) the project recovery decision package and (b) per the revised specification of project scope and objectives contained in the new project definition statement
  - *Cost*: Specifies reestimated project cost figures resulting from more precise use of project cost estimating tools and techniques
  - *Schedule*: Specifies reestimated project timelines resulting from application of more-accurate time-estimating tools and techniques
  - *Resource utilization*: Specifies reestimated project resource utilization requirements resulting from more effective use of staff-estimating tools and techniques
- Updated project risk management plan:
  - Includes (a) a review of the original risk assessment and associated response strategies and (b) the preparation of a new plan to address the elements of the revised project work plan
  - Specifies (a) the general risk management responsibilities of all project team members and (b) the specific responsibilities of selected managers and technical leaders assigned to the project recovery team
  - Identifies (a) the likely increased frequency for conducting project risk reviews and (b) specifies the need for immediate reporting of results to the project recovery manager

- ■ Updated quality assurance plan:
  - – Integrates steps to rectify quality issues cited in the project recovery decision package
  - – Includes, where possible, enhanced quality control activities to improve deliverables and offset any negative perceptions resulting from project failure, i.e., making a good deliverable better as a means of demonstrating success and positive influence of the project recovery effort
  - – Specifies opportunities for increased middle- and senior management technical review and approval of project deliverables, as is necessary to the recovery effort
- ■ Revised project communication plan:
  - – Introduces the enhanced need for close collaboration of plans and progress among project team members and, as appropriate to individual roles, with other stakeholders, e.g., senior management, customer, vendors and contractors
  - – Identifies the project recovery manager and other new participants on the project recovery team, and outlines their roles and responsibilities
  - – Presents revised requirements for reporting project status — content, frequency, and distribution — and progress to senior management
  - – Highlights adjusted, presumably tighter thresholds for reporting cost, schedule, and resource utilization variations and for elevating issues and problems encountered in a timely manner
  - – Reiterates the required change-control process and provides guidance for the coordination and distribution of revised project plans, technical documents, and other correspondence and reference materials

The PMO can prescribe these four primary documents to provide fundamental guidance to the project recovery effort. However, it can also recommend or require the development (or revision) and implementation of additional technical and project supporting plans, as necessary.

The nature and impact of the particular project recovery effort may warrant creation of additional guidance either for inclusion in or separate from the project recovery plan. This refers to the preparation of planning elements that address the business interests of the relevant organization. The PMO will need to collaborate with senior management and the project recovery manager to better define the need and the content, but the following are a few examples of additional project planning elements associated with project recovery that the PMO can consider in support of the current and ongoing capability to respond to project recovery efforts within the relevant organization.

- Customer relationship management plan
- Internal incident (rumor) control plan
- Public information and media management plan
- Senior management activity and response plan
- Business unit reorganization/realignment plan
- Shareholder communication plan
- Project management methodology update plan
- Project team member training plan
- Project management governance policies review plan

The concept of project recovery necessitates that the project recovery plan be reviewed at high levels in the relevant organization and be approved for implementation. The level of review may vary from organization to organization — some will have the newly assigned project recovery manager as the final authority, and others will want senior management to demonstrate that they are active participants in the recovery process, with final review and approval authority placed at that senior level. In reality, there likely will be several levels of review, and concurrence at all levels should be sought as a basis for proceeding with implementation of the project recovery plan.

Finally, the PMO should examine the situation of each individual recovery effort as a means of determining which stakeholders need to receive copies of the project recovery plan or any of its components. To that end, the PMO can facilitate distribution, consistent with its overall role in the project recovery effort.

Stabilize Project Using Recovery Solution

Once the project recovery plan has been prepared and distributed to the project team and other appropriate stakeholders, there can be a formal project restart or transition to project recovery mode. The project recovery work plan, in particular, will enable the project recovery team to begin rectifying problems and continue with the development of project deliverables per the revised project schedule. The critical event here is to implement the revised and refined project solution to demonstrate that control has been reestablished and that project success is imminent.

The implementation of the project recovery plan and its prescribed solution is highlighted by the close attention paid to several essential project management actions, which incidentally represent the same primary project management actions that are applied to routine projects, but with added focus under project recovery conditions:

■ *Recovery solution implementation*: The elements of the project recovery work plan are followed to achieve scheduled tasks and deliverables. The work plan is closely monitored to ensure that all activities are accomplished according to established technical requirements and deliverable specifications. Technical review and decision meetings are specified in the work plan and are conducted to include appropriate participation by members of the project team, senior management, and vendors and contractors; and meetings are monitored for attendance and achievement of desired results. The work plan is updated to reflect new risk response strategies (risk management is performed on an ongoing basis) and to incorporate bona fide changes from other project plan components.

■ *Stakeholder communication management*: Collaboration and participation of project stakeholders are managed to ensure that individual and business commitments are honored. Project documents and materials distributed for review and comment or decision are tracked, and timeliness of individual responses is monitored. Attention is given to effective meeting management; advance notification and meeting preparation instructions are given, an agenda is prepared, and individual action items are captured and tracked to completion. senior management decisions are facilitated by timely presentation of information and reports, and follow-on contact to provide clarification is conducted as critical decision dates draw close. Customer participation in key activities and critical decision points is particularly monitored, and professional reminders of the customer's role and responsibilities in project recovery are conveyed, as appropriate.

■ *Project tracking and controlling*: The three primary elements of the project work plan are tracked and controlled relative to planned versus actual:
  – Cost tracking and controlling: The revised project budget is closely monitored at frequent intervals for any discernable variation and for the cause of that variation. Cost variations outside of an extremely small tolerance range require immediate application of corrective actions. Project expenditures are closely managed, and expense approval and spending authority is limited to the project recovery manager (and possibly a few delegates) during the recovery effort. Virtually all expenses, particularly incoming invoices from vendors and contractors, are scrutinized for accuracy and validated for acceptance. New and additional funding is monitored for receipt and inclusion in the project budget.

- Schedule tracking and controlling: The revised project schedule is closely monitored at frequent intervals for any discernable variation and for the cause of that variation. Schedule variations outside of an extremely small tolerance range require immediate application of corrective actions. Project task performance is closely managed at shorter-interim review intervals. Task completion is verified. The project's critical path is frequently examined for progress and to identify potential delays or roadblocks, sometimes on a daily basis.
- Resource utilization tracking and controlling: The revised staffing plan is closely monitored at frequent intervals for any discernable variation and for the cause of that variation. Resource assignments and resource manager commitments are monitored for timely fulfillment. Individual resource participation is managed relative to the completion of assigned tasks. New and additional resource allocations are monitored for fulfillment and inclusion in the project staffing plan.

■ *Change management*: Changes to project scope, plans, specifications, and customer contracts or agreements are closely monitored and strictly controlled. The project recovery manager normally serves as the single point of approval for such changes and will usually collaborate and convey approved changes directly with affected stakeholders. The PMO should be proactive in establishing and monitoring the use of a project recovery change-management process. Essentially, this means using any current change-management process already included in the project management methodology, adjusting its procedures and content for the recovery effort at hand, and ensuring that it is used to track and manage changes encountered during project recovery. A rigorous change-management process is implemented to avoid casual decisions and to ensure proper coordination and collaboration of bona fide change requests, including performing the following general change-management process steps:

- Request: Specifying the details of a needed change and forwarding it for consideration in a project-change request
- Analyze: Analyzing the needs, benefits, and impacts of the change request, and preparing a recommended response for acceptance or rejection of the change request
- Review: Conducting a review of the recommended response by the project recovery manager and any other key stakeholders
- Approve: Approving the change request by the project recovery manager, senior management, or other designated authority

– Implement: Implementing the approved change, which includes (a) modifying the content of the project work plan, other project supporting plans, and technical and contractual documents and (b) announcing the implemented changes to members of the project team and other relevant stakeholders (per the project communication plan)

The PMO, as a prime stakeholder in project recovery efforts, needs to develop the capability to monitor the performance and results of these project management actions under project recovery conditions. In some project management environments, the PMO may be called upon to conduct these activities. In either case, the PMO should act in a supportive role during the transition to project recovery mode and should facilitate the accomplishment of project management actions that lead to a successful project recovery effort.

Conclude Project Recovery

Project recovery can be concluded when the project recovery manager deems the project has been stabilized and can demonstrate that essential project management indicators — usually cost, schedule, and resource utilization — are under sufficient control to ensure that the project will be successful in producing required customer deliverables, achieving customer satisfaction, and achieving its business objectives for the relevant organization. Other project management indicators can be specified for inclusion in the determination of project health and viability. The PMO should be a participant in constructing the indicators for use on project recovery efforts and in preparing guidance for their application.

The PMO will also need to develop the process that enables a project in recovery mode to transition back to routine or normal operations. The following elements are highlighted for consideration and inclusion in that transition process:

- *Compile recovery project data*: As a determination is made that transition to routine project operations appears warranted, a data collection point in time is specified, and a final compilation of key project management indicators and project recovery data is accomplished. This includes collecting collateral project recovery data from vendors and contractors and surveying the customer for input of project performance indicators.
- *Prepare project analysis and recommendation report*: A report is prepared by the project recovery manager to convey the project management improvements made, to specify the trends and current

status of acceptable project management indicators, and to show that project stabilization has been accomplished. Included in this report is the project recovery manager's recommendation for project transition, which inherently represents that the project is now viable and problem free according to widely accepted business and project management standards and practices, as applied within the relevant organization.

■ *Specify transition activities*: A separate document, or one attached to the analysis and recommendation report, should be prepared by the project recovery manager to show the activities that will be accomplished to facilitate the transition to routine project operations. This essentially equates to developing a transition plan that includes:

- Specification of final review, coordination, and approval activities
- Designation of the project manager (current project recovery manager continuation, assignment of a new project manager, or return of authority to the original project manager)
- Dispersal of the project recovery team (which members of the project team are leaving, which will be retained as part of a core team needed to complete the project, what new resources will be assigned or returned to this project assignment)
- Redesignation of roles and responsibilities for the remaining members of the project team
- Designation of the approach to project recovery document and material collection, including plans for a final examination of the project recovery effort (lessons learned) prior to archiving the data and materials
- Specification of planned internal information announcements, including recognition of project recovery team and customer satisfaction statements
- Specification of recommended public information and media announcements

■ *Obtain approval for transition*: The project analysis and recommendation report, along with the transition plan, are provided to key project stakeholders — prominently senior management and the customer — for review and approval decisions to proceed with transition to routine project operations. This process may include a personal appearance and presentation by the project recovery manager to substantiate the recommendation for transition.

■ *Conduct transition to routine operations*: Upon receipt of the approval to proceed, all project stakeholders are notified, and the transition plan is implemented.

■ *Archive project recovery documents and materials*: All project recovery documents and materials are collected and stored.

Conducting project recovery is presumably both a cost burden and an inefficient use of valuable resources for most organizations. Therefore, it is in their better business interest to rectify the problems of the troubled project as quickly as possible so that the routine practice of project management can resume. The PMO, having facilitated a large potion of the project recovery activities — if not directly leading them — will also benefit from a reduction in the demand for resources and in the urgency of project recovery support requirements as the project returns to normal operations.

However, not all projects will necessarily return to normal operations after being in recovery mode. In some cases, business interests may dictate continuing the enhanced attention and detailed management of the project recovery effort for the duration of the project. In other cases, it may be found that even the project recovery effort does not sufficiently rectify the troubled project, and project termination again becomes an option for consideration.

Capture Recovery Lessons Learned

The completion of a project recovery effort is a significant undertaking that warrants review to determine what went well; what could have been done better; and what should be done in future, similar efforts. The PMO should be a facilitator of information collection and analysis as well as a repository for lessons learned from project recovery.

There are four recommended areas in which the PMO can focus its efforts to obtain maximum benefit from its review of the project recovery experience, as described in the following subsections.

Examine Project Management Indicators

The need for the project recovery effort was originally identified because of project management indicators that were found to exceed specified acceptable thresholds. The PMO can examine the relevant project recovery assessment report, as well as the approach used to monitor project management indicators during the recovery effort, to determine whether new indicators or threshold criteria are needed.

The result of this examination should be (a) to validate that current project management and project performance indicators and criteria are still acceptable or (b) to specify that new indicators and criteria are needed. This activity does not actually develop any new or revised indicators and criteria, which is actually done in conjunction within the PMO's "standards and metrics" function (see Chapter 3). However, those involved in this examination (the PMO or others) are free to recommend specific modifications that can be considered during a separate development effort.

Examine Project Selection Criteria

The troubled project presumably started its life cycle by successfully passing through the project selection process — a process of close scrutiny relative to strategic business interests, technical performance competency, and overall perceived value within the relevant organization. The PMO can examine the business case used to select this project, with particular focus on the project's achievement of specified selection criteria. The results of this examination should provide some indication of whether or not the selection process could have precluded selection of the troubled project at the onset, or whether the project was selected despite selection indicators and criteria to the contrary. The results of this examination should be immediately forwarded to the executive control board, or other project selection authority, for inclusion in considerations for pending project selections. In the bigger picture, the PMO can recommend and revise the established project selection process and associated criteria per the validation of findings from this project recovery effort.

In addition to examining the selection criteria that represent the business case element of project selection, the PMO should also examine any associated resource allocation impacts. In particular, it should identify, from a retrospective position, whether all resource allocation commitments were fulfilled as prescribed during the selection process. It can also review early project selection negotiations that possibly reduced or modified the number or types of resources actually needed to ensure project success. Again, any preliminary findings resulting from this examination should be forwarded to the project control board (or other project selection authority) for inclusion in considerations for pending project resource allocation decisions. The PMO can resolve any existing resource allocation process issues as a separate effort from this examination.

Examine Project Recovery Process

The PMO can enhance the capability to conduct project recovery by reviewing application of its current project recovery process relative to the just-completed recovery effort.

The following list highlights a few of the areas that the PMO can examine to determine whether the prescribed project recovery process was effective or whether it contributed to project management difficulties during the project recovery effort:

- *Project recovery process utilization*: Did all key project recovery team members have access to and use the prescribed project recovery methods?
  - Process availability
  - Process familiarity
  - Process applicability
- *Project recovery process effectiveness*: Was the process comprehensive enough to provide sufficient guidance to enable users to initiate and conduct the project recovery effort?
  - Description of roles for project recovery participants
  - Description of procedures and activities for project recovery
  - Management tools and templates for project recovery
- *Project recovery support*: Does the process provide adequate guidance for obtaining (and giving) technical and business support during project recovery?
  - PMO guidance and support
  - Senior management guidance and support
  - Project recovery manager guidance and support

The PMO can examine the project recovery process in a manner similar to that used for the project management methodology. The objective is to identify what worked well and what did not work well. The examination can be based on a combination of PMO observations captured during the recovery effort and user comments solicited through surveys and interviews conducted during and after the recovery effort.

The PMO can use the findings of this examination to plan revisions to the project recovery process for future enhancement of project recovery capability.

Update Routine and Project Recovery Remedies

In conjunction with the earlier examinations of the project recovery effort, the PMO should receive considerable insight into the project management strategies and tactics used to rectify the problems encountered by the project in recovery mode. Indeed, the PMO may be a contributor of corrective action guidance for the project recovery manager and project team. The project recovery effort, in turn, provides an opportunity to validate the effectiveness of corrective actions implemented to achieve project recovery objectives.

Along the way, the lessons learned during project recovery will also provide some new insights into corrective actions that can be applied to routine project management efforts. In particular, it would be ideal to identify the corrective actions that do not work very well and then replace them with more-effective means of resolving routine project problems and issues and, of course, of reducing project variance across cost, schedule, and resource utilization indicators.

To that end, the lessons learned in project recovery efforts can be used to formulate standard remedies that can then be applied by project managers who encounter various project ailments and project management difficulties. The ultimate goal is to develop and implement remedies during routine project operations so that the project never veers so far as to require a project recovery effort.

The remedies developed can be incorporated by the PMO into both the project management methodology process as well as the project recovery process.

POSTSCRIPT FOR THE SMALLER PMO

The smaller PMO is likely to provide technical support rather than technical or business leadership for this PMO "project recovery" function. The PMO's primary role should be to reduce or remove the causes of troubled projects, thereby minimizing the likelihood of any need for project recovery. It can accomplish this role through regular reviews of project status and by assisting the project manager in identifying any indicators of weak project performance.

The PMO should be proactive — in conjunction with its "methodology development" function (see Chapter 1) and its "standards and metrics" function (see Chapter 3) — in identifying those indicators of weak project performance that best serve the relevant organization. Such indicators can be incorporated into the content of recurring project status and progress reports prepared by project managers. The most prominent indicators include the results of variance measurements for project cost, schedule, and resource utilization. The PMO can also develop other indicators that have significance within its project management environment.

Finally, the PMO can be of service to project managers, not to mention the business interests of the relevant organization, by constructing prescribed remedies that can be applied in response to weak project performance indicators. These remedies represent corrective actions that a project manager can take when specific problems or issues are encountered in the course of project management. For example, standard remedies can be prescribed to bring project variance to within acceptable thresholds, to reduce extensive product development time, or to manage scope creep through the use of more-stringent change-management procedures.

In summary, the smaller PMO should do what it can to facilitate development of project problem indicators, to facilitate routine examination of those indicators, and to prepare the preferred response or corrective actions that can be applied by project managers when problems are identified.

V

BUSINESS ALIGNMENT

17

PROJECT PORTFOLIO MANAGEMENT

The PMO has fundamental responsibility for coordinating project management activities across the designated organization it serves. A project portfolio is the collection of all projects under the purview of the senior managers of that designated organization. The project portfolio identifies all of the organization's current and pending projects, allowing each project to be viewed and examined individually and relative to all other projects in the portfolio collection.

Project portfolio management is inherently a responsibility of executive and senior managers. Establishing a project portfolio management capability enables the PMO to facilitate the involvement of executives and senior managers in project oversight. It allows the PMO to manage and coordinate ongoing executive and senior manager guidance and participation in processes, deliberations, and business decisions related to:

- Alignment of projects with business strategy
- Approval of the project "business plan" and funding
- Allocation of organizational resources for project work
- Prioritization of projects in the portfolio collection
- Review of ongoing project and portfolio performance

These responsibilities can be assumed by individual executives, such as department heads, or by a group of senior managers comprising a project portfolio review board.

The PMO can develop and implement processes and procedures for each of these project portfolio management activities, consistent with its level of responsibility and maturity. The nature of portfolio management suggests that any portfolio management capability pursued by the PMO will be accomplished in collaboration with the relevant executive or management team.

PROJECT ENVIRONMENT INTERFACE CONCEPTS

The project environment benefits from the implementation of an effective project portfolio management capability primarily due to ongoing executive and senior manager involvement in project oversight activities. Portfolio management is essentially a top-down function. It requires senior management to demonstrate strategic insight, apply sound business judgment, provide functional guidance, and make critical project continuation decisions. Conversely, in order to be successful in achieving top-down responsibilities, senior management also must ensure that the necessary bottom-up capability exists within the project environment, i.e., adequate project management methods for planning and tracking project performance, timely project communication and reporting procedures, proper system interfaces for data exchange and collaboration, an effective project resource management capability, and project manager competency to execute portfolio decisions.

In order to have an effective portfolio management capability, the organization must have an effective project management capability that underlies and supports the process of project portfolio management. This presents the need for executives and senior managers to recognize that portfolio management will only be as good as the information generated at the project level, since it is this information that is elevated to the portfolio management process, where it provides the basis for making project portfolio decisions. This should prompt senior management to commit to building and maintaining an effective project management environment when it establishes a "project portfolio management" function.

BUSINESS ENVIRONMENT INTERFACE CONCEPTS

A department or enterprise that generates revenue or otherwise conducts its business through the accomplishment of projects is well served by establishing a project portfolio management capability. Using this approach, project decisions become business decisions, and such decisions warrant the examination of project progress and performance on an ongoing basis by the individuals who make relevant business decisions.

The output of a well-constructed "project portfolio management" function is pertinent data that is available for exchange and review across the relevant organization and across the enterprise. In particular, project portfolio management information will be interspersed with related information in accounting, contracts, and human resource management departments. In an organization where project portfolio management is an advanced function, the data obtained or derived from the project portfolio management process may become the primary source of such business information. In turn, the financial calculations performed and the business decisions made can be returned to the portfolio management process and to the individual projects for implementation.

PORTFOLIO MANAGEMENT ACTIVITIES ACROSS THE PMO CONTINUUM

The PMO is an ideal organizational entity to lead in the establishment of a project portfolio management capability. Its dual ability to view the status of all current projects and to offer assistance in initiating and planning future projects positions it well for the job at hand. In structuring a "project portfolio management" function, its primary responsibilities will be to facilitate the involvement of senior management, to create processes envisioned by senior management, and to manage process implementation.

The stages of PMO evolution along the PMO competency continuum are characterized by an increasing capability to influence and manage senior management participation in the processes of project portfolio management. As well, the PMO's progressive ability to integrate projects with the organization's business interests is a factor in its project portfolio management maturity.

Table 17.1 presents an overview of the range of prescribed PMO project portfolio management activities according to each level in the PMO competency continuum.

The *project office* at the low end of the continuum has minimal direct concern for project portfolio management, except to ensure that accurate project performance information is conveyed in a timely manner. Portfolio management decision makers will rely on this information from every project as a basis for managing the organization's business interests.

It is at the *mid-range PMO* levels of the continuum that a viable portfolio management function is formulated and implemented. This is where the PMO establishes its ability to collect, manage, and sometimes provide preliminary analysis of the project performance information that is made available to executives and senior managers for review and deliberation associated with the project portfolio management process. The mid-range PMO's efforts also can include some level of collaboration and coordination, which is particularly needed when the project portfolio review authority is a board or committee that crosses

Table 17.1 Range of Project Portfolio Activities across the PMO Continuum

Project Office	Basic PMO	Standard PMO	Advanced PMO	Center of Excellence
Provides project data to a higher level PMO or other oversight authority for consolidation	Introduces the fundamental concepts of project portfolio management ■ Develops a process and criteria for project selection ■ Establishes senior managers project reviews ■ Compiles and compares performance data from multiple projects	Establishes and manages collaborative processes for project portfolio management ■ Aligns projects with business strategy ■ Establishes project business case review gateways ■ Implements a process for resource review and allocation ■ Develops methods to prioritize projects	Creates a comprehensive project portfolio management capability ■ Convenes formal portfolio review boards or other authority on a recurring basis ■ Enables real-time project data use in decision making ■ Establishes early project termination process	Develops policies and guidance for project portfolio management ■ Pursues an environment that supports effective portfolio management ■ Examines and manages business issues affecting portfolio management

organizational boundaries. The PMO can serve to facilitate executive and senior manager participation in project and portfolio reviews, deliberations, and decisions — usually by arranging or otherwise specifying needed meetings, review periods, and decision deadlines. Then, the PMO carries out the direction and guidance of the portfolio review authority's decisions and implements the associated actions at the project level and within the project management environment.

The *center of excellence* has primary added responsibility for ensuring that the project environment is supportive of the relevant organization's portfolio management activities. To that end, it monitors the effectiveness of other PMO functions already in place and, where needed, implements function expansion and process improvements to better serve the "project portfolio management" function. It also ensures that cross-functional business interests are achieved by this function.

The fundamental objective of the PMO's "project portfolio management" function across this continuum is to involve senior management in the project management process. By ensuring their ability to know what is going on in the collection of current and pending projects, and by enabling them to make relevant business decisions against that knowledge of status, progress, and performance of the project portfolio, the PMO will achieve the requisite senior management participation in project management.

PROJECT PORTFOLIO MANAGEMENT FUNCTION MODEL

This function model addresses the responsibility of the PMO to establish and manage processes and activities that give the relevant organization a capability to accomplish project portfolio management. This model illustrates one way in which a PMO can implement the essential steps of project portfolio management. The relative maturity of the PMO will be a factor in the depth and extent to which the prescribed activities are implemented.

The primary activities of this PMO "project portfolio management" function model are depicted in Figure 17.1. Each activity is described in the following subsections.

Set Up Project Portfolio Management

A foundation for project portfolio management must be established within the relevant organization and its project environment. Several preparation activities are presented to ensure that a solid basis for conducting project portfolio management is established.

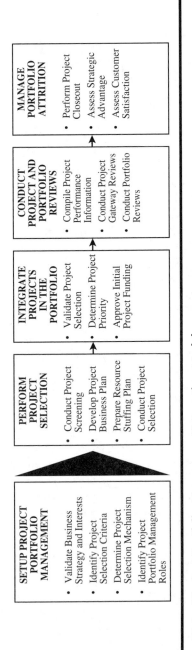

SETUP PROJECT PORTFOLIO MANAGEMENT

- Validate Business Strategy and Interests
- Identify Project Selection Criteria
- Determine Project Selection Mechanism
- Identify Project Portfolio Management Roles

PERFORM PROJECT SELECTION

- Conduct Project Screening
- Develop Project Business Plan
- Prepare Resource Staffing Plan
- Conduct Project Selection

INTEGRATE PROJECTS IN THE PORTFOLIO

- Validate Project Selection
- Determine Project Priority
- Approve Initial Project Funding

CONDUCT PROJECT AND PORTFOLIO REVIEWS

- Compile Project Performance Information
- Conduct Project Gateway Reviews
- Conduct Portfolio Reviews

MANAGE PORTFOLIO ATTRITION

- Perform Project Closeout
- Assess Strategic Advantage
- Assess Customer Satisfaction

Figure 17.1   "Project Portfolio Management" Function Model

Validate Business Strategy and Interests

Executives are responsible for establishing the strategic direction of the organization. The strategy provides the purpose, expectations, goals, and action steps necessary to guide business pursuits. Day-to-day application of the business strategy narrows the range of possible business opportunities to only those distinctly aligned with business objectives. It also ensures that valuable resources are assigned only to those efforts that further the objectives set forth in the strategic business plan.

It is essential that a well-conceived and well-articulated strategic context is available within the PMO in order to align project management activities with top level business direction. In this preparation activity, the PMO examines the existing business strategy documentation and guidance for the relevant organization and collaborates with senior management to verify that it is valid and current. This activity is particularly needed if there has been a long period since the organization's business strategy was last formulated.

If the PMO represents a business unit, e.g., a department or agency, then the parts of the strategic plan that are relevant to the organization should be considered in lieu of the overall organizational business plan. Keep in mind that a "business strategy" exists in some form in any viable organization, although it may be called by different names. Part of this PMO effort may be to discern what business-strategy documents exist, and this effort could include discussions with senior management to identify and locate whatever documentation is available. In any case, the PMO must identify and validate the business objectives of the relevant organization, as they will serve as the basis for establishing the selection criteria used in the project portfolio management process. Table 17.2 presents an abbreviated checklist that can be used to validate business strategy and interests.

For established "project portfolio management" functions, this validation activity should be performed on a recurring basis, perhaps annually or biannually, or whenever the strategic business plan or other relevant document is revised or updated. This examination and validation can be done either independently by the PMO or, ideally, in a facilitated review meeting with the executives and senior managers responsible for project portfolio management.

If, by some chance, the PMO discovers that there are no strategic plans, business goals and objectives document, or other business guidance, it will be imperative to facilitate or otherwise arrange a senior management working session to formulate and document the business strategy. This guidance is distinctly needed before project portfolio management can be accomplished.

Table 17.2   Project Portfolio Strategy Review Checklist

- *Vision statement*: Review for comprehension and understanding
  - Is it current?
  - Is it known, understood, and supported across the organization?
- *Mission statement*: Review for comprehension and understanding
  - Is it current?
  - Is it known, understood, and supported across the organization?
- *Business goals*: Review for comprehension and understanding
  - Are they current?
  - Are they known, understood, and supported across the organization?
  - Do they clearly support the organization's vision and mission?
  - Are performance measures aligned to support their achievement?
  - Does each goal have an "owner"?
  - Does each goal have relevant objectives that are "SMART": specific, measurable, agreed to, realistic, and time-based?
- *Strategy deployment*: Examine how well the business strategy is accepted and applied within the organization
  - Are strategic goals and objectives positioned, communicated, and routinely addressed within the organization?
  - Does senior management reinforce commitment to strategic goals and objectives on a continual basis?
  - Are projects currently tabulated with relevant data and with indications of alignment to specific goals and objectives?

If projects are already being aligned with strategic business goals and objectives, this provides a distinct advantage and suggests that some form of portfolio management may already be in place. If this is the case, the PMO can concentrate on examining the current process to identify areas of alignment with project management rather than initiating a brand new "project portfolio management" function.

Identify Project Selection Criteria

The process of project selection is that of choosing which project initiatives will be pursued and which will not. The alignment of a project opportunity with the organization's business strategy usually makes it a candidate for selection, but it does not guarantee its selection. Conversely, a project opportunity that is not aligned with the organization's business strategy should never be selected. Project selection criteria should be identified to provide guidance that supports project selection decisions.

The strategic nature of this consideration warrants executives and senior managers be involved in deliberating project selection criteria. To that end, the PMO can facilitate a workshop or similar session to determine what criteria will be used for project selection. Alternatively, the PMO can convene an appropriate senior level panel, executive control board, or even develop and present its own project selection criteria recommendations for review and approval by senior managers.

Projects are initiated in response to a specific business need, condition, or situation that is aligned with the strategic direction of the organization. The PMO can facilitate the examination of four project selection criteria perspectives to help determine the criteria that will ensure project alignment with the business strategy. These are described in the following subsections. The PMO can expand this fundamental list per the nature of business and the needs of the relevant organization.

Business Perspective

The business strategy is supported by particular business objectives that consider sales and revenue objectives, market position, and competitive strategies. Therefore, project selection criteria for this strategy alignment perspective can be developed relative to such factors as:

- *Project costs*: Projects are selected based on criteria for achievement of:
  - Project cost reduction initiatives
  - Product/service pricing strategies that cover specific incurred project costs
  - Product/service pricing strategies that attract new, expanded, or specialized business
  - Cost management objectives associated with resource use and optimization
- *Product and service quality*: Projects are selected based on criteria for achievement of:
  - Product/service-quality measures and objectives
  - Entry of high-quality products/services in the marketplace
  - Delivery of the highest-quality products/services in the industry
- *Customer satisfaction*: Projects are selected based on criteria for achievement of:
  - Fulfillment of customer needs and requirements
  - Development of customer business relationships
  - Acceptance of customer product and service deliverables
  - Reorders and retention of customers
- *Business advantage*: Projects are selected based on criteria for achievement of:
  - Increased revenue objectives
  - Enlarged customer base objectives

- Expanded market share objectives
- Increased marketplace recognition objectives
- Global business expansion objectives
■ *New products/technology*: Projects are selected based on criteria for achievement of:
  - New product/service development opportunities and objectives
  - New technology introduction objectives

The criteria developed for project selection using business perspective factors will show how well a project fulfills or otherwise supports the organization's business objectives.

Financial Perspective

Each organization and industry has different requirements for the financial returns that are necessary for a project to be considered or approved. These requirements normally are based on the perceived risk and rewards inherent to that industry. Executives must examine the financial parameters of their business and determine what financial factors weigh into the criteria for selecting projects. Project selection criteria for this strategy alignment perspective can be developed relative to such factors as:

■ *Investment commitment*: Projects are selected based on criteria for achieving the specified limit of the investment amount allowed by type of project. For example, only IT projects under $250,000 will be considered; only construction projects under $1 million will be considered; etc.

■ *Investment returns*: Projects are selected based on criteria for achieving the specified acceptable range of investment return or objectives for increased investor value. For example, one type of project may require a minimum 12% return, while another high-risk effort can be started only if the return falls into the 15% to 20% range.

■ *Investment period*: Projects are selected based on criteria for achieving the desired returns within specific acceptable time frames per organizational standards or general industry constraints. For example, a short capital project may be expected to pay back in 3 to 5 years, while a new product launch will be given as long as 5 to 7 years.

■ *Investment allocation*: Projects are selected based on criteria for achieving the objectives specified by financial funding pools that are established and available for allocation to project work. For example, specified funding pools may be used to allocate investment funds to only a certain classification of projects.

The criteria developed for project selection using financial perspective factors will show that a project has the capability to achieve the specified financial aspects of the business strategy.

Performance Perspective

Projects are selected when general project performance indicators reflect the likelihood of successful outcomes. Executives specify or otherwise influence these criteria against which all projects are evaluated, and they emphasize these criteria at every decision gateway. These criteria inherently expand on the previously discussed business and financial perspectives criteria, and they provide more detail to the project selection effort. Criteria for this strategy alignment perspective can be developed relative to such factors as:

- *Nature of work (competency)*: Projects are selected based on criteria that confirm the application of existing competencies within the organization to achieve project objectives. Such criteria could specify competency within one or more technical or professional disciplines. It also could specify competency in conducting a particular business process, developing a particular product, or providing a particular service. For example, a checklist could be developed to identify which of the organization's core competencies are being applied to the project under consideration.
- *Extent of work (capability)*: Projects are selected based on criteria that confirm the organization's capability to fulfill project performance requirements. While an organization has fundamental competency in a technical or professional discipline, it must ascertain its capability (and its limitations) — within the constraints of a particular type of client or industry — to accomplish projects at various and necessarily advanced or higher levels of monetary value, duration, risk, technical or professional discipline diversity, and complexity. For example, an organization may develop criteria that specify selecting a highly complex project of 6-month duration, but not one of 2-year duration.
- *Extent of risk or opportunity*: Projects are selected based on the type and amount of technical work performance and business risk the organization is prepared to accept. Therefore, criteria should be created to specify the thresholds of risk that could be encountered as a result of project selection. For example, criteria could be specified for prominent categories of project risk and include the thresholds for project selection.

■ *Resource availability*: Projects are selected based on the organization's ability to perform the specified work through the assignment of qualified resources. Criteria are formulated to ensure that resource availability — primarily in terms of numbers and necessary skills — is addressed and confirmed prior to project selection.

Nonnumerical Perspective

Projects are selected when business needs warrant them. Executives and senior managers need to identify the criteria that will introduce projects for purposes that are generally outside the first three project selection perspectives. As well, these criteria are often characterized not by using numerical thresholds, but by business decisions. Criteria for this strategy alignment perspective can be developed relative to such factors as:

■ *Executive mandate or directive*: Projects are selected based on the executive's purview to require them. In such cases, a project is selected and performed because the executive perceives some business value or benefit to be gained by the effort. Often, the executive applies some unspecified "numeric criteria" to such a mandate, and normally such criteria can be found to be an expansion or extension of one or more of the existing criteria in the previous three project selection criteria perspectives. When applied to the project selection process, the executive-mandate criterion simply specifies that when an executive project decision is received, just do it.

■ *Operating necessity/infrastructure*: Projects are selected to maintain or achieve certain levels of operational efficiency or effectiveness. These types of projects are sometimes selected as part of a larger organizational program or initiative, but often they are selected because of the inherent operational benefits to be received from the proposed project activities, including process development and implementation; infrastructure upgrades; software and computer network system upgrades and implementation; and facility construction, maintenance, and refurbishment. Criteria for this project selection perspective are usually aligned with the need to achieve operating-capability objectives that are specified elsewhere in an organizational initiative or business plan.

■ *Competitive necessity*: Projects are selected based on the need to maintain business advantage, if not business parity. Project criteria are usually prescribed per specific business, market, or industry indicators. Such criteria include the introduction of new technology, the emergence of new industry or technical-practice standards, and sometimes the need to respond to competitor actions and activities in the marketplace. For example, an organization might select a project when it provides a "facility certification" that its customers require as a basis for ongoing association.

■ *Regulatory requirement*: Projects are selected based on the need to fulfill external mandates that facilitate business performance or otherwise enable the organization to continue as a viable business entity. Often, government agencies are the source of the regulatory requirements that must be addressed for such purposes as: receiving government-sponsored contracts and business considerations, obtaining business licenses and authorizations, and complying with new or revised laws and regulations. The criteria in this area are simply that of weighing the business impact of nonselection of a fulfillment project versus the benefit of selecting a project for compliance with the imposed mandate.

Determine Project Selection Mechanisms

Once project selection criteria are established, the PMO can construct or use established mechanisms to evaluate the criteria for selecting candidate projects. The mechanisms suggested in this section can be applied to go/no-go decisions at the initial project screening, at project selection, and at each subsequent project decision point.

The six project selection mechanisms presented in the following subsections illustrate a range of project selection mechanisms available to the PMO. The PMO can choose one of these fundamental mechanisms, develop a combined mechanism, develop its own approach, or seek a more comprehensive mechanism from among a variety of advanced tools and techniques available today.

New Project Classification Mechanism

This mechanism is a framework for project selection and evaluation that considers projects in four strategic classifications:

■ *Breakthrough*: Projects that move the organization to new markets, a new competitive position, or new competencies
■ *Evolutionary/extension*: Projects that support the internal operational needs of the organization, such as human-resource management systems, financial systems, information management, and decision support

■ *Infrastructure*: Projects that are an iteration of what the organization is currently doing, capitalizing on a core competency or extending current product lines
■ *Customer service and support*: Projects that focus on customer expectations, requirements, and improvements to improve competitive advantage

An organization can use these classifications to delineate the nature of work associated with each project and to determine what efforts are being pursued against specific strategic business objectives. Each ongoing and candidate project is listed by its focus and alignment within one of the four classification areas. Then, each project is ranked by importance relative to the achievement of strategic objectives within each of the classifications. This ranking can be supported or adjusted by further examination of subcriteria within each classification (e.g., risk, resource utilization, and investment returns). Table 17.3 illustrates a matrix depicting the new-project classification mechanism. The organization can adapt these classifications to provide better alignment with the strategic nature of its project efforts.

Financial Calculations Mechanism

This project selection mechanism is an approach to project selection that considers financial aspects of the project investment and that uses quantifiable metrics and mathematical formulas to distinguish and determine the appropriateness of project selection (and retention). The mechanism simply considers the relevant organization's preferred methods and formulas for cost and financial analysis. Ongoing and candidate projects are scrutinized, and forecasts or results of competing projects are examined. Management can select either a specified number of top project contenders or all projects meeting specified criteria. Table 17.4 presents several representative financial calculations that could be applied to an organization's project selection and retention process.

The organization will likely already have robust financial analysis models in place as a fundamental aspect of business management. The PMO should prompt consideration by executives and senior managers to identify financial analysis models that can be applied to project portfolio management, and specifically to project selection and retention.

Table 17.3 New Project Classification Matrix

Breakthrough		
Projects that move the organization to new markets, new competitive position, or new competencies		
Risk	*Resource*	*Returns*
High	Variable	High
Project 1		
Project 2		
Project 3		

Infrastructure		
Projects that support the internal operational needs of the organization, such as human-resource management systems, financial systems, information management, and decision support		
Risk	*Resource*	*Returns*
Low	Normal	Variable
Project 4		
Project 5		
Project 6		

Evolutionary/Extension		
Projects that are an iteration of what the organization is currently doing, capitalizing on a core competency or extending current product lines		
Risk	*Resource*	*Returns*
Low	Normal	High
Project 7		
Project 8		
Project 9		

Customer Service and Support		
Projects that focus on customer expectations, requirements, and improvements to provide competitive advantage		
Risk	*Resource*	*Returns*
Medium-Low	Variable	Medium-High
Project 10		
Project 11		
Project 12		

Table 17.4 Financial Calculations

Benefit–cost ratio analysis	Financial evaluation that contrasts the benefits to be realized per the varying level of investment cost
Economic analysis	Process of establishing project value in relation to other corporate standards, project profitability, benchmarks, financing, interest rates, and acceptance criteria
Feasibility study	Method or technique used to examine technical and cost data to determine the economic potential or practicality of the project, such as time-value of money
Financing analysis	Techniques and methods related to providing the sources of monies and methods to raise funds for the project
Prospectus review	Evaluation of profitability studies and all pertinent technical data in a report presented for acceptance by the sponsor and funding managers of a project
Project investment analysis	Evaluation of all the cost elements (capital and operating) of a project as defined by an agreed-upon scope of work that includes costs incurred during the period from the completion of the project to the beginning of normal revenue earnings on operations
Inflation/escalation allowance analysis	Evaluation of the factor in cost evaluation that must be predicted to account for price changes with time
Cash-flow analysis	Evaluation of monthly in/out and accumulated project cash flow data to measure actual versus budget, allowing for funding at lowest carrying charges and measured spending; includes techniques providing the measure and means to assess total income relative to expended monies (e.g., present value, return on investment, discounted cash flow, internal rate of return, etc.)

Balanced-Scorecard Mechanism

This mechanism is a framework for project selection based on the balanced-scorecard evaluation approach developed by Kaplan and Norton.* It presents a "whole organization" perspective in four evaluation areas:

- *Financial perspective*: Links financial objectives to organizational strategy for improvement of financial performance, and addresses timely and accurate reporting and management of organizational expenses and assets within the project management environment. It includes project management metrics that deal with increasing revenues, lowering costs, improving productivity, upgrading asset utilization, and reducing risk.
- *Business process perspective*: Entails specification of internal business processes and activities necessary to support product and service value for customers and shareholders. Measures associated with project management can include such elements as project management and technical performance process time; process quality and process cost; and vendor and supplier selection, performance, and management processes.
- *Customer perspective*: Considers the customer and market segments that will deliver the revenue to meet the organization's financial objectives, and specifies the value proposition that will be applied to target customers and segments. Measures associated with project management that help an organization retain and expand its business with targeted customers include such things as product and service quality, timeliness of project deliverables, degree of satisfaction in customer business relationships, and image and reputation in the marketplace and industry.
- *Learning and growth perspective*: Provides the infrastructure and capability that enables the other three perspectives to be achieved. This includes a particular focus on capability to implement change for business advantage. For project management, this perspective considers such metrics and measures as tool implementation and utilization, training, quality elements of planning and performance, and application of lessons learned.

This mechanism for project selection focuses on project value relative to these four dimensions of business. Organizational goals are listed for each of the four dimension categories, and measures for attaining the specified goals are added to the matrix. Then, the projects that are under

---

* Kaplan, R. and Norton, D., "The Balanced Scorecard-Measures That Drive Performance," *Harvard Business Review*, Jan/Feb 1992, pp. 71–79.

Table 17.5 Balanced-Scorecard Matrix

Financial Perspective			Business Process Perspective		
Goals	*Measures*	*Projects*	*Goals*	*Measures*	*Projects*

Customer Perspective			Learning and Growth Perspective		
Goals	*Measures*	*Projects*	*Goals*	*Measures*	*Projects*

consideration or under way are listed according to the business goals they will achieve. The measures of the projects should match or be related to the measures of the business goals.

Table 17.5 provides an example of the balanced-scorecard matrix used in the project management environment to select or retain projects.

Rank-Order Matrix Mechanism

This mechanism is a framework for project selection based on a method developed by Buss.* It provides a benefit-cost approach that does not rely on quantitative data but, rather, examines and ranks project benefits in four areas that could be interpreted as follows:

- *Financial benefits*: Cost versus such metrics as revenue returned and cash flow impacts resulting from the project effort, expense reduction (or increase) resulting from the project management approach, and further business opportunities resulting from project success (or failure)
- *Technical benefits*: Cost versus such metrics as opportunity for the introduction of new product(s) and the potential for technical innovation or breakthrough

---

* Buss, M., "How to Rank Computer Projects," *Harvard Business Review*, Jan/Feb 1983, pp. 118–124.

Table 17.6   Rank-Order Matrix

Financial Benefits				Technical Benefits			
	High benefit	Medium benefit	Low benefit		High benefit	Medium benefit	Low benefit
High cost				High cost			
Medium cost				Medium cost			
Low cost				Low cost			

Core Competency Enhancement				Harmony with Corporate Culture			
	High benefit	Medium benefit	Low benefit		High benefit	Medium benefit	Low benefit
High cost				High cost			
Medium cost				Medium cost			
Low cost				Low cost			

- *Core competency enhancement*: Cost vs. such metrics as demonstration of new or enlarged performance capability and expansion of project manager and project-team member skill and experience
- *Harmony with corporate culture*: Cost vs. such metrics as achievement of business objectives that endorse or enhance organizational customs, traditions, and values; fit and impact on the cultural aspects of the organization; and validation of individual affiliation with the organization

Table 17.6 presents a version of the rank-order matrix. While metrics have been suggested for the rank-order matrix, the value of this project selection mechanism is found in the more intuitive nature of evaluating the project cost vs. the discernable benefits to be gained.

Pairwise Comparison Mechanism

Many executives have difficulty making choices when a whole list of options are offered, but they have less difficulty making a selection when pairs of choices are presented. The pairwise comparison method reduces the need to make a choice from a long list of projects. This mechanism

Table 17.7 Pairwise Comparison

PROJECT A	PROJECT A			
PROJECT B	B / A	PROJECT B		
PROJECT C	C / A	C / B	PROJECT C	
PROJECT D	D / A	D / B	D / C	PROJECT D
PROJECT E	E / A	E / B	E / C	E / D	PROJECT E

facilitates review and prioritization of projects under consideration. Table 17.7 illustrates the grid used for pairwise connection project selection mechanism.

In a grid pattern, list all the projects on the left side of the page and copy the same list in diagonal boxes to the right. The project at the top left is compared for preference (or another criterion) to the second project named across the right-hand diagonal. If the project on the left is preferable to the project listed in the diagonal, circle the favored one in the "comparison box" between the two projects. Then tally the number of times each project is selected. Rank the projects according to the highest-to-lowest tally numbers resulting from the group effort.

Peer/Oversight Committee Review Mechanism

Whether an individual or group has made project selections, and regardless of the selection method, selected projects should be examined rigorously before they are ultimately entered into the portfolio. A peer/oversight committee review is a means used to challenge each project. The reviewers, comprising either a peer group or a cadre of stakeholders, should convene (a) to confront all assertions and claims of progress, of resources, and of schedules and (b) to address the alignment with strategic objectives. They should look for gaps, overreaching, and unclear detail in each project. Each project sponsor and project manager who has put the project forward should be ready to defend the project. Table 17.8 demonstrates

Table 17.8 Peer/Oversight Committee Review

Project	Sponsor/Project Manager	Argument/Criteria
Project 1 Lab upgrade		☐ Business case review ☐ Resource allocation plan review
Project 2 New building		☐ Business case review ☐ Resource allocation plan review
Project 3 Regulatory fix		☐ Business case review ☐ Resource allocation plan review
Project 4 X-10 system		☐ Business case review ☐ Resource allocation plan review
Project 5 Method update		☐ Business case review ☐ Resource allocation plan review
Project 6 Golf tourney		☐ Business case review ☐ Resource allocation plan review

one simple method for approaching and documenting the peer/oversight committee review.

The peer/oversight committee review has two important additional benefits beyond evaluating and clarifying projects. First, each reviewed project is challenged by a fresh perspective and a broad array of expertise; and second, the sponsor, project managers, and reviewer all become more committed to the projects evaluated as a result of delving into the details of each project. Ultimately, key personnel gain knowledge and commitment for all of the projects within the relevant organization.

Identify Project Portfolio Management Roles

Project portfolio management is a business alignment function of the PMO that requires coordination and collaboration across the relevant organization. The activities of project portfolio management will naturally transcend the boundaries of the PMO. However, in the context of its functional responsibility, the PMO must ensure that all participants in project portfolio management know and understand the range of their responsibilities and the extent of their authority to make or implement project portfolio decisions.

Unless specified otherwise, the PMO's primary role is to facilitate the process of project portfolio management. It is possible, and in some organizations likely, that the PMO will take on primary responsibility for conducting project portfolio management activities, sometimes even fulfilling the review and approval role for the organization. Any responsibility in that regard should be identified in the PMO charter.

Beyond the PMO, there are various roles and responsibilities that are needed to support the "project portfolio management" function. A brief description of key portfolio management roles and responsibilities are presented for consideration below. These are practical, generic roles and names that can be adjusted, adapted, or customized for use in an organization pursuing an effective project portfolio management capability.

Executive Review Board

This is the senior management team that serves as the guiding force in developing and implementing an effective portfolio management process. It oversees the portfolio management process and makes go/no-go decisions about the mix, scope, resource allocations, and continuation of projects at specified intervals. This team may include the president/CEO, chief financial officer (budget director), vice presidents, and business unit directors. In some instances in smaller organizations or business units, a single executive may take on this role and associated responsibilities.

The primary responsibilities of the executive review board include:

■ Validate the organization's strategic direction
■ Participate in the development of portfolio management concepts
■ Conduct project screening
■ Review and assess projects at decision points
■ Identify and correct business gaps in projects
■ Balance projects to support the desired mix of business interests
■ Allocate resources (and resolve resource allocation issues)
■ Conduct regular examinations of the organization's competitive position
■ Make decisions on business direction and project funding

Portfolio Management Team

This is the team that serves as the managers of the portfolio management process on an ongoing, operational basis. This team is usually cross functional and provides recommendations to the executive review board for project selection and continuation. This team also compiles project and portfolio information and performs preexecutive reviews as a basis for making portfolio recommendations to the executive review board. The PMO is ideally situated and often assigned to perform in this role or to lead activities for portfolio management team participants.

The primary responsibilities of the portfolio management team include:

- Conduct project prescreening
- Ensure completeness of project business plans at selection and decision points
- Ensure completeness of resource staffing plans at selection and decision points
- Conduct ongoing examination of projects for compliance with project plans
- Develop project selection and continuation recommendations at decision points
- Develop resource utilization and allocation recommendations at decision points

Portfolio Manager

This is a senior manager who serves as the project portfolio administrator within the relevant organization. This is a responsibility that is normally found within the more mature PMO, and therefore is a collateral responsibility of the PMO director. It is a role that represents the essence of the PMO's portfolio management function. This position usually represents the head of the portfolio management team described just above. In smaller organizations, this position alone may perform some or all of the suggested activities of the portfolio management team. Conversely, in larger organizations, some of the portfolio manager's responsibilities may be delegated to the portfolio management team.

The primary responsibilities of the portfolio manager include:

- Facilitate executive team participation and involvement in establishing portfolio management concepts in the organization
- Set schedules for project selection meetings and project decision-point reviews
- Monitor portfolio performance; manage portfolio attrition
- Manage issues and changes to business plans and resource allocations
- Facilitate project reporting and communication to the executive review board
- Link portfolio management information requirements with project management information systems (PMIS) using data included in each project business plan

Project Sponsor

This is the individual who serves as the executive level advocate for the project and represents the interests of the project to the executive team. The sponsor may be an executive team member or a key senior manager who takes responsibility for the project. Typically, there is a project sponsor for every project. This manager could also be a sponsor for multiple projects, possibly a separate subportfolio of projects.

The primary responsibilities of the project sponsor include:

- Confirm project prescreening results sent to the executive review board
- Validate initial project business plan and any subsequent changes
- Validate initial resource staffing plan and any subsequent changes
- Advocate project selection before the executive team and at decision points
- Issue the project charter upon project selection and funding approval (or direct the PMO to issue it)
- Monitor project performance, project risk, and key project objectives, thus ensuring adherence to strategic alignment
- Serve as the initial point of escalation for resource resolution, negotiating at higher levels for resources that may be needed unexpectedly

Project Manager

This is the individual assigned to lead a specific project with responsibility for that project's outcome. Presumably, there is a project manager for every project in the organization.

The primary responsibilities of the project manager include:

- Develop the project definition document for integration into the business plan
- Develop the project business plan with the assistance of the project team and project sponsor
- Develop the project resource staffing plan with the assistance of the project team and project sponsor
- Manage project performance on a day-to-day basis, thus ensuring adherence to the project work plan, fidelity to the project business plan, and alignment with strategy
- Develop and present project performance reports and forecasts of future performance for consideration at decision-point reviews
- Communicate with all project stakeholders, as necessary

- Identify and negotiate for timely assignment of resources to conduct the project
- Continually assess what personnel and financial resources are needed to implement the project plan; make adjustments as necessary

Establish a Supportive Project Environment

The PMO, as the representative of an organization's project management environment, needs to ensure that the project management environment has the capability to support the interests of the PMO's project portfolio management function.

For the most part, portfolio management support needs are established and maintained through the PMO's other functional responsibilities. However, relative to the "project portfolio management" function, the PMO must ensure that such support is fine-tuned to the critical and time-sensitive activities of the relevant organization. In the event that other applicable PMO functions have not been established or matured, the PMO can begin their introduction as elements of the "project portfolio management" function.

The following activities warrant consideration for their benefit in support of an organization's "project portfolio management" function.

- *Methodology deployment*: The early project opportunity analysis — including preparation of the project definition and business plan — is normally created consistent with project management methodology guidance. Implementing a project management methodology precludes having a separate process that is used by only a few portfolio management participants.
- *Project reporting*: The practices used to collect and report project progress information are important to project selection and for use at project and portfolio reviews. This activity enables preparation of project and portfolio progress reports for distribution to senior management for review.
- *Business policy development*: This governance factor is needed to demonstrate executive support and commitment to the portfolio management process. It conveys senior management expectations and may specify responsibilities of the portfolio management participants within the project environment. It can also identify the role of the PMO in project portfolio management.
- *Standards and metrics*: This PMO oversight function will contribute to initial development and updates of project selection criteria.
- *Information systems*: The established project management information system (PMIS) may require a component to handle project portfolio management data. The interconnection of organizational

databases and relevant applications are also considered under this PMO function as a means to support data transfer used in project portfolio management.

The features identified above highlight some of the more prominent activities desired in a supportive project environment. This should not negate consideration of other PMO or organizational functions that warrant early implementation as a means of enhancing portfolio management capability.

Perform Project Selection

The organization's project selection process ensures that all projects are bona fide business efforts and that every project is selected and conducted to implement a business strategy or to support a business objective.

There are four fundamental activities of project selection:

- *Conduct project screening*: This activity is conducted to provide an indication of whether or not initial project planning (business plan development) should be pursued.
- *Develop project business plan*: This activity is used to identify and examine the project opportunity and customer needs and interests. It collects and compiles the information used in the previous project screening activity, and it includes preparation of the project definition, which specifies the scope and work effort to be undertaken.
- *Develop resource allocation plan*: This activity is used to identify resource requirements for the candidate project and to specify the financial and resource allocations that will be needed to fulfill project requirements.
- *Conduct project selection*: This activity applies established criteria and prescreening results to the information compiled in the business plan and project resource allocation plan to analyze and examine the candidate project for final selection.

Each of these action steps can be performed as a matter of process contained within the organization's project management methodology, or they can be a separate activity performed only by the portfolio management team.

As well, organizational culture, existing practices and procedures, or applicable policy guidance should be considered and applied to rearrange the order of these action steps, if necessary, to fit the organization. Some organizations may prefer to do more-detailed business planning prior to any context of project screening, and that becomes a "built in" feature of the process. Others may not require as rigorous an effort to initiate a project, but simply a few indicators of business fit. Consider introducing these steps relative to the overall purpose of project selection. Perform all or parts of these action steps in the order and in a way that best fits the relevant organization's needs. A description of each activity is presented in the following subsections.

Conduct Project Screening

The continual application of the same criteria lets managers in the organization know what is important, and ensures that rational decision making is applied when all projects are measured by the same criteria.

Suggested project screening criteria elements include:

- *Customer readiness*: Validated need, availability of funding, and effort priority
- *Nature of work*: Application of core business competency
- *Return on investment*: Project contribution to the overall portfolio
- *Break-even time*: Reasonableness of time to payback
- *Competitive position*: Project contribution to business pursuits and interests
- *Internal impacts*: Project contribution to business lines and organizational interests
- *Market position and market share*: Project contribution to market expansion
- *Risk*: Benefits to be gained versus potential threats of loss
- *Resource requirements*: Application and availability of necessary skills
- *Cost of ownership*: Costs of project deliverables

Through activities of the portfolio management team, portfolio manager, or the PMO, the executive participants can review these criteria elements and identify any other specific criteria to be applied to the project screening process.

Screening provides a preliminary examination of the project opportunity and enables the organization to determine whether the opportunity warrants further consideration. The premise that a project must be aligned with business strategy is a focus of project screening. In particular, the criterion established to examine strategic fit is applied here. Opportunities that satisfy the criterion will go forward to further planning and final project selection.

Some organizations may consider this activity to be their project selection step and therefore will conduct project screening as a more rigorous process. This emphasizes the importance of business strategy alignment as the prominent criterion for project selection. As well, it suggests that the organizational project management processes require project selection before any relevant project business plans are prepared. This approach also may warrant a subsequent go/no-go decision to confirm this earlier selection decision.

Develop Project Business Plan

The project business plan identifies and supports the business reasons for conducting the project. In some organizations, this item is known as the "business case." It integrates the project's strategic alignment information, and it introduces the project definition information elements. The project business plan is the governing document in the portfolio management process by which project selection and project continuation decisions can be made.

Business plan development may be a part of a larger process created by the PMO. Once created, project business plan development then can be conducted and managed by the PMO or by a portfolio management team (or portfolio manager).

The project business plan is constructed to contain certain business-relevant project information, which is updated continuously throughout the project management life cycle. Initial and interim reviews of this plan facilitate validation of business purpose (per selection criteria), recurring determination of consistency with the organization's business strategy, and decisions about project continuation.

This activity includes three primary action steps that facilitate the development of the initial project business plan and enable timely updates during the project life cycle.

Identify Project Opportunity

A preliminary examination of the project opportunity must be accomplished in association with business plan development. The following information elements can be considered when identifying the project opportunity:

- Customer identification
- Customer point of contact
- Nature of customer business
- Type of project
- Customer's level of interest and pursuit
- Customer's project funding status

Prepare Project Definition

The project definition provides a complete understanding of the project and serves to guide the project manager and project team in planning and implementation. It also provides the basis of decision making for executives who need to evaluate the potential for project success and completion on time, within budget, and according to performance specifications.

The project definition document can stand alone, but it is presented here as an integral part of the business plan. The project definition contains the information and initial guidance used by the project team when conducting detailed project planning activities. In some organizations, the project definition is completed as an activity contained within the project management methodology process.

The organization should give consideration to the preparation of the following information elements for inclusion in the project definition document. As much detail can accompany each information element as is required by the organization, and more or fewer elements can be included in the project definition.

Key Project Resources. Key project resources include the following:

- *Project manager:* The individual responsible for initial and detailed planning and for managing project performance to achieve project objectives.
- *Project sponsor:* An individual or group within the organization that provides and manages financial resources, either in cash or in kind, and makes financial decisions to support the project.
- *Project stakeholders:* The individuals or groups either actively involved or somewhat associated in the project, and whose interests may be positively or negatively affected as a result of the project outcome. Each individual or group and their interests should be identified.
- *Team resources:* An early estimate of resources needed to conduct project work; an element closely coordinated with examining project costs and entails determining what people, equipment, and materials are required by the project.

Project Work Elements. Project work elements include the following:

- *Project objectives:* The quantifiable criteria that must be achieved for the project to be considered a success, typically expressed in terms of cost, schedule, and performance measures. Qualitative objectives, such as customer satisfaction, entail high risks and should be restated in a quantifiable manner, if possible.

- *Scope statement*: A description of the nature and boundaries of the work to be performed to achieve project objectives.
- *Project justification statement*: A statement of the business need or purpose that the project was undertaken to address. Justification points must be carefully considered because they provide a basis for evaluating future project trade-offs or opportunities.
- *Project deliverables*: The project outcomes or performance results of the project effort, with consideration of how well each deliverable meets the needs and requirements of the customer and identified business objectives.
- *Preliminary project schedule*: An early estimate of the project duration.
- *Preliminary project costs*: An early estimate of project costs, usually with emphasis on resource costs.
- *Project milestones*: The identifiable points in a project that represent a reporting requirement or completion of a large or important set of activities.

The project definition also may include project manager review comments per an examination of other projects to determine how costing has performed on projects of similar nature and duration.

Project Assumptions and Constraints. Assumptions are factors considered to be true, real, or certain for the purposes of making project decisions. Assumptions involve a degree of risk. Examples of assumptions to be considered include specifications or statements of:

- Date(s) when a key person is available
- Budget and resource availability
- Time requirements
- Organizational structure and culture
- Staff availability, training requirements, and experience
- Number and identity of stakeholders
- Level of project complexity
- Size and duration of the project
- External needs
- Extent of risks
- Level of technical capabilities

Constraints are factors that limit the project's options. Specifically, constraints may restrict the planning of project cost, schedule, and resources needed to achieve the project scope; affect when or how an activity can be scheduled; or lead to team pressure to complete the project on time, within budget, and according to specification. Examples of constraints include:

- Cost
- Schedule
- Staffing requirements or availability
- Funding availability
- Available technology
- Contractual factors
- Government regulations
- Risk factors
- Scope expectations and feasibility
- Market or economic factors
- Organizational structure
- Organization's culture
- Collective bargaining agreements
- Preferences of the project management team

Preliminary Project Risks.   Preliminary project risks include the following:

- *Schedule risks*: Risks that can affect the project's completion time, such as the availability of resources and funding, and changing project requirements.
- *Financial risks*: Risks that involve cash flow and profitability, including the level of competition, cash flow interruptions, cost overruns, and underestimating the project budget.
- *Technical risks*: Risks that relate to the development or operation of the deliverable and involve the level of technological maturity, complexity, and customization needed to develop the deliverable, including problems associated with existing, new, or evolving technology in which the problems or consequences are largely unforeseen.
- *Legal risks*: Risks that involve licensing requirements, ambiguous contract language, lawsuits, bankruptcies, and other legal challenges associated with the project.
- *External risks*: Risks outside the immediate control or influence of the project manager that may be predictable or unpredictable, including government regulations and mandates, natural hazards, environmental occurrences, changes in public interest, market changes, currency changes, inflation, and taxation.

Integrate and Expand Business Basis Information

The integration of relevant business information is the final step in preparing the project business plan. If prescreening was completed prior to this step, then initial strategy alignment data should be available for incorporation. Otherwise, this information will need to be compiled and included as part of the important business basis information.

The specific content and format of the project business plan is a matter of the organization's established documentation practices or preferences. The practical consideration of this component is to provide all necessary information to enable a detailed opportunity evaluation for project selection. This includes consideration for incorporating the following information elements:

- Strategy alignment/business objectives
- Business interest
- Financial analyses
- Customer analyses

In addition to considering these information elements, any other information needed to make a decision regarding opportunity examination and project selection should be incorporated into the project business plan.

Develop Project Resource Staffing Plan

Projects can go forward only with adequate resources to support them. Ordinarily, an organization has limits on resources and must make choices about which projects to support. Project selection, nonselection, termination, or adjustment is dependent, ultimately, on the availability of resources to support projects. Consequently, considerations for allocation of the organization's resources are an integral part of project selection.

This plan can be developed separately or incorporated as part of the project business plan. It also should be noted that this activity step might be performed as a part of project initiation activities conducted by the project manager as guided by the project management methodology process. Three primary activity steps can be applied to create a resource allocation plan, and these are described in the following subsections.

Identify Financial Impacts of Staffing Requirements

Each project opportunity must be reviewed for anticipated financial impacts of staffing requirements. This review can include the examination of the following elements:

- *Resource requirements*: The project business plan may provide a preliminary determination of resource requirements. Review that preliminary information and formulate additional information to ensure that both financial and personnel issues have been considered. Note that the development of project resource requirements can be done in conjunction with and using the tools of an established project methodology process step. Relevant considerations regarding resource requirements include:
  - What resources are currently required? What is projected for the future?
  - What personnel can be assigned to this project? What is the cumulative impact of all personnel requirements?
  - Is resource availability within our current capability? Are external resources needed? Are financing and partnering capabilities available?
  - Are resources available to achieve the current project scope? Are scope adjustments needed to better utilize resources?
  - How will project schedules impact workload? Are adjustments needed?
  - Are personnel overutilized or underutilized? Are certain resource skill types overburdened? Do current personnel need additional training to meet anticipated project requirements?
- *Project cost and schedule impacts*: Costs for specific skills, unique specialties, or turnovers during the project — all of which raise the costs of projects over time — should be evaluated. Information to be examined includes:
  - Are all necessary skills available within the company, or is external resource acquisition necessary?
  - Are the skills necessary to complete the project part of the core competency, or is this a new business area?
  - What is the time dimension for the project under evaluation and for all projects using the same resources? Will the deadline or the cumulative impact of all affected projects require funding of outside assistance?
- *Quality management*: Both anticipated and unexpected changes in the quality factors of the project and in the people required to ensure quality may incur cost adjustments as the project goes forward. This warrants examination of:
  - What quality specifications in the project might generate personnel costs?
  - Will a different level of product or service quality expectation require a new level of effort that will affect resource allocations and costs?

– Does the required resource level for quality expectations exist within the organization?

■ *Supplier, contractor, or subcontractor agreements*: External agreements and arrangements may affect pricing, over time. Identifying and accessing external resources can save costs:
   – What agreements have been made with external organizations?
   – Are firm commitments needed early in this project?
   – What external supplier, contractor, or subcontractor costs for products and services stay the same or increase over the life of the project?

■ *Costing methods*: The use of different costing methods can produce different results, and these must be normalized. Alternatively, the organization can use standard methods across all projects. Note that the financial and personnel resource requirements developed in this step will be included in the resource allocation plan. A review of methods helps to ensure costing method accuracy:
   – What cost methods have been used? Hours versus dollars? Are the methods consistent across the period of project work?
   – Will the skill mix required on the project change over time? Will that change affect costs and internal or external personnel utilization?
   – Have all costs been accounted for in each project? (For example, have administrative and support costs been included in all projects?)
   – Have previous projects' cost data been used to estimate costs here?
   – What technology enhancements might be utilized to reduce personnel costs across all projects?

Review Organizational Resource Utilization Impacts

Resource requirements for the current project opportunity should be evaluated against the total portfolio of projects. This examination can be presented using a spreadsheet or other analytical tool. It includes examination of other projects' resource allocation plans (or extracted summaries), and it provides for a review of the total financial commitments and staffing requirements tallied across all projects. The following considerations can be deliberated:

■ Are the resource projections within the limits of the organization if this project is added to the portfolio?
■ Are changes to project scope or outside financing needed to do this project?

- Is the pending resource utilization commitment financially sound? Is there flexibility to handle unanticipated changes?
- What is the total impact on resource availability relative to the number and types of particular skills available?
- Do interests in applying resources to this project make any other projects stand out to be adjusted or eliminated?
- Relative to resource skill and availability, is this project too big? Too risky? Too unknown? Of marginal benefit?
- Can project schedules be adjusted or scope scaled differently to have a different impact on financial resources or on resource utilization?
- Can personnel be grouped or clustered so that several projects can be supported simultaneously?

Key points of this examination of the impact on organizational resources should be included in the resource allocation plan.

Develop Resource Staffing Plan

Once the financial and resource impacts are specified, resource allocations can be developed and finalized. In general, the following should be specified in a resource allocation plan for each project:

- Project resource requirements by skill and experience levels required (including financial commitments)
- Internal resource allocations by major time increments (e.g., quarterly), including the planned approach to identifying and acquiring individuals, by name, and the schedule for internal resource acquisition activities
- External resource allocations by major time increments (e.g., quarterly), including the planned approach to identifying and establishing contracts for external participants and the schedule of external resource acquisition activities
- Identifiable resource allocation conflicts (within the portfolio)
- General and specific resource training required to increase individual skill and competency, and to address the use of any new technology or processes
- Oversight required for resource allocation management for this project, i.e., issues to monitor, recommended frequency of resource allocation review, etc.

The resource staffing plan becomes the ongoing portfolio level budgeting document for this project in the project portfolio management process. The resource allocation plan is reviewed (a) when this and other projects move into new phases or undergo plan revision and (b) as projects are added to or terminated from the portfolio.

Conduct Project Selection

The PMO should ensure that a viable project selection process is developed and implemented. This begins with consideration of several principles that can be applied to the decision-making process to support better project choices:

- Principle 1: Be explicit about the selection criteria and ensure that all projects are held to the same standard no matter how many interesting options may be available.
- Principle 2: Be clear about the procedure for choosing projects and ensure that all projects are selected by the same method.
- Principle 3: Be prepared to challenge (and defend) all assertions in a project business plan, since overly rosy or incomplete predictions do not promote success.
- Principle 4: Convene a review group of diverse stakeholders to review project selections, since the impact of all projects will cross the organization and have impacts outside it.
- Principle 5: Include the project management staff, as is consistent with organizational practices, in the project selection process.

In the past, organizations have typically emphasized financial goals as indicators of performance, almost to the exclusion of other values in the organization. Benefit-cost ratios, return-on-investment, and stockholder value have been typical quantitative measures employed. Increasingly, organizations are realizing that they need a broader decision framework than just financial performance for the organization to continue to survive and thrive in a more holistic but fast-paced business environment.

In general, project selection methods range from simple paper and pencil calculations to highly analytical and mathematical models, to value-driven and performance-based methods, to decision software packages. A thorough review of selection framework models should be conducted before a single framework is adopted to ensure that a method is chosen that matches the strategic intention and business operations of the organization.

The executive review board should conduct project screening, with the portfolio management team (ideally with PMO leadership) as the next-best group for this task. Participants begin with an individual and independent review of the selection materials created to date. The team then convenes to deliberate and discuss the merits of the business and resource allocation plans, making any adjustments deemed appropriate through consensus, and then examining the project opportunity. Areas of team review should focus on:

- Consistency with strategic objectives (with project screening)
- Project opportunity business evaluation (using the established screening method)
- Business and project risk indicators
- Point(s) of executive participation in business plan review
- Subsequent decision points for further project examination
- Recommended project position within the portfolio
- Decision appeal options (for project sponsor or project manager)

This activity is best achieved through an expert-led facilitation that the PMO can provide. This activity should lead to a decision toward one of the following actions:

- Select project and proceed with detailed project planning
- Select project and hold, pending a project start date to be determined
- Withhold selection, pending a request for more information and further review
- Nonselect project and discontinue opportunity evaluation

This activity determines whether or not a project is selected for inclusion in the relevant organization's project portfolio. The results of this deliberation can be either a mandate to proceed or a recommendation of project selection to the relevant executive authority. A project that is not selected is normally not reported to the executive authority.

Integrate Projects in the Portfolio

The practice of effective project portfolio management inherently requires the participation of the executive portfolio owner. If that individual executive review team (portfolio owner) has not yet been involved in the initial selection activities, it is essential that executive participation begin at this juncture in the project portfolio management process.

There are three activities performed to achieve project integration:

- *Validate project selection*: A final executive level reviewer signs off on the business plan as the approved approach for conducting the project. The executive reviewer also signs off on the resource allocation plan, if presented as a separate document, as the approved approach for staffing the project.

■ *Determine project priority*: The executive portfolio owner assigns a project ranking within the portfolio of projects.
■ *Approve initial project funding*: The executive portfolio owner signs off on project funding to enable the project to be "booked" and to authorize the expenditure of money for the specified initial project planning effort.

It should be noted that this activity can be performed as a part of the project selection effort conducted by members of the executive review board, or it can be conducted as a separate activity performed by the portfolio management team (or portfolio manager), with participation and sign-off by the relevant executive owner. A discussion of the concepts for accomplishing these action steps is presented in the following subsections.

Validate Project Selection

The project business plan and project resource allocation plan are subjected to a final review by either individual executives or in conjunction with a meeting of an executive review board. If project selection actions precede executive review, the relevant executive may opt to examine an abbreviated project selection document or selection recommendation document, with access to the actual project business plan and resource allocation plan, as needed.

The designated executive reviewer signs the business plan (and resource allocation plan) to assert the following:

■ Project consistency with the organization's business objectives and interests
■ An awareness of business issues and risks associated with the project
■ Approval of the high level approach to conducting the project
■ Approval of the specified resource allocations
■ Frequency of review and the next scheduled project review date
■ Approval to proceed with the project

These validated elements serve as the basis for developing the project charter, which is normally prepared by the project sponsor or project manager under guidance contained in the organization's project management methodology.

Determine Project Priority

When project opportunities are being considered for selection, a resource calculation is made, and each project is prioritized or adjusted based on its fit in the portfolio. As projects are introduced into the portfolio, each project should be ranked in order of priority. This allows senior management to maximize support to critically important projects and to perform ongoing evaluation of other projects, sometimes terminating projects of lesser importance or value to allow higher priority projects to enter the portfolio and be sustained.

If the relevant organization has discrete business units, this prioritization and ranking is particularly important, because projects initiated within a business unit may require adjustments relative to other projects in other business units across the whole organization. The position of all projects within the portfolio should be reevaluated at portfolio reviews and with every new project addition or project termination. The position within the portfolio provides a guide to the relevant organization about intent and means to achieve strategic goals.

In this activity step, the executive examines the fit of each newly selected project and assigns it a priority within the portfolio. This assignment will likely affect the position of all other projects already in the portfolio; therefore, part of this effort includes realignment of project priorities across the entire portfolio. The PMO can assist in this effort when there are established formulas for project prioritization.

Approve Initial Project Funding

This action step authorizes funds for conducting at least initial project planning, if not for conducting the entire project. Essentially, the relevant executive signs the authorization to release funds and start the project. The nature and duration of the project may warrant initial full funding. Otherwise, funding approval can be incremental, and additional fund authorizations can be accomplished at project and portfolio review points.

Funding approval can be part of the sign-off of the project's business and resource staffing plans, or it can be conducted as a separate act. There may be a preference to have a separate funding approval document that can be prepared and distributed to other departments in the organization that require notification of funding approval but that do not have a need for copies of the project's business and resource allocation plans.

Like the project business and resource staffing plans, funding authorization is passed for inclusion in the project charter.

Conduct Project and Portfolio Reviews

The essence of project portfolio management is reflected in the ongoing participation of executives and senior managers in reviewing individual projects and the overall portfolio on a recurring basis. These reviews are key to keeping projects and related activities on course toward the achievement of strategic business objectives. Review activities must demonstrate sufficient rigor to enable serious business decisions to be made. In particular, project level reviews must present adequate examination to make decisions about project continuation or project termination. Portfolio level reviews must provide the necessary information to judge business results for the collection of projects in the portfolio.

There are three primary activities to accomplish in conducting project and portfolio reviews:

■ *Compile project performance information*: A process linked to the project collaboration and project status reporting capabilities is implemented to ensure that appropriate information is collected and compiled for use in project and portfolio reviews.

■ *Conduct project gateway reviews*: The practice of when and how to evaluate active projects is established.

■ *Conduct portfolio reviews*: The practice of when and how to examine the total collection of projects in the relevant organization's portfolio is established.

A suggested approach for accomplishing each of these action steps is provided in the following subsections.

Compile Project Performance Information

The PMO is the communication link between senior management and the project environment. The PMO specifically facilitates organizing reports to management, although this responsibility could be delegated to a portfolio manager or portfolio management team. Nevertheless, it is likely that the PMO will play a role in establishing the project reporting capability within the relevant organization. Therefore, it must coordinate and perhaps facilitate report content development with the executive review board or other designated portfolio management authority.

A progress or status report developed for use in project and portfolio management reviews must be generated at the project level, by the project manager, on a recurring basis. This very well may be the single monthly report that is produced under guidance contained in the project management methodology. This is recommended as a matter of maximizing the efficiency of reporting project progress. This report already provides the essential project information needed to ascertain the state of project performance, and it normally includes the following or similar data elements:

- Indication of project status (e.g., green, on track; yellow, issues; red, troubled)
- Significant accomplishments
- Open action items
- Milestone/deliverables status
- Cost, schedule, and resource utilization status
- Key project issues
- Scope-change status

The PMO should work with key stakeholders to specify and format the desired content. The frequency and timing of such project level reports to management should be established to accommodate portfolio management review activities. If required, supplementary reports can be established to satisfy "off-cycle" project reporting needs, but such reports should be an exception rather than standard practice for the sake of efficiency.

The process of compiling project information for portfolio level reviews may warrant an additional reporting step. That step is the intermediate examination of compiled project data by the PMO, portfolio manager, or portfolio management team. This examination will be performed by middle to senior managers with a focus on interpreting project status report information, including calculating additional financial indicators used by executives, verifying project alignment with strategy (as specified in the project business plan), and checking resource utilization against resource allocations. This "special" report can be designed for use in either project reviews or portfolio reviews, or both.

Conduct Project Gateway Reviews

Ongoing executive reviews and decisions ensure that each project within the portfolio continues to contribute to the overall strategic business interests of the organization. A standard decision-making process should be adopted, and project gateway decision points should be implemented to occur at project life cycle phase-transition junctures or at other points deemed appropriate by the executive review team.

The standardization of portfolio decisions ensures that all projects are examined from a common frame of reference and that the entire portfolio can be viewed from that frame of reference. The specification of decision points ensures that each project is revalidated regularly throughout its life cycle and that all key stakeholders know when those reevaluation decisions are scheduled and made.

The project gateway review process comprises the following five activities:

- Validate business plan
- Assess project performance
- Evaluate resource allocation
- Confirm position within the portfolio project
- Make continuation decision

These activities are performed by the executive review team or other designated portfolio management authority to ensure that an effective project review is accomplished. These five activities are described in the following subsections.

Validate the Business Plan

The business plan review has a focus on different elements as it progresses through the portfolio management process. These different elements support the different decision requirements of a particular project management phase. In general, after initial selection, the validation of the business plan is accomplished according to a review of elements associated with the project phase decision points encountered:

- *Solution planning phase:* The business plan review has a focus on any changes to scope, cost, risk, and other initial selection criteria.
- *Solution implementation phase:* The business plan review has a focus on project financial performance and resource utilization (assignment) consistent with the Resource Staffing Plan.
- *Project closure phase:* Projects can be closed for a variety of reasons. The business plan review has a focus on the achievement of project objectives and lessons learned that can be applied to business decisions on similar future projects.

The executive review team, depending on the length of each project phase, may request interim progress reports or updates as a means to conduct additional business plan reviews not specifically associated with project phase decision points.

Assess Project Performance

Ideally, executives will personally review all projects at all phase decision points. However, based on the size and complexity of the organization and the number of projects involved, executives may delegate this to a PMO manager, a portfolio manager, or a cross-functional portfolio management team to provide continuous project monitoring. Notwithstanding this support, executives are inherently responsible for assuring satisfactory project performance, and for providing guidance and influence to ensure success.

The process surrounding an assessment of project performance should include:

- Review of status and progress reports for projects currently under way
- Review of project performance indicators, looking for gaps in plan implementation and scope or resource requirement changes
- Review of project deliverable quality and customer acceptance — and customer satisfaction.

Portfolio management decision points are opportunities for executive leadership to address the results of project work and to make project continuation decisions based on accomplishments to date.

Evaluate Resource Allocations

A resource review must be conducted at each decision point associated with gateway review phases and at other times deemed necessary. Resource staffing plan review activities are generally conducted throughout the project, normally as an inherent responsibility of the project manager. As resource assignment and allocation issues arise during the project, they are elevated to the PMO or portfolio management team and, as necessary, to executives. However, there should be planned executive level involvement in resource allocation reviews at every decision point of the project.

These reviews are conducted in conjunction with business plan reviews and enable the responsible executive and project sponsor to evaluate the status of resource allocation for a particular project and the status of resource allocation for the entire portfolio. The reviews described in the following four subsections should be accomplished according to the decision point encountered at project phases.

Conduct Project Initiation Resource Review. When a project is offered as a possible opportunity for selection and initiation, resource requirements are identified. At this point in the project, the resource request is at its most negotiable because the project is uncommitted and its scope and scale are open. At this early juncture, executive portfolio managers and the project manager and sponsor have an opportunity to develop pertinent information about resource requirements for the intended project. At the same time, executive reviewers have the greatest potential for shaping projects through adjustments in personnel, budget, or schedule. The following items are part of the resource allocation review at project initiation:

- Skills necessary
- Skill match to current competencies
- Staffing plan
- Number of personnel necessary
- Geographic requirements for staffing
- Staffing schedules required
- Alliances and partnerships available
- Risks anticipated
- Project materials list
- Special equipment needs
- Space requirements
- Geographic requirements for anticipated staffing

The collective consequence of these considerations will affect decisions to undertake a particular project as all project opportunities and ongoing projects are reviewed within and among categories.

Conduct Solution Planning Resource Review. Detailed project planning begins during the solution planning phase, and adjustments are made to the project business plan and resource requirements based on the refined project scope. Further definition and specificity are provided, and the following considerations should be part of the resource allocation review at the project solution planning point:

- Skills necessary
- Skill match to current competencies
- Staffing plan
- Number of personnel necessary
- Project organization structure
- Geographic requirements for staffing
- Anticipated resource schedules
- Alliances and partnerships available
- Risks anticipated
- Project materials list
- Special equipment needs
- Space requirements
- Geographic requirements for locations

- Skill and personnel requirements anticipated for implementation
- Budget requirements anticipated based on work breakdown structure

Conduct Solution Implementation Resource Review. The actual performance of project work enables managers to know more about resource utilization. This phase is characterized by more-specific budgets and more-detailed estimates. However, the overall ability to affect a particular project is reduced; the field of decision making is smaller because the resources are already committed. The following considerations should be part of the resource-allocation review at the project solution implementation point:

- Skills necessary
- Extra skills required beyond current competency
- Training requirements
- Number of personnel necessary
- Geographic requirements for staffing
- Planned resource schedules
- Alliances and partnerships committed
- Budget commitment based on projected versus actual expenditures
- Project expenses budget
- Risks encountered and overcome
- Special equipment budget
- Space requirements budget
- Geographic location commitments and budget
- Additional impacts on current staffing
- Additional organizational impacts anticipated

Conduct Project Closure Resource Review. When a project is closed, the resource reports resulting from all phases become part of the project file. These reports stand as a final record of the conduct of the project, serve as estimating models for new projects, and are a source of lessons learned to the organization. The final resource allocation review should address the following considerations:

- Final budget and expenditures of the project by fiscal year and WBS element
- Review of final close out of all supporting accounts and costs, including leases and other contractual obligations
- Final personnel budget and resource utilization numbers
- Development of lessons learned from the resource allocation point of view

Additional project closure activities such as dispersing and releasing team members and returning material resources must be conducted. These activities may be conducted during or as a result of the events of the project management methodology.

Confirm Project Position in the Portfolio

Projects in the portfolio are examined and considered on their own merit as decisions made regarding the business plan, project performance, and resource allocation. Now the executive must examine each project to determine whether its current project position in the portfolio is still valid.

It should be rare when two or more current projects significantly change portfolio positions relative to each other. However, newly selected projects could very well influence discernable adjustments to current project portfolio positions. Therefore, as a matter of focus, projects under review should be contrasted primarily with those that have just entered the portfolio.

Executive reviewers should then confirm or prepare to change the position of the project under review within the portfolio. At this project level review, the possibility of project position changes is identified. Unless there are extenuating circumstances, actual changes in portfolio positions are made during the portfolio review described later.

Make Project Continuation Decision

Establishing or confirming a project's position within the portfolio inherently invokes a decision to allow the project to continue on to the next project phase, and it represents an expectation that it will continue through completion.

A significant downward change in a project's priority and portfolio position warrants an additional examination regarding a decision to continue. Similarly, a project portfolio position that has been changed to a significantly higher priority may also warrant examination regarding its continuation. This second instance of priority change warrants further consideration for possible project termination because there may be borderline influences that affect a decision to either raise the project's priority or to discontinue the project.

Conduct Portfolio Reviews

The executive (or executive review team) is the final authority on which projects are pursued and when. This is because they inherently have the answer to why every project is being performed — achievement of strategic business objectives, of course. To that end, that authority is used to manage and decide on the makeup and evolution of projects in the portfolio from the holistic perspective of all projects working together to pursue the business objectives of the organization. This perspective also warrants a routine examination of the collection of projects in the relevant organization's portfolio, as a whole.

Although individual project status information has been developed and reviewed separately, all project information should be updated and standardized for a comprehensive review and evaluation by the executive review team or by the portfolio management team. Reviewers should examine both in-progress projects and new projects together. The following elements provide a recommended, fundamental focus for the portfolio review:

- Progress against projections
  - What has been the progress and history of each project?
  - Are projects over- or underperforming based on projections?
- Current and projected resource utilization
  - Are the projections for resource allocations on target?
  - What financial and personnel resources are being consumed by each project?
  - Are resources performing to expected standards and skill levels?
  - What resource changes will be needed as projects go forward?
  - Have commitments allowed for continuation of those resources?
  - Are any projects indicating a need for increased costs that were unforeseen at the last portfolio review?
- Potential for success
  - Are all projects in the portfolio likely to be successful?
  - Will the successful project results move the organization forward in the desired business direction?
- Project status
  - Relative to project level gateway review points in the portfolio management process, at what gateways are these projects?
  - What is the general schedule for completion of each project?
  - Will resources used by these projects be freed to support new projects (of equal or higher priority) as a result of timely project completion?
  - Are any new directions (e.g., scope changes) anticipated for any projects?
- Continuation issues
  - Does each project warrant continuation (are any questionable)?
  - Are increased or reduced resource requirements predicted for any projects?

- Are additional contracts or new alliances necessary for continuation?
- Is there ongoing customer support for each project underway?
■ Consequences of project close out
- If any project is discontinued, what are the consequences to the organization?
- If any project is discontinued, what is at risk?
- If any project is discontinued, will other projects be jeopardized?
- If any project is discontinued, are additional closedown costs anticipated?
- If any project is discontinued, is that consistent with customer expectations?
■ Alignment with core competencies
- Do all projects match the current capabilities of the relevant organization?
- Has new technology on any project produced the predicted results?
- Has staff training on any project demonstrated the successful expansion of technical competency?
- Are new staff skills that are currently out of the core competencies of the organization required in order to complete any project?
- Would additional skills or capabilities boost future capability, or is this a direction that would not support the general direction of the organization?

Manage Portfolio Attrition

The projects that come to make up the portfolio are first selected and then managed through a series of project gateway review points that facilitate examination and then a decision to either continue or terminate the project.

The project attrition funnel depicts how projects progress in a standard life cycle from initial selection, through various gateway review points, and then final disposition. This means that it is expected, as a natural course of business decision making, that only the most favorable projects will be performed and survive to completion. The remaining projects will be eliminated, ideally as early as possible, through attrition. Figure 17.2 illustrates a project attrition funnel.

Generally, the rate of project attrition through the project management life cycle can be expected to occur as depicted in Figure 17.2. This diagram shows that the rate of attrition early in the project life cycle, beginning with the project selection screening, can be as much as 75% of the original

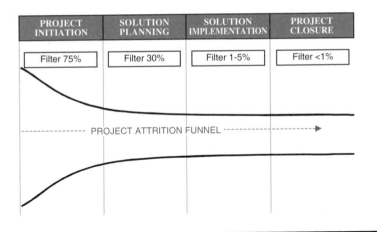

PROJECT INITIATION	SOLUTION PLANNING	SOLUTION IMPLEMENTATION	PROJECT CLOSURE
Filter 75%	Filter 30%	Filter 1-5%	Filter <1%

------------- PROJECT ATTRITION FUNNEL ------------------------▶

Figure 17.2   Project Attrition Funnel

project opportunities identified. This is because of the rigorous evaluation and selection criteria applied at each decision point to all projects. During the project initiation phase, the diagram indicates that as many as 30% of the in-progress projects can be terminated as decision makers gather more information about the effort, weigh resource utilization, and examine strategic alignments. This rate then decreases dramatically as "accepted" projects progress into the solution planning and solution implementation phases. The actual rate of project attrition is determined by the criteria established by the executives responsible for project portfolio management — as facilitated by the PMO.

When a project is either selected for termination or comes to an end through the natural completion of its life cycle, there are three primary activities that should be performed to manage project attrition:

■ Perform project close out
■ Assess strategic advantage
■ Determine level of customer satisfaction

Each of these action steps is described in the following subsections.

Perform Project Close Out

A project coming to conclusion, and thus on the verge of being removed from the portfolio, must be reviewed to identify the purpose for closure. This is generally either a matter of a termination decision or the result of a successfully completed project effort.

The prominent action, from the perspective of the portfolio management team, is to examine the decisions made to prematurely close out a project as a termination action. In these cases, the close out purpose should be specified with accompanying information concerning:

- Accuracy of the initial selection decision
- What has changed since the initial project selection decision
- Identification of the influences that warranted a project discontinuation decision as internal or external
- Determination if the discontinuation influences were quick deliberation actions or anticipated over time
- Determination of what, if anything, could have been done at an earlier gateway review point to enable the project to continue

This specification of close out purpose, and the associated influences or causes, can be conveyed to the project selection process for application during the next new project selection activity.

In addition to this particular action step, the PMO must convey any early project termination decision to the appropriate project manager for immediate action. The PMO also should monitor and assist the project manager in conducting project closure. The project manager should use guidance contained in the project management methodology to perform project level close out activities. When these activities are completed, a formal report of project closure should be reported through the PMO to the executive review team.

Assess Strategic Advantage

Projects being removed from the portfolio collection should be examined for their impact on the organization's business strategy, beneficial or otherwise. This means looking at what was achieved over the course of the project management life cycle relative to the following considerations:

- Did the project complete its full life cycle, and were all of the project's objectives achieved?
- Did the project scope change or stay the same; what influenced any change?
- Did the project stay within the established criteria for which it was selected, thereby maintaining its alignment with business purpose and objectives?
- What business needs or interests were affected by project performance?
  - Profitability and ROI

- Achievement of strategic goals
- Expansion of organizational visibility within the industry
- Expansion of organization visibility in the marketplace
- Attainment of client satisfaction
■ If the project terminated early, how does the cause of early project termination affect the organization's strategic position?

By incorporating "lessons learned," the results of this examination can be conveyed for incorporation into the selection process for the next new project as well as into project gateway review points.

Assess Customer Satisfaction

This final activity step of project portfolio management is essentially an extension of the previous activity step. In this case, however, the focus is on the customer's perspective of any benefits obtained as a result of the project that is being closed out. The customer's perspective is obtained through compilation of various forms of feedback.

It is important for the relevant organization to examine how well the different projects placed within the portfolio are responding to customer needs. To that end, the PMO should conduct or otherwise facilitate the creation of processes that enable customer feedback and evaluation of customer satisfaction.

The following customer information can be compiled, deliberated, and communicated (a) to enhance future business decisions about project selection and project continuation and (b) to improve the overall project portfolio management capability:

■ Executive level examination:
  - General comments of direct or indirect awareness of customer satisfaction at project close out
  - Executive guidance addressing the desired course of any follow-on business relationship with the customer
  - Executive guidance addressing the desired course of business relationships with other customers based on results and reactions of this customer
■ Customer survey and feedback:
  - Completion of a customer end-of-project service/project satisfaction survey
  - Completion of a customer interim service/project satisfaction survey
  - Compilation of customer feedback based on discussions at close out meetings

- Review of customer feedback as presented by comments in quality and deliverable acceptance/sign-off documents
- Review of customer issues and problem resolution actions during the project
■ Project manager/PMO evaluation:
    - Evaluation of customer satisfaction
    - Examination of customer's participation in the project
    - Identification and review of issues and problems encountered

POSTSCRIPT FOR THE SMALLER PMO

An effective project portfolio management process is complex and comprehensive. It is not a very common undertaking for the smaller PMO, which presumably has limited resources, not to mention limited business influence. However, the point of focus here is for the PMO to ensure some level of executive involvement in project management. To reiterate the point: projects directly or indirectly produce revenue, executives are responsible for revenue, and therefore executives should be involved in project decisions.

The smaller PMO can begin to influence project portfolio management activities in a number of ways:

■ Examine existing oversight processes, including any formal and informal processes used by executives and senior managers to monitor projects. Perhaps there is some type of portfolio management performed by the accounting and finance department that is not evident within the project management environment. Review these processes to ensure that good project management information is being applied to executive business decisions. Prepare and submit recommendations for improved executive project review.

■ Establish a formal project selection process that includes an executive level review and approval step. This ensures that all projects undertaken are bona fide business efforts, and it introduces project selection as a preliminary activity toward development of project portfolio management. If necessary, and within allowable policies and practices of the business, construct and begin to manage project selection from the purview of the PMO until executives or other stakeholders can be brought into the process.

■ Prepare reports to senior management that compile results across projects and have strategic significance. Remember, program management is not portfolio management. If program management is conducted, a separate strategic level report is still needed.

- Develop a solid business case, including funding and resource requirements, that demonstrates the value of project portfolio management, and then present it to senior managers and executives for review and consideration. Properly constructed, such a business case could be the PMO's early entry for achieving business integration.

Anything the PMO does to enhance executive level business decisions regarding project management will be a step forward.

18

CUSTOMER RELATIONSHIPS

Every project has an internal or external customer who is relying on project fulfillment. Most external customers have a financial investment in the project effort. Internal customers often seek greater operational effectiveness and efficiency as a result of the product or service delivered by the project effort. Along with these considerations of *revenue* and *efficiency*, the third common element of the project–business equation is *customer satisfaction*. These elements need to be managed from both a business and a project management perspective. To the extent that the PMO is responsible for project–business integration, managing customer relationships within the project management environment is an important element of the PMO's efforts.

Most customers will have some level of participation in project activities. At a minimum they will initiate a request for the project effort and execute the associated project contract or agreement. Some customers will be more involved than others in project performance and project management oversight. Any level of customer involvement in the project effort warrants that the PMO also be involved in managing those customer relationships.

This PMO function addresses the essentials of managing customer relationships, and most prescribed activities can be applied to both internal and external customers. However, there will be a distinct inclination toward the external business customer who has an investment commitment to one or more project efforts conducted by the relevant organization. To that end, the PMO should evaluate internal project management customer relationships and then translate as much of the prescribed customer relationship management approach as possible for internal use.

This "customer relationships" function enables the PMO to:

- Establish customer relationship practices within the project management environment
- Develop guidance for managing the business aspects of customer projects
- Conduct customer satisfaction measurements related to project performance

These activities can be designed and developed in conjunction with the introduction of an overall customer relationship management (CRM) system within the relevant organization, or they can be developed and implemented solely within the project management environment. In either case, these activities will always be in collaboration with relevant managers and other participants in the business environment.

PROJECT ENVIRONMENT INTERFACE CONCEPTS

The project manager has inherent responsibility for managing the customer relationship for the duration of the project. The PMO can lead development of the preferred approach that project managers can use to properly represent the relevant organization to the customer. The PMO can further examine opportunities and develop the means to maintain a business relationship with customers after the project is completed. This can be reflected in follow-up customer contact to evaluate customer satisfaction with the completed project, explore new project and business opportunities, or just extend appreciation for recent business. This type of follow-up activity is essential for external customer business relationships. It would enhance project management professionalism if similar considerations could be extended to internal customers as well.

Managing the customer relationship relative to the project effort presents a range of interactions that can be adequately conducted only by those directly involved in the project management effort. Therefore, the PMO and project manager are ideally suited to fulfill such customer interactions. The project manager certainly can convey insight and information related to technical performance and project management performance, and the PMO can prominently contribute to the third dimension, business performance. This approach will keep the customer appropriately informed and involved in the project while also ensuring that business performance aspects of the project — particularly contract administration — are accomplished as routine activities of project management. Moreover, the customer's project and business experience can be enhanced when the customer has ongoing access to qualified professionals in project management who can answer technical questions as well as resolve business issues solely within the project management environment.

BUSINESS ENVIRONMENT INTERFACE CONCEPTS

The business units of the relevant organization that have customer relationship responsibilities will normally find an increase in efficiency and sometimes a reduction in workload when the PMO and project managers have been assigned with responsibility for customer relationship management. This includes such departments as business development, finance and accounting, legal/contracts management, and the like. Professionals in these business areas can focus on more-prominent duties or possibly problem areas associated with customer projects when the PMO and project managers are able to contribute to developing and managing effective customer relationships as a natural part of the project management effort.

The project management methodology should be ideally suited to incorporate business practices for critical customer relationship activities associated with projects and project management. This includes such things as initial examination of customer requirements, development of technical solutions and proposals, management of contracts and agreements, acceptance of project deliverables and associated invoice management, and evaluations of customer satisfaction at interim project points and at project close out. This integration enables the PMO and project managers to implement the existing business processes and preferred approach for customer relationship management within the relevant organization.

CUSTOMER RELATIONSHIPS ACTIVITIES ACROSS THE PMO CONTINUUM

The "customer relationships" function along the PMO competency continuum represents the development of capability within the project management environment to establish and manage an effective customer relationship process. This begins with emphasis on the customer's interest and involvement in specific project efforts, and it expands with PMO functional capability into business areas associated with projects conducted by the relevant organization.

Table 18.1 presents an overview of the range of prescribed PMO customer relationships activities according to each level in the PMO competency continuum.

The *project office* has fundamental responsibility for implementing the established customer relationship management process, usually as such

Table 18.1 Range of Customer Relationships Activities across the PMO Continuum

Project Office	Basic PMO	Standard PMO	Advanced PMO	Center of Excellence
Applies customer relationship process guidance	Manages customer relationship and project information ■ Monitors customer relationship information ■ Monitors customer project information	Manages customer relationships across project duration ■ Prescribes customer project participation ■ Manages customer project proposals ■ Administers customer project contracts ■ Evaluates customer project satisfaction	Manages customer relationships across business interests ■ Manages pre- and postproject customer activity ■ Conducts forums and interactions for customer relationship development ■ Examines and implements customer partner arrangements	Evaluates customer relationships for business benefits ■ Analyzes customer base ■ Evaluates trends in customer relationships ■ Recommends customer relationship improvements

process steps are incorporated into the project management methodology. The focus at this level is normally on the relationship established with the customer's project manager or other designated customer business representative. In the absence of formal guidance or process steps, the project office will simply ensure that prescribed project deliverables are presented on time and to the customer's satisfaction for acceptance. It will also manage any customer issues or problems associated with project performance.

Mid-range PMO levels develop and implement a comprehensive customer relationship management capability in the project management environment. This includes establishing practices that proactively manage customer participation in project performance, facilitate customer contract administration, and provide serious attention to customer satisfaction issues and conditions. In conjunction with these activities, the mid-range PMO is collecting and using pertinent customer information to examine and develop a broader business perspective in key customer relationships.

The *center of excellence* provides an additional business capability in its detailed examination and analysis of customer business relationships within the project management environment and across the relevant organization.

Customer relationship management represents a business approach developed and applied in the course of conducting project management. Therefore, concepts and considerations for customer relationship management can be introduced in the PMO "project management methodology" function (see Chapter 1). The business nature of this function will also be influenced by policies created under the PMO "project governance" function (see Chapter 5), strategies applied in the PMO "project portfolio management" function (see Chapter 17), and executive guidance prescribed by the PMO "business performance" function (see Chapter 20).

CUSTOMER RELATIONSHIPS FUNCTION MODEL

The PMO's overall responsibility for project management and business alignment is supported by this PMO function. In many project management environments, the external customer represents the business of the relevant organization. The closer that customers are likewise aligned with the project effort, the greater is the opportunity for business success. This PMO function model enables the PMO to achieve that alignment from both business and project management perspectives.

The prominent activities of the PMO's "customer relationships" function model are depicted in Figure 18.1. Each activity is described in the following subsections.

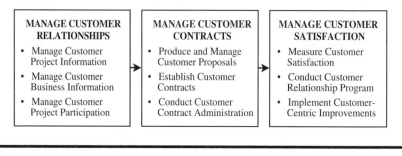

Figure 18.1 "Customer Relationships" Function Model

Manage Customer Relationships

The PMO's role in managing customer relationships is not a replacement for the several (if not many) activities accomplished within the business environment toward that end. Rather, the PMO is responsible for ensuring that the customer's business experience as a recipient of project-based product and service solutions equals or exceeds the standards for service prescribed by the relevant organization. As well, when PMO responsibility is discussed in this function, it is implied that the concepts and practices it establishes will be properly used by the project manager and members of the project team, who inherently have associated responsibility for managing customer relationships.

In the context of project management, the PMO will have to establish the capability to learn about the customer's needs, requirements, expectations, etc. and to achieve business objectives associated with each customer project. Moreover, the PMO has the added responsibility to appropriately include customers in the project effort simply as a matter of demonstrating effective project management practices.

The PMO can consider the following three activities when establishing its capability to manage customer relationships within the project management environment.

Manage Customer Project Information

The PMO should examine information requirements needed to initiate and conduct projects and project management activities for each customer. These project information elements are primarily associated with technical needs, but they may include other types of information as well. The following list describes four primary areas of customer project information that will assist not only in project delivery, but also in customer relationship management:

- *Project requirements and specifications:* This set of information represents the customer's perspective of what needs to be achieved by the project. Presumably, associated information items are prepared and presented by the customer as a part of the request for project assistance. In some cases, initial efforts in project management or external sales and business development activity may provide a measurable amount of assistance in preparing this information. However, in the context of this activity, the customer's view of what is to be achieved is paramount. (Note that additional information elements of project requirements and specifications are described in greater detail in Chapter 14, the PMO "planning support" function model.) A few sample information elements include:
  - Request for proposal (RFP)
  - Statement of work (SOW)
  - Business/technical needs analysis
  - Technical specifications document
  - Technical survey document
  - Technical design document
- *Project definition:* This set of information represents the translation of customer requirements into a description of the project effort. This information is aligned with the customer's needs but represents the perspective of the relevant organization regarding what needs to be achieved by the project. This of course is collaborated with the customer. In some cases, the project definition is contained as an element of the project business case document. (Note that additional information elements of project definition are described in greater detail in Chapter 14, the PMO "planning support" function model.) A few sample information elements include:
  - Project scope statement
  - Project objectives
  - Project deliverables and milestones
  - Project assumptions and constraints
- *Customer contract:* This set of information establishes the formal business relationship between the customer and the relevant organization. It sets forth the agreement between the two parties, specifies their obligations to one another, and presents the terms and conditions under which the agreement and obligations are upheld. Often, the customer contract will append or reference the project information materials mentioned in the previous two items.
- *Customer management plan:* This set of information is used by the project manager and the members of the project team to guide their interactions with the customer. This information is sometimes

incorporated into the project communications plan, which represents the communication practices and protocols to be used on the project. This information specifies points of contact for business and technical collaboration, coordination, and decision making. In particular, it will identify the individuals and preferred interactions with any customer project manager or customer project team.

The PMO can consider these and other information elements in establishing and managing customer project information.

Manage Customer Business Information

Project information elements will not necessarily present a comprehensive depiction of the customer, but rather they will focus on customer technical needs for the project effort at hand. Therefore, the PMO will also have to acquire and manage customer business information as a means of understanding the current status of the customer relationship. This includes the following three types of customer business information:

- *Customer business profile:* The customer's business profile contains any relevant information the PMO deems is needed to gain an adequate understanding of the nature of the customer's business. Fundamental information elements in the customer business profile can include:
  - Customer business description (e.g., product, service, industry, etc.)
  - Customer business size (e.g., number of employees)
  - Customer business location(s) (e.g., local, regional, national, global, etc.)
  - Customer business status (e.g., sales, revenue, stock position and outlook, etc.)
  - Customer business management (e.g., executives, directors, private owners, etc.)
  - Customer business affiliations (e.g., partnerships, industry memberships, etc.)
- *Customer relationship history:* Information on customer relationship history examines past business dealings with the customer. Its focus is on being able to review past business with the customer, but it can also look at the customer's other dealings in the industry and in the marketplace. Fundamental information elements in the customer relationship history package can include:
  - Major business transaction history with the customer, and the outcomes

- Project work history with the customer, and the outcomes
- Partnership or business affiliation history with the customer, and the outcomes
- Key customer participants in projects and business transactions
- Sales and revenue history with the customer
- Customer invoice payment history
- Prominent types of products and services outsourced by customer
- *Customer business approach:* Information about the customer's business approach may well be included in the customer relationship history, but it is separated here to distinguish the nature of the information compiled. The primary information elements collected are based primarily on the discernment and judgment of managers in the relevant organization vs. absolute factual data. This information set helps to examine the customer and associated business opportunities from a business-interest perspective of the relevant organization. Fundamental information elements in the customer business approach package can include:
  - Management perspective on alignment of customer business objectives and interests
  - Management perspective on customer's business decisions and outcomes
  - Management perspective on impacts of customer's business values
  - Management perspective on demonstrated customer loyalty
  - Management perspective on importance of particular customer retention

These three areas of customer business information can be comprehensive or basic, per established business needs and the capacity to manage it. It is likely that most commercial organizations will already have this type of information, and the PMO's role is to facilitate its transfer and use within the project management environment. To the extent that the project knowledge management system is established, that would be a primary mechanism for introducing customer information for use by the PMO and by project managers.

Manage Customer Project Participation

The third component of establishing an effective customer relationship capability is to identify points of opportunity and necessity for customer involvement in projects and in project management. The PMO can play an instrumental role in (a) collaborating with project managers to prescribe these points and (b) developing the means to optimize customer involvement for the purposes of business interest (i.e., achievement of relevant organization business objectives and obligations), technical performance (i.e., achievement of quality technical-solution delivery), and project management interest (i.e., achievement of customer satisfaction).

In some cases, customer relationship management means introducing the customer to project manager and associated project technical leader activities. In other cases, it considers PMO, business unit, and executive involvement with the customer. The following are several areas the PMO can examine as a means of incorporating customer project participation as a basis for achieving the desired customer relationship results:

- *Project management activities:* The customer can participate on projects in association with a variety of activities aligned with phases of the project management life cycle:
  - Business needs collaboration
  - Technical requirements specification/statement of work
  - Project planning and technical solution development
  - Project tracking and controlling
  - Project team status reports
  - Project manager progress reviews
  - Change-management process (project scope management)
  - Project close out
- *Project technical activities:* The customer can be a part of the progressive development of the project deliverable(s) at appropriate junctures in the technical effort:
  - Technical solution implementation
  - Configuration management process
  - Interim test and acceptance (quality control and assurance)
  - Delivery and acceptance
- *Project business activities:* The customer should participate in several business-related activities associated with the project effort:
  - Contract or agreement negotiation
  - Contract modification process
  - Executive and senior management collaboration
  - Project business reports
  - Invoice receipt and payment

The nature and extent of customer involvement will also consider the particular type of project work, industry and marketplace influences, and associated norms for customer involvement under these conditions.

Completion of this customer relationship activity description warrants a side note. The particular prescription for PMO consideration of customer information and involvement presented above has a distinct commercial tone to it. However, the PMO can also examine these concepts relative to noncommercial project efforts, and specifically internally conducted projects. The PMO should ensure that internal customers and end-users receive equal value from a professional project management capability within the relevant organization as do customers and end-users in the external marketplace.

Manage Customer Contracts

A major shift in the project manager's role is emerging in association with the implementation of concepts and practices in modern project management. The responsibility for customer contract management is one of the more prevalent considerations of project manager role expansion. This is consistent with one definition of a contract, i.e., a relationship between a buyer and a seller. Therefore, the project manager would be appropriately positioned to be the contract manager relative to the established customer relationship. A second definition of a contract — an agreement about rights and responsibilities — leads to the consideration of contract administration. The individual who administers the contract can be a member of the project team, a business unit support person, or a PMO that assists the project manager in managing and achieving contractual obligations. However, the project manager could also administer the contract on smaller projects.

It is sometimes said that while every contract is not a project, every project is a contract. Therefore, lest we forget, there will be a need for a contract on every project, including internal projects. Often, such contracts are referred to as internal memoranda of agreement or simply agreements. While internal agreements may not have significant legal implications, they nevertheless have obligations that a professional project management organization should properly manage and fulfill.

Then comes the consideration of what the PMO can do to oversee and support customer contract management within the project management environment. Fundamentally, if it exists under project manager influence, the PMO should ensure that complete and comprehensive contract management and contract administration practices are being used. If this function has not yet made its way to the project management environment, the PMO should (a) ensure that complete and comprehensive contract management and contract administration practices are being used relative to the projects within its purview and (b) facilitate the introduction of appropriate contract management responsibilities to individuals within the project management environment.

This PMO function model prescribes a three-prong approach to achieving customer contract management within the project management environment. Each is described in the following subsections.

Produce and Manage Customer Proposals

The PMO should establish a viable process for preparing and managing the customer proposal. This represents the business offering of the relevant organization. In many cases, sales or business development managers perform this activity, and the PMO can provide support to the business development effort to ensure that an adequate business and technical solution will be presented to the customer. The activities of this effort, developed in collaboration with business unitbusiness unit responsibilities, should be incorporated into the initiation phase of the project management methodology.

The following four subsections describe the primary elements of customer proposal preparation and management that warrant attention and intervention of the PMO and project management environment.

Opportunity Qualification

Opportunity qualification is inherently a function of the expertise that will be applied to the anticipated project effort. Therefore, the intended project manager and technical experts should be involved in determining the customer's needs and in defining the project. Even when proposal responsibility resides within the project management environment, someone should be designated to attend to the business perspectives of the proposal offering. Usually the PMO can represent business interests, or it can collaborate with internal business-development professionals.

Opportunity qualification includes the following general activities:

- Identify the customer by conducting a customer business information review
- Identify the opportunity by conducting a customer project information review
- Develop the project business case, in part to determine:
  Is there business interest to do this project?
  Is there technical capability to do this project?
  Is there a reason to do this project?
- Assess business risk and opportunity

When an opportunity has been qualified and the business case approved, the next step in the proposal process can be addressed.

Proposal Preparation

The PMO should prescribe the components and general content for a proposal that is prepared within the project management environment as a business offer for conducting a customer project. It can examine the variety of formats that are prevalent in its industry or customer marketplace to establish its recommended approach to proposal development.

In the absence of any industry affiliation that provides a standard proposal format, the PMO can consider introducing a proposal preparation process that includes the following proposal components:

- *Technical solution:* This proposal component presents the technical approach that the project manager will use to achieve project objectives and fulfill customer deliverables. It normally includes a WBS and project task schedule, a description of each task, and the project resources that will be assigned to perform each task. It represents the relevant organization's response to the customer's RFP or statement of work and shows how those and other customer requirements and specifications will be fulfilled.
- *Business solution:* This proposal component presents the business pricing offered for the accomplishment of the technical solution. For smaller project efforts, the business solution component may be combined with the technical solution component. This component is often separated to allow the customer to review the technical solution independent of the cost to be incurred. This component contains such elements as the list of contract terms and conditions, assumptions and constraints, costs associated with each project deliverable, and the proposed customer payment schedule.
- *Management solution:* This proposal component is generally needed primarily on larger project proposals. It represents the organization and structure to be used to manage the project effort, and it usually demonstrates the scope of resource control afforded the project manager for each important customer project. It allows the customer to identify the different project management and technical team leaders and to gain confidence and comfort that project management and technical leadership is appropriately aligned to ensure project success.

Again, a proposal is still preferred, even for internal project work. This allows the project manager and the internal customer to establish a common understanding and agreement of what is to be accomplished by the project effort. Usually, an internal project proposal will focus only on the technical solution component, unless there is an interdepartmental cost-transfer requirement that the internal customer must consider. In turn, this proposal can easily become the project agreement or "contract" under which the project is conducted.

Proposal content can be as elaborate or as simple as is needed by the customer and warranted by the technical nature and complexity of work proposed. The PMO should consider development of proposal content guidance that addresses the variety of customers and needs encountered.

Proposal Submittal

The proposal submittal activities presented here are fundamental, but the PMO should establish the detailed process and responsibilities associated with presenting the project proposal to the customer for review and consideration.

The following are a few of the primary activities to be accomplished as a part of proposal submittal:

- *Proposal presubmittal meetings:* Prior to the proposal being finalized and presented to the customer, there could be opportunities to meet with the customer to clarify requirements and specifications. The PMO and project manager should participate in such meetings.
- *Proposal presentation:* The proposal is presented to the customer in a written document or in an oral presentation, or both.
- *Proposal clarification:* The PMO and project manager stand by during the customer's proposal review period to answer questions or to clarify points of technical, business, or management being offered. This could include participating in postsubmittal meetings with the customer.
- *Proposal management:* The project manager monitors specific proposals, and the PMO monitors all proposals currently offered and in the hands of customers for review and acceptance. Most proposals should include at least an overview schedule and an offer closing date. These two information elements are important because they represent the readiness of the relevant organization to initiate and conduct the project effort as offered. The PMO's proposal-monitoring activities ensure that readiness. This activity can also prompt follow-up contact with the customer as the proposal closing date approaches to determine current interest and to extend the proposal closing date, if necessary.
- *Proposal modification:* The project manager and PMO meet with the customer to address changes to the proposed technical approach to accommodate the customer's interests, but sometimes

proposal modifications can result from internal decisions for proposal adjustments that are initiated by the relevant organization and coordinated with the customer. Of course, such changes could also influence the need for adjustments in the business (pricing) proposal.

In some industries and internal business environments, the proposal management process will not be as elaborate as outlined above. Rather, the process may simply require the PMO to track what proposals are pending with each specified customer and maintain readiness to begin the project upon notification of customer acceptance. This also would be the case where a business unit in the relevant organization, and not the PMO or project manager, has primary responsibility for proposal submittals and management. The PMO should then conduct its proposal management activities in collaboration with the applicable business unit.

Contract Negotiation

The need for contract negotiation usually represents customer acceptance of the technical solution but also indicates the customer's desire to achieve an adjusted price for the proposed effort. The contract negotiation process can be simple or complex, as is appropriate to the level of the proposed project effort and business importance to both the customer (buyer) and the relevant organization (seller). Some basic steps for conducting contract negotiations from the seller's perspective are presented below, and the PMO can determine the level of complexity or detail to be implemented in its project management environment:

- *Plan the contract negotiation:* Less-formal contract negotiations, usually one-on-one discussions with the customer, generally require less preparation, but the authorized latitude to adjust proposal offers must be known by an authorized negotiator. Conversely, more-formal and more-complex contract negotiations warrant additional preparation, usually by a small team of experienced negotiators, ideally including the project manager and the PMO. The following are a few points of consideration in planning for contract negotiations, with consideration for the fact that the customer usually has control over the negotiation agenda.
  - Form a qualified team of individuals who have experience in contract negotiations to plan and conduct the negotiations; ensure that the capability to discuss technical concepts and considerations is included in the team makeup, usually represented by the PMO, project manager, or technical leader.

- Review any known points of customer contention and review customer project and business information. Confirm the strategic business importance of this customer and this project. Examine leeway in proposed cost, schedule, and resource utilization based on estimates presented in the customer proposal.
- Prepare the negotiation strategy. Specify and prioritize negotiation objectives; identify fair pricing standards; examine alternatives to be encountered during negotiation (best case, most likely, worst case). Determine negotiation tactics and countertactics to be used.
- Prepare a negotiation authorization plan that specifies the negotiation bottom-line price and other factors authorized for contract agreement.

■ *Conduct the negotiation:* Meet with the customer to identify negotiation points and to deliberate, debate, and discuss negotiable options for the proposed project effort. This usually includes learning about the customer's negotiation objectives and sharing the resolution objectives of the relevant organization. It includes examining the customer's initial offers and presenting any counteroffers. In particular, it requires the determination and discussion of differences, as perceived by each party. Ideally, this effort results in a settlement and agreement that enables the contract and associated project effort to be conducted.

■ *Document the negotiated agreement:* A memorandum of agreement (MOA) should be prepared and signed by both parties, which will serve to identify the changes and adjustments that will be incorporated into the final contract. The MOA should include:
- Date of the agreement
- Customer RFP/SOW reference and contract title
- Identification of the negotiators
- Adjusted project schedule
- Adjusted financial details (e.g., contract price, type, and payment terms)
- Discussion summary of other changes to the initial proposal or anticipated contract

In some cases, there could be multiple meetings required for negotiation of large-value contracts or complex technical project efforts. The negotiation team should remain intact to manage such an extended negotiation effort, revisiting the negotiation preparation steps prior to each contract negotiation session.

Establish Customer Contracts

The contract or agreement is the essential document that enables a project to be initiated and conducted. It confirms the customer's request for the project and represents the relevant organization's intent to achieve project deliverables and objectives. In the commercial environment, the contract or agreement further stipulates the monetary considerations of payment by the customer for the products delivered or services rendered. Therefore, it is particularly important to have a valid, executed contract if customer payments for project performance are expected.

The PMO should ensure that a contract or agreement, including internal agreements, is in place for every project under way in the relevant organization. It can do this simply by managing a list of current contracts, by maintaining and monitoring the files of all active contracts in association with performance of contract administration, or in conjunction with activities associated with the PMO "project portfolio management" function (see Chapter 17).

The PMO should establish the process by which customer proposals become official projects within the relevant organization. There are just a few key steps the PMO should consider in establishing each customer contract:

- *Verify contract documents:* This step represents verification that all contract documents are complete and accurate and that they reflect the results of any ensuing contract negotiations. It particularly includes a review and incorporation of project plans and technical documents that were adjusted as a result of contract negotiations.
- *Obtain contract approvals (and signatures):* The project manager, PMO, or business unit representative leading the negotiation team or customer contracting effort will present the contract or agreement for review, including a review by the legal department. Then, final review and an authorized signature within the relevant organization will be obtained. For internal projects, this authorization can reside within the PMO. The PMO will need to facilitate or otherwise monitor customer review and approval of the contract as well.
- *Book the contract:* Contract booking is the process of accepting a contract or order into the business system and the project repository. An account number is established for the project (contract), and the baselines for scope, schedule, and costs are validated in the accounting or project management information system. This process allows work orders to be issued, project work to begin, and invoices to be submitted to the customer.

■ *Transfer contract responsibility to the project manager:* The project officially begins when the contract is passed to the project manager for execution.

The PMO should also identify, through the established organization and structure or through a basic stakeholder analysis, which other stakeholders in the business and project management environments should receive a copy of the customer contract that will guide the project effort.

Many business environments have a dedicated contract management business unit that serves as the repository for all contracts and agreements. If this is the preferred contract management solution, the PMO can collaborate with that business unit in conjunction with oversight of contracts associated with projects. Otherwise, the PMO can become the repository for customer contracts and agreements associated with project work. In either case, if the knowledge management system in the project management environment is sufficiently advanced, the contract can be placed on that system for authorized individual access and review.

Conduct Customer Contract Administration

The principal objective of contract administration is to ensure the fulfillment of the contractual obligations by all parties to the contract. Ideally, a project contract manager is assigned. However, on small projects, the project manager or a member of the project team can hold responsibility for contract administration. On the other hand, an appropriately advanced PMO can assist project managers by developing a customer contract administration capability.

A key aspect of contract administration is managing the interfaces among the players. All members of the project team must be aware of the legal implications of actions taken when administering the contract. To that end, the PMO should incorporate important contract administration activities into the project management methodology for easy reference by all project participants.

The PMO can examine the following contract administration activities for applicability within the business and project management environments. It can then develop and implement preferred processes to enable contract administration to positively influence the customer relationship. The contract administration activities presented for PMO consideration are divided into three primary areas: contract administration planning, contract performance management, and contract close out.

Contract Administration Planning

The PMO should provide guidance to ensure that contractual obligations that impact the project effort are identified and appropriately addressed during detailed project planning conducted following award of the contract. The PMO can establish a staff position to perform contract administration planning; it can assist the project manager in this activity; or it can simply provide guidance incorporated into the project management methodology for use by the project manager and project team members. The following are a few of the more prominent planning activities that can be considered for implementation within the project management environment:

- *Establish a meetings schedule:* The meetings schedule specified in the contract and the internal meetings schedule should be established and communicated to all stakeholders. The schedule should include preliminary meetings, such as the customer's kickoff or initial planning meetings. It is important to the customer relationship that project team members demonstrate awareness of and preparation for all customer meetings.
- *Establish deliverables, reports, and reporting schedules:* All contractually required external and internal (team and management) deliverables, reports, and reporting schedules should be identified and communicated so that members of the project team and other project stakeholders know the required schedules for providing project deliverables and project reports to the customer in a timely manner.
- *Establish contract documentation oversight:* The PMO or a specified business unit may be the primary repository for contract documentation, but the project manager, and some members of the project team, will need access to critical contract documents. As well, the project manager and project team members may also need to document ongoing interactions of the customer relationship. Documentation is essential to provide proof of performance, management of changes, justification for claims, and evidence in the unlikely event of litigation. The purpose of documentation is to record facts and reduce reliance on human memory. Efforts to maintain documentation must be thorough and consistent. These documents can be made accessible to a variety of authorized stakeholders on the knowledge management system developed for use within the project management environment. Contract documentation should include:

- Official copy of the contract
- Contract modifications
- Conformed or adjusted working copies of the contract
- External and internal correspondence
- Invoices
- Change orders
- Meeting minutes
- Project plans
- Progress reports
- Project diaries
- Telephone logs
- Photographs and videotapes

■ *Establish a contract communication control system:* Communication is an essential part of contract administration. Compliance with contract terms and conditions requires effective communication about contract performance. The project manager must establish not only the communication procedures to ensure that project team members and all stakeholders know what to do, but also the controls to ensure that the procedures are used. In addition to developing an internal communications system, the project manager must ensure that effective communication with the customer is practiced.

■ *Establish procedures to solve contract issues and problems:* The means for project team members to use an issues log to identify, handle, report, and track project (contract) issues and problems should be implemented.

■ *Establish contract-change control procedures:* The PMO must ensure that acceptable change-control procedures are established for each project effort having contractual obligations and that all members of the project team know how to use it. Change-control procedures normally provide guidance to:

- Ensure that only authorized people negotiate or agree to contract changes
- Estimate the effect of a change on cost and schedule and gain approval for any additional expense and time before proceeding with a change
- Notify project team members that they must promptly report any action or inaction by the customer that does not conform to the contract terms and conditions
- Notify the customer in writing of any action or inaction that is inconsistent with the established contract terms and conditions
- Instruct team members to document and report in writing both the actions taken to comply with authorized changes and the cost and time required to comply

- Promptly seek compensation for increases in cost or time required to perform, and negotiate claims for such compensation from the customer in good faith
- Document all changes in writing and ensure that both parties have signed the contract or contract change; such written documentation should be completed before work under the change begins, if practical

■ *Set up procedures for claim and dispute resolution:* The PMO must ensure that project managers and other stakeholders responsible for achieving contract obligations are well versed in contract claim and dispute resolution procedures. Disagreements are inevitable and should be expected as a normal part of contract management. However, all contract parties must commit themselves to resolving disputes amicably. Although claims and disputes cannot be avoided, they can be resolved effectively, fairly, and without rancor and litigation. To that end, only professionally trained contract managers or legal counsel should initiate and conduct formal contract conflict and dispute resolution actions. The PMO's primary responsibility in dispute resolution is to work with each project manager to identify and attempt to resolve disputes when they are minor and showing only the earliest signs of disagreement. The project manager must seek the advice of the PMO, senior management, and legal counsel at the first indication that a customer dispute is emerging or escalating. The PMO should ensure that each project manager and project team are familiar with the range of common resolution issues and the techniques that can be used to avoid escalation of contractual conflicts and disputes. Prominent techniques include:

- *Negotiation:* Similar to the negotiation conducted for award of the contract, this interaction between the involved parties seeks to compromise on issues leading to resolution of a conflict.
- *Mediation:* Legal counsel is involved in this effort led by an impartial third-party participant, who facilitates a compromise on issues leading to resolution from an unbiased perspective.
- *Arbitration:* The disputed issues are submitted to a disinterested third party for a final decision. This approach is usually considered to be more expedient, less expensive, and a less-formal resolution method that is often preferred over litigation.
- *Litigation:* A highly formal and potentially lengthy process for resolving contractual disputes through the courts and applicable legal system. Litigation always involves lawyers.

All of these planning actions and determinations can be compiled into a contract administration plan for use by the project manager and members of the project team and for oversight by the PMO. In some cases, depending on content, elements of a contract administration plan can be shared with the customer.

Contract Performance Management

The PMO should provide guidance to ensure that the achievement of contractual obligations is a pertinent theme within the project management environment. The following steps are prescribed for PMO consideration in establishing a contract performance capability that advances the customer business relationship and the success of the project:

- *Manage commitments to the customer:* Ensuring that commitments made to the customer are accomplished within the approved scope of work is critical. The project manager is responsible for all such commitments. A customer commitment log can be used to document and monitor all authorized commitments to the customer.
- *Monitor the contract for compliance:* Contracting parties should know and understand the terms of their contracts and keep their promises to comply in good faith. To ensure that this premise is achieved, active management of contract compliance must be pursued, including compliance with the terms and conditions, contractual dates, costs, schedule, and deliverables in the contract. Often, those individuals who have negotiated or otherwise established the terms and conditions of the customer contract are not those who subsequently perform the work that achieves the contract objectives. Therefore, the project manager must ensure that all key personnel involved in managing technical performance are also advised and become familiar with contractual obligations associated with project performance. One means to accomplish this objective is to use the contract administration plan created in contract administration planning to train all members of the project team and other relevant project stakeholders, as appropriate.
- *Manage customer acceptance of deliverables:* Many contracts have specified acceptance procedures. However, if that is not the case on a particular project, controversies can still be avoided by using a formalized acceptance procedure. The PMO should implement the prescribed process for presentation of deliverables to the customer. The following are particularly important steps to include in the customer delivery and acceptance process:
  - Notifications to the customer
  - Acceptance meetings
  - Customer sign-off for acceptance

■ *Manage project cash:* The PMO must ensure that management practices are established to ensure proper oversight of the cash flow and to facilitate reduction in the cash-to-cash cycle, thus improving cash flow. Ideally, the PMO is involved in early proposal preparation and any negotiations to evaluate project cash flow issues. However, it also must institute proper cash management procedures for use by the project manager in conjunction with project performance. Some considerations for the PMO include:

   – *Obtain partial customer funding:* If a contract is funded in phases, ensure that the customer is aware of funding requirements with sufficient time to take funding action.

   – *Monitor billing and receipt of payments:* Take actions to provide timely delivery of goods and services that enable early customer payments; examine ways in which the project schedule can be renegotiated to improve cash flow; remove blocks to the customer's payment approval process; track customer invoice receipt; hand-carry large-value invoices; and facilitate review meetings for incentive payments.

   – *Monitor payments to subcontractors:* Where possible, establish subcontractor payment schedules that match the customer's billing cycle.

   – *Perform effective change management:* Provide prompt attention to customer-directed changes and early identification of constructive changes, particularly those that require additional funding to be accomplished.

   – *Expedite shipments:* Conduct shipping on schedule; complete conversion of inventory into receivables and cash as quickly as possible; and seek authority for accelerated delivery and early payment where possible.

   – *Maximize use of project equipment and residual material:* Manage and dispose of project equipment and used materials promptly to avoid costs resulting from extended equipment and material retention. Transfer customer-owned property back to the customer or to follow-on and related contracts, when possible, to avoid the need for equitable adjustment of costs specified in the contract.

   – *Reduce impact of liquidated and consequential damages clauses:* Continuously monitor the circumstances that cause payment of liquidated or consequential damages, and eliminate these clauses or obtain incentive clauses to offset the risk of penalties.

   – *Protect proprietary data:* Ensure protection of all proprietary data, including those of the third parties; monitor data submissions to ensure proper markings; and use appropriate nondisclosure

agreements. Proper attention and care will ensure that contingency funds for potential litigation are not needed.
- *Manage stop-work orders and termination:* Attend to customer orders to stop work in a timely manner. Likewise, discontinue contractor and subcontractor work at the direction of the customer. Following the stop-work response, ensure that the customer addresses valid partial payments and cost-recovery actions. Per the conditions encountered, consider whether legal counsel is needed to respond to customer work-stop or termination actions.

Contract Close Out

Contract close out is an integral part of contract administration and represents project completion. Close out includes the last important project tasks for which the project manager is responsible, and it requires the same level of attention as tasks encountered earlier in the project management life cycle. Following are key steps in the contract close out process:

- *Obtain customer acceptance sign-off:* Obtain official signatures for sign-off from the customer indicating final acceptance of the products and deliverables of the project. Consider the following activities:
  - Ensure that all project deliverables have been fulfilled and accepted by the customer.
  - Resolve any performance issues or problems that develop in association with warranty or guarantee provisions of the contract being closed.
  - Resolve any remaining open questions or issues.
- *Conduct contract close out actions:* Contract close out is performed during the closure phase of the project management life cycle. To formally close out the contract with the customer:
  - Ensure that contract terms and conditions have been fulfilled and that any final project reports have been prepared and submitted.
  - Prepare and distribute written instructions to all project team members and project stakeholders that the contract is completed and that no further charges should be incurred for that project account.
  - Manage the disposition of the customer's property.
  - Provide notice to the responsible business unit advising that action be taken to close out any associated subcontracts that remain open.

- Ensure that final invoices have been sent to the customer and that the customer's final payment has been received.
- Forward formal notification of contract completion to the customer.

■ *Prepare the postcontract summary report* — At completion of the contract, the project manager, contract manager, and project team jointly develop a postcontract summary. It should include a lessons-learned section, which describes the major positive and negative aspects of the contract. The postcontract summary provides general information, and the lessons-learned section focuses on sharing best practices with other company's project teams, warning them of potential problems, and suggesting methods to mitigate risks to ensure success. To prepare the postcontract summary report:
  - Evaluate the customer.
  - Evaluate the effectiveness of the processes and tools used.
  - Incorporate any approved improvements to processes and tools.
  - Identify lessons learned.
  - Write and archive the final report.

The completion of contract close out activities should be monitored by the PMO. In turn, contract close out leads to project close out activities, which has bearing on the utilization of resources within the project management environment and the achievement of business objectives within the relevant organization.

Manage Customer Satisfaction

The achievement of customer satisfaction is a genuine contribution to ongoing opportunities associated with the customer business relationship. However, customer satisfaction issues and information also tend to surface in the marketplace to reflect on and communicate the project management capability of the relevant organization. Therefore, the PMO has to ensure that the customer's experience with project performance conducted by the relevant organization is one that meets the customer's business needs and expectations. It can do this by establishing the means to monitor and respond to customer satisfaction issues on a nearly continuous basis.

The PMO should develop the processes and procedures needed by the project manager and project team members to gauge customer satisfaction throughout the project management life cycle and to respond to any indications of customer dissatisfaction. In turn, the PMO can play a key role in helping to discern customer satisfaction levels and in defining and implementing responses that can be used across projects within the relevant organization.

The PMO should pursue three primary activities, as prescribed in the following subsections.

Measure Customer Satisfaction

The only way to know the level of customer satisfaction achieved is to measure it — on each and every project. The PMO can be instrumental in developing measurements for use by the project manager and project team, but it can also actively participate in conducting customer satisfaction measurements and analyzing results across all projects.

Most customer satisfaction measurement actions can be performed by the project manager and can be included as an integral part of the project management methodology. However, the PMO or senior managers within the relevant organization also can perform measurement actions, sometimes independent of project performance. The following are a few examples of customer satisfaction measurements that can be conducted in association with the PMO's responsibilities for project performance:

- *Business manager follow-up:* The individual responsible for the customer account and associated customer business generation can maintain contact with the customer to ascertain how well the customer is responding to project performance and progression. This type of feedback can be collected across all projects and compiled by the PMO for further evaluation.
- *PMO and executive follow-up:* The business importance of the customer relationship will determine whether PMO and executive involvement with the customer is warranted. If so, an executive level relationship (i.e., contact and conversation) could be pursued with the customer at the executive level to obtain a senior management perspective on the progress of the project effort. The PMO can perform a similar role, as a representative of senior management within the relevant organization, in communicating with customer senior managers to ensure that project performance is meeting customer expectations.
- *Informal customer contact:* The project manager will likely be in continuous contact with a customer who desires such ongoing interaction. Otherwise, the contact will merely be frequent. This presents an ideal opportunity to discuss project progress and performance with customer representatives on an informal basis to obtain insight into customer perspectives and satisfaction with the project effort. These insights should be documented for subsequent examination, with recognition that they are obtained informally.

■ *Formal customer satisfaction surveys:* The PMO and project manager can collaborate to determine the appropriate junctures in the project to conduct formal surveys of customer satisfaction. The surveys can be administered by the PMO or by the project manager, depending on the nature of the business relationship with the customer. The PMO should (a) determine which formal customer satisfaction surveys would be most valuable to the relevant organization and then (b) obtain professional assistance to develop and implement the prescribed surveys for use within the project management environment. As a side note, on-line surveys are coming of age and should be considered as a means for increasing the PMO's efficiency in the survey administration and management process. The PMO can consider accomplishing customer surveys at the following points in the project:

– *Postcontract survey:* An evaluation of customer satisfaction relative to the business development and contracting processes encountered to initiate the project

– *Interim surveys:* An evaluation of customer satisfaction at specific junctures in the project management life cycle, when a determination of customer satisfaction is deemed critical, e.g., transition to the next project or technical phase, introduction of a new concept or practice, subcontractor performance, etc.

– *Test and acceptance evaluation:* An evaluation of customer satisfaction in association with the customer's inspection and acceptance of project deliverables

– *Evaluation of end-users:* An evaluation, which could be pursued on an informal basis as well, that considers the responses and reactions of end-users in the customer's environment to the technical solution delivered by the project

– *Postproject review:* An evaluation of customer satisfaction with both project performance and the associated business relationship

■ *Project status meetings:* The project manager should include customer representatives as participants in a recurring meeting to review project status and progress. This provides the opportunity to obtain direct customer feedback, which should be documented as a part of the review of all customer satisfaction results.

■ *Customer feedback report:* The PMO and project manager can jointly determine the applicability of using an impromptu customer satisfaction feedback form. This would be valuable when an extremely large project effort is conducted in a customer environment that spans a number of geographical locations, possibly global. This report allows customer managers and end-users throughout the customer's organization to provide feedback regarding all aspects of project performance, but likely focusing on satisfaction with project deliverables. This type of survey may be created for a specific project and specific customer effort.

The PMO should be a recipient of all customer satisfaction measurement and feedback results. It can then examine these results against the individual performance of project managers, the group performance of project teams, and the overall performance of all projects within the relevant organization. This will enable the PMO to prescribe corrective actions for individuals and for teams, where needed, but particularly to devise and implement actions for use across the project management environment to improve customer satisfaction indicators.

Conduct Customer Relationship Programs

Customer satisfaction is distinctly associated with projects that produce the desired deliverables and achieve the prescribed customer business objectives. Customer satisfaction with project performance can be determined in direct alignment with project success. However, there are other means that the PMO can use to complement project success as a primary reason for customer satisfaction and to induce customer satisfaction beyond the completion of the project effort.

The PMO should collaborate with project managers and business unit managers within the relevant organization and then lead the effort to determine what types of customer relationship programs can be developed and implemented to contribute to customer satisfaction — before, during, and after each project effort.

The following are a few examples of customer relationship programs that the PMO can consider developing and implementing within the relevant organization:

- *Customer interest surveys:* This is a survey of all or a portion of current and past customers to obtain their perspectives on business and technology, particularly as it pertains to the nature of project work conducted by the relevant organization. Customer comments and opinions can be used to evaluate new project management practices or to examine new technology or technical solutions. They can also be used to ascertain any emerging opportunities within the customer's industry or within the established customer base of the relevant organization.
- *Customer technical and business forums:* The PMO can arrange and present single or multiday programs for attendance by selected

current and past customers. These forums can be used to facilitate collaboration and communication among customers using the products or services delivered by the relevant organization through project efforts.

- *Customer postproject correspondence:* The PMO and project managers can "keep in touch" with customers through use of general and specific correspondence. Such correspondence could be more informal and personal, or it could represent an official follow-up at some time beyond project completion to inquire about project deliverable performance, business results achieved, and the state of customer satisfaction over the passage of time.
- *Customer postproject contact:* Similar to correspondence, this program represents personal contact by phone or in person. It demonstrates continued interest in the customer by the project manager or PMO and uncommon business interest and commitment to the customer by the relevant organization.
- *Customer newsletters:* The PMO can collaborate with leaders in the technical disciplines to design and publish a relevant newsletter to communicate with current and past customers. It can highlight technical trends and innovations, particularly those introduced by the professionals within the project management environment.

These follow-on customer programs help to build the customer relationship over time and, hopefully, contribute to extending each business customer relationship beyond a single project effort. However, as these programs are considered, the PMO must also be prepared and have the capability to respond to any adverse customer feedback. Of course, the key is to ensure excellence in the delivery of project management and the technical solution for which the customer will have no lingering doubts of success or loss of satisfaction over time.

The PMO's interest in these customer relationship programs is directly tied to its responsibility for business integration. As the project management environment achieves greater capability, and as the relevant organization becomes more mature in concepts and practices of modern project management, the PMO will inherently be positioned to address business practices such as customer relationship management programs within the project management environment.

Implement Customer-Centric Improvements

Managing customer satisfaction includes addressing improvement actions that the PMO can take to increase the likelihood of customer satisfaction. Some improvement actions will be a result of inherent business sense, while others will be more subtle — a result of discovery and analysis regarding how customers perceive the efficiency and effectiveness of the project management environment.

The PMO should be privy to virtually all feedback and survey results from customer satisfaction measurements. It must compile and analyze such information, from a business perspective, to identify indicators within the project management environment that can be adjusted to improve upon general and specific customer satisfaction results. The PMO's analyses should identify improvements that can be implemented in the integration of project management, technical, and business practices to increase individual and overall customer satisfaction. This means examining the project management environment from a customer's perspective and then determining what PMO influence can be applied to engender a mutually rewarding customer business relationship.

The specific examination of the project performance from the customer's perspective makes this a customer-centric activity. It extends and expands the traditional customer business relationship into the project management environment, and it seeks customer input and feedback to better position project management capability for achievement of results and benefits from the customer's point of view.

The PMO can develop and implement improvements to achieve greater customer satisfaction associated with project performance. The following are a few improvement areas to consider:

- Customer perceptions of project manager performance:
  - Project management skill and qualifications
  - Leadership capability and experience
  - Technical capability and experience
  - Customer relationship skills
- Customer perceptions of project management practices:
  - Communication of plans and documentation
  - Inclusion of the customer in key project decisions
  - Timeliness of project reporting
  - Collaboration and resolution of issues and problems
  - Scope and change-management effectiveness
  - Project stakeholder management
  - Contract administration (including invoice management)
- Customer perceptions of technical performance:
  - Technical skill and qualifications of the project team
  - Inclusion of the customer in key technical decisions
  - Achievement of technical specifications
  - Timeliness of project deliverables
  - Quality of project deliverables

- Effectiveness of configuration management
■ Customer perceptions of business performance:
  - Skill and qualification of the business manager
  - Attention given to the customer by executives and senior managers
  - Recognition of the customer's ongoing business relationship
  - Competitive pricing in the marketplace
  - Value of products and services obtained

The PMO can examine these points and incorporate additional improvement indicators to its evaluation of customer satisfaction. It can then develop and implement improvements to its processes and practices according to the particular PMO function area guidance it has established.

POSTSCRIPT FOR THE SMALLER PMO

The business nature of this PMO function precludes the smaller PMO from many of the more comprehensive prescribed activities. However, there are a few points on which the smaller PMO can focus to assist the relevant organization in achieving customer satisfaction through efforts pursued within the project management environment:

■ *Identify the customer:* Research and compile business, project experience, and any other historical information about the customer, and share that in a timely manner with the project manager. Examine each customer's business nuances, determine customer expectations in given circumstances, and identify allies among customer stakeholders.
■ *Facilitate customer involvement:* Collaborate with project managers to identify areas where customer participation in project management and technical activities can be encouraged and mutually beneficial. Incorporate standard customer-participation points into existing processes or into the project management methodology for use across all projects.
■ *Recommend executive participation:* Examine the nature of the customer project and its business value to the relevant organization. If warranted, induce executives and senior managers to demonstrate their interest in the customer's business by participating in critical meetings and project activities, particularly those at which customer executives and senior managers are also slated to be present.
■ *Informally evaluate customer satisfaction:* The vantage point of the PMO will likely produce contact with project managers, members

of the project team, and some customer representatives. Use these contact opportunities to obtain general insights into customer satisfaction. Use this approach across all current projects to gain an overview perspective of any particular strengths or weaknesses in customer relationship management within the relevant organization.

■ *Formally evaluate customer satisfaction:* Develop or influence the development and use of at least one significant survey instrument to measure customer satisfaction with the project effort. The administration of a sole measurement would normally be a project close out activity, and that can be incorporated into the project management methodology. Access and examine customer satisfaction survey results from all projects to identify significant points that warrant improvement in customer relationship practices pursued within the project management environment.

The primary consideration for the smaller PMO is to ensure that project management practices contribute to the customer relationship component of business conducted within the relevant organization.

19

VENDOR/CONTRACTOR RELATIONSHIPS

The management of external resources working on projects or otherwise influencing project performance is the focus of the "vendor/contractor relationships" function. These resources represent valuable contributions to a wide range of projects across many industries. Vendors and contractors bring specialized skill, knowledge, and capability to the technical nature of project work. They also fill temporary professional resource and skilled-laborer gaps; serve as advisors to the project manager and project team members; and provide supplies, equipment, and materials needed to accomplish the project effort.

There are as many combinations of names for these resources as there are industries. This includes such descriptions as "supplier and provider," "consultant and advisor," "distributor and manufacturer representative," and "subcontractor and partner." This PMO function captures the essence of all such resources under the term "vendor/contractor," indicating that they provide a product or service in support of the project effort, per an established contract or agreement, and undoubtedly for some remuneration.

The PMO's interest in vendor/contractor relationships is one that endeavors to maximize their value on projects and optimize their availability and use within the project management environment. The PMO can provide oversight and guidance that includes vendor/contractor performance management as an inherent component of project management.

This "vendor/consultant relationships" function enables the PMO to:

- Identify and qualify vendors and contractors who add value to project efforts
- Develop guidance for managing vendor/contractor participation on projects
- Develop guidance for managing vendor/contractor contracts within the relevant organization

The PMO is generally recognized as having oversight responsibility for project performance, and vendor/contractor participation represents a critical performance component — sometimes even as a member of the project team — that warrants appropriate attention.

PROJECT ENVIRONMENT INTERFACE CONCEPTS

The PMO can develop standard guidance for use and management of vendors and contractors within the project management environment. This precludes the need for project managers to figure out a different system for each vendor/contractor. In turn, preferred vendors and contractors will become familiar with the contract and performance management practices applied to their participation on projects within the relevant organization.

The PMO also can be proactive in identifying general and specific project needs for external vendor/contractor participation. It can be instrumental in prequalifying vendors and contractors for various types of project work, making them available for selection by project managers, who no longer are burdened with finding the right resource in a short period of time.

BUSINESS ENVIRONMENT INTERFACE CONCEPTS

The PMO can collaborate with business units that facilitate the introduction of vendors and contractors into the relevant organization — contracts, procurement, etc. Additionally, the PMO brings the necessary expertise in project management and technical capability to assist business units in accurately preparing requirements documents, RFPs, and qualifications to expedite the vendor/contractor review and acquisition process.

The PMO can adapt the project management methodology to incorporate essential business steps and practices associated with vendor/contractor acquisition and management. This enables preferred business practices to be applied by project managers across all projects within the relevant organization.

VENDOR/CONTRACTOR RELATIONSHIPS ACTIVITIES ACROSS THE PMO CONTINUUM

The "vendor/contractor relationships" function along the PMO competency continuum represents the progressive capability to apply and manage external resources within the project management environment. This begins with a focus on properly qualifying vendor/contractor candidates, then making them available as a project resource, and finally managing their performance.

Table 19.1 provides an overview of the range of prescribed PMO vendor/contractor relationships activities according to each level in the PMO competency continuum.

The *project office* has direct responsibility for managing vendor/contractor performance on projects. It uses established guidance to accomplish all required oversight actions.

Mid-range PMO levels introduce processes and practices to acquire and manage vendor/contractor participation on projects for maximum business value and project management effectiveness. They prescribe vendor/contractor roles and responsibilities and prepare guidance for project managers to oversee vendor/contractor plans and accomplishments. An advanced PMO examines opportunities for closer vendor/contractor relationships that offer a distinct business advantage.

The *center of excellence* supports the use of vendors and contractors by examining business results of vendor/contractor participation.

The PMO's role in this function model is to determine where vendor/contractor products and services are used or needed and to ensure that properly qualified vendors and contractors are selected for project assignments. Further, the PMO assumes responsibility for overseeing vendor/contractor performance management by developing processes and practices that can be incorporated into the project management methodology for use by project managers, as prescribed in the PMO "project methodology management" function (see Chapter 1).

VENDOR/CONTRACTOR RELATIONSHIPS FUNCTION MODEL

The introduction of vendor/contractor support in the project management environment creates a requirement to manage that participation. This is primarily a responsibility for the project manager, but the PMO can establish the foundation for vendor/contractor management and provide the necessary support for vendor/contractor relationships across all projects.

Table 19.1 Range of Vendor/Contractor Relationships Activities across the PMO Continuum

Project Office	Basic PMO	Standard PMO	Advanced PMO	Center of Excellence
Manages vendor/contractor project participation	Introduces vendor/contractor management ■ Monitors vendor and contractor business and relationship information ■ Develops vendor and contractor management guidance	Manages vendor/contractor acquisition ■ Identifies and qualifies vendors and contractors ■ Develops vendor and contractor responsibilities ■ Monitors vendor and contractor performance	Manages vendor/contractor relationships ■ Establishes preferred vendor and contractor programs ■ Develops vendor and contractor partnerships	Evaluates vendor/contractor performance ■ Analyzes vendor and contractor business value ■ Examines vendor and contractor participation and effectiveness across industries

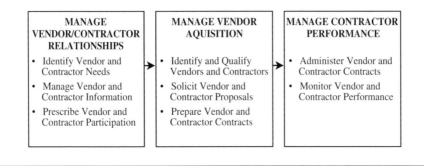

Figure 19.1 "Vendor/Contractor Relationships" Function Model

The prominent activities of the PMO's "vendor/contractor relationships" function model are depicted in Figure 19.1. Each activity is described in this section.

Manage Vendor/Contractor Relationships

The PMO's role in managing vendor/contractor relationships is focused on oversight and support; the project manager should focus on control of vendor/contractor participation. The PMO should grow its capability to identify vendor/contractor value and capability to support the various types of project efforts performed within the relevant organization. It can then develop guidelines and recommendations for establishing vendor/contractor relationships.

When establishing its capability to manage vendor/contractor relationships within the project management environment, the PMO can consider the three activities described in the following subsections.

Identify Vendor and Contractor Needs

The PMO should collaborate with project managers to determine the nature of vendor/contractor support needed within the project management environment. This entails discussion and deliberation about the type of vendors and contractors needed, the frequency of those needs, and the preferred business relationship for each type of vendor/contractor.

The following list can be reviewed to facilitate the PMO's examination of vendor and contractor needs within the relevant organization. It indicates the types of vendor/contractor relationships that can be established, allowing the PMO to specify those likely to be needed within the project management environment.

■ *Vendor/contractor partnerships:* This is a formal business relationship that is established to facilitate the mutual pursuit and achievement of common business objectives. The partnership relationship is used for vendors and contractors having frequent and close business alignment within the relevant organization. The vendor/contractor is often an active and visible participant on the project team and has vested interest in achieving overall project objectives. It is usually characterized by a written agreement put in effect for a period of time and reconfirmed at intervals that enables vendor/contractor participation on many or all projects within the relevant organization. Partnerships can be established to create a more permanent relationship from any of the other types of vendor/contractor relationships listed later in this section. The partnership relationship can range across a number of different business pursuits that support project efforts, for example:
  – Joint research and development (mutual business investment)
  – Business affiliation (joint sales and marketing)
  – Exclusivity of product or service use (sole vendor/contractor status)
  – Business referral activity (preferred vendor/contractor status)
  – Information system connectivity (business and sales information exchange)
  – Just-in-time product and service delivery (collaborated business processes)
■ *Vendor/contractor affiliations:* This is a formal business relationship that is established to enable prequalified vendors and contractors to be identified and positioned for use on projects as their products and services are required. This type of relationship is used to prepare for anticipated vendor/contractor needs across multiple projects. It is usually characterized by a general contract or agreement that is prepared to (a) identify the nature and standard costs of products and services that can be delivered by the prequalified vendor/contractor and (b) specify the contractual obligations to be applied when and if the vendor/contractor is selected for assignment to any projects. This affiliation removes the burden of having to solicit, negotiate, and establish a contract for every project on which the vendor/contractor will participate, and it expedites vendor/contractor availability to begin project work when needed. The contract is usually established for a period of time, perhaps one or more years, and is activated by issuing a vendor/contractor work order that specifies the technical details of the work to be performed.

▪ *Project-specific relationships:* This is a formal business relationship that is established to obtain vendor/contractor participation on one or more specific projects. It represents the need to solicit and qualify vendors and contractors for selection, and then to prepare a separate contract or agreement for their participation on each project. This relationship is characterized either by direct association of the vendor/contractor as a project team participant, or by responsibility for independent work associated with achieving project deliverables and objectives. The business relationship and responsibilities of each party are concluded upon completion of the assignment or at project close out.

▪ *Service provider relationships:* This is a business relationship that may be formally or informally established, but it does not necessarily warrant a formal contract or agreement. Instead, it represents some level of prequalification and selection of service providers, perhaps by establishing a recognized business account with each provider. Then, as project teams require relevant services, this type of business relationship is established to handle those requirements. The service provider relationship is characterized by (a) vendor/contractor recognition of the relevant organization as an established account and (b) the use of some work-order process to provide a timely response and fulfillment of service requests originating from each authorizing project manager or project team. Payment for services can be attributable to specific projects, or it can be a shared cost within the project management environment. A few examples of service provider relationships include:
  – Technical help desk services
  – Reference and research services
  – Equipment and tool calibration services
  – On-line information management services
  – Communication and conferencing services
  – Courier and shipping services
  – Transportation services (e.g., airlines, railways, taxis, etc.)
  – Selected consulting and auditing services

▪ *Supplier relationships:* This is a business relationship similar to that of the service provider, but it deals with prequalification and selection of sources of products, supplies, and equipment needed to accomplish the project effort. Like service providers, this type of relationship is initiated by establishing a recognized business account with each supplier. Then, as project teams need to make relevant purchases or when payment is attributed to specific projects, the preferred supplier is contacted and the established

account is referenced. A few examples of supplier relationships include:
- Office supplies and equipment
- Leased vehicles providers
- Leased equipment providers
- Leased housing providers
- Raw material providers
- Food service and meal providers

Manage Vendor and Contractor Information

Vendor/contractor information management is sometimes an administrative burden that can be reduced by effectively organizing its collection and use. Peak vendor/contractor information management efficiency can be achieved when the PMO centralizes the information database within the project management environment.

The PMO should undertake an initiative to acquire and manage vendor/contractor information as a basis for deliberating and establishing the preferred vendor/contractor relationship and as a means to recommend vendors and contractors for project work assignments. A comprehensive information management capability will examine vendor/contractor relationships from three perspectives:

- *Vendor/contractor presence:* What vendors and contractors exist in the market place, and what are their capabilities to contribute to project efforts within the relevant organization? This knowledge produces a general awareness of the products and services available to the PMO in support of project performance requirements.
- *Vendor/contractor qualification:* Which of the vendors and contractors, who have a viable presence and offerings that fit with needs in the project management environment, can be pursued in a business relationship?
- *Vendor/contractor performance:* What are the contributions and value of those vendors and contractors selected for a short- or long-term business relationship?

Vendor/contractor information collection can be either an exhaustive or a simple process, depending on the nature of project needs and the potential for a business relationship. The PMO will need to determine the specific information needed for its interests in vendor/contractor relationships. The information collected for vendors/contractors can be very similar to that collected for business customers. It includes consideration of the following elements:

■ *Vendor/contractor business profile:* The vendor/contractor business profile contains any relevant information that the PMO deems necessary to gain an adequate understanding of the nature of the vendor/contractor business. Fundamental information elements in the vendor/contractor business profile can include:
  – Description (e.g., product, service, industry, etc.)
  – Size (e.g., number of employees)
  – Location(s) (e.g., local, regional, national, global, etc.)
  – Status (e.g., sales, revenue, stock position and outlook, etc.)
  – Management (e.g., executives, directors, private owners, etc.)
  – Affiliations (e.g., partnerships, industry affiliations, etc.)

■ *Vendor/contractor relationship history:* Information on vendor/contractor relationship history examines past business dealings with each vendor/contractor. Its focus is on reviewing the business given to each vendor/contractor and the resulting performance achievements. It can also look at other vendor/contractor dealings in the industry and in the marketplace. Fundamental information elements in the vendor/contractor relationship history package can include:
  – Major business transaction history and the outcomes
  – Project work history and the outcomes
  – Partnership or business affiliation history and the outcomes
  – Key participants in projects and business transactions
  – Contract award and financial history
  – Invoice management history
  – Prominent types of products and services

■ *Vendor/contractor business fit:* Information about the vendor/contractor's business fit warrants review from time to time. The primary information elements collected are based on the discernment and judgment of managers within the relevant organization versus absolute factual data. This information set helps to examine the vendor/contractor and associated business opportunities from a business-interest perspective of the relevant organization. Fundamental information elements associated with vendor/contractor business fit can include management perspectives on:
  – Alignment of vendor/contractor business objectives and interests
  – Vendor/contractor's business decisions and outcomes
  – Impacts of vendor/contractor's business values
  – Demonstrated vendor/contractor loyalty
  – Importance of particular vendor/contractor retention

These three areas of vendor/contractor information can be comprehensive or basic, per established business needs and the capacity to manage it. To the extent that the project knowledge management system is established, that would be an excellent mechanism for introducing vendor/contractor information for use by the PMO and by project managers.

Prescribe Vendor and Contractor Participation

The third component of establishing an effective vendor/contractor relationship is to identify how they will be introduced and used on projects and within the project management environment. As is common in most situations where there is direct project manager oversight and involvement, processes and procedures applicable to vendor/contractor participation that are managed by the project manager can be incorporated into the project management methodology.

The PMO can consider a wide range of vendor/contractor participation issues by examining the following points:

- *Vendor/contractor sourcing responsibility:* The project manager is responsible for acquiring necessary vendor/contractor resources to achieve project objectives. The PMO will need to determine if it will serve as a clearinghouse for vendor/contractor acquisition or just as a resource for vendor/contractor information.
- *Vendor/contractor oversight responsibility:* The project manager is responsible for managing vendor/contractor task assignments and performance. In collaboration with project managers, the PMO will need to determine any PMO involvement in managing vendor/contractor participation. Determinations here will also indicate and influence the role of the PMO in managing individual and collective vendor/contractor business relationships.
- *Vendor/contractor project affiliation:* The PMO in collaboration with relevant project managers should determine the approach to vendor/contractor management on projects, relative to each type of vendor engaged. In particular, it would be good to specify whether the vendor/contractor will be performing its assigned role and tasks as a member of the project team or will be working independent of the project team.
- *Vendor/contractor project management responsibility:* The PMO should establish common activities and expectations for vendor/contractor participation in project management activities and performance of their own project management efforts, per each vendor/contractor type. This deliberation also results in establishing the project manager's role in overseeing vendor/contractor project participation and performance from a project management perspective. The vendor/contractor can contribute and participate in a

variety of activities aligned with phases of the project management life cycle, as warranted by the established vendor/contractor role:

- Vendor/contractor collaboration — needs, requirements, and technical specifications
- Vendor/contractor project planning and technical solution development
- Vendor/contractor project management methodology deployment
- Vendor/contractor tracking and reporting requirements

■ *Vendor/contractor technical performance responsibility:* The PMO should establish guidance for vendor/contractor use of acceptable technical performance standards and technical competency requirements that will be applied to vendor/contractor efforts within the project management environment. This deliberation also results in establishing the project manager's role in overseeing vendor/contractor project participation and performance from a technical perspective. PMO oversight of vendor/contractor performance can include the following:

- Fulfillment of qualifications for vendor/contractor technical team members
- Presentation of required technical plans, designs, and solutions for timely review
- Demonstration of a viable configuration management process, as needed
- Implementation of project deliverable quality control and -assurance measures
- Development of an acceptable timetable for delivery of products and services

■ *Vendor/contractor business management responsibility:* The PMO should establish guidance for vendor/contractor business activity management, which is generally translated to mean putting mechanisms in place to ensure that the vendor/contractor has the capability to manage its contractual obligations. This can include:

- Capability to lead and control vendor/contractor technical team work efforts
- Acceptance of the prescribed contract modification process
- Receptiveness to executive and senior management collaboration, as needed
- Presentation of preferred project progress and associated business reports
- Adherence to invoice submittal practices

The nature and type of vendor/contractor involvement will influence the particular type of roles and responsibility guidance that the PMO needs to create. In general, the PMO can begin defining vendor/contractor participation guidance in areas where project managers are expressing concerns or inquiries for assistance.

Manage Vendor/Contractor Acquisition

This activity specifies the means by which the PMO can recommend or establish the process by which vendors and contractors are introduced into the project management environment. The PMO should consider constructing a process for vendor/contractor acquisition according to the guidance contained in the following three subsections.

Identify and Qualify Vendors and Contractors

The identification and qualification of vendors and contractors should be accomplished according to the business relationship to be established. The process for vendor/contractor introduction is generally the same for all vendor/contractor types, but it is usually the urgency of need that dictates the depth and schedule of process deployment.

The following vendor/contractor acquisition steps are recommended for PMO consideration in establishing its own vendor/contractor acquisition process:

- *Identify vendor/contractor requirements:* Customer requirements are evaluated to determine whether accomplishing the work using vendor/contractor support is needed, cost effective, and in the relevant organization's best interest. The value of using vendor/contractor services may lie in the expertise to be gained, the need for resources, or the cost to be saved. Vendor/contractor requirements can be identified with reference to a specific project or for a broader support need anticipated within the project management environment. This step is usually accomplished in collaboration with the project manager's development of resource requirements and associated staffing plans.
- *Perform make-or-buy analysis:* A make-or-buy analysis is a general management concept and technique that is used to determine whether it is more cost effective for a particular product or service to be produced internally by the relevant organization, or whether the product or service should be obtained from external vendor/contractor sourcing. Simply stated, the PMO can provide guidance to help the project manager ascertain whether a

vendor/contractor should be pursued to perform certain project tasks.

■ *Qualify vendors and contractors:* The PMO's established vendor/contractor information database can be accessed to identify relevant vendors and contractors. Once identified, a review of their capabilities and expertise is used to create a "short list" of qualified candidates. The resulting vendor/contractor candidates on the "short list" for a particular project effort are then included in the distribution of the relevant proposal. Factors for vendor/contractor qualification can include:
  - Technical capability, including certifications and licenses
  - Staff experience, including résumé review
  - Familiarity with the vendor/contractor's products and services
  - Vendor/contractor familiarity with the organization
  - Geographic location and coverage
  - Previous similar jobs completed, including references
  - Financial stability, including bonding capacity

■ *Determine pricing arrangements:* The objective of vendor/contractor pricing arrangements is to negotiate a contract type and price that will result in reasonable vendor/contractor risk and provide the vendor/contractor with the greatest incentive for efficient and economical performance. Different types of contracts provide various ways to share risk between the buyer and the seller, particularly cost risk. The contract type continuum (fixed price to cost reimbursement) places the risk for fixed-price contracts directly on the vendor/contractor (seller), whereas cost-reimbursement contracts place the risk on the relevant organization (buyer).

■ *Develop the independent cost estimate:* An independent cost estimate should be developed for all major vendor/contractor acquisition efforts. This represents the relevant organization's estimate of the cost of the effort to be undertaken. It is used in the acquisition planning process and is generally required when examining vendor/contractor proposals. The pricing for vendor/contractor solutions should fall within an acceptable range of the costs presented in the independent cost estimate. In some cases the PMO will be adequately staffed to offer this step as a support activity to project managers.

■ *Write the vendor/contractor plan:* The project vendor/contractor plan, sometimes referred to as the procurement plan, contains a compilation of the previously prepared elements, plus guidance for conducting vendor/contractor acquisition activities. In particular, it specifies a schedule of key procurement/acquisition events, including:

- Vendor/contractor acquisition decision
- Independent cost estimate preparation
- Vendor/contractor solicitation preparation
- Vendor/contractor candidate identification
- Vendor/contractor proposal review period
- Vendor/contractor contract discussion and negotiation period
- Contract award date

The PMO can incorporate these planning steps into a template for use by project managers, or for its own use if it retains responsibility for vendor/contractor acquisition.

Solicit Vendor and Contractor Proposals

The following steps are recommended for PMO consideration in establishing guidance for preparing vendor/contractor solicitations, managing their distribution, and reviewing responses (proposals) toward selecting a qualified vendor/contractor:

- *Prepare internal requisition material:* The requirements in the vendor/contractor plan are reviewed and matched with existing and approved vendor/contractor sources. The requisitioning and purchasing requests are prepared in accordance with the policies and procedures established for using the particular vendor/contractor sources. The requisition authorizes the solicitation of vendor/contractor support and covers basic information such as a description of the item or service (statement of work), the quantity, the delivery date(s) or performance period, any special delivery or performance requirements, the funds, the funding source, any special progress or status reports required, the deliverables, the points of contact, and any other special terms and conditions.
- *Determine type of solicitation:* The proposal process to be used by the potential bidders (vendor/contractor) must be determined. Simply stated, the choices are either sole source or competitive bid.
- *Prepare solicitation:* Identified or prequalified vendor/contractor candidates are informed about the work opportunity through the distribution of a request for proposals (RFP) or request for quotes (RFQ) package. This information in the RFP (or RFQ) must be compiled for distribution and is usually readily transferred from the internal requisition material. The PMO can apply standards used by the relevant organization to create a template for the solicitation package, which typically contains the following elements:

- Scope of work
- Technical requirements
- Schedule
- Proposal format requirements
- Terms and conditions
- Subcontract type
- Evaluation criteria

■ *Specify optional proposal actions:* In conjunction with the preparation of the solicitation package, the following actions, although optional, are typically specified to ensure a successful vendor/contractor proposal response for major projects:

- *Prepare a draft solicitation:* A draft document can be used for unusual or complex bid packages to obtain feedback from potential vendors and contractors before issuing the final solicitation. This document can be of tremendous help in clarifying vendor/contractor requirements.

- *Conduct preproposal conferences and a site survey:* Meetings can be conducted for potential vendors/contractors in cases of unusual or complex bid packages. This can include vendor/contractor candidate visits to the actual performance site for services, construction, or installation work. These meetings ensure that all vendor/contractor candidates have a clear and common understanding of both the technical and contract requirements of the solicitation.

- *Respond to bidder inquiries and questions:* A time period is established in which potential bidders may submit questions in writing. All identified bidders receive a list of all questions and the respective answers from the relevant organization. In some cases, responses to questions may be incorporated into solicitation documents as amendments.

■ *Distribute the solicitation and manage vendor/contractor responses:* The solicitation package is distributed to vendor/contractor candidates on the qualified-source list. Vendor/contractor responses should be tracked and managed. Deadlines for receipt should be adhered to or, if necessary, extended as a distinct proposal management action. The PMO in conjunction with established practices may provide notice of the approaching deadline to all vendor/contractor participants. Similarly, the PMO may request the courtesy of receiving replies of "no-bid" from those vendor/contractor candidates who choose not to submit a proposal, and these too should be tracked for current and future reference.

■ *Evaluate vendor/contractor responses:* Vendor/contractor selection may be as simple as reviewing the proposal business elements and determining which competing set of prices is the lowest. On the other hand, it may involve weeks or even months of proposal analysis, on-site visits, prototype development, and testing. One person may accomplish vendor/contractor proposal review and selection, or it may require an extended effort by a panel of evaluators. The industry trend appears to lean toward more comprehensive screening and selection of fewer vendors and contractors for longer duration contracts. The vendor/contractor evaluation process typically includes the following actions:

– *Receive and evaluate proposals:* Oral vendor/contractor presentations of their proposals tend to improve and expedite the vendor/contractor selection process. However, proposal document review is still an acceptable means of examining the vendor/contractor candidates under consideration. Either way, proposals must be evaluated using the evaluation criteria stated in the solicitation regarding management, technical expertise, and price. The PMO can help to establish the practices of the relevant organization used to guide and facilitate vendor/contractor selection, and a weighting system should be used to determine which evaluation criteria are most important. Past vendor/contractor performance information should also be used to evaluate and verify the accuracy of information presented in the vendor/contractor proposal. Use of independent cost estimates, price realism, and competitive price analyses are part of the evaluation process. Use of qualified consultants to assist in this vendor/contractor proposal review is also a method for PMO consideration.

– *Hold vendor/contractor discussions:* Interactions with vendor/contractor candidates provide the opportunity to clarify ambiguities in proposals received. The PMO must also determine if conditions warrant an opportunity for vendor/contractor candidates to revise their proposals and submit a best and final offer.

– *Receive and evaluate best and final offers:* The receipt of revised, best and final offers from vendor/contractor candidates should be monitored, followed by a final evaluation of their revised proposed solutions. Normally, the focus of a best and final offer is on pricing. However, inasmuch as pricing affects performance, there also could be changes in the technical solution to be considered. Each vendor/contractor should highlight the revisions contained in their best and final offer presented to the relevant organization. As well, it should be noted that the best and final offer does not necessarily represent the outcome of negotiations. Vendor/contractor discussions may be used for business negotiations, or they can be used solely to request adjustment of technical aspects of the proposal.

■ *Conduct vendor/contractor negotiations:* The contract negotiation process comprises planning, conducting, and documenting the negotiations. It involves clarification and mutual agreement on the structure and requirements of the contract prior to the award. To the extent possible, final contract language should reflect all agreements reached. Generally, vendor/contractor negotiations include, but are not limited to, the following subjects:
  – Responsibilities and authorities
  – Applicable terms and law
  – Technical and business management approaches
  – Contract financing and price

■ *Select vendor/contractor:* This step represents the selection and notification of the successful vendor/contractor and is characterized by the following events:
  – *Vendor/contractor selection:* A formal vendor/contractor selection decision is made. If the associated customer contract is a major one, the final decision may require some coordination with the customer and possibly customer approval. The customer can be included in the vendor/contractor selection and decision process to preclude the need for post vendor/contractor selection confirmation.
  – *Award of vendor/contractor contract or agreement:* A final contract document, incorporating any negotiated modifications to the proposed offer and any customer-required directives, is prepared. Obtain appropriate approvals, sign the contract, and provide a copy for the vendor/contractor.
  – *Debriefing:* Notify unsuccessful vendors and contractors and debrief them on the selection outcome. Hold discussions appropriate to the proposal effort with each unsuccessful bidder to present at least general vendor/contractor selection results as a means to promote and refine future proposals. The courtesy extended by offering this discussion also refines or builds any future business relationship opportunities with unsuccessful vendors and contractors.

Prepare Vendor and Contractor Contracts

The PMO should establish the process by which vendor/contractor contracts are introduced in the relevant organization. The following are a few prominent steps the PMO can consider in establishing vendor/contractor contracts. They are not dissimilar to the process recommended for establishing customer contracts:

- *Verify contract documents:* This step represents verification that all vendor/contractor contract documents are complete and accurate, and reflects the results of any ensuing contract negotiations. It particularly includes a review and incorporation of subsequently received vendor/contractor project plans and technical documents that were adjusted as a result of contract negotiations.
- *Obtain vendor/contractor contract approvals (and signatures):* The project manager, PMO, or business unit representative leading the vendor/contractor contracting effort will present the contract or agreement for review, including a review by the legal department. Then, final review and an authorized signature within the relevant organization will be obtained.
- *Book the contract:* Booking the vendor/contractor contract is the process of accepting a vendor/contractor contract or work order into the business system and the project repository. An account number is established for the vendor/contractor contract, and the baselines for scope, schedule, and costs are validated in the accounting or project management information system. This process allows work orders to be issued, project work to begin, and invoices to be accepted from the vendor/contractor.
- *Transfer vendor/contractor responsibility to the project manager:* The work to be performed under the vendor/contractor contract officially begins when the contract is passed to the project manager for execution.

The PMO should also identify, through the established organization and structure or through a basic stakeholder analysis, which other stakeholders in the business and project management environments should receive a copy of the vendor/contractor contract.

Manage Vendor/Contractor Performance

The PMO may or may not have a direct role for oversight associated with any vendor/contractor efforts. That is a determination that must be made within the relevant organization, and presumably the points of PMO intervention will be obvious. However, the PMO is responsible for ensuring that project managers have a process for managing vendor/contractor performance, and that is addressed in this activity.

Vendor/contractor performance management is a matter of ensuring that contractual obligations are fulfilled, that roles and responsibilities associated with the project are outlined and understood, and that technical work is assigned and accomplished. The following three subsections offer insight to the PMO in establishing this capability.

Administer Vendor and Contractor Contracts

The principal objective of vendor/contractor contract administration is to ensure the fulfillment of the contractual obligations by all parties to the contract. The required level of effort for vendor/contractor contract administration depends on the magnitude and importance of the contract. On larger projects with multiple product and service vendors and contractors, a key aspect of contract administration is managing the interfaces among the various participants along with all other contract administrative activities.

It is critical that all members of the project team be aware of the legal implications of actions taken when administering the contract. For vendors and contractors, the effort needs to focus on vendor/contractor delivery management rather than personal interfaces.

The following are the recommended actions associated with vendor/contractor contract administration:

- *Verify vendor/contractor contract booking:* After the vendor/contractor contract has been awarded, the project manager must ensure that the vendor/contractor contract data are entered into the project and business databases. Critical vendor/contractor information areas are anything impacting on cost, schedule, meetings, and deliverables. The PMO can arrange for this action to be accomplished when the contract is established, but it is a good rule to have the project manager verify that through a notification by the accounting department.
- *Organize vendor/contractor contract files:* The project manager must retain critical vendor/contractor contracting documents in a file created for each vendor/contractor. This process should be an integral part of the project management information system, a component of the project knowledge management system. Vendor/contractor contract files typically contain the following information:
  - RFP/RFQ package
  - Vendor/contractor proposal (including related inquiries, preproposal meeting notes, and negotiation notes)
  - Vendor/contractor planning documents and modifications
  - Vendor/contractor performance management evaluations
  - Correspondence

- Meeting minutes
- Reports
- Invoices
- Change orders
- Vendor/contractor deliverable tracking and management logs

■ *Establish procedures for contract claims and dispute resolution:* The project manager should work closely with the PMO and procurement personnel on this highly legalistic area and ensure that project team personnel are aware of the procedures to be followed.

■ *Establish procedures to solve issues and problems:* The PMO should establish recommended procedures for use by project managers in identifying, managing, and reporting vendor/contractor issues and problems. The goal is to achieve early and effective resolution of any detriment to project success.

■ *Establish communication guidance:* The project manager should clearly identify all members of the project team, specify their responsibilities relative to vendor/contractor management, and convey authorization for communication with the vendor/contractor.

■ *Monitor vendor/contractor performance:* Vendor/contractor performance should be monitored, to include observing actual performance, conducting regular meetings and discussions, and reviewing written reports. As well, deliverables presented by vendors and contractors should be examined for accuracy and achievement of specifications.

■ *Manage vendor/contractor relations:* The participation of each vendor/contractor should be examined and management styles leveraged to maximize vendor/contractor strengths and minimize weaknesses. The subcontractor should be held responsible for compliance with technical and contractual matters. Working with vendors/contractors who demonstrate loyalty and indicate a potential for long-term relationships should be encouraged. Relationships with major vendors and contractors should be more actively managed than relationships with subcontractors who provide off-the-shelf items.

■ *Conduct meetings with vendor/contractor representatives:* An initial meeting should be conducted with vendor/contractor managers and representatives for the purposes of introduction and to establish protocols associated with the project effort. Ongoing progress and status meetings should be held with the key members of the vendor/contractor project team as required by the project effort.

■ *Manage vendor/contractor contract changes:* The project manager must establish a subcontract change-control system based on PMO guidance that defines the process by which any vendor/contractor contract can be modified. Managing change ensures that changes are authorized and their effects estimated and provided for, that changes are promptly identified, that the other party is properly notified, that compliance and impact are reported, that compensation is provided, and that the entire transaction is properly documented. The contract change-control system must be integrated with the overall change-control system prescribed by the project management methodology.

■ *Monitor vendor/contractor contract compliance:* The project manager has responsibility for vendor/contractor contract compliance to ensure that the vendor/contractor is authorized to perform work at the appropriate time and that any special terms and conditions are complied with. Project engineers or technical personnel usually manage the technical portion of the vendor/contractor contract, whereas procurement or financial personnel (who may or may not be assigned as project team members) manage the business portion. The project manager must ensure that an effective vendor/contractor contract administration plan is prepared for any major vendor/contractor contract to ensure internal collaboration on vendor/contractor contract compliance.

■ *Manage acceptance of vendor/contractor deliverables:* The project manager must ensure the management of vendor/contractor deliverables by members of the project team. It is critical that an effective quality control program be established and implemented to inspect and verify the adequacy of the vendor/contractor product. Acceptance of deliverables (goods, services, progress reports, documents) must be performed in accordance with both the prime contract and the vendor/contractor contract, and it must be accomplished before invoices are authorized to be paid.

■ *Manage vendor/contractor payments:* The vendor/contractor contract should contain provisions on invoicing and payment schedules. Payment terms should be defined within the contract and should involve a specific linkage between progress made and compensation paid. Vendors and contractors should be required to submit an invoice to receive payment. This ensures the ability to track and trace invoices, which is particularly important if there are multiple vendor/contractor participants. The vendor/contractor invoice should contain at least the following information: subcontract identification number, subcontractor payment amount requested, and identification of the work performance associated with the requested payment. The project manager should also establish a plan specifying who is authorized to approve the invoices that are submitted in accordance with the relevant contracts. Frequently, invoices are tied to deliverables, and acceptance must be authorized before payment can be made. Following are several types of payments:

- Progress payments tied to measurable progress in work or based on cost incurred, with some determination of actual work. Progress payments should be used only if the costs can be recovered by the project.
- Payments aligned with the achievement of specific milestones or deliverables.
- Payments based on the "pay when paid" concept, i.e., the vendor/contractor gets paid when the relevant organization receives payment from the customer.

■ *Review and close out vendor/contractor contract:* Vendor/contractor contract close out may occur at any time during the project, but it should be performed at least during the project closure phase. The following steps are normally performed to close out a subcontract:

- Verify that all requirements are completed and accepted. Resolve any open or pending questions and issues.
- Confirm that all subcontractor submittals and deliveries have been received. Ensure that deliverables have been accepted in accordance with the prescribed test and inspection procedures and that the customer has accepted the deliverables.
- Ensure that the subcontractor issues a final invoice accompanied by any other required documentation, including final lien waivers, warranty documents, or certificates of completion.
- Approve the final invoice, and monitor and verify the subcontractor's receipt of the final payment.

■ *Manage vendor/contractor resource departures:* Ensure that vendor/contractor staff departures are managed and that material resources are disposed of appropriately if no longer needed on the project. This includes managing turn-in of project equipment provided to vendor/contractor staff for use during the project, reallocation of work space, and removal of vendor/contractor staff access to facilities and documents, as appropriate.

■ *Prepare a postproject vendor/contractor performance report:* Review vendor/contractor performance, contributions, and contract compliance, and then prepare and archive a final report. This report can be prepared in collaboration with the vendor/contractor, or a copy of the postproject performance report can be conveyed to the vendor/contractor upon completion. The final report should include the following:

- Evaluation of the effectiveness of vendor/contractor staff and managers
- Evaluation of the effectiveness of vendor/contractor processes and tools
- Preparation of lessons learned from the vendor/contractor business relationship
- Recommendations for appropriate recognition of vendor/contractor staff and manager

The PMO must refine these activities for use within the relevant organization, which may or may not already have a basis for vendor/contractor contract administration. If one does exist, the PMO can simply incorporate existing practices into processes deployed within the project management environment. If one does not exist, a vendor/contractor contract administration process development effort is warranted. Moreover, if there is no existing process, the PMO may need to facilitate buy-in of managers who are unaccustomed to such scrutiny of vendor/contractor participation. That can be accomplished with relative ease by demonstrating the benefits to be achieved by effective vendor/contractor management, e.g., receipt of quality vendor/contractor work products and services, proper payment of invoices and release of project funds based on validation and acceptance of vendor/contractor work products and services, and fulfillment of the primary customer contract through oversight and management of timely delivery of vendor/contractor work products and services.

Monitor Vendor and Contractor Performance

It has been reiterated that the project manager is responsible for vendor/contractor performance management and oversight. Conversely, this activity examines ways in which the PMO can support the project manager in achieving that responsibility. In particular, it specifies review and assessment activities that the PMO can perform across all vendor/contractor participants to ascertain the individual and collective value and effectiveness brought into the project management environment by these external resources. In some cases vendor/contractor performance review and assessment results will serve business decisions regarding the current or proposed business relationship with a particular vendor/contractor. In other cases, PMO review and assessment findings can be conveyed to project managers for their consideration in selecting the next vendor/contractor needed for a particular project effort.

The range of PMO responsibilities will determine the depth of vendor/contractor assessment and analysis that is performed. The following are a few examples of the reviews the PMO can conduct to monitor vendor/contractor performance and ensure that value is being achieved by the introduction of vendor/contractor products and services within the project management environment:

- *Price variation analysis:* This review looks at how vendor/contractor pricing varies across projects, for the same vendor/contractor and for different vendors and contractors, particularly those performing the same or similar work. It will help determine if there are pricing inconsistencies among the vendor/contractor resources used or inconsistencies in pricing for a particular vendor/contractor. Significant variations should be identified, challenged, and rectified.

- *Deliverable performance analysis:* This review examines the trends in the technical quality of vendor/contractor work products and services. It should ascertain any adverse trends in vendor/contractor deliverables, where the product or service routinely does not meet objectives, specifications, or expectations. This includes an examination of rework frequency, timeliness of product and service delivery, vendor/contractor responsiveness to requests for fixes, and ultimate endurance and usability of the delivered product or service. Conversely, this analysis also could identify positive trends in vendor/contractor deliverable performance. The PMO can use these analysis results to identify preferred vendor/contractor relationships for future project work and business opportunities.

- *Contract add-on/extension analysis:* This review is used to identify any particular vendor/contractor having a recurring need to request or negotiate work extensions, with or without additional costs incurred. This could be an indication of weak estimating practices, either within the relevant organization or by the vendor/contractor, or possibly vendor/contractor underpricing in their proposals in anticipation of obtaining subsequent increases after work has begun. It could also be an indicator of vendor/contractor staff competency or vendor/contractor management attention and capability. Once indicators are identified, the PMO can determine the cause and implement rectifying actions.

- *Billing practices analysis:* This review can be applied to examine the accuracy of individual and collective vendor/contractor invoices and to ensure that prescribed billing practices are adhered to by each vendor/contractor, i.e., timely submittal, appropriate description of work performed, etc. As well, this examination looks at internal handling of vendor/contractor invoices, particularly project manager approval, which serves as verification of product receipt and work performed. The PMO can then act to correct any discrepancies identified.

■ *Management retention analysis:* This review addresses vendor/contractor manager assignments and associated effectiveness. It examines preferred vendor/contractor manager retention for subsequent or recurring efforts as a matter of developing their familiarity and experience within the relevant organization. It also identifies the frequency of vendor/contractor manager turnovers on individual projects and across multiple projects for which the vendor/contractor is involved. The PMO can review vendor and contractor manager retention and turnover issues in terms of any project effectiveness issues that require attention and resolution.

■ *Customer satisfaction analysis:* The PMO should review any indicators of customer satisfaction or dissatisfaction with any vendor/contractor. This is usually associated with vendor/contractor work that is visible to the customer. This examination should be distinguished from finding vendor/contractor blame, because the relevant organization has inherent responsibility to select and manage qualified vendor/contractor participants, and is doing itself a disservice in suggesting vendor/contractor blame to any customer. Rather, the PMO needs to obtain customer perspectives, if not approval, regarding the vendor/contractor products and services used, and this is a measure of customer feedback in that regard.

■ *Project manager oversight analysis:* This review solicits project manager input to vendor/contractor performance, and it can be accomplished in conjunction with the preparation of a vendor/contractor postproject evaluation report. However, here the PMO examines the input of multiple project managers, or multiple reports, to ascertain project manager perspectives on the vendor/contractor. In particular, this review focuses on the level of vendor/contractor management attention required, with the goal of identifying any undue burdens placed on the project manager resulting from vendor/contractor oversight requirements. The PMO will need to identify any vendor/contractor that presents an unacceptable burden on project manager time and effort.

■ *Business and investment posture:* This review is conducted relative to the nature of the relationship with each vendor/contractor type. Closer business relationships, i.e., partnerships, will have a different focus than do simple vendor/contractor relationships established for project-specific work. Some of the points that can be examined to ascertain business and investment posture in vendor/contractor relationships include:

- Financial contributions to partnering initiatives
- Resource investments in the relationship
- Demonstrated actions to introduce and use prescribed technical practices
- Investments in new technology
- Investments in communication and information-sharing tools
- Information sharing

The results from each of these examinations should be entered into the appropriate vendor/contractor information file and be made available through the project knowledge management system used in the project management environment. Analysis results also should be considered in mid- and long-term planning for vendor/contractor support as well as in the vendor/contractor acquisition process when obtaining new or renewed vendor/contractor contracts. The primary objective of this monitoring effort is to maximize business value from vendor/contractor participation within the project management environment.

POSTSCRIPT FOR THE SMALLER PMO

The accomplishment of vendor/contractor oversight should be a distinct activity in every project management environment: for large PMOs, small PMOs, and no PMOs. Vendor/contractor activity must be managed as a means of achieving the prescribed business interests and objectives of the relevant organization. Vendor/contractor activity that is not managed only achieves vendor/contractor business interests and objectives. To that end, there are a few activities that the smaller PMO can contribute with regard to managing the vendor/contractor relationship.

The smaller PMO should formally or informally pursue the following basic vendor/contractor relationship management activities:

- *Identify and categorize vendor/contractor project participation:* This activity is useful to identify current vendor/contractor participation and activities within the project management environment. It could provide discovery of redundant vendor/contractor contracts, make project managers aware of vendor/contractor availability for their projects, and account for costs associated with one or more project efforts.
- *Compile vendor/contractor information:* Establish information on current and prospective vendor/contractor relationships. The more that is known, the better the vendor/contractor selection decisions will be. In particular, compile historical information on current vendor/contractor relationships. The smaller PMO may not have

the responsibility or capability to conduct detailed vendor/contractor analyses, but having pertinent vendor/contractor relationship information will still provide fundamental insight to vendor/contractor performance. The PMO should incorporate all information collected into the project knowledge management system for access by project managers having needs for vendor/contractor products and services.

■ *Develop vendor/contractor management guidance:* The PMO should develop and document the prescribed common process for vendor/contractor acquisition and management, ideally for incorporation in the project management methodology. This can be accomplished in collaboration with project managers and business unit representatives within the relevant organization. The initial elements of early process development should include:
  - Determination of vendor/contractor needs
  - Vendor/contractor selection
  - Vendor/contractor performance management
  - Vendor/contractor contract administration

The PMO should facilitate the introduction and use of the established vendor/contractor relationship management process as a single project management activity or as a part of the overall project management methodology deployment effort.

20

BUSINESS PERFORMANCE

The PMO's role transcends multiple professional disciplines in its effort to integrate project management practices with business performance objectives. Project management provides a variety of tools that can be used for managing business performance. In many ways, project management *is* business performance management. At the PMO level, project management concepts and practices are applied to integrate technical and business functions within the relevant organization, with executive level oversight of business interests and strategy implementation. To that end, the PMO's effort to establish project management capability within the relevant organization effectually represents business performance management.

The PMO can be successful in contributing to business performance management only if the essential project management capabilities have been implemented within the relevant organization. Key activities within each of the PMO functions need to be examined, and essential capabilities need to be positioned to facilitate and maximize business performance management. Executives and senior managers can be effective in managing business performance decisions and actions only if they understand and apply those essential capabilities, which, by any other name, is still project management.

This "business performance" function enables the PMO to:

- Institute an enterprisewide business collaboration capability
- Consolidate project management practices for distinct business value
- Establish measures and controls for business productivity

- Develop executive understanding of project management processes and practices
- Facilitate the achievement of core business goals: revenue, operational efficiency, and customer satisfaction

The PMO will need sufficient internal recognition and executive sponsorship to achieve this strategic level capability. However, it can begin to introduce components of this capability with fundamental senior management support and implementation of critical PMO functions.

PROJECT ENVIRONMENT INTERFACE CONCEPTS

The PMO can represent executive and senior management interests within the project management environment of the enterprise — a concept indicating a broader role and range of responsibility within the relevant organization. This role includes a capability to coordinate and collaborate business interests and activities across multiple project management environments, perhaps representing global or multinational components of the relevant organization.

The existence of multiple project management environments, for example in a technical or geographic sense, could also suggest the need for multiple mid level PMOs. These distributed PMOs could be developed, evolve, or otherwise become aligned with and receive guidance from the "central PMO," possibly a center of excellence, which has responsibility for contributing to business performance management and collaborating its efforts across the enterprise.

As business performance becomes a function of PMO responsibility, fundamental capabilities in project management cannot be discarded. The PMO will need to continue its *oversight role* to ensure that all components of business operations, possibly represented by PMO functions or other business unit activities, achieve the prescribed level of capability and maturity in project management. This role alone should inherently accomplish many business performance objectives. However, it will also need to continue its *control role* to measure capability and effectiveness of processes and procedures across the enterprise and to recommend remedies or intervene to rectify weak performance areas. Finally, the PMO will need to continue its *support role* to facilitate the introduction and application of effective project management practices and principles in all business units relying on its expertise. When optimized, this PMO effort should facilitate a consistent and integrated business performance approach across the enterprise that brings uncommon value to the business and its stakeholders.

BUSINESS ENVIRONMENT INTERFACE CONCEPTS

The mature PMO can serve as the enterprisewide clearinghouse for integration of technical and business interests and objectives within one or several project management environments. Its functionality will contribute to alignment of business operations and business objectives within the relevant organization, and its role will facilitate coordination and collaboration of integrated business solutions across the enterprise.

The relevant organization usually establishes a PMO because it wants to improve project management capability; it seeks more-effective project management processes, practices, and tools. As improved project management performance is achieved and project contributions to business success are realized, the relevant organization begins to recognize how closely modern project management is aligned with, well, normal business management practices. It sees how improved project management effectiveness is achieved through the introduction of effective business principles and practices within the project management environment. Conversely, it will also note some incidences of project management performance requirements driving business processes and procedures. The moment at which the relevant organization recognizes that this integration of business and project management practices represents business performance management can be profound. The PMO can then begin to facilitate and manage a broader range of activities for business performance improvement and increased business success.

BUSINESS PERFORMANCE ACTIVITIES ACROSS THE PMO CONTINUUM

The "business performance" function along the PMO competency continuum represents a progressive expansion of the PMO's role and responsibility as an implementer of business strategy. In particular, the advanced implementation capabilities along the PMO continuum focus on contributions to business fulfillment across the enterprise.

Table 20.1 presents an overview of the range of prescribed PMO business performance activities according to each level in the PMO competency continuum.

The *project office* is predominantly a beneficiary of business performance management conducted by higher level PMOs. It conducts project management with awareness that business principles and practices have been incorporated into its primary activities within the project management environment. It does not usually independently conduct wide-reaching business performance management initiatives.

Table 20.1 Range of Business Performance Activities across the PMO Continuum

Project Office	Basic PMO	Standard PMO	Advanced PMO	Center of Excellence
Applies established business practices to conduct project management	Facilitates business practice integration ■ Examines PMO business function implementation ■ Validates project management processes for business use	Introduces business collaboration ■ Integrates business performance ■ Consolidates central project management authority ■ Coordinates and deploys project management-based business solutions	Expands business collaboration ■ Serves as project management and business advisor to executives ■ Accomplishes business performance measurements ■ Implements PMO functionality at multiple business locations and levels	Manages business performance ■ Analyzes project performance for business results ■ Evaluates productivity of project and business teams ■ Asserts control for business performance improvement

Mid-range PMO levels will be more and more involved in business performance management, alongside other business units and in response to applicable executive deliberations and decisions. Its role becomes one of taking the established project management capabilities to broad-reaching areas of the relevant organization, including a possible national, multinational, or global scope of influence. In conjunction with this effort, it integrates both enterprisewide and regionally specific business practices into each project management environment encountered. It also introduces project management practice solutions into each business environment encountered. The mid-range PMO, particularly one with more advanced functionality, will play an active role in business fulfillment. It will use such mechanisms as project management methodology deployment to define, measure, and forecast the achievement of business objectives within each aligned project management environment. It will use such mechanisms as an expanded project knowledge management system to collaborate business information, inform decision makers, and measure and achieve customer and stakeholder satisfaction across the enterprise. It will use such mechanisms as project portfolio management to improve business position, ascertain returns on investments, and facilitate timely business decisions in a constantly evolving global marketplace. The mid-range PMO's "business performance" function ensures that the established capability within the project management environment enables and does not restrict the fulfillment of business purposes.

The *center of excellence* represents the essence of global business performance management across the broadest stretch of the enterprise. It distinctly addresses business issues from the perspective of implementing executive business decisions and supporting strategic business objectives. In some cases, it can help deliberate and develop executive positions and strategic goals related to business performance management. In turn, it also provides business performance oversight, control, and support to any established mid level PMOs across the enterprise.

A major feature of this PMO function is the development and implementation of key components of all the other PMO functions to enable business performance to be measured and managed. The primary variable encountered is the breadth and depth of influence the PMO will assert relative to the relevant organization or the enterprise. To that end, this PMO function model will sometimes reference activities associated with particular PMO functions. It does this from a perspective of integrating business practices into the project management environment and project management practices into the business environment.

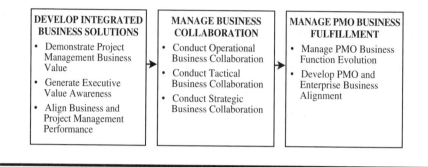

Figure 20.1 "Business Performance" Function Model

BUSINESS PERFORMANCE FUNCTION MODEL

The introduction of project management as a component of business performance involves the integration of collaborative project management and business processes, the implementation of mechanisms and measures that facilitate business decisions, and the development of PMO capability for the attainment of strategic business objectives.

The prominent activities of the PMO's "business performance" function model are depicted in Figure 20.1. Each activity is described in the following subsections.

Develop Integrated Business Solutions

The PMO can contribute to business performance improvement in a variety of ways, but it can achieve more in a formal business role than it can through informal means. However, informal contributions to business performance may be the appropriate initial means to draw attention to the robust application of project management principles and practices within the business environment. The PMO needs to not only devise the integrated solution, but also to devise the approach that will enable that integrated solution to be accepted and implemented within the relevant organization and within the enterprise. This activity prescribes such an approach to demonstrate the business value of project management, boost executive awareness of PMO value, and present the benefits of aligning project management and business performance solutions.

The PMO can consider the three activities in the following subsections to promote and manage its prescriptions for business integration within the project management environment.

Demonstrate Project Management Business Value

It has been reiterated several times in this handbook that business value is recognized in three primary ways: achievement of revenue generation, achievement of operational efficiency, and achievement of customer satisfaction. To the extent that projects contribute to any of these factors, project management can be used and integrated with business practices to provide additional value to the business effort. Each of these three factors is considered in the following subsections.

Project Management and Revenue Generation

The achievement of revenue generation is a fundamental purpose for business existence. The concepts of business provide for creating the organization, infrastructure, and methods for selling and delivering products and services in the marketplace as a means to produce revenue.

There is distinct alignment between revenue generation and revenue management, i.e., achieving a profit after accounting for expenses associated with the cost of doing business. There is also a relationship between revenue generation and the capability to make critical and timely business decisions regarding the presentation of products and services in the marketplace — pricing, marketing and sales strategies, business partnerships and industry affiliations, etc.

The following list represents a few concepts and considerations for PMO review relative to identifying and demonstrating project management value in generating business revenue:

- *Project planning:* This project management activity represents the specification of what will be done, when it will be done, and the associated costs (including resource utilization costs). It will assist in determining both cash flow (project funding) and any other financial investments required for each project. As project planning becomes more accurate and reliable, per staff experience and the use of estimating tools and techniques, projects can be evaluated to forecast the revenue to be realized by each effort. In association with project planning, project costs are identified relative to the preferred technical or business solution to be delivered. This allows sales and business managers to construct pricing that will be a part of the offer submitted to customers — the initial business indicator for anticipated revenue.
- *Project scope management:* This project management activity ensures that resource efforts and project funding are maintained to achieve primary business objectives, as represented by the scope

of the project. It allows project work to be monitored and ensures that only authorized scope changes are made following due consideration of impact and authorized adjustments for any additional costs or resources. With such oversight, project cost and resource utilization do not erode profit associated with anticipated revenue.

■ *Project risk management:* This project management capability examines possible risk events that could impair project performance and impose a financial burden on the project if not contained or otherwise managed. The project can still be pursued under such risk conditions, but this activity normally provides sufficient insight to allow managers to make informed decisions. This includes the examination of business risks as well as technical risks.

■ *Project tracking and controlling:* This project management effort provides for the timely collection of project status and progress information so that project and business decisions can be made. In particular, financial considerations are normally included in project reports to alert management to marginal or unacceptable conditions, thus enabling them to implement management actions that rectify the financial position of projects that could otherwise affect associated revenue.

■ *Project information management:* This project management capacity allows project stakeholders at all levels, particularly executives and senior managers, to access the project knowledge management system to ascertain individual and collective status of project performance relative to business performance indicators, including contributions to revenue.

■ *Project portfolio management:* This "project management methodology" function (see Chapter 1) introduces executive and senior management involvement in project oversight. If "casual" review of business indicators using the project knowledge management system is not regularly pursued, this aspect of project management is routinely conducted. It enables revenue options to be evaluated and business decisions to be made regarding revenue goals associated with project selection, project continuation, and project termination.

■ *Project contract administration:* This project management process provides for oversight of contracts associated with projects, but it particularly addresses monitoring and management of contractual obligations. This has direct bearing on vendor/contractor invoice management (outgoing project expenses) and customer invoice management (incoming project revenue).

- *Project close out activities:* This project management feature facilitates project closure and associated financial account closure. It includes activities that verify payments for project expenses and receipt of payment for products or services rendered. Across a collection or portfolio of projects, project close out activities allows revenue to be recognized and management focus to be redirected to active revenue pursuits.

The business perspective of project management warrants that the PMO address these issues not only to show project management contributions to revenue generation, but also as information needed by project managers and project team members to enable them to manage business factors within the project management environment.

Project Management and Operational Efficiency

Business advantage is achieved when all business units within the relevant organization apply efficient processes and implement effective executive decisions regarding business strategy and direction. Project management practices generally impose process rigor and repeatability, both of which are attributes of project performance that inherently define efficiency. In addition, when properly constructed and deployed as a comprehensive methodology, those processes can be used across different business units. Thus, comprehensive project management processes can also be instrumental in addressing efficiency needs within the business environment.

Beyond individual decision-making skill, executive decisions are most likely to be effective when accurate and timely information is made available. Effectiveness is enhanced when decisions are conveyed to implementers in an accurate and timely manner. Formal and informal collaboration is needed so that managers at all levels have the opportunity to understand the prescribed strategy and the means to implement it in their business areas. Project management practices and PMO functionality can prescribe the necessary collaboration and monitor its effectiveness.

The following list represents a few concepts and considerations for PMO review relative to identifying and demonstrating project management value that contributes to operational efficiency within the enterprise:

- *Communication and collaboration:* This feature of project management ensures that project stakeholders are appropriately informed and that they apply skill and information toward achieving the same project objectives. This capability can be used by the PMO to communicate and collaborate across all projects in the relevant organization, and when elevated to the enterprise level, it becomes a business enabler. The communication and collaboration processes of effective project management offer efficiency for business interactions in the enterprise.

■ *Project knowledge management system:* This feature represents the mechanism by which communication and collaboration can be expanded across the enterprise. To the extent that projects are the business of the relevant organization, this is the information and knowledge center for that business. The project knowledge management system of course contains the project management information system, but it also contains the data and information needed to manage business operations on a real-time basis. It can provide access to the standard processes for business, technical, and project management application. It can provide a project management library that inherently includes business as well as technical topics. It can provide electronic forums to facilitate business-group collaboration. It can provide an "executive dashboard" feature that summarizes project and business information for real-time use by senior managers and other business stakeholders. This feature offers efficiency in having one central business knowledge center that can be accessed by users who contribute real-time updates and use stored information to make real-time decisions to support the achievement of business interests and objectives. It is a feature that facilitates fast and accurate decision making.

■ *Common business approach:* This feature represents the mechanism for integrating business and project management processes throughout the enterprise. Through the PMO's efforts, common practices and standards for business performance can be established for application in every business unit, thereby avoiding the replication of critical process development several times over and hoping that all business units are properly aligned. Efficiency is achieved when each business uses a common approach to business. Greater efficiency is achieved when all business units apply a common understanding of a common process.

■ *Training programs:* This feature is used by the PMO to identify needs and to specify the training requirements within the project management environment. To the extent that modern project management concepts are applied within the relevant organization, it will be seen that many of the learning programs characterized as "project management" training actually include significant topics of business interest, particularly in organizations where a comprehensive project management curriculum is available. The PMO "training and education" function (see Chapter 10) also prescribes related technical training. As business and project management processes become integrated, the PMO can similarly address business training. Efficiency is achieved by having the training designated for the project managers and other project stakeholders become a component of the overall organizational training program. In an organization that has advanced project management maturity, nearly everyone in all business units are project stakeholders.

- *Organizational structure and alignment:* This feature addresses efficiency from the perspective of business unit relationships and associated resource alignment and utilization within the project management environment. The PMO can develop its "organization and structure" function (see Chapter 7) to include examination of efficiency at the enterprise level. It can evaluate how structure affects business unit and resource assignment efficiency. It can then make recommendations for organizational and structure design that facilitates timely interactions and decisions about business unit contributions to project efforts.

Project Management and Customer Satisfaction

Customers are the lifeblood of the enterprise. Business success is achieved when a sufficient number of customers are acquired and retained to generate the desired business revenue. Customer satisfaction is a business indicator that represents the ability to attract customers, expand the customer base, and achieve repeat customer business. As one of three primary factors associated with business value, customer satisfaction warrants attention and scrutiny.

Project management activities often are characterized as the business conducted with customers. To that end, project manager and project team member competencies are developed and honed to ensure achievement of customer satisfaction objectives. Similarly, project management practices can be used to incorporate processes for managing the customer business relationship.

Thus, customer business relationship management, the means to achieving customer satisfaction, is a process that is already in place in any relevant organization having a comprehensive project management capability. Furthermore, the project manager often serves as the key point of customer contact in many environments, along with business managers in some environments, and this prepositions the relevant organization toward achieving business results through implementation of the customer satisfaction functionality that is applied within the project management environment.

The following list represents a few concepts and considerations for PMO review relative to identifying and demonstrating project management value that contributes to customer satisfaction within the enterprise:

■ *Problem identification/issue resolution:* Project management capability can include a defined process for handling problems and issues arising with the customer or having customer satisfaction implications. It addresses matters of technical performance, contractual obligations, and customer expectations for business value of project deliverables. This "front-line" process can be expanded to routinely inform executives and senior managers of customer relationship conditions and to elevate major customer problems and issues to allow them to make business decisions when higher level intervention is needed to ensure ongoing customer satisfaction.

■ *Coordination of customer participation:* This activity is inherently a part of every project effort. Some customers desire more project involvement than others; some customers require more project management oversight than others. The project manager will be able to provide a flexible approach to accommodate the different participation needs of customers. Likewise, customer business activities can be naturally incorporated into each project effort according to the needs of the customer and the interests of the relevant organization.

■ *Specification of customer requirements:* Project management is based upon the specification of requirements, which lead to a statement of project objectives and scope. This information has significant business value that is often bypassed in the rush to accomplish each project effort. The achievement of customer requirements defines the business of the relevant organization. Across multiple projects, it indicates the breadth of products and services being offered in the marketplace, the nature of professional and technical skill required within the project management environment, and the type of customers being attracted by the relevant organization. This is an aspect of customer satisfaction that indicates what types of customers achieve business fulfillment by what is delivered, and this warrants review at executive and senior levels within the relevant organization.

■ *Management of business obligations:* Project management is widely accepted to represent a condition of contract or agreement between the customer and the relevant organization conducting the project. The project manager has responsibility for contract management and administration associated with the project effort and thus can contribute valuable insight to business aspects of the relationship.

An unhappy customer inherently results from an unattended contract or agreement. The established approach to managing contracts that accomplish business obligations of both parties can be expanded to include direct and indirect involvement of business units to ensure that customer satisfaction is achieved relative to contract management and administration.

■ *Creation of customer partnerships:* Project management practices can be adapted to facilitate business relationships with customers for mutual business advantage. The deliberation or requirements for these business relationships can be considered in the context of customer satisfaction points, and existing project management processes can facilitate their implementation. This aspect of customer satisfaction is one in which such a partnership accomplishes:
  - The preferred level of project oversight and control for the customer
  - A desired public demonstration of business affiliation between the customer and the relevant organization
  - The necessary involvement and participation of the customer in the project or business effort
  - The required business relationship for pursuit of mutually beneficial business opportunities

Generate Executive Value Awareness

Project management practices can inherently account for a large part of business performance. If projects are the means by which products and services are delivered, the contribution of project management to business performance is significantly increased. It would seem appropriate for executives and senior managers in the relevant organization to be well informed regarding project performance and associated project accomplishments, as that represents the pursuit of business for which they have responsibility.

Similarly, as projects enable the delivery of products and services, they present an approach to business that should be controlled at the highest management levels in the relevant organization. Executives have ultimate responsibility for the achievement of strategic business objectives and interests, and that suggests that they should have significant interest and participation in key project decisions — project selection, continuation, and termination — the primary activities of project portfolio management. To that end, executives and senior managers should have a demonstrated interest in project performance as a primary indicator of business performance. If they are interested in revenue, and projects are the means to revenue, then they should be "managing" projects from a strategic perspective.

The preceding consideration suggests a distinct link between project management practices and traditional business management practices that converge in the domain of business performance. Some organizations do not readily recognize the business performance capability that can be achieved through the implementation of comprehensive project management practices. In particular, it is the infrastructure established by the PMO to define the project management environment and implement PMO functionality that creates the capability to address business performance requirements. This is the perspective that needs to be conveyed to executives and senior managers who see project management as a lesser contributor to business performance.

The following are a few areas that the PMO can examine in creating heightened executive level awareness and support for project management and business process integration:

- *Business decisions:* Executives need access to fundamental project information in a timely manner in order to make accurate business decisions. This type of information is not generated solely from the advice and guidance of business managers. In some instances, that is just speculation and conjecture, and business units who are part-time or inactive project stakeholders cannot be expected to generate this information. Rather, this type of information is generated at the project team level, tracked at the project management level, compiled across all projects and analyzed at the PMO level, and then presented for executive review and deliberation. Project information used at the executive level is a business solution. Executives need to support, endorse, and fund the development and implementation of processes, procedures, and tools that provide this type of business solution.
- *Strategy implementation:* Executives need to convey business strategies and decisions to the project management environment for implementation. This is readily achieved when the PMO's role and responsibilities extend into the business environment, where strategy is initially communicated. In turn, the PMO can focus on the people and processes affected by executive direction, recognize the business performance impacts, and serve as a single strategy-implementation point rather than having the project management environment bombarded from all sides by business unit managers attempting to introduce executive direction from a variety of perspectives. Executives need to recognize not only the benefits of the PMO serving as a representative of the project management environment, but also as an entity serving as a business performance leader within the project management environment.

■ *Resource acquisition and allocation:* Executives need to have an ongoing awareness of project resource requirements. Possibly the largest expense in the project management environment, project resources need to be managed at mid levels according to the direction provided by the executive level. Therefore, executives need to understand the implications of their resource allocation decisions — a function of business performance. Fundamentally, this means ensuring that necessary resources are available to conduct each project that is pursued in conjunction with the prescribed business strategy. It also means attending to peripheral considerations such as resource training, qualification, assignment selection, performance management, professional development, recognition, and termination. The processes created for resource management on projects can well serve the business needs of executives. The PMO, serving as a project resource clearinghouse, can compile resource information that is needed to make resource acquisition and allocation decisions at the executive level. It can identify current resource utilization and prepare resource requirement forecasts — information the executive needs to ensure that business pursuits are not impaired by gaps in resource availability or resource management issues. Executives need to use PMO expertise and established capability in the project management environment to examine resource requirements relative to business performance.

■ *Technical performance:* Executives need to review and recognize the effectiveness and value associated with technical performance from a perspective of customer satisfaction and from a perspective of business advantage or industry competitiveness. The alignment of technical processes and project management practices can provide such business performance insight. The PMO can establish functionality to capture and analyze technical performance results across all projects internally and to compare them to industrywide results. This is business information that has its origins in the project management environment. Executives need to recognize that the PMO, at an interim management level, can establish functionality to evaluate technical performance conditions and provide routine and exception reports that will bring value to executive business deliberations and decision making. Analysis results can be conveyed to executives for examination relative to the following business interests:
  – State of core technical competencies
  – Perceived value of technical capability in the marketplace
  – Quality–cost comparisons of products and services

- Technical resource competency
- Technical management capability
- Reliance on vendor/contractor technical resources

■ *Centralized oversight, control, and support:* Executives need to understand the formal and informal boundaries of the project management environment and then maximize the effectiveness of that condition on business performance. The formal project management environment that conducts project management under PMO guidance is normally an efficient and effective means for conducting business. In contrast, the informal project management environment, usually represented by business unit intervention, is not always aligned with central PMO guidance or oversight. Therefore, such part-time interventions in project management could introduce different business perspectives and possibly different business objectives. In a sense, project management processes can be used to manage business performance, but business processes cannot necessarily be used to manage projects, particularly when there are variations for each business unit having influence. The PMO can be instrumental in coordinating a common approach to managing project contributions to business performance, integrating multiple business unit processes and procedures into a standard approach and leading collaboration among business unit participants in their ongoing contributions to the formal project management environment. Executives need to establish the PMO as a single point of reference that enables their decisions on oversight, control, and support to be implemented not only in the project management environment, but also across the relevant organization.

These are but a few of the concepts for the PMO to consider relative to achieving the desired level of executive awareness and support for project management and business integration. Each PMO should examine the pertinent issues in its relevant organization to formulate the ways in which (a) executive recognition of PMO capability to support business performance can be conveyed and (b) executive support for consolidation of many business performance activities can be achieved.

Align Business and Project Management Performance

Concepts and activities of this PMO "business performance" function presented to this point have described a significantly enlarged role for the PMO within the relevant organization, and it is one that is not readily found in many business environments. Therefore, it is important to understand that this PMO model is not prescribing PMO takeover of business-performance management! Instead, this PMO function model presents what is believed to be several compelling indications that the relevant organization could benefit from alignment of business and project management processes as well as from PMO participation in structuring and contributing to business performance management. The PMO does not create the critical business processes; it introduces, integrates, and implements them in the project management environment with consideration for project management efficiency and effectiveness, and toward maximizing project management contributions to business performance. This role warrants and possibly requires alignment of the PMO at the business unit level in order to conduct necessary cross-business unit collaboration and facilitate business unit discussions and deliberation relative to business performance management accomplished within the project management environment.

Now it is time to examine some of the specific areas of business and project management performance alignment. The following list is by no means exhaustive, but it does present some business–project management interface areas the PMO can consider for process or practice consolidation if PMO functionality is established:

- Customer account management:
  - Customer opportunity management
  - Customer information management
  - Customer relationship management
  - Customer contact and collaboration management
  - Customer contract administration
  - Customer evaluation management
- Project delivery management:
  - Project estimating: cost, schedule, and resource utilization
  - Project classification
  - Financial tracking and analysis
  - Change management
  - Project reporting
  - Administrative project close out
- Business management:
  - Strategic business interest evaluation
  - Business capability evaluation
  - Cost–benefit analysis
  - Business risk analysis
  - Product and service quality assurance
  - Proposal management
  - Contract negotiation management
  - Contract management

- – Customer invoice and payment management
- ■ Project resource management:
  - – Project resource recruiting, acquisition, and assignment
  - – Project resource training program management
  - – Project resource qualification and career development
  - – Project resource performance management
- ■ Vendor/contractor management:
  - – Vendor/contractor identification, evaluation, and selection
  - – Vendor/contractor contract management
  - – Vendor/contractor performance management
  - – Vendor/contractor invoice and payment management
- ■ Senior management oversight
  - – Project sponsorship (chartering) and funding authority
  - – Project management governance and policy development
  - – Executive control board participation
  - – Project portfolio management

Each PMO will have a different consideration of the items on this list. In some business environments, many of these activities are already an inherent part of either project management activities or PMO responsibilities. In other business environments, this list presents some novel concepts. The PMO working within the cultural norms of the relevant organization will have to decide the appropriate fit of business processes and practices in the project management environment. Note, however, that these project management performance areas can be considered not only from a perspective of process integration and consolidation, but also from a perspective of reducing or eliminating redundancy, removing confusion, and implementing common, repeatable practices for more efficient business operations within the relevant organization.

Manage Business Collaboration

Business collaboration involves conveying business information and guidance for implementation and use within the project management environment, coordinating project participation and performance results across business units and business locations, and exchanging essential business information among all internal and external project stakeholders. The alignment of business and project management interests requires responsible organizations and individuals to collaborate in order to achieve timely and appropriate business performance decisions.

The PMO should facilitate business collaboration within the relevant organization among the resident business units and across regional and global business locations. It should also facilitate vertical collaboration in those entities, and particularly within the project management environment. Furthermore, business collaboration can be accomplished relative to three business levels: operational, tactical, and strategic.

The PMO can establish business collaboration practices using its own functionality, or it can facilitate collaboration as an inherent part of its business interactions across the relevant organization. The three business collaboration areas the PMO can address are discussed in the following subsections.

Conduct Operational Business Collaboration

Operational business collaboration conveys and relates to the exchange of business requirements, information, and guidance at the staff level. This business level can generally be associated with project team efforts, but it also includes comparable staff roles in business units as well as in customer and vendor/contractor environments. Staff members at this business level are responsible for preparing and executing plans and processes to achieve specified business objectives. In the project management environment, that includes the accomplishment of project deliverables. In other business environments, this could include the accomplishment of requisite activities and conveyance of information contributing to project performance, or it could include deriving project output and information for application to business operations.

The PMO will need to examine business information sharing and collaboration conducted by operational staff to determine specific interests or needs. The following list highlights a few of the operational collaboration areas affecting both project and business performance that the PMO can consider for inclusion in integrated processes and practices:

- Task performance guidance and supervision:
  - Staff receipt and acknowledgement of tasking and work assignments
  - Staff tasking and work assignment clarification and assistance requests
  - Interstaff/interlocation work effort coordination and collaboration
  - Staff task performance management
- Task performance capability:
  - Staff/team reliance on predecessor task completion
  - Staff/team reliance on collateral task input
  - Staff/team reliance on design, quality review, or funding decisions
- Business and project information management:
  - Information system data sources and data entry responsibility
  - Information system access, availability, and performance
  - Information database completeness, accuracy, and timeliness

- Material, supplies, and equipment transfer and delivery management:
  - Interoffice/cross-location materials transfer and delivery
  - Vendor/contractor materials transfer and delivery
  - Customer-contributed materials transfer and delivery
- Staff business interface activities:
  - Customer service activities
  - Vendor/contractor affiliation activities
  - Management interface activities
  - Issue and problem identification, resolution, and elevation
- Personnel actions:
  - Staff recruitment actions
  - Staff qualification actions
  - Staff assignment, transfer, and termination actions
  - Staff training actions

Operational collaboration activities provide for calibration within the project and business environments. Collaboration ensures that everyone is working toward the same business objectives, provides interim indicators of progress toward those objectives, and conveys notification of completed actions.

The PMO can implement processes and practices that facilitate direct interactions by staff members, or it can set up procedures for action, information, and knowledge capture through project managers, business unit managers, and the PMO. This activity can be achieved by extending the capability of the "project knowledge management" function (see Chapter 4) to introduce a focus on operational level business interests and information.

Conduct Tactical Business Collaboration

Tactical business collaboration conveys and relates to the exchange of business performance information and oversight activities at the business unit level. This business level can generally be associated with business unit manager efforts, including the PMO. Managers at this business level are responsible for developing and implementing the processes, practices, and procedures that achieve specified strategic business objectives. In the project management environment, this role is generally fulfilled by the PMO with responsibility for project management capability and its own functionality. In some cases, project managers may be considered as a part of this tactical business level as well. In other business environments, this will include business unit heads and their designees and delegates who have some affiliations with the project management environment relative to their own specific business-function responsibility.

The PMO will need to examine business information sharing and collaboration conducted by tactical managers to determine specific interests or needs. The following list highlights a few of the tactical collaboration areas affecting both project and business performance that the PMO can consider for inclusion in integrated practices and processes:

- Business performance oversight:
  - Business strategy implementation
  - Business process development, integration, and implementation
  - Business performance measurement
  - Business regulatory guidance implementation
  - Business analysis and report management
- Project performance oversight:
  - Resource management
  - Facilities management
  - Task management
  - Contract management
  - Methodology management
  - Capability and maturity management
- Technical performance oversight:
  - Specifications and standards utilization
  - Technical process development, integration, and implementation
  - Quality control and assurance
  - Technical competency development
- Staff performance oversight:
  - Professional staff development
  - Performance review management
  - Staff recognition and rewards management
  - Staff acquisition and assignment management
- Customer relationship oversight:
  - Customer acquisition and retention management
  - Customer satisfaction management
  - Customer partnering management
- Vendor/contractor relationship oversight:
  - Vendor/contractor selection management
  - Vendor/contractor contract management
  - Vendor/contractor performance management
  - Vendor/contractor partnering management

Tactical collaboration activities provide for business navigation within the project and business environments. This means that business strategy is translated into actions in the workplace to achieve business objectives.

The PMO can implement processes and practices that facilitate cross-business unit manager interactions. This activity can be achieved by extending the capability of the "project knowledge management" function (see Chapter 4) to introduce a focus on strategic level business interests and information.

Conduct Strategic Business Collaboration

Strategic business collaboration conveys and relates to the exchange of business policies and guidance within the relevant organization and across the enterprise. This business level can generally be associated with executives and senior managers formulating business strategy and setting the course for business pursuits. In the project management environment, this is represented by the PMO charter and subsequent development of PMO functionality to serve the business interests of the relevant organization. In other environments, it represents the approval and implementation of business unit operating and business plans.

The PMO will need to examine business information sharing and collaboration conducted by strategic managers to determine specific interests or needs. The following list highlights a few of the strategic collaboration areas affecting both project and business performance that the PMO can consider for inclusion in integrated practices and processes:

- Business strategy implementation and fulfillment:
  - Project portfolio management
  - Business performance management
- Financial analysis and management:
  - Financial performance indicators
  - Investment initiatives
  - Owner/stockholder reports
- Operational capability analysis and management:
  - Internal business process deployment
  - Productivity and efficiency measures
  - New technology initiatives
  - Core competency maintenance and expansion
  - Maturity and continuous-improvement initiatives
- Marketing and sales analysis and management:
  - Industry posture and alignment review
  - Competitive analysis
  - Product and service offerings review

     – Sales forecasts
     – Customer account analysis

Strategic collaboration activities provide for business consultation within the project and business environments. This means that business strategy implementation is monitored and managed to achieve business objectives.

The PMO can implement processes and practices that facilitate executive and senior management interactions. This activity can be achieved by extending the capability of the "project knowledge management" function (see Chapter 4) to introduce a focus on tactical level business interests and information.

Manage PMO Business Fulfillment

The PMO's role in business performance management is one that can expand based on its contributions to business growth in the areas of revenue generation, operational efficiency, and customer satisfaction. Such expansion rarely results merely from an executive mandate but, rather, from an evolving capability within the relevant organization to achieve business objectives.

This section examines points whereby the PMO can consider ways in which it can contribute to business performance management. This discussion begins with a review of the PMO functions that can be constructed to include business responsibilities. Then, the introduction of PMOs at various levels within the relevant organization and across the enterprise is presented. These PMO activities are described in the following two subsections.

Manage PMO Business Function Evolution

The preceding sections of this chapter presented a high level perspective of how the PMO can demonstrate that the relevant organization's capabilities in project management provide business value. This section prompts the PMO to conduct an internal examination of its PMO-function development plans to ascertain how it can build PMO capability that provides business value.

PMO business function evolution is considered from the perspective of the five PMO function categories that served as the framework for this book:

- Practice management
- Infrastructure management

- Resource integration
- Technical support
- Business alignment

Practice Management

The practice management functions — project methodology management (Chapter 1), project management tools (Chapter 2), standards and metrics (Chapter 3), and project knowledge management (Chapter 4) — enable the project manager and the project team to effectively manage and conduct the project. The content of practice management guidance is inherently representative of the technical nature of business of the relevant organization, but that usually happens as a matter of default, not by design.

The PMO can begin to examine business performance impacts during early project management capability implementation associated with process and methodology development. The project management methodology and aligned supporting functions should always be geared toward helping project managers to achieve project performance success. However, there are a few features that can be included in this functional area to help middle and senior managers achieve associated business performance success. Generally, that is a matter of collecting, analyzing, and reporting the project-related information that is needed to make business decisions. For the most part, standard project information handling will suffice. However, the PMO can add early business value by ensuring that work done by project managers and members of the project team addresses important aspects of business performance within the relevant organization.

The PMO can consider the following areas when integrating business performance features into its practice management functions (see Chapter 1 to Chapter 4):

- Ensure the collection of project management information to produce comprehensive status and progress reports that can be aggregated across projects, cross-referenced to business performance, and utilized to make business decisions.
- Incorporate appropriate senior management review and approval points in the project management methodology process to facilitate senior manager involvement and input to project direction associated with business performance.
- Acquire or develop and implement automated project management tools that provide project and cross-project critical information summaries for use by executives and senior managers, including

the use of an "executive dashboard" for access to the project knowledge management system.

■ Construct project knowledge management system features that present project business case information access for the project manager and project team members to enable them to gain additional insight about their project efforts. Include additional features that present general business news and information about their project, thus providing an external, industry perspective of their accomplishments.

■ Specify standards and metrics that help to achieve business objectives. In particular, examine and incorporate technical and business standards in criteria for project management performance, and be sure to include any special business objectives aligned with achieving industry certifications or awards.

Infrastructure Management

The infrastructure management functions — project governance (Chapter 5), assessment (Chapter 6), organization and structure (Chapter 7), and facilities and equipment support (Chapter 8) — enable the PMO to provide cross-project oversight and support to projects. This functional capability is established so that (a) individual project managers are not burdened with infrastructure setup for every project effort encountered and (b) the relevant organization gains benefit from centralized deployment of project oversight activities that could otherwise be repeated with dissimilar approaches by each project manager.

The PMO can begin to examine business performance impacts as project management infrastructure planning is performed, primarily along the lines of business efficiency but also with attention to project management capability.

The PMO can consider the following areas when integrating business performance features into its infrastructure management function:

■ Solicit senior management involvement and input to project governance activities — the primary means by which executives and senior managers directly influence the capability established in the project management environment — particularly including the specification of policy guidance to achieve business performance within the project management environment.

■ Select and use project management capability and maturity assessments that include the examination of business practices and business contributions within the project management environment. This will enable project management capability improvements to likewise contribute to improved business performance.

■ Cultivate and implement a structure within the relevant organization that enables project management to be an efficient contributor to the achievement of business interests and responsive to business requirements, i.e., project team alignment to facilitate speedy project initiation, project team assignment to optimize staff availability, and project team readiness to maximize project performance capability.

■ Define and collaborate overall project management facility and equipment needs across business units to establish management efficiency and cost control as contributions to business performance.

Resource Integration

The resource integration functions — resource management (Chapter 9), training and education (Chapter 10), career development (Chapter 11), and team development (Chapter 12) — enable the PMO to identify requirements and establish capability for the deployment of staff competencies within the project management environment. This function allows the PMO to represent project staff interests within the relevant organization. It also allows the PMO to define and manage project staff needs within the project management environment. It normally will interface with the human resources (HR) department to acquire and assign resources, but that effort begins with facilitating deliberation with senior managers to obtain resource acquisition approval and allocation — a function of business performance.

The PMO can begin to examine business performance impacts through evaluation of the resource alignment and assignment processes and conditions. It will need to define the current state, develop the recommended state, and then demonstrate the increased business value to be achieved by the recommended state.

The PMO can consider the following areas when integrating business performance features into its resource integration function (see Chapter 9 to Chapter 12):

■ Determine the current allocation and assignment of resources within the project management environment — define prominent roles and responsibilities, examine assignment coverage across projects, and ascertain the effectiveness of current staff strength. This fundamental analysis will support the resource planning needed to ensure that the business interests of the relevant organization are not adversely impacted by project resource availability relative to current and forecast resource utilization requirements.

- Examine ways to develop requisite skill and competency in project management for all project resources and active stakeholders within the project management environment. The greater the number of individuals who comprehend the concepts and practices of modern project management, regardless of their role, the more efficient and effective they will be in their participation on projects and in their contributions to business achievement.
- Qualify and certify project managers in the relevant organization as a means to achieve business advantage, including industry and customer recognition of professional competency; colleague recognition and associated project manager motivation to achieve business objectives; role and position clarification to expedite project management activities and conduct projects more efficiently; and increased project manager capabilities, based on qualification criteria, to achieve successful project and business performance.
- Develop capability to conduct team building for noncohesive project teams. Even fundamental, short-period work sessions can go a long way toward improving team performance and thereby business performance.

Technical Support

The technical support functions — mentoring (Chapter 13), planning support (Chapter 14), project auditing (Chapter 15), and project recovery (Chapter 16) — enable the PMO to help project managers bring in successful projects with forecasted reliability and regularity. This function provides focused support at the project level, but it does so in conjunction with distinct business interest. To the extent that projects represent the business of the relevant organization, technical support functions (see Chapter 13 to Chapter 16) ensure that business is accomplished in a timely and professional manner and in compliance with contractual and regulatory obligations.

The PMO can begin to examine business performance impacts first by developing a close professional relationship with project managers to identify general and specific support needs within the project management environment, and then by providing unencumbered project management support services. A large part of this PMO functional area will include (a) advising and making project managers aware of business impacts resulting from project performance and (b) working in collaboration with them to resolve or rectify conditions that present adverse business impacts.

The PMO can consider the following areas when integrating business performance features into its technical support functions (see Chapter 13 to Chapter 16):

- Identify where project managers most need assistance in managing project performance, and develop PMO support services in response to those needs. Use mentoring and project team facilitation to convey concepts and transfer project management skill and knowledge to the project manager and members of the project team.
- Introduce a fundamental project management auditing capability to enable examination of project impacts on business performance. Conduct routine project management reviews and audits across all projects to ascertain any trends or indications of project influence on business performance.
- Develop the capability to identify and rectify troubled projects as a business decision that usually comes from executive and senior managers because of the redirection of manager time and attention as well as the added cost and concentration of resources needed to conduct project recovery activities.

Business Alignment

The business alignment functions — portfolio management (Chapter 17), customer relationships (Chapter 18), vendor relationships (Chapter 19), and business performance (Chapter 20) — enable the PMO to receive business performance guidance and translate it for application within the project management environment. This function represents a range of PMO activities from the distinct alignment of business strategy with project performance to the sometimes more subtle direction and policy guidance that emanates from the executive board room.

The PMO can begin to examine business performance impacts by evaluating the current depth of business integration within the project management environment and contrasting that to the business advantages that could be gained with more-complete and comprehensive business process and practice integration. Early PMO involvement in defining the need for business alignment requirements and information is presented in the practice management functions (Chapter 1 to Chapter 4).

The PMO can consider the following areas when integrating business performance features into its business alignment functions:

- Determine the current depth of project and business strategy alignment processes and practices. Specify how project selection occurs; identify the project selection decision makers; ascertain whether they implement business strategies as a normal part of their role and responsibilities; and examine the extent to which they recognize project performance as a contributing factor to business performance. This effort will provide insight to the PMO in deliberating and positioning its recommendations for conducting and managing processes associated with project portfolio management.

■ Examine how well business units within the relevant organization collaborate on efforts toward achieving strategic business objectives. Business operations, business culture, and business interests will determine how an effective, collaborated approach to customers, vendors and contractors, and marketplace influences can be introduced into the project management environment.

■ Ascertain senior level interest in centralized project management oversight, control, and support as a prominent means of achieving improved business performance. Construct plans for PMO functional evolution according to direction and insights gained from executives and senior managers.

Develop PMO and Enterprise Business Alignment

The PMO works under the sponsorship and in support of the business purposes of a particular relevant organization. The relevant organization could be an entity that ranges in size from a small business unit tasked to provide project management oversight for a few projects to the enterprise, a global network of departments and divisions that represent a comprehensive business capacity to manage multinational projects.

In fact, there could be multiple relevant organizations within a business enterprise, each requiring its own level and depth of PMO support. To that end, there could be multiple levels of PMO activity within the enterprise, each with its own distinct purpose and particular business objectives associated with the sponsoring relevant organization. The consideration of multilayered PMO capability within the enterprise has been a recurring consideration briefly alluded to at junctures throughout this handbook. It is now time to consider multilayer PMO options and opportunities.

If there is going to be more than one PMO in the relevant organization, business needs will likely dictate their alignment. The following represents five very general PMO alignment models that establish multiple PMO presence and affiliations within the relevant organization. Variations on these models can be constructed to achieve a more accurate alignment of PMO functions with business organization needs and interests:

■ *Business unit affiliation:* The PMO supports the business interests of an operating unit within the relevant organization. The business unit has a particular business purpose for which it conducts projects, and a PMO is established and aligned to help it achieve that purpose. The full range of PMO capability can be applied here because business units can range from specific operational entities to comprehensive business departments and divisions.

■ *Product/service affiliation:* The PMO supports the design, manufacture, and delivery of products and services in the marketplace. It will have organizational alignment with a particular business unit, but its efforts will likely extend across business unit boundaries to support and manage project and business performance associated with a particular product/service development life cycle.

■ *Technical discipline affiliation:* The PMO support services and activities focus on the technical performance aspects of project efforts. This often represents a special case of business unit affiliation, where the PMO is aligned with a department, division, or other entity that has a specific technical performance purpose. Generally, this PMO will provide oversight, guidance, and support to the management of technical processes and procedures, with some responsibility for incorporating effective project management practices but usually with limited responsibility for business process integration.

■ *Business region affiliation:* The PMO has responsibility for project management oversight, control, and support in one or more designated geographical areas in which the relevant organization conducts business. This could be characterized by alignment with specific business unit activities across multiple regions, or it could represent direct alignment with all of the business operations of one or more regions. The PMO's purpose is focused on achieving effective project management capability in support of business objectives within the specified region.

■ *Enterprise affiliation:* The enterprise level PMO normally has as much responsibility for business performance as it does for project management performance. It can be aligned within the enterprise that is itself the relevant organization, or it can be aligned with an enterprise that oversees multiple component organizations that have their own PMO capability. The enterprise PMO's focus is normally on establishing the project management capability and maturity for the entire enterprise. To that end, there will be a need for the PMO to understand the business interests of each component as well as the strategic direction of the enterprise.

Here is a final thought on the matter of PMO affiliation in a multiple-PMO business environment. Each PMO should have established working relationships with every other PMO in the enterprise. They can be designated as peers, subordinates, enterprise level PMOs, or some other preferred naming convention that fits best within the relevant organization. As well, each PMO that is not a peer should have specific and distinct roles and responsibilities that are not replicated at other PMO levels above or below it.

POSTSCRIPT FOR THE SMALLER PMO

There is no specific role defined for the smaller PMO relative to the prominent activities of this "business performance" function. It is primarily intended for use by larger, more advanced PMOs who have responsibility for business performance. However, this does not limit the smaller PMO from taking initiative to improve business performance through its efforts within the project management environment.

The following represents a few simple examples of the initiatives that a smaller PMO can take to contribute to business performance management within the relevant organization:

- Identify needs and facilitate collaboration of project management performance results and information for use by managers in making business decisions related to project efforts.
- Coordinate business unit contributions to project management efforts, and seek ways in which to integrate business practices into the project management methodology.
- Identify project management contributions to business performance; examine project management effectiveness in those areas; and recommend and implement improved processes and practices.

INDEX

Training and education, *see also*
    Certification; Courses;
    Mentoring; Mentoring
    function model; Training and
    education function model
  automated methodology deployment,
    34
  basics, xviii, 271–272
  business environment interface,
    272–273
  business performance, 602–603
  business unit managers, 38
  career development, 316
  competency, 172–173, 273, *274,* 275
  methodology implementation, 38–39,
    42–43
  new technology, 264
  oversight responsibility, 160
  plans, 123, 410
  position descriptions and
    qualifications, 312
  project environment interface, 272
  project management, 264
  project managers, 38
  resource management, 263–264
  senior managers, 38
  smaller PMOs, 293–294
  teams, 38, 339, 347
  technical skills, 264
  tools, 63, 64–65
  virtual teams, 339
Training and education function model,
    see also Career development
    function model
  basics, 275–276, *276*
  courses development, 283–286
  evaluation, 290–293
  external training resources, 282
  implementation, 291
  in-house training resources, 281
  management of program, 286–290
  needs assessment, 277–278
  plans, 283–286
  program establishment, 276–286
  project management training,
    289–290
  promotion of program, 288–289
  public training resources, 282
  registration, 286–287

  requirements, 278–279
  resources, 279–282, 291–292
  updating program, 292–293
Transfers
  close out phase, 268
  facilities and equipment, 239,
    244–245
Transition activities
  career path integration, 313–315
  implementation transition, 39–40
  methodology implementation, 39–42
  plans, 410
  PMIS, 123
  project recovery, 471
  tools, 64
Transportation plan, 124, 410
Travel arrangements, 261, 265
Trial-and-error approaches, 355
Triggered project audit point, 433–434
Troubled projects, 440, *see also* Recovery
    function model, project
Trust issues, management, 338

U

Updating, process, 292–293, 474–475
User feedback, *see* Feedback
Users
  assistance, 37
  capability improvement plans, 179
  knowledge management framework,
    106–107, 120
  stakeholder participation, 215
Users group, 36
User training, *see* Training and education
Utilization, *see also* Resource utilization
  facilities and equipment, 235–237
  management plan, 410
  methodology platform, 17
  policy, 18
  portfolio management, 512–513
  project recovery, 474
  tools, 66

V

Validation plan, 125
Value